THE DIARY OF
SAMUEL PEPYS

THE DIARY
OF
SAMUEL PEPYS

A new and complete
transcription edited by

ROBERT LATHAM
AND
WILLIAM MATTHEWS

CONTRIBUTING EDITORS
WILLIAM A. ARMSTRONG · MACDONALD EMSLIE
SIR OLIVER MILLAR · T. F. REDDAWAY

VOLUME IX · 1668–1669

HarperCollins*Publishers*

University of California Press
Berkeley and Los Angeles

Published in the UK by
HarperCollins*Publishers*
77–85 Fulham Palace Road
Hammersmith, London W6 8JB
www.**fire**and**water**.com

UK paperback edition 1995
Reissued 2000

Published in the USA by
University of California Press
Berkeley and Los Angeles, California

First US paperback edition 2000

1 3 5 7 9 8 6 4 2

First published by Bell & Hyman Limited 1971

ISBN 0 00 499029 3 (UK)
ISBN 0 520 22701 8 (USA)

Library of Congress Catalog Card No. 70-96950

Printed and bound in Great Britain by
Clays Ltd, St Ives plc

CONTENTS

LIST OF ILLUSTRATIONS

READER'S GUIDE

This section is meant for quick reference. More detailed information about the editorial methods used in this edition will be found in the Introduction and in the section 'Methods of the Commentary' in vol I, and also in the statements preceding the Select Glossary at the end of each text volume and the Large Glossary in the *Companion*.

I. THE TEXT

The fact that the MS. is mostly in shorthand makes exact reproduction (e.g. of spelling, capitalisation and punctuation) impossible.

Spelling is in modern British style, except for those longhand words which Pepys spelt differently, and words for which the shorthand indicates a variant pronunciation which is also shown by Pepys's longhand elsewhere. These latter are given in spellings which reflect Pepys's pronunciations.

Pepys's capitalisation is indicated only in his longhand.

Punctuation is almost all editorial, except for certain full-stops, colons, dashes and parentheses. Punctuation is almost non-existent in the original since the marks could be confused with shorthand.

Italics are all editorial, but (in e.g. headings to entries) often follow indications given in the MS. (by e.g. the use of larger writing).

The **paragraphing** is that of the MS.

Abbreviations of surnames, titles, place names and ordinary words are expanded.

Single **hyphens** are editorial, and represent Pepys's habit of disjoining the elements of compound words (e.g. Wh. hall/White-hall). Double hyphens represent Pepys's hyphens.

Single **angle-brackets** mark additions made by Pepys in the body of the MS.; double angle-brackets those made in the margins.

Light **asterisks** are editorial (see below, Section II); heavy asterisks are Pepys's own.

Pepys's **alterations** are indicated by the word 'replacing' ('repl.') in the textual footnotes.

II. THE COMMENTARY

1. Footnotes deal mainly with events and transactions. They also identify MSS, books, plays, music and quotations, but give only occasional and minimal information about persons and places, words and phrases. The initials which follow certain notes indicate the work of the contributing editors. Light asterisks in the text direct the reader to the Select Glossary for the definition of words whose meanings have changed since the time of the diary.

2. The **Select List of Persons** is printed unchanged in each text volume. It covers the whole diary and identifies the principal persons, together with those who are described in the MS. by titles or in other ways that make for obscurity.

3. The **Select Glossary** is printed at the end of each text volume. It gives definitions of certain recurrent English words and phrases, and identifications of certain recurrent places.

4. The **Companion** (vol. X) is a collection of reference material. It contains maps, genealogical tables, and a Large Glossary, but consists mainly of articles, printed for ease of reference in a single alphabetical series. These give information about matters which are dealt with briefly or not at all in the footnotes and the Select Glossary: i.e. persons, places, words and phrases, food, drink, dress etc. They also treat more systematically than footnotes can the principal subjects with which the diary is concerned: Pepys's work, interests, health etc. References to the *Companion* are given only rarely in the footnotes.

III. DATES

In Pepys's time two reckonings of the calendar year were in use in Western Europe. Most countries had adopted the New Style – the revised calendar of Gregory XIII (1582); Britain until 1752 retained the Old Style – the ancient Roman, or Julian, calendar, which meant that its dates were ten days behind those of the rest of Western Europe in the seventeenth century. 1 January in England was therefore 11 January by the New Style abroad. On the single occasion during the period of the diary when Pepys was abroad (in Holland in May 1660) he continued to use the Old Style, thus avoiding a break in the run of his dates. In the editorial material of the present work dates relating to countries which had adopted the new reckoning are given in both styles (e.g. '1/11 January') in order to prevent confusion.

It will be noticed that the shortest and longest days of the year occur in the diary ten days earlier than in the modern calendar. So, too, does Lord Mayor's Day in London – on 29 October instead of 9 November.

For most legal purposes (from medieval times until 1752) the new year in England was held to begin on Lady Day, 25 March. But in accordance with the general custom, Pepys took it to begin on 1 January, as in the Julian calendar. He gives to all dates within the overlapping period between 1 January and 24 March a year-date which comprehends both styles – e.g. 'January 1 16$\frac{59}{80}$.' In the present commentary a single year-date, that of the New Style, has been used: e.g. '1 January 1660'.

THE DIARY
1668–1669

1. Up, and all the morning in my chamber making up some accounts against this beginning of the new year; and so about noon abroad with my wife, who was to dine with W. Hewer and Willett at Mrs. Pierce's; but I had no mind to be with them, for I do clearly find that my wife is troubled at my friendship with her and Knepp, and so dined with[a] my Lord Crew, with whom was Mr. Browne, Clerk of the House of Lords, and Mr. John Crew.[1] Here was mighty good discourse, as there is alway; and among other things, my Lord Crew did turn to a place in the *Life of Sir Ph. Sidny*, wrote by Sir Fulke Grevill, which doth foretell the present condition of this nation in relation to the Dutch, to the[b] very degree of a prophecy; and is so remarkable that I am resolved to buy one of them, it being quite through a good discourse.[2] Here they did talk much of the present cheapness of Corne,[c] even to a miracle; so as their[d] farmers can pay no rent, but do fling up their lands – and would pay in corne;[3] but (which I did observe to my Lord, and he liked well of it) our gentry are grown so ignorant in everything of good husbandry, that they know not how to bestow this corn; which, did they understand but a little trade, they would be able to joyne together, and know what markets there are abroad and send it thither, and thereby ease their tenants and be able to pay themselfs. They did talk much of the disgrace the Archbishop is fallen

a	repl. 'at'	*b*	repl. 'to'
c	repl. 'br'-	*d*	repl. 'the'

1. John Browne (*recte* Clerk of the Parliaments) was Lord Crew's brother-in-law; John Crew his second son.

2. The French attack on the Spanish Netherlands was now driving England and Holland together (the alliance between them being concluded this month) just as they had been driven together in Sidney's time in common resistance to Spain. Cf. Sir Fulke Greville (Lord Brooke), *Life of the renowned Sir Philip Sidney* (1652), pp. 25, 68, 227. Pepys acquired a copy of the 1652 edition: PL 214.

3. Cf. above, viii. 158, n. 1.

under with the King, and the rest of the Bishops also.[1]   Thence
I after dinner to the Duke of York's playhouse, and there saw
Sir Martin Marrall, which I have seen so often;[2] and yet am
mightily pleased with it and think it mighty witty, and the fullest
of proper matter for mirth that ever was writ.[a]   And I do clearly
see that they do improve in their acting of it.   Here a mighty
company of citizens, prentices and others; and it makes me
observe that when I begin first to be able to bestow a play on
myself, I do not remember that I saw so many by half of the
ordinary prentices and mean people in the pit, at 2s-6d apiece,
as now; I going for several years no higher then the 12d, and
then the 18d places,[3] and though I strained hard to go in then
when I did – so much the vanity and prodigality of the age is to
be observed in this perticular.   Thence I to White-hall, and there
walked up and down the House a while and do hear nothing of
anything done further in this business of the change of Privy-
counsellors.[4]   Only, I hear that Sir G. Savill, one of the Parliament committee of nine for examining the accounts, is by the
King made a Lord, the Lord Hallifax; which I believe will
displease the Parliament.[5]   By and by I met with Mr. Brisban;
and having it[b] in my mind this Christmas to (do what I never
can remember that I did) go to see the manner of the gaming at
the Groome porter's[6] (I having in my coming from the playhouse

a repl. 'in'   *b* repl. 'in'

---

1. Because of their defence of
Clarendon: see above, viii. 532 & n.
3.
2. Pepys had already seen Dryden's
comedy (q.v. above, viii. 387, n. 1),
in whole or in part, five times. (A).
3. 1s. and 1s. 6d. were the prices of
admission to the upper gallery and the
middle gallery respectively. (A).
4. See above, viii. 596 & n. 1.
5. By a vote of 2 December none
of the Brooke House committee (q.v.
above, viii. 559, n. 2) was to be

a member of either House. But
Halifax played no great part in the
committee's work, and no parliamentary criticism of his appointment
seems to have been made. The
warrant for his peerage was issued
on 31 December; the patent on 13
January.
6. A court official at Whitehall Palace: for his duties as controller of the
gaming at court, see above, iii. 293,
n. 1. The post was now held by
Thomas Offley.

stepped into the two Temple-halls,[1] and there saw the dirty prentices and idle people playing – wherein I was mistaken in thinking to have seen gentlemen of quality playing there, as I think it was when I was a little child,[a] that one of my father's servants, John Bassum I think, carried me in his armes thither), I did tell him of it and he did lead me thither; where after staying an hour, they[b] begin to play at about 8[c] at night – where to see how differently one[d] man took his losing from another, one cursing and swearing, and another only muttering and grumbling to himself, a third without any appearing discontent at all – to see how the dice will run good luck in one hand for half an hour together – and another have no good luck at all. To see how easily here, where they play nothing but guinnys, 100*l* is won or lost. To see two or three gentlemen come in there drunk, and putting their stock[e] of gold together – one 22 pieces, the second 4, and the third 5 pieces; and these to play one with another, and forget how much each of them brought, but he that brought the 22 think that he brought no more then the rest. To see the different humours of gamesters to change their luck when it is bad – how ceremonious they are as to call for new dice – to shift their places – to alter their manner of throwing; and that with great industry, as if there was anything in it. To see how some old gamesters, that have no money now to spend as formerly, do come and sit and look on; as among others, Sir Lewes Dives,[2] who was here and hath been a great gamester in his time. To hear their cursing and damning to no purpose; as one man, being to throw a seven if he could[f] and failing to do it after a great many throws,[g] cried he would be damned if ever he flung seven more while he lived, his despair of throwing it

a repl. 'boy'   *b* repl. 'or two'   *c* repl. '9'
     d s.h. repl. '1'   *e* repl. 'gold'
     f repl. 'doth'   *g* l.h. repl. s.h.

---

1. The Halls of the Inner and Middle Temple, where (as in college halls at Oxford and Cambridge) gaming was permitted during the twelve days of Christmas. When the floorboards of Middle Temple Hall were taken up c. 1764 nearly 100 pairs of dice were found: J. Ashton, *Hist. gambling in Engl.*, p. 27.

2. Sir Lewis Dyve (1599–1669), of Bromham, Beds. He had lost heavily in serving the royalist cause during the civil wars.

being so great, while others did it as their luck served, almost every throw. To see how persons of the best quality do here sit down and play with people of any, though meaner; and to see how people in ordinary clothes*a* shall come hither and play away 100, or 2 or 300 guinnys, without any kind of difficulty. And lastly, to see the formality of the Groome-porter, who is their judge of all disputes in play and all quarrels that may arise therein;[1] and how his under-officers are there to observe true play at each table and to give new dice, is a consideration I never could have thought had been in the world, had I not now seen it. And mighty glad I am that I did see it; and it may be will find another evening, before Christmas be over, to see it again; when I may stay later, for their heat*b* of play begins not till about 11 or 12 a-clock; which did give me another pretty observation, of a man that did win mighty fast when I was there: I think he won 100*l* at single pieces in a little time; while all the rest envied him his good fortune, he cursed it, saying, "A pox on it that it should come so earely upon me! For this fortune two hours hence would be worth something to me; but then, God damn me, I shall have no such luck." This kind of profane, mad entertainment they give themselfs. And so I having enough for once, refusing to venture, though Brisband pressed me hard and tempted me with saying that no man was ever known to lose the first time, the devil being too cunning to discourage a gamester; and he offered me also to lend me ten pieces to venture, but I did refuse and so went away – and took coach and home about 9 or 10 at night; where, not finding my wife come home, I took the same coach again; and leaving my watch behind for fear of robbing, I did go back and to Mr. Pierce's, thinking they might not have broken up yet, but there I find my wife newly gone; and not going out of my coach, spoke only to Mr. Pierce in his nightgown* in the street; and so away back again home, and there to supper with my wife and to talk about their dancing and doings at Mrs. Pierce's today; and so to bed.

a repl. 'know'   *b* MS. 'height'

---

1. Cf. the example (22 June 1666) in *Savile Corr.* (ed. W. D. Cooper), p. 10.

2. Up, and with Sir Jo. Minnes by coach to White-hall; and there attended the King and the Duke of York in the Duke of York's lodgings with the rest of the officers and many of the commanders of the fleet and some of our maister-Shipwrights, to discourse the business of having the topmasts of ships made to lower abaft of the mainmast[1] – a business I understood not, and so can give no good account; but I do see that by how much greater the Council and the number of councillors is, the more confused the issue is of their counsels; so that little was said to the purpose regularly, and but little use was[a] made of it, they coming to a very broken conclusion upon it: to make trial in a ship or two. From this they fell to other talk about the fleet's fighting this late war, and how the King's ships have been scattered; though the King said that the world would not have it that above[b] ten or twenty ships in any fight did do any service, and that this hath been told so to him himself by ignorant people. The Prince, who was there, was mightily surprized at it, and seemed troubled; but the King told him that it was only discourse of the world; but Mr. Wren whispered me in the eare, and said that the Duke of Albemarle had put it into his Narrative for the House, that not above 25 ships fought in the engagement wherein he was, but that he was advised[c] to leave it out; but this he did write from sea, I am sure, or words to that effect[2] – and did displace many commanders; among others,[d] Captain Batts,[3] who the Duke of York said was a very stout man, all the world knew; and that another was brought into his ship that had been turned off his place when he was a bosun not long before for being a Drunkerd: this the Prince took notice of, and would

a repl. 'came'   b MS. 'about'
c followed by -'ed' struck through   d repl. same symbol badly formed

---

1. The established practice was to lower them before the mainmast.

2. See Albemarle to Coventry, the *Royal Charles*, 6 June 1666: 'I assure you I never fought with worse officers than now in my life, for not above twenty of them behaved themselves like men' (Smith, i. 110). The reference was to the Four Days Battle. For his narrative, see above, viii. 514 & n. 1.

3. George Batts of the *Unicorne*; Coventry had thought him capable of becoming a good commander: above, iv. 196. He never held another command.

have been angry, I think, but they let their discourse fall; but the Duke of York was earnest in it and the Prince said to me, standing by me, "God damn me, if they will turn out every man that will be drunk, he must turn out all the commanders in the fleet. What is the matter if [he] be drunk, so when he comes to fight he doth his work? At least, let him be punished for his drunkenness, and not put out of his command presently." This he spoke, very much concerned for this idle fellow, one Greene.[1] After this, the King begin to tell stories of the Cowardize of the Spaniards in Flanders when he was there at the siege of Mardike and Dunkirke[2] – which was very pretty, though he tells them but meanly. This being done, I to Westminster-hall and there stayed a little; and then home, and by the way did find with difficulty the *Life of Sir Ph. Sidny* (the book I mention*a* yesterday); and the bookseller told me that he had sold four within*b* these week or two, which is more then ever he sold in all his life of them and he could not imagine what should be the reason of it. But I suppose it is from the same reason, of people's observing of this part therein, touching his prophesying our present condition here in England in relation to the Dutch – which is very remarkable. So home to dinner, where Balty's wife is come to town; she came last night and lay at my house, but being weary, was gone to bed before I came home and so I saw her not before. After dinner I took my wife and her and girl out to the New Exchange, and there my wife bought herself a lace for a handkercher, which I do give her, of about 3*l*,[3] for a ⟨new⟩ year's gift, and I did buy also a lace for a band for myself; and so home, and there to the office busy late; and so

a repl. 'mentioned'   *b* repl. 'in'

---

1. Levi Greene, later (1672) dismissed by court martial.

2. In the winter of 1657–8, when the King had served under Turenne with a Franco-English force at the siege of Mardyck. It was generally thought that the Spaniards had abandoned the town's defence too soon. The loss of Dunkirk in the following summer was due to other reasons – principally to the Spanish defeat in June at the battle of the Dunes (in which the Dukes of York and Gloucester had fought). Cf. Duke of York, *Memoirs* . . . *1652–60* (ed. A. Lytton Sells), pp. 243+; Clarendon, *Hist.*, vi. 33+, 81+.

3. The lace was of gold- or silver-thread.

home to my chamber, where busy on some accounts, and then to
supper and to bed. This day my wife shows me a Locket of
Dyamond's, worth about 40*l*, which W. Hewer doth press her to
accept,*ᵃ* and hath done for a good while, out of his gratitude for
my kindness and hers to him. But I do not like that she should
receive it, it not being honourable for me to do it; and so do
desire her to force him to take it back*ᵇ* again, he leaving it
against her will yesterday with her. And she did this evening
force him to take it back, at which she says he is troubled; but
however, it becomes me more to refuse then to let her accept of
it – and so I am well pleased with her returning it him. It is
generally believed that France is endeavouring a firmer league
with us then the former, in order to his going on with his business
against Spayne the next year; which I am, and so everybody
else I think, very glad of, for all our fear is of his invading us.¹

This day at White-hall I overheard ⟨Sir W. Coventry⟩ propose to the King his ordering* of some perticular*ᶜ* thing in the
Wardrobe; which was of no great value, but yet, as much as it
was, it was of profit to the King and saving to his purse. The
King answered to it with great indifferency, as a thing that it
was no great matter whether it was done or no. Sir W. Coventry
answered: "I see your Majesty doth not remember the old
English proverb*ᵈ*, 'He that will not stoop for a pin, will never be
worth a pound' ", and so they parted, the King bidding him do
as he would – which methought was an answer not like a King*ᵉ*
that did entend ever to do well.

a repl. ? 'replace'   *b* repl. 'bad'   *c* repl. 'thing'
          d MS. 'provert'   *e* repl. 'thing'

---

1. France was busy isolating her
enemy Spain, and had already in
December concluded agreements with
Brandenburg and the Emperor. Her
attempt to bring off a bargain with
England was now on the brink of
failure. Her last offer had been made
on 25 December/4 January, and
England switched courses to join
Holland and Sweden in the anti-
French Triple Alliance on 13/23
January. (See Feiling, pp. 248+.)
The previous Anglo-French treaty
was that of 8 April 1667 in which
England and France had agreed not
to ally with each other's enemies:
Feiling, p. 218. For the fear of a
French invasion of England, see
below, pp. 18, 30; newsletters (10,
31 December 1667) in BM, Add.
36916, ff. 42, 56.

3.   At the office all the morning with Mr. Willson and my clerks, consulting again about a new contract with the Victualler of the Navy;[1] and at noon*a* home to dinner and thence to the office again, where busy all the afternoon, preparing something for the Council about Tanger this*b* evening; so about 5 a-clock away with it to the Council, and there do find that the Council hath altered its times of sitting to the mornings, and so I lost my labour; and back again by coach presently, round by the City wall, it being dark; and so home and there to the office, where till midnight with Mr. Willson and my people to go through with the Victualler's contract and the considerations about the new one; and so home to supper and to bed – thinking my time very well spent.

4.   Up, and then*c* to the office, where we sat all the morning. At noon home to dinner, where my clerks and Mr. Clerke the Sollicitor with me; and dinner being done, I to the office again, where all the afternoon till late busy; and then home, with my mind pleased at the pleasure of despatching my business; and so to supper and to bed – my thoughts full, how to order*d* our design of having some dancing at our house on Monday next, being Twelfth-day.

It seems worth remembering that this day I did hear my Lord Anglesy at the table, speaking touching this new Act for Accounts,[2] say that the House of Lords did pass it because it was a senseless, impracticable, ineffectual, and foolish Act; and that my Lord Ashly having*e* shown this that it was so to the House of Lords, the Duke of Buckingham did stand up and told the Lords that [they] were beholden to my Lord Ashly, that*f* having first commended them for a most grave and honourable assembly, he thought it fit for the House to pass this Act for Accounts because it was a foolish and simple Act.   And it seems it was passed with but a few in the House, when it was intended to

| *a* repl. 'home' | *b* repl. 'tonight' | *c* MS. 'there' |
| *d* repl. 'ordering' | *e* repl. 'after' | *f* repl. same symbol |

1. For Gauden's contract, see above, viii. 567 & n. 3; below, p. 316 & n. 1, pp. 317–18 & n.
2. The act establishing the Brooke

House Committee which was to enquire into the war finances: above, viii. 559, n. 2.

have met in a Grand Committee upon it.[1]   And it seems that in
itself it is not to be practised till after this session of Parliament,
by the very words of the Act which nobody regarded, and
therefore cannot come in force yet, unless the next meeting[a]
they do make a new Act for the bringing it into force sooner –
which is a strange omission.[2]   But I perceive my Lord Anglesy
doth make a mere laughing-stock of this act, as a thing that
can do nothing considerable for all its great Noise.

5.   *Lords=day*. Up; and being ready, and disappointed of a
coach, it breaking a wheel[b] just as [it] was coming for me, I
walked as far as the Temple, it being dirty.   And as I went out
of my doors, my cousin Anth. Joyce met me and so walked part
of the way with me; and it was to see what I would do upon
what his wife a little while since did desire, which was to supply
him with 350*l*, to enable him to give[c] to build his house again:[3] I
(who in my nature am mighty unready to answer Noe to anything, and thereby wonder that I have suffered no more in my life
by my easiness in that kind then I have) answered him that I would
do it; and so I will, he offering me good security.   And so it
being left for me to consider the manner of doing it, we parted –
taking coach, as I said before, at the Temple; I to Charing-cross
and there went into Unthankes to have my shoes wiped, dirty
with walking; and so to White-hall, where I visited the vice-
chamberlain, who tells me, and so I find by others, that the
business of putting out of some of the Privy-council[d] is over, the
King being at last advised to forbear it;[4] for whereas he did
design it to make room for some of the House of Commons that
are against him, thereby to gratify them, it is believed that it will
but so much the more fret the rest that are not provided for,
and raise a new stock of enemies by them that are displaced.
And so all they think is over.   And it goes for a pretty saying

a repl. 'sitting'   *b* repl. same symbol
    c possibly 'go'   *d* repl. 'great'

---

1. On 18 December 1667 it had
been remitted to a select committee
instead of to a Committee of the
Whole: *LJ*, xii. 175–6.

2. A mistake; the Committee

began work later in the month:
below, p. 34.

3. See above, viii. 586 & n. 1.

4. Cf. above, viii. 596 & n. 1.

of my Lord Anglesy's up and down the Court, that he should lately say to one of them that are the great promoters of this putting him and others out of the Council – "Well," says he, "and what are we to look for when we are outed; will all things be set right in the nation?" The other said that he did believe that many things would be mended: "but," says my Lord, "will you and the rest of you be contented to be hanged, if you do not redeem all our misfortunes and set all right, if the power be put into your hands?" The other answered No, he would not undertake that. "Why then," says my Lord, "I, and the rest of us that you are labouring to put out, will be contented to be hanged if we do not recover all that is passed, if the King will put the power into our hands and adhere wholly to our advice" – which saying,*a* as it was severe,*b* so generally people have so little opinion of the people that are now likely to be uppermost, that they do mightily commend my Lord Anglesy for this saying.

From the Vicechamberlain, up and down the House till Chapel done, and then did speak with several that I had a mind to; and so, intending to go home, my Lady Carteret saw and called me out of her window, and so would have me home with her to Lincoln's Inne-fields to dinner; and there we met with my Lord Brereton and several other strangers, to dine there; and I find him a very sober and serious, able man, and was in discourse too hard for the Bishop of Chester,[1] who dined there; and who, above all books lately wrote, commending the matter and style of a late book called *The Causes of the Decay of Piety*,[2]

a repl. 'true'   *b* repl. 'so'

---

1. George Hall was Bishop of Chester, 1662–68. Brereton was chairman of the Brooke House Committee. For his roughness in argument, see Bryant, ii. 21+.

2. *The causes of the decay of Christian piety . . . written by the author of The whole duty of man* was published anonymously in 1667; another edition appeared in 1668 and many others later. *The whole duty of man* (1658), also published anonymously, was one of the most popular devotional books of its time. They were possibly, though not certainly, by the same author, usually identified as Dr Richard Allestree, the Oxford theologian. They were published (with other works from the same pen) as *The works of the learned and pious author of The whole duty of man* at Oxford in 1684. PL 1086 (*Causes*, 1694 ed.); PL 1083 (*Whole duty*, 1702 ed.). See P. Elmen in *The Library* (ser. 5), 6/19+.

I do resolve at his great commendation to buy it. Here dined also Sir Ph. Howard, a Barkeshire Howard,[1] whom I did once hear swear publicly and loud in the Matted Gallery, that he had not been at a wench in so long time. He did take occasion to tell me at the table that I have got great ground in the Parliament by my ready answers to all that was asked me there about the business of Chatham,[2] and they would never let me be out of imployment – of which I made little,[a] but was glad to hear him, as well as others, say it. And he did say also, relating to Comissioner Pett, that he did not think that he was guilty of anything like a fault that he was either able or concerned to amend, but only the not carrying up of the ships higher[b] (he meant – but he said three or four times "lower" down to Rochester bridge; which is a strange piece of ignorance in a Member of Parliament, at such a time as this and after so many examinations in the House of this business); and did boldly declare that he did think the fault to lie in my Lord Middleton, who had the power of the place to secure the boats that were made ready by Pett and to do anything that he thought fit – and was much, though not altogether, in the right, for Spragg, that commanded the River, ought rather to be charged with the want of the boats and the misimploying of them. After dinner my Lord Brereton very gentilely went to the Organ and played a verse very handsomely. Thence after dinner away with Sir G. Carteret to White-hall (setting down my Lord Brereton at my Lord Bruncker's) and there up and down the House and on the Queenes side to see the ladies; and there saw the Duchesse of York, whom few pay the respect they used, I think, to her;[3] but she bears all out with a very great deal of greatness, that is the truth of it. And so it growing night, I away home by coach, and there set my wife to read; and then comes Pelling, and he and I to sing a little; and then sup and so to bed.

a repl. same symbol   *b* l.h. repl. s.h.

---

1. I.e. a son of the Earl of Berkshire. He was M.P. for Carlisle and Colonel of Albemarle's troop of the Life Guard.

2. See above, viii. 494–6.

3. Her father Clarendon had been dismissed in the previous autumn.

6.*ᵃ*   Up, leaving my wife to get her ready and the maids to get a supper ready against night for our company; and I by coach to

《*Twelfe day*》   White-hall and there up and down the House; and among others, met with Mr. Pierce, by whom I find (as I was afeared from the folly of my wife) that he understood that he and his wife was to dine at my house today, whereas it was to sup; and therefore I having done my business at Court, did go home to dinner, and there find Mr. Harris[1] by the like mistake come to dine with me.   However, we did get a pretty dinner ready for him; and there he and I to discourse of many things, and I do find him a very excellent person, such as in my whole [life] I do not know another better qualified for converse, whether in things of his own trade or of other kinds, a man of great understanding and observation, and very agreeable in the manner of his discourse, and civil as far as is possible. I was mightily pleased with his company; and after dinner did take coach with him and my wife and girl to go to a play and to carry him thither to his own house.   But I light*ᵇ* by the way to return home, thinking to have spoke with Mrs. Bagwell, who I did see today in our entry, come from Harwich, whom I have not seen these twelve months I think and more, and voudrais haver hazer algo with her, sed she was gone; and so I took coach, and away to my wife at the Duke*ᶜ* of York's House in the pit; and so left her, and to Mrs. Pierce and took her and her cousin Corbet, Knipp, and little James, and brought them to the Duke's House; and the House being full, was forced to carry them to a box, which did cost me 20*s* besides oranges; which troubled me – though their company did please me.   Thence, after the play, stayed till Harris was undressed (there being Acted *The Tempest*) and so he withal, all by coaches home, where we find my house with good fires and candles ready, and our office the like, and the two Mercers, and Betty Turner, Pendleton, and W. Batelier; and so with much pleasure we into the house and there fell to dancing, having extraordinary music, two violins and a bass viallin and Theorbo (four hands), the Duke of Buckingham's

a repl. '5'   *b* repl. 'little'   *c* repl. 'play'

---

1. Henry Harris, a leading actor at the Duke of York's Theatre.   (A).

Musique, the best in Towne, sent me by Greeting;[1] and there we set in*a* to dancing. By and by to my house to a very good supper, and mighty merry and good music playing; and after supper to dancing and singing till about 12*b* at night; and then we had a good sack-posset for them and an excellent Cake,[2] cost me near 20*s.* of our Jane's making,*c* which was cut into twenty pieces, there being by this time so many of our company by the coming in of young Goodyer and some others of our neigh-bours, young men that could dance, hearing of our dancing; and anon comes in Mrs. Turner the mother and brings with her Mrs. Hollworthy,[3] which pleased me mightily; and so to dancing again*d* and singing with extraordinary great pleasure, till about 2 in the morning; and then broke up, and Mrs. Pierce and her family and Harris and Knip by coach home, as late as it was; and they gone, I took Mrs. Turner and Hollworthy home to my house and there gave them*e* wine and sweetmeats; but I find Mrs. Hollworthy but a mean woman, I think, for understanding; only, a little conceited and proud and talking, but nothing extraordinary in person or discourse or understanding. How-ever, I was mightily pleased*f* with her being there, I having long longed for to know her; and they being gone, I paid the fiddler 3*l* among the four, and so away to bed, weary and mightily pleased; and have the happiness to reflect upon it as I do some-times on other things, as going to a play or the like, to be the greatest real comforts that I am to expect in the world, and that it is that that we do really labour in the hopes of; and so I do really enjoy myself, and understand that if I do not do it now, I shall not hereafter, it may be, be able to pay for it or have health to take pleasure in it, and so fool myself with vain expecta-tion of pleasure and go without it.

7. Up, weary, about 9 a-clock; and then out by coach to

a repl. 'into'   *b* repl. 'one in the morning'   *c* preceded by smudge
     d MS. 'a again'   *e* repl. 'her'   *f* MS. 'pleased and'

1. Pepy's flageolet master. (E).
2. A Twelfth-Night cake: cf.
above, i. 10, n. 3.

3. A widow and 'a woman of state and wit and spirit': above, viii. 141.

White-hall to attend the Lords of the Treasury about Tanger with Sir St. Fox;[1] and having done with them, I away back again home by coach, time enough to despatch some business; and after dinner, with Sir W. Penn's coach (he being gone before with Sir D Gawden) to White-hall to wait on the Duke of York; but I finding him not there, nor the Duke of York within, I away by coach to the Nursery,[2] where I never was yet, and there to meet my wife and Mercer and Willet as they promised; but the House did not act today and so I was at a loss for them, and therefore to the other two playhouses into the pits to gaze up and down to look for them, and there did by this means for nothing see an Act in *The Schoole of Compliments* at the Duke of York's House and *Henery the 4th* at the King's House;[3] but not finding them, nor liking either of the plays, I took my coach again and home, and there to my office to do business; and by and by they came home, and had been at the King's House and saw me, but I could [not] see them; and there I walked with them in the garden a while, and to sing with Mercer there a little; and so home with her and taught her a little of my *It is decreed*,[4] which I have a mind to have her learn to sing, and she will do it well; and so after supper she went away, and we to bed and there made amends by sleep for what I wanted last night.

8. Up; and it being dirty, I by coach (which I was forced to go to the Change for) to White-hall, and there did deliver the Duke of York a Memoriall for the Council about the case of

---

1. Sir Stephen Fox was Paymaster-General to the army. He and Pepys were called in about the assignments on the country excise for the garrisons. 'Mr. Pepys will return answer as soon as may be': *CTB*, ii. 218.

2. A minor theatre opened in 1667 at Hatton Garden for the training of the young actors of the two patent theatres. Nominally licensed to Capt. Edward Bedford, it was controlled by Thomas Killigrew and

Davenant, managers of the patent theatres. In the prologue to John Dover's *The Roman Generalls* (licensed for publication in 1667) it is referred to as 'both the Houses *Nursery*'. (A).

3. A comedy by Shirley, and Pt I of Shakespeare's play respectively: see above, viii. 375, n. 2; i. 325, n. 1. Theatregoers could see one act free if they undertook to leave at the end of it or to pay if they stayed. (A).

4. See above, vii. 91, n. 4. (E).

Tanger's want of money,[1] and I was called in and there my paper was read; I did not think fit to say much, but left them to make what use they pleased of my paper; and so went out and waited without all the morning, and at noon hear[a] that there is something ordered towards our help; and so I away by coach home, taking up Mr. Prin[2] at the Court-gate (it raining) and setting him down at the Temple. And by the way did ask him about the manner of holding of Parliaments, and whether the number of Knights and Burges's were alway the same; and he says that the latter were not, but that for aught he can find, they were sent up at the discretion, at first, of the Sheriffes, to whom the writs are sent to send up generally the[b] Burges's and Cittizens of their county; and he doth find that heretofore, that Parliament-men being paid by the country,* several Burroughs have complained of the Sheriffes putting them to the charge of sending up Burges's;[3] which is a very extraordinary thing to me that knew not this but thought that the number had been known, and always the same.

Thence home[c] to the[d] office, and so with my Lord Brouncker and his mistress, Williams, to Captain Cocke's to dinner, where was Temple and Mr. Porter – and a very good dinner, and merry. Thence with Lord Brouncker to White-hall to Commissioners of Treasury, at their sending for us to discourse about the paying of tickets;[4] and so away, and I by coach to the Change and

a repl. 'do'   *b* repl. 'all'
c repl. same symbol badly formed   *d* repl. 'dinner'

1. 'Upon a Memoriall of Mr. Pepys . . . concerning his Maties Garrison of Tangier (this day read at the Board) It was Ordered . . . That the seventy thousand pounds per Annum formerly Established . . . be continued till the 25th. of March': PRO, PC 2/60, p. 112. The memorandum has not been traced.

2. William Prynne, lawyer and antiquarian; M.P. for Bath; author of what was then the principal book on the history of parliamentary elections, the *Brief register of parliamentary writs* (1659–64).

3. This had been a common complaint in the 13th and early 14th centuries. See Prynne's *Fourth part of a brief register . . .* (1664), p. 7 etc. Cf. M. McKisack, *Parl. representation of Engl. boroughs during the Middle Ages*, esp. c. 1.

4. The Navy Board was asked at this meeting to draw up rules for the issue of pay-tickets and to submit them to the Treasury: *CTB*, ii. 220. The government had been especially troubled about this matter since the enquiries of the Commons' Committee on Miscarriages into the conduct of the war: cf. above, viii. 485, n. 1; 538, n. 1; 545–6 & n.

there took up my wife and Mercer and the girl by agreement; and so home, and there with Mercer to teach her more of *It is decreed*, and to sing other songs and talk all the evening; and so after supper, I to even my Journall since Saturday last, and so to bed.

Yesterday, Mr. Gibson, upon his discerning by my discourse to him that I had a willingness, or rather do*a* desire to have him stay with me then go, as he designed, on*b* Sir W. Warren's account to sea, he resolved to let go that design and wait his fortune with me, though I laboured to make him understand the uncertainty of my condition or service; but however, he will hazard it, which I take mighty kindly of him, though troubled lest he may come to be a loser by it; but it will not be for want of my telling him what he was to think on and expect. However, I am well pleased with it with regard to myself, who find him mighty understanding and acquainted with all things in the Navy, that I should, if I continue in the Navy, make great use of him.[1]

9.   Up and to the office, having first been visited by my Cosen Anth. Joyce about the 350*l* which he desires me to lend him; and which I have a mind fain to do, but would have it in my power to call it out again in a little time – and so do take a little further time to consider it.   So to the office, where all the morning busy; and so home at noon to dinner with my people, where Mr. Hollier came and dined with me; and it is still mighty pleasant to hear him talk of Rome and the Pope, with what hearty hatred and zeal he talks against him.   After dinner to the office again, where busy till night, very busy; and among other things wrote to my father about lending Anth. Joyce the money he desires; and I*c* declare that I would do*d* it as part of Pall's

a	MS. 'to'	*b*	repl. 'with'
c	symbol blotted	*d*	MS. 'day

---

1. Richard Gibson (Pepys's clerk since 1667) had been a purser. He stayed in the service of the Navy, becoming Purser-General to the Straits fleet (1670–2), chief clerk to three successive Clerks of the Acts (1672–7), and Pepys's clerk at the Admiralty (1680–9). His hand-writing (perhaps significantly) was very like that of Pepys.

portion, and that Pall should have the use of the money till she be married; but I do propose to him to think of Mr. Cumberland rather then this Jackson that he is upon;[1] and I confess I have a mighty mind to have a relation to so able a man and honest, and so old an acquaintance, as Mr. Cumberland. I shall hear his answer by the next. At night home and to cards with my wife and girl, and to supper late; and so to bed.

10. Up, and with Sir Denis Gawden, who called* me to White-hall; and there to wait on the Duke of York with the rest of my brethren, which we did a little in the King's green room while the King was in Council; and in this room we found my Lord Bristoll walking alone; which wondering at, while the Council was sitting, I was answered that, as being a Catholique, he could not be of the Council; which I did not consider before. After, broke up and walked a turn or two with Lord Brouncker, talking about the times; and he tells me that he thinks, and so doth everybody else, that the great business of putting out some of the Council, to make room for some of the Parliament men to gratify and wheadle them, is over – thinking that it might do more hurt then good, and not obtain much upon the Parliament neither.[2] This morning there was a Persian in the country dress, with a Turban, waiting to kiss the King's hand in the Vane-room against he came out; it was a comely man as to features, and his dress methinks very comely.[3] Thence in Sir W. Penn's coach alone (he going with Sir D. Gawden) to my new bookseller, Martin's;[4] and there did meet with Fournier, the Frenchman that hath wrote of the Sea=Navigation,[5] and I could not but buy him; and also bespoke an excellent book which I met with there,

1. For the match with John Jackson, see above, viii. 539 & n. 1. Richard Cumberland (an old Magdalene friend) later became Bishop of Peterborough. Nothing came of this proposal about the portion.

2. See above, pp. 9–10.

3. Possibly 'Pietro Cisii', a Persian educated at Rome, who was in England this year and helped Evelyn

to compose his *History of the three . . . impostors* (1669): Evelyn, iii. 516, 522 & n.

4. John Martin of St Paul's Churchyard.

5. Père Georges Fournier, *Hydrographie* (Paris, 2nd ed., 1667; PL 2678); a compendious work on sea matters.

of China.[1]   The truth is, I have bought a great many books
lately, to a great value; but I think to ⟨buy⟩ no more till Christmas next, and these that I have will so fill my two presses, that
I must be forced to give away some to make room for them, it
being my design to have no more at any time for my proper
Library then to fill them.   Thence home and to the Exchange,
there to do a little business; where I find everybody concerned
whether we shall have out a fleet this next year or no, they
talking of a peace concluded between France and Spayne, so
that the King of France will have nothing to do with his Army
unless he comes to us.[2]   But I do not see in the world how we
shall be able to set out a fleet, for want of money to buy stores
and pay men, for neither of which we shall be any more trusted.
So home to dinner, and there with my wife and Deb to the
King's House to see *Aglaura*,[3] which hath been always mightily
cried up; and so I went with mighty expectation, but do find
nothing extraordinary in it at all, and but hardly good in any
degree.   So home, and thither comes to us W. Batelier and sat
with us all the evening, and to Cards and supper, passing the
evening pretty pleasantly; and so late at night parted, and so to
bed.   I find him mightily troubled at the Lords Comissioners
[of the] Treasury opposing him in the business he hath a patent
for, about the business of Impost on Wine; but I do see that the
Lords have reason for it, it being a matter wherein money might
be saved to his Majesty; and I am satisfied that they do let
nothing pass that may save money, and so God bless them.[4]   So
he being gone, we to bed.

   This day I received a letter from my father and another from
my Cosen Roger Pepys, who have had a view of Jackson's
evidences of his estate and do mightily like of the man and his

1. Probably Athanasius Kircher,
China monumentis . . . illustrata
(Amsterdam, 1667); a folio with
numerous engravings: PL 2683.
   2. Peace negotiations had begun,
but were not concluded until April.
See below, p. 176 & n. 3.
   3. By Sir John Suckling; originally
a tragedy and awkwardly trans-
formed into a tragicomedy: see
above, iii. 204, n. 5.   (A).

4. The Treasury was reducing the
number of privileged persons (diplomats, officeholders and noblemen)
who were allowed annually a quota
of wine free of customs-duty: *CTB*,
ii. 218, 225, 247.   Will Batelier was
a wine merchant who had in 1667
succeeded his father as clerk and paymaster of the bills of impost on wines.

condition and estate, and do advise me to accept of the match for my sister and to finish it as soon as I can; and he doth it so as I confess I am contented to have it done, and so give her her portion; and so I shall be eased of one care how to provide for her. And do in many respects think that it may be a match proper enough to have her married there,[1] and to one that may look after my concernments if my father should die and I continue where I am. And there[fore] I am well pleased with it. And so to bed.

11. Lay some time talking with my wife in bed[a] about Pall's business, and she doth conclude to have her married here[b] and to be merry at it; and to have W. Hewer and Batelier, and Mercer and Willet bridemen and bridemaids, and to be very merry; and so I am glad of it and do resolve to let it be done as soon as I can. So up and to the office, where all the morning busy; and thence home to dinner, and from dinner with Mercer (who dined with us) and wife and Deb to the King's House, there to see *The Wildgoose chase*,[2] which I never saw but have long longed to see, it being a famous play; but as it was yesterday, I do find that where I expect most I find least satisfaction, for in this play I met with nothing extraordinary at all, but very dull inventions and designs. Knipp came and sat by us, and her talk pleased me a little, she telling me how Mis Davis[3] is for certain going away from the Duke's House, the King being in love with her; and a house is taken for her and furnishing and she hath a ring given her already, worth 600*l*. That the King did send several times for Nelly, and she was with him, but what he did she knows not; this was a good while ago, and she says that the King first spoiled Mrs. Weaver[4] – which is very mean

a MS. 'dead'   *b* repl. same symbol

---

1. In Huntingdonshire.
2. A comedy by John Fletcher, acted in 1621 and published in 1652. (A).
3. Mary Davis, an actress. According to Downes (pp. 23–4) it was her singing of 'My Lodging it is on the Cold Ground' in *The Rivals* which so charmed the King that 'it

rais'd her from her Bed on the Cold Ground, to a Bed Royal'. She bore him a daughter in 1673. (A).
4. Elizabeth Farley, later known as Mrs Weaver, had been the King's mistress briefly c. 1660. She played secondary roles at the Theatre Royal. (A).

methinks in a prince, and I am sorry for it – and can hope for no good to the State from having a prince so devoted to his pleasure. She told me also of a play shortly coming upon*ᵃ* the stage of Sir Ch. Sidly's, which she thinks will be called *The Wandring Ladys*, a comedy that she thinks will be most pleasant; and also another play, called *The Duke of Lerma*; besides *Catelin*,[1] which she thinks, for want of the clothes which the King promised them,[2] will not be acted for a good while. Thence home, and there to the office and did some business; and so with my wife for half an hour walking by moonlight and, it being cold frosty weather, walking in the garden; and then home to supper, and so by the fireside to have my head combed, as I do now often do, by Deb, whom I love should be fiddling about me; and so to bed.

12. *Lords day.* Up and to dress myself, and then called in to my wife's chamber, and there she without any occasion fell to discourse of my father's coming to live with us when my sister marries. This, she being afeared of declaring an absolute hatred to him since his falling out with her about Coleman's being with her,[3] she declares against his coming hither; which I not presently agreeing to, she declared if he came, she would not live with me but would shame me all over the City and Court; which I made slight of, and so we fell very foul; and I do find she doth keep very bad remembrances of my former unkindnesses to her, and doth mightily complain of her want of money and liberty; which I will rather hear and bear the complaint of then grant the contrary, and so we had very hot work a great while; but at last I did declare as I intend, that my father shall not come and that

a repl. 'out of Sir which'

1. The first of these plays was probably Sedley's comedy *The mulberry garden*, acted on 18 May 1668 and published in the same year. The others were Sir Robert Howard's tragedy *The great favourite, or The Duke of Lerma*, acted and published in 1668; and Ben Jonson's tragedy *Catiline*, q.v. above, v. 3 49, n. 4. (A).

2. See above, viii. 575. (A).

3. Coleman was an army officer ('as very a rogue for women as any in the world') who had met Mrs Pepys on a coach journey: above, viii. 588 & n. 1.

he doth not desire and intend it; and so we parted with pretty good quiet, and so away I; and being ready, went to church, where first I saw Alderman Backewell and his lady come to our church, they living in Mark-lane; and I could find my heart to invite her to sit*a* with us – she being a fine lady. I*b* came in while they were singing the 119 Psalm, while the Sexton was gathering to his box,[1] to which I did give 5s. And so after sermon home, my wife, Deb, and I all alone, and very kind, full of good discourse; and after dinner, I to my chamber, ordering my Tanger accounts to give to the Auditor in a day or two, which should have been long ago with him. At them to my great content all the afternoon till supper and after supper (with my wife, W. Hewer and Deb, pretty merry) till 12 at night, and then to bed.

13. Up, and Mr. Gibbs comes to me and I give him instructions about the writing fair my Tanger accounts against to-morrow. So I abroad with Sir W. Penn to White-hall, and there did with the rest attend the Duke of York, where nothing extraordinary; only I perceive there is nothing yet declared for the next year what fleet shall be abroad. Thence homeward by coach and stopped at Martins my bookseller, where*c* I saw the French book which I did think to have had for my wife to translate, called *L'escholle de Filles*;[2] but when*d* I came to look

a repl. ? 'sent' *b* repl. 'And so after sermon'
c repl. 'who' *d* repl. 'when'

---

1. This psalm (of 176 verses) was chosen so that the collection made for the sexton should not be skimped. Cf. above, ii. 6.

2. *L'escolle des filles, ou La philosophie des dames, divisée en deux dialogues*; usually attributed to Michel Millot and Jean L'Ange. A conversation between an experienced woman and a virgin, with a simple plot added (first published Paris, 1655; other editions 1659, 1667 and 1668; several later editions and translations).

Millot was condemned and the book burnt in Paris in 1655; English translations were the subject of prosecutions in 1677, 1688 and 1744–5. See D. Foxon, *Libertine literature in Engl.*, *1660–1745*, pp. 5–6; cf. Horner in Wycherley's *The country wife* (I, i), written c. 1670–1: 'I have brought over [from France] not so much as a bawdy picture, no new postures, nor the second part of the *Ecole des Filles* . . .'.

into it, it is the most bawdy, lewd book that ever I saw, rather worse then *putana errante*[1] – so that I was ashamed of reading in it; and so away home, and there to the Change to discourse with Sir H. Cholmly and so home to dinner; and in the evening, having done some business, I with my wife and girl out, and left them at Unthankes while I to White-hall to the Treasury-chamber for an order for Tanger; and so back, took up my wife, and home, and there busy about my Tanger accounts against tomorrow, which I do get ready in good condition; and so with great content to bed.

14. At the office all the morning, and at noon home to dinner; and after dinner, with Mr. Clerke and Gibson to the Temple (my wife and girl going further by coach), and there at the Auditors[2] did begin the examining my Tanger account, and did make a great entry into it and with great satisfaction, and am glad I am so far eased. So appointing another day for further part of my accounts, I with Gibson to my bookseller Martin, and there did receive my book I expected of China, a most excellent book with rare Cutts;[3] and there fell into discourse with him about the burning of Pauls when the City was burned, his house being in the churchyard; and he tells me that it took fire first upon the end of a board that, among others, was laid upon the roof instead of lead, the lead being broke off – and thence down, down lower and lower; but that the burning of the goods under St. Fayths arose from the goods taking fire in the churchyard, and so got*a* into St. Faith's church; and that they first took fire from the Drapers side, by*b* some timber of

a repl. 'came'   *b* repl. full stop

---

1. *La puttana errante*; a prose dialogue, on which *L'escolle des filles* was based, famous largely because of the plates published with it; possibly by Niccolo Franco; wrongly attributed to Aretino, first appearing in his *Ragionamenti* in 1584. There is also a poem of the same title, from which the dialogue derives, which has been shown to be by Lorenzo Veniero, a pupil of Aretino. Neither is in the PL. See Foxon, op. cit.; L.-J. Hubaud, *Dissertation littéraire . . . sur deux petits poèmes.*

2. John Wood's: see below, p. 42. He was an Auditor of the Exchequer.

3. See above, p. 18, n. 1.

the houses that were burned falling into the church. He says
that one ware-house of books was saved under Paul's; and he
says that there was several dogs found burned among the goods
in the churchyard, and but one man; which was an old man
that said he would go and save a blanket which he had in the
church; and being a weak old man, the fire overcame him, and
was burned. He says that most of the booksellers do design to
fall a-building again the next year; but he says that the Bishop of
London doth*a* use them most basely, worse then any other land-
lords, and say he*b* will be paid to this day the rent, or else he will
not come to treat with them for the time to come; and will not,
on that condition neither, promise them anything how he will
use them. And the Parliament sitting, he claims his privilege,
and will not be cited before the Lord Chief Justice as others are,
there to be forced to a fair dealing.[1]

Thence by coach to Mrs. Pierce's, where my wife and Deb is;
and there they fall to discourse of last night's work at Court,
where the ladies and Duke of Monmouth and others acted *The
Indian Emperour*[2] – wherein they told me these things most
remarkable: that not any woman but*c* Duchesse of Monmouth
and Mrs. Cornwallis did anything like, but like fools and sticks;
but that these two did do most extraordinary well – that not any
man did anything well but Captain Obryan, who spoke and did

a   repl. 'or the Deane of Pauls, I know not which'
b   repl. 'they'   c   MS. 'of'

1. The Court of Claims set up
under Chief Justice Kelynge to deal
with the complicated interests in real
property destroyed by the Fire,
usually remitted arrears of rent
accruing after 1 September 1666,
provided the tenant paid for rebuilding. Only where the rent was
a ground rent or little more, and a
substantial fine had been paid many
years before, was rent often exacted as
suggested here. Cf. above, vii. 357 &
n. 2. The Bishop of London,
Humphrey Henchman, was said to
have been harsh in dealing with the
booksellers and mercers of Paternoster
Row, and to have claimed his parliamentary privilege as a peer to protect
himself against citation to the Court:
Bell, *Fire*, pp. 246–7.

2. The heroic tragedy by Dryden
(see above, viii. 14, n. 2), now acted
in the Great Hall, Whitehall, which
had been converted into a theatre;
see above, vi. 85. Amateur performances of plays at Court were rare;
see E. Boswell, *Restoration court stage*,
pp. 128–9. (A).

well; but above all things, did dance most incomparably[1] – that she did sit near the players of the Dukes House; among the rest, Mis Davis, who is the most impertinent slut she says in the world, and the more now the King doth show her countenance and is reckoned his mistress, even to the scorn of the whole world, the King gazing on her, and my Lady Castlemayne being melancholy and out of humour all the play, not smiling once. The King, it seems, hath given her a ring of 700*l*, which she shows to everybody, and owns that the King did give it her. And he hath furnished a house for her in Suffolke-street most richly for her, which is a most infinite shame. It seems she is a bastard of Collonell Howard, my Lord Barkeshire, and that he doth pimp to her for the King, and hath got her for him.[2] But Pierce says that she is a most homely jade as ever she saw, though she dances beyond anything in the world. She tells me that the Duchesse of Richmond doth not yet come to the Court, nor hath not seen the King, nor will not; nor doth he own his desire of seeing her, but hath used means to get her to Court, but they do not take.

Thence home, and there I to my chamber, having a great many books brought me home from my bookbinder's; and so I to the new setting of my books against the next year, which costs me more trouble then I expected; and at it till 2 a-clock in the morning and then to bed, the business not being yet done to my mind. This evening came Mr. Mills and his wife to see and sit and talk with us, which they did till 9 a-clock at night, and then parted, and I to my books.[a]

15. Up, and to the office, where all the morning. At noon home to dinner and then to the office again, where we met about

a last sentence added in smaller hand

---

1. This was an accomplishment which Pepys later held against him, for it was 'his quallity & Guift of Daunceing' that brought him (through the favour of Monmouth and his duchess) naval promotion: NWB, p. 221.

2. She was also said to have been the daughter of a Wiltshire black-smith. The truth is not known. Burnet (i. 483-4) alleges that the pimp was Buckingham, who wanted to get rid of Lady Castlemaine's influence.

some business of D. Gawden's till candle-light; and then, as late as it was, I down to Redriffe and*ª* so walked by moonlight to Deptford, where I have not been a great while; and my business I did there was only to walk up and down about la casa of Bagwell,*ᵇ* but could not see her; it being my intent to have spent a little time con her, she being newly come from her husband.*ᵇ* But I did lose my labour, and so walked back again, but with pleasure by the walk; and I had the sport to see two boys swear and stamp and fret for not being able to get their horse over a stile and ditch, one of them swearing and cursing most bitterly; and I would fain, in revenge, have persuaded him to have drove his horse through the ditch, by which I believe he would have stuck*ᶜ* there. But the horse would not be drove, and so they were*ᵈ* forced to go back again; and so I walked away homeward, and there reading all the evening; and so to bed. This after-noon, my Lord Anglesy tells us that it is voted in Council to have a fleet of 50 ships out[1] – but it is only a disguise for the Parliament to get some money by; but it will not take I believe, and if it did, I do not think it will be such as he will get any of, nor such as will enable us to set out such a fleet.[2]

16. Up, after talking with my wife with pleasure about her learning on the Flag[el]ette a month or two again this winter,*ᵉ*[3] and all the rest of the year her painting, which I do love. And so to the office, where sat all the morning. And here Lord Anglesy tells us again that a fleet is to be set out; and that it is generally, he hears, said that it is but a Spanish Rhodomontado; and that he saying so just now to the Duke of Albemarle, who came to town last night (after the thing was ordered), he told*ᶠ*

---

a repl. 'by w'-   *b–b* garbled s.h.: see above, viii. 244, note *a*
     c MS. 'stick'   *d* repl. same symbol badly formed
     e repl. 'year'   *f* repl. 's'-

---

1. PRO, PC 2/60, p. 124; an order to the Admiral to have a fleet of 50 sail ready by the spring. Fifty ships of the 4th rate and upwards were to be repaired.

2. A supply of £300,000 was in fact voted on 26 February (below, pp. 92–3 & n.); for its expenditure, see *CSPD 1667–8*, p. 424.

3. Her lessons with Greeting were not resumed until 13 August of this year. (E).

him a story of two seamen: one wished all the guns of the ship were his, and that they were Silver; "Nay," says the other, "you are [a] fool, for if you can have it for wishing, why do you not wish them gold?" "So," says he, "if a Rodomontado will do any good, why do you not say 100 ships?" And*a* it is true; for the Duch and French are said to make such preparations as 50 sail will do no good.

At noon home to dinner with my gang of clerks, in whose society I am mightily pleased, and mightily with Mr. Gibsons talking; he telling me so many good stories relating to the Warr and practices of commanders, which I will find a time to recollect; and he will be an admirable help to my writing a history of the Navy, if ever I do.[1]

So to the office, where busy all the afternoon and evening, and then home. My work this night with my clerks till midnight at the office was to examine my list of ships I am making for myself, and their dimensions,[2] and to see how it agrees or differs from other lists; and I do find so great a difference between them all, that I am at a loss which to take; and therefore think mine to be as much depended upon as any I can make out of them all. So little care there hath been to this day to know or keep any history of the Navy.

17. Up, and by coach to White-hall to attend the Council there; and here I met, first by Mr. Castle the shipwright whom I met there, and then from the whole House, all the discourse of the Duell yesterday between the Duke of Buckingham, Holmes, and one Jenkins on one side, and my Lord of Shrewsbury, Sir Jo. Talbot, and one Bernard Howard, on the other side;

a repl. 'at'

---

1. For Pepys's projected history, see above, v. 178 & n. 1. Gibson had been a purser, 1655–65. He made a collection of naval material, covering 1650–1702; now BM, Add. 11602.

2. Untraced; possibly conflated with later lists: cf. the greatest of

them (1688) printed in *Cat.*, i. 253+. There is a small list (18 July 1666), beautifully neat, partly in Pepys's hand, in Rawl. A 174, ff. 219+. For the difficulties of representing dimensions (especially tonnage), see above, v. 357–8 & n.

and all about my Lady Shrewsbury, who is a whore and is at this time, and hath for a great while been, a whore to the Duke of Buckingham; and so her husband challenged him, and they met yesterday in a close near Barne Elmes and there fought; and my Lord Shrewsbury is run through the body from the right breast through the shoulder, and Sir Jo. Talbot all along up one of his arms, and Jenkins killed upon the place, and the rest all in a little measure wounded.[1] This will make the world think*a* that the King hath good councillors about him, when the Duke of Buckingham, the greatest man about him, is a fellow of no*b* more sobriety then to fight about a whore. And this may prove a very bad accident to the Duke of Buckingham, but that my Lady Castlemaine doth rule all at this time as much as ever she did, and she will, it is believed, keep all matters well with the Duke of Buckingham; though this is a time that the King will be very backward, I suppose, to appear in such a business. And it is pretty to hear how that the King had some notice of this challenge a week or two ago, and did give it to my Lord Generall[2] to confine the Duke, or take security that he should not do any such thing as fight; and the Generall trusted to the King that he, sending for him, would do it, and the King trusted to the Generall; and so between both, as everything else of the greatest moment doth, doth fall between two stools. The whole House full of nothing but the talk of this business; and it is said that my Lord Shrewsbury's case is to be feared, that he may die too, and that may make it much the worse for the Duke of Buckingham;

---

a repl. 'th'-   *b* repl. symbol rendered illegible

---

1. This formidable duel (fought at Barn Elms) was perhaps the most notorious of the period in England. For an account, see Gramont, pp. 300–2. The Countess was Buckingham's mistress from 1666 to 1674. Shrewsbury died two months later, perhaps as a result of his wounds. With Buckingham he had received the royal pardon. The King salved his conscience by appointing a committee of Council to suppress duelling (HMC, *Le Fleming*, p. 55). The surgeons later certified that Shrewsbury's death was caused by a disease of the heart or liver. Buckingham's seconds were Sir Robert Holmes, the naval commander, and Capt. William Jenkins, an officer in the Horse Guards.

2. Albemarle.

and I shall not be much sorry for it, that we may have some soberer man come in his room to assist in the government. Here*a* I waited till the Council rose and talked the while with Creed, who tells me of Mr. Harry Howards giving the Royall Society a piece of ground next to his house to build a College on, which is a most generous Act.[1]   And he tells me he is a very fine person, and understands and speaks well; and no rigid papist neither, but one that would not have a protestant servant leave his religion, which he was going to do, thinking to recommend himself to his maister by it – saying that he had rather have an honest protestant then a knavish catholique.   I was not called into the Council; and therefore home, first informing myself that my Lord Hinchingbrook ⟨hath⟩ been*b* married this week to my Lord Burlington's daughter; so that that great business is over,[2] and I mighty glad of it – though I am not satisfied that I have not a favour sent me – as I see Atturny Mountagu and the vice-chamberlain have.   But I am mighty glad that the thing is done. So home, and there alone with my wife and Deb to dinner; and after dinner comes Betty Turner, and I carried them to the New Exchange; and thence I to White-hall and did a little business at the Treasury, and so called them there and so home and to Cards and supper; and her mother came and sat at Cards with us till past 12 at night, and then broke up and to bed, after entering my journall, which made it one before I went to bed.

a repl. 'Thence'   *b* repl. 'is'

---

1. See below, p. 146 & nn. Henry Howard was the second son of the Earl of Arundel, and became 6th Duke of Norfolk in 1677. He received the thanks of the Society on 25 January: Birch, ii. 242. The ground consisted of 400 sq. ft in Arundel Gardens. Difficulties arose about the conveyance of the property, and the scheme was postponed in the autumn, only to be later abandoned. C. R. Weld, *Hist. Roy. Soc.* (1848), i.

211; Birch ii. 242, 299–300, 313. Wren, Hooke and Howard himself had prepared designs for the new college: *Pub. Wren Soc.*, 13/48–9; Weld, i. 212–13. The society did not acquire a building of its own until 1710, when it purchased two houses in Crane Court, Strand: Weld, i. 389–91.

2. The wedding had taken place (according to a newsletter) on the 13th: *Bulstrode Papers*, i. 19.

18. At the office all the morning, busy sitting. At noon home to dinner, where Betty Turner dined with us; and after dinner carried my wife, her and Deb, to the Change, where they bought some things while I bought *The Mayden Queene*, a play newly printed which I like at the King's House so well, of Mr. Dryden's; which he himself in his preface seems to brag of, and endeed is a good play.[1] So home again, and I late at the office and did much business; and then home to supper and to bed.

19. *Lords day.* My wife the last night very ill of those, and waked me early and her people, and I up and to church, where a dull sermon of our lecturer;[2] and so home to dinner in my wife's chamber, which she is a little better. Then after dinner with Captain Perryman[3] down to Redriffe; and so walked to Deptford, where I sent for Mr. Shish out of the church to advise about my vessel the *Maybolt*; and I do resolve to sell presently for anything rather then keep her longer – having already lost 100*l* in her value, which I was once offered and refused, and the ship left without anybody to look to her, which vexes me.[4] Thence ⟨Perryman⟩*a* and I back again, talking of the great miscarriages in the Navy; and among the principal, that of having gentlemen-commanders.[5] I shall hereafter make use of his and others' help to reckon up and put down in writing what is fit to be mended in the Navy, after all our sad experiences therein.[6] So home, and there sat with my wife all the evening; and Mr. Pelling a while talking with us, who tells me that my Lord Shrewsbury is likely to do well, after his great wound in the late Duell. He

a repl. 'he'

---

1. It was a heroic drama, now first published; not in the PL. Cf. above, viii. 91, n. 2. In his preface Dryden said that he rated it 'above the rest of my follies of this kind'. (A).

2. Unidentified.

3. John Perriman, the Navy Board's river agent.

4. For the *Maybolt*, see above,

viii. 465, n. 1. The diary has no mention of the sale nor has any trace of it been found in Pepys's papers.

5. Cf. above, vii. 11, n. 1.

6. In the following August Pepys produced a scheme for the reform of the Navy Office: see below, p. 289 & n. 1.

gone, came W. Hewer and supped with me; and so to talk of
things, and he tells me that Mr. Jessop is made Secretary to the
Commissioners of Parliament for Accounts; and I am glad, and
it is pretty to see that all the Cavalier party were not able to find
the Parliament nine Commissioners, or one Secretary, fit for the
business.[1]   So he gone, I to read a little in my chamber, and so
to bed.

20.   Up, and all the morning at the office very busy; and at
noon by coach to Westminster to the Chequer about a warrant
for Tanger money.   In my way, both coming and going, I did
stop at Drumbleby's the pipe-maker, there to advise about the
making of a flagelette to go low and saft;[2] and he doth show me a
way which doth do, and also a fashion of having two pipes of the
same note fastened together, so as I can play of one and then echo
it upon the other; which is mighty pretty.[3]   So to my Lord
Crew's to dinner, where we hear all the good news of our making
a league now with Holland against the French power coming
over them or us,[4] which is the first good act that hath been done a
great while, and*a* done secretly and with great seeming wisdom;
and is certainly good for us at this time, while we are in no
condition to resist the French if he should come over hither;
and then a little time*b* of peace will give us time to lay up something; which these Commissioners of the Treasury are doing,
and the world doth begin to see that they will do the King's work

a repl. 'nor'   *b* repl. 'peace'

---

1. William Jessop had been a
distinguished public servant during
the Civil War and Interregnum,
serving as Secretary to the Admiralty
Commissioners 1645–53; Clerk to
the Council of State 1654–9 and 1660,
and Assistant-Clerk to the Con-
vention Parliament. He was described as a 'rigid' enemy to monarchy
on the eve of the Restoration:
CSPClar., iv. 675. For the appointment of Commonwealthsmen to the

commission of accounts, see above,
viii. 577 & n. 1.
2. A flageolet bought for £1 at
about this time appears in Pepys's
accounts in Rawl. A 185, f. 23*r*.
3. The pipes being presumably of
different timbre and volume.   (E).
4. Signed on the 13th/23rd and
within three days broadened into the
Triple Alliance between Britain,
Holland and Sweden.

for him if he will let them. Here dined Mr. Case the Minister, who, Lord, doth talk just as I remember he used to preach;[1] and did tell a pretty story of a religious lady, the Queen of Navarre;[2] and my Lord also a good story of Mr. Newman, the minister in New England who wrote the Concordance, of his foretelling his death and preaching his funeral sermon, and did at last bid the Angells do their office, and died.[3]

It seems there is great presumption that there will be a Toleration granted; so that the presbyters do hold up their heads, but they will hardly trust the King or the Parliament where to yield to them – though most of the sober party be for some kind of allowance to be given them.[4] Thence and home, and then to the Change in the evening; and there Mr. Cade told me how my Lord Gerard*a* is likely to meet with trouble the next

a repl. 'Grer'-

---

1. Thomas Case was a leading London Presbyterian. Pepys had probably heard too much of him in the 1650s; there is no sermon of his recorded in the diary.

2. Marguerite de Valois (d. 1549), sister of Francis I of France, and Queen of Navarre, patroness of the French reformers.

3. Samuel Newman, author of the *Large and complete concordance to the Bible* (first published in London in 1643; PL 2535) had in 1663 died in Massachusetts, whither he had emigrated in 1637. The story of his death was well known at the time. It is told in a letter of Henry More to Lady Conway, 17 March 1666: 'Whyle he was well [he] did many moneths predict his own death, the very hour of it, and that day that he dyde, rose very well, and after some meditations and studious fitts in his study, and after some exhortations to his Family, and praying with them, when he had rose from his prayers,

and sett himself down in his chaire, he having said these words, Now good Angel, do thy office, he presently gave up the Ghost' (M. H. Nicolson, ed., *Conway Letters*, pp. 269–70).

4. Since the fall of Clarendon in the autumn of 1667, the government had encouraged discussion of a scheme of comprehension (for Presbyterians) and indulgence (for Independents and others). A bill had been drafted before Christmas; a second draft was now in preparation for the parliamentary session due to begin on 10 February. But the Commons proved hostile, and the bill was never passed. The number of Pepys's references to this subject shows both his interest in it and its importance. Details of the bill in BM, Add. 19526, f. 157v (and below, p. 51 & n. 4); accounts in N. Sykes, *From Sheldon to Secker*, ch. iii; G. F. Nuttall and O. Chadwick (eds), *From uniformity to unity, 1662–1962*, pp. 196+ (by R. Thomas).

sitting of Parliament, about   being set in the pillory; and
I am glad of it.¹   And it is mighty acceptable to the world to
hear that among other reductions, the King doth reduce his
Guards;² which doth please mightily.   So to my bookbinder's³
with my boy, and there did stay late to see two or three things
done that I had a mind to see done; among other, my Tanger
papers of accounts; and so home to supper and to bed.

21.   Up, and while at the office comes news from Kate Joyce
that if I would see her hus[band] alive, I must come presently;
so after the office was up, I*a* to him, and W. Hewer with me,
and find him in his sick bed (I never was at their house, this Inne,
before),⁴ very sensible in discourse and thankful for my kindnesses to him; but his breath rattled in his throate and they did
lay pigeons to his feet⁵ while I was in the house; and all despair of
him, and with good reason.   But the sorrow is that it seems on
Thursday last he went sober and quiet out of doors in the morning
to Islington, and behind one of the Inns, the White Lion, did
fling himself into a pond –*b* was spied by a poor woman and got
out by some people binding up Hay in a barn there, and set on his
head and got to life; and known by a woman coming that way,
and so his wife and friends* sent for.   He confessed his doing the
thing, being led by the Devil; and doth declare his reason to be
his trouble that he found in having forgot to serve God as he
ought since he came to this new imployment; and I believe
that, and the sense of his great loss by the fire, did bring him to it,

---

a MS. 'and'   *b* punctuation mark repl. 'was'

---

1. For this case, see above, viii. 581
& n. 1.   The missing name is that of
Carr.

2. The committee of council for
retrenchments set up on 29 July 1667
had reported on 3 January. The
King accepted their recommendations
and took steps to reduce the expense of his guards and garrisons to
c. £168,000 p.a. from Lady Day 1668.
Warrants to this effect were issued on

16 March: *CSPD 1667–8*, p. 291.
For a list of the new figures of
expenditure, see ib., p. 296.

3. Unidentified: possibly William
Richardson (above, viii. 237).

4. Anthony Joyce, once a tallow
chandler in Newgate, was now an
innkeeper in Clerkenwell. He had
moved there after the Fire.

5. Cf. above, iv. 339, n. 2.

and so everybody concludes. He stayed there all that night, and came home by coach next morning; and there grew sick, and worse and worse to this day. I stayed a while among the friends that were there; and they being now in fear that the goods and estate would be seized on, though he lived all this while, because of his endeavouring to drown himself,[1] my cousin did endeavour to remove what she could of plate out of the house, and desired me to take her*ᵃ* flagons; which I was glad of, and did take them away with me, in great fear all the way of being seized; though there was no reason for it, he not being dead; but yet so fearful I was. So home and there eat my dinner, and busy all the afternoon, and troubled at this business. In the evening, with Sir D Gawden to Guild hall to advise with the Towne Clerke about the practice of the City and nation in this case, and he thinks it cannot be found Selfe-murder; but if it be, it will fall, all the estate, to the King.[2] So we parted, and I to my cousin's again; where I no sooner came but news*ᵇ* was brought down from his chamber that he was departed. So at their entreaty I presently took coach and to White-hall, and there find W. Coventry and he carried me to the King, the Duke of York being with him, and there told my story which I had told him; and the King without more ado granted that if it was found [self-murder]*ᶜ* the estate should be to the widow and children. I presently to each Secretary's office and there left Caveats,[3] and so away back again to my cousin's – leaving a Chimny on fire at White-hall in the King's closet, but no danger. And so when I came thither, I found her all in sorrow, but she and the rest mightily pleased with my doing this for them; and endeed, it was a very great courtesy, for people are looking out for the

---

a MS. 'my'   *b* repl. 'he'   *c* no blank in MS.

---

1. Until 1870 the property of suicides was forfeit to the Crown.
2. In such a case the King would normally pass on the property to the Lord Almoner to be applied to 'charitable uses', which could mean the surviving members of the family. Joyce had left a widow and three children. His will, made this day, is in Whitear, p. 23.
3. Summary in *CSPD 1667–8*, p. 179 (Pepys to Williamson, 21 January). The effect would be to prevent creditors and others from distraining on the estate.

estate,[1] and the Coroner will be sent to and a jury called to examine his death.   This being well done, to my and their great joy, I home and there to my office; and so to supper and to bed.

22.   Up, mighty busy all the morning at the office.   At noon with Lord Brouncker to Sir D. Gawden's at the Victualling Office to dinner, where I have not dined since he was Sheriffe; he expected us, and a good dinner and much good company; and a fine house, and especially two rooms very fine, he hath built there.   His Lady a good lady; but my Lord led himself and me to a great absurdity in kissing[a] all the ladies but the finest of all the company, leaving her out I know not how; and I was loath to do it since he omitted it.   Here little Chaplin dined, who is like to be Sheriffe the next year; and a pretty humoured little man he is.[2]   I met here with Mr. Talents the younger of Magdalen College, chaplain here to the Sheriff; which I was glad to see, though not much acquainted with him.[3] This day came the first demand[b] from the Commissioners of Accounts to us, and it contains more then we shall ever be able to answer while we live,[4] and I do foresee we shall be put to much trouble and some shame; at least, some of us.   Thence stole away after dinner to my Cousin' Kate's, and there find the Crowner's jury sitting; but they could not end it, but put off the business to Shrove Tuesday next, and so do give way to the[c] burying of him, and that is all; but they all encline to find it a natural death – though there are mighty busy people to have it go otherwise, thinking to get his estate; but are mistaken.   Thence, after sitting with her and company a while, comforting her: though I can find she can, as all other women, cry and yet talk of

a repl. 'not'   b repl. 'mem'-   c repl. 'b'-

---

1. They were hopeful of getting a grant of it from the King.

2. Francis Chaplin (like Gauden, a provision merchant) was Sheriff in 1668–9 and Lord Mayor in 1677–8.

3. Philip Tallents had been senior to Pepys at Magdalene by three years. Both he and his elder brother Francis were briefly fellows of the college.

4. They wrote on the 21st asking for an account of naval expenses, stores, contracts, and the hiring of ships during the late war. The questions were referred to the various officers concerned. BM, Add. 9311, ff. 160+. For the Board's answers, see below, p. 42, n. 1, p. 442, n. 1.

other things all in a breath.[1]   So home, and there to cards with
my wife, Deb, and Betty Turner and Batelier; and after, supper
and late to sing; but Lord, how did I please myself to make
Betty Turner*a* sing, to see what a beast she is as to singing, not
knowing how to sing one note in tune; but*b* only for the experiment I would not for 40*s* hear her sing a tune – worse then my
wife a thousand times, so that it doth a little reconcile me to her.
So, late to bed.

23.   At the office all the morning and at noon find the Bishop
of Lincolne[2] come to dine with us; and after him comes Mr.
Brisban, and there mighty good company; but the Bishop a
very extraordinary good-natured man and one that is mightily
pleased, as well as I am, that I live so near Bugden, the seat of his
Bishopricke, where he is like to reside;[3] and endeed I*c* am glad of
it.   In discourse, we think ourselfs safe for this year by this league
with Holland, which pleases everybody, and they say vexes*d*
France; insomuch that De lestrade the French Imbassador in
Holland, when he heard it, told the States that he would have
them*e* not forget that his Maister is in the head of 100000 men,
and is but 28 years old – which was a great speech.[4]   The Bishop
tells me he thinks that the great business of Toleration will not,
notwithstanding this talk, be carried this Parliament;[5] nor for

---

a name in s.h.   *b* repl. ?'that'
c repl. 'of'   *d* repl. 'vexed'   *e* repl. 'not not'

---

1. Cf. Pepys's similar observation
(about Lady Batten), above, viii. 483.
2. Pepys's friend, William Fuller,
appointed to Lincoln in the previous
September.
3. Buckden, Hunts., the country
seat of the bishops, had been used
since 1660 as their main residence, the
episcopal palace in Lincoln having
been destroyed in the Civil War.
Fuller soon settled in a house in
Lincoln close. VCH, *Lincs.*, i. 69.
4. Louis had already announced to
the Dutch that he would shortly
attack Flanders; d'Estrades's two

despatches of 16/26 January make it
clear that he used strong words when
shown the Anglo-Dutch treaty by
de Witt: *Letters and negotiations of the
Comte d'Estrades* (1711), pp. 509–12.
Sir William Temple, English ambassador to the United Provinces,
reported to Arlington (14/24 January)
that d'Estrades remarked to him that
some of the terms of the treaty were
not 'very proper to be digested by a
king of twenty-nine years old, and
at the head of eighty thousand men':
Temple, *Works* (1814), i. 305.
5. See above, p. 31 & n. 4.

the King's taking away the Deanes and Chapters' lands to supply
his wants, they signifying little to him – if he had them for his
present service.[1]   He gone, I mightily pleased with his kindness,
I to the office, where busy till night; and then to Mrs. Turners,
where my wife and Deb and I and Batelier spent that night and
supped and played at Cards, and very*a* merry; and so I home to
bed.   She is either a very prodigal woman or richer then she
would be thought, by her buying of the best things and laying
out much money in new-fashioned pewter; and among other
things, a new-fashion case for a pair of Snuffers, which is very
pretty, but I could never have guessed what it was for had I not
seen the snuffers in it.

24.   Up before day to my Tanger accounts; and then out and
to a committee on Tanger, where little done but discourse about
reduction of the charge of the garrison; and thence to Westminster about orders at the Exchequer; and at the Swan I drank,
and there met with a pretty ingenious young Doctor of physic
by chance, and talked with him; and so home to dinner, and
after dinner carried my wife to the Temple; and thence, she to a
play and I to St. Andrewe's Church in Holburne at the Quest-
house, where the company meets to the burial of my cousin
Joyce;[2] and here I stayed with a very great rabble of 4 or 500
people of mean condition, and I stayed in the room with the
kindred till ready to go to church, where there is to be a sermon
of Dr. Stillingfleete and thence carry to Sepulchers;[3] but it being
late, and endeed not having a black cloak to lead her with or
fallow the Corps, I away, and saw endeed a very great press of
people fallow the corpse; I to the King's playhouse to fetch my
wife, and there saw the best part of *The Mayden Queene*,[4] which

a repl. 'so'

---

1. This was one of Buckingham's
hare-brained schemes: cf. Starkey's
newsletter, 18 January (BM, Add.
36916, f. 58r). An unsuccessful
motion to this effect was made in the
Commons on 7 March: Grey, i. 108.
See below, p. 347 & n. 3.

2. Presumably because the Quest
House of Joyce's own parish, St
Sepulchre's, had suffered in the Fire.
For Quest Houses, see above, v. 158,
n. 2. (R).

3. St Sepulchre's, Newgate St.

4. See above, p. 29, n. 1. (A).

the more I see the more I love, and think one of the best plays I ever saw; and is certainly the best acted of anything ever that House did, and perticularly, Becke Marshall[1] to admiration. Found my wife and Deb, and saw many fine ladies; and sat by Collonell Reames, who understands and loves a play as well as I, and I love him for it; and so thence home; and after being at the Office, I home to supper and to bed, my eyes being very bad again with over-working with them.

25. Up and to the office, where busy all the morning; and then at noon to the Change with Mr. Hater, and there he and I to a tavern to meet Captain Minors; which we did, and dined; and there happened to be Mr. Prichard (a ropemaker of*a* his acquaintance, and whom I know also and did once mistake for a fiddler;[2] which sung well, and asked him for such a song*b* that I had heard him sing); and after dinner did fall to discourse about the business of the old contract between the King and East India Company for the ships of the King's that went thither,[3] and about this did beat my brains all the afternoon; and then home and made an end of that account to my great content; and so late home, tired and my eyes sore, to supper and to bed.

26. *Lords day.* Up, and with my wife to church; and at noon*c* home to dinner, no strangers there; and all the afternoon and evening very late doing serious business of my Tanger accounts and examining my East India account with Mr. Poynter, whom I imployed all this day to transcribe it fair; and so to supper, W. Hewer with us; and so the girl to comb my head till I slept, and then to bed.

27. It being weather like the beginning of a frost, and the

---

a repl. closing bracket   *b* repl. 'sun'   *c* repl. 'home'

---

1. She played the Queen of Sicily. (A).
2. See above, iii. 36, n. 3. (E).
3. This was a dispute about the amount owed by the Company to the government for the transport of goods in the King's ships sent out to Bombay in 1662. Richard Minors had brought the squadron home. See above, iv. 368 & n. 3.

ground dry, I walked as far as the Temple and there took coach
and to White-hall; but the Committee not being met, I to
Westminster; and there I do hear of the letter that is in the
pamphlet this day of the King of France, declaring his design to
go on against Flanders and the grounds of it – which doth set
us mightily at rest.¹   So to White-hall, and there a committee of
Tanger met, but little done there; only, I did get two or three
little Jobs done to the perfecting two or three papers about my
Tanger accounts.   Here Mr. Povy doth tell me how he is like
to lose his 400*l* a year pension of the Duke of York, which he
took in consideration of his place which was taken from him.²
He tells me the Duchesse is a devil against him, and doth now
come like Queen Elizabeth and sits with the Duke of York's
Council and sees what they do;³ and she crosses out this man's
wages and prices as she sees fit for saving money, but yet he
tells me she reserves 5000*l* a year for her own spending; and my
Lady Peterborough by and by tells me that the Duchesse doth
lay up mightily Jewells.   Thence to my Lady Peterborough, she
desiring to speak with me; she loves to be taken dressing herself,
as I always find her; and there, after a little talk to please her
about her husband's pension,*ᵃ*⁴ which I do not think he will ever
get again, I away thence home; and all the afternoon mighty
busy at the office and late preparing*ᵇ* a letter to the Comissioners of Accounts, our first letter to them.⁵   And so home to
supper, where Betty Turner was (whose Brother Franke did set
out toward the East Indys this day, his father and mother gone

a repl. 'pro'-   *b* repl. 'and then home'

---

1. The 'pamphlet' was the *London
Gazette* of this day, which printed a
letter of Louis XIV announcing that
on 1 February he would invade
Franche-Comté in order to force
Spain to make peace and to prevent
the Emperor from attacking
Burgundy. The letter was sent to
Britain and the United Provinces who
were acting as mediators.

2. On 27 September 1666 Thomas

Povey had been replaced by Sir Allen
Apsley as Treasurer and Receiver-
General to the Duke.   In December
1669 he was granted £2000 in
compensation, through the interven-
tion of the Queen Mother: HMC,
Rep., 8/1/280.

3. For her pride, see above, iii. 64
& n. 1.

4. See above, viii. 459, n. 3.

5. See below, p. 42 & n. 1.

down with*a* him to Gravesend); and there was her little brother
Moses, whom I examined, and he is a pretty good scholar for a
child; and so after supper to talk and laugh, and to bed.

28. Up, and to the office, and there with W. Griffin talking
about getting a place to build a coach-house or to hire one, which
I now do resolve to have, and do now declare it; for it is plainly
for my benefit for saving money.[1]

By and by the office sat, and there we concluded on our letter
to the Commissioners of Accounts and to the several officers of
ours about the work they are to do to answer their late great
demands. At noon home to dinner, and after dinner set my
wife and girl down at the Change, and I to White-hall; and by
and by the Duke of York comes and we had a little meeting,
Anglesey, W. Penn*b* and I there and none else; and among other
things, did discourse of the want*c* of discipline in the fleet, which
the Duke of York confessed and yet said that he, while he was
there, did keep it in a good measure, but that it was now lost
when he was absent; but he will endeavour to have it again.
That he did tell the Prince and Duke of Albemarle they would
lose all order by making such and such men commanders, which
they would because they were stout men; he told them that it
was a reproach to the nation, as if there were no sober men
among us that were stout to be had. That they did put out some
men for cowards that the Duke of York had put in but little
before for stout men and would now, were he to go to sea
again, entertain them in his own division to choose. And did
put in an idle fellow, Greene, who was hardly thought fit for a
bosun by him; they did put him from being a lieutenant to
a captain's place of a second-rate ship;[2] as idle a drunken fellow,
he said, as any was in the fleet. That he will now desire the
King to let him be what he is, that is, Admirall, and he will put
in none but that that he hath great reason to think well of;
and perticularly says that though he likes Collonell Legg well, yet

---

a repl. 'to'   *b* repl. 'Brouncker'   *c* ? 'breach'

---

1. Pepys bought his coach on 24   2. See above, pp. 5–6 & n.
October.

his son that was, he knows not how, made a Captain after he had been but one voyage at sea, he should go to sea another[a] apprentiship before ever he gives him a command.[1] We did tell him of the many defects and disorders among the Captains, and I prayed we might do it in writing to him; which he liked, and I am glad of an opportunity of doing it.[2] Thence away and took up wife and girl and home, and to the office, busy late; and so to supper and to bed. My wife this day hears from her father and mother; they are in France at paris; he, poor good man I think he is, gives her good counsel still, which I always observed of him, and thankful for my small charities to him. I could be willing to do something for them, were I sure not to bring them over again hither. ⟨Coming home, wife and I went and saw Kate Joyce, who is still in mighty sorrow; and the more from something that Dr. Stillingfleete[b] should simply say in his sermon of her husband's manner of dying, as killing himself.⟩[3]

29. Up betimes and by coach to Sir W. Coventry, whom I found in his chamber; and there stayed an hour and talked with him about several things of the Navy and our want of money; which they[4] endeed do supply us with a little, but in no degree likely to enable[c] us to go on with the King's service. He is at a stand where to have more, and is in mighty pain for it, declaring that he[d] believes there never was a Kingdom so governed as this was in the time of the late Chancellor and the Treasurer, nobody minding or understanding anything how things went, or what the King had in his Treasury or was to have; nothing in the world of it minded. He tells me that there

a repl. 'an'   *b* repl. 'Hool'-
c repl. 'go'   *d* repl. 'they have found'

---

1. George Legge, son of Col. William Legge of the Ordnance Office, had commanded the *Pembroke* in 1667 at the age of 19. There is no record of his serving as lieutenant before receiving his next command in 1672. He became Baron Dartmouth in 1682 and in 1683-4 led the Tangier expedition (on which Pepys also served) sent to dismantle the fortress and evacuate the town.

2. No such report has been traced. Cf. above, p. 29 & n. 6.

3. See below, p. 49.

4. The Treasury Commissioners.

are still people desirous to overthrow him, he resolving to stick at nothing nor no person that stands in his way*a* against bringing the King out of debt, be it to retrench any man's place or profit; and that he cares not, for rather then be imployed under the King and have the King continue in this condition of indigence, he desires*b* to be put out from among them, thinking it no honour to be a minister in such a government. He tells me he hath no friends in the whole Court but my Lord Keeper and Sir Jo. Duncum. He tells me they have reduced the charges of Ireland above 70000*l* a year, and thereby cut off good profits from my Lord-Lieutenant; which will make a new enemy, but he cares not.[1] He tells me that Townsend of the Wardrobe is the veriest knave and bufflehead that ever he saw in his life, and wonders how my Lord Sandwich came to trust such a fellow;[2] and that now Reames and   [3] are put in to be overseers there and do great things and have already saved a great deal of money in the King's Liverys; and buy linen so cheap, that he will have them buy the next cloth he hath for shirts – but then, this is with ready money, which answers all. He doth not approve of

a MS. 'wife'   *b* repl. 'thinks'

---

1. The existing Irish establishment had been in force since 1 April 1666. On 15 January 1668 Coventry had secured the appointment of a joint committee of English and Irish privy councillors to reduce expenditure which had reported on the 27th. When their proposals were effected in Michaelmas 1669, the total saving was only c. £13,000 p.a. It had been found impossible to cut the costs severely without dangerously weakening the military establishment, far and away the biggest item of expense. See *CSP Ireland, 1666–9*, pp. 7–9; ib., *1669–70*, pp. 7–9; *CTB*, ii. 232, 236, 238; HMC, *Ormonde*, n.s. iii, pp. x–xiii. For Ormond's hostility to Coventry, see HMC, op. cit., p. 262.

2. Thomas Townshend, sen. (Sandwich's deputy at the Wardrobe) was in trouble over his accounts with Capt. Henry Cooke of the Chapel Royal, and on the 24th had been examined by Coventry and the rest of the Treasury Commissioners on the subject: *CTB*, ii. 238. He was suspended from his office in March: PRO, SP29/253, f. 28*v*.

3. On 16 January warrants were issued for the appointment of Col. Bullen Reymes as Surveyor and Andrew Newport as Controller of the Great Wardrobe: *CSPD 1667–8*, p. 170. For the reorganisation of the department at this time, see ib., pp. 64–5.

my letter I drew, and the office signed yesterday, to the Commissioners of Accounts, saying that it is a little too submissive and grants a little too much and too soon our bad managements; though we lay on want of money, yet that it will be time enough to plead it when they object it – which was the opinion of my Lord Anglesy also, so I was ready to alter it; and did presently, going from him, go home and there transcribed it fresh as he would have it and got it signed;[1] and to White-hall presently and showed it him, and so home and there to dinner; and after dinner, all the afternoon and till 12 a-clock at night with Mr. Gibson at home upon my Tanger accounts, and did end them fit to be given the last of them to the Auditor tomorrow, to my great content.   This evening came Betty Turner and the two Mercers and W Batelier, and they had fiddlers and danced and kept a quarter; which pleased me (though it disturbed me) but I could not be with them at all.   Mr. Gibson lay at my house all night, it was so late.

30.   Up, it being fast-day for the King's death;[2] and so I and Mr. Gibson by water to the Temple, and there all the morning with Auditor Wood; and I did deliver in the whole of my accounts and run them over in three hours, with full satisfaction; and so with great content thence, he and I and our clerks and Mr. Clerke the solicitor, to a little Ordinary in Hercules-Pillars-Ally, the Crowne (a poor sorry place, where a fellow in twelve year hath gained ⟨an estate of, as⟩ he says, 600*l* a year, which is very strange)[3] and there dined and had a good dinner, and very good discourse between them old men belonging to the law.   And here first I heard that my Cosen Pepys of Salsbury Court was Marshall to my Lord Cooke when he was Lord Chief Justice;[4] which beginning of his I did not know to be so low,

1. Copies in NMM, LBK 8/523 (28 January, in Hewer's hand); BM, Add. 9311, f. 161 *v* (28 January); PRO, Adm. 106/2886, pt I (29 January).   The letter merely recites the questions which had been referred to the appropriate officers; see above, p. 34 & n. 4.

2. See above, ii. 26, n. 1.
3. Pepys remarks on the fortunes made by other innkeepers at 25 February 1665. The landlord was William King.
4. John Pepys (d. ?1652) had later become Coke's secretary and man of business.

but so it was it seems. After dinner, I home, calling*a* at my bookbinder's, but he not within.*b* When come home, I find Kate Joyce hath been there with sad news, that her house stands not in the King's Liberty[1] but the Dean of Pauls; and so, if her estate be forfeited, it will not be in the King's power to do her any good. So I took coach and to her, and there find her in trouble, as I cannot blame her. But I do believe this arises from somebody that hath a mind to fright her into a composition for her estate, which I advise her against; and endeed, I do desire heartily to be able to do her service, she being methinks a piece of care I ought to take upon me for our fathers' and friends'* sake – she being left alone, and no friend so near as me or so able to help her. After having given her my advice, I home; and there to my office and did business, and hear how the Committee for Accounts are mighty active and likely to examine*c* everything; but let them do their worst. I am to be before them with our contract books tomorrow.*d* So home from the office, to*e* supper and to bed.

31. Up and by coach, with W Griffin with me and our contract-books, to Durham Yard to the Commissioners for Accounts – the first time I ever was there; and staying a while before I was admitted to them, I did observe a great many people attending about complaints*f* of seamen concerning tickets; and among others, Mr. Carcasse and Mr. Martin my purser. And I observe a fellow, one Collins, is there, who is imployed by these Commissioners perticularly to hold an office*g* in Bishops-gate-street, or somewhere thereabouts, to receive complaints of all people about tickets – and I believe he will have work enough. Presently I was called in, where I found the whole number of Commissioners, and was there received with great respect and kindness and did give them great satisfaction, making it my endeavour to inform them what it was they were to expect from me and what was the duty of other people, this being my only way to preserve myself after all my pains and trouble. They did ask many questions and demand other books of me; which I

a repl. 'and there'   *b* repl. 'with in'   *c* repl. 'spy'
d repl. 'night'   *e* repl. 'at'   *f* repl. 'conpl'-   *g* repl. 'of'-

1. 'Liberty' (=jurisdictional enclave) is here incorrectly used for 'jurisdiction'.

did give them very ready and acceptable answers to; and upon the whole, I observe they do go about their business like men resolved to go through with it, and in a very good method, like men of understanding.[1]   They have Mr. Jessop their secretary; and it is pretty to see that they are fain to find out an old-fashion man of Cromwell's to do their business for them, as well as the Parliament*a* to pitch upon such for the most part in the list of people that were brought into the House for Commissioners.[2]   I went away with giving and receiving great satisfaction; and so away to White-hall to the Commissioners of Treasury*b* – where waiting some time, I met there with Collonell Birch and he and I fell into discourse, and I did give him thanks for his kindness to me in the Parliament-house, both before my face and behind my back; he told me he knew me to be a man of the old way for taking pains,[3] and did always endeavour to do me right and prevent anything that was*c* moved that might tend to my injury – which I was obliged to him for, and thanked him.   Thence to talk of other things and the want of money and he told me of the general want of money in the country; that land sold for nothing, and the many pennyworths he knew of lands and houses upon them with good titles in his country, at 16 years' purchase.[4]   "And," says he, "though I am in debt,

---

a repl. 'Parl'-   *b* repl. 'Accounts'   *c* repl. 'might'

---

1. For the Brooke House Committee, see above, viii. 559, n. 2. Their reputation now stood high: cf. above, viii. 586; M. Sylvester, *Reliq. Baxt.*, 1696, pt iii. 21. But Pepys later attacked their report.

2. See above, p. 30 & n. 1.

3. Birch was a Presbyterian and like Pepys had served the Commonwealth.

4. Birch's 'country' was Herefordshire – he was M.P. for Leominster. In June 1669 a Leominster estate was offered at 16 years' purchase: HMC, *Portland*, iii. 311. Birch had a great

reputation as a shrewd business man. The shortage of money and (in many places) the drop in rents had been progressive since the beginning of the war. (Cf. above, viii. 158 & n. 1.) According to a witness before the Lords' Committee on the Decay of Trade, appointed in October 1668, the capital value of land generally was then, and had been for some time, calculated at 16 years' purchase.   In 1665 Petty had rated it at 18, and in better times it stood at 20: HMC, *Rep.*, 8/133-4; W. R. Scott, *Joint Stock Companies*, i. 264.

yet I*ᵃ* have a mind*ᵇ* to one, and that is a Bishop's lease;" "But," said I, "will you choose such a lease before any other?" – "Yes," says he plainly, "because I know they*ᶜ* cannot stand, and then it will fall into the King's hands, and I in possession shall have an advantage by it – and," says he, "I know they must fall, and they are now near it, taking all the ways they can to undo themselfs and showing us the way;"[1] and thereupon told me a story of the present quarrel between the Bishop and Deane of Coventry and Lichfield; the former of which did excommunicate the latter and caused his excommunication to be read in the church while he was there; and after it was read, the Deane made the service be gone through with, though himself, an excommunicate, was present (which is contrary to the Canon), and said he would justify the Quire therein against the Bishop; and so they are at law in the Arches about it – which is a very pretty story.[2] He tells me that the King is for Toleration, though the Bishops be against it; and that he doth not doubt but it will be carried in Parliament but that he fears some will stand for the tolerating of papists with the rest; and that he knows not what to say to, but rather thinks that the sober party will be without it rather

---

a MS. 'says I'   *b* repl. 'm'-   *c* MS. 'not they'

---

1. This was an extension of the rumour about deans and chapters reported at 23 January. There were stories in May 1669 that the bishops were going to surrender their lands in exchange for salaries settled on the revenue: *CSPD 1668–9*, p. 320; cf. also Marvell, i. 165. Birch had invested heavily in church lands during the Interregnum.

2. During the recent rebuilding of Lichfield Cathedral the Bishop, Dr John Hacket, had had constant trouble with the Dean, Dr Thomas Wood. The excommunication had been pronounced in 1667, but there appears to be no trace of the dispute in the records of the Court of Arches. Wood was an eccentric. He courted his wife for 30 years before marrying her, and after marriage threatened to 'lie alone because . . . [she] putts her arms out of bed, & lets the cold into it': G. D. to Sancroft, 2 March 1667, Tanner 45, f. 153*r*. He was made bishop of the see on Hacket's death in 1670, but lived mostly at his native Hackney, where he spent his time sawing wood in order to save money (though he was very rich). On being told by the Primate in July 1681 to pay a visit to his diocese, he replied that he would go 'when the weather was somewhat cooler'. He was thereupon suspended, and at his death in 1692 was buried without any inscription on his tomb: T. Harwood, *Lichfield* (1806), p. 156; W. Beresford, *Lichfield*, pp. 250+.

then have it upon those terms – and I do believe so.[1]   Here we broke off, and I home to dinner; and after dinner set down my wife and Deb at the Change, and I to make a visit to Mr. Godolphin at his lodgings; who is come late from Spain from[a] my Lord Sandwich,[2] and did the other day, meeting me in White-hall, compliment me mightily; and so I did offer him this visit, but missed him.   And so back and took up my wife and set her at Mrs. Turner's, and I to my bookbinder's and there till late at night, binding up my second part of my Tanger accounts; and I all the while observing his working and his manner of gilding of books with great pleasure; and so home and there busy late, and then to bed.

This day Griffin did in discourse in the coach put me in the head of the little house by our garden, where old goodman Taylor[3] puts his brooms and dirt, to make me a stable of; which I shall improve, so as I think to be able to get me a stable without much charge; which doth please me mightily.   He did also in discourse tell me that it is observed, and is true, in the late Fire of London, that the fire burned just as many parish-churches as there were hours from the beginning to the end of the fire; and next, that there were[b] just[c] as many churches left standing as there were[d] taverns left standing in the rest of the City that was not burned; being, I think he told me, thirteen in all of each – which is pretty to observe.

---

a repl. 'from'   *b* repl. 'was'   *c* repl. 'with'   *d* repl. 'are taverns'

---

1. For the scheme of comprehension and indulgence, see above, p. 31, n. 4. Birch had been in charge of the abortive bill introduced before Christmas: G. F. Nuttall and O. Chadwick (eds), *From uniformity to unity, 1662–1962*, p. 198. At the opening of the new session the King made a strong appeal to parliament to 'think of some course to beget a better union and composure in the minds of my Protestant subjects': *LJ*, xii. 181. Charles in fact favoured toleration for all peaceable subjects, Catholic as well as Protestant.

2. William Godolphin, Secretary to the English embassy at Madrid, had been sent by Sandwich to bring news of the Spanish-Portuguese treaty (q.v. below, p. 80, n. 1), and to discuss with the government proposals for an Anglo-Spanish alliance. Sandwich MSS, Letters to Ministers, f. 45.

3. Matthew Taylor, Navy Office handyman and messenger.

FEBRUARY.

1. Up and to the office pretty betimes; and the Board not meeting as soon as I wished,[a] I was forced to go to White-hall in expectation of a Committee for Tanger; but when I came it was put off, and so home again to the office and sat till past 2 a-clock; where at the Board some high words passed between Sir W. Penn and I, begun by me and yielded to by him; I being in the right in finding fault for his[b] neglect of duty.[1] At noon home to dinner; and after dinner, out with my wife, thinking to have gone to the Duke's playhouse; but was, to my great content in the saving my vow,[2] hindered by coming a little too late; and so it being a fine day, we out to Islington, and there to the old house[3] and eat cheese-cakes[c] and drank and talked; and so home in the evening, the ways being mighty bad, so as we had no pleasure in being abroad at all almost, but only the variety of it. And so to the office, where busy late; and then home to supper and to bed – my head mighty full of business now on my hand: *viz*., of finishing my Tanger accounts – of auditing my last year's accounts – of preparing answers to the Comissioners of Accounts – of drawing up several important letters to the Duke of York and Commissioners of Treasury – the marrying of my sister – the building of a coach and stables against summer. And the setting many things in my office right – and the drawing up a new form of contract with the Victualler of the Navy – and several other things; which pains, however, I will go through with – among others, the taking care of Kate Joyce in the trouble she is in at present for saving her estate.

2. *Lords day*. Wife took physic this day. I all day at home,

a repl. 'would'   b MS. 'for his with his'
c repl. 'cates'

---

1. Cf. below, p. 377 & n. 3.   3. The King's Head.
2. See above, viii. 527. (A).

and all the morning setting my books in*a* order in my presses for
the fallowing year, their number being much encreased since the
last, so as I am fain to lay by several books to make room for
better, being resolved to keep no more then just my presses will
contain.*b1*   At noon to dinner, my wife coming down to me; and
a very good dinner we had, of a powdered leg of pork and a loin
of lamb roasted – and with much content, she and I and Deb.
After dinner, my head combed an hour together, and then to
work again – and at it, doing many things towards the setting
my accounts and papers in order; and so in the evening, Mr.
Pelling supping with us, to supper and so to bed.

3.   Up and to the office, where with my clerks all the morning
very busy about several things there wherein I was behindhand.
At noon home to dinner; and thence after dinner to the Duke
of York's House to the play, *The Tempest*, which we have often
seen; but yet I was pleased again, and shall be again to see it,
it is so full of variety; and perticularly, this day I took pleasure
to learn the ⟨tune of the⟩ Seamans dance – which I have much
desired to be perfect in, and have made myself so.² So home with
my wife and Deb, and there do at the office meet, to my trouble,
with a warrant from the Commissioners of Accounts for my
attending them and Cocke two days hence; which I apprehend,
by Captain Cockes being to go also, to be about the prizes.³
But however, there is nothing of crime can be laid to my charge,
and the worst that can be is to refund my 500*l* profit;⁴ and who
can help it.   So I resolve not to be troubled at it, though I fear
I cannot bear it so – my spirit being very poor and mean as to
the bearing with trouble, that I do find of myself.   So home,
and there to my chamber and did some business; and thence to
supper and to bed.

a repl. 'ready for the'   *b* repl. 'cont'-

---

1. He now had two presses: above,
p. 18.   They would hold about 500
books.

2. See above, viii. 521 & n. 4.
Pepys had already seen the play four
times.   (A).

3. The prize-goods scandal of
1665: see above, vi. 230-1 & n.

4. Pepys had sold his share of the
goods to Cocke for this amount:
above, vi. 297.

4. Up and to the office, where a full Board sat all the morning, busy, among other things, concerning a solemn letter we intend to write to the Duke of York about the state of the things of the Navy for want of money, though I doubt it will be to little purpose.[1] After dinner, I abroad by coach to Kate Joyces, where the Jury did sit where they did before about her husband's death; and their verdict put off for fourteen days longer at the suit of somebody under pretence of the King, but it is only to get money out of her to compound the matter. But the truth is, something they will make out of Stillingfleet's sermon which may trouble us; he declaring like a fool in his pulpit, that he did confess*a* that his losses in the world did make him do what he did. This doth vex me, to see how foolish our protestant divines are, while the papists do make it the duty of a confessor to be secret, or else nobody would confess their sins*b* to them.

All being put off for today, I took my leave of Kate, who is mightily troubled at it for her estate sake; not for her husband, for her sorrow for that I perceive is all over. I home, and there to my office busy till the evening and then home; and there my wife and Deb and I and Betty Turner, I imployed in the putting new Titles to my books,[2] which we proceeded on till midnight; and then*c* being weary and late, to bed.

5. Up, and I to Captain Cockes, where he and I did discourse of our business that we are to go about to the Comissioners of Accounts, about our prizes. And having resolved to conceal nothing but confess the truth, the truth being likely to do us most good, we parted; and I to White-hall, where missing of the Commissioners of the Treasury, I to the Commissioners of

---

a repl. 'that' *b* repl. full stop
c followed by 'at [struck through] but'

---

1. Untraced.

2. Mr H. M. Nixon writes: 'Few of Pepys's books at this time had binders' titles, and Pepys and his companions may now have been pasting paper labels on to the spines. If so, it is odd that no trace of the labels remains. He refers again, at 15 February, to "titleing" the books. The words used in both entries make it clear that he was dealing with his new books, and it is difficult to believe that he was merely listing them. On the 16th he made a new catalogue.'

Accounts, where I was forced to stay two hours I believe before I was called in; and when came in, did take an oath to declare the truth to*ᵃ* what they should ask me (which is a great power, I doubt more then the Act doth, or as some say can, give them: to force a man to swear against himself);¹ and so they fell to enquire about the business of prize-goods, wherein I did answer them as well as I could answer them, to everything the just truth, keeping myself to that.　I do perceive at last that that they did lay most like a fault to me was that I did buy goods upon my Lord Sandwiches declaring that*ᵇ* it was with the King's allowance, and my believing it without seeing the King's allowance² – which is a thing I will own, and doubt not to justify myself in. That that vexed me most was their having some watermen by to witness my saying that they were rogues, that they had betrayed my goods; which was upon some discontent with one of the watermen that I imployed at Greenwich, who I did think did discover* the goods sent from Rochester to the Custome-house officer – but this can do me no great harm.　They were inquisitive into the meanest perticulars, and had had great information; but I think that it can do me no hurt, at the worst more then to make me refund, if it must be known, what profit I did make of my agreement with Captain Cocke.³　And yet though this be all, yet I do find so poor a spirit within me, that it makes me almost out of my wits, and puts me to so much pain that I cannot think of anything, nor do anything but vex and fret and imagine myself undone – so that I am ashamed of myself to myself, and do fear what would become of me if any real affliction should come upon me.　After they had done with me, they called in Captain Cocke, with whom they were shorter. And I do fear he may answer foolishly, for he did speak to me foolishly before he went in; but I hope to preserve myself, and let him shift for himself as well as he can.　So I away; walked

a repl. 'about the bus'–　　*b* repl. 'me'

---

1. They had been given statutory powers to compel witnesses to answer questions: 19–20 Car. II, c. 1, section 1. ●

2. See above, p. 48 & n. 3.
3. See above, p. 48 & n. 4.

to my flagelette-maker in the Strand[1] and there stayed for Captain Cocke, who took me up and carried me home; and there coming home and finding dinner done and Creed there (and Mr. Cooke, who came for my Lady Sandwiches plate, which I must part with and so endanger the losing of ⟨my⟩ money, which I lent upon my thoughts of securing myself by that plate:[2] but it is no great sum, but 60*l*; and if it must be lost, better that then a greater sum), I away back again to find a dinner anywhere else; and so I first to the Ship tavern, thereby to get a sight of the pretty mistress of the house, with whom I am not yet acquainted at all; and I do always find her scolding, and do believe she is an ill-natured devil, that I have no great desire to speak to her. Here I drank, and away by coach to the Strand, there to find out Mr. Moore;[3] and did find him at the Bell Inne and there acquainted him with what passed between me and the Commissioners today about the prize goods, in order to the considering what to do about my Lord Sandwich; and did conclude to own the thing to them, as done by the King's allowance and since confirmed. Thence to other discourse. Among others, he mightily commends my Lord Hinchingbrooke's match and Lady, though he buys her 10000*l*[a] dear – by the jointure and settlement his father makes her.[4] And that the Duke of York and the Duchess of York did come to see them in bed together on their wedding-night, and how my Lord had 50 pieces of gold taken out of his pocket that[b] night after he was in bed. He tells me that an Act of Comprehension is likely to pass this Parliament, for admitting of all persuasions in religion to the public observation of their perticular worship, but in certain places and the persons therein concerned to be listed of this or[c] that Church[5] – which it is thought

a figure blotted *b* repl. full stop *c* repl. 'and'

---

1. Drumbleby: above, p. 30. (E).
2. See above, viii. 573 & n. 2, 579.
3. Sandwich's lawyer.
4. For the current ratio of jointure to settlement, see above, iii. 231, n. 1.
5. For the bill (which provided for toleration as well as for 'comprehension'), see above, p. 31, n. 4. The unusual clause requiring registration of members of congregations, as well as of their ministers, was included in original draft proposals put forward by Dr John Owen, the Independent leader: G. F. Nuttall and O. Chadwick (eds), *From uniformity to unity, 1662–1962*, p. 200.

will do them more hurt then good, and make them not own their persuasion. He tells me that there is a pardon passed to the Duke of Buckingham, my Lord of Shrewsbury and the rest for the late Duell and murder; which he thinks a worse fault then any ill use my late Lord Chancellor ever put the Great Seal to, and will be so thought by the Parliament – for them to be pardoned without*ᵃ* bringing them to any trial.[1] And that my Lord Privy-Seale therefore would not have it pass his hand, but made it go by immediate warrant; or at least, they knew that he would not pass it and so did direct it to go by immediate warrant, that it might not come to him.[2] He tells me what a Character my Lord Sandwich hath sent over of Mr. Godolphin, as the worthiest man, and such a friend to him as he may be trusted in anything relating to him in the world; as one whom he says he hath infallible*ᵇ* assurances that he will remain his friend; which is very high, but endeed, they say the gentleman is a fine man.[3] Thence, after eating a lobster for my dinner, having eat nothing today, we broke up, here coming to us Mr. Townsend of the Wardrobe; who complains of the Commissioners of the Treasury as very severe against my Lord Sandwich, but not so much as they complain of him for a fool and a knave,[4] and so I let him alone. And home, carrying Mr. Moore as far as Fanchurch-street, and I home; and there, being vexed in my mind about my prize businesses, I to my chamber, where my wife and I had much

a repl. 'before'　　　*b* repl. 'in'-

---

1. For the duel, see above, pp. 26–7 & n. For the warrants for the pardons (27, 27 January), see *CSPD 1667–8*, pp. 192, 193; *London Gazette*, 27 February. Pardons were not normally issued before trial and sentence (cf. E. Wright to Pepys, 12 November 1696: *Priv. Corr.*, i. 130), and their use in this manner in the case of Danby's impeachment (1678) led to the statutory prohibition of the procedure in 1701.

2. Immediate warrants were authorised to Chancery by the King's sign-manual alone, thus by-passing the Signet and Privy Seal. The Keeper of the Privy Seal was Lord Robartes.

3. William Godolphin (after an apprenticeship as secretary to Arlington) had served Sandwich as secretary to the Madrid embassy, taking a leading part in the conclusion of the recent Anglo-Spanish treaty. He was knighted in August 1668 and became envoy-extraordinary to Spain in 1669 and ambassador there in 1671.

4. Cf. above, p. 41 & n. 2.

talk of W Hewers, she telling me that he is mightily concerned for my not being pleased with him, and is herself mightily concerned; but I have much reason*a* to blame him for his little assistance he gives me in my business, not being able to copy out a letter with sense or true spelling, that makes me mad; and endeed, he is in that regard of as little use to me as*b* the boy – which troubles me and I would have him know it – and she will let him know it. By and by to supper, and so to bed and slept but ill all night, my mind running like a fool on my prize business, which according to my reason ought not to trouble me at all.

6. Up and to the office, where all the morning; and among other things, Sir H. Cholmly comes to me about a little business and there tells me how the Parliament (which is to meet again today) are likely to fall heavy on the business of the Duke of Buckingham's pardon;[1] and I shall be glad of it. And that the King hath put out of the Court the two Hides, my Lord Chancellor's two sons, and also the Bishops*c* of Rochester and Winchester,[2] the latter of which should have preached before him yesterday, being Ashwendsdy; and had his sermon ready, but was put by – which is great news. He gone, we sat at the office all the morning, and at noon home to dinner; and my wife being gone before, I to the Duke of York's playhouse, where a new play of Etheriges called *She*_d_ *would if she could*.[3] And

---

a repl. 'fault'   *b* repl. 'almost'
c l.h. repl. l.h. 'Deans'   *d* MS. 'Shew'

---

1. The attack was made on 18 March in the debates on an unsuccessful bill against duelling: Milward, pp. 230–1.

2. These now fell victim to Clarendon's enemies. His sons Henry, Viscount Cornbury, and Laurence Hyde – respectively Lord Chamberlain to the Queen and Master of the Robes to the King – were dismissed the court, but, thanks to the Duke of York, did not lose their posts. The bishops – Dolben of Rochester (Clerk of the Closet) and Morley of Winchester (Dean of the Chapel Royal) – were both dismissed from their court offices: Morley's successor (Crofts, Bishop of Hereford) was sworn in on the 8th. PRO, LC 3/73, n.p.; *N. & Q.*, 3 July 1937, p. 8.

3. A comedy by Sir George Etherege, first acted and published in 1668. This is one of the earliest references to a performance. (A).

though I was there by 2 a-clock,[1] there was 1000 people put back that could not have room in the pit; and[a] I at last, because my wife was there, made[b] shift to get into the 18*d* box[2] – and there saw; but Lord, how full was the house and how silly the play, there being nothing in the world good in it and few people pleased in it. The King was there; but I sat mightily behind, and could see but little and hear not all. The play being done, I into the pit to look* my wife; and it being dark and raining, I to look my wife out, but could not find her;[c] and so stayed, going between the two doors[3] and through the pit an hour and half I think, after the play was done, the people staying there till the rain was over and to talk one with another; and among the rest, here was the Duke of Buckingham today openly sat in the pit; and there I found him with my Lord Buckhurst and Sidly and Etherige the poett – the last of whom I did hear mightily find fault with the Actors, that they were out of humour and had not their parts perfect,[4] and that Harris did do nothing, nor could so much as sing a Ketch in it, and so was mightily concerned: while all the rest did through the whole pit blame the play as a silly, dull thing, though there was something very roguish and witty; but the design of the play, and end, mighty insipid. At last I did find my wife staying for me in the entry, and with her was Betty Turner, Mercer, and Deb; so I got a coach, and a humour took us and I carried them to Hercules pillers and there did give them a kind of a supper of about 7*s*, and very merry; and home round the town, not through the ruines; and it was pretty how the coachman[a] by mistake drives

---

a symbol smudged   *b* repl. 'go'   *c* repl. 'here'
                  d repl. 'fellow'

---

1. An hour and a half before the usual time of commencement. (A).

2. The middle gallery. (A).

3. These admitted to the pit, and were at either side of the theatre and close to the apron stage. (A).

4. The cast listed by Downes (pp. 28–9) includes Smith as Courtall, Harris as Sir Joslin Jolly, Mrs Davis as Gatty and Mrs Shadwell as Lady Cockwood. The imperfect memorising of parts was not uncommon in Restoration productions, partly because of the frequent changes of programme, but the actors seem to have been exceptionally faulty on this occasion: they are severely criticised on this score by Thomas Shadwell in his preface to his comedy *The Humorists* (1671). (A).

us into the ruines from London-wall into Coleman-street, and would persuade me that I lived there; and the truth is, I did think that he and the linkman had contrived some roguery, but it proved only a mistake of the coachman; but it was as^a cunning a plot to have done us a mischief in as any I know, to drive us out of the road into the ruins and there stop, while nobody could be called to help^b us. But we came safe home; and there, the girls being gone home, I to the office, where a while busy; my head not being free of my trouble about my prize business, I home to bed. This evening coming home I did put my hand under the coats^c of Mercer and did touch her thigh, but then she did put by my hand^c and no hurt done, but talked and sang and was merry.

7. Up, and to the office to the getting of my books in order to carry to the Commissioners of Accounts this morning. This being done, I away, first to Westminster-hall and there met my Cosen Rogr. Pepys by his^d desire (the first time I have seen him since his coming to town, the Parliament meeting yesterday and adjurned to Monday next); and here he tells me that Mr. Jackson, my sister's servant,* is come to town and hath this day suffered a Recovery on his estate, in order to the making her a settlement. The young man is gone out of the Hall, so I could not now see him; but here I walked a good while with my cousin and among other things do^e hear that there is a great Tryall between my Lord Gerard and Carr today, who is endicted for his life at the King's Bench for running from his colours; but all do say that my Lord Gerard, though he designs the ruin of this man, will not get any thing by it.[1] Thence I to the Comissioners of Accounts and there presented my books, and was made to sit

a M.S. 'a'   *b* repl. incomplete symbol
c–c garbled s.h.: see above, viii. 244, note *a*
d repl. 'des'-   *e* MS. 'to'

1. For Gerard's persecution of Carr, see above, viii. 581 & n. 1. Carr was now indicted on three charges: one of felony (for desertion) and two of forgery. He was acquitted of all three, and came off with credit: HMC, *Rep.*, 14/4/81; BM, Add. 36916, f. 66r.

down and used with much respect, otherwise then the other day
when I came to them as a Criminall about the business of the
prizes.[1] I sat here with them a great while, while my books
were inventoried;[2] and here do*a* hear from them by discourse
that they are like to undo the Treasurer's instruments of the
Navy[3] by making it a rule that they shall repay all money paid
to wrong parties;[4] which is a thing not to be supported by these
poor creatures, the Treasurer's instruments; as it is also hard
for seamen to be ruined by their paying money to whom they
please. I know not what will be the issue of it. I find these
gentlemen to sit all day and only eat a bit of bread at noon and a
glass of wine; and are resolved to go through their business with
great severity and method. Thence I about 2 a-clock to Wesminster-hall by appointment, and there met my cousin Roger
again and Mr. Jackson, who is a plain young man, handsome
enough for her; one of no education nor discourse, but of few
words, and one altogether that I think will please me well
enough. My cousin hath got me to give the od*b* sixth, 100*l*,[5]
presently, which I intended to keep to the birth of the first child:
and let it go, I shall be eased of that care; and so after little talk
we parted, resolving to dine all together at my house tomorrow.
So there parted, my mind pretty well satisfied with this plain
fellow for my sister, though I shall I see have no pleasure nor
content in him, as if he had been a man of breeding and parts
like Cumberland.[6] And to the Swan I, and there sent for a bit
of meat and eat and drank; and so to White-hall to the Duke of
York's chamber, where I find him and ⟨my⟩ fellows at their

a MS. 'to'   *b* l.h. repl. s.h.

---

1. See above, pp. 50–1.

2. The inventory is in PRO, Adm.
106/2886, pt I, s.d.   There were 194
books.

3. The clerks of the Treasurer of
the Navy.

4. They had paid off tickets to the
wrong individuals. Impersonation
was a common occasion for a mistake
of this sort. Anglesey's statement on
this matter (8 February) is in *CSPD*

Add. 1660–85, pp. 253–4.

5. Pepys was to settle £600 on his
sister at her marriage; see below, p.
61.

6. For Pepys's hopes of Richard
Cumberland, see above, p. 17 & n. 1.
Pepys found his brother-in-law in-
corrigibly improvident. He came
to avoid direct dealings with him,
preferring to correspond only with
Paulina.

usual meeting, discoursing about securing the Medway this year; which is to shut the door after the horse is stole – however, it is good. Having done here, my Lord Brouncker and W. Penn and I, and with us Sir Arnold Breames, to the King's playhouse, and there saw a piece of *Love in^a a Maze*,[1] a dull, silly play I think; and after the play, home with W. Penn and his son Lowther, whom we met there. And there home, and sat most of the evening with my wife and Mr. Pelling talking, my head being full of business of one kind or other, and most such as doth not please me. And so to supper and to bed.

8. Up and to the office, where sat all day; and at noon home and there find Cosen Roger and Jackson by appointment come to dine with me, and Creed – and very merry; only, Jackson hath few words, and like him never the worse for it. The great talk is of Carr's coming off in all his trials; to the disgrace of my Lord Gerard^b to that degree, and the ripping up of so many notorious rogueries and cheats of my Lord's, that my Lord it is thought will be ruined; and above all things, doth show the madness of the House of Commons, who rejected the petition of this poor man by a combination of a few in the House; and much more, the base proceedings (just the epitome of all our public managements in this age) of the House of Lords, that ordered him to stand in the pillory for those very things, without hearing and examining, which he hath now, by the seeking of my Lord Gerard himself, cleared himself of in open Court, to the gaining himself the pity of all the world and shame for ever to my Lord Gerard. We had a great deal of good discourse at table; and after dinner we four men took coach, and they set me down at the Old Exchange and they home, having discoursed nothing today with cousin or Jackson about our business. I to Captain Cocke's and there discoursed over our business of prizes; and I think I shall go near to state the matter so as to secure myself without wrong to him, doing nor saying anything but the very truth. Thence away to the Strand to my book-seller's, and there stayed an hour and bought that idle, roguish

---

a l.h. '*Love in*' repl. s.h.   *b* MS. 'Gerald'

---

1. See above, iii. 88, n. 4. (A).

book, *L'escholle des Filles*;[1] which I have bought[a] in plain binding
(avoiding the buying of it better bound) because I resolve, as soon
as I have read it, to burn it, that it may not stand in the list of books,
nor among them, to disgrace them if it should be found.   Thence
home, and busy late at the office; and then home to supper and
to bed. My wife well pleased with my sister's match, and
designing how to be merry at their marriage. And I am well at
ease in my mind to think that that care will be over.   This night,
calling at the Temple at the Auditors,[2] his man told me that
he heard that my account must be brought to the view of the
Commissioners of Tanger before it can be passed; which though
I know no hurt in it, yet it troubled me, lest[b] there should be
any or any designed by them who put this into the head of the
Auditor; I suppose Auditor Beale or Creed, because they saw
me carrying my account another way then by them.

9. *Lords day.*   Up, and at my chamber all the morning and
the office, doing business and also reading a little of *L'escolle des
Filles*, which is a mighty lewd book, but yet not amiss for a sober
man once to read over to inform himself in the villainy of the
world.   At noon home to dinner, where by appointment Mr.
Pelling came, and with him three friends: Wallington that sings
the good bass, and one Rogers, and a gentleman, a young man, his
name Tempest, who sings very well endeed and understands
anything in the world at first sight.[3]   After dinner, we into our
dining-room and there to singing all the afternoon (by the way,
I must remember that Pegg Pen was brought to bed yesterday
of a girl;[4] and among other things, if I have not already set it
down, that hardly ever was remembered such a season for the
smallpox as these last two months have been, people being seen
all up and down the streets, newly come out after the smallpox):[5]
but though they sang fine things, yet I must confess that I did
take no pleasure in it, or very little, because I understood not the

----

a repl. 'bound'   *b* repl. 'there'

1. See above, p. 21, n. 2.
2. John Wood's.
3. For the singers, see above, viii.
437 & n. 4. (E).
4. See below, p. 84 & n. 2.

5. Cf. C. Creighton, *Hist. epi-
demics in Britain*, ii. 452–3. The Duke
of York had had it in the previous
November: *CSPD 1667–8*, e.g. p.
51.

words; and with the rests that the words are set, there is no sense nor understanding in them, though they be English – which makes us weary of singing in that manner, it being but a worse sort of instrumental music.[1] We sang till almost night, and drank my good store of wine; and then they parted and I to my chamber, where I did read through *L'escholle des Filles*; a lewd book, but what doth me no wrong to read for information sake (but it did hazer my prick*a* para stand all the while, and una vez to decharger); and after I had done it, I burned it, that it might not be among my books to my shame; and so at night to supper and then to bed.

10. Up, and by coach to Westminster and there made a visit to Mr. Godolphin[2] at his chamber; and I do find him a very pretty and able person, a man*b* of very fine parts and of infinite zeal to my Lord Sandwich, and one that says he is, he believes, as wise and able a person as any prince in the world hath. He tells me that he meets with unmannerly usage by Sir Robt. Southwell in Portugall, who would sign with him in his negotiations there, being a forward young man, but that my Lord maister[ed] him in*c* that point, it being ruled for my Lord here at a hearing of a committee of the Council.[3] He says that if my Lord can compass

---

  a garbled s.h.: see above, viii. 244, note *a*
  b repl. 'very'   *c* repl. 'therein' and full stop

---

1. Cf. above, viii. 437–8. (E).
2. See above, p. 46, n. 2.
3. The dispute concerned the peace negotiations between Spain and Portugal conducted under English mediation. The treaty was signed on 3/13 February. Sandwich had travelled from Spain to Lisbon and (with Arlington's agreement) had excluded Southwell, the English envoy there, both from the conferences and from the signing of the treaty on the ground of his own superior status as an ambassador-extraordinary. The chagrined Southwell (who had done valuable work in preparing the way for the treaty) sailed for home on the 9th, leaving Sandwich to deal with the exchange of ratifications. The treaty itself was almost wrecked at the last moment by a similar dispute over punctilio between the Portuguese and Spanish signatories, the one a marquess and the other a duke; and Sandwich was himself criticised in England for allowing the Spanish ambassador's signature to precede his own. See Sandwich MSS, Journals, vi. 436–40, 442–3, 444–7; ib., Letters to Ministers, f. 60*v*; ib., Letters from Ministers, ii, ff. 116+, 140+; Southwell's letters in PRO, SP 89/9, ff. 3, 10–11, 32, 38. Cf. Harris, ii. 136–9.

a peace between Spain and Portugall, and hath the doing of it
and the honour himself, it will be a thing of more honour then*a*
ever any man hath, and of as much advantage. Thence to
Westminster-hall, where the Hall mighty full; and among other
things, the House begins to sit today, and the King came. But
before the King's coming, the House of Commons met; and
upon information given them of a*b* Bill intended to be brought in,
as common report said, for Comprehension, they did mightily
and generally inveigh against it, and did vote that the King
should be desired by the House, and the message delivered by the
Privy-counsellors of the House, that the laws against breakers of
the Act of Uniformity should be put in execution.[1]　And it was
moved*c* in the House that if any people had a mind to bring
any new laws into the House about*d* religion, they might come as
a proposer of new laws did in Athens, with ropes about their
necks.[2]　By and by the King comes to the Lords' House and
there tells them of his league with Holland – and the necessity of
a fleet, and his debts and therefore want of money; and his desire
that they would think of some way to bring in all his protestant
subjects to a right understanding and peace one with another,
meaning the Bill of Comprehension.[3]　The Commons coming
to their House, it was moved that the vote passed this morning
might be suspended, because of the King's speech,*e* till the House
was full and called over two days hence; but it was denied, so
furious they are against this Bill; and thereby a great blow either
given to the King and presbyters; or, which is the rather of the
two, to the House itself, by denying a thing desired by the King
and so much desired by much the greater part of the nation.

　　a　repl. 'and advantage then'　　　*b*　repl. 'an'
　c　repl. 'said'　　　*d*　repl. 'that'　　　*e*　repl. 'speak'

---

1. *CJ*, ix. 44; for the comprehension bill, see above, p. 31, n. 4.
2. The motion has not been traced
elsewhere. It was erroneously conceived or is here erroneously reported:
the analogy should have been not with
Athens, but with Locri (S. Italy). Its
law-code (devised by Zaleucus, c.

660 B.C.) was the earliest of all European codes, and until the 4th century
was protected by this means. The
proposer was strangled if his proposal
was defeated by the Council.
3. The speech is in *LJ*, xii. 181.
For the Dutch (Triple) alliance, see
above, p. 30, n. 4.

Whatever the consequence be, if the King be a man of any stomach and heat, all do believe that he will resent this vote.

Thence with Creed home to my house to dinner, where I met with Mr. Jackson and find my wife angry with Deb, which vexes me. After dinner by coach away to Westminster, taking up a friend of Mr. Jacksons, a young lawyer; and parting with Creed at White-hall, they and I to Westminster-hall; and there met Roger Pepys and with him to his chamber and there read over and agreed upon the deed of Settlement to our minds: my sister to have 600*l* presently and she to be joyntured in 60*l* per annum – wherein I am very well satisfied.[1] Thence I to the Temple to Charles Porter's lodgings, where Captain Cocke met me; and after long waiting we to one Pemmerton, an able lawyer, about the business of our prizes and*a* left the matter with him to think of – against to-morrow – this being a matter that doth much trouble my mind, though there be no fault in it that I need fear the owning that I know of. Thence with Cocke home to his house and there left him; and I home and there got my wife to read a book I bought today and came out*b* today, licensed by Joseph Williamson for Lord Arlington, showing the state of England's affairs relating to France at this time; and the whole body of the book very good and solid, after a very foolish introduction as ever I read – and doth give a very good account of the advantage of our league with Holland at this time.[2] So, vexed in my mind with the variety of cares I have upon me, and so to*c* bed.

> *a* repl. 'business'   *b* repl. 'at
> *c* repl. 'home' and full stop

---

1. The payment of the £600 is noted in Pepys's accounts in Rawl. A 185 (f. 20*v*). 10% (the proportion of jointure to dowry) was a good rate: cf. above, p. 51, n. 4.

2. *The buckler of state and justice against the design manifestly discovered of the universal monarchy, under the vain pretext of the Queen of France her pretensions*; PL 841: a translation of a pamphlet (published in French in 1667) usually attributed to Lisola,

the Imperial diplomatist. The imprimatur of the licenser (dated 19 September 1667) is printed opposite the title-page. The preface which Pepys finds foolish is an attack on Louis XIV's claims to Flanders and to a European hegemony which concludes by absolving him from blame and fastening responsibility on 'those mean Incendiarie Writers' who promoted his case.

11. At the office all the morning, where comes a damned summons to attend the Committee of Miscarriges*ᵃ* today; which makes me mad that I should by my place become the hackney of this Office, in perpetual trouble and vexation, that need it least. At noon home to dinner, where little pleasure, my head being split almost with the variety of troubles upon me at this time and cares. And after dinner by coach to Westminster-hall and sent my wife and Deb to see *Mustapha*¹ acted. Here I brought a book to the Committee, and do find them, and perticularly Sir Tho. Clerges, mighty hot in the business of tickets; which makes me mad, to see them bite at the stone and not at the hand that flings it. And here my Lord Bruncker unnecessarily orders it that he is called in, to give opportunity to present his*ᵇ* report of the state of that business of paying by ticket;² which I do not think will do him any right, though he was made believe that it did operate mightily, and that Sir Fresh. Hollis did make a mighty harangue and to much purpose in his defence; but I believe no such effects of it, for going in afterward I did hear them speak with prejudice of it, and that his pleading of the Admirall's warrant for it now was only an evasion, if not an aspersion upon the Admirall, and therefore they would not admit of this his report, but go on with their report as they had resolved before. The orders they sent for this day was the first order that I*ᶜ* have yet met with about this business, and was of my own single hand warranting; but I do think it will do me no harm, and therefore do not much trouble myself with it – more then to see how much trouble I am brought to who have best deported myself in all the King's business. Thence with Lord Brouncker and set him down at Bowstreete, and so to the Duke of York's playhouse and there saw the last Act for nothing;³ where I never saw such good acting of any creature as Smith's*ᵈ* part of Zanger; and I do also,

a l.h. repl. s.h. 'privileges'   *b* MS. 'is'
  c repl. 'we'   *d* repl. 'H'-

1. A tragedy by Roger Boyle, Earl of Orrery (see above, vi. 73, n. 1); now performed at the LIF. (A).
2. See below, p. 69 & n. 2.

3. Playgoers commonly claimed this privilege although it had been prohibited by the Lord Chamberlain on 7 December 1663. (A).

though it was excellently acted by[a]   , do yet want
Betterton mightily.[1]   Thence to the Temple to Porter's chamber,
where Cocke met me; and after a stay there some time, they
two and I to Pemerton's chamber and there did read over the
act of calling people to account[2] and did discourse all our business
of the prizes; and upon the whole, he doth make it plainly appear
that there is no avoiding to give these Commissioners satisfaction
in everything they will ask; and that[b] there is fear lest they may
find reason to make us refund for all the extraordinary profit
made by those bargains; and doth make me resolve rather to
declare plainly and once for all the truth of the whole and what
my profit hath been, then be forced at last to do it and in the
meantime live in pain – as I must always do.   And with this
resolution on my part, I departed with some more satisfaction of
mind, though with less hopes of profit then I expected.   It[c] was
pretty here to see the heaps of money upon this lawyer's table;
and more to see how he had not since last night spent any time
upon our business, but begin with telling us that we were not
at all concerned in that Act; which was a total mistake, by his
not having read over the Act at all.   Thence to Porter's chamber,
where Captain Cocke had fetched my wife out of the coach;
and there we stayed and talked and drank, he being a very
generous, good-humoured man; and so away by coach, setting
Cocke at his house,[3] and we with his coach home; and there I
to the office and there[d] till past one in the morning; and so home
to supper and to bed – my mind at pretty good ease, though full
of care and fear of loss.

   This morning, my wife in bed told me the story of our Tom
and Jane; how the rogue did first demand her consent to love
and marry him and then, with pretence of displeasing me, did

a repl. 'do yet'	*b* repl. 'therefore'
c repl. 'so'	*d* repl. 'so'

---

1. Betterton usually played Soly-
man the Magnificent. William
Smith, a tall, handsome actor, was a
leading member of the company.
(A).
   2. The act establishing the Brooke
House Committee: see above, viii.
559, n. 2.
   3. Close by Gresham College; he
also had a country house at Greenwich.

slight her; but both he and she have confessed the matter*a* to her, and she hath charged him to go on with his love to her and be true to her, and so I think the business will go on; which, for my love to her because she is in love with him, I am pleased with, but otherwise I think she will have no good bargain of it; at least, if I should not do well in my place. But if I do stand, I do entend to give her 50*l* in money and do them all the good I can in my way.[1]

12. Up and to my office, where all the morning drawing up my Narrative of my proceedings and concernments in the buying of Prize-goods, which I am to present to the Committee for Accounts.[2] And being come to a resolution to conceal nothing from them, I was at great ease how to draw it*b* up without any inventions or practice to put me to future pain or thoughts how to carry on; and now I only discover what my profit was,*c* and at worst I suppose I can be made but to refund my profit – and so let it go. At noon home to dinner, where Mr. Jackson dined with me; and after dinner I (calling at the Excise Office, and setting my wife and Deb at her tailor's) did with Mr. Jackson go to find my Cosen Rog. Pepys, which I did in the Parliament-house, where I met him and Sir Tho. Crew and Mr. George Mountagu, who are mighty busy how to save my Lord's name from being in the report for anything which the Committee is commanded to report to the House of the Miscarriages of the late war.[3] I find they drive furiously still in the business of Tickets, which is nonsense in itself and cannot come to anything. Thence with Cosen Rogr. to his lodgings and there sealed the writings

a repl. 'meter'
b repl. symbol rendered illegible
c repl. 'at'

---

1. Jane Birch and Tom Edwards were married in the following March, and Pepys gave them £80. When c. 1682 Jane was left a widow with two children, she turned to Pepys for help in getting the elder admitted to Christ's Hospital: Smith, i. 284–5.

2. Copy (12 February; in Hayter's hand) in Rawl. A 174, f. 301.

3. Neither Crew nor Mountagu was on the committee. For its report (in which Sandwich escaped censure), see below, p. 69, n. 2.

with Jackson about my sister's marriage;[1] and[a] here my Cosen Rogr. told me the pleasant passage of a fellow's bringing a bag of letters today into the Lobby of the House, and left them and withdrew himself with[out] observation. The bag being opened, the letters were found all of one size and directed with one hand; a letter to most of the Members of the House. The House was acquainted with it, and voted they should be brought in and one opened by the Speaker; wherein, if he found anything unfit to communicate, to propose a committee to be chosen for it. The Speaker opening one, found it only a Case with a Libell in it, printed – a Satyr most sober and bitter as ever I read – and every letter was the same; so the House fell a-scrambling for them like boys; and my cousin Rogr. had one directed to him, which he lent me to read.[2] So away and took up my wife; and setting Jackson down at Fetter-lane end, I to the Old Exchange to look Mr. Houblon; but not finding him, did go home and there late, writing a letter to my Lord Sandwich, and to give passage to a letter of great moment from Mr. Godolphin to him; which I did get speedy passage for by the help of Mr. Houblon, who come late to me, and there directed the letters to Lisbon under Covers of his;[3] and here we talked of the times, which look very sad and distracted, and made good mirth at this day's passage in the House; and so parting and going to the gate with him, I found his[b] lady and another fine lady sitting an hour together,

a repl. 'and so away'   b MS. 'is'

---

1. Abstract (12 February) in Magd. Coll., Jackson MSS 1; between John Jackson on the one part and John Pepys, sen., and Samuel Pepys on the other.

2. Probably *Vox et lacrimae Anglorum: or The true Englishmen's complaints to their representatives in parliament, humbly tendered to their serious consideration at their next sitting*; dated 6 February; summarised in *CSPD 1667–8*, p. 217; 'a little book in verse, a foolish libel': Milward, p. 183. Not in the PL. It complained of everything from heavy taxation to the King's mistresses, and called for the abolition of monopolies, the relief of debtors, encouragement of husbandry, and justice against 'perfidious Clarendon'. A committee was appointed on the following day to discover the author, printer and publisher (*CJ*, ix. 48), but nothing seems to have come of it.

3. None of these letters has been traced.

late at night, in their coach while he was with me; which is so like my wife that I was mighty taken with it, though troubled for it. So home to supper and to bed. This day Captain Cocke was with the Commissioners of Accounts to ask more time for his bringing in his answer about the prize-goods; and they would not give him fourteen days as he asks, but would give only two days – which was very hard I think, and did trouble me for fear of their severity, though I have prepared my matters so as to defy it.

13. Up, and to the office, where all the morning. At noon home to dinner, and thence with my wife and Deb to White-hall, setting them at her tailor's; and I to the Commissioners*a* of the Treasury, where myself alone did argue the business of the East India-Company against their whole company on behalf of the King before the Lords-Commissioners; and to very good effect I think, and with reputation.[1] That business being over, the Lords and I had other things to talk about; and among the rest, about our making more Assign[m]ents on the Exchequer since*b* they bid us hold; whereat they were extraordinary angry with us, which troubled me a little, though I am not concerned in it at all.[2] Waiting here some time without, I did meet with several people; and among others, Mr. Brisbanke,[3] who tells me in discourse that Tom Killigrew hath a fee out of the wardrobe for cap and bells, under the title of the King's foole or Jester, and may with privilege revile or jeere anybody, the greatest

---

a repl. 'Council'   *b* repl. full stop

---

1. The dispute was about the hiring of ships: see above, p. 37 & n. 3. Nothing was now settled. The Treasury demanded £7600, but in 1672 the government agreed to accept 2000 gns paid into the Privy Purse. *CTB*, ii. 253; *Cal. court mins E. India Co.*, *1668–70* (ed. E. B.

Sainsbury), pp. 26–8; ib., *1671–3*, p. 172.

2. *CTB*, ii. 254.

3. John Brisbane, later (1680–4) Secretary to the Admiralty, seems now to have been employed by Carteret.

person, without offence, by the privilege of his place.[1]   Thence took up my wife and home, and there busy late at the office writing letters; and so home to supper and to bed.   The House was called over today.[2]   This morning Sir G. Carteret came to the office to see and talk with me; and he assures me that to this day the King is the most kind man to my Lord of Sandwich in the whole world – that he himself[a] doth not now mind any public business, but suffers things to go on at Court as they will, he seeing all likely to come to ruin – that this morning the Duke of York sent to him to come to make up one of a committee ⟨of the Council⟩ for Navy[b] affairs; where when he came, he told the Duke of York that he was none of them; which shows how things are nowadays ordered, that there should be a committee for the Navy and the Lord Admirall not know the persons of it, and that Sir G. Carteret and my Lord Anglesy should be left out of it and men wholly improper put into it.[3]   I do hear of all hands that there is great difference at this day between my Lord Arlington and Sir W. Coventry; which I am sorry for.[4]

14.   *Valentine's-day.*   Up, being called up by Mercer, who came to be my Valentine; and so I rose, and my wife, and were merry a little, I staying to talk; and did give her a Guinny in gold for her Valentine's gift.   There comes also my Cosen Rogr. Pepys betimes, and comes to my wife for her to be his Valentine, whose Valentine I was also, by agreement to be so to her every year; and this year I find it is likely to cost 4 or 5*l* in a ring for

a MS. 'him himself'   *b* repl. 'the'

1. Killigrew had served as King's Jester since at least 1661: Wood, *L. & T.*, iii. 38; R. W. Lowe, *Betterton*, p. 70.   M. Summers (*Playhouse of Pepys*, p. 66) has suggested that he was made jester in compensation for the loss of his office of Master of the Revels.   The place of jester was not, like the latter, an established office in the Household.   Killigrew was witty and outspoken, and even Charles felt the edge of his tongue at times: see above, vii. 400.   (A).

2. *CJ*, ix. 49.

3. In fact both Carteret and Anglesey were members.   It had just been reconstituted (as a standing committee) on the 12th.   PRO, PC 2/60, p. 176.

4. They had been allies in the attack on Clarendon, but now, faced by the parliamentary enquiry into the war, began to quarrel.   See V. Barbour, *Arlington*, p. 116.

her which she desires.   Cosen Rogr. did come also to speak
with Sir W. Pen; who was quoted, it seems, yesterday by Sir
Fr. Hollis to have said that if my Lord Sandwich had done so
and so, we might have taken all the Dutch prizes at that time when
he stayed and let them go.[1]   But Sir W. Penn did tell us he
should say nothing in it but what*ª* would do my Lord honour –
and he is a knave I am able to prove, if he do otherwise.   He
gone, I to my office to perfect my Narrative about prize-goods;[2]
and did carry it to the Comissioners of Accounts, who did
receive it with great kindness – and express great value of and
respect to me; and my heart is at rest that it is lodged there in so
full truth and plainness, though it may hereafter prove some loss
to me.   But here I do see they are entered into many enquiries
about prizes by the great attendance*ᵇ* of commanders and others
before them, which is a work I am not sorry for.   Thence I
away, with my head busy but my heart at pretty good ease, to
the Old Exchange; and there met Mr. Houblon and prayed him
to discourse with some of the merchants that are of the Committee
for Accounts, to see how they do resent* my paper, and in general
my perticular in the relation to the business of the Navy; which
he hath promised to do carefully for me and tell me.   Here it
was a mighty pretty sight to see old Mr. Houblon, whom I
never saw before, and all his sons about him, all good merchants.[3]
Thence home to dinner, and had much discourse with W. Hewer
about my going to visit Collonell Thomson, one of the Committee of Accounts; who among the rest, is mighty kind to me
and is likely to mind our business more then any, and I would be
glad to have a good understanding with him.[4]   Thence after

a repl. 'do my'   *b* repl. same symbol badly formed

1. In September 1665 Sandwich had
allowed most of the Dutch E. India
fleet, with its escort, to sail home unscathed: above, vi. 218, 231. He put
the blame on the weather and shortage of provisions: above, vi. 277, n.
1; Harris, i. 338+.
  2. See above, p. 64, n. 2.
  3. James Houblon, sen., and his
five sons were merchants remarkable

both for their commercial success and
their mutual affection. Cf. above,
vii. 36 & n. 1.
  4. Thomson (one of the Commonwealthsmen appointed to the Committee: see above, viii. 569–70 & n)
proved a severe critic, harping always
on the virtues of the 1650s – 'those
pure Angelicall times', as the King
called them: PL 2874, pp. 415–16,428.

dinner to White-hall to attend*a* the Duke of York; where I did let him know the troublesome life we lead, and perticularly myself, by being obliged to such attendances every day as I am, on one committee or other. And I do find the Duke of York himself troubled, and willing not to be troubled with occasions of having his name used among the Parliament; though he himself doth declare that he did give direction to Lord Brouncker to discharge the men at Chatham by ticket; and will own it if the House call for it, but not else. Thence I attended the King and Council, and some of the rest of us, in a business to be heard about the value of a ship of one Dorrington's.[1] And it was pretty to observe how, Sir W. Penn making use of this argument against the validity of one Oath against the King, being made by the Maisters mate of the ship, who was but a fellow of about 23 years of age – the Maister of the ship against whom we pleaded did say that he did think himself at that age capable of being master's mate of any ship at that age; and doth know that he himself, Sir W. Penn, was so himself, and in no better degree at that age himself – which word did strike Sir W. Penn dumb and made him open his mouth no more; and I saw the King and Duke of York wink at one another at it. This done, we into gallery and there I walked with several people; and among others, my Lord Brouncker, who I do find under much trouble still about the business of the Tickets, his very case being brought in, as is said, this day in the report of the Miscarriages; and he seems to lay much of it on me, which I did clear and satisfy him in, and would be glad with all my heart to serve him in, and have done it more then he hath done for himself, he not deserving the least blame, but commendations, for this.[2] I met with

a repl. same symbol

1. The *Leicester*, owned by Francis and John Dorington, had been sunk and used as a blockship at Blackwall in June 1667: *CSPD 1667*, p. 493; ib., *1667–8*, pp. 206, 409, 538. The Board was at this meeting required to restore to the owners the cables and everything else recoverable, and to fix a reasonable sum in compensation for the loss.

2. Cf. above, viii. 538 & n. 1. For the report of the House's Committee on Miscarriages, see above, viii. 485, n. 1; *CJ*, ix. 49–51; debate in Grey, i. 70–1; Milward, p. 184. The committee stated that their information about Brouncker had been provided by Pepys. A copy of Brouncker's defence (partly in Hewer's hand) is in Rawl. A 191, ff. 237+.

Cosen Roger Pepys and Creed; and from them understand that
the Report was read today of the Miscarriages, wherein my Lord
Sandwich is [blamed] about the business I mentioned this morning;[1]
but I will be at rest, for it can do him no hurt.

Our business of Tickets is soundly up, and many others; so
they went over them again and spent all this morning on the
first, which is the dividing of the Fleete;[2] wherein hot work was,[a]
and that among great men, Privy-Councillors, and they say Sir
W. Coventry; but I do not much fear it, but do hope that it
will show a little of the Duke of Albemarle and the Prince to
have been advisers in it. But whereas they ordered[b] that the
King's speech should be considered today, they took no notice of
it at all, but are really come to despise the King in all possible
ways of showing it.[3] And it was the other day a[c] strange
saying, as I am told by my Cosen Pepys, in the House, when it
was moved that the King's speech should be considered, that
though the first part of the speech, meaning the league that is
there talked of,[4] be the only good public thing that hath been
done since the King came into England, yet it might bear with
being put off to consider till Friday next, which was this day.
Secretary Morris did this day in the House, when they talked of
intelligence, say that he was allowed but 700*l* a year for intelligence, whereas in Cromwell's time he did allow 70000*l* a year
for it; and was confirmed therein by Collonell Birch, who said
that thereby Cromwell carried the secret of all the princes of

a MS. 'will'   *b* repl. 'entend'
      c repl. 'when'

---

1. The Committee in fact condemned Sandwich for quitting the
fleet in early October, when the
Dutch were on our coasts, and not for
the events of September mentioned
at p. 68.

2. See above, vii. 144, n. 1.

3. On the 10th the House had
resolved to consider the King's
speech after first hearing the report of
the Committee on Miscarriages: *CJ*,
ix. 41+.

4. The Triple Alliance.

Europ at his girdle.[1] The House is in a most broken condition; nobody adhering to anything, but reviling and finding fault; and now quite mad at the "Undertakers", as they are commonly called, Littleton, Lord Vaughan, Sir R. Howard, and others that are brought over to the Court and did undertake to get the King money; but they despise and will not hear them in the House, and the Court doth do as much, seeing that they cannot be useful to them as was expected.[2] In short, it is plain that the King will never be able to do anything with this Parliament and that the only likely way to do*ᵃ* better (for it cannot do worse) is to break this and call another Parliament; and some do*ᵇ* think that it is intended. I was told tonight that my Lady Castlemayne is so great a gamester as to have won 15000*l* in one night and lost 25000*l* in another night at play, and hath played 1000*l* and 1500*l* at a cast. Thence to the Temple, where at Porter's chamber I met Captain Cocke, but lost our labour, our counsellor

---

a repl. 'day'   *b* MS. 'to'

---

1. Grey (i. 79) places these statements in the next day's debate on the same subject. He gives the amount of Morice's grant as £750 p.a. (as does Pepys below, p. 74). According to P. Fraser, *Intelligence of Secretaries of State* (esp. p. 30), the efficiency of the Cromwellian secret service, under Secretary Thurloe, has been exaggerated, both by partisans (like John Birch in this instance) and by later historians. Certainly the amount spent on it was not £70,000 but c. £2000 p.a.: *EHR*, 12/528. Morice's annual grant (itself only half the normal total available in the 1660s to the two secretaries) was supplemented by special grants. The amounts for 1660–2 (BM, Egerton 2543, ff. 115+, 129*v*) show an annual grant for intelligence and secret service of £6000 (apart from what was occasionally available from the

Post Office), plus certain allowances amounting to c. £700 p.a. Possibly it is these 'allowances' to which Morice here referred. In the economies which began on Lady Day 1668 the main grant was cut to £4000 p.a.: *CSPD 1667–8*, p. 296. Charles II's secret service was administered to great effect, both in domestic and foreign affairs, by Joseph Williamson, one of the greatest public servants of the century. See J. Walker in *TRHS* (ser. 4), 15/211–42.

2. This was a scheme hatched in the previous autumn by which a group of Buckingham's lieutenants in the Commons 'undertook' management – i.e. promised to get a grant of supply in return for office. Edward Seymour and Sir Richard Temple were also involved. For its failure, see C. Roberts, *Growth of responsible government in Stuart Engl.*, pp. 174–5.

not being within, Pemberton; and therefore home and I late at my office, and so home to supper and to bed.

15. Up betimes, and with Captain Cocke by coach to the Temple to his Counsel again about the prize-goods, in order to the drawing up his answer to them; where*a* little done but a confirmation that our best interest is for him to tell the whole truth; and so parted, and I home to the office, where all the morning. And at noon home to dinner; and after dinner, all the afternoon and evening till midnight almost, and till I had tired my own backe and my wife's and Deb's, in titleing of my books for the present year and in setting them in order;[1] which is now done to my very good satisfaction, though not altogether so completely as I think they were the last year, when*b* my mind was more at leisure to mind it.[2] So about midnight to bed, where my wife taking some physic overnight it wrought with her; and those coming upon her with great gripes, she was in mighty pain all night long; yet God forgive me, I did find that I was more*c* desirous to take my rest then to ease her; but there was nothing I could do to do her any good with.

16. *Lords day*. Up and to my chamber, where all the*c* morning making a Catalogue of my books;[3] which did find me work, but with great pleasure, my chamber and books being now set in very good order and my chamber washed and cleaned, which it had not been in some months before – my business and trouble having been so much. At noon Mr. Hollier put in and dined with my wife and me, who was a little better today. His company very good; his story of his love and fortune, which hath been very good and very bad in the world, well worth hearing. Much discourse also about the bad state of the church, and how the clergy are come to be men of no worth in the

---

a repl. 'thence'   *b* repl. 'where'
c MS. 'most'   *d* repl. 'the afternoon

---

1. See above, p. 49, n. 2.
2. Cf. above, vii. 412 & n. 2.

3. None of Pepys's early catalogues survives.

world[1] – and, as the world doth now generally discourse, they must be reformed; and I believe the Hierarchy will in a little time be shaken, whether they will or no – the King being offended with them and set upon it as I hear.

He gone, after dinner to have my head combed; and then to my chamber and read most of the evening till pretty late, when, my wife not being well, I did lie below stairs in our great chamber, where I slept well.

17. Up and to the office, where all the morning till noon getting some things more ready against the afternoon for the Committee of Accounts – which did give me great trouble, to see how I am forced to dance after them in one place and to answer committees of Parliament in another. At noon thence toward the committee; but meeting with Sir W. Warren in Fleet-street, he and I to the ordinary by Temple-bar and there dined together, and to talk, where he doth seem to be very high now in defiance of the Board: now he says that the worst is come upon him, to have his accounts brought to the Committee of Accounts, and he doth reflect upon my late coldness to him;[2] but upon the whole, I do find that he is still a cunning fellow, and will find it necessary to be fair to me; and what hath passed between us of kindness, to*a* hold his tongue*a* – which doth please me very well. Thence to the Committee, where I did deliver the several things they expected from me[3] with great respect and show of satisfaction, and my mind thereby eased of some care. But thence I to Westminster-hall and there spent till late at night, walking to and again with many people; and there in

a–a garbled s.h.

---

1. Hollier was a Puritan, but this was a view taken by some strong Anglicans: cf. John Eachard, *Grounds . . . of the contempt of the clergy* (1670). For Pepys's anti-clericalism, see above, iii. 135 & n. 2; iv. 372 & n. 5; cf. also J. H. Overton, *Life in Engl. Church*, pp. 302+.

2. For his accounts, see below, p. 378 & n. 2; for his quarrel with

Pepys, above, viii. 31 & n. 3. The Committee had ordered him on 10 February to attend them this day to answer questions: PRO, Adm. 106/2886, pt I, s.d.

3. These were a number of contracts: the list drawn up by Hayter and signed by Jessop (Clerk to the Committee of Accounts) is in Rawl. A 184, f. 287r.

general I hear of the great high words that was in the House on Saturdy last, upon the first part of the Committee's Report about the dividing of the fleet;[1] wherein some would have the[a] counsels of the King to be declared, and the reasons of them and who did give them; where Sir W. Coventry lay open to them the consequences of doing that, that the King would never have any honest and wise men ever to be of his Council. They did here in the House talk boldly of the King's bad counsellors, and how they must be all turned out, and many of them, and better brought in; and the proceedings of the Long-Parliament in the beginning of the war were called to memory. And the King's bad intelligence was mentioned, wherein they were bitter against my Lord Arlington; saying, among other things, that whatever Morrices was, who declared he had but 750*l* a year allowed him for intelligence, the King paid too dear for my Lord Arlington's in giving him 10000*l* and a Barony for it.[2]

Sir W. Coventry did here come to his defence in the business of the letter that was sent to call back Prince Rupert after he was divided from the fleet[3] – wherein great delay was objected; but he did show that he sent it at one in the morning, when the Duke of York did give him the instructions after supper that night. And did clear himself well of it; only it was laid as a fault, which I know not how he removes, of not sending it by an express – but by the ordinary post; but I think I have heard he[b] did send it to my Lord Arlington's, and that there it lay for some hours, it coming not to Sir Ph. Honiwoods hand at Portsmouth till 4 in the afternoon that day, being about fifteen or sixteen hours in going; and about this, I think I have heard of a falling-out between my Lord Arlington heretofore, and W. Coventry. Some mutterings I did hear of a design of dissolveing

---

a MS. 'a'   *b* repl. same symbol badly formed

---

1. Reports of debate in Grey, i. 70–9; Milward, pp. 185–7. This was the committee on the miscarriages of the war. For the dividing of the fleet, see above, vii. 144, n. 1.

2. This point was made by Andrew Marvell (member for Hull), who had served in the Secretary's office during the Protectorate. Grey (i. 71) reports the speech under the 14th; Milward (p. 185) agrees with Pepys in dating it the 15th. Milward gives '£1000' instead of £10,000.

3. See above, vii. 144, n. 1.

the Parliament, but I think there is no ground for it yet, though Oliver would have dissolved them for half the trouble and contempt these have put upon the King and his councils. The dividing of the fleet, however, is I hear voted a miscarriage, and the not building a fortification at Sherenesse;*a* and I have reason every hour to expect that they will vote the like of our paying men off by ticket;[1] and what the consequence of that will be I know not, but am put thereby into great trouble of mind. I did spend a little time at the Swan, and there did kiss*b* the maid Sarah.*b* At night home, and there up to my wife, who is still ill, and supped with her, my mind mighty full of trouble for the office and my concernments therein; and so to supper and talking with W. Hewer in her chamber about business of the office, wherein he doth well understand himself and our case, and it doth me advantage to talk with him and the rest of my people. I to bed below, as I did last night.

18. Up by break of day, and walked*c* down to the Old Swan, where I find little Michell building, his Booth[2] being taken down and a foundation laid for a new house, so that that street is like to be a very fine place. I drank, but did not see Betty. And so to Charing-cross stairs, and thence walked to Sir W. Coventry and talked with him; who tells me how he hath been prosecuted, and how he is yet well come off in the business of the dividing of the fleet and the sending of the letter. He expects next to be troubled about the business of bad officers in the fleet, wherein he will bid them name whom they call*d* bad and he will justify himself – having never disposed of any but by the Admiral's liking. And he is able to give an account of all them, how they came recommended, and more will be found

---

a MS. 'Sherenesses' with final 's' struck through   *b–b* garbled s.h.
    c repl. 'was'   *d* repl. 'can'

---

1. The vote about the division of the fleet was passed on the 14th; that about Sheerness on the 17th; that about the payment by tickets on the 22nd: *CJ*, ix. 51, 52, 55.

2. The temporary building put up after the Fire. He kept a strong-water house.

to have been placed by the Prince and Duke of Albemarle then by the Duke of York during the war. And as a no bad instance of the badness of officers, he and I did look over the list of commanders, and found that we could presently recollect 37 commanders that have been killed in actuall service this war.[1] He tells me that Sir Fr. Hollis is the main man that hath prosecuted him hitherto in the business of dividing the fleet, saying vainly that the want of that letter to recall the Prince hath given him that that he shall remember it by to his grave; meaning the loss of his arme – when, God knows, he is as idle and insignificant a fellow as ever came into the fleet. He tells me that in discourse on Saturday, he did repeat Sir Rob. Howard's words about*a* "rowling out" of counsellors; that for his part he*b* neither cared who they rowled in nor who they rowled out, by which the word is become a word of use in the House, the "Rowling out" of officers.[2] I will remember what in mirth he said to me this morning when upon this discourse he said, if ever there was another Dutch war, they should not find a Secretary; "Nor," said I, "a Clerk of the Acts, for I see the reward of it; and thanked God I have enough of my own to buy me a good book and a good fiddle, and I have a good wife;" – "Why," says he, "I have enough to buy me a good book, and shall not need a fiddle,[3] because I have never a one*c* of your good wifes." I understand by him that we are likely to have our business of tickets voted a miscarriage; but cannot tell me what that will signify, more then that he thinks they will report them to the King and there leave them. But I doubt they will do more.

Thence walked over St. James's park to White-hall; and thence to Wesminster-hall and there walked all the morning and did speak with several Parliament-men; among others, Birch, who

---

a repl. 'that he'   *b* MS. 'of'
c repl. same symbol

---

1. The Duke of York gave Pepys a copy of the list of 39 commanders killed in the war: Rawl. A 191, ff. 108–9.

2. The expression did not survive long, and is not noticed in the con-temporary dictionaries or in the *OED* or its *Supplement*.

3. A *double-entendre*. (Cf. 'My master's lost his fiddling stick,/And doesn't know what to do.')

is very kind to me and calls me, with great respect and kindness, a man of business, and he thinks honest; and so, long will stand by me and every such man to the death. My business was to instruct them to keep the House from falling into any mistaken vote about the business of tickets before they were better informed. I walked in the Hall all the morning with my Lord Brouncker, who was in great pain there; and the truth is, his business is, without reason, so ill resented by the generality of the House, that I was almost troubled to be seen to walk with him, and yet am able to justify him in all that he is under so much scandal for. Here I did get a copy of the report itself, about our*a* paying off men by tickets;[1] and am mightily glad to see it now, knowing the state of our case and what we have to answer to, and the more for that the House is like to be kept by other business today and tomorrow; so that against Thursdy I shall be able to draw up some defence to put into some members' hands to inform them; and I think we may [make] a very good one, and therefore my mind is mightily at ease about it. This morning they are upon a Bill brought in today by Sir Rd. Temple, for obliging the King to call Parliaments every three years; or if he fail, for others to be obliged to do it; and to keep him from a power of dissolving any Parliament in less then 40 days after their first day of sitting[2] – which is such a Bill as doth speak very high proceedings to the lessening of the King; and this they will carry, and whatever else they desire, before they will give any money; and the King must have money, whatever it cost him.

a repl. 'us'

---

1. This would be a MS. copy obtained at the office of the Clerk of the House of Commons. Pepys retained a copy (13 February) in Hewer's hand (Rawl. A 191, ff. 229–30), and also a copy of the petition presented on the 18th to the Commons: *The humble petition of many poor distressed sea-mens wives, and widows* (ib., A 195a, f. 76r).

2. This was an attempt (by Temple, Littleton, Howard and others) to re-introduce the terms of the Triennial Act of 1641 which the King had taken care to have repealed in 1664: see above, v. 94 & n. 1. The Commons now ordered the bill to be withdrawn: *CJ*, ix. 52. Reports of debate in Grey, i. 82–4; Milward, pp. 189–90. For Temple's opposition to the act of 1664, see above, v. 99 & n. 3.

I stepped to the Dog tavern, and thither come to me Doll Lane and there we did drink together, and she tells me she is my valentine; and there I did tocar sa cosa and might have done whatever else yo voudrais, but there was nothing but only chairs*a* in the room and so we*a* were unable para hazer algo. Thence, she being gone, and having spoke with Mr. Spicer here, whom I sent for hither to discourse about the security of the late Act of eleven-months Tax, on which I have secured part of my money lent to Tanger,[1] I to the Hall and there met Sir W Pen; and he and I to the Beare in Drury-lane, an excellent ordinary after the French manner,[2] but of Englishmen, and there had a little fricasse, our dinner coming to 8s; which was mighty pretty, to my great content; and thence he and I to the King's House, and there in one of the upper boxes saw *Flora's vagarys*,[3] which is a very silly play; and the more, I being out of humour, being at a play without my wife and she ill at home, and having no desire also to be seen and therefore could not look about me. Thence to the Temple and there we parted; and I to see Kate Joyce, where I find her and her friends in great ease of mind, the Jury having this day given in their verdict that her husband died of a Feaver.[4] Some opposition there was, the foreman*b* pressing them to declare the cause of the Feaver, thinking thereby to obstruct it; but they did adhere to their verdict and would give no reason. And so all trouble is now over, and she's safe in her estate, which I am mighty glad of; and so took leave and home and up to my wife, not owning my being at a play; and there she shows me her ring, which [is] of a Turky-stone set with little sparks of Dyamonds, which I am to give her as my valentine, and I am not much troubled at it, it will cost me near 5l– she costing me but little compared with other wifes, and I have

a–a garbled s.h.   b l.h. repl. l.h. 'Coroner'

1. Sc. the money lent to Pepys as Treasurer for Tangier. He had £15,000 and £6000 registered on orders on this tax. Backwell advanced him £6000 on 9 July 1668. PRO, E 403/2430.

2. I.e. with the courses served separately.

3. A comedy by Richard Rhodes: see above, v. 236, n. 2. (A).

4. Cf. above, pp. 32–4 & nn.

not many occasions to spend on her.   So to my office, where late,
and to think up my observations tomorrow upon the report of
the committee to the Parliament about the business of tickets,
whereof my head is full.   And so home to supper and to
bed.

19.   Up, and to the office, where all the morning drawing
up an answer to the Report of[a] the Committee for Miscarriages
to the Parliament, touching our paying men by tickets[1] – which
I did do in a very good manner I think.   Dined with my clerks[b]
at home, where much good discourse of our business of the Navy
and the troubles now upon us, more then we expected.   After
dinner, my wife out with Deb to buy some things against my
sister's wedding and I to the office to write fair my business I did
in the morning;   and in the evening to White-hall, where I find
Sir W. Coventry all alone a great while with the Duke of York
in the King's drawing-room,[c] they two talking together all alone,
which did mightily please me;   then I did get W. Coventry (the
Duke of York being gone) aside, and there read over my paper;
which he liked and corrected, and tells me it will be hard to
escape, though the thing be never so fair, to have it voted a
miscarriage;   but did advise me and my Lord Brouncker, who
coming by did join with us, to prepare some members in it;
which we shall do.   Here I do hear how La Roche, a French
captain who was once prisoner here, being with his ship at
Plymouth, hath played some reakes there;[2]   for which, his men
being beat out of the town, he hath put[d] up his flag of defiance;
and also, somewhere thereabout, did land with his men and go a
mile into the country and did some prank;   which sounds pretty

---

a   repl. symbol rendered illegible   b   MS. 'clerk'
c   repl. 'bed-chamber'   d   repl. 'p'-

---

1. Office copy in Hayter's hand, 21
February, entitled in Pepys's hand:
'Considerations offered by the
Principal Officers & Comissioners
of the Navy touching theyr dis-
charging Seamen by Ticket': Rawl.
A 191, ff. 233–5; signed by Pepys and
Mennes. On the flyleaf Pepys has
written a note that unsigned copies
were sent to Col. Birch, Sir John
Lowther and Mr. Jolliffe.

2. See the account of his raids
below, pp. 96–7 & n. He had been
taken prisoner by Rupert in 1666.

odd, to our disgrace, but we are in condition now to bear anything. But blessed be God, all the Court is full of the good news
of my Lord Sandwiches having made a peace between Spain and
Portugall; which is mighty great news, and above all, to my
Lord's honour, more then anything he ever did;[1] and yet I do
fear it will not prevail to secure him in Parliament against
incivilities there.[2] Thence took up my wife at Unthankes and
so home; and there, my mind being full of preparing my paper
against tomorrow for the House, with an*a* address from the office
to the House, I to the office, there late, and then home to supper
and to bed.

20. Up and to the office a while; and thence to White-hall*b*
by coach, with Mr. Batelier with me, whom I took up in the
street. I thence by water to Westminster-hall, and there with
Lord Brouncker, Sir T. Harvey, Sir J. Mennes, did wait all the
morning to speak to members about our business, thinking our
business of Tickets would come before the House today; but we
did alter our minds about the petition to the House or sending in
the paper to them. But the truth is, we were in a great hurry,
but it fell out that they were most of the morning upon the
business of not prosecuting the first victory; which they have
voted one of the greatest miscarriages of the whole war; though
they cannot lay the fault anywhere yet, because Harman is not
come home.[3] This kept them all the morning, which I was

a repl. 'a'   *b* repl. 'Wesminster'

1. This was the treaty of Lisbon
(signed 3/13 February) ending the
twenty-six years war between Spain
and Portugal. See above, p. 59 &
n. 3.
2. In the matter of the prize-goods
scandal, now being investigated by
the Commons' Committee on Miscarriages.
3. For the debate and vote, see
Grey, i. 86–7; Milward, pp. 193–4;
CJ, ix. 53–4. For the controversy
over the conduct of the Battle of
Lowestoft (June 1665), see above,
viii. 490, 491–2 & nn. Sir John
Harman had commanded the *Royal
Charles*, carrying the Duke of York,
and had obeyed what he took to be
the Duke's orders to shorten sail. He
was now ordered to attend the House.
On his return from the W. Indies in
early April he was committed to the
Tower, and examined by the Commons on the 17th: *CJ*. ix. 82.

glad of. So down to the Hall, where my wife by agreement stayed for me at Mrs. Michell's; and there was Mercer and the girl, and I took them to Wilkinson's, the cook's in King's-street (where I find the maister of the house hath been dead for some time) and there dined; and thence by one a-clock[1] to the King's Play-[house], a new play, *The Duke of Lerma*, of Sir Rob. Howard's, where the King and Court was there; and Knepp and Nell spoke the prologue[2] most excellently, especially Knepp, who spoke beyond any creature I ever heard. The play designed to reproach our King with his mistress;[3] that I was troubled for it, and expected it should be interrupted; but it ended all well, which salved all. The play a well-writ and good play; only, its design I did not like, of reproaching the King – but altogether, a very good and most serious play. Thence home, and there a little to the office; and so home to supper, where Mercer with us, and sang and then to bed.

21. At the office all the morning to get a little business done, I having, and so the whole office, been put out of doing any business there for this week by our trouble in attending the Parliament. Hither comes to me young Captain Beckford the slopseller, and there presents me a little purse with gold in it, it being, as he told me, for his present ⟨to me⟩ at the end of the last year. I told him I had not done him any service I knew of; he persisted and I refused, but did at several[a] denials; and telling him that it was not an age to take presents in, he told me he had

a MS. 'service'

---

1. I.e. two and a half hours before the customary time of commencement. (A).
2. Their joint delivery of the prologue receives special mention in the first edition of the play (1668). For the play, see above, p. 20, n. 1. (A).
3. Nell Gwyn played the part of Maria, with whom the King of Spain falls in love, but she is never represented as his mistress, and there is little in the text to prompt Pepys's assumption except an episode in Act IV, Scene i, in which certain characters ascribe 'lust' and 'luxury' to Maria and the King. These accusations are baseless, however. (A).

reason to present me with something, and desired me to accept of it; which, at his so urgeing me, I did; and so fell to talk of his business, and so parted.[1] I do not know of any manner of kindness I have done him this last year – nor did expect anything. It was therefore very welcome to me, but yet I was not fully satisfied in my taking it, because of my submitting myself to the having it objected against me hereafter; and the rather, because this morning Jacke Fen came and showed me an order from the Commissioners of Accounts, wherein they demand of him an account upon oath of all the sums of money that have been by him defalked or taken from any man since their time[a] of enquiry upon any payments; and if this should, as it is to be feared, come to be done to us, I know not what I shall then do; but I shall take counsel upon it. At noon by coach toward Westminster, and met my Lord Brouncker and W. Penn and Sir T. Harvey in King's-street, coming away from the Parliament House; and so I to them and to the French ordinary at the Blue Balls in[b] Lincoln's Inn fields and there dined and talked; and among other things, they tell me how the House this day is still as backward for giving any money as ever, and do declare they will first have an account of the disposals of the last Pole bill and Eleven-Months Tax; and it is pretty odde that the very first sum mentioned in the account brought in by Sir Rob. Long of the disposal of the Poll-bill money is 5000*l* to my Lord Arlington for intelligence; which was mighty unseasonable, so soon after they had so much cried out against his want of intelligence.[2] The King doth also own but 250000*l*[3] or thereabout yet paid on the

a repl. 'enq'—   *b* repl. 'at'

---

1. The purse contained 50 gns: Rawl. A 185, f. 23*v*. On 6 March Beckford sent to Pepys a petition on behalf of all victualling contractors desiring payment: Rawl. A 195a, f. 231*r*. Some years later (c. 1676) Beckford was accused of serving in 'tobacco, brandy and other things under the name of clothes': *CSPD Add. 1660–85*, pp. 457–8.

2. See above, p. 74 & n. 2. The effect of this debate would be to decide whether or not there would be a summer fleet. See below, pp. 92–3, 216. Long was Auditor of the Receipt in the Exchequer.

3. Milward (p. 194) gives £237,000.

Poll-bill, and that he hath charged 350000*l* upon it. This makes them mad; for that the former Poll-bill, that was much less in its extent then the last, which took in all sexes and qualities, did come to 350000*l*.[1] Upon the whole, I perceive they are like to do nothing in this matter to please the King or relieve the State, be the case never so pressing; and therefore it is thought*a* by a great many that the King cannot be worse if he should dissolve them; but there is nobody dares advise it, nor doth he consider anything himself. Thence, having dined for 20*s*, we to the Duke of York at White-hall and there had our usual audience, and did little*b* but talk of the proceedings of the Parliament; wherein he is as much troubled as we, for he is not without fears that they do ayme at doing him hurt; but yet he declares that he will never deny to owne what orders he hath given to any man to justify him, notwithstanding their having sent to him to desire his being tender to take upon him the doing anything of that kind. Thence with Brouncker and T. Harvey to Wesminster-hall; and there met with Collonell Birch and Sir Jo. Lowther and did there in the Lobby read over what I have drawn up for our defence,[2] wherein they own themselfs mightily satisfied; and Birch, like a perticular friend, doth take it upon him to defend us, and doth mightily do me right in all his discourse. Here walked in the Hall with them a great while and discoursed with several members, to prepare them in our business against to-morrow. And meeting my Cosen Rogr. Pepys, he showed me Grangers written confession of his being forced by imprisonment ⟨by my Lord Gerard⟩ &c. most barbarously to confess his forging of a deed in behalf of Fitton in the great case between

a repl. 'wish'   *b* repl. 'all'

---

1. The former poll-bill was that of 1660; the 'last' that of 1667. The 1660 bill yielded £252,167; that of 1667, c. £500,000: S. Dowell, *Hist. Taxation*, ii. 29. On this day a Committee of the Whole had considered a motion for supply made on the 19th: *CJ*, ix. 53, 55. Reports of debate in Grey, i. 89, 90; Milward, pp. 194–5.

2. See above, p. 79, n. 1.

him and my Lord Gerard;[1] which business is under examination, and is the foulest against my Lord Gerard that ever[a] anything in the world was, and will, all do believe, ruine him – and I shall be glad of it. Thence with Brouncker and T. Harvey as far as New Exchange, and there at a draper's shop drawing[b] up a short note of what they are to desire of the House for our having a hearing before they determine anything against us, which paper is for them to show to what friends they meet against to-morrow, I away home to the office, and there busy pretty late; and here comes my wife to me, who hath been at Pegg Pen's christening,[2] which she says hath made a flutter and noise, but was as mean as could be and but little company – just like all the rest that that family do. So home to supper and to bed, with my head full of a defence before the Parliament tomorrow; and therein content myself very well, and with what I have done in preparing some of the members thereof in order thereto.

---

a repl. 'every'   *b* MS. 'dropping'

---

1. This was a dispute over the descent of the property of Sir Edward Fitton of Gawsworth, Cheshire (d. 1643), between his kinsman Alexander Fitton (cr. Baron Fytton of Gosworth, co. Limerick, 1689) who had possessed it during the Interregnum, and Lord Gerard of Brandon (the late owner's nephew), who had claimed it at the Restoration. (For Gerard's reputation for unscrupulousness, see above, viii. 574 & n. 1.) A Chancery award of 27 November 1662 in Gerard's favour had been challenged by Fitton in a 'libel' for which the House of Lords had imprisoned him. Fitton had now addressed a petition to the Commons, on which a committee reported on 22 February 1668. Fitton claimed that Gerard had bribed Abraham Gowry (*alias* Granger), a 'notorious cheat', then a pri-

soner in the Gatehouse, to state that he had forged the deed on which Fitton's case in 1662 had rested. Litigation continued into James II's reign, but Gerard remained in possession. *LJ*, xi. 554, 555; *CJ*, ix. 54, 55; Milward, pp. 195–6; *A true narrative of the proceedings in the severall suits in law that have been between the Right Hon. Charles Lord Gerard of Brandon and A. Fitton Esq.*, . . . (The Hague, 1663); *A true account of the unreasonableness of Mr Fitton's pretences* . . . (1685); R. North, *Life of* . . . *Guilford* (1742), pp. 206–8; G. Ormerod, *Hist. Cheshire* (1882 ed.), iii. 551 n.

2. The daughter of Anthony and Peg Lowther (*née* Penn) was now named Margaret: *Harl. Soc. Reg.*, 46/75.

22. Up, and by coach through Ducke lane; and there did buy Kircher's *Musurgia*, cost me 35s, a book I am mighty glad of, expecting to find great satisfaction in it.[1] Thence to West-minster-hall and the Lobby, and up and down there all the morning; and to the Lords' House and heard the Sollicitor generall plead very finely, as he always doth; and[a] this was in defence of the East India Company against a man that complains of wrong from them.[2] And thus up and down till noon, in expectations of our business coming on in the House of Commons about Tickets; but they being busy about my Lord Gerard's business, I did give over the thoughts of ours coming on; and so with my wife and Mercer and Deb, who came to the Hall to me, I away to the Beare in Drury-lane and there bespoke a dish of meat and in the meantime sat and sung with Mercer; and by and by dined with mighty pleasure, and excellent meat, one little dish enough for us all, and good wine, and all for 8s. And thence to the Duke's playhouse and there saw *Albumazar*,[3] an old play, this the second time of acting; it is said to have been the ground of B. Johnson's *Alchymist*;[4] but saving the ridiculous-nesse of Angell's part, which is called Trinkilo,[5] I do not see any-thing extraordinary in it; but was endeed weary of it before it was done. The King here, and indeed all of us, pretty merry at

a repl. 'and thus it was'

1. Athanasius Kircher, *Musurgia Universalis, sive Ars magna consoni et dissoni* (Rome, 1650); PL 2467–8; now bought unbound (see below, pp. 89, 101–2 & nn). (E).

2. For the case (Thomas Skinner *v.* E. India Company), see below, pp. 182–3 & n. It was the occasion of a long dispute between the Commons and the Lords, and became a leading case in the matter of the original jurisdiction of the Lords in civil cases. The Solicitor-General was Sir Hene-age Finch.

3. A comedy by Thomas Tomkis, performed at Trinity College, Cam-bridge on 9 March 1615 and pub-lished in the same year. (A).

4. This erroneous assumption de-rives from the prologue written by Dryden for the 1668 revival of Tomkis's comedy. *The Alchemist* was acted in 1610, five years before what was almost certainly the first performance of *Albumazar*. (A).

5. Trincalo, a blustering farmer, is the chief comic role in *Albumazar*, and was played by Edward Angel, one of the original members of the Duke of York's Company. (A).

the mimique tricks of Trinkilo. So home, calling in Ducke-
lane for the book I bought this morning; and so home and wrote
my letters at the office, and then home to supper and to bed.

23. *Lords day.* Up, and being desired by a messenger from
Sir G. Carteret, I by water over to Southwarke, and so walked
to the Falkon on the Bankside and there got another boat; and
so to Westminster,*a* where I would have gone into the Swan,
but the door was locked and the girl could not let me in;[1] and
so to Wilkinson's in King-street and there wiped my shoes, and
so to Court – where sermon not yet done; I met with Brisbanke
and he tells me first that our business of tickets did come to
debate yesterday (it seems after I was gone away) and was voted
a miscarriage in general.[2] He tells me in general that there is
great looking after places, upon a presumption of a*b* great many
vacancies; and he did show me a fellow at Court, a brother of
my Lord Fanshaw's, a witty but rascally fellow without a penny
in his purse, that was asking him what places there were in the
Navy fit for him;[3] and Brisbank tells me in mirth, he told him
the Clerk of the Acts; and I wish he had it, so I were well and
quietly*c* rid of it, for I am weary of this kind of trouble, having I
think enough whereon to support myself. By and by, chapel
done, I met with Sir W. Coventry and he and I walked awhile
together in the Matted Gallery and there he told me all the proceedings yesterday: that the matter[4] is found in general a miscarriage, but no persons named; and so there is no great matter
to our prejudice yet, till, if ever, they come to perticular persons.
He told me Birch was very industrious to do what he could,
and did like a friend; but they were resolv[ed] to find the thing

---

a l.h. repl. s.h. 'White'-   *b* repl. 'all'
    c repl. same symbol badly formed

---

1. Taverns were forbidden to serve
customers during divine service.
2. *CJ*, ix. 55; debate in Milward,
pp. 196–7.
3. This was Henry Fanshawe, brother of the 2nd Viscount. He had a
minor post in the Exchequer ('keeping, sorting and ordering' hearth-tax
returns) for which he had a salary of
£20 p.a.: *CTB*, iii. 215; H. C.
Fanshawe, *Fanshawe Family*, p. 121.
4. Of tickets.

in general a miscarriage; and says that when we shall think fit to desire its being heard as to our own defence, it will be granted.[1] He tells me how he hath with advantage cleared himself in what concerns himself therein, by his servant Robson; which I am glad of. He tells me that there is a letter sent by conspiracy to some of the House, which he hath seen, about the matter of selling of places, which he doth believe he shall be called upon tomorrow for and thinks himself well prepared to defend himself in it; and then neither he, nor his friends for him, are afeared of anything to his prejudice.[2] Thence[a] by coach with Brisband to Sir G. Carteret's in Lincoln's Inn fields, and there dined – a good dinner and good company; and after dinner he and I alone, discoursing of my Lord Sandwiches matters; who hath in the first business before the House[3] been very kindly used, beyond expectation, the matter being laid by till his coming home; and old Mr. Vaughan did speak for my Lord,[4] which I am mighty glad of. The business of the prizes[5] is the worst that can be said, and therein I do fear something may lie hard upon him – but against this, we must prepare the best we can for his defence. Thence with G. Carteret to White-hall, where I finding a meeting of the[b] committee of the Council for the Navy,[6] his Royal Highness there and Sir W. Penn, and some of the Brethren of Trinity-house to attend, I did go in with them; and it was to be informed

<hr/>

a repl.? 'come'   *b* repl. 'a'

<hr/>

1. See below, p. 95 & n. 1.
2. The petition was presented on the 24th by Sir Robert Brooke, but since it accused nobody by name the House did not allow it to be read: Grey, i. 92; Milward, p. 197. Presented again in April, it named Coventry: Rawl. A 195a, f. 74 (copy). For Coventry's reply (13 April), see Milward, pp. 320–1. He had been accused of the same offence in 1663 (see above, iv. 170, 330 & nn.), and made both then and now a considerable collection of papers in his own defence (Longleat, Coventry MSS 101, ff. 104–244).

Cf. V. Vale in *Camb. Hist. Journ.*, 12/114+.
3. The charge against Sandwich of quitting the fleet in October 1665. See above, p. 70 & n. 1.
4. Writing about a later debate, Creed told Sandwich (1 June) that John Vaughan had been very helpful to Sandwich's interest: Sandwich MSS, Letters from Ministers, ii, f. 111r.
5. See above, vi. 230–1 & n.
6. For the committee, see above, p. 67, n. 3. Report of meeting in *HMC, Rep.*, 8/1/1/253*b*.

of the practice heretofore, for all foreign nations at enmity one
with another to forbear any acts of hostility one to another in
the presence of any of the King of England's ships; of which
several instances was given[1] and is referred to their further enquiry,
in order to the giving instructions accordingly[a] to our ships now
during the war between Spain and France – would to God we
were in the same condition as heretofore, to challenge and maintain this our Dominion.   Thence with W. Penn homeward and
quite through to Mile end for a little ayre, the days being now
pretty long but the ways mighty dirty.   And here we drank at
the Rose,[2] the old house, and so back again, talking of the Parliament and our trouble with them, and what passed yesterday.
Going back again, Sir R. Brookes[3] overtook us coming to town;
who hath played the Jacke with us all and is a fellow that I must
trust no more, he quoting me for all he hath said in this business of
tickets; though I have told him nothing that either is not true
or I afeared to own.   But here talking, he did discourse in this
style – " Wee", and "wee" all along, "will not give any money,
be the pretence never so great; nay, though the enemy was in
the River of Thames again, till we know what became of the
last money given;" and I do believe he doth speak the mind of
his fellows – and so let them, if the King will suffer it.   He gone,
we home and there I to read, and my belly being full of my
dinner today, I anon to bed and there, as I have for many days,
slept not an hour quietly, but full of dreams of our[b] defence to
the Parliament and giving an account of our doings.   This
evening, my wife did with great pleasure show me her stock of
Jewells, encreased by[c] the ring she had made lately as my Valen-

----

a   repl. same symbol badly formed
b   repl. 'my'   c   repl. 'my'

----

1. 'The Master [of Trinity House]
instanced a passage when King
Charles the 1st returned from Spain
and found some Dutch men-of-war
fighting with Ostenders, which were
parted, and though they did im-
portune the King, then prince, for
liberty to fight, he would not permit
them, but kept some of the commanders on board till the others
sailed away.': HMC, op. cit., loc.
cit.

2. The Rose and Crown: cf.
below, p. 255.

3. Chairman of the Commons'
Committee on Miscarriages.

tine's gift this year, a Turky-stone set with Diamonds; and with this and what she had, she reckons that she hath above 150*l* worth of Jewells*a* of one kind or other. And I am glad of it, for it is fit the wretch*should have something to content herself with.

24. Up, and to my office, where most of the morning entering my Journall for the three days past. Thence about noon with my wife to the New Exchange, by the way stopping at my bookseller's and there leaving my Kircher's *Musurgia* to be bound,*b1* and did buy *L'illustre Bassa*2 in four volumes for my wife. Thence to the Exchange and left her; while meeting Dr. Gibbons3 there, he and I to see an Organ at the Deane of Westminister's lodgings at the Abby, the Bishop of Rochester's, where he lives like a great prelate, his lodgings being very good, though at present under great disgrace at Court, being put by his Clerk of the Closet's place.4 I saw his lady, of whom the *Terrae filius* of Oxford was once so merry5 – and two children, whereof one very pretty little boy like him, so fat and black. Here I saw the organ; but it is too big for my house and the fashion* doth not please me enough, and therefore will not have it.6 Thence to the Change back again, leaving him, and took my wife and Deb home and there to dinner alone; and after dinner I took them to the Nursery,7 where none of us ever was before; where the house is better and the Musique better then we looked for, and*c* the acting not much worse, because I expected as bad as could: and

a repl. 'one k'-   *b* MS. 'found'   *c* repl. 'but'

---

1. For the book and its binding, see above, p. 85, n. 1.
2. *Ibrahim, ou L'illustre Bassa*, a lengthy and fashionable romance by Madeleine de Scudéri, first published at Paris in 1641; not in the PL.
3. Christopher (son of Orlando) Gibbons, organist of Westminster Abbey. (E).
4. Cf. above, p. 53 & n. 2.
5. His wife was Catherine Sheldon, niece of Archbishop Sheldon. She and her husband had lived in St Aldate's Oxford, c. 1657–60. The *Terrae Filius* was the licensed jester who performed at university ceremonies. I have not discovered the reason for his making fun of her.
6. For Pepys's intention to buy an organ, see above, viii. 532 & n. 1. (E).
7. See above, p. 14, n. 2. (A).

I was not much mistaken, for it was so. However, I was pleased well to see it once, it being worth a man's seeing to discover the different ability and understanding of people, and the different growth of people's abilities by practice. Their play was a bad one, called *Jeronimo is Mad Again*[1] – a tragedy. Here was some good company by us who did make mighty sport at the folly of their Acting, which I could not neither refrain from sometimes, though I was sorry for it. So away thence home, where to the office to do business a while, and then home to supper and to read, and then to bed. I was prettily served this day at the playhouse-door; where giving six shillings into the fellow's hand for us three, the fellow by legerdemain did convey one away, and with so much grace face me down that I did give him but five, that though I knew the contrary, yet I was overpowered by his so grave and serious demanding the other shilling that I could not deny him, but was forced by myself to give it him.[2] After I came home this evening comes a letter to me from Captain Allin, formerly Clerk of the Ropeyard at Chatham and whom I was kind to in those days, who in recompense of my favour to him then doth give me notice that he hears of an accusation likely to be exhibited against me, of my receiving 50*l* of Mason the timber merchant, and that his wife hath spoke it. I am mightily beholden to Captain Allin for this, though the thing is to the best of my memory utterly false, and I do believe it to be wholly so;[3] but yet it troubles me to have my name mentioned in this business, and more to consider how I may be liable to be accused where I have endeed taken presents, and therefore puts me upon an enquiry into my actings in this kind and prepare against a day of accusation.

25. Up, having lain this last night the first night that I have lain with my wife since she was last ill, which is about eight days.

---

1. The famous Elizabethan play, *The Spanish tragedy, or Hieronymo is mad again*, by Thomas Kyd, first acted c. 1586 and published in 1592. (A).

2. Theatre door-keepers were notorious for sharp practices. Prices at a 'nursery' were lower than those at the major theatres; 6*s.* may have been the cost of three seats in the pit. (A).

3. It was Hewer who had received Mason's present: below, p. 283.

To the office, where busy all the morning. At noon comes W How to me to advise what answer to give to the*a* business of the Prizes; wherein I did give him the best advice I could, but am sorry to see so many things wherein I doubt it will not be prevented but Sir Rogr. Cuttance and Mr. Pierce will be found very much concerned in goods beyond the distribution, and I doubt my Lord Sandwich too – which troubles me mightily. He gone, I to dinner; and thence set my wife at the New Exchange, and I and Mr. Clerke my solicitor to the Treasury-chamber; but the Lords did not sit, so I by water with him to the New Exchange and there he parted, and I took my wife and Deb up, and to the Nursery, where I was yesterday, and there saw them act a comedy, a Pastorall, *The Faythfull Shepheard*,[1] having the curiosity to see whether they did a comedy better then a Trajedy; but they do it both alike in the meanest manner, that I was sick of it but only for to satisfy myself once in seeing the manner of it – but I shall see them no more I believe.

Thence to the New Exchange to take some things home that my wife hath bought, a dressing-box and other things for her chamber and table, that cost me above 4*l*. And so home, and there to the office and tell W. Hewer of the letter from Captain Allen last night, to give him caution if anything should be discovered of his dealings with anybody which I should, for his sake as well or more then for my own, be sorry for. And with great joy I do find, looking over my Memorandum-books,[2] which are now of great use to me and do fully reward me for all my care in keeping them, that I am not likely to be troubled for anything of that kind but what I shall either be able beforehand to prevent,

a repl. 'his'

---

1. A pastoral play based upon Battista Guarini's *Il pastor fido* (1590). The first of several 17th-century English translations; published in 1602. (A).

2. The office memorandum-books which survived in 1688 (but are no longer extant) consisted of a series of four, beginning in January 1666: BM, Add. 9303, f. 124*r*. Pepys also kept two more comprehensive memorandum-books: 'Memorandums and Conclusions of the Navy Board' [1660–8] (PRO, Adm. 106/3520); and his 'Navy White Book' [1663–72] (PL 2581: q.v. above, v. 116 & n. 1).

or if discovered, be able to justify myself in. And I do perceive by Sir W. Warren's discourse that they[1] do all they can possibly to get out of him and others what presents they have made to the Officers of the Navy. But he tells me that he hath denied[a] all, though he knows that he is forsworn as to what relates to me. So home to supper and to bed.

26. Up, and by water to Charing-cross stairs, and thence to W. Coventry to discourse concerning the state of matters in the Navy, where he perticularly acquainted me again with the trouble he is like to meet with about the selling of places, all carried on by Sir Fr. Hollis; but he seems not to value it, being able to justify it to[b] be lawful and constant practice, and never by him used in the least degree since he upon his own motion did obtain a salary of 500*l* in lieu thereof.[c2] Thence to the Treasury-chamber about a little business and so home by coach; and in my way did meet W How going to the Commissioners of Accounts; I stopped and spoke to him, and he seems well resolved what to answer them, but he will find them very strict and not easily put off. So home and there to dinner; and after dinner comes W How to tell me how he sped; who says he was used civilly and not so many questions asked as he expected, but yet I do perceive enough to show that they do entend to know the bottom of things and where to lay the great weight of the disposal of these East India goods,[3] and that they entend plainly to do upon my Lord Sandwich. Thence with him by coach, and set him down at the Temple and I to Westminster-hall; where, it being now about 6 a-clock, I find the House just risen and met with Sir W. Coventry and the Lieutenant of the Tower, they having sat all day and with great difficulty have got a vote for giving the King 300000*l*, not to be raised by any

---

a repl. 'forsworn'   *b* repl. 'to'   *c* MS. 'of thereof'

---

1. The Brooke House Committee.
2. This was in September 1664. See above, iv. 331 & n. 4.

3. The prize-goods taken by Sandwich in 1665: see above, vi. 231, n. 1.

land-tax.[1] The sum is much smaller then I expected and then the King needs; but is grounded upon Mr. Wren's reading our estimates the other day of 270000*l* to*a* keep the fleet abroad, wherein we demanded nothing for setting and fitting of them out, which will cost almost 200000*l* I do verily believe – and do believe that the King hath no cause to thank Wren for this motion.[2] I home to Sir W. Coventry's lodgings with him and the Lieutenant of the Tower, where also was Sir Jo Coventry and Sir Jo Duncum and Sir Job. Charleton; and here a great deal of good discourse, and they seem mighty glad to have this vote passed; which I did wonder at, to see them so well satisfied with so small a sum, Sir Jo. Duncum swearing (as I perceive he will freely do) that it was as much as the nation could beare. Among other merry discourse about spending of money and how much more chargeable a man's living is now, more then it was heretofore, Duncum did swear that in France he did live off 100*l* a year, with more plenty and wine and wenches then he believes can be [had] now for 200*l* – which was pretty odd for him, being a Committee-man's son,[3] to say. Having done here and supped, where I eat very little, we home in Sir Jo. Robinson's coach and there to bed.

27. All the morning at the office, and at noon home to dinner; and thence with my wife and Deb to the King's House to see *Virgin Martyr*, the first time it hath been acted a great while,

a MS. 'for'

---

1. This was the recommendation of a committee, and was not voted by the House until 6 March: *CJ*, ix. 62; below, pp. 120–1. The House was so thin at one point that the government was in danger of defeat: Grey, i. 93–4; Milward, p. 198. The government hoped for £500,000: BM, Add. 36916, f. 77*r*. Cf. Marvell, ii. 66.

2. The cost of setting out the summer fleet had been debated in a Committee of the Whole on 21 February: Milward, pp. 194–5. Matthew Wren's speech has not been traced. He was secretary to the Duke of York and M.P. for St Michael's, Cornwall.

3. 'Committee-men' were members of the committees which had during most of the puritan revolution displaced J.P.'s, the traditional governors of the shires. But Pepys was mistaken in thinking that Duncombe's father was one of them: see above, viii. 245, n. 1.

and it is mighty pleasant; not that the play is worth much, but it is finely Acted by Becke Marshall;[1] but that which did please me beyond anything in the whole world was the wind-musique when the Angell comes down,[2] which is so sweet that it ravished me; and endeed, in a word, did wrap up my soul so that it made me really sick, just as I have formerly been when in love with my wife; that neither then, nor all the evening going home and at home, I was able to think of anything, but remained all night transported, so as I could not believe that ever any music hath that real command over the soul of a man as this did upon me; and makes me resolve to practise wind-music and to make my wife do the like.[3]

28. Up and to the office, where all the morning doing business; and after dinner with Sir W. Penn to White-hall, where we ⟨and the rest of us⟩ presented a great letter of the state of our want of money to his Royal Highness.[4] I did also present a demand of mine for consideration for my travelling-charges of coach and boat-hire during the war[5] – which though his Royal Highness and the company did all like of, yet contrary[a] to my expectation I find him so jealous now of doing anything extra-

a repl. ? 'the'

---

1. She played the part of St Dorothea. The play was a tragedy by Dekker and Massinger: q.v. above, ii. 37, n. 3. (A).

2. The part of the angel was probably played by Nell Gwyn: J. H. Wilson in *N. & Q.*, 27 February 1948, pp. 71-2. Spectacular descents in Restoration theatres were managed by means of ropes and pulleys. Pepys is probably referring to the episode in V, i, in which Angelo appears to Theophilus. As in the Elizabethan theatre, the descent of a supernatural being in the Restoration theatre was usually accompanied by music. The music played on this occasion (presumably on recorders) has not been traced. (A).

3. Pepys started to learn the recorder on 16 April, and his wife resumed lessons on the flageolet on 13 August: below, pp. 164, 279. (E).

4. Untraced; in preparation since 4 February: above, p. 49.

5. Copy (in Hewer's hand) in NMM, LBK/8, p. 528; printed in *Further Corr.*, p. 191. Pepys informed the Duke that he had kept 'a dayly accompt' of all expenses incurred through travel on official business 'in a booke distinct from what ever like expences he hath been at on his perticuler occasions', and had frequently spent 6s. 8d. per day.

ordinary, that he desired the gentlemen that they would consider it and report their minds in it to him.   This did unsettle my mind a great while, not expecting this stop: but however, I shall do as well I know, though it causes me a little stop.   But that that troubles me most is that while we were thus together with the Duke of York, comes in Mr. Wren from the House, where he tells us another storm hath been all this day almost against the Officers of the Navy upon this complaint: that though they have made good rules for payment of tickets, yet that they have not observed them themselfs; which was driven so high as to have it urged that we should presently be put out of our places – and so they have at last ordered that we be heard at the bar of the House upon this business on Thursdy next.[1]   This did mightily trouble me and us all; but me perticularly, who am least able to bear these troubles, though I have the least cause to be concerned in it. Thence therefore to visit Sir H. Chomly, who hath for some time been ill*a* of a cold; and thence walked towards Westminster and met Collonell Birch, who took me back to walk with him and did give me an account of this day's heat against the Navy officers, and an account of his speech on our behalfs, which was very good;[2] and endeed, we are much beholden to him, as I, after I parted with him, did find by my Cosen Roger, whom I went to; and he and I to his lodgings and there he did tell me the same over again, and how much Birch did stand up in our defence – and that he doth see that there are many desirous to have us out of the office; and the House is so furious and passionate that he thinks nobody can be secure, let him deserve never so well; but how[ever] he tells me we shall have a fair hearing from*b* the House, and he hopes justice of them.   But upon the whole, he doth agree with me that I should hold my hand as to making any purchase of land, which I had formerly discoursed with

a repl. 'all'   *b* MS. 'for' (? 'fore)

---

1. *CJ*, ix. 58; reports of debate in Grey, i. 98; Milward, p. 201. The Board had established an order of priorities for payment – first the dead, second the wounded and thereafter according to length of service – but were alleged to have observed it for only one week.   For Pepys's speech in defence of the Board on 5 March, see below, pp. 102–4.

2. Grey and Milward summarise only the speeches of the critics; no printed account I have seen mentions Birch's defence.

him about, till we see a little further how matters go. He
tells me that that that made them so mad today first, was several
letters in the House about the Fanatickes in several places coming
in great bodies and turning people out of the churches and there
preaching themselfs and pulling the surplice over the parsons'
heads: this was confirmed from several places, which makes them
stark mad, especially the hectors and bravados of the House –
who show all the zeal on this occasion.[1]   Having done with him,
I home, vexed in my mind and so fit for no business; but sat
talking with my wife and supped with her, and Nan Mercer came
and sat all the evening with us – and much pretty discourse,[a]
which did a little ease me.   And so to bed.

29.   Up and walked to Captain Cock's, where Sir G Carteret
promised to meet me, and did come to discourse about the prize
business of my Lord Sandwiches, which I perceive is likely to be
of great ill consequence to my Lord, the House being mighty
vehement in it.   We could say little, but advise that his friends
should labour to get it put off till he comes.   We did here talk
many things over, in lamentation[b] of the present posture of affairs
and the ill condition of all people that have had anything to do
under the King – wishing ourselfs a great way off.   Here they
tell me how Sir Tho. Allen hath taken the Englishmen out of
La Roche, and taken from him a Ostend prize which La Roche
had fetched out of our harbours.   And at this day La Roche
keeps upon our coasts; and had the boldness to land some men
and go a mile up into the country, and there took some goods
belonging to this prize out of a house there – which our King
resents and they say hath wrote to the King of France about;
and everybody doth think a Warr will fallow – and then, in what

a   repl. same symbol badly formed
b   repl. same symbol badly formed

1. *CJ*, ix. 58; reports of debate in
Grey, i. 97; Milward, p. 201.   One
allegation (of riotous behaviour at
Betley, Staffs.) was referred to a
committee on 5 March and is denied
by the biographer of Philip Henry,
one of the nonconforming ministers
involved: M. Henry, *Account of . . .
P. Henry* (1712), pp. 90–1; cf. *CJ*, ix.
61.

a case we shall be for want of money, nobody knows.[1] Thence to the office, where we sat all the morning; and at noon home to dinner, and to the office again in the afternoon, where we met to consider of an answer to the Parliament about the not paying of tickets according to our own Orders, to which I hope we shall be able to give a satisfactory answer – but that the design of the House being apparently to remove us, I do question whether the best answer will prevail with them. This done, I by coach with my wife to Martin my bookseller's, expecting to have had my Kercher's *Musurgia*; but to my trouble and[a] loss of time,[b] it was not done. So home again, my head full of thoughts about our troubles in the office, and so to the office; wrote to my father this post, and sent him now Colvill's note for 600*l*[2] for my sister's portion, being glad that I shall, I hope, have that business over before I am out of play; and I trust I shall be able to save a little of what I have got, and so shall not be troubled to be at ease, for I am weary of this life; so home to supper and to bed.

So ends this month, with a great deal of care and trouble in my head about the answerings of the Parliament, and perticularly in our payment of seamen by tickets.

---

a repl. 'it'   *b* MS. 'trouble'

---

1. Louis de la Roche, in the *Jules César*, commanded a small French squadron which had been attacking the lines of communication between Spain and the Netherlands in the Channel. He had captured a company of English soldiers in Plymouth under Capt. Bevill Skelton destined for the service of Spain, and was transporting them to France. At Torquay he had attacked an Ostend ship (the *Sainte Marie*) in the harbour itself, and had landed an armed party to secure its cargo, which had been hidden in a private house. Charles II had made a vigorous protest to the French king about these violations of English soil and waters, and had instructed Sir Thomas Allin to intercept de la Roche if he found himself with a superior force. Allin had come up with the French off Spithead on the 25th, and after an exchange of civilities, had secured the release of the English troops and the Ostend prize. See Allin, ii. 9–10; *CSPD 1667–8*, passim; C. H. Hartmann, *The King my brother*, pp. 213–14; *Bulstrode Papers*, i. 26, 27.

2. 'This appears to be the earliest definite case recorded of the use of a goldsmith's note for making a payment': A. E. Feavearyear, *Pound Sterling*, p. 98.

MARCH.

1. *Lords day.* Up very betimes and by coach to Sir W. Coventry, and there, largely carrying with me all my notes and papers, did run over our whole defence in the business of Tickets, in order to the answering the House on Thursday next; and I do think, unless they be set without reason to ruin us, we shall make a good defence.[1] I find him in great anxiety, though he will not discover* it, in the business of the proceedings of Parliament; and would as little as is possible have his name mentioned^a in our discourses to them; and perticularly the business of selling places is now upon his hand to defend himself in – wherein I did help him in his defence about the Flaggmaker's place which is named in the House.[2] We did here do the like about the complaint^b of want of victuals in the fleet in the year 1666,[3] which will lie upon me to defend also; so that my head is full of care and weariness in my imployment. Thence home; and there, my mind being a little lightened by my morning's work in the arguments I have now laid together in better method for our defence to the Parliament, I^c to talk with my wife; and in lieu of a Coach this year, I have got my wife to be contented with her closet being made up this summer and going into the country this summer for a month or two to my father's, and there Mercer and Deb and Jane shall go with them; which [I] the rather do for the entertaining my wife, and preventing^d of fallings-out between her and my father or Deb – which uses to be the fate of her going into the country. After dinner, by coach to Westminster and there to St. Margaretts church, thinking to have

---

a repl. symbol rendered illegible   b repl. same symbol badly formed
c repl. 'though'   d repl. 'keeping'

---

1. Pepys's 'several collections' of notes for the defence of the office are in Rawl. A 191, ff. 179–93.
2. This was probably the charge made by Sir Robert Brooke in a debate in Committee of Supply on 24 February: Grey, i. 92. 'His aim was at Sir William Coventry, as was thought': Milward, p. 197.
3. Cf. above, viii. 512, n. 2.

seen Betty Michell, but she was not there; but met her father and mothers and with them to her father's house, where I never was before, but was mighty much made of, with some good strong waters which they have from their son Michell; and mighty good people they are. Thence to Mr[s]. Martin's, where I have not been also a good while, and with great difficulty, company being there, did get*ᵃ* an opportunity to hazer what I would con her.*ᵃ* And here*ᵇ* I was mightily taken with a Starling which she hath, that was the King's, which he kept in his bedchamber, and doth whistle and talk the most and best that ever I heard anything in my life. Thence to visit Sir H Cholmly, who continues still sick of his cold; and thence calling, but in vain, to speak with Sir G. Carteret at his house in Lincoln's Inn field, where I spoke with nobody; but home, where spent the evening talking with W Hewers about business of the House, and declaring my expectation of all our being turned out. Hither comes Carcasse*ᶜ* to me about business, and there did confess*ᵈ* to me of his own accord his having heretofore discovered as a complaint against Sir W. Batten, W. Penn and me, that we did prefer the paying of some men to man the *Flying Greyhound* to others, by order under our hands. The thing upon recollection I believe is true, and do hope no great matter can be made of it; but yet I would be glad to have my name out of it, which I shall labour to do. In the meantime, it lies as a new trouble upon my mind – and did trouble me all night. So without supper to bed, my eyes being also a little overwrought of late, that I could not stay up to read.

2. Up and betimes to the office, where I did much business and several came to me; and among others, I did prepare Mr. Warren, and by and by Sir D Gawden, about what presents I have had from them, that they may not publish them; or if they do, that in truth I received none on the account of the Navy but Tanger. And this is true to the former, and in both, that I never asked anything of them. I must do the like with the rest. Mr. Moore was with me, and he doth tell me, and so W Hewers

a–a   garbled s.h.: see above, viii. 244, note *a*   *b*   repl. 'so'
c   following page of the MS. headed 'Febr' and corrected to 'March'
d   repl. 'tell me'

tells me, he hears this morning that all the town is full of*a* the
discourse that the Officers of the Navy shall be all turned out but
honest Sir Jo. Minnes – who, God knows, is fitter to have been
turned out himself then any of us, doing the King more hurt by
his dotage and fally than all the rest can do by their knavery if
they had a mind to it.   At noon home to dinner, where was
Mercer, and very merry as I could be with my mind so full of
business; and so with my wife, her and the girl, to the King's
House to see *The Virgin Martyr* again; which doth mightily please
me, but above all the Musique at the coming down of the Angell [1] –
which at this hearing the second time doth so still command me
as nothing ever did, and the other music is nothing to it.   Thence
with my wife to the Change; and so calling at the Cocke ale-
house, we home, and there I settle to business and with my people
preparing my great answer to the Parliament for the office
about tickets, till past 12 at night; and then home to supper and
to bed – keeping Mr. Gibson all night with me.   ⟨This day I
have the news that my sister was married on Thursday last to
Mr. Jackson; so that work is I hope well over.⟩*b*[2]

3.   Up betimes to work again, and then met at the Office,
where to our great business of this answer to the Parliament;
where to my great vexation I find my Lord Brouncker prepared
only to excuse himself, while*c* I that have least reason to trouble
myself, am preparing with great pains to defend them all; and
more, I perceive he would lodge the beginning of discharging
ships by ticket upon me – but I care not, for I believe I shall get
more honour by it when the Parliament, against my will, shall
see how the whole business of the office was done by me.   At
noon rose and to dinner; my*d* wife abroad with Mercer and Deb
buying of things, but I with my clerks home to dinner, and thence
presently down with Lord Brouncker, W. Penn, T. Harvy,
T. Middleton, and Mr. Tippets, who first took his place this day

a MS. 'on'   *b* addition crowded in between entries
        c repl. 'why'   *d* repl. 'and present'

---

1. Cf. above, p. 94 & nn. 1, 2.   2. They were married at Brampton.
(A).

at the table as a Commissioner in the room of Comissioner Pett,[1] down by water to Deptford, where the King, Queene, and Court are to see launched the new ship built by Mr. Shish, called the *Charles*: God send her better luck then the former.[2] Here some of our Brethren, who went in a boat a little before my*ᵃ* boat, did by appointment take opportunity of asking the King's leave that we might make full*ᵇ* use of the want of money in our excuse to the Parliament for the business of tickets and other things they will lay to our charge, all which arose from nothing else. And this the King did readily agree to, and did give us leave to make our full use of it. The ship being well launched, I back again by boat, setting T. Middleton and Mr. Tippets on shore at Ratcliffe; I home and there to my chamber with Mr. Gibson, and up late till midnight, preparing more things against our*ᶜ* defence on Thursdy next to my content, though vexed that all this trouble should lie on me. So to supper and to bed.

4. Up betimes and with*ᵈ* Sir W. Penn in his coach to White-hall, there to wait upon the Duke of York and the Commissioners of the Treasury, W. Coventry and Sir Jo. Duncombe – who do declare that they cannot find the money we demand; and we, that less then what we demand will not set out the fleet intended; and so broke up with no other conclusion then that they would let us have what they could get, and we would improve that as well as we could.[3] So God bless us and prepare us against the consequences of these matters. Thence, it being a cold wet day, I home with Sir J. Mennes in his coach, and called by the way at my bookseller's and took home with me Kercher's *Musica*,

     a   repl. 'us'   *b*   repl. 'use'
    c   MS. 'on'   *d*   repl. same symbol

---

1. John Tippets had been appointed Commissioner in charge of Chatham yard on 28 February.

2. The new ship (a 1st-rate) was built to replace the *Royal Charles* captured by the Dutch in 1667. The launch is mentioned in *London Gazette*, 5 March, where the ship is called *Charles the Second*.

3. The official minute of the meeting (*CTB*, ii. 269) does not record any decision on this matter.

very well bound.[1]   But I had no comfort to look upon them, but as soon as I came home fell to my work at the office, shutting the doors that we, I and my clerks, might not be interrupted; and so, only with room for a little dinner, we very busy all the day till night, that the officers met for me to give them the heads of what I intended to say; which I did, with great discontent to see them all rely on me that have no reason at all to trouble myself about it, nor have any thanks from them for my labour; but contrarily, Brouncker looked mighty dogged, as thinking that I did not intend to do it so as to save him.   This troubled me so much, as together with the shortness of the time and muchness of the business, did let me be at it till but about 10 at night; and then, quite weary and dull and vexed, I could go no further, but resolved to leave the rest to tomorrow morning; and so in full discontent and weariness did give over and went home with[out] supper, vexed and sickish, to bed – and there slept about three hours; but then waked, and never in so much trouble in all my life of mind, thinking of the task I have upon me, and upon what dissatisfactory grounds, and what the issue of it may be to me.   With these thoughts I lay troubling myself till 6 a-clock, restless, and at last getting my wife[a] to talk to me to comfort me; which she at last did, and made me resolve to quit my hands of this office and endure the trouble [of] it no longer

《5.》   then till I can clear myself of it.   So, with great trouble but yet with some ease from this discourse with my wife, I up and to my office, whither came my clerks; and so I did huddle up the best I could some more notes for my discourse today; and by 9 a-clock was ready and did go down to the Old Swan, and there by boat, with T. Hater and W. Hewer with me, to

a   repl. 'self'

---

1. For the book and its cost, see above, p. 85 & n. 1. Of the binding Mr H. M. Nixon writes: 'The volumes are in thick calf, with gold tooling on the spines; bound in Style F (see the forthcoming official *Catalogue* of the PL). But there is nothing else in the PL uniform with them. Bought in sheets for 35*s.* from Shrewsbury or Allestree, they were now bound by (or for) Martin, the bookseller. Pepys has a note (on the flyleaf of the first volume) of the total cost ($£3$), which would make the binding-costs 12*s.* 6*d.* per vol.'

Wesminster, where I found myself come time enough and my
Brethren*a* all ready.   But I full of thoughts and trouble touching
the issue of this day; and to comfort myself did go to the Dogg
and drink half a pint of mulled sack, and in the Hall did drink a
dram of brandy at Mrs. Howletts, and with the warmth of this
did find myself in better order as to courage, truly.   So we all
up to the Lobby; and between 11 and 12 a-clock were called in,
with the Mace before us, into the House; where a mighty full
House, and we stood at the Barr – *viz.*, Brouncker, Sir J. Mennes,
Sir T. Harvey and myself – W. Penn being in*b* the House as a
Member.   I perceive the whole House was full, and full of
expectation of our defence what it would be, and with great
præjudice.   After the Speaker had told us the dissatisfaction of the
House, and read the report of the Committee, I begin our defence
most acceptably and smoothly, and continued at it without any
hesitation or losse but with full scope and all my reason free
about me, as if it had been at my own table, from that time till
past 3 in the afternoon; and so ended without any interruption
from the Speaker, but we withdrew.[1]   And there all my fellow-
officers, and all the world that was within hearing, did congratulate me and cry up my speech as the best thing they ever
heard, and my fellow-officers overjoyed in it.   We were called
in again by and by to answer only one question, touching our
paying tickets to ticket-mongers – and so out; and we were in
hopes*c* to have had a vote this day in our favour, and so the
generality of the House was; but my speech being so long, many
had gone out to dinner and come in again half drunk, and then
there are two or three that are professed enemies to us and
everybody else; among others, Sir T. Littleton, Sir Tho. Lee,
Mr. Wiles (the coxcomb whom I saw heretofore at the cock-
fighting)[2] and a few others; I saw these did rise up and speak

a l.h. 'B' repl. s.h. 'brethern'   *b* repl. 'one'
      c repl. same symbol badly formed

1. *CJ*, ix. 61; Pepys's speech is
summarised in Milward, pp. 207–9;
Grey, i. 71–4 (misdated 15 February).
Pepys's notes for the speech were
drawn up from the crossed-out passages in his 'collections' on the subject,
now in Rawl. A 191, ff. 179–93 (cf.
above, p. 98 & n. 1) ; see f. 193 *v.*
2. George Weld (Wild), M.P. for
Much Wenlock, Salop. For the
cock-fight, see above, iv. 427–8.

against the coming to a vote now, the House not being full, by reason of several being at dinner but most because that the[a] House was to attend the King this afternoon about the business of Religion (wherein they pray him to put in force all the laws against nonconformists and papists);[1] and this prevented it, so that they put it off to tomorrow come sennit.   However, it is plain we have got great ground; and everybody says I have got the most honour that any could have had opportunity of getting. And so, with our hearts mightily overjoyed at this success, we all to dinner to Lord Brouncker; that is to say, myself, T. Harvey, and W. Penn, and there dined; and thence with Sir Anth. Morgan,[2] who is an acquaintance of Brouncker's, a very wise man, we after dinner to the King's House and there saw part of *The Discontented Colonell*[3] – but could take no great pleasure in it because of our coming in in the middle of it.   After the play, home with W. Penn and there to my wife, whom W. Hewer had told of my success; and she overjoyed, and I also as to my perticular.   And after talking awhile, I betimes to bed, having had no quiet rest a good while.

6.   Up betimes, and with Sir D. Gawden to Sir W. Coventry's chamber, where the[b] first word he said to me was, "Good-morrow Mr. Pepys, that must be Speaker of the Parliament-house" – and did protest I had got honour for ever in Parliament. He said that his brother,[4] that sat by him, admires me; and another gentleman said that[c] I could not get less than 1000*l* a year if I would put on a gown and plead at the Chancery-bar.   But what pleases me most, he tells me that the Sollicitor generall[5] did protest that he thought I spoke the best of any man in England. After several talks with him alone touching his own businesses,

a repl. 'they were'   *b* repl. 'he'   *c* repl. 'he'

---

1. This meeting was arranged for 3 p.m. in the Banqueting Hall, Whitehall: *CJ*, loc. cit.

2. A soldier, physician and one of the original Fellows of the Royal Society.

3. A tragicomedy by Sir John Suckling; see above, ii. 139, n. 4. (A).

4. Henry Coventry, the diplomat; Secretary of State 1672–9.

5. Sir Heneage Finch, whose own oratory Pepys admired: cf. above, v. 140 & n. 2.

he carried me to White-hall and there parted; and I to the Duke of York's lodging and find him going to the parke,*a* it being a very fine morning; and I after him, and as soon as he saw me, he told me with great satisfaction that I had converted a great many yesterday, and did with great praise of me go on with the discourse with me. And by and by overtaking the King, the King and*b* Duke of York came to me both, and he said, "Mr. Pepys, I am very glad of your success yesterday;" and fell to talk of my well speaking; and many of the Lords there, my Lord Berkely did cry me*c* up for what they had heard of it; and others, Parliament[-men] there about the King, did say that they never heard such a speech in their lives delivered in that manner. Progers of the Bedchamber swore to me afterward before Brouncker in the afternoon, that he did tell the King that he thought I might teach*d* the Sollicitor generall. Everybody that saw me almost came to me, as Joseph Williamson and others, with such eulogys as cannot be expressed. From thence I went*e* to Westminster-hall, where I met Mr. G. Mountagu; who came to me and kissed me, and told me that he had often heretofore kissed my hands, but now he would kiss my lips, protesting that I was another Cicero, and said all the world said the same of me. Mr. Ashburnham, and every creature I met there of the Parliament or that knew anything of the Parliament's actings, did salute me with this honour – Mr. Godolphin,[1] Mr. Sands,[2] who swore he would go twenty mile at any time to hear the like again, and that he never saw so many sit four hours together to hear any man in his life as there did to hear me. Mr. Chichly, Sir Jo. Duncom, and everybody doth say that the Kingdom will ring of my ability, and that I have done myself right for my whole life; and so Captain Cocke, and other of my friends, say that no man had ever such an opportunity of making his abilities known. And, that I may cite all at once, Mr. Lieutenant of the

---

a l.h. repl. s.h. 'par'-   *b* repl. 'called'   *c* repl. 'mi'
    d repl. 'speak'   *e* repl. 'walk'

---

1. William Godolphin, diplomat.   2. William Sandys, M.P. for Evesham, Worcs.

Tower did tell me that Mr. Vaughan[1] did protest[a] to him, and that in his hearing it, said[b] so to the Duke of Albemarle and afterward to W. Coventry, that he had sat 26 years in Parliament and never heard such a speech there before – for which the Lord God make me thankful, and that I may make use of it not to pride and vainglory, but that now I have this esteem, I may do nothing that may lessen it.

I spent the morning thus, walking in the Hall, being complimented by everybody with admiration; and at noon stepped into the Legg with Sir W. Warren, who was in the Hall, and there talked about a little of[c] his business; and thence into the Hall a little more, and so with him by coach as far as the Temple almost, and there light to fallow my Lord Brouncker's coach, which I spied; and so to Madam Williams,[2] where I overtook him and agreed upon meeting this afternoon; and so home to dinner; and after dinner, with W. Penn, who came to my house to call me, to White-hall to wait on the Duke of York; where he again and all the company magnified me, and several in the Gallery; among others, my Lord Gerard, who never knew me before nor spoke to me, desires his being better acquainted with me; and [said] that at table where he was, he never heard so much said of any man as of me in his whole life.

We waited on the Duke of York; and thence into the Gallery, where the House of Lords waited the King's coming out of the park, which he did by and by; and there in the Vane Roome my[d] Lord Keeper delivered a message to the King, the Lords being about him, wherein the Barons of England, from many good arguments very well expressed in the part he read out of, do demand precedence in England of all noblemen of either of the King's other two kingdoms, be their title what it will; and did show that[e] they were in England reputed but as commoners and sat in the House of Commons, and at conferences with the Lords did stand bare. It was mighty worth my hearing. But

---

a repl. 'say'   b repl. 'told'
c repl. 'bus'-   d repl. 'the'   e repl. 'them'

---

1. John Vaughan, himself a powerful orator.

2. Brouncker's mistress; she lived in the Piazza, Covent Garden.

the King did say only that he would consider of it, and so dismissed them.[1] Thence Brouncker and I to the Committee of Miscarriages sitting in the Court of Wards, expecting with Sir D. Gawden to have been heard against Prince Rupert's complaints for want of victuals.[2] But the business of Holmes's charge against Sir Jer. Smith,[3] which is a most shameful scandalous thing for flag-officers to accuse one another, and that this should be heard here before men that understand it not at all, and after it hath been examined and judged in before the King and Lord High Admiral and other able seamen to judge – it is very hard. But this business did keep them all the afternoon; so we not heard but put off to another day. Thence with the Lieutenant of the Tower in his coach home; and there with great pleasure with my wife, talking and playing at Cards a little, she and I and W. Hewer and Deb.; and so after a little supper, I to bed.

7. Up, and to the office, where all the morning. At noon home to dinner, where Mercer with us; and after dinner, she, my wife, Deb and I to the King's playhouse and there saw *The Spanish Gipsys*,[4] the second time of acting, and the first that I saw it – a very silly play; only, great variety of dances, and those most excellently done, especially one part by one Hanes, only lately come thither from the Nursery, a understanding fellow that yet they say hath spent 1000*l*[a] a year before he came thither.[5]

a repl. '50'

---

1. The objection was to the habit of those Irish and Scottish peers who were English by birth and residence, of claiming equality of rank and place with English peers: PRO, SP 29/253, f. 23*v*. A petition had been drawn up by the Lords' Committee of Privileges and agreed to by the House on the 4th: *LJ*, xii. 197, 198, 199. No reply from the King is reported in the *Journals* this session. The anomaly ceased with the acts of union with Scotland and Ireland in 1707 and 1801.

2. In 1666: cf. above, viii. 512, n. 2.
3. Smith was accused of allowing the Dutch fleet to escape after the Battle of St James's Day, July 1666: see above, vii. 339-40 & n.
4. A tragicomedy by Thomas Middleton and William Rowley: see above, ii. 123 & n. 1. (A).
5. Joseph Haynes, a popular comedian until his death in 1701, had been at Queen's College, Oxford, before he became an actor. For the 'Nursery', see above, p. 14 & n. 2. (A).

This day my wife and I full of thoughts about Mrs.*ᵃ* Pierce's sending me word this day that she and my old company, Harris and Knep, would come and dine with us next Wednesday, how we should do to receive or put them off – my head being at this time so full of business and my wife [in] no mind to have them neither, and yet I desire it. Came to no resolution tonight. Home from the playhouse to the office, where wrote what I had to write; and among others, to my father to congratulate my sister's marriage;[1] and so home to supper a little, and then to bed.

8. *Lords day.* At my sending to desire it, Sir Jo. Robinson, Lieutenant of the Tower, did call me with his coach and carried me to White-hall – where met with very many people still that did congratulate my speech the other day in the House of Commons – and I find all the world almost rings of it. Here spent the morning walking and talking with one or other; and among the rest, with Sir W. Coventry, who I find full*ᵇ* of care in his own business, how to defend himself against those that have a mind to choque him; and, though I believe not for honour and for the keeping his imployment, but for his safety and reputation sake, is desirous to preserve himself free from blame. And among other mean ways, which himself did take notice to me to be but a mean thing, he desires me to get information against Captain Tatnell, thereby*ᶜ* to diminish his testimony, who it seems hath a mind to do W. Coventry hurt – and I will do it with all my heart, for Tatnell is a very rogue.[2] He would be glad too that I could find anything proper for his taking notice

a repl. 'an'   *b* repl. 'in'   *c* repl. 'to'

---

1. This letter has not been traced.

2. In April a petition was presented to the House of Commons accusing Coventry of selling places: see above, p. 87 & n. 2. Coventry regarded Valentine Tatnell as his principal enemy among the naval officers, and as chiefly responsible for the petition:

Longleat, Coventry MSS 101, pp. 157–8, 214–15; Rawl. A 195a, f. 74. Pepys wrote to Coventry on 9 March giving details of frauds committed by Tatnell. He had once, for instance, been imprisoned for tampering with seamen's tickets: Longleat, Coventry MSS 97, f. 111r.

against Sir Fr. Hollis.[1] At noon, after sermon, I to dinner with
Sir G. Carteret to Lincoln's Inn fields, where I find mighty deal
of company, a solemn day for some of his and her friends, and
dine in the great dining-room above stairs, where Sir G. Carteret
himself and I and his son at a little table by, the great table being
full of strangers. Here my Lady Jem doth promise to come,
and bring my Lord Hinchingbrooke and his Lady some day this
week to dinner to me – which I am glad of.[a] After dinner I up
with her husband, Sir Ph. Carteret, to his closet; where beyond
expectation, I do find many pretty things wherein he appears to
be ingenious, such as in painting and drawing and making of
watches and such kind of things, above my expectation; though
when all is done, he is a shirke, who owns his owing me 10*l* for
his Lady two or three year ago, and yet cannot provide to pay
me.[2] The company by and by parted, and G. Carteret and I to
White-hall, where I set him down and took his coach as far as
the Temple, it raining; and there took a hackney and home and
there to read and talk with my wife; and so had my head
combed, and then to bed.

9. Up betimes, and anon with Sir W Warren, who came to
speak with me, by coach to White-hall; and there met Lord
Brouncker and he and I to the Commissioners of the Treasury,
where I find them mighty kind to me, more, I think, then was
wont.[3] And here I also met Colvill the goldsmith, who tells me
with great joy how the world upon the Change talks of me
and how several Parliament-men, *viz.* Boscawen and Major
Walden of Huntington, who it seems doth deal with him, do
say how bravely I did speak, and that the House was ready to
have given me thanks for it; but that I think is a vanity. Thence
I with Lord Brouncker and did take up his mistress, Williams;

a followed by 'it' struck through

---

1. His other principal enemy; a
member of Rupert's faction at court.

2. The debt does not appear to be
mentioned in the diary, nor is it
entered in Pepys's rough notes of his
accounts for 1667–9 (Rawl. A 185).

For Carteret's improvidence, see
above, viii. 600 & n. 1.

3. The business concerned tickets
and payment of the yards: *CTB*, ii.
271.

and so to the Navy Office, where did a little business, and so to
the Change, only to show myself, and did a little business there;
and so home to dinner, and then to the office, busy till the evening;
and then to the Excise Office, where I find Mr. Ball in a mighty
trouble that he is to be put out of his place at Midsummer, the
whole Commission being to cease.[1] And the truth is, I think
they are very fair dealing men, all of them. Here I did do
a little business; and then to rights home and there dispatched
many papers, and so home late to supper and to bed[a] – being[b]
eased of a great many thoughts, and yet have a great many more
to remove as fast as I can, my mind being burdened with them,
having been so much imployed on the public business of the
office in their defence before the Parliament of late and the further
cares that do attend it.

10.[c] Up, and to the office betimes, where all the morning. At
noon home[d] to dinner with my clerks; and after dinner comes
Kate Joyce, who tells me she is putting off her house,[2] which I
am glad of. But it was pleasant that she came on purpose to
me about getting a ticket paid,[3] and in her way hither lost her
ticket, so that she is at a great loss what to do. There comes in
then Mrs. Mercer the mother, the first time she hath been here
since her daughter lived with us – to see my wife. And after a
little talk, I left them and to the office; and thence with Sir
D Gawden to Westminster-hall, thinking to have attended the
Committee about the victualling business, but they did not
meet. But here we met Sir R. Brookes, who doth mightily
cry up my speech the other day, saying my fellow-officers[e] are
obliged to me, as endeed they are. Thence with Sir D. Gawden

---

a repl. same symbol badly formed   *b* MS. 'having'
c From here to the end of this volume of the MS. (i.e. the end of April)
the s.h. is smaller than usual and more lines are crowded into each page.
              d repl. 'came'   *e* repl. 'officers'

---

1. A new Excise commission was
appointed at midsummer. John Ball
(Receiver-General) was awarded a
pension of £200 p.a.: *CSPD 1667–8*,
p. 467.

2. An inn at Clerkenwell: for her
husband's death, see above, pp. 32–3.
3. Innkeepers often acted as ticket-
brokers for seamen.

homeward, calling at Lincolns Inn fields, but my Lady Jemimah was not within. And so to Newgate, where he stopped to give direction to the Jaylor about a Knight, one Sir Tho. Halford, brought in yesterday for killing one Collonell Temple, falling out at a taverne.[1] So thence as far as Leaden-hall, and there I light and back by coach to Lincolns Inne fields; but my Lady was not come in, and so I am at a great loss whether she and her brother Hinchingbrooke and sister will dine with me tomorrow or no; which vexes me. So home; and there comes Mr. Moore to me, who tells me that he fears my Lord Sandwich will meet with very great difficulties to go through about the prizes, it being found that he did give order for more then the King's letter doth justify.[2] And then for the act of Resumption, which he fears will go on and is designed only to do him hurt – which troubles me much.[3] He tells me he believes the Parliament will not be brought to do anything in matters of religion, but will adhere to the Bishops. So he gone, I up to supper, where I find W. Joyce and Harman come to see us, and there was also Mrs. Mercer and her two daughters; and here we were as merry as that fellow Joyce could make us with his mad talking, after the old wont, which tired me. But I was mightily pleased with his singing, for the rogue hath a very good eare and a good voice. Here he stayed till he was almost drunk, and then away at about 10 at night; and then all broke up, and I to bed.

11. Up and betimes to the office, where*a* busy till 8 a-clock

a repl. 'whither came'

---

1. Halford, a baronet (not a knight) of Wistow, Leics., and once sheriff of his county, was shortly afterwards convicted of the manslaughter of Edmund Temple, but pardoned by the King: *CSPD 1667-8*, pp. 273, etc. Gauden was Sheriff of London, 1667-8.

2. For the King's pardon, see above, vii. 260 & n. 2.

3. Cf. above, viii. 530 & n. 3. A Commons' committee of enquiry into the disposal of crown lands had been appointed on 27 February 1668, but by the time the session ended on 9 May, no report (according to the *Journals*) had been made, and the proposed bill was dropped: *CJ*, ix. 57, 93. Letters to Sandwich on the subject (6 April, 1 June) are in Sandwich MSS, App., f. 160r; ib., Letters from Ministers, ii, ff. 110-11.

and then went forth; and meeting Mr. Colvill, I walked with
him to his building, where he is building a fine house where he
formerly lived in Lumbar-street; and it will be a very fine
street.   Thence walked down to the Three Crane and there took
boat to White-hall, where by direction I waited on the Duke of
York about office business; and so by water to Wesminster,
where walking in the Hall most of the morning, and up to my
Lady Jem. in Lincoln fields to get her to appoint the day certain
when she will come and dine with me; and she hath appointed
Saturday next.   So back to Westminster and there still walked,
till by and by comes Sir W. Coventry and with him and Mr.
Chichly and Mr. Andr. Newport I to dinner with them to Mr.
Chichly's in Queen-street in Covent-garden; a very fine house,
and a man that lives in mighty great fashion, with all things in a
most extraordinary manner noble and rich about him, and eats
in the French fashion all; and mighty nobly served with his
servants, and very civil – that I was mighty pleased with it; and
good discourse.[1]   He is a great defender of the Church of England,
and against the act for Comprehension, which is the work of this
day, about which the House is like to sit*a* till night.   After dinner,
away*b* with them back to Westminster, where about 4 a-clock
the House rises and hath done nothing more in the business then
to put off the debate to this day month.[2]   In the meantime, the
King hath put out his proclamations this day, as the House
desired, for the putting in execution the act against nonconformists and papists.[3]   But yet it is conceived that for all this, some
Liberty must be given, and people will have it.   Here I met

---

a repl. same symbol   *b* MS. 'among'

---

1. Thomas Chicheley was M.P.
for Cambridgeshire; later (1670)
Master-General of the Ordnance and
a knight.   He was rich but extravagant, and in 1686 was forced to sell
his country house at Wimpole,
Cambs.   For the French style of
eating, see above, viii. 211 & n. 1.
Great Queen St was one of the most
fashionable quarters of town.

2. *CJ*, ix. 65: reports of debate in
Grey, i. 110–15; Milward, pp. 214–
22.   For the bill, see above, p. 31,
n. 4.

3. A proclamation enforcing the
laws against conventicles etc. was
issued on 10 March: Steele, no. 3514.
For the Commons' request (4 March),
see *CJ*, ix. 60.   Cf. above, p. 96 &
n. 1.

with my Cosen Roger Pepys, who is come to town[1] and hath
been told of my performance before the House the other day,
and is mighty proud of it. And Captain Cocke met me here
today and told me that the Speaker says he never heard such a
defence made in all his life in the House; and that the Sollicitor
generall doth commend me even to envy. I carried Cosen
Rogr. as far as the Strand; where spying out of the coach Collonell
Charles George Cocke,[2] formerly a very great man and my
father's customer whom I have carried clothes to, but now
walks like a poor sorry sneake, he stopped and [I] light to him.
This man knew me, which I would have willingly avoided, so
much pride I had; he being a man of mighty heighth and
authority in his time but now signifies nothing. Thence home,
where to the office a while and then home, where W. Batelier
was and played at cards and supped with us, my eyes being out of
order for working; and so to bed.

12. Up, and to the office, where all the morning. At noon
home; and after dinner with wife and Deb, carried them to
Unthankes;[3] and I to Westminster-hall, expecting our being with
the Committee this afternoon about Victualling business, but
once more waited in vain. So after a turn or two with Lord
Brouncker, I took my wife up and left her at the Change, while I
to Gresham College, there to show myself,[4] and was there greeted
by Dr. Wilkins, Whistler, and others, as the patron of the Navy
Office and one that got great fame by my late speech to the
Parliament. Here I saw a great trial of the goodness of a burning-
glass, made of a new figure, not Sphæricall (by one Smithys,
I think they call him),[5] that did burn a glove of my Lord
Brouncker's from the heat of a very little fire – which a burning-
glass of the old form, very much bigger, could not do – which
was mighty pretty. Here I heard Sir Rob. Southwell give an

---

1. As a supporter of the comprehension bill, he may have come up for
this day's debate.
2. A High Court judge under the
Commonwealth. His daughter had
on 4 April 1663 attended Pepys's
'stone feast'.
3. Mrs Pepys's tailor.

4. According to the diary, Pepys
does not appear to have attended
meetings of the Royal Society since
30 November 1667.
5. The designer was Francis Smeth-
wick; a concave glass was used:
Birch, ii. 253, 255; *Philos. Trans.*, iii.
631–2.

account of some things committed to him by the Society at his
going to Portugall, which he did deliver in a mighty handsome
manner.[1] Thence went away home, and there at my office as
long as my eyes would endure; and then home to supper and to
talk with Mr. Pelling, who tells me what a fame I have in the
City for my late performance; and upon the whole, I bless God
for it, I think I have, if I can keep it, done myself a great deal of
repute. So by and by to bed.

13. Up betimes to my office, where to fit myself for attending the Parliament again; not to make any more speeches, which
while my fame is good I will avoid for fear of losing of it, but
only to answer to what objections shall be made against us.
Thence walked to the Old Swan and drank at Michell's, whose
house is going up apace; here I saw Betty, but could not besar la;
and so to Westminster, there to the Hall, where up to my Cosen
Rogr. Pepys at the Parliament door, and there he took me aside
and told me how he was taken up by one of the House yesterday[a]
for moving for going on with the King's supply of money without regard to the keeping pace therewith with the looking into
miscarriages, and was told by this man privately that it arose
because that he had a kinsman concerned therein and therefore
he would prefer the safety of his kinsman to the good of the
nation.[2] And that there was great things against us, and against
me, for all my fine discourse the other day. But I did bid him
be at no pain for me, for I knew of nothing but[b] what I was

a repl. 'the other'   b repl. 'them'

---

1. On going on his embassy in
1665, Southwell had conveyed an
astronomical quadrant on behalf of
the Society to 'a body of men at
Lisbon, who had applied themselves,
among other kinds of literature, to
Mathematics': Birch, ii. 256. It was
usual for the Royal Society to ask
favours of this sort from diplomats
serving abroad. As Oldenburg
wrote, in a letter to Boyle about the

departure of Sandwich and Godolphin
to Spain in 1666, 'They both have
receaved as well Philosophicall as
Politicall Instructions': A. R. and
M. B. Hall (ed.), *Corresp.*, iii. 46.
2. On the 12th a debate on the miscarriages of the war had been postponed to the 14th, and a vote for the
grant of £100,000 passed: *CJ*, ix. 65;
report of debates in Milward, pp.
222–4.

very well prepared to answer; and so I think I am, and therefore was not at all disquieted by this. Thence, he to the House and I to the Hall, where my Lord Brouncker and the rest waiting till noon and not called for by the House, they being upon the business of money again; and at noon, all of us to Chatelin,[1] the French house in Covent-garden, to dinner, Brouncker, J. Mennes, W. Penn, T. Harvey, and myself; and there had a dinner cost us 8*s* 6*d* apiece, a damned base dinner, which did not please us at all – so that I am not fond of this house at all, but do rather choose the Beare.[2] After dinner, to White-hall to the Duke of York and there did our usual business, complaining of our standing still in every respect for want of money; but no remedy propounded, but so I must still be. Thence with our company to the King's playhouse, where I left them; and I, my head being full of tomorrow's dinner, I to my Lord Crews, there to invite Sir Tho. Crew; and there met with my Lord Hinchingbrooke and his Lady, the first time I spoke to her.[3] I saluted her, and she mighty civil; and with my Lady Jem do all resolve to be very merry tomorrow at my house. My Lady Hinchingbrooke I cannot say is a beauty, nor ugly; but is alto-gether a comely lady enough, and seems very good-humoured, and I mighty glad of this occasion of seeing her before tomorrow. Thence home; and there find one laying of my napkins against tomorrow in figures of all sorts, which is mighty pretty; and it seems it is his trade*ª* and gets much money by it, and doth now*ᵇ* and then furnish tables with plate and linen for a feast at so much – which is mighty pretty – and a trade I could not have thought of. I find my wife upon the bed, not very well, her breast being broke out with heate; which troubles her, but I hope it will be for her good. Thence I to Mrs. Turner and did get her to go along with me to the French pewterers, and there did buy some new pewter against tomorrow. And thence to White-hall to have got a cook of her acquaintance, the best in England as she

a repl. 'tr'-   *b* repl. same symbol badly formed

---

1. A well-known eating-house: cf. R. North, *Life of . . . Baron Guilford* (1742), p. 51.

2. In Drury Lane: where Pepys had eaten well and cheaply on 18 February.

3. Cf. above, p. 28 & n. 2.

says. But after we have with much ado found him, he could not come; nor was Mr. Gentleman in town, whom next I would have had; nor would Mrs. Stone[1] let her man Lewis come, whom this man recommended to me; so that I was at a mighty loss what in the world to do for a Cooke, Philips being out of town. Therefore, after staying here at Westminster a great while, we back to London and there to Phillips's and his man directed us to Mr. Levetts,[2] who could not come; and he sent to two more, and they could not; so that at last, Levett, as a great kindness, did resolve he would leave his business and come himself, which set me in great ease in my mind; and so home, and there with my wife and people setting all things in order against tomorrow, having seen Mrs. Turner at home; and so late to bed.

14. Up very betimes, and with Jane to Levetts, there to conclude upon our dinner; and thence to the pewterers to buy a pewter Sestorne,[3] which I have ever hitherto been without. And so up and down upon several occasions to set matters in order. And that being done, I out of doors to Westminster-hall and there met my Lord Brouncker, who tells me that our business is put off till Monday, and so I was mighty glad that I was eased of my attendance here and of any occasion that might put me out of humour, as it is likely if we had been called before the Parliament. Therefore, after having spoke with Mr. Godolphin and Cosen Roger, I away home and there do find everything in mighty good order; only, my wife not dressed, which troubles me. Anon comes my company, *viz.*, my Lord Hinchingbrooke and his Lady, Sir Ph. Carteret and his Lady, Godolphin and my Cosen Roger, and Creed, and mighty merry; and by and by to dinner, which was very good and plentiful (I should have said, and Mr. George Mountagu, who came at a very little warning, which was exceeding kind of him): and there among other things, my Lord had Sir Samuel Morland's late invention for casting up of sums of 0*l*. 0*s*. 0*d*.; which is very pretty, but not

---

1. Probably the wife of Thomas Stone, landlord of the Leg in New Palace Yard. (R).
2. Probably William Levitt who kept an eating house (the 'Ship') in Bartholomew Lane. (R).

3. Cisterns of this sort were used on grand occasions for washing the plates during the meal.

very useful.[1]   Most of our discourse was of my Lord Sandwich and his family, as being all of us of that family;* and with extra-ordinary pleasure all the afternoon thus together, eating and looking over my closet: and my Lady Hinchingbrooke I find a very sweet-natured and well-disposed lady, a lover of books and pictures and of good understanding.   About 5 a–clock they went, and then my wife and I abroad[a] by coach into Moorefields, only for a little ayre; and so home again, staying nowhere, and then up to her chamber, there to talk with pleasure of this day's passages, and so to bed.   This day I had the welcome news of our prize being come safe from Holland, so as I shall have hopes, I hope, of getting my money of my Lady Batten – or good part of it.[2]

15.   *Lords day.*   Up and walked, it being fine dry weather, to Sir W. Coventry's, overtaking[b] my Boy Ely[3] (that was) by the way; and he walked with me, being grown a man, and I think a sober fellow.   He parted at Charing-cross, and I to W. Coventry and there talked with him about the Commissioners of Accounts, who did give in their report yesterday to the House,[4] and do yet lay little upon us to[c] aggravate anything at present; but only do give an account of the dissatisfactory account they receive from Sir G. Carteret;[d] which I am sorry for, they saying that he tells them not any[e] time when he paid any sum – which is fit for them to know for the computing of interest – but I fear he is hardly able to tell it.[5]

---

a repl. 'ab'-   *b* repl. 'being'
c MS. 'so'   *d* repl. 'G.C.'s'   *e* repl. 'when'

---

1. A calculating machine, described in Morland's *A new and most useful instrument for addition and subtraction of pounds, shillings, pence and farthings, without charging the memory, disturbing the mind, or exposing the operator to any uncertainty . . . invented and presented to . . . Charles II [in] 1666* (1672; PL 293), and in his *The description and use of two arithmetick instruments . . .* (1673). See also Gunther, vol. i, pt ii. 41.

2. In October 1667 her husband had died owing Pepys c. £666 from the sale of prize goods: above, viii. 477 & n. 2.

3. Eliezer Jenkins, who had served Pepys on the Dutch voyage, 1660.

4. *CJ*, ix. 67; Milward, p. 226. This was an interim report; the final report was delivered in October.

5. Cf. above, viii. 448, n. 4; below, p. 214, n. 5.

They promise to give them an account of the imbezzlement of prizes, wherein I shall be something concerned, but nothing that I am afeared of, I thank God.[1]   Thence walked with W. Coventry into the park, and there met the King and the Duke of York and walked a good while with them; and here met Sir Jer. Smith, who tells me he is like to get the better of Holmes[2] – and that when he is come to an end of that, he will do Hollis's business for him in the House for his blasphemies; which I shall be glad of.

So to White-hall and there walked with this man and that man till chapel done and the King dined; and then Sir Tho. Clifford the Controller[3] took me with him to dinner to his lodgings, where my Lord Arlington and a great deal of good and great company – where I very civilly used by them – and had a most excellent dinner.   And good discourse of Spain, Mr. Godolphin[4] being there – perticularly of the removal of the bodies of all the dead Kings of Spain that could be got together, and brought to the Pantheon at the Escuriall ⟨(when it was finished)⟩ and there placed before the Alter, there to lie for ever.   And there was a sermon made to them upon this text, *Arida ossa, audite verbum dei* – a most eloquent sermon as they say who say they have read it.[5] After dinner, away thence; and I to Mrs. Martin's and there spent the afternoon and did hazer con ella; and here was her sister and Mrs. Burrows; and so in the evening got a coach and home, and there find Mr. Pelling and W. Hewer, and there talked and

1. See below, p. 165 & n. 1.   The report on the prize-goods affair led to the impeachment of Penn.

2. Cf. above, p. 107 & n. 3.

3. Comptroller of the King's Household.

4. William Godolphin, late secretary to Sandwich's embassy in Madrid.   Arlington (another of the guests) had been Charles II's agent in Madrid, 1658–60.

5. The Pantéon was a vault under the high altar of the chapel of the Escorial.   Description (1665) in Lady Fanshawe, *Mem.* (1829), pp. 225+.

It was completed in 1654, when, in the presence of Philip IV 'and with the most awful services of mass and burial imaginable', a monk of the order of St Jerome (Fray Juan de Avellaneda, chaplain to the King) preached a sermon on this text (Ezek., xxxvii. 4). The sermon had been printed in Fray Francisco de los Santos, *Descripcion breve del monasterio de S. Lorenzo el real del Escorial* . . . (Madrid, 1667), ff. 182v–183r; part of it is translated in Edward Clarke, *Letters concerning the Spanish nation* (1763), pp. 141–8.

supped ⟨(Pelling*ᵃ* being gone)⟩; and mightily pleased with a picture that W. Hewer brought hither of several things painted upon a deal Board, which board is so well painted that in my whole*ᵇ* life I never was so pleased or surprized with any picture, and so troubled that so good pictures should be painted upon a piece of bad deale; even after I knew*ᶜ* that it was not board, but only the picture of a board, I could not remove my fancy.[1] After supper to bed, being very sleepy and, I bless*ᵈ* God, my mind at very good present rest.

16. Up, to set my papers and books in order and put up my plate since my late feast. And then to Westminster by water with Mr. Hater; and there in the Hall did walk all the morning, talking with one or other, expecting to have our business in the House; but did now a third time wait to no purpose, they being all this morning upon the business of Barker's petition about the making void the Act of Settlement in Ireland,[2] which makes a great deal of hot work. And at last, finding that by all men's opinion they could not come to our matter today, I with Sir W. Penn home, and there to dinner; where I find by Willet's crying that her mistress had been angry with her, but I would take no notice of it. Busy all the afternoon at the office, and then by coach to the Excise Office; but lost my labour, there being nobody there, and so back again home; and after a little at*ᵉ* the office, I home and there spent the evening with my wife talking and singing; and so to bed with my mind pretty well at ease.

This evening W. Penn and Sir R. Ford and I met at the first's house to talk of our prize that is now at least come safe over from Holland, by which I hope to receive*ᶠ* some, if not all, the benefit of my bargain with W. Batten for my share in it; which if she had miscarried, I should have doubted of my Lady Batten being left little able to have paid me.

a name in s.h.   *b* repl. same symbol badly formed   *c* repl. 'know'
d repl. same symbol   *e* repl. 'after'   *f* repl. 'save what'

1. The picture has not been identified. For *trompe l'oeuil* paintings, now in vogue, see Whinney and Millar, pp. 281–2; cf. above, iv. 18, n. 1 (OM).

2. *CJ*, ix. 67–8; cf. above, viii. 420 & n. 2.

17.   Up betimes and to the office, where all the morning busy; and then at noon home to dinner; and so again to the office awhile, and then abroad to the Excise Office, where I met Mr. Ball and did receive the paper I went for; and there fell in talk with him, who being an old Cavalier doth swear and curse at the present state of things: that we should be brought to this; that we must be undone and cannot be saved – that the Parliament is sitting now and will till night to find how to raise this 300,000*l*,[1] and doubts they will not do it so as to be seasonable for the King. But doth cry out against our great men at Court, how it is a fine thing for a Secretary of State to dance a Jigg,[2] and that it was not so heretofore; and above all doth curse my Lord of Bristoll, saying that the worst news that ever he heard*a* in his life, or that the Devil could ever bring us, was this*b* Lord's coming to prayers the other day in the House of Lords, by which he is coming about again from being a papist, which will undo this nation;[3] and he says he ever did say, at the King's first coming in, that this nation could not be safe while that man was alive.   Having done there, I away towards Westminster; but seeing by the coaches the House to be up, I stopped at the Change ⟨⟨where I met Mrs. Turner and did give her a pair of gloves)⟩ and there bought several things for my wife; and so to my bookseller's and there looked*c* for Montaigne's *essays*, which I heard by my Lord Arlington and Lord Blany so much commended, and entend to buy it but did not now.[4]   But home, where at the office did some business, as much as my eyes would give leave; and so home to supper, Mercer with us talking and singing; and so to bed.   The House, I hear, have this day concluded up[on] raising 100000*l* of the 300000*l* by wine, and the rest by a pole, and have resolved to excuse the Church, in expectation that they will do

---

a repl. 'word'   *b* repl. 'like'   *c* same symbol badly formed

---

1. Cf. above, pp. 92–3 & n.   They sat until 6 p.m.

2. A reference to the courtly accomplishments of Arlington.

3. Bristol had been converted to Rome just before the Restoration, and had reverted to Anglicanism once before, in 1664, but only temporarily. (Cf. above, v. 59 & n. 1.) There was no truth in the suggestion that he had now reverted again. As a Catholic peer he normally attended and voted in the House without going to prayers.

4. See below, p. 121 & n. 3.

the more of themselfs at this juncture.[1]   And I do hear that Sir W. Coventry did make a speech in behalf of the Clergy.[2]

18.   Up betimes to Westminster, where met with Cosen Rogr. and Creed and walked with them, and Rogr. doth still continue of the mind that there [is] no other way of saving this nation but by dissolving this Parliament and calling another; but there are so many about the King that will not be able to stand, if a new Parliament come, that they will not persuade the King to it. I spent most of the morning walking with one or other, and anon met Doll Lane*a* at the Dog*b* tavern,*c* and there yo did hazer what I did desire with her and did it backward, not having convenience to do it the other way.   And I did give her,*b* as being my valentine, 20*s* to buy what ella would.   Thence away by coach to my booksellers and to several places to pay my debts and to Ducke lane, and there bought Montagne's *essays* in English,[3] and so away home to dinner; and after dinner with W. Penn to White-hall, where we and my Lord Brouncker attended the Council to discourse about the fitness of entering of men presently for the manning of the fleet, before one ship is in condition to receive them.   W. Coventry did argue against it; I was wholly silent, because I saw the King, upon the earnestness of the Prince, was

---

a   name in s.h.   *b–b*   garbled s.h.: see above, viii. 244, note *a*
           c   repl. same symbol badly formed

---

1. These were votes in committee, confirmed by the House on the following day: *CJ*, ix. 68, 69. Reports of debates in Grey, i. 116–17; Milward, pp. 228–9. The clergy were normally included in poll-taxes (e.g. in 1660), but on this occasion, when only the dignified clergy (bishops and cathedral clergy) were apparently to be affected, it was decided to leave them to tax themselves in Convocation: Marvell, ii. 67; Milward, p. 231. But this expectation died with the abandonment of the proposed poll-tax itself at the end of the month.   In

fact the clergy never taxed themselves in Convocation after 1663.
    2. There is a similar speech reported under 26 March in Grey (i. 121 n.): 'That the Bishops, Deans and Chapters, and Prebends, in repairs, abatements of fines, redemption of captives, and other charitable uses, have disbursed [since 1660] 413,800*l*'.
    3. John Florio's translation, first published in 1603 and several times reissued.   Pepys retained the version by Charles Cotton (1693): PL 1018–20.

willing to it, crying very sillily, "If ever you intend to man the fleet without being cheated by the Captains and pursers, you may*a* go to bed and resolve never to have it manned." And so it was, like other things, over-ruled that all volunteers should be presently entered. Then there was another great business, about our signing of ⟨new⟩ Certificates to the Exchequer for goods upon the 1250000*l* Act, which the Commissioners of the Treasury did all oppose, and to the laying fault upon us; but I did then speak*b* to the justifying what we had done, even to the angering of Duncomb and Clifford, which I was vexed at: but for all that, I did the office and myself right and went away with the victory, my Lord Keeper saying that he would not advise the Council to order us to sign no more certificates.[1] But before I begin to say anything in this matter, the King and the Duke of York, talking at the Council-table before all the Lords of the Committee of Miscarriages how this entering of men before the ships would be ready would be reckoned a miscarriage; "Why," says the King, "it is then but Mr. Pepys making of another speech to them" – which made all the Lords, and there was by also the Atturny and Sollicitor generall, look upon me. Thence Sir W. Penn*e* and I by hackney-coach to take a little ayre in Hide-park, the first time I have been there this year; and we did meet many coaches going and coming, it being mighty pleasant weather; and so coming back again, I light in the Pell Mell and there went to see Sir H. Cholmly, who continues very ill of his cold; and there came in Sir H. Yelverton, whom Sir H. Cholmly com-

---

a repl. 'will'   *b* repl. 'make'   *c* repl. 'Coventry'

---

1. The Treasury claimed that the Navy Board was allowing charges which could not be met by advances under the Additional Aid of 1665 to become a first charge on the Eleven Months Tax of 1667. Pepys's answer seems to have been a defence of the practice in so far as it concerned payment of interest to creditors rather than payment for goods. The difficulty, however, was that the Exchequer had not accounted for any interest, and only £28,000 remained from the first act when the second was passed. The matter was this day referred to the law officers who on 3 April, contrary to Pepys's expectation, reported in the Treasury's favour. A council order forbidding the issue of more certificates followed on 22 April. PRO, PC 2/60, ff. 116*r*, 126*v*; *CTB*, ii. 292, 293, 307.

mended me to his acquaintance; which the other received, but without remembering to me, or I him, of our being school-fellows together;[1] and I said nothing of it. But he took notice of my speech the other day at the bar of the House; and endeed, I perceive he is a wise man – by his manner of discourse. And here he doth say that the town is full of it that now the Parliament hath resolved upon 300000*l*, the King instead of 50 will set out but 25 ships, and the Duch as many – and that Smith is to command them – who is allowed to have the better of Holmes in the late dispute[2] and is in good esteem in the Parliament, above the other. Thence home; and there, in favour to my eyes, stayed at home reading the ridiculous history of my Lord Newcastle wrote by his wife,[3] which shows her to be a mad, conceited, ridiculous woman, and he an asse to suffer*a* [her] to write what she writes to him and of him. Betty Turner sent my wife the book to read; and it being a fair print, to ease my eyes, which would be reading, I read that. Anon comes Mrs. Turner and sat and talked with us, and most about the business of Ackworth,[4] which comes before us tomorrow, that I would favour it; but I do not think, notwithstanding*b* all the friendship I can show him, that

a repl. 'let'   *b* repl. 'as'

---

1. Sir Henry Yelverton, Bt (scholar of St Paul's in Pepys's time) was now M.P. for Northampton borough.

2. See above, p. 107 & n. 3.

3. *The life of the thrice noble, high, and puissant prince, William Cavendishe, Duke . . . of Newcastle . . . written by the thrice noble, illustrious and excellent princess, Duchess of Newcastle, his wife . . .*; first published 1667; not in the PL. In the preface the authoress says that she writes 'in my own plain Style, without elegant Flourishings, or exquisit Method, relying intirely upon Truth, in the expressing where-of, I have been very circumspect'. In bk iii she gives translations of all her husband's patents of nobility, and comprehensive encomiums, under several heads. Newcastle was still alive, and was unpopular among royalists for his quitting the country (his wife called it his 'banishment') after Marston Moor.

4. William Acworth, Storekeeper at Woolwich, had in January been accused of embezzling naval stores. He had asked for time in which to prepare his accounts and had been given until 19 March: *CSPD 1667–8*, pp. 197, 279. For the progress of the case, see below, pp. 145, 281, 382; for Pepys's references to his dishonesty on earlier occasions, see above, v. 130 & n. 2; ib., p. 156.

he can escape; and therefore it had been better he had fallowed the advice I sent him the other day by Mrs. Turner, to make up the business. So parted and I to bed, my eyes being very bad – and I know not how in the world to abstain from reading.

19. Up, and betimes to the Old Swan and by water to White-hall; and thence to W. Coventry, where stayed but a little to talk with him and thence by water back again, it being a mighty fine, clear Spring morning. Back to the Old Swan and drank at Michells, whose house goes up apace, but I could not see Betty; and thence walked all along Thames-street, which I have not done since it was burned, as far as Billings-gate and there do see a brave street likely to be, many brave houses being built, and of them a great many by Mr. Jaggard. But the raising of the street will make it mighty fine.¹   So to the office, where busy all the morning. At noon home to dinner; and thence to the office, very busy till 5 a-clock; and then to ease my eyes I took my wife out and Deb to the Change, and there bought them some things; and so home again and to the office, ended my letters, and so home to read a little more in last night's book with much sport, it being a foolish book.   And so to supper and to bed.

This afternoon I was surprized with a letter without a name to it, very well writ in a good style, giving me notice of my Cosen Kate Joyces' being likely to ruin herself by marriage and by ill reports already abroad of her; and I do fear that this keeping*ᵃ* of an Inne may spoil her, being a young and pretty comely woman and thought to be left well.   I did answer the letter with thanks and good liking, and am resolved to take the advice he gives me, and go see her and find what I can; but if she will ruin herself, I cannot help it – though I shall be troubled for it.

a repl. 'being'

---

1. Thames St was a main thorough-fare and was now widened as well as raised.   The old street had been in places only 11 ft wide: now it was to be 30 ft. See T. F. Reddaway, *Rebuilding of London*, pp. 105, 299.

Abraham Jaggard was a wealthy grocer who often supplied navy victualling. At his death in 1694 he owned houses in both Thames St and Love Lane, Billingsgate: PCC, Box, 42.

20. Up betimes and to my*a* office, where we had a meeting extraordinary to consider of several things; among others, the sum of money fit to be demanded ready money to enable us to set out 27 ships,[1] everybody being now in pain for a fleet and everybody endeavouring to excuse themselfs for the not setting out of one, and our true excuse is lack of money. At it all the morning; and so at noon home to dinner with my clerks, my wife and Deb being busy at work above in her chamber, getting things ready and fine for her going into the country a week or two hence. I away by coach to White-hall, where we met to wait on the Duke of York; and as soon as prayers were done, it being Good Friday, he came to us and we did a little business and presented him with our demand of money, and so broke up; and I thence by coach to Kate Joyces, being desirous and in pain to speak with her about the business that I received a letter yesterday, but had no opportunity of speaking with her about it, company being with her; so I only invited her to come and dine with me on Sunday next; and so away home, and for saving my eyes, at my chamber all the evening, pricking down some things and trying some conclusions upon my viall, in order to the inventing a better theory of Musique then hath yet been abroad; and I think verily I shall do it.[2] So to supper with my wife, who is in very good humour with her working, and so am I; and so to bed. This day at Court I do hear that Sir W. Penn doth command this summer's fleet;[3] and Mr. Progers*b* ⟨of the Bedchamber⟩, as a secret, told me that the Prince Rupert is troubled at it, and several friends of his have been with him to know the reason of it; so that he doth pity Sir W. Penn, whom he hath great kindness

a repl. 'the'   *b* '21' (struck through) in margin

1. This was in response to an enquiry from the Admiral (M. Wren to Navy Board, 20 March: PRO, Adm. 106/15, f. 407r). The Board's estimate was £45,000 but the Council allowed only £24,000: PRO, PC 2/60, ff. 119r, 125r.

2. For Pepys's interest in this subject, see e.g. above, viii. 574–5.

There are 'Loose notes & Queries Musicall' (undated; in Hewer's hand) among Pepys's MSS in the Bodleian which include ideas about a simpler scale: Rawl. A 312, ff. 143–6, esp. 144v. (E).

3. Penn never took up this appointment. Within a month he was impeached in parliament.

for, that he should not at any desire of his be put to this service, and thereby make the Prince his enemy and contract more envy from other people.   But I am not a whit sorry if it should be so; first for the King's sake, that his work will be better done by W. Penn then the Prince; and next, that Pen, who is a false rogue, may be bit a little by it.

21.   Up betimes to the office, and there we sat all the morning. At noon home with my clerks, a good dinner, and then to the office and wrote my letters, and then abroad to do several things and pay what little scores I had; and among others, to Mrs. Martins and there did give 20*s.* to Mrs. Cragg her landlady, who was my valentine in*a* the house, as well as Doll Lane.   Here*b* yo did hazer la cosa with Mrs. Martin backward.*c*   So home and to the office, there to end my letters; and so home, where Betty Turner was to see my wife; and she being gone, I to my chamber to read a little again, and then after supper to bed.

22.   *Easter day*.   I up and walked to the Temple; and there got a coach and to White-hall, where spoke with several people, and find by all that Pen is to go to sea this year with this fleet. And they excuse the Prince's going by saying that it is not a command great enough for him.   Here I met with Brisban; and after hearing the service at the King's chapel, where I heard the Bishop of Norwich, Dr. Reynolds the old presbyterian, begin a very plain sermon,[1] he and I to the Queen's chapel and there did hear the Italians sing; and endeed, their music did appear most admirable to me, beyond anything of ours – I was never so well satisfied in my life with it.   So back to White-hall, and there met Mr. Pierce and adjousted together how we should spend

a   repl. full stop   b   repl. 'In coming'
c   repl. 'bal'- (garbled s.h.)

1. Edward Reynolds had been the only one of the moderate Presbyterian leaders to accept a bishopric in 1661, when offers of preferment were made to several.   The sermon he preached on this occasion (on Hebrews, xiii. 20–1) was published.   As a preacher he was given to excessive quotation: W. Fraser Mitchell, *Engl. pulpit oratory*, p. 104.

tomorrow together. And so by coach, I home to dinner, where Kate Joyce was, as I invited her; and had a good dinner, only she and us; and after dinner, she and I alone to talk about her business as I designed; and I find her very discreet, and assures me she neither doth nor will incline to the doing anything towards marriage without my advice, and did tell me that she had many offers,*a* and that Harman and his friends* would fain have her but he is poor and hath poor friends, and so it will not be advisable. But*b* that there is another, a Tobacconist, one Holinshed, whom she speaks well of to be a plain, sober*c* man and in good condition, that offers her very well; and submits to me my examining and inquiring after it – if I see good – which I do like of it, for it will be best for her to marry I think as soon as she can; at least, to be rid of this house – for the trade will not agree with a young widow that is a little handsome; at least, ordinary people think her so. Being well satisfied with her answer, she anon went away; and I to my closet to make a few more experiments of*d* my notions in Musique; and so then my wife and I to walk in the garden, and then home to supper and to bed.

23. Up, and after discoursing with my wife about many things touching this day's dinner, I abroad; and first to the tavern to pay what I owe there, but missed of seeing the mistress of the house. And there bespoke wine for dinner; and so away thence and to Bishopsgate*e*-street, thinking to have found a Harpsicon-maker that used to live there before the fire,[1] but he is gone; and I have a mind forthwith to have a little Harpsicon made me – to confirm and help me in my music notions, which my head is nowadays full of, and I do believe will come to something that is very good. Thence to White-hall, expecting to have heard the Bishop of Lincolne,[2] my*f* friend, preach, for so I understood he would do yesterday, but was mistaken; and therefore away presently back again and there find everything in good order

---

a MS. 'officers' b repl. 'that' c repl. same symbol
d repl. 'up'- e repl. 'Grac'- f repl. 'f'-

---

1. ? Cf. above, ii. 44. 2. William Fuller.

against dinner; and at noon come Mr. Pierce and she, and Mrs. Manuel the Jew's wife, and Mrs. Corbett, and Mrs. Pierce's boy and girl. But we are defeated of Knepp by her being forced to act today, and also of Harris; which did trouble me, they being my chief guests. However, I had an extraordinary good dinner, and the better because dressed by my own servants – and were mighty merry; and here was Mr. Pelling, by chance came and dined with me. And after sitting long at dinner, I had a barge ready at Tower wharfe to take us in; and so we went, all*a* of us, up as high as Barne elmes, a very fine day, and all the way sang; and Mrs. Manuel sings very finely and is a mighty discreet, sober-carriaged woman, that both my wife and I are mightily taken with her; and sings well, and without importunity or the contrary. At Barne-Elms we walked round; and then to the barge again and had much merry talk and good singing; and came before it was [dark] back to the New Exchange stairs, and there landed and walked up to Mrs. Pierce's, where we sat awhile and then up to their dining-room; and so having a violin and theorbo, did fall to dance, here*b* being also Mr. Floyd come thither, and by and by Mr. Harris. But there being so few of us that could dance, and my wife not being very well, we had not much pleasure in the dancing (there was Knepp also, by which with much pleasure we did sing a little); and so about 10 a-clock I took coach with my wife and Deb, and so home and there to bed.

24. Up pretty betimes; and so there comes to me Mr. Shish to desire my appearing for him to succeed Mr. Chr. Pett, lately dead, in his place of Maister-Shipwright of Deptford and Woolwich; which I do resolve to promote when I can.[1] So by and by to*c* White-hall and there to the Duke of York's chamber, where I understand it is already resolved by the King and Duke of York that Shish shall have the place. From the Duke's chamber, Sir W. Coventry and I to walk in the Matted Gallery;

a repl. 'and'   *b* MS. 'hearing'
c repl. 'out of the Duke of York'

---

1. Pett had died on 22 March; Jonas Shish, his assistant, was appointed to succeed him on the 25th.

and there, among other things, he tells me of the wicked design that now is at last contriving against him, to get a petition presented from people, that the money they have paid to W. Coventry for their places may be repaid them back. And that this is set on by Temple and Hollis of the Parliament and among other mean people in it, by Captain Tatnell. And he prays me that I will use some effectual way to sift Tatnell what he doth, and who puts him on on this business; which I do undertake, and will do with all my skill for his service – being troubled that he is still under this difficulty.[1] Thence up and down Westminster, by Mrs. Burroughes*a* her mother's shop, thinking to have seen her, but could not; and therefore back to White-hall, where great talk of the tumult*b* at the other end of the town about Moore-fields among the prentices, taking the liberty of these holidays to pull down bawdy-houses.[2] And Lord, to see the apprehensions which this did give to all people at Court, that presently order was given for all the soldiers, horse and foot, to be in armes; and forthwith alarmes were beat by drum and trumpet through Westminster, and all to their colours and to horse, as if the French were coming into the town. So Creed, whom I met here, and I to Lincolnes Inn fields, thinking to have gone into the fields to have seen the prentices; but here we found these fields full of soldiers all in a body, and my Lord Craven commanding of them, and riding up and down to give orders like a madman. And some*c* young men we saw brought by soldiers to the guard at White-hall, and overheard others that stood by

a   name in s.h.   *b*   repl. 'mutult'   *c*   MS. 'I some'

---

1. Cf. above, p. 108 & n. 2.
2. These were the most serious London riots of the diary period. They began in Poplar and continued for three days. No lives were lost, but much property was damaged, and the composition of the mobs, together with the character of their slogans ('Liberty of Conscience!', 'Reformation and Reducement!'), show that there was something more involved than the high spirits of apprentices. The tone of Pepys's account becomes perceptibly more serious on 25 March. Cf. *State Trials* (ed. Howell), vi. 879–914; *CSPD 1667–8*, pp. 306, 310–11; HMC, *Le Fleming*, p. 56; J. C. Jeaffreson (ed.), *Middlesex county records*, vol. iv, pp. xiii+, 8–12; M. Beloff, *Public Order, 1660–1714*, pp. 30–1; below, p. 152 & n. 2.

say that it was only for pulling down of bawdy-houses. And none of the bystanders finding fault with them, but rather of the soldiers for hindering them. And we heard a Justice of Peace this morning say*a* to the King that he had been endeavouring to suppress this tumult, but could not; and that imprisoning some in the new prison at Clerkenwell, the rest did come and break open the prison and release them. And that they do give out that they are for pulling down of bawdy-houses, which is one of the great grievances of the nation. To which the King made a very poor, cold, insipid answer: "Why, why do they go to them, then?", and that was all, and had no mind to go on with the discourse. Mr. Creed and I to dinner to my Lord Crew, where little discourse, there being none but us at the table and my Lord and my Lady Jemimah. And so after dinner away, Creed and I, to White-hall, expecting a committee of Tanger, but came too late. So I to attend the Council, and by and by were called in with Lord Brouncker and Sir W. Penn to advise how to pay away a little money to most advantage to the men of the yards, to make them despatch*b* the ships going out; and there I did make a little speech, which was well liked. And after all, it was found most satisfactory to the men and best for the King's despatch, that what money we had should be paid weekly to the men for their week's work, until a greater sum could be got to pay them their arreares and then discharge them.[1] But Lord, to see what shifts and what cares and thoughts there was imployed in this matter, how to do the King's work and please the men and stop clamours, would make a man think the King should not eat a bit of good meat till he hath got money to pay the men – but I do not see the least print of care or thoughts in him about it at all. Having done here, I out and there met Sir Fr. Hollis, who doth still tell me that above all things in the world he wishes he had my tongue in his mouth; meaning, since my speech in Parliament. He took Lord Brouncker and me down to the guards, he and his company being upon the guards today; and

a repl. 'come to'   *b* repl. 'this'

---

1. In June £8,000 was borrowed from Backwell the banker for pay- ment of the arrears: *CTB*, ii. 354, 357.

there he did, in a handsome room to that purpose, make us drink, and did call for his Bagpiper;^a which, with pipes of ebony tipped with silver, he did play beyond anything of that kind that ever I heard in my life. And with great pains he must have obtained it, but with pains that the instrument doth not deserve at all; for at the best, it is mighty barbarous music. So home, and there to my chamber to prick out my song, *It is decreed*,[1] intending to have it ready to give Mr. Harris on Thursdy when we meet for him to sing, believing that he^b will do it more right then a woman that sings better, unless it were Knipp – which I cannot have opportunity to teach it to.

This evening I came home from White-hall with Sir W. Penn, who fell in talk about his going to sea this year and the difficulties that arises to him by it, by giving offence to the Prince and occasioning envy to him, and many other things that make it a bad matter at this time of want of money and necessaries, and bad and uneven counsels at home, for him to [go] abroad. And did tell me how much with the King and Duke of York he had endeavoured to be excused, desiring the Prince might be satisfied in it, who hath a mind to go; but he tells me they will not excuse him; and I believe it, and truly do judge it a piece of bad fortune to W. Penn.

25. Up and walked to White-hall, there to wait on the Duke of York, which I did; and in his chamber there, first by hearing the Duke of York call me^c by my name, my Lord Burlington did come to me and with great respect take notice of me and my relation to my Lord Sandwich,[2] and express great kindness to me; and so to talk of my Lord Sandwiches concernments. By and by the Duke of York is ready, and I did wait for an opportunity of speaking my mind to him about Sir J. Mennes his being unable to do the King any service; which I think doth become me to do in all respects, and have Sir W. Coventry's concurrence therein; which I therefore will seek a speedy opportunity to do – come what will come of it.

---

a l.h. repl. s.h. 'bagpipe'   *b* MS. 'it'   *c* repl. 'my'

---

1. See above, vii. 91 & n. 4. (E).
2. Burlington's daughter had recently married Sandwich's son, Viscount Hinchingbrooke.

The Duke of York and all with him this morning were full of the talk of the prentices, who are not yet down, though the Guards and militia of the town have been in arms all this night and the night before; and the prentices have made fools of them, sometimes by running from them and flinging stones at them. Some blood hath been spilt, but a great many houses pulled down; and among others, the Duke of York was mighty merry at that of Damaris Page's, the great bawd of the seamen. And the Duke of York complained merrily that he hath lost two tenants by their houses being pulled down, who paid him for their wine licences 15*l* a year.[1] But here it was said how these idle fellows have had the confidence to say that they did ill in contenting themselfs in pulling down the little bawdy-houses and did not go and pull down the great bawdy-house at White hall. And some of them have the last night had a word among them, and it was "Reformation and Reducement!" This doth make the courtiers ill at ease to see this spirit among people, though they think this matter will not come to much; but it speaks people's mind. And then they do say that there are men of understanding among them, that have been of Cromwell's army; but how true that is I know not.

Thence walked a little to Westminster, but met with nobody to spend any time with; and so by coach homeward, and*a* in Seething-lane met young*b* Mrs. Daniel, and I stopped; and she had been at my house but found nobody within, and tells me that she drew me for her valentine this year; so I took her into the coach, and was going to the other end of the town with her, thinking to have taken her abroad; but remembering that I was to go out with my wife this afternoon, I only did hazer her para tocar my prick*c* con her hand,*c* which did hazer me hazer; and so to a milliner at the corner*d* shop going into Bishopsgate and Leadenhall-street, and there did give her eight pair of gloves,

a repl. 'in'   *b* repl. 'Mr.'
c garbled s.h.   *d* repl. 'end'

---

1. Since 1661 the Duke had enjoyed all the profits from the sale of licences for the retailing of wines: *CTB*, i. 269–70.

and so dismissed her; and so I home and to dinner, and then with my wife to the King's playhouse to see *The Storme*; which we did, but without much pleasure, it being but a mean play compared with *The Tempest* at the Duke of York's, though Knipp did act her part of grief very well.[1] Thence with my wife and Deb by coach to Islington to the old house,[2] and there eat and drank till it was almost night; and then home, being in fear of meeting*a* the prentices, who are many of them yet, they say, abroad in the fields. But we got well home, and so I to my chamber a while; and then to supper and to bed.

26. Up betimes to the office, where by and by my Lord Brouncker and I met and made an end of our business betimes; so I away with him to Mrs. Williams's and there dined, and thence I alone to the Duke of York's House to see the new play called *The Man is the Maister*,[3] where the house was, it being not above one a-clock, very full; but my wife and Deb being there before with Mrs. Pierce and Corbett and Betty Turner, whom my wife carried with her, they*b* made me room; and there I sat, it costing me 8*s* upon them in oranges, at 6*d* apiece. By and by the King came and we sat just under him, so that I durst not turn my back all the play.[4] The play is a translation out of French, and the plot Spanish;[5] but not anything extraordinary at all in it, though translated by Sir W Davenant; and so I found the King and his company did think meanly of it, though

a repl. 'being'   *b* repl. 'and was'

---

1. Mrs Knepp played the part of Aminta: Genest, i. 81. The play was *The sea voyage*, a comedy by Fletcher and Massinger (see above, viii. 450, n. 4). *The Tempest* was Shakespeare's play as altered by Dryden and Davenant (see above, viii. 521, n. 4). (A).

2. The King's Head.

3. A comedy, Davenant's last play; published in 1668. This is the first record of a performance. One

o'clock was two-and-a-half hours before the usual time of commencement. (A).

4. Pepys was sitting on the rearmost bench of the pit and the royal box was situated in the centre of the boxes. (A).

5. It was based upon two plays by Paul Scarron: *Jodelet, ou Le maître-valet* and *L'héritier Ridicule*. The scene was set in Madrid. (A).

there was here and there something pretty; but the most of the mirth was sorry, poor stuffe, of eating of sack-posset and slabbering themselfs, and mirth fit for Clownes.* The prologue but poor; and the epilogue, little in it but the extraordinariness of it, it being sung by Harris and another in the form of a ballet.[1] Thence by agreement, we all of us to the Blue Balls hard by, whither Mr. Pierce also goes with us, who met us at the play; and anon comes Manuel and his wife and Knipp and Harris, who brings with him Mr. Banester, the great maister of Musique.[2] And after much difficulty in getting of Musique, we to dancing and then to a supper of some French dishes (which yet did not please me) and then to dance and sing; and mighty merry we were till about 11 or 12 at night, with mighty great content in all my company; and I did, as I love to do, enjoy myself in my pleasure, as being the heighth of what we take pains for and can hope for in this world – and therefore to be enjoyed while we are young and capable of these joys. My wife extraordinary fine today in her Flower tabby suit, bought a year and more ago, before my mother's death put her into mourning, and so not worn till this day – and everybody in love with it; and endeed, she is very fine and handsome in it. I having paid the reckoning, which came to almost 4*l*, we parted: my company and Wm. Batelier, who was also with us, home in a coach round by the Wall, where we met so many stops by the Waches that it cost us much time and some trouble, and more money to every watch to them to drink – this being encreased by the trouble the prentices did lately give the City, so that the militia and watches are very strict at this time; and we had like to have met with a stop for all night at the Constables watch at Mooregate, by a pragmatical Constable. But we came well home at about 2 in the morning, and so to bed.

This noon, from Mrs. Williams, my Lord Brouncker sent to Somerset-house to hear how the Duchess of Richmond doth; and word was brought him that she is pretty well, but mighty

---

1. Harris played Don John; his partner was Sandford. According to Downes (p. 30) they sang the epilogue 'like two Street Ballad-Singers'. (A).

2. John Banister, leader until recently of the King's band. (E).

full of the smallpox[1] – by which all do conclude she will[a] be wholly spoiled; which is the greatest instance of the uncertainty of beauty that could be in this age. But then, she hath had the benefit of it, to be first married – and to have kept it so long, under the greatest temptation in the world from a King, and yet without the least imputation.

This afternoon at the play, Sir Fr. Hollis spoke to[b] me, as a secret and matter of confidence in me and friendship to Sir W. Penn, who is now out of town, that it were well he were made acquainted that he finds in the House of Commons, which met this day, several motions made for the calling strictly again upon the miscarriages; and perticularly in the business of the prizes and the not prosecuting of the first victory, only to give an affront to Sir W. Penn, whose going to sea this year doth give them matter of great dislike;[2] so though I do not much trouble myself for him, yet I am sorry that he should have this fall so unhappily, without any fault, but rather merit of his own that made him fitter for this command then anybody else; and the more for that this business of his may happily occasion their more eager pursuit against the whole body of the office.

27. Up and walked to the waterside, and thence to Whitehall to the Duke of York's chamber; where he being ready, he went to a Committee of Tanger, where I first understand that my Lord Sandwich is in his coming back from Spayne, to step over thither to see in what condition the place is – which I am glad of,[c] hoping that he will be able to do some good there for the good of the place – which is so much out of order.[3] Thence to walk a

---

a MS. 'be will'   *b* repl. 'm'-   *c* repl. same symbol

---

1. There was an epidemic: above, p. 58 & n. 5. One of her eyes was badly affected: Harris, ii. 182.

2. The Committee on Miscarriages was now revived, and an enquiry into the conduct of officers of the fleet was ordered: *CJ*, ix. 69. For the attempt to prevent Penn from taking up this command, see Arlington to Sandwich,

16 April: Sandwich MSS, Letters from Ministers, ii, f. 81r.

3. In August Sandwich visited Tangier and conducted a thorough enquiry, particularly into the disputes between the military and civil authorities. Sandwich MSS, Letters from Foreign Ministers, ff. 81–118; Harris, ii. 153–9.

little in Westminster-hall, where the Parliament I find sitting, but spoke with nobody to let me know what they are doing, nor did I enquire. Thence to the Swan and drank, and did besar Frank; and so down by water back again and to the Exchange a turn or two, only to show myself; and then home to dinner, where my wife and I had a small squabble; but I first this day tried the effect of my silence and not provoking her when she is in an ill humour, and do find it very good, for it prevents its coming to that heighth on both sides, which used to exceed what was fit between us. So she became calm by and by, and fond; and so took coach, and she to the mercer's to buy some lace, while I to White-hall but did nothing; but then to Westminster-hall and took a turn, and so to Mrs. Martins and there did sit a little and talk and drink and did hazer con her; and so took coach and called my wife at Unthankes, and so up and down to the Nursery, where they did not act; then to the New Cockepitt[1] and there missed, and then to Hide parke, where many coaches, but the Dust so great that it was troublesome; and so by night home, where to my chamber and finished my pricking out of my song for Mr. Harris (*It is decreed*); and so a little supper, being very sleepy and weary since last night, and so by 10 a-clock to bed – and slept well all night.

This day at noon comes Mr. Pelling to me and shows me[a] the stone cut lately out of Sir Tho. Adam's (the old comely Alderman) body, which is very large endeed, bigger I think then my fist, and weighs above 25[b] ounces – and which is very miraculous, never in all his life had any fit of it, but lived to a great age without pain, and died at last of something else, without any sense of this in all his life.[2]

---

a repl. 'the'　　　*b* repl. '25 oun -

1. In Holborn: below, p. 154 & n. 3. For the Nursery, see above, p. 14, n. 2. (A).

2. Adams had died on 24 February after a fall from his coach. The stone had been exhibited at the Royal Society on 26 March: Birch, ii. 260. In a report made to the Society on 27 February it was said that the stone had 'in the midst a gutter, through which the urine had probably passed', with the result that 'the patient had not been heard to make any great complaint of inconvenience': ib., p. 254. The suffering from stone is caused by the small stones which travel from the kidneys to the bladder, not by those which are too large to move.

This day, Creed at Whitehall in discourse told me what information he hath had, from very good hands, of the cowardize and ill-government of Sir Jer. Smith and Sir Tho. Allen, and the repute they have, both of them, abroad in the Streights, from their deportment when they did at several times command there.[1] And that above all Englishmen that ever was there, there never was any man that behaved himself like poor Charles Wager,[2] whom the very Moores do mention with teares sometimes.

28. Up and to the office, where all the morning busy; and at noon home to dinner with my clerks; and though my head full of business, yet I had a desire to end this holiday week with a play; and so with my wife and Deb to the King's House and there saw *The Indian Emperour*,[3] a very good play endeed. And thence directly home and so to my writing of my letters; and so home to supper and to bed for fearing my eyes. Our greatest business at the office today is our want of money for the setting forth of these ships that are to go out, and my people at dinner did tell me that they[a] do verily doubt that the want of men will be so great as we must press; and if we press, there will be mutinies in the town, for the seamen are said already to have threatened the pulling down of the Treasury Office – and if they once come to that, it will not be long before they come to ours.

29. *Lords day.* Up, and I to church, where I have not been these many weeks before;[4] and there did first find a strange Reader, who could not find in the service-book the place for churching of women, but was fain to change books with the

a repl. 'he'

---

1. Smith had commanded a squadron in the Mediterranean in 1666. Allin in 1664 had run ashore near Gibraltar, with the loss of two ships, when chasing the Dutch Smyrna fleet: above, vi. 8 & n. 3.

2. Wager (a popular commander

with his men, being himself the son of a mariner) had command of the *Crown* in Allin's fleet. He had died on active service in February 1666.

3. See above, viii. 14, n. 2. (A).

4. The last occasion was on 26 January.

Clerke. And then a stranger preached, a seeming able man; but said in his pulpit that God did a greater work in raising of a oake-tree from an*ª* akehorne than a man's body raising it at the last day from his dust (showing the possibility of the Resurrection); which was methought a strange saying. At home to dinner, whither comes and dines with me W How, and by invitation Mr. Harris and Mr Banister, most extraordinary company both, the latter for music of all sorts, the former for everything. Here we sang, and Banister played on the Theorbo. And afterward Banister played on his flagelette and I had very good discourse with him about music, so confirming some of my new notions about music that it puts me upon a resolution to go on and make a Scheme and Theory of music not yet ever made in the world.[1] Harris doth so commend my wife's picture of Mr. Hales's, that I will have him draw Harris's head;[2] and he hath also persuaded me to have Cooper draw my wife's; which though it cost 30*l*, yet I will have done.[3] Thus spent the afternoon most deliciously, and then broke up, and I walked with them as far as the Temple; and there parted and I took coach to Westminster, but there did nothing, meeting nobody that I had a mind to speak with; and so home, and there find Mr. Pelling, and then also comes Mrs. Turner and sup and talk with us; and so to bed. I do hear by several that Sir W. Penn's going to sea doth dislike the Parliament mightily, and that they have revived the Committee of Miscarriages to find something to prevent it;[4] and that he being the other day with the Duke of Albemarle to ask his opinion touching his going to sea, the Duchesse overheard and came in to him, and asks W. Penn how he durst have the confidence to offer to go to sea again, to the endangering the nation, when he

a repl. 'a'

---

1. Cf. above, p. 125, n. 2; below, p. 157, n. 5. (E).
2. Nothing (apart from the diary's information) appears to be known of these portraits of Mrs Pepys and of Henry Harris: above, vii. 42–3, 74; below, p. 175. The latter was portrayed in the title role of Orrery's *Henry V*. (OM).

3. Samuel Cooper (d. 1672), the miniaturist, was now at the height of his powers, and had an international reputation. This portrait is not known to survive. (OM).
4. See above, p. 135, n. 2.

knew himself such a coward as he was – which, if true, is very
severe.

30. Up betimes and so to my office, there to do business –
till about 10 a-clock; and then out with my wife and Deb and
W Hewers by coach to Common-garden Coffee-house, where
by appointment I was to meet Harris; which I did, and also
Mr. Cooper the great painter and Mr. Hales; and thence presently
to Mr. Cooper's house[1] to see some of his work; which is all in
little, but so excellent, as though I must confess I do think the
colouring of the flesh to be a little forced, yet the painting is so
extraordinary, as I do never expect to see the like again. Here I
did see Mrs. Stewards picture as when a young maid, and now
again done just before her having the smallpox; and it would
make a man weep to see what she was then, and what she is like
to be, by people's discourse, now. Here I saw my Lord Generalls
picture, and my Lord Arlington and Ashlys, and several others;[2]
but among the rest, one Swinfen, that was Secretary to my Lord
Manchester, Lord Chamberlain (with Cooling), done so admirably as I never saw anything; but the misery was, this
fellow died in debt and never paid Cooper for his picture;[3] but it
being[a] seized on by his creditors among his other goods after his

a repl. 'is'

---

1. Cooper had been established in
Henrietta St., Covent Garden, since
at least 1650. (OM).

2. Of the miniatures mentioned
here, the later one of the Duchess of
Richmond ('Mrs. Steward') may be
the portrait in male attire, signed and
dated '166–' in the Royal Library,
Windsor (a variant in the Uffizi is
dated 1669 and one in The Hague
1666: Roy. Acad., *The Age of
Charles II*, 1960–1, nos 585, 646, 654);
that of Albemarle may be the large
unfinished miniature in the Royal
Library (or one of the smaller deriva-
tions from it: D. Foskett, *Cooper*, nos

80, 91); that of Arlington may be the
large miniature at Castle Howard
(Foskett, p. 120, pl. 74) which may
have been left unfinished by Cooper;
that of Ashley may be the large
miniature at St Giles's House, Cranborne, Dorset, which shows the
sitter in official robes (Roy. Acad., op.
cit., nos 566, 563). The Grand Duke
of Tuscany, visiting Cooper's house
in 1669, was impressed by miniatures
of Albemarle and of the Duchess of
Richmond: Magalotti, p. 343; *Burl.
Mag.*, 99/16+. (OM).

3. This miniature is unknown.
(OM).

death, Cooper himself says that he did buy it, and gave 25*l* out
of his purse for it, for what he was to have had but 30*l*. Being
infinitely satisfied with this sight, and resolving that my wife
shall be drawn by him when she comes out of the country, I away
with Harris and Hales to the Coffee-house (sending my people
away) and there resolve for Hales to begin Harris's head for me –
which I will be at the cost of. After a little talk, I away to
White-hall and Westminster, where I find the Parliament still
bogling about the raising of this money – and everybody's mouth
full now; and Mr. Wren himself tells me that the Duke of York
declares to go to sea himself this year, and I perceive it is only on
this occasion of distaste of the Parliament against W Pen's going,
and to prevent the Prince's; but I think it is mighty hot counsel
for the Duke of York at this time to go out of the way; but
Lord, what pass are all our matters come to. At noon by
appointment to Cursiters-alley in Chancery-lane to meet Captain
Cocke and some other creditors of the Navy and their counsel
(Pemmerton, North, Offly, and Ch. Porter); and there dined
and talk of the business of the assignments on the Exchequer on
the 1250000*l* on behalf of our creditors;[1] and there I do perceive
that the counsel had*a* heard of my performance in the Parliament-
house lately, and did value me and what I said accordingly.
At dinner we had a great deal of good discourse about parliaments
their number being uncertain and always at the will of the
King to encrease, as he saw reason to erect a new burrow.[2] But
all concluded*b* that the bane of the Parliament hath been the leaving off the old custom of the places allowing wages to them that
served them in Parliament, by which they chose men that understood their business and would attend it, and they could expect
an account from, which now they cannot; and so the Parliament

a repl. 'do'   *b* repl. 'conclude'

---

1. See above, p. 122 & n. 1.
2. Pepys had learnt this fact fairly
recently from Prynne: above, p. 15.
But the Commons now objected to
this exercise of the prerogative.
Newark (in 1675) was the last

parliamentary borough to be created
by charter, and the number of M.P.'s
then remained unaltered at 513 until
the parliamentary union with Scotland in 1707.

is become a company of men unable to give account for the interest of the place they serve for.[1]

Thence, the meeting of the Council with the King's counsel this afternoon being put off by reason of the death of Serjeant Maynards lady, I to White-hall, where the Parliament[2] was to wait on the King; and they did, and it was to be told that he did think fit to tell them that they might expect to be adjourned at Whitsontide, and that they might make haste to raise their money. But this I fear will[a] displease them, who did expect to sit as long as they pleased; and whether this be done by the King upon some new counsels I know not, for the King must be beholding to them till they do settle this business of money. Great talk today as if Beaufort was come into the Channel with about 20 ships,[3] and it makes people apprehensive – but yet the Parliament doth not stir a bit faster in the business of money.

Here I met with Creed, expecting a Committee of Tanger, but the Committee met not, so he and I up and down, having nothing to do, and perticularly to the New Cockpitt by the King's Gate in Holborne; but seeing a great deal of rabble, we did refuse to go in, but took coach and to Hide-park and there till all the Tour[4]

a MS. 'will be'

---

1. The medieval custom whereby constituencies paid wages to their M.P.'s – usually 2s. a day in the case of boroughs and 4s. in the case of counties – had been greatly weakened from the 16th century onwards by competition among parliamentary candidates and by the tenure of borough seats by 'strangers'. Almost all members now served without wage, and sometimes under the terms of a bargain by which they promised not to claim any. A few of the larger cities (London among them) continued to pay wages, though not regularly: the last-known case being that of Bristol in 1696. See *EHR*, 66/27÷.

2. *Recte* the Commons. They met the King in the Banqueting Hall, Whitehall, at 3 p.m.: *CJ*, ix. 71, 72.

3. The French fleet under the Duc de Beaufort had left Brest on the 18th and had been sighted off Ushant on the night of the 25th–26th: Allin, ii, pp. xxxvii, 18. The Duke of York on the King's orders this day instructed Allin to retreat to the Downs if outnumbered: *CSPD 1667–8*, p. 314; Duke of York, *Mem. (naval)*, pp. 147–8.

4. The 'Ring' around which coaches were driven, especially at Easter time: see above, iv. 95, n. 3.

was empty; and so he and I to the Lodge[1] in the park and there eat and drank till it was night, and then carried him to Whitehall, having had abundance of excellent talk with him in reproach of the times and managements we live under; and so I home and there to talk and to supper with my wife, and so to bed.

31. Up pretty betimes and to the office, where we sat all the morning; and at noon I home to dinner, where[a] my Uncle Tho dined with me, as he doth every quarter, and I paid him his pension;[2] and also comes Mr. Hollier, a little fuddled and so did talk nothing but Latin and laugh, that it was very good sport to see a sober man in such a humour, though he was not drunk to scandal. At dinner comes a summons for this[b] office and the Victualler to attend a committee of Parliament this afternoon with Sir D Gawden, which I accordingly did, with my papers relating to the sending of victuals to Sir Jo. Harman's fleet; and there, Sir R. Brookes in the chair, we did give them a full account; but Lord, to see how full they are and immovable in their jealousy that some means are used to keep Harman from coming home,[c3] for they have an implacable desire to know the bottom of the not improving the first victory,[4] and would lay it upon Brouncker.[5] Having given them good satisfaction, I away thence up and down, wandering a little to see whether I could get Mrs. Burroughs[d] out, but[e] ella being in the shop[f] ego did speak con her, but she could not then go foras.[f] And so I took coach, and away to Unthankes and there took up my wife

a repl. same symbol badly formed   b repl. 'me to'   c repl. 'in'
    d name in s.h.   e repl. 'that'   f-f garbled s.h.

---

1. The Keeper's Lodge (later, in the 18th century, known as Cheesecake House) at which milk, whey, cheesecakes, etc. were sold. Account (with illustration) in J. Ashton, *Hyde Park*, pp. 29-30.

2. An annuity of £20 payable under the will of his brother Robert Pepys: above, ii. 135 & n. 1.

3. On the 30th the House had appointed two members to ask the Duke of York to renew his order to Harman to hasten home from the W. Indies: *CJ*, ix. 72. He was in fact already on his way and arrived in the Downs on 9 April. Cf. above, p. 80, n. 3.

4. The battle of Lowestoft, 3 June 1665.

5. See above, viii. 490 & n. 1.

and Deb and to the parke; where being in a Hackny and they undressed, I was ashamed to go into the Tour, but went round the park; and so with pleasure home, where Mr. Pelling came and sat and talked late with us; and he being gone, I called Deb to take pen, ink, and paper and write down what things came into my head for my wife to do, in order to her going into the country; and the girl writing not so well as she would do, cried, and her mistress construed it to be sullenness and so was angry, and I seemed angry with her too; but going to bed, she undressed me, and there I did give her good*ᵃ* advice and beso la,*ᵇ* ella weeping still; and yo did take her, the first time in my life, sobra mi genu*ᵃ* and did poner mi mano sub her jupes and toca su thigh, which did hazer me great pleasure; and so did no more, but besando-la went to my bed.*ᶜ*

> *a–a* garbled s.h.   *b* repl. same symbol badly formed
>   *c* repl. 'rest'; followed by one blank page

APRILL.

1. Up and to dress myself; and called, as I use, Deb to brush and dress me and there I did again as I did the last night con mi mano, but would have tocado su thing; but ella endeavoured to prevent me con much modesty by putting su hand there about, which I was well pleased with and would not do too much, and so con great kindness dismissed la; and I to my office, where busy till noon, and then out to bespeak some things against my wife's going into the country tomorrow. And so home to dinner, my wife and I alone, she being mighty busy getting her things ready for her journey. I all the afternoon with her looking after things on the same account, and then in the afternoon out and all alone to the King's House; and there sat in an upper box to hide myself and saw *The Blacke prince*, a very good play, but only the fancy; most of it the same as in the rest of my Lord Orery's plays – but the dance very stately.[1] But it was pretty to see, how coming after dinner and no company with me to talk to, and at a play that I had seen and went to now not for curiosity but only idleness, I did fall asleep the former part of the play but afterward did mind it and like it very well. Thence called at my bookseller's and took Mr. Boyles book of Formes, newly imprinted, and sent my brother my old one.[2] So home, and there to my chamber, till anon comes Mr. Turner and his wife and daughter and Pelling to sup with us and talk of my wife's journey tomorrow,[a] her daughter going with my wife; and after

a repl. same symbol badly formed

---

1. The play was a tragedy by Roger Boyle, Earl of Orrery (see above, viii. 487 & n. 2), and like most of his plays was concerned with the commonplace theme of the conflict between love and honour. The dance was part of a highly spectacular episode at the outset of Act II, when men and women descended from cloud-machines, danced, and returned 'into the Clouds'. (A).

2. Robert Boyle's *The origin of formes and qualities* had been first published in 1666; the second edition, enlarged (Oxford, 1667), is still in the PL: PL 1160.

supper to talk with her husband about the office and his place, which by Sir J. Mennes's age and inability is very uncomfortable to him, as well as without profit or certainty what he shall do when Sir J. Mennes [dies]; which is a sad condition for a man that hath lived so long in the office as Mr. Turner hath done; but he aymes, and I advise him to it, to look for Mr. Ackworth's place in case he should be removed.[1] His wife afterward did take me into my closet and give me a cellar of waters of her own distilling for my father, to be carried down with my wife and her daughter tomorrow; which was very handsome. So broke up and to bed.

2. Up, after much pleasant talk with my wife and upon*a* some alterations I will make in my house in her absence, and I do intend to lay out some money thereon.[2] So she and I up, and she got her ready to be gone; and by and by comes Betty Turner and her mother and W Batelier, and they and Deb, to*b* whom I did give 10*s* this morning to oblige her to please her mistress (and yo did besar her mucho) and also Jane; and so in two coaches set out about 8 a-clock toward the carrier, there for to take coach for my father's (that*c* is to say, my wife and Betty Turner, Deb and Jane); but I meeting my Lord Anglesy going to the office, was forced to light in Cheapside, and there took my leave of them (not besando Deb, which yo had a great*d* mind to); left them to go to their coach,*e* and I to the office, where all the morning busy. And so at noon with my other clerks (W. Hewer being a day's journey with my wife) to dinner, where*f* Mr. Pierce came and dined with me; and then with

---

a repl. 'when'   *b* preceded by opening bracket
c repl. 'but'   *d* garbled s.h.: see above, viii. 244, note *a*
e repl. 'car'-   *f* repl. 'and after dinner'

---

1. William Acworth, Storekeeper at Woolwich, now under a charge of embezzlement, was in fact acquitted: below, p. 382, n. 3. Thomas Turner, clerk to Mennes and Purveyor of Petty Provisions, was appointed Storekeeper at Deptford in the following October: below, p. 327, n. 4.

2. No work of any importance appears to have been done. The office had its windows painted and its walls whited (below, pp. 202, 244), but at the King's expense. Mrs Pepys did not return until 20 June.

Lord Brouncker (carrying his little kinswoman on my knee, his coach being full) to the Temple, where my Lord and I light and to Mr. Porter's chamber, where Cocke and his counsel; and so to the Atturnys, whither the Sollicitor generall came, and there their cause about their Assignments on the 1250000*l* Act was argued[1] – where all that was to be said for them was said, and so answered by the Sollicitor generall, beyond what I expected, that I said not one word all the time, rather choosing to hold my tongue and so mind my reputation with the Sollicitor generall (who did mightily approve of my speech in Parliament) then say nothing against him to no purpose. This I believe did trouble Cocke and those gentlemen, but I did think this best for me. And so I do think that the business will go against them – though it is against my judgment, and I am sure against all justice to the men, to be invited to part with their goods and be deceived afterward of their security for payment. Thence with Lord Brouncker to the Royall Society, where they were just done; but there I was forced to subscribe to the building of a College, and did give 40*l*. And several others did subscribe, some greater and some less sums;[2] but several I saw hang off, and I doubt it will spoil the Society – for it breeds faction and ill will, and becomes burdensome to some that cannot or would*a* not do it. Here to my great content I did try the use of the Otacousticon,[3] which was only a great glass bottle broke at the bottom, putting the neck to my eare; and there I did plainly hear the dashing*b* of the oares of the boats in the Thames to Arundell gallery window; which without it I could not in the least do, and may I believe be improved to a great heighth – which I was mighty glad of. Thence with Lord Brouncker and several of

---

a repl. 'will'   *b* MS. 'danshing'

---

1. See above, p. 122 & n. 1.

2. Altogether £1075 was contributed by 24 Fellows out of a membership of 207; C. R. Weld, *Hist. Roy. Soc.* (1848), i. 211. The scheme (for a building in Arundel Gardens) was abandoned. See above, p. 28 & n. 1.

3. See Birch, ii. 261-2. Hooke appears to have been the inventor, and at the request of the Society produced on 9 April two larger and better models – one of latten and the other of glass: ib., p. 263. There were other varieties by other inventors.

them to the King's Head tavern by Chancery-lane, and there did drink and eat and talk; and above the rest, I did desire of Mr. Hooke and my Lord an account of the reason of Concords and Discords in music – which they say is from the æquality of the vibrations; but I am not satisfied in it, but will at my leisure think of it more and see how far that doth go to explain it.[1] So late at night by coach home with Mr. Colwell,[2] and parted, and I to the office and then to Sir W. Penn to confer with him and Sir R Ford and Young about our *St. Jo. Baptist* prize;[3] and so home, without more supper, to bed – my family being now little, by the departure of my wife and two maids.

3. Up, and Captain Perryman came to me to tell me how Tatnell told him that this day one How is to charge me before the Comissioners of Prizes to the value of 8000*l* in prizes;[4] which I was troubled to hear, so fearful I am, though I know that there is not a penny to be laid to my charge that I dare not own or that I have not owned under*[a]* my hand; but upon recollection, it signifies nothing to me and so I value it not – being sure that I can have nothing in the world to my*[b]* hurt known from that business. So to the office, where all the morning to despatch business. And so home to dinner with my clerks, whose company is of great pleasure to me for their good discourse in anything of the Navy I have a mind to talk of. After dinner, by water from the Tower to White-hall, there to attend the Duke of York as usual, and perticular[ly] in a fresh complaint the Comissioners of the Treasury do make to him, and by and by to the Council this day, of our having prepared Certificates on*[c]* the Exchequer to the further sum*[d]* of near 50000*l*. And as soon as we had done with the Duke of York, we did attend the

a repl. ? 'up'-   *b* repl. 'be'
c repl. 'to the'   *d* MS. 'of sum'

---

1. For a similar discussion with Hooke, see above, vii. 239 & n. 1.

2. Daniel Colwall, Treasurer of the Royal Society, who lived on the n. side of Tower Hill. (R).

3. Taken in 1667 by their privateer the *Flying Greyhound*. Pepys has a summary of the accounts concerning her in Rawl. A 174, ff. 291–3.

4. See below, p. 204 & n. 1.

Council; and there were called in and did hear Mr. Sollicitor make his report to the Council in that business; which he did in a most excellent manner of words, but most cruelly severe against us, and so were some of the Lords-Commissioners of the Treasury, as men guilty of a practice with the tradesmen to the King's prejudice.[1] I was unwilling to enter into a contest with them, but took advantage of two or three words last spoke, and brought it to a short issue in good words: that if we had the King's order to hold our hands, we would; which did end the matter and they all resolved we should have it, and so it ended. And so we away; I vexed that I did not speak more in a cause so fit to be spoke in, and wherein we had so much advantage; but perhaps I might have provoked the Solicitor and the Commissioners of the Treasury; and therefore, since, I am not sorry that I forbore. Thence my Lord Brouncker and I to the Duke of York's playhouse and there saw the latter part of *The Maister is the Man.*[2] And thence by coach to Duck lane to look for Marsenne[3] in French, a man that hath writ well of music, but it is not to be had; but I have given order for its being sent for over, and I did here buy Des Cartes his little treatise of music;[4] and so home, and there to read a little and eat a little, though I find that my having so little taste doth make me so far neglect eating, that unless company invite, I do not love to spend time upon eating, and so bring emptiness and the Cholique. So to bed. This day I hear that Prince Rupert and Holmes do go to sea; and by this there is a seeming friendship and peace among all our great seamen, but the devil a bit there is any love among them, or can be.

4. Up betimes, and by coach towards White-hall; and took Aldgate-street in my way[a] and there called upon one Hayward

---

a MS. 'wife'

---

1. The report is in PRO, PC 2/60, p. 252; the Treasury minute in *CTB*, ii. 289–90. See above, p. 122 & n. 1.
2. *The man's the master*, a comedy by Davenant; see above, p. 133 & n. 3. (A).
3. Marin Mersenne, *Harmonie Uni-* *verselle* (first published Paris, 1633–7). For its purchase, see below, p. 216. (E).
4. René Descartes, *Musicae Compendium* (first published Rheims, 1650). Not in the PL. (E).

that makes virginalls, and did there like of a little Espinettes and will have him finish them for me; for I had a mind to a small Harpsicon, but this takes up less room and will do my business as to finding out of Chords – and I am very well pleased that I have found it. Thence to White-hall; and after long waiting did get a small running Committee of Tanger, where I stayed but little; and little done but the correcting two or three egregious faults in the Charter for Tanger, after it had so long lain before the Council and been passed there and drawn up by the Atturny general, so slightly are all things in this age done.[1]

Thence home to the office by water, where we sat till noon; and then I moved we might go to the Duke of York and the King presently, to get out their order in writing that was ordered us yesterday about the business of Certificates, that we might be secure against the tradesmen who (Sir Jo. Bankes by[a] name) have told me this day that they will complain in Parliament against us for denying to do them right.[2] So we rose all of a sudden, being mighty sensible of this inconvenience we are liable to should we delay to give them them longer, and yet have no order for our indemnity. And I did dine with Sir W. Penn, where my Lady Batten did come with desire of meeting me there and speaking with me about the business of the 500*l* we demand of her for the Chest.[3] She doth protest before God she never did see the account, but that it was as her husband in his life-time made it, and he did often declare to her his expecting 500*l*

a repl. closing bracket

---

1. The charter was issued on 4 June: Routh, p. 117. It had been in preparation for about a year.

2. See Banks to Pepys, Lee, 4 April: PRO, SP 29/237, no. 206; summary in *CSPD 1667–8*, p. 326. He wrote on behalf of two neighbours who were creditors of the navy. On 3 April the Council had ordered the Navy Board to issue no more certificates on the Eleven Months Tax: above, p. 122, n. 1.

3. Batten had claimed this sum (and presumably been paid it) for managing and accounting for an extraordinary fund set up to buy off certain pensions awarded to seamen and their dependants in 1660–3. The accounts (endorsed by Pepys, 31 January 1668) are in Rawl. A 171, ff. 345–52.

and that we could not deny it him for his pains in that business, and that he hath left her worth nothing of his own in the world, and that therefore she could pay nothing of it, come what will come, but that he hath left her a beggar; which I am sorry truly for, though it is a just judgment upon people that do live so much beyond themselfs in house-keeping and vanity, as they did. I did give her little answer but general words that might not trouble her, and so to dinner; and after dinner, W. Penn and I away by water to White-hall, and there did attend the Duke of York and he did carry us to the King's lodgings; but he was asleep in his closet, so we stayed in the Green-roome, where the Duke of York did tell us what rules he had of knowing the weather, and did now tell us we should have rain before tomorrow (it having been a dry season for some time);[1] and so it did rain all night*a* almost. And pretty rules he hath, and told Brouncker and me some of them; which were such as no reason seems ready to be given. By and by the King*b* comes out,*c* and he did easily agree to what we moved and would have the Commissioners of the Navy to meet us with him tomorrow morning. And then to talk of other things; about the Quakers not swearing, and how they do swear in the business of a late election of a Knight of the Shire of Hartfordshire in behalf of one they have a mind to have[2] – and how my Lord of Pembroke will now and then, he says he hath heard him at the tennis-Court, swear to himself when he loses. And told us what pretty notions my Lord Pembroke hath of the first chapter of Genesis – how

a repl. 'of'   *b* MS. 'Duke of York'   *c* repl. 'and'

---

1. January and February had been unusually warm, and March unusually dry. A long warm summer followed.

2. Their candidate has not been identified. Little is known of this bye-election (in which Viscount Cranborne was returned by a writ dated this day), but presumably there had been a close contest, a poll had been held and the qualifications of certain voters challenged. They would have had to swear that they were properly qualified as forty-shilling freeholders. In the general election of 1690 a Hertfordshire candidate was disqualified by the Commons because his majority had so largely consisted of Quakers who for reasons of conscience had refused to swear: *CJ*, x. 395–6. The Quakers were strong in Hertfordshire: cf. above, ii. 148–9 & n.

Adam's sin was not the suckeing (which he did before) but the swallowing of the apple; by which the contrary elements begun to work in him and to stir up evil passions – and a great deal of such fooleries, which the King made mighty mockery at.[1] Thence, my Lord Brouncker and I into the park in his coach and there took*a* a great deal of ayre, saving that it was mighty dusty and so a little unpleasant. Thence to Common-garden with my Lord, and there I took a hackney and home; and after having done a few letters at the office, I home to a little supper and so to bed – my eyes being every day more and more weak and apt to be tired.

5. *Lords day.* Up, and to my chamber and there to the writing fair some of my late music notions;[2] and so to church, where I have not been a good while.[3] And thence home, and dined at home with W Hewers with me; and after dinner, he and I a great deal of good talk touching this office: how it is spoilt by having so many persons in it, and so much work that is not made the work of any one man but of all, and so is never done; and that the best way to have it well done were to have the whole trust in one (as myself) to set whom I pleased to work in the several businesses of the Office, and me to be accountable for the whole; and that would do it, as I would find instruments. But this is not to be compassed; but something I am resolved to do*b* about Sir J. Mennes before it be long. Then to my chamber again, to my music, and so to church; and then home, and thither comes Captain Silas Taylor to me, the Storekeeper of Harwich; where much talk, and most of it against Captain

a repl. 'saw'   *b* repl. 'day'

1. In 1665 Pembroke had told the King that the end of the world would come that year, and bade him prepare for it. Whereupon the King had offered him seven years' purchase for his manor of Wilton, but Pembroke replied, 'No and please your Majesty it shall die with me': HMC, *Rawdon*

Hastings, ii. 120-1. He was a Quaker (of a sort). For his belief in prophecies, see J. J. Jusserand, *French Ambassador*, p. 118.
2. See above, p. 125, n. 2. (E).
3. He had attended church on the previous Sunday. But see above, p. 137 & n. 4.

Deane,[1] whom I do believe to be a high, proud fellow; but he is an active man, and able in his way, and so I love him. He gone, I to my music again and to read a little and to sing with Mr. Pelling, who came to see me and so spent the evening; and then to supper and to bed. I hear that eight of the ringleaders in the late tumults of the prentices at Easter are condemned to die.[2]

6. Betimes, I to Alderman Backewell and with him to my Lord Ashly's, where did a little business about Tanger and to talk about the business of Certificates; wherein, contrary to what I could have believed,[a] the King and Duke of York themselfs in my absence did call for some of the Commissioners of the Treasury and give them direction about that business; which I, despairing to do anything on a Sunday and not thinking that they would think of it themselfs, did rest satisfied; and stayed at home all yesterday, leaving it to do something in this day. But I find that the King and Duke of York had been so pressing in it, that my Lord Ashly was more forward for the doing of it this day then I could have been; and so I to White-hall with Alderman Backwell in his coach, with Mr. Blany my Lord's Secretary, and there did draw a rough draft of what order I would have and did carry it in and had it read twice and approved of before my Lord Ashly and three more of the Commissioners of the Treasury; and then went up to the Council-chamber, where the Duke of York and Prince Rupert and the rest of the Committee of the Navy were sitting, and I did get some of them to read it there; and they would have had it passed presently, but Sir Jo. Nichollas[3] desired they would first have it approved by a full Council; and therefore a Council-extraordinary was readily

a   repl. 'could beheve'

---

1. Anthony Deane, Master-Ship-wright, Harwich.

2. For the riots, see above, pp. 129–30, 132 & nn. Fifteen ringleaders had been indicted for high treason (in that the riots amounted to levying war on the King). Against eight the jury re-turned special verdicts (i.e. left it to the court to decide if treason had been committed); and on 9 May four were condemned and executed, the rest being pardoned. *London Gazette*, 11 May.

3. A clerk of the Council.

summoned against the afternoon, and the Duke of York run presently to the King, as if now they were really set to mind their business; which God grant. So I thence to Westminster and walked in the Hall and up and down, the House being called over today; and little news, but some talk as if the agreement between France and Spain were like to be; which would be bad for us.[1] And at noon with Sir Herb. Price to Mr. George Mountagu's to dinner, being invited by him in the Hall; and there mightily made of, even to great trouble to me to be so*a* commended before my face, with that flattery and importunity that I was quite troubled with it – yet he is a fine gentleman truly, and his Lady a fine woman. And among many sons that I saw there, there was a little daughter that is mighty pretty, of which he is infinite fond; and after dinner did make her play on the Gittarr and sing, which she did mighty prettily and seems to have a mighty musical soul, keeping time with most excellent spirit.[2] Here I met with Mr. Brownlow my old schoolfellow, who came thither I suppose as a suitor to one of the young ladies that were there, and a sober man he seems to be.[3] But here Mr. Mountagu did tell me how Mr. Vaughan in that very room did say that I was a great man and had great understanding, and I know not what, which I confess I was a little proud of, if I may believe him.[4]

Here I do hear as a great secret, that the King and the Duke of York and Duchess and my Lady Castlemaine are now all agreed in a strict league, and all things like to go very current, and that it is not impossible to have my Lord Clarendon in time here

a repl. same symbol

---

1. For the peace, see below, p. 176 & n. 3.

2. Mountagu (lawyer and M.P., a cousin of Sandwich) had in 1645 married Elizabeth, daughter of Sir Anthony Irby, of Whaplade, Lincolnshire. They lived in Cannon Row, Westminster, and had seven sons and four daughters.

3. William, second son of Sir William Brownlow, a Lincolnshire baronet, was at St Paul's School with Pepys, and went to Cambridge (to Sidney Sussex) in 1650, a year ahead of Pepys. He was married on 9 July to Margaret Brydges, daughter of Lord Chandos.

4. John Vaughan, a prominent M.P., was member for Cardiganshire. He was presumably referring to Pepys's parliamentary triumph on 5 March.

again. But I do hear that my Lady Castlemaine is horribly
vexed at the late Libell, the petition of the poor whores about the
town whose houses were pulled down the other day.[1] I have
got one of them, and it is not very witty; but devilish severe
against her and the King. And I wonder how it durst be printed
and spread abroad – which shows that the times are loose, and
come to a great disregard of the King or Court or Government.
Thence to White-hall to attend the Council; and when the
Council rose, did find my order mightily enlarged by the Sollicitor
general, who was called thither, making it more safe for him and
the Council; but their order is the same in*a* the command*b* of it
that I drew, and will I think defend us well.[2] So thence, meeting
Creed, he and I to the new Cocke pitt by the King's gate,[3] and
there saw the manner of it and the mixed rabble of people that
came thither; and saw two battles of cocks, wherein is no great
sport, but only to consider how these creatures without any
provocation do fight*c* and kill one another – and aim only at one
another's heads, and by their good wills not leave till one of them
be killed. And thence to the park in a hackney-coach, so would*d*
not go into the Tour, but round about the park and to the House,[4]
and there at the door eat and drank; whither came my Lady
Kerneagy, of whom Creed tells me more perticularly: how her
Lord, finding her and the Duke of York at the King's first coming
in too kind, did get it out of her that he did dishonour him;
and so he bid her continue to let him, and himself went to the
foulest whore he could find, that he might get the pox; and did,
and did give his wife it on purpose, that she (and he persuaded
and threatened her that she should) might give it the Duke of
York; which she did, and he did give it the Duchesse; and since,

a   repl. 'that'   b   repl. 'com'-
c   repl. 'fine'   d   repl. 'durst'

1. *The poor-whores petition to the
most splendid, illustrious, serene, and
eminent lady of pleasure, the Countess of
Castlemayne* . . .; 25 March 1668; a
mock appeal from the leading bawds
and drabs of the town; reprinted
(together with *The gracious answer of*
the . . . *Countess of Castlem* . . ., 24
April) in G. S. Steinman, *Mem* . . . .
Cleveland, pp. 101–11.
2. See above, p. 122 & n. 1.
3. In Holborn. (R).
4. The Keeper's Lodge. Cf. above,
p. 142 & n. 1.

all her children are thus sickly and infirm – which is the most pernicious and foul piece of revenge that ever I heard of.[1] And he at this day owns it with great glory, and looks upon the Duke of York and the world with great content in the ampleness of his revenge. Thence (where*a* the place was now by the last night's rain very pleasant, and no dust) to White-hall and set Creed down, and I home and to my chamber; there about my music notions again, wherein I take delight and find great satisfaction in them; and so after a little supper, to bed.

This day in the afternoon, stepping with the Duke of York into St. James's park, it rained and I was forced to lend the Duke of York my cloak, which he wore through the park.

7. Up and at the office all the morning, where great hurry to be made in the fitting forth of this present little fleet; but so many rubs by reason of want of money and*b* people's not believing us in cases where we have money unless (which in several cases cannot be ⟨as in hiring of vessels⟩) they be paid beforehand, that everything goes backward instead of forward. At noon comes Mr. Clerke my solicitor and the Auditors men, with my account drawn up in the Exchequer way with their queries, which are neither many nor great, or hard to answer upon it;[2] and so dined with me, and then I by coach to the King's playhouse and there saw *The English Monsieur*[3] (sitting for privacy sake in an upper box): the play hath much mirth in it as to that perticular humour. After the play done, I down to Knipp and did stay her undressing herself[4] and there saw the several players,

a repl. 'set'   *b* repl. 'of'

---

1. Robert Carnegie, 3rd Earl of Southesk, had married Lady Anne Hamilton, daughter of the Duke of Hamilton. The story was often told: Burnet (i. 406) has an almost indentical version (under 1665); Gramont (p. 167) a briefer and different version (under 1669). Cf. [Anon.,] *An historicall poem*, ll. 5-6: 'But now Yorkes Genitalls grew over hot /

With Denham and Coneig's infected pot': Marvell, i. 202.

2. For this enquiry, see above, p. 122 & n. 1.

3. A comedy by James Howard: see above, vii. 401 & n. 2. (A).

4. Actresses often allowed this privilege to their friends and patrons. (A).

men and women, go by; and pretty, to see how strange they are all one to another after the play is done. Here I saw a wonderful pretty maid of her own that came to undress her, and one so pretty that she says she intends not to keep her, for fear of her being undone in her service by coming to the play-house.

Here I hear that Sir W Davenant is just now dead – and so [who] will succeed him in the mastership of that House is not yet known.[1]   The eldest Davenport is it seems gone from this House to be kept by somebody; which I am glad of, she being a very bad actor.[2]   I took her then up into a coach, and away to the park, which is now very fine after some rain.   But the company was going away most, and so I took her to the Lodge[3] and there treated her and had a great deal of good talk, and now and then did besar la, and that was all, and that as much or more then I had much mind to, because of her paint.   She tells me mighty news, that my Lady Castlemayne is mightily in love with Hart of their House and he is much with her in private,[4] and she goes to him and doth give him many presents; and that the thing is most certain, and Becke Marshall ⟨only⟩ privy to it and the means of bringing them together – which is a very odd thing; and by this means she is even with the King's love to Mrs. Davis.   This done, I carried her and set her down at Mrs. Manuel's, but stayed not there myself nor went in; but straight home and there to my letters, and so home to bed.

8.   Up and at my[a] office all the morning doing business; and then at noon home to dinner all alone.   Then to White-hall with Sir J. Mennes in his coach to attend the Duke of York upon our usual business, which was this day but little; and thence with

a   repl. 'the'

---

1. He had died on this day, and was succeeded by his widow.   (A).
2. This was Frances Davenport, eldest of three actress sisters.   She played minor roles.   The name of her protector is unknown.   (A).

3. See above, p. 142, n. 1.
4. For this affair, see G. S. Steinman, *Mem. Cleveland*, pp. 98–9; cf. Burnet, i. 475–6.

Lord Brouncker to the Duke of York's playhouse, where we saw
The Unfortunate Lovers,[1] no extraordinary play methinks;[a] and
thence I to Drumbleby's and there did talk a great deal about
pipes and did buy a Recorder which I do intend to ⟨learn to⟩
play on, the sound of it being of all sounds in the world most
pleasing to me.   Thence home and to visit Mrs. Turner; where
among other talk, Mr. Foly and her husband being there, she did
tell me of young Captain Holmes's marrying[b] of Pegg Lowther
last Saturday by stealth; which I was sorry for, he being an
idle rascal and proud, and worth little I doubt, and she a mighty
pretty, well-disposed lady, and good fortune.[2]   Her mother and
friends* take on mightily;[3] but the sport is, Sir Rob. Holmes
doth seem to be mad too with his brother and will disinherit
him, saying that he hath ruined himself, marrying below himself
and to his disadvantage; whereas, I said in this company that I
had married a sister lately with little above half that portion[4]
that he should have kissed her breech before he should have had
her – which, if R. Holmes should hear, would make a great
quarrel; but it is true, and I am heartily sorry for the poor girl
that is undone by it.   So home to my chamber, to be fingering
of my Recorder and getting of the scale of Musique[5] without book,
which I at last see is necessary, for a man that would understand
music as it is now taught, to understand, though it be a ridiculous
and troublesome way and I know I shall be able hereafter to
show the world a simpler way.[6]   But like the old[c] Hypotheses
in philosophy,* it must be learned, though a man knows a

---

a   repl. symbol rendered illegible   b   repl. 'running away'
                    c   repl. 'od'

---

1. A tragedy by Davenant; see
above, v. 77 & n. 2.   (A).

2. The bridegroom was John
Holmes, younger brother of Sir
Robert, the admiral, and himself later
a knight and admiral.   The bride was
the daughter of the late Ald. Robert
Lowther of London, and sister of
Anthony, who had married Peg Penn.

3. But the marriage certificate records her mother's consent.

4. Paulina, married to John Jackson
on 27 February, with a portion of
£600.

5. The gamut: the contemporary
method of naming the notes of the
scale.   (E).

6. Cf. above, p. 125, n. 2.   (E).

better. Then to supper and to bed. ⟨This morning Mr. Chr. Pett's widow and daughter came to me to desire my help to the King and Duke of York, and I did promise, and do pity her.⟩¹

9. Up and to the office, where all the morning sitting. Then at noon home to dinner with my people. And so to the office again, writing of my letters, and then abroad to my bookseller's and I up and down to the Duke of York's playhouse, there to see, which I did, Sir W Davenant's corps carried out toward Westminster, there to be buried.² Here were many coaches and six horses and many hackneys, that made it look, methought, as if it were the burial of a poor poett.³ He seemed to have many children by five or six in the first mourning-coach, all boys.⁴ And there I left them coming forth, and I to the New Exchange, there to meet Mrs. Burroughs; and did tomar her*ᵃ* in a carosse and carry ella toward the park, kissing her and tocando su breast, so as to make myself do; but did not go into any house, but came back and set her*ᵃ* down at White-hall; and did give her wrapped in paper, for my Valentine's gift for the last year before this, which I never did yet give her anything for, twelve half-crowns; and so I back home and there to my office, where came a packet from the Downes from my brother Balty, who with Harman is arrived there – of*ᵇ* which this day came the

a–a garbled s.h.   b repl. ? 'which'

---

1. Pett, the navy shipwright at Woolwich, had died on 22 March. Ann, his widow, had written to Pepys on the 26th: *CSPD 1667-8,* p. 308. She had many debts to face and claimed £500 in arrears of pay due to her husband.
2. His house adjoined his theatre in Lincoln's Inn Fields. He was buried in Westminster Abbey. (A).
3. He died heavily in debt: T. L.

Chester, *Reg. Westminster Abbey,* p. 168 n. But his coffin was of walnut, and Sir John Denham is said to have remarked that it was 'the finest . . . that ever he sawe': Aubrey, i. 208.
4. He had seven surviving sons, all by his third and last marriage. The youngest was born in 1668: hence the 'five or six' attending his funeral. (A).

first news.[1]   And now the Parliament will be satisfied, I suppose, about the business they have so long desired between Brouncker and Harman, about not prosecuting the first victory.[2]   Balty is very well, and I hope hath performed his[a] work well – that I may get him into further imployment.   I wrote to him this night; and so home, and there to the perfecting my getting the scale of music without book; which I have done to perfection, backward and forward; and so to supper and to bed.

a repl. 'is'

---

1. Balty St Michel was Muster-Master and Deputy-Treasurer of the fleet of 20 ships just come from the W. Indies. For the news of its arrival, see *CSPD 1667–8*, pp. 335, 337.

2. See above, p. 80 & n. 3.

[Here eight pages (with top and left-hand margins in red) are left blank for the entries for 10–19 April.   The entries were never inserted, and in their place the rough notes from which they were to be constructed (together with a few notes for the 20th) were bound into the volume.   These were written in ink on three foolscap leaves folded so as to form six pages, and numbered in Pepys's hand. The leaves have been misfolded, so that page 5 follows page 2.   The notes are the best evidence we have about Pepys's method of composition.   They include, for instance, accounts of expenditure which he normally transferred to his account-books.   They are here reproduced as exactly as possible, except that the mistake in the page sequence has been rectified, and that where necessary the abbreviations of personal and place names are extended within editorial square brackets.   Italics are used for words and abbreviations written in longhand.]

~~Mony~~   ~~March.~~
~~Eastwood 100!~~[1] ~~M°. Aprill.~~
~~M! Rayner.   Young Lyon 200!~~[2]
~~Cap!: Cabbins.~~
~~Wollw!ᶜʰ Master Attend! carry Fr[ench] Ruby~~
~~where she may lie afloat and take in men and~~
~~provisions.~~
~~Young Lyon.   buy 200!~~
~~Elizabeth Ketch~~[3] ~~17!~~
~~Wren's vessell~~[4] ~~39~~
~~Goldsmith's~~[5] _____

================

Fr. 10 All morning at office.
      At noon with *W P[enn]*
      to *D[uke of] Y[ork]* and
      attended council.   So to
      piper's.[6]   And Duck-lane

1. Roger Eastwood (assistant-ship-wright at Deptford and Woolwich) was now fitting the *Ruby* (a French prize) with masts.   His requests for money are in *CSPD 1667–8*, pp. 233, 342.

2. The *Young Lyon* was a 6th-rate recently sold to Rayner and now bought back for £200: *CSPD Add. 1660–85*, pp. 266, 267.

3. Untraced.
4. Untraced.
5. Ralph Goldsmith, a ship's captain of Rotherhithe, was reported to the Navy Board on 18 April for keeping money and clothes belonging to a seaman: *CSPD 1667–8*, p. 347.
6. Drumbleby's,   the   flageolet-maker's.

and there kissed book-
seller's wife and bought
Legend[1] —————— 0–14–0
So home coach——— 0–4–0 to S[r]. *W P[enn]*
                 Carrier. Mrs *Hann*[2]
                 dead.

S. 11 ~~gloves~~ —————— 0–6–6
     ~~bacon and anchoves~~ —— 0–13–0
     ~~*Cicero*[3]~~ —————— 2–10–0 News of peace.[4]
     ~~coach~~ —————— 0–1–0 Conning my gamut.
     ~~play~~ —————— 0–4–0
     ~~coach home~~ —————— 0–2–0
     ~~letters~~ —————— 0–0–6

      12   4
Sundy   ~~spent at Chequer~~ —— 0–0–6 Dined at *Br[ouncker's]*
       ~~*Lord Br[ouncker's]* coach~~   and saw the new[s]-
       ~~from park~~ —————— 0–2–6 book. Peace.[5]
       ~~hackney~~ —————— 0–1–0 Cutting away sails.
       ~~*W P[enn']s* coach~~ —— 0–1–0
       ~~spent at Swan Frank~~[6] —— 0–0–6[a]

Monday
   ~~M~~ 13 spent at *Michells* ————————— 0– 0– 6
      ~~oyster~~ in the *Folly*[7] ————————— 0– 1– 0
      oysters ————————————— 0– 1– 0

a   end of page 1

———————

1. The bookseller was William Shrewsbury: cf. below, p. 260 & n. 4. The *Legenda Aurea* (compiled by Jacques de Voragine, a 13th-century Dominican) was the most popular collection of lives of the saints in the late Middle Ages. It is likely (from the number of shelf-marks on the flyleaf) that PL 2040 (an English version published by Wynkyn de Worde in 1527) is the copy Pepys now bought.

2. Mary Hammond, sister of Sir John Mennes.

3. All copies of Cicero in the PL are of editions later than 1668: cf. above, ii. 6, n. 4.

4. See below, n. 5.

5. The *London Gazette* (9 April) printed Louis XIV's terms for a peace with Spain. See below, p. 176 & n. 3.

6. Frances Udall.

7. A large floating house of entertainment moored on the Thames, off Somerset House. (R).

coach to *W C[oventry]* about Mr *Pett*[1] _____   0- 1- 0√
Thence to Commissioners Treasury and so⎤   0- 0- 6√
to *W[estminste]r* hall by water _____⎦   0- 0- 6√
with *G Mountagu* and *R P[epys]* and spoke⎤
with *Vaughan* and *Birch* all in trouble about the⎮
prize business.[2]   And so to *Ld Crews* (calling⎬   0 -1- 0√
for a low pipe by the way where *Creed* and⎮
G M[ountagu] and *G C[arteret]* came _____⎦
So with *Creed* to a play Little Thief_____   0- 4- 0[3]
Thence ~~into the~~ towards the park by coach __   0- 2- 6√
Came home met with order of Commissioners
of Accounts[4] which put together with the rest
vexed me and so home to supper and to bed.

14
Tuesd.   Up betimes by water to Temple. In the way
read the Narrative about prizes[5] and so to Lord
Crews bedside. And then to *W[estminste]r*
where I hear *Pen* is sent for by messenger last
night.   Thence to Commissioners of Accounts
and there examined.   And so back to *W[est-
minste]r*-hall where all the talk of committing
all to the Tower. And *Creed* and I to the
Quakers[6] dined together. Thence to the
House, where^a rose about 4 a'clock and with
much ado *Pen* got to Thursday to bring in his
answer^b so my Lord ~~pray~~ escapes today.
Thence with *Godolph[in]* and *G M[ountagu]* to
G C[arteret]'s and there sat their dinner time.
And hear myself by many Parliament men
mightily commended. Thence to a play
~~and so~~ *Loves* Cruelty.[7]   And so to my Lord
Crew who glad of this day's time got, and so

a   preceded by blot   b   preceded by blot

---

1. See above, p. 158 & n. 1.
2. All named here were M.P.'s.
For the prize business, see above, vi.
231, n. 1.
3. A seat in the boxes cost 4s.   For
the play (by John Fletcher and James
Shirley), see above, ii. 65, n. 1. (A).
4. See below, p. 169 & n. 1.

5. Produced by the Brooke House
Committee: *CJ*, ix. 80, 81. Copy
(in hands of Gibson and Hewer) in
BM, Harl. 7170, ff. 72–84.
6. An eating-house.
7. A tragedy by Shirley (see above,
viii. 598, n. 4); probably staged at
the TR. (A).

home and there office a little and then home to
supper and to bed my *eyes* being bad but better
upon leaving drinking at night.

water___	0–1–0√	play part_____	0– 2– 0[1]
porter___	0–0–6	oranges_____	0– 1– 0[2]
water___	0–0–6√	home coach___	0– 1– 6
dinner___	0–3–6.*a*		

15

*W*___ *Apr.* ~~16.~~ 1668_____

After playing a little upon*b* my new little
flagelette that is so soft that pleases me mightily[3]
betimes to my office – where most of the
morning. Then by coach_____ 0– 1– 0√
and meeting L[ord] Br[ouncker] light at the
Exchange and thence by water to Wh[ite] hall 0– 1– 0√
and there to the Chapel expecting wind music
and to the Harp and Ball and drank all alone___ 0– 0– 2
Back and to the fiddling concert and heard a
practice mighty good of *Grebus*[4] and thence to
W[estminste]r hall where all cry out that the
House will be severe with *Pen* but do hope
well concerning the *buyers*[5] that we shall have
no difficulty which God grant. Here met
Creed and about noon he and I and S[r] *P. Neale*
to the Quakers and there dined with a silly
executor of *Bp Juxon*[6] and *Cos. Roger P[epys]*.
Business of money goes on slowly in the House.
Thence to White hall by water _____ 0– 0– 6√
and there with D[uke of] Y[ork] a little but
stayed not but see him and his lady at his

a end of page 2   *b* repl. 'to'

---

1. Pepys probably arrived late at
the theatre.   He appears to have paid
half-price for a seat in the boxes. (A).
2. Usually 6*d*. each. (A).
3. The 'low pipe' bought on the
14th: above, p. 162.   (E).
4. Louis Grabu, 'Master of the Eng-
lith Chamber Musick' to the King.
(E).

5. Of prize goods.
6. Probably Sir William Juxon,
nephew of the late Archbishop (d.
1663). He was now promoting a
private bill to enable him to recover
part of the estate from a fraudulent
steward who had fled overseas: *CJ*,
ix. 95; Milward, pp. 184, 297.

little pretty chapel where I never was before
but silly devotions God knows.[1]   Thence I
left *Creed* and to the King's playhouse into a
corner of the 18^d box and there saw The
Maid's Tragedy[2] a good play.   Coach_____   1^s-0√
Play & *oranges*   0- 2- 6
Creed came dropping presently here but he did
not see me and came to the same place nor
would I be seen by him.   Thence to my Lord
Crews and there he came also after and there
with S^r *T Cr[ew]* bemoaning my Lord's folly
in leaving his old interest[3] by which he hath
now lost all.   An ill discourse in the morning
of my Lord's being killed but this evening
Godolphin tells us here that my Lord is well.
Thence with *Creed* to the Cock alehouse and
there spent   6^d
And so by coach home _____   0- 2- 6
And so to bed.

16
Th.   *Greetings* book[4]   0- 1- 0
       Begin this day to learn the *Recorder*.   To the
       office where all the morning.   Dined with my
       clerks and merry at S^r *W P[enn]'s* crying
       yesterday as they say to the king that he was
       his martyr.^{a}
       So to White hall by coach to Commissioners
       Treas[ur]y about certificates but they met not[5]_ 0- 2- 0√

a   end of page '5'

---

1. They were soon afterwards (c.
1669-70) received into the Roman
church. The location of the chapel
has not been determined.
2. A tragedy by Beaumont and
Fletcher; see above, ii. 100, n. 4.   A
seat in the middle gallery cost 18*d*.
(A).
3. That of the political Presby-

terians, to which both Sandwich and
Crew had belonged.
4. Probably a MS. primer. (E).
5. On the 13th the Treasury
Commissioners had directed the Navy
Board to attend on this day: *CTB*, ii.
299. For the certificates, see above,
p. 122 & n. 1.

To *W[estminste]r* by water to *W[estminste]r*-
hall where I hear *W P[enn]* is ordered to be
impeached[1]   0– 0– 6√
There spoke with many and particularly with
G M[ountagu] and went with him and *Creed*
to his house where he told me how *W P[enn]*
hath been severe to *L.ᵈ Sandw* but the *Coventrys*
both labouring to save him by laying it on
L Sand b which our friends cry out upon and I
am silent but do believe they did it as the only
way to save him. It could not be carried to
commit him. It is thought the House doth
Coole. *W C[oventry]*'s being for him provoked *S.ʳ R Howard* and his party. *Court* all
for *W P[enn]*.[2] Thence to White hall but no
meeting of the Commissioners and there met
Mr *Hunt* and thence to Mrs *Martin* and there
did what I would she troubled for want of
imploy for her husband. Spent on her_____   0– 1– 0
Thence to the Hall to walk a while and ribband
spent   0– 1– 0
So Lord *Crews* and there with *G C[arteret]*
and my lord to talk and they look upon our
matters much the better and by this and that
time is got   0– 1– 0
So to the Temple late and by water by moon-
shine home   0– 1– 0
                                                    *books*_____   0– 0– 6
Wrote my letters to my Lady *Sandwᶜʰ* and so
home where displeased to have my maid[3]
bring her brother a countryman to lie there
So to bed

              17
Fridy   Called up by *Balty's* coming who gives me a
           good account of his *voyage* and pleases me well
           and I hope hath got something. ~~So to~~ This
           morning paid *R.ˡˡ Society* _____   1– 6– 0[4]

1. *CJ*, ix. 81–2. The charge concerned his part in the prize-goods
scandal (q.v. above, vi. 231 & n. 1).
2. Cf. the reports of the debate in
Grey, i. 136–9; Milward, pp. 259–60.

3. Bridget, the cook-maid.
4. Fellows of the Society paid 1s.
weekly 'towards the defraying of
occasional charges': Birch, i. 237.

And so to the office all the morning.   At noon
home to dinner with my people.   And there h
much pretty discourse of Balty's.   So by
coach to White hall the coachman on Ludgate
hill light and beat a fellow with a sword.____   0- 2- 6√
Did little business with D[uke of] Y[ork].
Hear that the House is upon the business of
Harman who they say takes all on himself.[1]
Thence with Br[ouncker] to the King's House
and saw The Suprizall where base singing only
Knepp.[2]   Who came after her song on the
clouds[3] to me in the pit and there oranges____   0- 2- 0
After the play she and I and Rolt by coach   0- 6- 6
To Kensington and there to the Grotto and
had admirable pleasure with their singing and
fine ladies listening to us with infinite pleasure
I enjoyed myself.   So to the tavern there[4] and
did spend   0-16- 6
And the gardener   0- 2- 0
Mighty merry and sang all the way to the
town a most pleasant evening moonshine and
set them at her house in Covent Garden and I
home and to bed.[a]

Saturday. 18th—Up and my booksellers brought home⎫   0-17- 6
books bound.   The binding comes to____⎭
Advanced to my maid Bridget_____   1[b]- 0- 0
S[r] W P[enn] at the office seemingly merry.
Do hear this morning that Harman is committed by the Parliament last night the day he
came up.   Which is hard but he took all upon
himself first and then when witness came in to
say otherwise he would have retracted and the

a   end of page '6'   b   repl. 'o'

_____

1. See below, p. 167, n. 1.   3. See above, p. 94 & n. 2.   (E).
2. The play was a comedy by Sir   4. ?The Talbot, at the Gravel
Robert Howard: see above, viii. 157,   Pits: B. Lillywhite, London Signs, no.
n. 3. Mrs Knepp played Emilia.   14411.
(A).

House took it so ill they would commit him.[1]
Thence home to dinner with my clerks and   1
so to White hall by ~~coach~~ ⟨water⟩_____   0– 2– 0√
And there a short committee for *Tanger*. And
so [to the King's playhouse_____   1.^s –0√
And to the play the *D[uke]* of *Lerma*_____   0– 2– 6²
And oranges   0– 1– 0
Thence by coach to *Westm.* and the House⎫   0– 1– 0√
again up having been about money business⎭
So home ⟨by coach ____ 0– 3– 0√/⟩ calling
in Duck Lane and did get *D. Cartes* music
in English³ and so home and wrote my letters
and then to my chamber to save my *eyes* and
to bed.

Sundy. 19^*th* Lay long. *Rog.* *P[epys]* and his son⁴ came
and to church with me where *W P[enn]* was
and did endeavour to show himself to the
church. Then home to dinner and *R P* ~~tell~~
did tell me the whole story of *Harman* how he
prevaricated and hath undoubtedly been im-
posed on and wheedled, and he is call[ed] the
Miller's Man that in *R.^d* the 3^*d* time was hanged
for his maister.⁵ So after dinner I took them

1. *CJ*, ix. 82. This was in the course of the enquiry into the escape of the Dutch fleet after the battle of Lowestoft, June 1665. Harman had at first concealed from the Commons the fact that he knew that the order to slacken sail was given to him in the Duke of York's name. His evidence was contradictory: he was said to have sat up the night before with his ship's company 'and was scarce sober . . . he looked disorderly': Grey, i. 140 n. He was acquitted and dis- charged on the 21st: *CJ*, ix. 86. See also Milward, p. 262; Marvell, ii. 72. Sandwich kept copies of Harman's examination and his answers: Sand- wich MSS, App, ff. 188+.

2. I.e. for a seat in the pit. The

play was a tragedy by Sir Robert Howard; see above, p. 20, n. 1. (A).

3. Lord Brouncker's translation of Descartes' *Compendium: Renatus Des- Cartes excellent compendium of musick: with . . . animadversions there-upon. By a Person of Honour* (1653); not in the PL. Pepys bought the original on 3 April: above, p. 148 & n. 4. (E).

4. Talbot, now a student at the Middle Temple.

5. This incident occurred not in Richard III's time, but in the Cornish rebellion of 1549, when a miller's man was tricked by the miller into posing as his master (a known rebel) and was hanged: R. Holinshed, *Chronicles* (1807–8), iii. 925–6. Cf. F. Rose- Troup, *Western rebellion of 1549*, ch. xx.

by water to White hall taking in a very pretty
woman at Paul's Wharf.   And there landed
we and I left *RP* and to S! *Marg!* church and
there saw Betty and so to walk in the Abbey
with S! *Jo. Talbot* who would fain have
pumped me about the prizes but I would not
let him.   And so to walk towards Mitchells
to see her but could not.   And so to Martin's
and her husband was at home.   And so took
coach and to the park and thence home and
to bed betimes.

Water	0– 1– 0
Coach	0– 5– 0
Balty borrowed	2– 0– 0[a]

Monday. 20.   Up and busy about answer to Committee
of Accounts this morning about several
questions which vexed me though in none I
have reason to be troubled.   But the business
of the Flying Greyhound begins to find me
some care, though in that I am wholly void
of blame.   Thence[b]

a   end of page '3'   b   rest of page '4' left blank

20. Up betimes and to the getting ready my answer to the Committee of Accounts to several questions;[1] which makes me trouble, though I know of no blame due to me from any; let them enquire what they can out. I to White-hall and there hear how Brouncker is fled,[2] which I think will undo him; but what good it will do Harman I know not, he hath so much befouled himself. But it will be good sport to my Lord Chancellor, to hear how this great enemy is fain to take the same course that he is. There met Robinson,[3] who tells me that he fears his maister, W. Coventry, will this week have his business brought upon the stage again, about selling of places – which I shall be sorry for, though the less since I hear his standing for Pen the other day, to the prejudice though not to the wrong of my Lord Sandwich; and yet I do think what he did, he did out of a principle of honesty. Thence*a* to Committee of Accounts, and delivered my paper and had little discourse; and was unwilling to stay long with them to enter into much, but away and glad to be from them, though very civil to me – but cunning* and close I see they are. So to Westminster-hall and there find the Parliament upon the Irish business;[4] where going into the Speaker's chamber, I did hear how plainly one Lawyer of counsel for the complainants did inveigh by name against all the late Commissioners[5] there. Thence with Creed, thinking, but failed, of dining with Lord Crew; and so he and I to Hercules Pillars and there dined, and thence home*b* by coach and so with Jacke Fenn to the Chamberlain of London to look after the state of some Navy Assignments that are in his hands;[6] and thence away, and meeting

---

a repl. same symbol   *b* repl. 'home ward'

---

1. These mostly concerned Sandwich's prize goods and Pepys's privateer. Copy of Pepys's answer (in Gibson's hand) in NMM, LBK/8, pp. 533–4; printed in *Further Corr.*, pp. 192–4.

2. Cf. above, viii. 489–90 & n. Henry Brouncker now fled to France, where he settled for a time at Rouen: *CSPD 1667–8*, p. 383.

3. Thomas Robson, Coventry's clerk.

4. *CJ*, ix. 84. This was the hearing of a petition from the Irish Adventurers: see above, viii. 420, n. 2.

5. I.e. those appointed under the acts of settlement to adjudicate in the land disputes in Ireland.

6. Presumably Treasury orders had been assigned to the Chamberlain (Sir Thomas Player, sen.) on which he was trying to raise money on behalf of the navy.

Sir Wm. Hooker the Alderman, he did cry out mighty high against Sir W. Penn for his getting such an estate and giving 15000*l* with his daughter, which is more by half then ever he did give;[1] but this the world believes, and so let them.   Thence took coach and I all alone to Hide parke (passing through Duck-lane among the booksellers only to get a sight of the pretty little woman that I did salute the other night)[2] and*a* did in passing; and so all the evening in the park, being a little unwilling to be seen there; and*b* at night home, and there to W. Penn's and sat and talked there with his wife and children a good while, he being busy in his closet I believe, preparing his defence in Parliament. And so home to bed.

21.   Up, and at the office all the morning.   At noon dined at home, and thence took Mrs. Turner out and carried her to the King's House and saw *The Indian Emperour*;[3] and after that done, took Knipp out, and to Kensington and there walked in the garden and then supped and mighty merry, there being also in the House Sir Ph. Howard and some company; and had a dear reckoning, but merry; and away, it*c* being quite night, home, and dark, about 9 a-clock or more; and in my coming had the opportunity, the first time in my life, to be bold*d* with Knepp by*e* putting my hand abaxo de her coats and tocar su thighs and venter – and a little of the other thing, ella but a little opposing me; su skin very douce and I mightily pleased with this; and so left her*e* at home, and*f* so Mrs. Turner and I home to my letters and to bed.

Here hear how Sir W. Penn's Impeachment was read and agreed to in the House this day, and ordered to be ingrossed – and he suspended the House – Harman set at Liberty – and Brouncker put out of the House; and a writ for a new election – and an Impeachment ordered to be brought in against him – he being fled.[4]

----

a repl. full stop   *b* repl. 'but'   *c* repl. same symbol
d repl. 'b'-   *e-e* garbled s.h.   *f* repl. 'and we home'

----

1. See above, viii. 63.

2. See above, pp. 160-1 & n.

3. See above, viii. 14, n. 2.   (A).

4. *CJ*, ix. 85-6.

22. Up, and all the morning at my office busy. At noon, it being washing day, I toward White-hall and stopped and dined all alone at Hercules pillers, where I was mightily pleased to overhear a woman talk to her counsel how she had troubled her neighbours with law, and did it very roguishly and wittily. Thence to White-hall, and there we attended the Duke of York as usual and I did present Mrs. Pett, the widow, and her petition to the Duke of York for some relief from the King.[1] Here was today a proposition made to the Duke of York by Captain van Hemskirke for 20000*l* to discover an art how to make a ship go two foot for one what any ship doth now – which the King enclines to try, it costing him nothing to try; and it is referred to us to contract with the man.[2] Thence to attend the Council about the business of Certificates to the Exchequer, where the Commissioners of the Treasury of different minds; some would, and my Lord Ashly would not, have any more made out – and carried it that there should not.[3]

After done here, and the Council up, I by water from the Privy-stairs to Westminster-hall; and taking water, the King and Duke of York were in the new buildings;[4] and the Duke of York called to me whither I was going and I answered aloud, "To wait on our Maisters at Westminster!" at which he and all the company laughed; but I was sorry and troubled for it afterward, for fear any Parliament-man should have been there, and will be a caution to me for the time to come. Met with R. Pepys, who tells me they have been on the business of money;

1. Cf. above, p. 158 & n. 1.
2. Laurens van Heemskerck and his partner claimed that their ship (whose qualities supposedly derived from the way the grain of the timber ran) would outsail any of the King's ships: *CSPD 1667–8*, p. 359. A frigate (the *Nonsuch*) was built by Anthony Deane at Portsmouth to their design, and her success earned Heemskerck a knight-hood and a life-pension: ib., *1668–9*, pp. 204, 399–40. He later offered the design also to the French: C. de la Roncière, *Hist. de la marine française*, v. 376. Pepys (who was from the

beginning sceptical of its virtues: below, p. 206) later pronounced the design a 'ridiculous proposition': *Naval Minutes*, p. 203; cf. also *Tangier Papers*, p. 301. See also *Bulstrode Papers*, i. 49, 79, 83; W. Westergaard (ed.), *First Triple Alliance*, pp. li, 23+.

3. For the council order, see PRO, PC 2/60, f. 142r. Cf. *CTB*, ii. 305. For the dispute about certificates, see above, p. 122, n. 1.

4. For the new buildings, see below, p. 251 & n. 4.

but not ended yet, but will take up much more time. So to the fishmonger's and bought a couple of lobsters, and over to the Spargus garden, thinking to have met Mr. Pierce and his wife and Knepp; but met their servant to bring me to Chatlins, the French house in Covent-garden;[1] and there with music and good company, Manuel and his wife, and one Swaddle, a clerk of Lord Arlington's, who dances and speaks French well but got drunk and was then troublesome. And here mighty merry till 10 at night, and then I away and got a coach and so home, where I find Balty and his wife come to town and did sup with them, and so they to bed. This night, the Duke of Monmouth and a great many blades were at Chatlins, and I left them there, with[a] a hackney-coach attending him.

23. Up and to the office, where all the morning. And at noon comes Knepp and Mrs. Pierce and her daughter, and one Mrs. Foster, and dined with me – and mighty merry; and after dinner carried them to the Tower and showed them all to be seen there; and among other things, the Crown and Scepters and rich plate, which I myself never saw before and endeed is noble – and I mightily pleased with it.[2] Thence by water to the Temple, and there to the Cocke ale-house and drank and eat a lobster and sang, and mighty merry. So, almost night, I carried Mrs. Pierce home, and then Knipp and I to the Temple again and took boat, it being darkish, and to Fox-hall, it being now night and a bonfire burning[b] at Lambeth for the King's Coronacion-day. And there she and I drank; and yo did tocar her corps all over and besar sans fin her, but did not offer algo mas; and so back and led her home, it being now 10 at night, and so got a link; and walking towards home, just at my entrance into the ruines at St. Dunstan's, I was met by two rogues with clubs, who came toward us; so I went back and walked home quite round by the Wall and got well home; and to bed, weary but pleased at my

a repl. 's'-   b repl. 'lit'

---

1. See above, p. 115, n. 1.
2. The Crown jewels at this time are listed and described in Sir Edward

Walker, *Circumstantial account of the . . . coronation of . . . Charles II* (1820), pp. 30+.

day's pleasure – but yet displeased at my expense and time I lose.

24. Up betimes, and by water to White-hall to the Duke of York and there hear that this day Hollis and Temple purpose to bring in the petition against Sir W. Coventry;[1] which I am sorry for, but hope he will get out of it. Here I*a* presented Mrs. Pett and her condition to Mr. Wren for his favour,[2] which he*b* promised us. Thence to Lord Brouncker and sat and talked with him, who thinks the Parliament will by their violence and delay in money matters force the King to run any hazard and dissolve them. Thence to Ducke-lane and there did overlook a great many of Monsieur Fouquet's Library, that a bookseller hath bought, and I did buy one Spanish, *Los illustres Varones*.[3] Here did I endeavour to see my pretty woman that I did besar in las tenebras a little while despues.[4] And*c* did find her sola in*d* the boutique, but had not la confidence para hablar a ella. So lost my pains – but will have another time; and so home to my office and then to dinner. After dinner, down to the Old Swan and by the way called at Michell's and there did see Betty; but that was all, for either she is shy or foolish, and su marido hath no mind para laisser me see su moher. To White*e*-hall by water and there did our business with the Duke of York, which was very little; only, here I do hear the Duke of York tell how Sir W Pen's impeachment was brought into the House of Lords today; and spoke with great kindness of him, and that the Lords would not commit him till they could find precedent

---

a repl. same symbol badly formed   *b* repl. 'is'   *c* repl. 'but'
            d repl. 'at'   *e* repl. 'W'-

---

1. See above, p. 87 & n. 1.
2. See above, p. 158 & n. 1.
3. Juan Sedeño, *Summa de varones illustres* (Toledo, 1590; PL 2149). It bears Fouquet's arms on the back. After Fouquet's disgrace and imprisonment in 1661 – he had been

minister of finance – most of his superb library of 30,000 volumes was confiscated by the King (and is now in the Bibliothèque Nationale); other items were sold.

4. See above, pp. 160–1.

for it – and did incline to favour him.¹ Thence to the King's playhouse and there saw a piece of *Begger's bush*, which I have not seen some years.² And thence home, and there to Sir W Pen's and supped and sat talking there late, having no where else to go and my eyes too bad to read right; and so home to bed.

25. Up, and with Sir J. Mennes to my Lord Brouncker and with him, all of us, to my Lord Ashly to satisfy him about the reason of what we do or have done in the business of the trades-men's certificates,³ which he seems* satisfied with, but*a* is not; but I believe we have done what we can justify,*b* and he hath done what he cannot, in stopping us to grant them; and I believe it will come into Parliament and make trouble. So home and there at the office all the morning. At noon home to dinner; and thence after dinner to the Duke of York's playhouse and there saw *Sir M. Marr all*, which the more I see, the more I like.⁴ And thence to Westminster-hall and there met with Rogr. Pepys; and he tells me that nothing hath lately passed about my Lord Sandwich, but only Sir Rob. Carr did*c* speak hardly of him.⁵ But it is hoped that nothing will be done more this meeting of Parliament – which the King did, by a message yesterday, declare ⟨again⟩ should rise the 4 of May, and then only adjourne for three months;⁶ and this message, being only adjournment, did please

a repl. 'is'   *b* repl. 'jus[t]ify'   *c* repl. full stop

---

1. See *LJ*, xii. 232–4. The Duke had been present at the debate, which ended in an order commanding Penn to appear before the House and answer the charges against him at 10 a.m. on 27 April. For precedents in the matter of commitment, see ib., p. 235.

2. A comedy by Fletcher and Massinger (q.v. above, i. 297, n. 2) which, according to the diary, Pepys last saw on 8 October 1661. (A).

3. See above, p. 122, n. 1.

4. Pepys had already seen Dryden's comedy (q.v. above, viii. 387, n. 1) in whole or in part, six times. (A).

5. It was Carr (M.P. for Lincoln-shire) who had proposed the revival of the enquiry into the miscarriages of the war on 26 March: Milward, p. 234. His attack on Sandwich may have been made on 16 April in the debate on Penn and the prize-goods, when unnamed speakers asserted that 'Sandwich had the greatest store in the good[s] and was most at fault': ib., p. 259.

6. *LJ*, xii. 231.

them mightily – for they are desirous of their power mightily. Thence homeward by the Coffee-house in Covent-garden, thinking to have met Harris here but could not; and so home, and there, after my letters, I home to have my hair cut by my sister Michell[1] and her husband; and so to bed. This day I did first put off my Wastecoate,* the weather being very hot; but yet lay in it at night, and shall for a little time.

26. *Lords day.* Lay long, and then up and to church; and so home, where there came and dined with me Harris, Rolt, and Bannester, and one Bland, that sings well also; and very merry at dinner; and after dinner, to sing all the afternoon. But when all was done, I did begin to think that the pleasure of[a] these people was not worth so often charge and cost to me as it hath occasioned me. They being gone, I and Balty walked as far as Charing-cross, and there got a coach and to Hales's the painter, thinking to have found Harris sitting there for his picture which is drawing for me.[2] But he and all this day's company, and Hales, were got to the Crown tavern at next door; and thither I to them and stayed a minute (leaving Captain Grant[3] telling pretty stories of people that have killed themselfs or been accessory to it, in revenge to other people and to mischief other people); and thence with Hales to his house and there did see his beginning of Harris's picture, which I think will be pretty like, and he promises a[b] very good picture. Thence with Balty away, and got a coach and to Hide Parke, and there up and down and did drink some milk at the Lodge;[4] and so home and to bed.

27. Up, and Captain Deane came to see me and he and I toward Westminster together; and I set him down at Whitehall, while I to Westminster-hall and up to the Lords' House

a repl. 'was'   *b* MS. 'he'

---

1. Esther St Michel, wife of Balty.
2. See above, p. 138 & n. 2. (OM).
3. John Graunt, the pioneer demo-

grapher; author of *Natural and political observations . . . upon the Bills of Mortality* (1661).
4. See above, p. 142, n. 1.

and there saw Sir W Pen go into the House of Lords; where his Impeachment was read to him and he used mighty civilly, the Duke of York being there. And two days hence, at his desire, he is to bring in his answer and a day then to be appointed for his being heard with counsel.[1] Thence down into the Hall, and with Creed and Godolphin walk and do hear that tomorrow is appointed, upon a motion on Friday last, to discourse the business of my Lord Sandwich, moved by Sir R. Howard, that he should be sent for home; and I fear it will be ordered.[2] Certain news come, I*a* hear this day, that the Spanish plenipotentiary in Flanders will not agree to the peace and terms we and the Dutch have made for him and the King of France; and by this means the face of things may be altered and we forced to join with the French against Spain, which will be an odd thing.[3] At noon, with Creed to my Lord Crews and there dined; and here was a very fine-skinned lady dined, the daughter of my Lord Roberts,[4] and also a fine lady, Mr. John Parkhurst his wife,[5] that was but a boy the other day. And after dinner there comes in my Lady Roberts herself, and with*b* her Mr.*c* Roberts's wife,*d* that was Mrs. Boddeville the great beauty,

a repl. 'this night'   *b* repl. same symbol badly formed
   c repl. 'her daughter'   *d* MS. 'daughter'

---

1. *LJ*, xii. 235.

2. No such motion by Howard has been traced, and certainly no such order was made. But Sandwich, even more than Penn, was implicated in the prize-goods scandal which had led to Penn's impeachment, as several M.P.'s had pointed out in the debates of 16 and 24 April: Milward, pp. 278–80; Grey, i. 136–9, 145–6. Sandwich returned from Spain in the following September.

3. The War of Devolution between France and Spain, which had started with the French invasion of the Spanish Netherlands in the spring of 1667, was now ending. The English mediators on 6/16 March had threatened to use force if Spain did not accept terms, but on 22 April/2 May peace was signed. The Spanish plenipotentiary was Castel Rodrigo, Governor of the Netherlands.

4. Laetitia Isabella, daughter of Lord Robartes, Lord Privy Seal; she married the 2nd Earl of Drogheda in 1669 and William Wycherley, the dramatist, in c. 1680.

5. Parkhurst (a nephew of Lord Crew) was 24, and in the previous year had married Catherine, daughter of John Dormer of Quainton, Bucks.

and a fine lady endeed – the first time I saw her.[1] My Lord
Crew and Sir Tho. and I and Creed all the afternoon debating
of my Lord Sandwiches business against tomorrow. And thence
I to the King's[a] playhouse and there saw most of *The Cardinall*,[2]
a good play; and thence to several places to pay my debts;
and then home and there took a coach and to Mile end to take a
little ayre; and thence home[b] and to Sir W. Penn's, where I
supped and sat all the evening; and being lighted homeward by
Mrs. Markham, I blew out the candle and kissed her, and so
home to bed.

28. Up betimes and to Sir W. Coventry's by water, but lost
my labour; so through the park to White-hall, and thence to
my Lord Crews to advise again with him about my Lord Sandwich; and so to the office, where till noon; and then I by coach
to Westminster-hall, and there do understand that the business
of religion and the act against[c] Conventicles[3] have so taken them
up all this morning, and doth still, that my Lord Sandwiches business is not like to come on today; which I am heartily glad of.
This law against Conventicles is very severe; but Creed, whom I
met here, doth tell me that it being moved that Papists meetings
might be included, the House was divided upon it and it was
carried in the negative;[4] which will give great disgust to the
people I doubt.[d] Thence with Creed to Hercules[e]-Pillars by the
Temple again, and there dined, he and I all alone; and thence
to the King's House and there did see *Love in a maze*; wherein

a repl. 'D'-   b repl. 'to'   c repl. 'for'
d repl. same symbol badly formed   e repl. 'the'

---

1. Pepys had seen and admired her
portrait in 1665: see above, vi. 84 &
n. 2. The elder Lady Robartes, her
mother-in-law, was also a remarkable
beauty
2. A tragedy by Shirley: see above,
iii. 211, n. 2. (A).
3. For the comprehension scheme
('the business of religion'), see above,
p. 31, n. 4. The Conventicle Bill

was designed to replace the Conventicle Act of 1664 which was due to
expire at the end of this session. It
later failed to pass the Lords.
4. By 84 votes to 69: *CJ*, ix. 90.
Some members argued against the bill
on the ground that it would be milder
than the existing laws against the
Papists: Milward, p. 283.

very good mirth of Lacy the clown* and Wintersell the country-knight, his maister.¹ Thence to the New Exchange to pay a debt of my wife's there, and so home; and there to the office and walk in the garden in the dark to ease my eyes; and so home to supper and to bed.

29. Up and to my office, where all the morning busy. At noon dined at home, and my clerks with me; and thence I to White-hall and there do hear how Sir W. Penn hath delivered in his answer; and the Lords have sent it down to the Commons,² but they have not yet read it nor taken notice of it – so as I believe they will by design defer it till they rise, that so, he, by lying under an impeachment, may be prevented in his going to sea; which will vex him and trouble the Duke of York. Did little business with the Duke of York, and then Lord Brouncker and I to the Duke of York's playhouse and there saw *Love in a tubb*.³ And after the play done, I stepped up to Harris's dressing-room, where I never was, and there I observe much company come to him, and the Witts to talk after the play is done and to assign meetings. Mine was to talk about going down to ᵃ see the *Resolution*;⁴ and so away, and thence I to Wesminster-Hall and there met with Mr. G Mountagu and walked and talked, who tells me that the best ᵇ fence against the Parliament's present fury is delay, and recommended it to me in my friends' business and my own, if I have any; and is that that W. Coventry doth take and will secure himself. That the King will deliver up all to the Parliament; and being petitioned the other day by Mr. Brouncker to protect him, with tears in his eyes the King did say he could not, and bid him shift for himself, at least till the House is up. Thence I away to White-hall and there took coach

a MS. 'to the'   *b* repl. 'perf'-

---

1. The play was a comedy by Shirley: see above, iii. 88, n. 4. John Lacy, a popular comedian, played Johnny Thump, and William Wintersell Sir Gervaise Simple. (A).

2. *LJ*, xii. 237-8.
3. A comedy by Etherege: see above, vi. 4, n. 2. (A).
4. A new 3rd-rate, then at Woolwich: *CSPD 1667-8*, p. 377.

home with a stranger I let into the coach, to club with me for it, he going into London; and set him down at the lower end of Cheapside and I home and to Sir W. Penn's and there sat; and by and by, it being now about 9 a-clock*a* at night, I heard Mercer's voice and my boy Tom's singing in the garden; which pleased me mightily, I longing to see the girl, having not seen her since my wife went; and so into the garden to her and sang and then home to supper, and mightily pleased with her company in talking and singing; and so parted and to bed.

30. Up, and at the office all the morning. At noon Sir J. Mennes and I to the Dolphin tavern, there to meet our neighbours, all of the Parish, this being procession-day[1], to dine – and did; and much very good discourse, they being most of them very able merchants, as any in the City – Sir Andr. Rickard, Mr. Vandeputt, Sir Jo. Fredricke, Harrington, and others. They talked with Mr. Mills about the meaning of this day and the good uses of it; and how heretofore, and yet in several places, they do whip a boy at every place they stop at in their procession.[2]

Thence I to the Duke of York's playhouse and there saw *The Tempest*,[3] which still pleases me mightily. And thence to the New Exchange, and then home; and in the way stopped to talk with Mr. Brisband, who gives me an account of the rough usage Sir G. Carteret and his counsel had the other day before the Commissioners of Accounts, and what I do believe we shall all of us have, in a greater degree then any we have had yet with them, before their three years are out; which are not yet begun, nor God*b* knows when they will, this being like to be no session of

a repl. '9 where'
b repl. 'God's'

---

1. Ascension Day, when parish bounds were beaten (cf. above, ii. 106 & n. 1) and parish dinners were held (cf. above, viii. 218).

2. The object was to imprint on the boys' memories a knowledge of the parish boundaries.

3. Shakespeare's play as altered by Dryden and Davenant; see above, viii. 521, n. 4. (A).

Parliament when they[1] now rise.[2]   So home, and there took up
Mrs. Turner and carried her to Mile-end and drank; and so back,
talking, and so home and to bed, I being mighty cold, this
being a mighty cold day and I had left off my waistcoat three or
four days.   This evening, coming home in the dusk, I saw and
spoke to our Nell,[a] Pain's daughter, and had I[b] not been very
cold, I should have taken[c] her to Tower-hill para talk together et
tocar her.[c]

Thus ends this month; my wife in the country.   Myself full
of pleasure and expense; and some trouble for my friends, my
Lord Sandwich by the Parliament, and more for my eyes, which
are[d] daily worse and worse, that I dare not write or read almost
anything.   The Parliament going in a few days to rise.   Myself,
so long without accounting now, for seven or eight months I
think or more, that I know not what condition almost I am in
as to getting or spending for all that time – which troubles me,
but I will soon do it.   The kingdom in an ill state through
poverty.   A fleet going out, and no money[e] to maintain it or
set it out.   Seamen yet unpaid, and mutinous when pressed to
go out again.   Our office able to do little, nobody trusting us nor
we desiring any to trust us, and yet have not money to [?do] anything but only what perticularly belongs to this fleet going out,
and that but lamely too.   The Parliament several months upon
an act for 300000*l*, but cannot or will not agree upon it – but do
keep it back, in spite of the King's desires to hasten it, till they
can obtain what they have a mind, in revenge upon some men
for the late ill managements; and he is forced to submit to[f] what
they please, knowing that without it he shall have no money;
and they as well, that if they give[g] the money, the King will
suffer them to do little more.   And then the business of religion

1. Parliament.
2. The Commissioners' term ran
for three years from the end of the
present session. If Parliament were
now to be adjourned instead of prorogued, their term would be so much
the longer. In fact, the session did
end now, on 9 May, and the Commissioners reported in October 1669.
See above, viii. 559, n. 2.

doth disquiet everybody, the Parliament being vehement against the nonconformists, while the King seems to be willing to countenance them: so we are all poor and in pieces, God help us; while the peace is like to go on between Spain and France, and then the French may be apprehended able to attack us. So God help us.[a]

[a] Here end the entries in the fifth volume of the MS. Five ruled and four unruled pages follow.

1. Up, and to my office, where all the morning busy. Then to Westminster hall and there met Sir W. Penn, who labours to have his answer to his impeachment, and sent down from the Lords' House, read by the House of Commons;[1] but they are so busy on other matters that he cannot, and thereby will, as he believes, by design be prevented in going to sea this year. Here met my Cosen Tho. Pepys of Deptford and took some turns with him; who is mightily troubled for this Act now passed against Conventicles,[2] and in few words and sober doth lament the condition we are in, by a negligent prince and a mad Parliament. Thence I by coach to the Temple and there set him down; and then to Sir G. Carteret's to dine, but he not being at home, I back again to the New Exchange a little; and thence back again to Hercules Pillars and there dined all alone, and then to the King's[a] playhouse and there saw *The Surprizall*; and a disorder in the pit by its raining in from the Copulo at top,[3] it being a very foul day and cold, so[b] as there are few I believe go to the Park today, if any.[4] Thence to Westminster-hall, and there I understand how the Houses of Commons and Lords are like to disagree very much about the business of the East India Company and one Skinner, to the latter of which the Lords have awarded 5000*l* from the former for some wrong done him heretofore – and the former appealing to the Commons, the Lords vote their petition

---

a repl. 'Duke of York's'   *b* repl. same symbol badly formed

---

1. Some of Penn's papers in defence of his conduct in the prize-goods affair are in NMM, Wyn 15/4.
2. The bill was not in fact passed until 1670: see above, p. 177, n. 3. For Thomas Pepys's puritanism, see above, vii. 114.
3. Pepys has more than one re-ference to the inadequate protection against bad weather given by this glazed cupola. The play was a comedy by Sir Robert Howard; see above, viii. 157, n. 3. (A).
4. On May Day all London usually took a jaunt in Hyde Park.

a libell; and so there is like to fallow very hot work.[1] Thence
by water, not being able to get a coach, nor boat but a sculler,
and that with company, it being so foul a day, to the Old Swan;
and so home and there spent the evening making Balty read to
me; and so to supper and to bed.

2. Up, and at the office all the morning. At noon with
Lord Brouncker in his coach as far as the Temple, and there light
and to Hercules Pillars and there dined; and thence to the Duke
of York's playhouse at a little past 12, to get a good place in the
pit against the new play; and there setting a poor man to keep
my place, I out and spent an hour at Martin's my bookseller's;
and so back again, where I find the house quite full; but I had
my place, and by and by the King comes and the Duke of
York; and then the play begins, called *The Sullen lovers or The
Impertinents*,[2] having many good humours in it; but the play
tedious and no design[a] at all in it. But a little boy, for a farce,[3]
doth dance Polichinelli[4] the best that ever anything was done in
the world by all men's report – most pleased with that, beyond

a repl. 'great'

---

1. This developed into a legal dispute of the first importance and
marked the last occasion on which the
Lords exercised an original civil
jurisdiction. Thomas Skinner, accusing the E. India Company of
having seized a ship of his, had
brought the case in the Lords and had
been awarded damages. Long debates followed in the Commons, 2–8
May, at the end of which Skinner was
put in custody. The Lords thereupon
declared these proceedings illegal and
arrested four of the Company.
Adjournment and prorogation of
parliament prevented a settlement,
and in 1670 both houses agreed to
expunge all record of the affair from
their journals. Since then the Lords

have tacitly accepted their incapacity
in such cases. Grey, i. 150–7; Milward, pp. 287+; HMC, *Rep.*,
8/107+, 165+; M. A. Thomson,
Const. hist. Engl. 1642–1801, pp.
147–8.
2. A comedy by Thomas Shadwell,
now first acted, and published in
1668. The cast listed by Downes
(p. 29) includes Harris as Sir Positive
At-all, Nokes as Ninny, Smith as
Stanford, and Mrs Shadwell as
Emelia. Performances usually began
at 3.30 p.m. (A).
3. A short comic playlet presented
after the main play. (A).
4. The leading character in the
popular Italian puppet play; see
above, vii. 257, n. 2. (A).

anything in the world, and much beyond all the play. Thence to the King's House to see Knipp, but the play done; and so I took a hackney alone, and to the park and there spend the evening, and to the Lodge and drank new milk; and so home to the office, ended my letters and, to spare my eyes, home and played on my pipes; and so to bed.

3. *Lords day.* Up, and to church, where I saw Sir A. Rickard, though he be under the Black Rod by order of the Lords' House, upon the quarrel between the East India Company and Skinner, which is like to come to a very great heat between the two Houses. At noon comes Mr. Mills and his wife, and Mr. Turner and his wife, by invitation to dinner, and we were mighty merry; and a very pretty dinner, of my Bridget and Nell's^a dressing, very handsome. After dinner to church again where I did please myself con mes ojos shut in futar in conceit the hook-nosed young lady, a merchant's daughter, in the upper pew in the church under the pulpit. So home, and with Sir W. Penn took a Hackny and he and I to Old-street, to a brew-house there to see Sir Tho. Teddiman, who is very ill in bed of a fever, got I^b believe by the fright the Parliament have put him into of late. But he is a good man, a good seaman, and stout. Thence he and I to Islington, and there at the old house[1] eat and drank and merry. And there by chance giving two pretty fat boys each of them a cake, they proved to be Captain Holland's children, whom^c therefore I pity.[2] So round by Hackny home, having good discourse, he being very open to me in his talk: how the King ought to dissolve this Parliament when this Bill of money is passed, they being never likely to give him more. How he hath a great opportunity of making himself popular by stopping this act against conventicles. And how my Lord Lieu-tenant of Irland, if the Parliament continue, will undoubtedly

a repl. 'Kn'-   b repl. same symbol badly formed
        c repl. full stop

---

1. The King's Head.   2. Philip Holland (a naval captain) was an old friend; he had deserted to the Dutch.

fall, he having managed that place with so much self-seeking
and disorder and pleasure, and some great men are designing to
overthrow [him]; as, among the rest, my Lord Orery – and
that this will try the King mightily, he being a firm friend to my
Lord Lieutenant.[1] So home and to supper a little, and then to
bed – having stepped, after I came home, to Alderman Backewell
about business and there talked a while with him and his wife,
a fine woman of the country, and how they had bought an estate
at Buckeworth, within four mile of Brampton.[2]

4. Up betimes and by water to Charing*a*-cross, and so to
W. Coventry and there talked a little with him; and thence
over the park to White-hall and there did a little business at the
Treasury;[3] and so to the Duke of York and there present Balty
to the Duke of York and a letter from the Board to him about
him; and the Duke of York is mightily pleased with him and I
doubt not his continuance in imployment[4] – which I am glad of.
Thence with Sir H: Cholmly to Westminster-hall, talking, and he
crying mightily out of the power the House of Lords usurp in
this business of the East India Company. Thence away home
and there did business, and so to dinner, my sister Michell and I;
and thence I to the Duke of York's House and there saw *The
Impertinents* again, and with less pleasure then before, it being
but a very contemptible play, though there are many little witty

a repl. 'Wh'-

---

1. Ormond, the Lord-Lieutenant,
was ultimately dismissed in March
1669, not because of any misconduct
in office, but because his influence
threatened that of Buckingham and
the anti-Clarendonian faction at
court. He now came to England
on 6 May to defend himself against
a possible impeachment. Orrery,
Lord President of Munster, once his
friend, was now his principal enemy
in Ireland, and came to England in
June to mount his attack. T. Carte,
Ormonde (1736), ii. 363-7; A. Browning, *Danby*, i. 63-4.

2. Ald. Edward Backwell's elder
brother John in 1666 had acquired a
share in the ownership of the manor
of Buckworth, Hunts., which was
later transferred to Edward Backwell
himself: VCH, *Hunts.*, iii. 24. His
(second) wife was Mary, daughter of
Richard Leigh of Warwickshire.

3. See *CTB*, ii. 312.

4. Cf. above, p. 159, n. 1.

expressions in it – and the pit did generally say that of it.[1]
Thence going out, Mrs. Pierce called me from the gallery; and
there I took her and Mrs. Corbet by coach up and down, and
took up Captain Rolt in the street; and at last, it being too late
to go to the park, I carried them to the Beare in Drury-lane and
there did treat them with a dish of Mackrell, the first I have seen
this year, and another dish, and mighty merry; and so carried
her home, and thence home myself, well pleased with this
evening's pleasure; and so to bed.

5. Up, and all the morning at the office. At noon home to
dinner, and Creed with me; and after dinner, he and I to the
Duke of York's playhouse; and there coming late, he and I up
to the Balcony-box,[2] where we find my Lady Castlemayne and
several great ladies and there we sat with them. And I saw *The
Impertinents* once more, now three times, and the three only
days it hath been acted; and to see the folly how the house doth
this day cry up the play more then yesterday; and I for that
reason like it, I find, the better too. By Sir Positive At=all, I
understand, is meant Sir Rob. Howard.[3] My Lady pretty well
pleased with it; but here I sat close to her fine woman, Willson,
who endeed is very handsome, but they say with child by the
King. I asked, and she told me this was the first time her Lady
had seen it, I having a mind to say something to her. One
thing of familiarity I observed in my Lady Castlemayne; she
called to one of her women, another that sat by this, for a little
patch off of her face, and put it into her mouth and wetted it
and so clapped it upon her own by the side of her mouth, I
suppose she feeling a pimple rising there. Thence with Creed
to Westminster-hall and there met with Cosen Roger, who tells
me of the great conference this day between the Lords and

---

1. But Downes records (p. 29) that
this play (q.v. above, p. 183, n. 2) 'had
wonderful Success, being Acted 12
days together', and on 24 June Pepys
describes it as 'a pretty good play'.
(A).

2. Probably a box close to the stage
like the 'side Balcone' mentioned
above, at viii. 521. (A).

3. Sir Positive was described in the
Dramatis Personae as 'a foolish Knight,
that pretends to understand everything in the world, will suffer no man
to understand anything in his Company; so foolishly Positive, that he
will never be convinced of an Error,
though never so gross.' Cf. Evelyn,
iv. 416. (A).

Commons about the business of the East India Company – as being one of the weightiest conferences that hath been, and managed*a* as weightily;[1] I am heartily sorry I was not there, it being upon a mighty point of the privileges of the subjects of England in regard to the authority of the House of Lords and their being condemned by them as the supreme court; which they*b* say ought not to be but by appeal from other courts.[2] And he tells me that the Commons had much the better of them in reason and history there quoted, and believes the Lords will let it fall. Thence to walk in the Hall; and there hear that Mrs. Martin's child, my god-daughter,[3] is dead. And so by water to the Old Swan; and thence home and there a little at Sir W. Penn's; and so to bed.

6. Up, and to the office; and thence to White-hall, but came too late to see the Duke of York, with whom my business was; and so to Westminster-hall, where met with several people and talked with them; and among other things, understand that my Lord St. Johns is meant by Mr. Woodcocke in *The Impertinents.*[4] Here met with Mrs. Washington, my old acquaintance of the Hall, whose husband hath a place in the Excise at Windsor, and it seems lives well. I have not seen her these eight or nine years, and she begins to grow old I can perceive, visibly. So time doth alter, and doth doubtless the like in myself. This morning*c* the House is upon the City Bill, and they say hath passed it[5] –

a repl. 'did'   *b* MS. 'we'   *c* repl. 'the'

---

1. See Milward, esp. p. 295. For the case, see above, p. 183, n. 1.

2. The Commons' principal objections were that the subject in such cases was deprived of the right to a trial by jury and of his right of appeal.

3. Catherine, born November 1666.

4. St John (later, 1675, 6th Marquess of Winchester) was a friend of Sir Robert Howard, who was also caricatured in the play. Woodcocke was 'a fulsome friend'.

5. The second Rebuilding Bill (not enacted till 1670) this day passed its third reading and was sent to the Lords. It suppressed a number of churches whose sites were needed for the carrying out of improvements, and united the parishes concerned with neighbouring ones. T. F. Reddaway, *Rebuilding of London*, p. 139, n. 4.

though I am sorry that I did not think to put somebody in mind of moving for the churches to be allotted according to the convenience of the people, and not to gratify this Bishop or that College. Thence by water to New Exchange, where bought a pair of shoe-strings; and so to Mr. Pierce's, where invited, and there was Knipp, Mrs. Foster, and here dined, but a poor, sluttish dinner as usual – and so I could not be heartily merry at it. Here saw her girl's picture, but it is mighty far short of her boy's, and not like her neither – but it makes Hales's picture of her boy appear a good picture.[1]   Thence to White-hall; walked with Brisban, who dined there also, and thence I back to the King's playhouse and there saw *The Virgin Martyr* – and heard the music that I like so well;[2] and entended to have seen Knipp, but I let her alone; and having there done, went to Mrs. Pierce's back again where she was, and there I*ᵃ* found her asleep on a pallet in the dark, where yo did poner mi manos under her jupe and tocar su cosa and waked her; that is, Knipp. And so to talk, and by and by did eat some Curds and cream and thence away home; and it being night, I did walk in the dusk up and down, round through our garden, over Tower Hill, and so through*ᵇ* Crutched Friars, three or four times; and once did meet Mercer and another pretty lady, but being surprized, I could say little to them, though I had an opportunity of pleasing*ᶜ* myself with them; but left them, and then I did see our Nell, Payne's daughter, and her yo did desear venga after migo, and so ella did seque me*ᵈ* to Tower-hill to our back entry there that comes upon the degres entrant into nostra garden; and there, ponendo the key in the door, yo tocar sus mamelles con*ᵉ* mi*ᶠ* mano and su*ᵈ* cosa with mi cosa et yo did dar-la a shilling; and so parted, and yo home to put up things against tomorrow's carrier for my wife; and among others, a very fine salmon-pie sent me by Mr. Steventon,[3] W. Hewer's uncle; and so to bed.

                 a repl. 'we'   *b* repl. 'up'
     c repl. full stop   *d–d* garbled s.h.: cf. above, viii. 244, note *a*
                 e MS. 'all'   *f* repl. 'su'

1. For Hayls's portrait of James   2. See above, pp. 93–4, 100.   (E).
Pierce, see above, viii. 439 & n. 5. 3. A purser, of Portsmouth.
(OM).

7. Up, and to the office, where all the morning. At noon home to dinner, and thither I sent for Mercer to dine with me; and after dinner, she and I called Mrs. Turner and I carried them to the Duke of York's House and there saw *The Man's the Maister*, which proves, upon my seeing it again,[1] a very good play. Thence called Knepp from the King's House; where going in for her, the play being done, I did see Becke Marshall come dressed off of the stage, and looks mighty fine and pretty, and noble – and also Nell in her boy's clothes, mighty pretty;[2] but Lord, their confidence, and how many men do hover about*a* them as soon as they come off the stage, and how confident they [are] in their talk. Here I did kiss the pretty woman newly come, called Pegg,[3] that was Sir Ch. Sidly's mistress – a mighty pretty woman, and seems, but is not, modest.* Here took up Knepp into our coach and all of us with her to her lodging, and thither comes Bannester with a song of hers that he hath set in Sir Ch. Sidly's play for her,[4] which is I think but very meanly set; but this he did before us, teach her; and it being but a slight, silly, short ayre, she learnt it presently. But I did here get him to prick me down the notes of the Echo in *The Tempest*,[5] which pleases me mightily. And here was also Haynes, the incomparable dancer of the King's house,[6] and a seeming civil man and sings pretty well. And they gone, we abroad to Marrowbone and there walked in the garden,[7] the first time I ever there, and a pretty place it is; and here we eat and drank and stayed till 9 at night; and so home by moonshine, I all the way having mi mano abaxo la jupe de Knepp*b* con much placer and freedom; but endeavouring afterward to tocar her con mi cosa, ella did strive against that, but yet I do not think that she*b* did find much*c* fault

---

a repl. 'up'   *b–b* garbled s.h.   *c* repl. same symbol badly formed

---

1. See above, p. 133 & n. 3. (A).

2. They had probably been playing St Dorothea and Angelo, respectively, in *The Virgin Martyr* which Pepys had seen the day before. (A).

3. Probably Margaret Hughes, later Prince Rupert's mistress: J. H. Wilson in *N & Q*, October 1956. (A).

4. *The mulberry garden*, a comedy; first performed on the following day. The song begins 'Ah, Chloris now that I could sit'. The music does not appear to have survived. (A).

5. See above, viii. 522 & n. 1. (E).

6. Joseph Haynes, who had recently joined the King's Company: see above, p. 107, n. 5. (A).

7. Marylebone Gardens. (R).

with it, but I was a little*a* moved at my offering it and not having it. And so set Mrs. Knepp at her lodging, and so the rest and I home, talking with a great deal of pleasure, and so home to bed.

8. Up, and to the office, where busy all the morning. Towards noon, I to Westminster and there understand that the Lords' House did sit till 11 a-clock last night about the business in difference between them and the Commons, in the matter of the East India Company. Here took a turn or two, and up to my Lord Crews and there dined – where Mr. Case the minister; a dull fellow in his talk, and all in the presbyterian manner, a great deal of noise and a kind of religious tone, but very dull.¹ After dinner, my Lord and I together. He tells me he hears that there are great disputes like to be at Court between the factions of the two women, my Lady Castlemaine and Mrs. Stewart, who is now well again² and the King hath made several public visits to her – and like to come to Court. The other is to go to Barkeshire-house, which is taken for her, and they say a Privy-Seal is passed for 5000*l* for it.³ He believes all will come to ruin. Thence I to White-hall, where the Duke of York gone to the Lords' House, where there is to be a conference on the Lords' side to the Commons this afternoon, giving in their reasons⁴ – which I would have been at, but could not; for going by direction to the Princes chamber, there Brouncker, W. Penn, and Mr. Wren and I met and did our business with the Duke of York. But Lord,*b* to see how this play*c* of *Sir Positive Att all*, in abuse of Sir Rob. Howard,⁵ doth take, all the Duke's and everybody's talk being of that, and telling more stories of him

a repl. 'm'-　　　*b* repl. 'now'　　　*c* repl. 'business'

---

1. Thomas Case, a leading Presbyterian; ejected from St Giles-in-the-Fields, 1662.

2. From her attack of smallpox.

3. *Recte* £4,000; lent by Backwell, the goldsmith, who received a warrant for that amount on the customs for the following January: *CTB*, ii. 264, 310,

316, 375. The house had been occupied by Clarendon for a short time until the spring of 1667.

4. This was a conference concerning Skinner's case: see above, p. 183, n. 1. There is a newsletter report in BM, Add. 36916, f. 97.

5. Cf. above, p. 183, n. 3. (A).

of the like nature, that it is now the town and country talk; and they say is most exactly true. The Duke of York himself [said] that of his ⟨playing at⟩ trapball is true,[1] and told several other stories of him. This being done, Brouncker, W. Penn, and I to Brouncker's house and there sat and talked, I asking*ᵃ* many questions in mathematics to my Lord; which he doth me the pleasure to satisfy me in. And here we drank and so spent an hour, and so W. Penn and I home. And after being with W. Penn at his house an hour, I home and to bed.

9. Up, and to the office, where all the morning we sat. Here I first hear that the Queene hath*ᵇ* miscarried of a perfect child, being gone about ten weeks; which doth show that she can conceive, though it be unfortunate that she cannot bring forth.[2] Here we are also told that last night the Duchesse of Monmouth, dancing at her*ᶜ* lodgings, hath sprained her thigh.[3] Here we are told also that the House of Commons sat till 5 a-clock this morning upon the business of the difference between the Lords and them, resolving to do something therein before they rise to assert their privileges.[4] So I at noon by water to Westminster, and there find the King hath waited in the Prince's chamber these two hours, and the Houses are not ready for him – the Commons having sent this morning, after their long debate therein the last night, to the Lords, that they do think the only expedient left to preserve unity between the two Houses is that they do put a stop to any proceedings upon their late judgment against the East India Company, till their next meeting – to

a repl. 'answering'   *b* repl. 'is come'
c repl. 'his'

---

1. Howard was represented in Act III as so 'eminent' at trap-ball as to offer to play it for a £5000 wager. The Duke of York was his political enemy.

2. She miscarried on the 7th: Charles II to Henrietta, 7 May (C. H. Hartmann, *The King my brother*, pp. 216–17); cf. HMC, *Rutland*, i. 10.

For the story of a previous miscarriage, see above, vii. 48–9.

3. She had dislocated a hip, and was lamed for life.

4. Cf. Milward, pp. 302–3. The authorities cited there (p. 303, n. 1) give both 4 and 5 a.m. as the time of the House's rising.

which the Lords returned answer that they would return answer
to them by a messenger*a* of their own.   Which they not presently
doing, they were all inflamed, and thought it was only a trick
to keep them in suspense till the King came to adjourne them;
and so rather then lose the opportunity of doing themselfs right,
they presently with great fury came to this vote: That whoever
should assist in the execution of the judgment of the Lords
against that Company, should be held betrayers of the liberties
of the people of England and of the privileges of that House.[1]
This the Lords have notice of, and were mad*b* at it; and so continued debating, without any design to yield to the Commons,
till the King came in and sent for the Commons.   Where the
Speaker made a short but silly speech, about their giving him
31000*l*, and then the several Bills their titles were read and the
King's assent signified in the proper terms, according to the
nature of the Bills – of which about three or four were public
Bills, and seven or eight private ones[2] (the*c* ⟨additional⟩ Bills
for the building of the City and the Bill against Conventicles
being*d* none of them): the King did make a short silly speech,
which he read, giving them thanks for the money, which now
he said he did believe would be sufficient, because there was peace
between his neighbours; which was a kind of a slur methought
to the Commons.   And that he was sorry for what he heard of
difference between the two Houses, but that he hoped their
recesse would put them into a way of accommodation; and so
adjourned them to the 9th of August; and then recollected himself
and told*e* them the 11th – so imperfect a speaker he is.[3]   So the
Commons went to their House and forthwith adjourned; and
the Lords resumed their House, the King being gone, and sat an
hour or two after; but what they did I cannot tell – but everybody expected they would commit Sir Andr. Rickard, Sir Sam.

  a repl. 'messeng'- *b* repl. symbol rendered illegible
  c repl. 'of neither of which' *d* repl. closing bracket
       e repl. 'made'

 1. Cf. the newsletter account in
BM, Add. 36916, f. 97.
 2. For these proceedings, see *LJ*,
xii. 247.   There were in fact seven

public, and eleven private bills.   For
the words of royal assent, see above,
iv. 249–50 & nn.
 3. Cf. above, iv. 250 & n. 4.

Bernardiston, Mr Boone, and Mr Wynne,[1] who were all there and called in upon their knees to the bar of the House. And Sir Jo. Robinson[2] I left there, endeavouring to prevent their being committed to the Tower, lest he should thereby be forced to deny their order because of this vote of the Commons, whereof he is one – which is an odde case. Thence I to the Rose tavern in Covent-garden and there sent for a pullet and dined all alone, being to meet Sir W. Penn; who by and by came, and he and I into the King's House, and there *The Mayd's Tragedy*,[3] a good play; but Knepp not there – and my head and eyes out of order, the first from my drinking wine at dinner, and the other from my much work in the morning. Thence parted, and I toward the New Exchange and there bought a pair of black silk stockings at the hosier's that hath the very pretty woman to his wife, about ten doors on this side the Change; and she is endeed very pretty – but I think a notable talking woman by what I heard to others there. Thence to Westminster-hall, where I hear the Lords are up; but what they have done I know not. And so walked toward White-hall and thence by water to the Tower; and so home and there to my letters, and so to Sir W. Penn's and there did talk with Mrs. Lowther, who is very kind to me, more then usual, and I will make use of it. She begins to draw very well, and I think doth as well, if not better, then my wife, if it be true that she doth it herself what she shows me. And so to bed, my head akeing all night with the wine I drank today, and my eyes ill. So lay long, my head*a* pretty well in the morning.*b*

10. *Lords day.* Up, and to my office, there to do business till church time, when Mr. Sheply, lately come to town, came to see me; and we had some discourse of all matters, and perticularly of my Lord Sandwiches concernments;[4] and here he did

---

a repl. 'w'-   *b* repl. 'morn and then'

---

1. Members of the E. India Company.
2. Lieutenant of the Tower.
3. By Beaumont and Fletcher; see above, ii. 100, n. 4. (A).
4. Edward Shipley was Sand-wich's steward at Hinchingbrooke. Pepys this day sent £20 to his father (presumably by Shipley's hand) for his wife's entertainment at Brampton: Rawl. A 185, f. 23r.

by the by, as he would seem, tell me that my Lady had it in her thoughts, if she had occasion, to borrow 100*l* of me – which I did not declare any opposition to, though I doubt it will be so much lost; but however, I will not deny my Lady if she ask it, whatever comes of it, though it be lost; but shall be glad that it is no bigger sum.[1]   And yet it vexes me though, and the more because it brings into my head some apprehensions what trouble I may hereafter be brought to when my Lord comes home, if he should ask me to come into bonds with him, as [I] fear he will have occasions to take up money.   But I hope I shall have the wit to deny it.

He being gone, I to church and so home; and there comes W. Hewer and Balty, and by and by I sent for Mercer to come and dine with me – and pretty merry.   And after dinner I fell to teach her *Canite Jehovæ*,[2] which she did a great part presently. And so she away, and I to church, and from church home with my Lady Pen; and after being there an hour or so talking, I took her and Mrs. Lowther, and old Mrs. Whistler her mother-in-law, by water with great pleasure as far as Chelsy; and so back to Spring-garden at Fox hall and there walked and eat and drank; and so to water again and set down the old woman at home at Durham-yard; and it raining all the way, it troubles us; but however, my cloak kept us all dry; and so home, and at the Tower wharf there we did send for a pair of old shoes for Mrs. Lowther, and there I did pull the others off and put them on, and did endeavour para tocar su thigh[a] but ella had drawers on, but yo did besar la and tocar sus mamelles, ella being poco shy but doth speak con mighty kindness to me that she would desire me por su marido if it were to be done.   Here stayed a little at Sir W. Penn's, who was gone to bed, it being about 11 at night; and so I home to bed.

a   garbled s.h. (repl. 'knee')

---

1. Pepys lent it (at 6%) on 8 June. It was still unpaid on 15 June 1670: Rawl. A 174, f. 437r.

2. One of Richard Dering's *Cantica*

Sacra (1662; PL 1972–5).   The book had been given to Pepys on 22 November 1662: above, iii. 263. (E).

11. Up, and to my*a* office, where alone all the morning. About noon comes to me my cousin Sarah and my aunt Licett,[1] newly come out of Gloucestershire, good woman, and come to see me; I took them home and made them drink, but they would not stay dinner, I being alone. But here they tell me that they hear that this day Kate Joyce was to be married to*b* a man called Hollinshed, whom she endeed did once tell me of and desired me to enquire after him.[2] But whatever she said of his being rich, I do fear, by her doing this without my advice, it is not as it ought to be; but as she brews,*c* let her bake. They being gone, I to dinner with Balty and his wife, who is come to town today from Deptford to see us. And after dinner, I out and took a coach and called* Mercer, and she and I to the Duke of York's playhouse and there saw *The Tempest*; and between two acts, I went out to Mr. Harris and got him to repeat to me the words of the Echo,[3] while I writ them down, having tried in the play to have wrote them; but when I had done it, having done it without looking upon my paper, I find I could not read the blacklead – but now I have got the words clear; and in going in thither, had the pleasure to see the Actors in their several dresses, especially the seamen and*d* monster,[4] which were very droll. So into the play again. But*e* there happened one thing which vexed me; which is, that the orange-woman did come in the pit and challenge me for twelve oranges*f* which she delivered by my order at a late play at night, to give to some ladies in a box, which was wholly untrue, but yet she swore it to be true; but however, I did deny it and did not pay her, but for quiet did buy 4*s* worth of oranges of her – at 6*d* a piece. ⟨Here I saw first my Lord Ormond since his coming from Ireland, which is now about eight days.⟩

a repl. 'the'   *b* MS. 'that'   *c* repl. same symbol badly formed
d repl. 'which'   *e* repl. 'but it p'-
f repl. symbol rendered illegible

---

1. Sarah Giles and her mother Lettice Howlett (sister of Pepys's mother).
2. See above, p. 127. He was a tobacconist.
3. See above, viii. 522, n. 1. (E).
4. Probably Caliban. (A).

After the play done, I took Mercer by water to Spring-garden and there with great pleasure walked and eat and drank and sang, making people come about us to hear us, and two little children ⟨of one of⟩ our neighbours that happened to be there did come into our Arbour and we made them dance prettily.

So by water, with great pleasure down to the Bridge, and there landed and took water again on the other side; and so to the Tower, and I saw her home, and myself home to my chamber and by and by to bed.

12. Up, and to the office, where we met and sat all the morning. Here Lord Anglesey was with us, and in talk about late difference between the two Houses he doth tell us that he thinks the House of Lords may be in an error, at least it is possible they may, in this matter of Skinner; and he doubts they may, and did declare his judgment in the House of Lords against their proceedings therein, he having hinder[ed] a hundred originall causes being brought into their House, notwithstanding that he was put upon defending their proceedings;[1] but that he is confident that the House of Commons are in the wrong in the method they take to remedy any error of the Lords, for no vote of theirs can do it; but in all like cases the Commons have done it by petition to the King, sent up to the Lords and by them agreed to and so redressed, as they did in the Petition of Right.[2] He says that he did tell them indeed what is talked of, and which did vex the Commons, that the Lords were *Judices nati* and *Conciliarii nati*, but all other Judges among us are under salary, and the Commons themselfs served for wages;[3] and therefore the Lords, in reason, the freer Judges.

1. Anglesey, a lawyer with a particular interest in jurisdictional matters, had acted as one of the managers of the inconclusive conferences recently held between the Lords and Commons in the case of Skinner *v.* E. India Company: Milward, pp. 296, 302; BM, Add. 25116, esp. ff. 40, 102.

2. In 1628; but this was the only occasion on which the method had

been used. Anglesey was referring to the Commons' resolutions of 8 and 9 May declaring that anyone aiding or abetting the execution of the Lords' sentence in the present case should be deemed 'a betrayer of the Rights and Liberties of the Commons . . .': Milward, p. 303, n.

3. Sc. in medieval parliaments. For parliamentary wages, see above, p. 141, n. 1.

At noon to dinner at home; and after dinner, where Creed dined with me, he and I by water to the Temple, where we parted; and I both to the King's and Duke of York's playhouses, and there went through the Houses to see what faces I could spy there that I knew; and meeting none, I away by coach to my house and then to Mrs. Mercer's, where I met with her daughters and a pretty lady I never knew yet, one Mrs. Sus. Gayet, a very pretty black lady, that speaks French well and is a Catholic and merchant's daughter by us, and here was also Mrs. Anne Jones; and after sitting and talking a little, I took them out and carried them through Hackny to Kingsland, and there walked to Sir G Whitmores house,[1] where I have not been many a day; and so to the old house at Islington[2] and eat and drank and sang, and mighty merry; and so by moonshine with infinite pleasure home; and there sang again in Mercer's garden and so parted, I having there seen[a] a Mummy in a merchant's ware-house there, all the middles of the man or woman's body black and hard; I never saw any before, and therefore pleased me much, though an ill sight; and he did give me a little bit, and a bone of an arme I suppose; and so home and there to bed.

13. Up and by water to White-hall, and so to Sir H. Cholmlys, who not being up, I[b] made a short visit to Sir W. Coventry, and he and I through the park to White-hall; and thence I back into the park and there met Sir H. Cholmly, and he and I to Sir St. Fox's; where we met and considered the business of the Excize, how far it is charged in reference to the payment of the Guards and Tanger.[3] Thence he and I walked to Westminster-hall and there took a turn, it being holiday;[4] and so back again, and I to the Mercers and my tailor's about a stuff suit that I am going to make; and thence at noon to Hercules

a repl. 'this'   *b* MS. 'and'

---

1. Baumes House, Hoxton, which Pepys had known as a child: see above, v. 272 & n. 2.

2. The King's Head.

3. In May–June a new farm of the Excise was in negotiation. For these payments, see *CTB*, vol. ii, p. xix.

4. The law courts had risen for the vacation on 4 May, and Parliament had been adjourned on the 9th.

Pillars and there dined alone.*ª* And so to White-hall, some of us, attended the Duke of York as usual and so to attend the Council about the business of Hemskirke's project of building a ship that shall [sail] two foot for one of any other*ᵇ* ship – which the Council did agree to be put in practice, the King to give him, if it proves good, 5000*l* in hand and 15000*l* more in seven years – which, for my part, I think a piece of folly for them to meddle with, because the secret cannot be long kept.¹ So thence after Council, having drunk some of the King's wine and water with Mr. Chevins,² my Lord Brouncker, and some others; I by water to the Old Swan and there to Michells and did see her and*ᶜ* drink there; but he being there, yo no puede besar la. And so back again by water to Spring-garden all alone, and walked a little; and so back again home and there a little to my viall; and so to bed, Mrs. Turner having sat and supped with me.

This morning, I hear that last night Sir Tho. Teddiman, poor man, did die by a thrush* in his mouth – a good man, and stout and able, and much lamented; though people do make a little mirth and say, as I believe it did in good part,*ᵈ* that the business of the Parliament did break*ᵉ* his heart, or at least put him into this fever and disorder that caused his death.

14. Up and to the office, where we sat all the morning; and at noon home to dinner with my people; but did not stay to dine out with them, but rose and straight by water to the Temple, and so to Penny's my tailor; where by and by, by agreement comes Mercer and she to my great content brings Mrs. Gayet, and I carried them to the King's House; but coming too soon, we out again to the Rose tavern and there I did give them a tankard of cool drink, the weather being very hot; and then into the playhouse again and there saw *The Country Captain*,³ a very

---

a repl. 'alone' badly formed   *b* repl. 'any'
c repl. 'dr'-   *d* repl. symbol rendered illegible   *e* MS. 'bring'

---

1. For the project, see above, p. 171 & n. 2. The money was granted this day to van Heemskirk and his partner (John de Moelyn): PRO, PC 2/60, pp. 300–1.

2. Will Chiffinch, page of the King's Bedchamber.

3. A comedy by the Duke of Newcastle: see above, ii. 202, n. 2. (A).

dull play that did give us no content; and besides, little company there, which made it very unpleasing. Thence to the waterside at Strand bridge, and so up by water and to Fox hall, where we walked a great while, and pleased mightily with the pleasure thereof and the company there; and then in and eat and drank, and then out again and walked; and it beginning to be dark, we to a Corner and sang, that everybody got about us to hear us; and so home, where I saw them both at their doors; and full of the content of this afternoon's pleasure, I home and to walk in the garden a little, and so home to bed.

15. Up, and betimes to White-hall and there met with Sir H. Cholmly at Sir St. Fox's; and there was also the Cofferer, and we did there consider about our money and the condition of the Excize; and after much dispute, agreed upon a state thereof and the manner of our future course of payments. Thence to the Duke of York and there did a little Navy business as we used to do; and so to a Committee for Tanger, where God knows how, my Lord Bellasses accounts passed,[1] understood by nobody but my Lord Ashly, who I believe was mad to let them go as he pleased. But here Sir H. Cholmly had his propositions read, about a greater price for his work of the Mole, or to do it upon account;[2] which being read, he was bid to withdraw; but Lord, to see how unlucky a man may be by chance; for taking an unfortunate minute when they were almost tired with other business, the Duke of York did find fault with it, and that made all the rest, that I believe he had better have given a great deal and had it had nothing said to it today; whereas, I have seen other things more extravagant pass at first hearing without any difficulty. Thence I to my Lord Brouncker's at Mrs. Williams's and there dined, and she did show me her closet; which I was sorry to see, for fear of her expecting something from

---

1. He had been Governor, 1665–7.
2. The cost of building the mole at Tangier had been badly under-estimated in the original contract of 1663. Cholmley (one of the contractors and also the engineer in charge of the work) later persuaded the Committee

to cancel the contract and to manage the work themselves, with himself as Surveyor-General – 'to do it', as he here proposed, 'upon account'. The new arrangements came into force in August 1669. See below, p. 364; Routh, pp. 344+, esp. p. 348.

me;[1] and here she took notice of my wife's not once coming to see her; which I am glad of, for she shall not – a prating, vain, idle woman. Thence with Lord Brouncker to Loriners-hall by Mooregate (a hall [I] never heard of before)[2] to Sir Tho. Teddiman's burial – where most people belonging to the sea were; and here we had rings,[3] and here I do hear that some of the last words that he said was: that he had a very good King, God bless him, but that the Parliament had very ill rewarded him for all the service he had endeavoured to do them and his country – so that for certain, this did go far towards his death.[4]   But Lord, to see among the young commanders and Tho. Killigrew and others that came, how unlike a burial this was, Obrian taking out some ballets[5] out of his pocket, which I read and the rest came about me to hear; and there very merry we were all, they being new ballets.

By and by the Corps went, and I with my Lord Brouncker and Dr Clerke and Mr. Pierce as far as the foot of London-bridge; and there we struck off into Thames-street, the rest going to Redriffe, where he is to be buried.   And we light at the Temple and there parted; and I to the King's House and there saw the last act of *The Committee*,[6] thinking to have seen Knepp there, but she did not act.   And so to my bookseller's and there carried home some books; among others, Dr. Wilkins's *Reall Character*.[7]   And thence to Mrs. Turner's, and there went and sat and she showed me her house from top to bottom, which I had not seen before – very handsome.[8]   And here supped; and

1. As a house-warming present: cf. above, vii. 237.

2. Until the Fire, the Lorimers (bit-makers) had had no hall of their own, but had used that of the Glaziers: Bell, *Fire*, p. 337. They were not incorporated until 1711.

3. For funeral rings, see above, ii. 74, n. 2.

4. Teddeman had been criticised for his conduct in the Bergen fiasco and accused of cowardice in the Four Days Battle.   See above, vi. 213; vii. 148 & n. 5.   He had held no command in 1667.

5. Street ballads.

6. A comedy by Sir Robert Howard; see above, iv. 181 & n. 1. (A).

7. John Wilkins, *An essay towards a real character, and a philosophical language* (1668); printed by order of the Royal Society; PL 2356. See above, vii. 12 & n. 6.

8. The house recently hired for the Turners by the Board: above, viii. 63 & n. 1.

so home and got Mercer, and she and I in the garden singing till
10 at night; and so home to a little supper, and then parted with
great content and I to bed.   The Duchess of Monmouth's hip is
I hear now set again, after much pain.   I am told also that the
Countesse of Shrewsbery*a* is brought home by the Duke of
Buckingham to his house; where his Duchess saying that it
was not for her and the other to live together in a house, he
answered, "Why, Madam, I did think so; and therefore have
ordered your coach to be ready to carry you to your father's;"
which was a devilish speech, but they say true; and my Lady
Shrewsbry is there it seems.

16.   Up; and to the office, where we sat all the morning.
And at noon home with my people to dinner; and thence to
the office all the afternoon, till, my eyes weary, I did go forth
by coach to the King's playhouse and there saw the best part of
The Sea Voyage, where Knepp I saw do her part of sorrow very
well.[1]   I afterward to her house, but she did not come presently
home; and here yo did besar her ancilla, which is so mighty
belle.   And I to my tailor's, and to buy me a belt for my new
suit against tomorrow.   And so home and there to my office,
and afterward late walking in the garden; and so home to supper
and to bed, after Nell's cutting of my hair close, the weather
being very hot.

17.   *Lords day.*   Up, and put on my new stuff-suit with*b*
a shoulder-belt, according*c* to the new fashion, and the hands
of my vest and tunic[2] laced*d* with silk lace of the colour of my
suit.   And so, very handsome, to church, where a dull sermon

---

a repl. 'Salsbury'   b MS. 'which'
c repl. 'to'   d repl. 'last with'

---

1. She played Aminta in this
comedy by Fletcher and Massinger;
q.v. above, viii. 450. n. 4.   (A).

2. Fashionable suits were now
made up of vest and tunic; cf. above,
vii. 324 & n. 3; Cunnington, p. 136.

The shoulder-belt carried a sword, and
went out of fashion c. 1700: ib.,
p. 168.   The bands were here presumably fastening-cords or 'points',
not neckbands.

of a stranger.   And so home and there I find W. How and aᵃ
younger brother of his come to dine with me;   and there comes
Mercer and brings with her Mrs. Gayet, which pleased me
mightily, and here was also W Hewers;   and mighty merry and
after dinner to sing psalms;   but Lord, to hear what an excellent
Base this younger brother of W How's sings, even to my
astonishment and mighty pleasant.   By and by Gayet goes away,
being a Catholique, to her devotions, and Mercer to church, but
we continued an hour or two singing, and so parted;   and I to
Sir W. Penn's, and there sent for a hackney-coach and he and
she and I out to take the ayre.   We went to Stepny and there
stopped at the Trinity-house, he to talk with the servants there
against tomorrow, which is a great day for the choice of a new
Maister.¹   And thence to Mile end and there eat and drank;   and
so home, and I supped with them;   that is, eat some butter and
radishes, which is my excuse for not eating of any other of their
victuals, which I hate because of their sluttery.   And so home
and made my boy read to me part of Dr.ᵇ Wilkins's new book of
the ⟨Real⟩ *Character*, and so to bed.

18.   Up and to my office, where most of the morning doing
business and seeing my window-frames new painted;   and then
I out by coach to my Lord Bellasses at his new house by my late
Lord Treasurer's;²   and there met him and Mr. Sherwin, Auditor
Beale, and Creed about my Lord's accounts;³   and here my Lord
showed me his new house, which endeed is mighty noble;
and good pictures, endeed not one bad one in it.⁴   Thence to my

---

a repl. 'his'   *b* repl. 'Mr.'

---

1. I.e. Trinity Monday. Col.
Thomas Middleton (Surveyor of the
Navy) was chosen.
2. Probably in Bloomsbury Sq.,
whose n. side was then occupied by
Southampton House, town house of
the late Lord Treasurer Southampton.
(R).
3. As Governor of Tangier, 1665–7.
4. Nothing appears to be known
about Lord Belasyse's collection. He

was apparently buying pictures in the
Interregnum: three pictures to the
value of £40 in all were sold to him
from the Earl of Pembroke's collection on 25 August 1652 (Hatfield
House, Private and Estate MSS,
Accts., 168/2). As a young man he
had been painted by Van Dyck;
portraits of the Belasyse family are
preserved at Newburgh Priory,
Yorks. (OM).

tailor's, and there did find Mercer come with Mrs. Horsfield and
Gayet according to my desire; and there I took them up, it
being almost 12 a-clock or little more, and carried them to the
King's playhouse, where the doors were not then open; but
presently they did open, and we in and find many people already
come in by private ways into the pit, it being the first day of
Sir Charles Sidly's new play, so long expected, *The Mulbery
guarden*;[1] of whom, being so reputed a wit, all the world doth
expect great matters. I having sat here a while and eat nothing
today, did slip out, getting a boy to keep my place; and to the
Rose tavern and there got half a breast of mutton off of the spit
and dined all alone; and so to the play again, where the King
and Queen by and by came, and all the Court, and the house
infinitely full. But the play when it came, though there was
here and there a pretty saying, and that not very many neither,
yet the whole of the play had nothing extraordinary in it at all,
neither of language nor design; insomuch that the King I did not
see laugh nor pleased the whole play from the beginning to the
end, nor the company; insomuch that I have not been less
pleased at a new play in my life I think.[2] And which made it
the worse was that there never was worse music played; that is,
worse*a* things composed; which made me and Captain Rolt, who
happened to sit near me, mad.*b* So away thence, very little
satisfied with the play, but pleased with my company: I carried*c*
them to Kensington to the Grotto,[3] and there we sang to my great
content; only, vexed in going in to see a son of Sir Heneage
Finche's beating of a poor little dog to death, letting it lie in so
much pain that made me*d* mad to see it; till by and by, the
servants of the house chiding of their young maister, one of
them came with a thong and killed the dog outright presently.

a repl. same symbol badly formed   *b* repl. 'm'-   *c* repl. 'to'
                       d repl. 'us'

1. A comedy published in 1668;
see above, p. 189, n. 4. Playhouses
usually opened at noon, though performances did not begin until 3.30
p.m. (A).

2. Despite Pepys's low opinion, the
play proved very popular. (A).

3. See above, p. 166, n. 4.

Thence to Westminster Palace and there took boat and to Fox-hall, where we walked and eat and drank and sang, and very merry; but I find Mrs. Horsfield one of the veriest citizen's wifes in the world, so full of little silly talk, and now and then a little sillily bawdy, that I believe if you had her*a* sola, a man might hazer algo with her. So back by water to Westminster Palace and there got a coach who carried us as far as the Minorys, and there something of the traces*b* broke, and we forced to light and walked to Mrs. Horsfields house, it being a long and bad way, and dark; and having there put her in a-doors, her husband being in bed, we left her; and so back to our coach, where the coachman had put it in order, but could not find his whip in the dark a great while, which made us stay long; at last, getting a neighbour to hold a candle out of their window, Mercer found it, and so away; we home at almost 12 at night; and setting them both at their homes, I home and to bed.

19. Up, and called on by*c* Mr. Pierce, who tells me that after*d* all this ado Ward is come to town, and hath appeared to the Commissioners of Accounts and given such answers as he thinks will do everybody right and let the world see that their great expectations and jealousies have been vain in this matter of the prizes.[1] The Commissioners were mighty inquisitive whether he was not instructed by letters or otherwise from hence from my Lord Sandwiches friends what to say and do, and perticularly from me – which he did wholly deny, as it was true, I not know-ing the man that I know of. He tells me also that for certain Mr. Vaughan is made Lord Chief Justice; which I am glad of.[2] He tells me too, that since my Lord of Ormond's coming over, the King begins to be mightily reclaimed, and sups every night

---

a   garbled s.h.   b   repl. 'k'-
  c   MS. 'my'   d   repl. 'at length'

---

1. For the dispute over the prize-goods, see above, vi. 231, n. 1. James Ward had been a lieutenant in Sandwich's flagship in 1665 and one of the three people to whom Sandwich gave his warrant to open up the cargo.

2. John Vaughan, M.P., was knighted and made Lord Chief Justice of Common Pleas on 19 and 20 May. He had praised Pepys's oratory (above, p. 153) and supported Sand-wich (above, p. 87 & n. 3).

with great pleasure with the Queene; and yet it seems he is
mighty hot upon the Duchess of Richmond; insomuch that
upon Sunday was sennit, at night, after he had ordered his guards
and coach to be ready to carry him to the park, he did on a
sudden take a pair of oars or sculler, and all alone, or but one
with him, go to Somerset-house and there, the garden-door not
being open, himself clamber over the walls to make a visit to her
where*a* she is; which is a horrid shame.

He gone, I to the office, where we sat all the morning. Sir
W Pen, sick of the gout, comes not out. After dinner at home,
to White-hall, it being a very rainy day. And there a Committee for Tanger, where I was mightily pleased to see Sir
W. Coventry fall upon my Lord Bellasses's business of the 3*d*
in every piece of eight,*b* which he would get to himself, making
the King pay 4*s*-9*d* while he puts them off for 4*s*-6*d*[1] – so that
Sir W. Coventry continues still the same man for the King's*c*
good. But here Creed did vex me with saying that I ought
first to have my account passed by the Commissioners of Tanger
before in the Exchequer. Thence, W. Coventry and I in the
Matted Gallery to talk; and there he did talk very well to me
about the way to save the credit of the Officers of the Navy,
and their places too, by making use of this intervall of Parliament
to be found to be mending of matters in the Navy, and that
nothing but this will do it; and gives an instance in themselfs
of the Treasury, whereof himself and Sir Jo. Duncombe all the
world knows have enemies, and my Lord Ashly a man obnoxious
to most, and Sir Tho. Clifford one that, as a man suddenly rising
and a creature of my Lord Arlington's, hath enemies enough
(none of them being otherwise but the Duke of Albemarle);
yet with all this fault, they hear nothing of the business of the
Treasury, but all well spoken of there. He is for the removal
of Sir J. Mennes, thinking that thereby the world will see a
greater change in the hands then now they do. And I will

---

a MS. 'which   *b* MS. 'it'   *c* repl. same symbol

---

1. Cf. the Treasury minute of 4
May 1668: 'Mr. Pepys says you may
have Pieces of Eight delivered at

Tangier for 4*s*. 6*d*. paying at a month's
usance' (*CTB*, ii. 312).

endeavour it, and endeavour to do some good in the office also. So home by coach and to the office, where ended my letters and then home; and there got Balty to read to me out of Sorbiere's observations in his voyage into*ᵃ* England;¹ and then to bed.

20. Up, and with Collonell Middleton in a new coach he hath made him, very handsome, to White-hall; where the Duke of York having*ᵇ* removed his lodgings for this year to St. James's,² we walked thither and there find the Duke of York coming to White-hall; and so back to the Council-chamber, where the*ᶜ* Committee of the Navy³ sat, and here we discoursed several things; but Lord, like fools, so as it was a shame to see things of this importance managed by a Council that understand nothing of them. And among other things, one was about this building of a ship with Hemskirkes secret, to sail a third faster then any other ship;⁴ but he hath got Prince Rupart on his side, and by that means I believe will get his conditions made better then he would otherwise, or ought endeed. Having done there, I met with Sir Rd. Browne⁵ and he took me to dinner with him to a new tavern above Charing-cross, where some Clients of his did give him a good dinner, and good company; among others, one Bovy,⁶ a solicitor* and lawyer and merchant all together, who hath travelled very much, did talk some things well, but only he is a Sir Positive;⁷ but the talk of their travels over the Alps very fine. Thence walked to the King's playhouse and there saw *The Mulbery-Garden* again;⁸ and cannot be reconciled to it, but only do find here and there an independent sentence of wit, and that is all. Here met with Creed and took him to Hales's, and there saw the beginnings of Harris's head which he draws for me and which I do not yet like.⁹ So he and I down to the New Ex-

a repl. 'to'   *b* MS. 'being'   *c* repl. 'a'

1. See above, v. 297 & n. 2.
2. It was his regular habit to go to St James's for the summer.
3. See above, p. 67, n. 3.
4. See above, p. 171, n. 2.
5. One of the four Clerks of the Privy Council.

6. James Boeve, a London merchant of Dutch extraction.
7. Cf. above, p. 186, n. 3. (A).
8. Sedley's comedy: see above, p. 203 & n. 1. (A).
9. Cf. above, p. 138, n. 2. (OM).

change and there cheapened ribbands for my wife, and so down to the Whey-house and drank some and eat some curds, which did by and by make my belly ake mightily. So he and I to White-hall and walked over the park to the Mulbery-garden,[1] where I never was before; and find it a very silly place, worse then Spring-garden, and but little company and those a rascally, whoring, roguing sort of people; only, a wilderness here is that is somewhat pretty, but rude. Did not stay to drink, but walked an hour, and so away to Charing-cross and there took coach and away home – in my way going into Bishopsgate-street to bespeak places for myself and boy to go to Cambridge in the coach this week, and so to Brampton to see my wife. So home and to supper and to bed.

21. Up, and busy to send some things into the country; and then to the office, where meets me Sir Rd. Ford; who among other things, congratulates me, as one or two did yesterday, my great purchase; and he advises me rather to forbear, if it be not done, as a thing that the world will envy me in. And what is it but my Cosen Tom Pepys's buying of Martin Abbey in Surry[2] – which is a mistake I am sorry for, and yet do fear that it may spread in the world to my prejudice. All the morning at the office, and at noon my clerks dined with me; and there do hear from them how all the town is full of the talk of a Meteor, or some fire that did on Saturday last to fly over the City at night;[3] which doth put me in mind that being then walking in the dark an hour or more myself in the garden after I had done writing,

---

1. A place of entertainment on part of the present site of Buckingham Palace and its grounds. (R).

2. Merton Priory, Surrey, was conveyed on 4–5 June 1668 to Thomas Pepys of Hatcham: O. Manning and W. Bray, *Hist. Surrey* (1804–14), ii. 255; VCH, *Surrey*, iv. 66.

3. Dr D. J. Schove writes: 'This meteor was observed by Wood (*L. & T.*, ii. 133) in Buckingham-shire: "May 16, Sat, between 9 and 10 of the clock at night being then at Borstall, com. Bucks, I saw a Draco volans [flying dragon] fall from the sky. It made the sky soe light that one might see to read. It seemed to me to be as long as All Saints Steeple, Oxon. It was long and narrow and when it came to the lower region it vanished in sparkles. Mr. Sanders of Hadnam whom I met at Notley on Monday following told me that with them it vanished with a report. Great rains and inundations followed."'

I did see a light before^a me come from behind me, which made me turn back my head and I did see a sudden fire or light running in the sky, as it were toward Cheapside-ward, and vanished very quick; which did make me bethink myself what holiday it was; and took it for some Rocket, though it was much brighter then any rocket, and so thought no more of it; but it seems Mr. Hater and Gibson, going home that night, did meet with many clusters of people talking of it, and many people of the towns about the City did see it, and the world doth make much discourse of it – their apprehensions being mighty full of the rest of the City to be burned, and the papists to cut our throats – which God prevent. Thence after dinner, I by coach to the Temple and there bought a new book of songs, set to music by one Smith of Oxford, some songs of Mr. Cowly's;[1] and so to Westminster, and there to walk a little in the Hall; and so to Mrs. Martin's, and there did hazer ce que yo voudrais mit her^b – and drank and sat most of the afternoon with her and her sister; and here she promises me her fine Starling, which was the King's and speaks finely, which I shall be glad of. And so walked^c to the Temple, meeting in the street with my cousin   Alcocke,[2] the young man that is a good sober youth I have not seen these four or five years, newly come to town to look for imployment. But I cannot serve him, though I think he deserves well. And so I took coach and home to my business; and in the evening took Mrs. Turner and Mercer out to Mile end and drank, and then home and sang and eat a dish of greene peese, the first I have seen this year, given me by Mr. Gibson – extraordinary young and pretty. And so saw them at home, and so home to bed. Sir W. Penn continues ill of the gout.

22. Up and all the morning at the^d office busy. At noon

a repl. 'against the'   b garbled s.h.
c repl. same symbol   d repl. same symbol

1. Music untraced; this is probably William King's *Poems of Mr. Cowley and others composed into songs and ayres* (Oxford, 1668): PL 1971. (E).

2. Probably Harry Alcock, of Cambridge.

home with my people to dinner, where good discourse and merry. After dinner comes Mr. Martin the purser and brings me his wife's Starling, which was formerly the King's bird, that doth speak and whistle finely; which I am mighty proud of, and shall take pleasure in it. Thence to the Duke of York's House to a play, and saw *Sir Martin Marr all*, where the house is full; and though I have seen it I think, ten times,[1] yet the pleasure I have is yet as great as ever, and is undoubtedly the best comedy ever was wrote. Thence to my tailor's and a mercer's for patterns to carry my wife, of cloth and silk for a bed, which I think will please her and me; and so home, and fitted myself for my journey tomorrow; which I fear will not be pleasant, because of the wet weather, it raining very hard all this day; but the less it troubles me because[a] the King and Duke of York and Court are at this day at Newmarket at a great horse-race; and proposed great pleasure for two or three days, but are in the same wet.[2] So from the office home to supper, and betimes to bed.

23. Up by 4 a-clock; and getting my things ready and recommending the care of my house to W. Hewer, I with the boy Tom, whom I take with me, to the Bull in Bishopsgate-street and there about 6 took coach, he and I and a gentleman and his[b] man – there being another coach also, with as many more I think in it. And so away to Bishops Stafford, and there dine and changed horses and coach at Mrs. Aynsworth's; but I took no knowledge of her.[3] Here this gentleman and I to dinner, and in comes Captain Foster, an acquaintance of his, he that doth belong to my Lord Anglesy, who had been at the late horse-races at Newmarket, where the King now is; and says that they had fair

a repl. 'for' *b* MS. 'in his'

---

1. According to the diary Pepys had seen Dryden's comedy (in whole or in part) seven times. (A).

2. They went on the 21st and returned on the 23rd: *London Gazette*, 25 May; below, p. 214.

3. She kept the Reindeer inn at Bishop's Stortford (Herts.) and had a doubtful reputation: see above, viii. 466 & n. 1.

weather there yesterday, though we here, and at London, had
nothing but rain, insomuch that the ways are mighty full of
water, so as hardly to be passed.   Here I hear Mrs. Aynsworth
is going to live at London; but I believe will be mistaken in it,
for it will be found better for her to be chief where she is then
to have little to do at London, there being many finer then she
there.   After dinner, away again and came to Cambridge, after
much bad way, about 9 at night; and there at the Rose[1] I met
my ⟨father's⟩ horses, with a man staying for me; but it is so
late, and the waters so deep, that I durst not go tonight; but after
supper to bed and lay very ill by reason of some drunken scholars
making a noise all night, and vexed for fear that the horses should
not be taken up from grass time enough for the morning.   ⟨Well
pleased all this journey with the conversation of him that went
with me, who I think is a lawyer; and lives about Lyn, but his
name I did not ask.⟩[a]

24.   *Lords day.*   I up at between 2 and 3 in the morning; and
calling up my boy and father's boy, we set out by 3 a-clock, it
being high day; and so through the waters with very good
success, though very deep almost all the way, and got to Brampton about   ,[b] where most of them in bed; and so I weary
up to my wife's chamber, whom I find in bed and pretended a
little not well, and endeed she hath those upon her, but fell to talk
and mightily pleased both of us; and up got the rest, Betty
Turner and Willet and Jane, all whom I was glad to see, and
very merry; and got me ready in my new stuff clothes that I
sent down before me; and so my wife and they got ready too,
while I to my father, poor man, and walked with him up and
down the house, it raining a little – and the waters all over Port-
holme and the meadows – so as no pleasure abroad.   Here I saw
my brothers[2] and sister Jackson, she growing fat, and since being
married, I think looks comelier then before.   But a mighty pert
woman she is, and I think proud, he keeping her mighty hand-

---

a addition crowded in at end of paragraph   *b* no blank in MS.

---

1. One of the principal inns: see   2. His brother John and his brother-
above, i. 68, n. 3.   in-law John Jackson, husband of Pall.

some, and they say mighty fond – and are going shortly to live at Ellington of themselfs, and will keep malting and grazing of cattle. At noon comes Mr. Phillips and dines with us, and a pretty odd-humoured man he seems to be – but good withal, but of mighty great methods in his eating and drinking, and will not kiss a woman since his wife's death.[1] After dinner, my Lady Sandwich sending to see whether I was come, I presently took horse and find her and her family at chapel; and thither I went in to them and sat out the sermon, where I heard Jervas Fullwood,[2] now their chaplain, preach a very good and seraphic kind of sermon, too good for an ordinary congregation. After sermon, I with my Lady and my Lady Hinchingbrooke and Paulina and Lord Hinchingbrooke to the dining-room, saluting none of them, and there sat and talked an hour or two, with great pleasure and satisfaction, to my Lady about my Lord's matters; but I think not[a] with that satisfaction to her or me that otherwise would, she knowing that she did design to borrow, and I remaining all the while in fear of being asked to lend her some money, as I was afterward (when I had taken leave of her) by Mr. Sheply, 100*l*;[3] which I will not deny my Lady, and am willing to be found when my Lord comes home to have done something of that kind for them. And so he riding to Brampton and supping there with me, he did desire it of me from my Lady; and I promised it, though much against my will, for I fear it is as good as lost. After supper, where very merry, we to bed, myself very weary, and to sleep all night.

25. Waked betimes, and lay long hazendo doz vezes con mi moher con grando pleasure to me and ella; and there fell to talking, and by and by rose, it being the first fair day, and yet not quite fair, that we have had some time; and so up and to walk with

a repl. 'with'

---

1. Lewis Phillips was a lawyer of Huntingdon. His wife had died in December 1665.

2. Fellow of St Catharine's, Cam-

bridge; Rector of Coton, Cambs., since 1662.

3. Cf. above, pp. 193–4.

my father again in the garden, consulting what to do with him
and this house when Pall and her husband goes away; and I
think it will be to let it and he go live with her,[1] though I am
against letting the house for any long time – because of having it
to retire to ourselfs.　So I do entend to think more of it before I
resolve.　By and by comes Mr. Cooke to see me, and so spent
the morning; and he gone by and by, at noon to dinner, where
Mr. Sheply came and we merry, all being in good humour
between my wife and her people about her; and after dinner
took horse, I promising to fetch her away about fourteen days
hence.　And so calling all of us, we men on horseback and the
women and my father, at Goody Gorum's and there in a frolic
drinking, I took leave, there going with me and my boy, my
two brothers, and one Browne, whom they call in mirth
"Collonell", for our guide, and also Mr. Sheply to the end of
Huntington, and another gentleman who accidentally came
thither, one Mr. Castle; and I made them drink at the Chequer,
where I observed the same Tapster, Tom, that was there when I
was a little boy; and so at the end of the town, took leave of
Sheply and the other gentleman, and so we away and got well to
Cambridge about 7 to the Rose, the waters not being now so high
as before.　And here lighting, I took my boy and two brothers
and walked to Magdalen College; and there into the Butterys as a
stranger and there drank my bellyfull of their beer, which pleased
me as the best I ever drank; and hear by the*a* butler's man, who
was son to Goody Mulliner over against the College that we used
to buy stewed prunes of, concerning the College and persons in it;
and find very few, only Mr. Hollins and Peachell I think, that
were*b* of my time.[2]　But I was mightily pleased to come in
this condition to see and ask; and thence, giving the fellow
something, away; walked to Chesterton to see our old walk;
and there into the church, the bells ringing, and saw the place I
used to sit in; and so to the ferry, and ferried over to the other

a repl. 'a'　　　*b* repl. 'was'

1. It appears that he did in fact go
to live with them: Whitear, pp. 41–2.
2. John Hollins (a physician) had

been an undergraduate in Pepys's
time; John Peachell (Master 1679–87,
1688–90) a fellow.

side and walked with great pleasure, the river being mighty high by Barnwell Abbey;[1] and so by Jesus College to the town, and so to our quarters and to supper; and then to bed, being very weary and sleepy, and mightily pleased with this night's walk.

26. Up by 4 a-clock; and by the time we were ready and had eat, we were called to the coach; where about 6 a-clock we set out, there being a man and two women of one company, ordinary people,[a] and one lady alone that is tolerable handsome, but mighty well spoken, whom I took great pleasure in talking to, and did get her to read aloud in a book she was reading in the coach, being the King's Meditations;[2] and then the boy and I to sing, and so about[b] noon came to Bishop's Stafford, to another house then what we were at the other day, and better used; and here I paid for the reckoning 11s, we dining all together and pretty merry. And then set out again, sleeping most part of the way, and got to Bishopsgate-street before 8 a-clock, the waters being now most of them down, and we avoiding the bad way in the Forrest[3] by a privy way which brought us to Hodsden,[4] and so to Tibalds[5] that road – which was mighty pleasant. So home, where we find all well, and Brother Balty and his wife looking to the house, she mighty fine in a new gold-laced juste-au-corps. I shifted myself, and so to see Mrs. Turner; and Mercer appearing over the way, called her in and sat and talked; and then home to my house by and by and there supped and talked mighty merry; and then broke up and to bed – being a

a repl. 's'   *b* repl. 'so'

---

1. A ruined Augustinian priory about one mile out of Cambridge on the Newmarket road. Only a chapel, now St Andrew the Less, and a fragment of wall have survived.
2. 'His Majesties prayers in the time of his restraint', printed at the end of Charles I's *Eikon Basilike*, first published in 1649, and reissued several times since. Charles II does not seem to have approved of their inclusion: F. F. Madan, *New bibliog. Eikon Basilike*, p. 80. PL 721 (octavo, 1648/9 ed.).
3. Waltham (now Epping) Forest.
4. Hoddesdon, Herts.
5. Theobalds palace (nr Cheshunt, Herts.), a royal residence then in the possession of Albemarle.

little vexed at what W Hewers tells me Sir Jo. Shaw did this day in my absence say at the Board, complaining of my doing of him injury and the board permitting it; whereas they had more reason to except against his attributing that to me alone which I could not do but with their consent and direction, it being to very good service to the King, and what I shall be proud [to] have imputed to me alone.[1]   The King,[a] I hear, came to town last night.[2]

27.   Up, and to the office, where some time upon Sir D. Gawden's accounts; and then I by water to Westminster for some Tanger orders;[3] and so meeting with Mr. Sawyer my old chamber-fellow,[4] he and I by water together to the Temple, he giving[b] me an account of the base rude usage which he and Sir G. Carteret had lately before the Commissioners of Accounts, where he was as counsel to Sir G. Carteret – which I was sorry to hear, they behaving themselfs like most insolent and ill-mannered men.[5]   Thence by coach to the Exchange and there met with Sir H. Cholmly at Colvills and there did give him some[c] orders; and so home, and there to the office again – where busy till 2 a-clock; and then with Sir D. Gawden to his house, with my Lord Brouncker and Sir J. Mennes, to dinner; where we dined very well, and much good company, among

a repl. 'hear'   b repl. 'tells'   c repl. 'small'

---

1. Of the consignment of 35 tons of hemp recently sent by Shaw to the Woolwich ropeyard, 15 or 16 had been rejected by the clerk: *CSPD 1667–8*, p. 387.

2. See above, p. 209 & n. 2.

3. Treasury orders for payment on the Tangier account.

4. Robert Sawyer, barrister; a fellow-student with Pepys at Magdalene.

5. The Commissioners investigating the expenditure of the moneys voted by parliament for the war criticised Carteret's slowness in producing his wartime accounts. Carteret, in reply, claimed that the delay was due to the fact that the Commissioners were demanding weekly accounts. It was August before he finished them. See HMC, *Rep. 8/1/128–33*; *CSPD 1667–8*, p. 462. In the end the Commissioners, in their report (25 October 1669) concluded that over £500,000 of the parliamentary grants for the war had been misapplied: PL 2874, pp. 392+, 431+.

others, a Dr.   , a fat*a* man, whom by face I know as
one that uses to sit in our church, that after dinner did take me
out and walked together, who told*b* me that he had now newly
entered himself into orders,[1] in the decay of the Church, and
did think it his*c* duty so to do, thereby to do his part toward
the support and reformation thereof; and spoke very soberly and
said that just about the same age, Dr. Donne did enter into
Orders.[2]   I find him a sober gentleman, and a man that hath seen
much of the world, and I think may do good.   Thence after
dinner to the office and there did a little business; and so to see Sir
W. Penn, who I find still very ill of the goute, sitting in his great
chair, made on purpose for persons sick of that disease, for their
ease; and this very chair he tells me was made for my Lady
Lambert.[3]   Thence by coach to my tailor's, there to direct about
the making of me another suit; and so to White-hall and through
St. James's park to St. James's, thinking to have met with Mr.
Wren, but could not; and so homeward toward the New Exchange; and meeting Mr. Creed, he and I to drink some whey
at the whey-house, and so into the Change and took a walk or
two; and so home, and there vexed at my boy's being out of
doors till 10 at night; but it was upon my brother Jackson's
business and so I was the less displeased; and then made the boy
to read to me out of Dr. Wilkins his *Real Character*, and perti-
ularly*d* about Noah's arke,[4] wherein he doth give a very good
account thereof, showing how few the number of the several
species of beasts and fowls were that were to be in the arke, and
that there was room enough for them and their food and dung;
which doth please me mightily – and is much beyond whatever
I heard of that subject.   And so to bed.

a MS. 'fam'   *b* rcpl. 'did'   *c* repl. 'is'   *d* repl. 'park'-

---

1. This was presumably Edward
Waterhouse, LL.D., F.R.S., a writer
on heraldry (cf. below, p. 432 & n. 4).
2. John Donne, the poet, was 42
when he took orders.
3. ?Viscountess Lambert (d. 1649),
an Irish acquaintance of Penn's, whom
Pepys may have mistaken for the wife

of the republican Maj. Gen. John
Lambert. Gout-chairs often had
wheels: cf. Evelyn, iii. 502 (Clarendon's chair).
4. Pt II, ch. v, of John Wilkins's
book (q.v. above, p. 200, n. 7) is
entitled: 'A digression concerning
the capacity of *Noah's* Ark'.

28.   Up, to set right some little matters of my Tanger accounts, and so to the office, where busy all the morning; and then home with my people to dinner, and after dinner comes   *a* about a petition for a poor woman whose ticket she would get paid.   And so talked a little and did besar her;*b* and so to the office – being pleased that this morning my*c* bookseller brings me home Marcennus's book*d* of music, which costs me 3*l.* 2*s.* 0*d* but is a very fine book.[1]   So to the office and did some business; and then by coach to the New Exchange and there by agreement at my bookseller's shop met Mercer and Gayette, and took them by water, first to one of the Neat-houses,[2] where walked in the garden; but nothing but a bottle of wine to be had, though pleased with seeing*e* the garden;*f* and so to Fox-hall, where with great pleasure we walked; and then to the upper end of the further retired walk and there sat and sang, and brought great many gallants and fine people about us; and upon the bench we did by and by eat and drank what we had, and very merry; and so with much pleasure to the Old Swan, and walked with them home and there left them; and so I home to my business at the office a little, and so to bed.

29.   Betimes up, and up to my Tanger accounts; and then by water to the Council-chamber and there received some directions from the Duke of York and the Committee of the Navy there, about casting up the charge of the present*g* summer's fleet, that so they may come within the bounds of the sum given by the Parliament.[3]   But it is pretty to see how Prince Rupert and other mad silly people are for setting out*h* but a little fleet, there being no occasion for it; and say it will be best to save the money for better uses; but Sir W. Coventry did declare that in wisdom it was better to do so, but that in obedience to the Parliament he

---

a no blank in MS. (omission occurs at end of page)   *b* garbled s.h.
      c repl. 'by'   *d* repl. 'mus'-   *e* repl. 'being'
      f repl. 'see'   *g* repl. same symbol   *h* repl. 'but'

---

1. See above, p. 148 & n. 3.   The book (PL 2494) has the price written by Pepys on the flyleaf.   (E).

2. In Chelsea.

3. See above, pp. 25, 92–3 & nn.

was setting out the 50 sail talked on, though it spend all the money and to little purpose; and that this was better then to leave it to the Parliament to make bad constructions of their thrift, if any trouble should happen. Thus wary the world is grown.[1]

Thence back again presently home, and did business till noon; and then to Sir G Carteret's to dinner, with*a* much good company, it being the King's birth*b*-day and many healths drunk; and here I did receive another*c* letter from*d* my Lord Sandwich; which troubles me, to see how I have neglected him, in not writing, or but once,[2] all this time of his being abroad. And I see he takes notice, but yet gently, of it, that it puts me to great trouble and I know not how to get out of it, having no good excuse, and too late now to mend, he being coming home. Thence home, whither by agreement by and by comes Mercer and Gayett, and two gentlemen with them, Mr. Montouth and Pelham, the former a swaggering young handsome gentleman – the latter a sober citizen merchant; both sing, but the latter with great skill; the other, no skill but a good voice*e* and a good basse – but used to sing only tavern tunes; and so I spent all this evening till 11 at night singing with them, till I tired of them because of the swaggering fellow with the basse, though the girl Mercer did mightily commend him before to me. This night yo had agreed para andar at Deptford, there para haber lain con the moher de Bagwell,*f* but this company did hinder me.

30. Up, and put on a new summer black bombazin suit, and so to the office; and being come now to an agreement with my barber to keep my perriwigs in good order at 20*s* a year, I am like to go very spruce, more then I used to do. All the morning at the office; and at noon home*g* to dinner, and so to the King's playhouse and there saw *Philaster*;[3] where it is pretty to see how

---

> a   MS. 'which'   b   l.h. repl. s.h. badly formed
>   c   repl. same symbol badly formed   d   repl. 'again from'
>   e   l.h. repl. l.h. 'voce'   f   garbled s.h.   g   repl. 'to my'

---

1. Sc. since the Chatham disaster of the previous summer.
2. See above, viii. 466.
3. A tragicomedy by Beaumont and Fletcher: see above, ii. 216 & n. 1. According to Genest (i. 82–3), Hart played Philaster and Nell Gwyn, Bellario. (A).

I could remember almost all along, ever since I was a boy,
Arethusa's part which I was to have acted at Sir Rob. Cooke's;[1]
and it was very pleasant to me, but more to think what a
ridiculous thing it would have been for me to have acted a
beautiful woman.   Thence to Mrs. Pierces, and there saw Knepp
also, and were merry;   and here[a] saw my little Lady Kath.
Mountagu, come to town about her eyes, which are sore, and
they think the King's Evil, poor pretty lady.[2]   Here I was freed
from a fear that Knepp was angry or might take advantage;
did parlar the esto that yo did the otra day quand yo was con her[b]
in ponendo her mano upon mi[b] cosa – but I saw no such thing;
but as pleased as ever, and I believe she can bear with any such
thing.

Thence to the New Exchange, and there met Harris and Rolt
and one Richards, a tailor and great company-keeper;   and with
these over to Fox-hall and there fell into the company of Harry
Killigrew, a rogue, newly come back out of France but still in
disgrace at our Court,[3] and young Newport[4] and others, as very
rogues as any in the town, who were ready to take hold of every
woman that came by them.   And so to supper in an[c] arbor;
but Lord, their mad bawdy talk did make my heart ake.   And
here I first understood by their talk the meaning of the company
that lately were called "Ballers", Harris[d] telling how it was by
a meeting of some young blades, where he was among them,

---

        a repl. 'to'   *b–b* garbled s.h.
        c preceded by blot   *d* repl. 'where'

---

1. Of Durdans, nr Epsom, Surrey;
d. 1653. Both he and his wife were
learned and cultivated; he had added
a hall to the house in 1639, in which
plays may have been produced.
(Pepys's part on this occasion was that
of one of the two heroines of the play.)
Pepys's relative John Pepys, who lived
nearby at Ashtead, in a house Pepys
often visited as a child, had been
secretary to Robert Coke's father,
Chief Justice Sir Edward Coke.

2. 'I have sent little Kat to London,
wrote Lady Sandwich, 'to Mr Pers
the Serg. that belongs to the Duke,
ther being they say the famostes Docr.
in Iingland for sore eies': Sandwich
MSS, App., f. 130r (qu. Harris, ii.
182).

3. For the occasion of his disgrace,
see above, vii. 336–7 & n.

4. Probably Richard, son of the 1st
Baron Newport; later (1708) 2nd
Earl of Bradford.

and my Lady Bennet[1] and her ladies, and there dancing naked, and all the roguish things in the world. But Lord, what loose cursed company was this that I was in tonight; though full of wit and worth a man's being in for once, to know the nature of it and their manner of talk and lives. Thence set Rolt and some of [them] at the New Exchange, and so I home; and my business being done at the office, I to bed.

31. *Lords day.* Up, and to church in the morning. At noon I sent for Mr. Mills and his wife and daughter to dine, and they dined with me and W. Hewer; and very good company, I being in good humour. They gone to church, comes Mr. Tempest, and he and I sang a psalm or two and so parted; and I by water to the New Exchange and there to Mrs. Pierces, where Knepp and she and W How and Mr. Pierce and little Betty over to Fox-hall and there walked and supped with great pleasure; here was Mrs. Manuell also and mighty good company, and good mirth in making How spend his 6 or 7*s*, and so they called him all together "Cully". So back, and at Summerset-stairs do*a* understand that a boy is newly drowned, washing*b* himself there, and they*c* cannot find his body.

So seeing them home, I home by water, W How going with me; and after some talk, he lay at my house, and all to bed. Here I hear that Mrs. Davis is quite gone from the Duke of York's House, and Gosnell comes in her room; which I am glad of. At the play at Court the other night, Mrs. Davis was there, and when she was to come to dance her Jigg, the Queene would not stay to see it; which people do think it was out of displeasure at her being the King's whore, that she could not bear it. My Lady Castlemaine is, it seems, now mightily out of request, the King coming little to her, and she mighty melancholy and discontented.*d*

     a MS. 'day'   *b* preceded by blot   *c* repl. 'these'
         d followed by one blank page

---

    1. A well-known procuress.

JUNE

1. Up, and with Sir J. Mennes to Westminster; and in the hall there I met with Harris and Rolt and carried them to the Rhenish wine-house, where I have not been in a morning, nor any tavern I think, these seven years and more. Here I did*a* get the words*b* of a song of Harris that I wanted.[1] Here was also Mr. Young and Whistler by chance met us and drank with us. Thence home and to prepare business against the afternoon; and did walk an hour in the garden with Sir W. Warren, who doth tell me of the great difficulty he is under in the business of his accounts with the Commissioners of Parliament, and I fear some inconveniences and troubles may be occasioned thereby to me. So to dinner, and then with Sir J. Mennes to White-hall; and there attended the Lords of the Treasury and also a committee of Council with the Duke of York about the charge of this*c* year's fleet;[2] and thence I to Westminster, and to Mrs. Martins and did hazer what yo would con her,*d* and did aussi tocar la thigh de su landlady. And thence all alone to Fox-hall and walked, and saw young Newport and two more rogues of the town seize on two ladies, who walked with them an hour with their masks on, perhaps civil ladies; and there I left them, and so home and thence*e* to Mr. Mills's,[3] where I never was before, and here find (whom I endeed saw go in, and that did make me go thither) Mrs. Halworthy and Mrs. Andrews; and here supped and extraordinary merry till one in the morning, Mr. Andrews coming to us: and mightily pleased with this

a repl. same symbol badly formed
b repl. 'order'   *c* repl. 'these'
d garbled s.h.: see above, viii. 244, note *a*   *e* repl. 'there'

1. Untraced. (E).

2. About £15,000–£20,000 was required e.g. for stores: *CTB*, ii. 338. See below, pp. 221–2 & n.

3. Daniel Milles, Rector of St Olave's.

night's company and mirth, I home to bed. Mrs. Turner too was with us.

2. Up, and to the office, where all the morning. At noon home to dinner, and there dined with me, besides my own people, W Batelier and Mercer, and we very merry. And after dinner, they gone, only Mercer and I to sing a while, and then parted; and I out and took a coach and called* Mercer at their back-door, and she brought with her Mrs. Knightly, [a] little pretty sober girl;[1] and I carried them to Old Ford,*a* a town by Bow where I never was before,[2] and there walked in the fields very pleasant, and sang; and so back again, and stopped and drank at the Gun at Mile-end; and so to the Old*b* Exchange door and did give them a pound of cherries, cost me 2*s*; and so set them down again, and I to my little*c* mercer's, Finch, that lives now in the Minories,[3] where I had left my cloak; and did here besar su moher,*d* a belle femme, and there*e* took my cloak which I had left there; and so by water, it being now about 9 a-clock, down to Deptford, where I have not been many a day; and there, it being dark, I did by agreement andar a la house*f* de Bagwell;*g* and there, after a little playing and besando, we did go up in the dark a su cama and there fasero la grand cosa upon the bed; and that being hecho, did go away and to my boat*f* again, and against the tide home; got there by 12 a-clock and to bed, taking into my boat for company,*h* a man that desired a passage, a certain western bargeman, with whom I had good sport, talking of the old woman of Woolwich and telling him the whole story.[4]

3. Up, and to the office, where busy till 9 a-clock; and then to White-hall to the Council-chamber, where I did present the

---

a l.h. repl. s.h.   *b* repl. 'New'   *c* repl. 'lady'
d garbled s.h.   *e* repl. 'so'   *f–f* garbled s.h.
      g name in s.h.   *h* MS. 'and a'

---

1. Possibly Mary, the eleven-year-old daughter of Pepys's neighbour, Robert Knightly.

2. But cf. above, v. 175.

3. Cf. above, viii. 224.

4. The story has not been traced. Western bargemen plied upriver from London Bridge; Woolwich lay in the territory of their rivals, plying downriver.

Duke of York with an account of the charge of the present fleet,
to his satisfaction;[1] and this being done, did ask his leave for my
going out of town five or six days; which he did give me, saying
that my diligence in the King's business was such, that I ought
not to be denied when my own business called me anywhither.
Thence with Sir D Gawden to Westminster, where I did take a
turn or two and met Rogr. Pepys, who is mighty earnest for me
to stay from going into the country till he goes,[2] and to bring my
people thither for some time; but I cannot, but will find another[a]
time this summer for it. Thence with him[b] home, and there
to the office till noon; and then with Lord Brouncker, J. Mennes,
and Sir G. Carteret, upon whose accounts they have been this
day, to the Three Tuns to dinner; and thence back again home;
and after doing a little business, I by coach to the King's House
and there saw good part of *The Scornfull Lady*;[3] and that done,
would have taken out Knepp, but she was engaged; and so to
my Lord Crews to visit him, from whom I learn nothing but
that there hath been some controversy at the Council-table about
my Lord Sandwiches signing where some would not have had
him, in the treaty with Portugall; but all, I think, is over in it.[4]
Thence by coach to Westminster to the hall; and thence to the
park, where much good company and many fine ladies; and in[c]
so handsome a hackney I was, that I believe Sir W. Coventry
and others who looked on me did take me to[d] be in one of my
own – which I was a little troubled for. So to the Lodge, and
drank a cup of new milk; and so home, and there to Mrs.

a repl. 'an'	*b* repl. 'home'
c repl. 'then'	*d* repl. 'for'

1. 'An Estimate of the Severall
Summs to bee charged on the Act for
300000 li.': PRO, SP 29/241 no. 41
(copy, 4 June, in Gibson's hand, with
an endorsement by Pepys); summary
in *CSPD 1667-8*, p. 424.

2. He lived at Impington, nr Cambridge.

3. A comedy by Beaumont and
Fletcher; see above, i. 303, n. 3. (A).

4. Cf. above, p. 59 & n. 3.
Sandwich had added his signature
after those of the Spanish and Portuguese plenipotentiaries. The Privy
Council made an enquiry on 29 May
and decided on the 30th that in the
instrument of ratification the signa-
tures of Charles II and of Sandwich
should come first. PRO, PC
2/60, p. 324; PRO, SP 29/253, f. 43r.

Turner's and sat and talked with her; and then home to bed, having laid my business with W Hewers to go out of town Friday next, with hopes of a great deal of pleasure.

4.*ᵃ* Up, and to the office, where all the morning. And at noon home to dinner, where Mr. Clerke the solicitor* dined with me and my clerks. After dinner I carried and set him down at the Temple, he observing to me how St. Sepulchers church steeple is repaired already a good deal, and the Fleet-bridge is contracted for by the City to begin to be built this summer; which doth please me mightily.¹ I to White-hall and walked through the park for a little ayre; and so back to the Council-chamber to the Committee of the Navy, about the business of fitting the present fleet suitable to the money given; which as the King orders it and by what appears, will be very little, and so as I perceive the Duke of York will have nothing to command, nor can intend to go abroad. But it is pretty to see how careful these great men are to do everything so as they may answer it to the Parliament – thinking themselfs safe in nothing but where the judges (with whom they often advise) do say the matter is doubtful; and so they take upon themselfs then to be the chief persons to interpret what is doubtful. Thence home; and all the evening to set matters in order against my going to Brampton tomorrow, being resolved upon my journey, and having the Duke of York's leave again today – though I do plainly see that I can very ill be spared now –*ᵇ* there being much business, especially about this which I have attended the Council about, and I the man that am alone consulted with; and besides, my Lord Brouncker is at this time ill, and Sir W. Penn. So things being put in order at the office, I home to do the like there, and to bed.

a repl. 'Up'   *b* repl. 'the'

---

1. This bridge (on the site of the modern Ludgate Circus) and Holborn Bridge were the only places at which wheeled traffic within the city could cross the river Fleet. Fleet Bridge was now rebuilt at a height of nine ft (instead of six) above the water, to facilitate the passage of boats. At the same time the gradient of the approach down Ludgate Hill was reduced. The work was completed in the following spring. PRO, PC 2/59, f. 172r; LRO, Rep. 74, f. 175v.

[Here ten pages (with top and left-hand margins ruled in red) are left blank for the entries for 5–17 June. The entries were never inserted, and in their place the rough notes from which they were to be constructed were bound into the volume. These were written in ink on 3½ foolscap leaves folded and refolded so as to form 8½ pages, all of which (except for the half-leaf) are larger than the pages of the diary volume. They were numbered by Pepys in two discontinuous series: 1, [unnumbered], 3 (altered from 4), 1, 2, 4 (altered from 3), 5 (altered from 1), 2, 3 and 6. The notes, like those for 10–19 April (above, pp. 160–8), include notes of expenditure which were meant for his account-books, not his diary; they also include the draft of part of a letter. They are here reproduced as exactly as possible, except that the mistakes made in the page sequence (due to the misfolding of the leaves by the binder) have been rectified. Pepys added asterisks and entry dates in pencil in order to indicate the correct order. Italics are here used for words and abbreviations written in longhand. *WH* represents Will Hewer.]

Friday—June 5. At Barnet for milk   00 . 00 . 06
            On the highway to menders of the high-
            way   00 . 00 . 06
            Dinner at Stevenage_____   00 – 05 – 06
  Saturd 6th Spent at *Huntington* ⟨with Bowles and
            Appleyard and *Shepley*⟩_____   00 – 02 – 00

  Sunday ~~6~~ 7. My father for money lent and horse hire   01 – 11 – 00

  Monday ~~8ᵃ~~ –8 Father's servants (father having in the ⎫
            garden told me bad stories of my wife's ⎬ 00 – 14 – 00
            ill words)   ⎭
            One that helped at the horses_____   00 – 01 – 00
            Menders of the highway_____   00 – 2 – 00
            Pleasant country to *Bedfᵈ* where while ⎫
            they stay I rode through the town and a ⎪
            good country town¹ and there drinking   ⎬ 00 – 01 – 00
            we on to ~~*Newport*~~ ⟨*Buckingham Newport*⟩² ⎪
            and there light and I and *WH* to the   ⎪
            church and there give the boy_____   ⎭
            So to ~~*Buckingh*~~ ⟨~~*Newport*~~ *Buckingh.*⟩ a
            good old town. ⁝. ·· ⁝·⁝ · ⁝⁝

a repl. '7'

1. A great town ... has in it 5 churches, and the ruins of an old castle': T. Baskerville (1681) in HMC, *Rep.*, 13/2/263. Description (c. 1698) in Celia Fiennes, *Journeys* (ed. Morris), pp. 340–1.

2. Newport Pagnell, Bucks.

~~in it only children~~. Here I to see the church which very good ~~like a cathedral~~ and the leads and a school in it.[1] Did give the sexton's boy _____   0– 1– 0
⟨A fair bridge here with many *arches*⟩.[2]
⟨Vexed at my people's making me lose so much time.⟩
Reckoning   0–13– 4
Mightily pleased with the pleasure of the ground all the day   At night to *Newp.!*
Pagnell[3] and there a good pleasant country town but few people in it.   A very fair and like a cathedral church and ~~therefore~~
I saw the leads.   And a vault that goes far under ground.   And here lay with Betty Turners sparrow.   The town ~~finely~~ and so most of this country well watered.
Lay here well and rose next day by 4 a-clock few people in the town.   And so away   Reckoning for supper_____.   0– 09– 6
Poor   0– 0– 6
Mischance to the coach but no time lost.
Tuesdy Paid our *Guide* ⟨when came to *Oxf.!* a
   9.th   very sweet place⟩[4]   01– 2– 6[5]
      barber   0– 2– 6

---

1. The Royal Latin school occupied a chantry chapel in St Peter's Church – the only church in Buckingham at that time. The church was rebuilt 1777–81 and again in the 19th century. Descriptions in R. Symonds, *Diary* (ed. Long), p. 20 [1644]; Browne Willis, *Hist. Buck.* (1745), ch. xii.

2. Celia Fiennes (c. 1694) remarked on the number and height of the arches: *Journeys*, p. 30. The river was liable to flood.

3. Presumably a slip for Bicester, which lay between Buckingham and Oxford. The description of the town and of the church, however, fits not Bicester but Newport, which Pepys had passed through earlier in the day.

4. For engravings of Oxford (illustrating all the buildings Pepys saw except Friar Bacon's study), see David Loggan, *Oxonia Illustrata* (1675). Descriptions in B. de Monconys, *Journal des voyages* (Lyon, 1665–6), ii. 48+ [1663]; James Yonge, *Journal* (ed. Poynter), pp. 168+ [1681]; Celia Fiennes, *Journeys* (ed. Morris), pp. 32+ [1694].

5. This charge probably included horse-hire. The guides were often used to conduct travellers over the rough and badly-defined roads. On 16 June Pepys's party, without a guide, lost its way between Newbury and Reading.

book *Stonheng*[1]   00– 4– 0

~~dinner~~   0– 1– 0

To dinner and then out with wife and⎫
people and landlord and to him that⎬ 0–10– 0
showed us the schools and library___⎭

To him that showed us All Souls College
and *Chichly's* pictures[2]_____   0– 5– 0

So to see Christ Church with my wife I⎫
seeing several others very fine alone with⎮
WH before dinner and did give the boy⎬ –0– 1– 0
that went with me ⟨before dinner⟩   ⎭

~~to the schools~~
Strawberries   0– 1[a]– 2
Dinner ⟨and servants⟩_____   1– 0[b]– 6

After came home from the schools I out⎫
with landlord to Brazen Nose College to⎮
the butteries and in the cellar find the⎬ 0– 2– 0
hand of the child of *Hales*[3]___Butler___⎭

Thence with coach and people to Physic
Garden[4]   0– 1– 0

a repl. figure rendered illegible   *b* repl. 'o – 19'

---

1. Probably Walter Charleton, *Chorea Gigantum* . . . (1663), a small work (64 pp.) criticising Inigo Jones's folio, *The most notable antiquity of Great Britain, vulgarly called Stoneheng* . . . (1655). Pepys kept Jones's book (PL 2010), but not Charleton's.

2. There was e.g. a three-quarter length portrait of Henry Chichele (Archbishop of Canterbury, d. 1443; founder of the college) by Sampson Strong, c. 1609: Mrs R. L. Poole, *Cat. of portraits in* . . . *Oxford*, ii. 181; ib., pl. xxiv. (OM).

3. John Middleton (d. 1623) of Hale, Lancs., was a giant wrestler, who in about 1617 had visited Brasenose (which had a strong Lancashire connection). Plot gives his height as 9 ft 3 in. – 'wanting but six

inches of the height of *Goliath*': *Natural hist. Staffs.* (1686), p. 295. Until c. 1880 there was an outline of his hand (made from an impression) painted on one of the doorposts of the cellar. Two pictures of it are still kept in the college. *Brasenose quatercentenary monographs* (Oxf. Hist. Soc., 1909–10), vii. 28, viii. 19.

4. A square walled garden established (in 1621) for the study of medicinal herbs – the oldest of its kind in Great Britain. Descriptions and engravings in *Collectanea* (Oxf. Hist. Soc., 1905), iv. 187–91; Evelyn, 12 July 1654; A. Wood, *Survey antiq.* . . . *Oxford* (ed. Clark), i. 291–2; Loggan, op. cit., pl. xii; R. T. Gunther, *Oxford Gardens*; VCH, *Oxf.*, iii. 49–50.

So to Friar *Bacons* study[1] I up and saw it
and give the man   0– 1– 0
Bottle of sack for landlord_____   0– 2– 0[a]
Oxford mighty fine place and well seated
and cheap entertainment.
At night came to *Abington* where had⎤
been a fair of custard[2] and met many⎟
people and scholars going home and there⎬ 0– 5– 0
did get some pretty good music and sang⎟
and danced till supper _____⎦

June Up and walked to the *Hospitall* very large
W 10th and fine and pictures of founders and the
history of the S Hospital and is said to be
worth 700[l] per an͞n͞ and that Mr. *Foly* was
here lately to see how their lands was
settled.[3] And here in old English the
story of the occasion of it and a *Rebus* at

a end of page 1

------

1. A tower on South (now Folly)
Bridge, which Roger Bacon (the
13th-century Franciscan philosopher)
was supposed to have used as an
observatory. Description (c. 1661–6)
in A. Wood, *Survey*, i. 425–6.

2. Several fairs were held at
Abingdon: this (founded in 1290 and
by the 17th century mainly a pleasure
fair) was the largest and longest and
lasted for a week. VCH, *Berks.*, iv.
441; description in W. Addison,
Engl. Fairs, pp. 134–5. Custard was
the dish served at it – cf. the 'Goose
fair' at Nottingham, and the 'Goose-
berry-pie fair' at Totnes.

3. This was Christ's (originally St
Helen's) Hospital, founded under
Henry V, refounded in 1553. See

A. E. Preston, *Christ's Hospital,
Abingdon, almhouses, hall and portraits*.
A list of the portraits is in E. Ashmole,
Antiq. Berks. (1719), i. 125–6. The
'history' was a manuscript ('A Monument of Christian Munificence')
written c. 1627 by Francis Brooke
alias Little, Master, 1596–8 (printed
1871 by C. D. Cobham); still in the
possession of the Hospital. Thomas
Foley (ironmonger to the navy) was
about to settle lands on a hospital in
Worcestershire; he bought an estate
for that purpose in 1668 and founded
the hospital (at Old Swinford) in 1670:
M. Sylvester, *Reliq. Baxt.* (1696), pt
iii. 93; VCH, *Worcs.*, iii. 202, 213,
269, n. 5.

the bottom.[1] So did give the poor
⟨which they would not take but in their
box.⟩[2]   0- 2- 6
So to the inn and paid the reckoning ⟨and
servants⟩   0-13- 0
So forth toward *Hungerford* led this good
way by our landlord one *Heart* a old but
very civil and well spoken man ⟨more
then⟩ as I ever heard of that quality.   He
gone we forward and I vexed at my
peoples not minding the way.   So came
to *Hungerford* where very good trouts eels
and cray fish dinner.[3] A bad mean town.
At dinner there   0-12- 0
Thence set out with a guide who saw us
to Newmarket heath[4] and then left us__   0- 3- 6
So all over the plain by the sight of the
steeple (the plain high and low) to *Salsbury* by night but before came to the town
I saw a great fortification and there light
and to it and in it and find it prodigious
so as to fright me to be in it all alone at
that time of night it being dark.   Understand I understand it since to be that that
is called *Old Sarum*.[5] Came to the town
George Inne[6] where lay in silk bed and
very good diet.   To supper.   Then to
bed.
Thursday And up and *WH* and I up and down the
11[th.] town and find it a very brave place with

1. The allusion here is to a set of
verses (c. 1458) by Richard Forman,
ironmonger and member of the
fraternity, written on vellum and dis-
played (with a rebus) in the hall of the
Hospital. They still survive, and are
described by Preston, pp. 54–5, and
reproduced in Ashmole, i. 127–34,
and Little, App. A.
2. The box is still there.
3. Hungerford (Berks.) was famous
for its trout and crayfish: cf. Evelyn,
4 July 1654; Celia Fiennes, *Journeys*
(ed. Morris), p. 23; J. Aubrey, *Nat.*

hist. Wilts. (ed. Britton, 1847), p. 62.
4. A mistake;   possibly Black
Heath, nr Bulford, Wilts.
5. There still remained fragments
of the walls of the medieval fortress
and city as well as Early Iron Age
earthworks: VCH, *Wilts.*, vi. 51+.
Salisbury (New Sarum), 1¼ miles to
the south, had been founded mostly
in the 13th century.
6. An old and large inn on the e.
side of High St: Sir R. Hoare, *Hist.
mod. Wilts.* (1822–37), iv. 598.

river go through every street[1] and a
most capacious market place. The city
great I think greater then Oxford. But
the minster most admirable[2] as ~~m~~ big I
think and handsomer then *Westm*.̂ And
a most large close about it and houses for
the officers thereof and a fine palace for
the *Bp*.[3] So to my lodging back and
took out my wife and people to show them
the town and church but they at prayers
could not be shown the *Quire*. A very
good *Organ* and I looked in and saw the
Bp. my friend *D*^r *Ward*.[4] Thence to the
Inne and there not being able to hire
coachhorses and not willing to use our
own we got saddle horses very dear.
Boy that fetched went to look for them⸺   0– 0– 6
So the three women behind *WH. Murf.*^{ds}[5]
and our guide, and I single, to *Stonehege*
over the plain and some prodigious great
hills even to fright us. Came thither and
them find them as prodigious as any tales
I ever heard of them and worth going

1. Water-courses through the
streets were a feature of Salisbury
until the 19th century. Evelyn (20
July 1654) remarked that they were
badly kept. Celia Fiennes (c. 1685)
thought they made the streets 'not so
clean or so easye to passe in': *Journeys*
(ed. Morris), p. 5.
2. Descriptions in Magalotti, pp.
151–4 [1669]; Celia Fiennes, *Journeys*
(ed. Morris), pp. 6–7 [c. 1685];
Aubrey, *Nat. hist. Wilts.* (ed. Britton,
1847), pp. 97–9. The building had
been kept in good repair throughout
the Interregnum: see Sir R. Hoare,
Hist. mod. Wilts. (1822–37), iv. 459;
VCH, *Wilts.*, iii. 193.

3. The palace, unlike the cathedral,
had suffered badly during the troubles:
the hall had been pulled down, a
passage opened up for public use
through the close wall, most of the
main building converted to an inn,
and the rest let out as tenements.
Seth Ward (Bishop, 1667–89) rebuilt
it at a cost of over £2,000: Walter
Pope, *Life* (1697), p. 63.
4. Ward was, like Pepys, a Fellow
of the Royal Society. He had taught
mathematics to Pepys's patron, Sandwich.
5. The Navy Office messenger who
accompanied them on this journey,
but whose presence has not been
mentioned before in the notes.

this journey to see.[1]   God knows what
their use was.   They are hard to tell but
yet may be told.   Give the shepherd
woman for leading our horses_____   0– 0– 4
So back by *Wilton* my Lord *Pembr's* house
which we could not see he being just
coming to town but the situation I do not
much like nor the house promise much
it being in a low but rich vall valley.[a 2]

June. So back home and there being light we
to the church and there find them at
prayers again so could not see the quire
but I sent the women home and I did go
in and see very many fine tombs and
among the rest some very ancient of the
Mountagus.[3]   So home to dinner and that
being done paid the reckoning which was
so exorbitant and perticularly in rate of
my horses and 7s-6d for bread and beer
that I was mad and resolve to trouble the
mistress about it and get something for
the poor.   And came away in that
humour   2– 5– 6
Servants   0– 1– 6
Poor   0– 1– 0
Guide to the stones _____   0– 2– 0
Poor woman in the street_____   0– 1– 0
Ribbands   0– 0– 9
Wash woman   0– 1– 0
⎧Seamstress for *WH*   0– 3– 0
⎩Lent *WH*   0– 2– 0

a   repl. 'value'; end of page '1'; entry for 11 June continues

---

1. Descriptions in Evelyn, 22 July
1654;   C. Fiennes, *Journeys* (ed.
Morris), pp. 15–16 [c. 1685].   Cf. also
the books by Inigo Jones and Charleton cited above, p. 226, n. 1.
2. Descriptions in Magalotti, pp.
150–1 [1669]; Aubrey, pp. 82–8.
3. *Recte* the Montacutes (Earls of
Salisbury) from whom Sandwich
claimed descent.   The tomb of Sir
John de Montacute (d. 1390), who
fought at Crecy and was King of the
Isle of Man, is now in the n. aisle of
the nave.   For the tombs, see R.
Symonds, *Diary* (ed. Long), p. 130.

Thence about 6 a'clock and with a guide
went over the ⟨smooth⟩ plain endeed till
night and then by a happy mistake and
that looked like an adventure we were
carried out of our way and with to a
town[1] where we would lie since we could
not not go as far as we would and there
with miser great difficulty came about
10 at night to a little inn where ~~f~~ we were
fain to go into a room where a pedlar was in
bed and made him rise and there wife and
I lay and in a truckle bed Betty Turner and
Willet but good beds and the master of
the house a sober understanding man and
I had pl[easant?] discourse with him about
⟨this⟩ country matters as *Wool* and *Corne*
and other things and he also merry and
made us mighty merry at supper about
manning the new ship at Bristol[2] with
men none but men whose wifes do master
them.   And it seems it is become in
reproach to some men of estate that are
such hereabouts that this is become
common talk.   By and by to bed glad of
this mistake because it seems had we gone
on as we pretended we could not have
passed with our coach and must have lain
on the plain all night. ⟨This day from
Salsb. I wrote by the post my excuse
for not coming home which I hope will
do for I am resolved to see the *Bath*[3] and it
may be Bristol.⟩

Friday
12 Up finding our beds good but we lousy.
Which made us merry we set out the
reckoning coming to and servants come
to   00. 9. 6
⟨My guide thither   00. 2. 0⟩

---

1. Chitterne, Wilts., near the
Wylye valley: see below, p. 234.
2. See below, p. 235, n. 1.

3. 'The Bath', not 'Bath', was a
common 17th-century form of the
name.

⟨*Coachman* advanced_____ oo – 10 . 0.⟩
So rode a very good way led to my great
content by our landlord to *Phillip's
Norton*[1] with great pleasure being now
come into Somerset-shire where my wife
and *Deb* mightily joyed thereat[2] I commending the country as endeed it deserves[a]

June. and the first time town we came to was
Brekington[3] where we stopping and drank
in for something of the horses we called
two or three little boys to us and pleased
ourselfs with their manner of speech and
did make one of them kiss *Deb* and
another say the Lord's Prayer (hallowed
be thy Kingdom come) at *Ph. Norton* I
walked to the church and there saw an
a very ancient tomb of some *K*! Templar
I think[4] and here saw the tombstone
whereon there were only two heads cut
which the story goes were the and credibly
were two sisters call the fair maids of
Foscott that had two bodies upward and
one below and there lie buried.[5]   Here is
also a very fine ring of six bells and
chimes mighty tuneable.   Having dined
very well ⟨   0 – 10 – 00⟩
we came before night to the *Bath*.
Where I presently stepped out with my
landlord and saw the baths with people in

a   end of page '1'; entry for 12 June continues

---

1. Norton St Philip.
2. Both being natives of the county.
3. Beckington; three miles north-
east of Frome.
4. It was in fact the tomb of an
unidentified lawyer, c. 1460, in
barrister's gown; now in the s. aisle;
illust. in J. C. Collinson, *Hist.
Somerset* (ed. Braikenridge), iii, pt 3,
p. 371.

5. One of the twins was said to have
died 'at a state of maturity' so that
'the survivor was constrained to drag
about her lifeless companion, till
death released her of her horrid
burden': Collinson, loc. cit. The
stone remains on the n. wall of the
Tower.

them.[1] They are not so large as I expected but yet pleasant and the town most
of stone and clean though the streets generally narrow. I home and being weary
went home to bed without supper the rest
supping.

*Sat_*Up at 4 a'clock being by appointment
13 called up to the ⟨Cross⟩ *Bath*[2] where we
were carried after one another myself and
wife and Betty Turner *Willet* and *WH.*
And by and by though we designed to
have done before company came much
company came very fine ladies and the
manner pretty enough only methinks it
cannot be clean to go so many bodies
together in to the same water. Good
conversation a among them that are acquainted here and stay together. Strange
to see how hot the water is and in s some
places though this is the most temperate
bath the springs so hot as the feet not to
endure. But strange to see what women
and men herein that live all the season in
these waters that cannot but be parboiled
and look like the creatures of the Bath.
Carried back wrap in a sheet and in a
chair[3] home and there one after another
thus carried (I staying above two hours in
the water) home to bed sweating for an
hour and by and by comes music to play

1. Descriptions of 17th-century
Bath are in BM Lansdowne 213, ff.
339+ [1634]; J. Childrey, *Britannia
Baconica* (1661), pp. 32–3; Mundy, iv.
7–8 [1639]; T. Guidott, *Discourse of
Bathe* (1676), ch. xii; James Yonge,
Journal (ed. Poynter), pp. 183–4
[1681]; C. Fiennes, *Journeys* (ed.
Morris), pp. 18+ [?1687]. Drawings
by Schellinks (1662) are in *Drawings
of Engl. in 17th cent.* (ed. P. H.

Hulton), ii, pls 19 (general), 20
(King's Bath). Cf. P. R. James, *The
baths of Bath in 16th & 17th centuries.*
2. A triangular bath so-called from
the cross in the middle; being the
coolest, it was the one most used in
summer. Gentlemen sat in seats
around the cross; ladies at the side
under the arches.
3. A bath-chair: cf. Fiennes, loc.
cit.

to me extraordinary good as ever I ever I⎱
heard at Landon almost anywhere_____ ⎰ 0– 5– 0

Up to go to *Bristoll* about 11 a'clock and⎫
paying my landlord that was our guide ⎬ 0–10– 0
from *Chiltren*[1]   ⎭

Set out to Bristow and the *Serj^t* of the
Bath   0–10– 0

and the man that carried us in chairs___   0– 3– 6

Set out toward Bristow and came thither
the way bad (in coach c hired to spare our
own horses) but country good about two
a'clock where set down at the Horse Shoe[2]
and there being trimmed ⟨by a very
handsome fellow⟩   0– 2– 0

walked with my wife and people through
the city which is in every^a respect another
London that one can hardly know it to
stand in the country no more then that.[3]
No carts it standing generally on *vaults*
only dog carts.[4] So to to the Three
Cranes tavern[5] I was directed but when I
came in the master told me that he had
newly given over selling of wine it
seems grown rich and so went to the
Sun[6] and there *Deb* going with *WH* and
Betty Turner to see her uncle[7] and leaving

a end of page '2'

---

1. Chitterne: see above, p. 231,
n. 1.
2. In Wine St.
3. Descriptions of the city in BM,
Lansdowne, ff. 335*v*+ [1634];
Mundy, iv. 8–11 [1639]; Evelyn, 30
June 1654 ('a citty emulating *London*,
not for its size, but manner of building,
shops, bridge . . .'); A. Jouvin de
Rochefort, *Le voyageur d'Europe*
(Paris, 1672), iii, pt 2, pp. 460–3;
Fiennes, op. cit, pp. 237–9 [c. 1698].
Plan with marginal pictures (by
J. Millerd, 1673) in *Trans. Bristol and*

Glouc. Arch. Soc., 44/203+; other
plans and views ib., pp. 325+;
Drawings of Engl. in 17th cent. (ed.
P. H. Hulton), ii, pl. 48.
4. Sleds drawn by dogs; similar
ones were in use in Southampton:
Fiennes, p. 54. The vaults were
mostly wine-cellars.
5. Untraced; possibly a mistake
for 'Three Crowns', a common sign
since it was the arms of the diocese.
6. In Christmas St.
7. William Butts, city broker.

my wife with mistress of the house I to
see the key which is a most large and
noble place and to see the new ship building by Bailey neither he nor *Furzer* being
in town.[1] It will be a fine ship. Spoke
with the foreman and did give the boys
that kept the cabin   0– 2– 0
Walked back to the *Sun* where I will find
Deb come back and with her her uncle a
sober merchant very good company and
is so like one of our sober wealthy London
merchants as pleased me mightily. Here
dined and much good talk with him⸺   0– 7– 6
⟨A messenger to *S.ʳ Jo. Knight*[2] who was
not at home   0– 0– 6
Then walked with him and my wife and
company to round the key and to the
ship and he showed me the Custom House[3]
and made me understand many things of
the place and led us through *Marsh* street
where our girl was born but Lord the joy
that was among the ⟨old⟩ poor people of
the place to see Mrs. *Willets* daughter it
seems her mother being a brave woman
and mightily beloved. And so brought
us a back way by surprize to his house
where a substantial good house and well
furnished and did give us good entertainment of strawberries a ⟨whole⟩ venison
pasty cold and plenty of brave wine and

1. This was the *Edgar*, launched on
29 July (*CSPD 1667–8*, p. 512); a
3rd-rate, costing over £6000. Francis Bailey was one of the few ship-
builders with yards large enough for
the construction of a warship (he
built two others in the '70s), but it was
contrary to normal policy to have
warships built elsewhere than in the
royal yards. See B. Pool, *Navy
Board contracts, 1660–1832*, pp. 13–14;

R. C. Anderson (comp.), *Lists of Men
of War, 1650–1700*, pt i (*Engl. Ships,
1649–1702*), nos 565, 609. Daniel
Furzer was also a shipbuilder.

2. Navy agent at Bristol. A rich
merchant, he was M.P. for the city
from 1660, an Alderman from 1662
and Lord Mayor 1663–4.

3. Newly built in 1666, on the
Welsh Back, by Bristol Bridge.

above all *Bristoll* milk.[1] Where comes
in another poor woman who hearing that
Deb was here did come running hither
and with her *eyes* so full of tears and heart
so full of joy that she could not speak
when she came in that it made me weep
too I protest that I was not able to speak
to her (which I would have done) to have
diverted her tears. His wife a good
woman and so sober and substantial as I
was never more pleased anywhere.
Servant maid   0– 2– 0
So thence took leave and he with us
through the city where in walking I find
the city pay him great respect and he the
like to the meanest which pleased me
mightily.   He showed us the place where
the merchants meet here[2] and a fine
cross[3] yet standing like Cheapside.   And
so to the Horse Shoe where paying the
reckoning   0– 2– 6
We back and by moonshine to the *Bath*
again about 10 a'clock bad way and
giving the coachman_____   0– 1– 0
went all of us to bed.[a]

Deare M[r] *Hill.*[4]
   *'Twill bee hard (I know) to make you
believe y*[t] *any thing lesse then a forgetfull-*

a   end of page '3' '4'

---

1. A sweet sherry. Cf. Fuller's
Worthies (ed. Nuttall, 1840), iii. 115:
'Though as many elephants are fed as
cows grassed within the walls of this
city, yet great plenty of this meta-
phorical milk, whereby *Xeres* or
sherry sack is intended. Some will
have it called milk because . . . such
wine is the first moisture given infants
in this city.'
   2. The Merchants' Tolzey, Corn
St.

3. A (?)13th-century cross (enlarged and beautified in 1633) which
stood at the junction of the four main
streets of the city; removed 1733;
now at Stourhead, Wilts. C. Pooley,
Old crosses of Glos., pp. 3+; *Proc.
Clifton Antiq. Club*, iii (1897), pp.
177+.
   4. Thomas Hill, merchant; now
in Lisbon.

nesse of my obligations to you could begett ⟨*make way for*⟩ ⟪*my*⟫ *soe long a silence. in mee. But soe well I am assured of y.ᵗ inclination to thinke well of mee, y.ᵗ I will not* despair of your making a better construction of it when I have ⟪frankly⟫ told you frankly and that the 'sh' ⟪shameful⟫ as well as sorrowfull successes of all our matters which have without any intermission attended issues ⟨which have without intermission attended the management and⟩ issue of the late war have kept me to this day under so chagrin a sense an apprehension of my share ⟨particular interest⟩ in the reproach ⟨due thereto⟩ (God though God knows (though without vanity (though I thank God (though the world hath been pretty favourable to myself (though I nevertheless (though I cannot by (though I cannot complain of (though the world hath ⟨not⟩ been very unkind to me in this matter) that I have taken joy little joy in the notice of my ⟪home⟫ friends at home but much less could find any content in appearing to them abroad who as they are more sensible have greater sense of the *Scandall* so by their distance are the they less ⟨able⟩ to distinguish between them that are and those that are not chargeable upon whose negligence or corruption favour to charge the same

but the opportunity of this worthy hand that brings us this (*S.ʳ Rob. Southewell*)[1] makes it ⟨as well⟩ safe as well as ⟨fit⟩ necessary for me to necessary for me to show myself now to you and (leaving all those public

---

1. Southwell, envoy-extraordinary to Portugal, was at Deal on 15 June, about to take sail for Lisbon: *CSPD 1667–8*, pp. 438, 441.

S. 14ᵗʰ Up and walked up and down the town
and saw a pretty good market place and
many good street and ⨍ very fair stone
houses and so to ⟨the great⟩ church and
there saw ·*Bp*. Montagu's tomb¹ and
when placed did there see many brave
people come and among other two men
brought in litters and set down in the
chancel to hear.   But I did not know one
face. Here a good *Organ* but a vain
pragmatic fellow preached a ridiculous
sermon affected that made me angry and
some *gent.* that sat next me and sang well.
So home walking round the walls of the
city which are good and the *battlemᵗˢ* all
whole.²

The sexton of the church_____   0– 1– 0
So home to dinner.**ᵃ

June ** and after dinner comes Mr. *Butts* again
14ᵗʰ to see me and he and I to church where
the same idle fellow preached. And I
slept most of the sermon.   Thence home
and took my wife out and the girls and
came to this church again to see it and
look over the monuments where among
others *Dʳ. Venner*³ and *Pelling*⁴ and a lady

a   end of page '4' '3'

---

1. James Mountagu, Bishop of
Bath and Wells 1608–16, was Sand-
wich's uncle. The tomb (by William
Cure and Nicholas Johnson) is on the
s. side of the n. aisle of the Abbey
Church. Contemp. illust. in T.
Dingley, *Hist. from marble* (ed.
Nichols), i. 48; cf. K. Esdaile, *Engl.
monumental sculpture*, p. 123.

2. Cf. plan in Guidott, op. cit.
3. Tobias Venner (d. 1660); a
Bath physician who published works
on the waters of the spa.
4. John Pelling (d. 1621), Rector of
Bath.

of S.' *W Wallers* he lying[a] with his face
broken.[1] So to the fields a little and
walked and then home and had my head
looked and so to supper and then comes
my landlord to me a ~~sorer~~ sober understanding man and did give me a ⟪a~~a~~
good account of the antiquity of this
town and *Wells* and of two heads on
two pillars in *Wells* church.[2] But he
a catholic. So he gone I to bed.⟫

Monday Up and with Mr. *Butts* to look into the
15. Baths and find the King and Queen's
full of a mixed sort of good and bad
and the Cross only almost for the
gentry. So home and did the like
with my wife and did pay my guides.

Two women	00– 5– 0
One man	0– 2– 6
Poor	0– 0– 6
Woman to lay my footcloth_____	0– 1– 0
So to our *Inne* and there eat and paid reckoning	1– 8– 6
Servants	0– 3– 0
Poor	0– 1– 0
Lent the *Coachman*	0–10– 0

a MS. 'living'

---

1. A monument of great beauty (by
Epiphanius Evesham) erected by Sir
William Waller (later the parliamentary general) to the memory of
his first wife Jane (d. 1633). It had
been defaced by royalist soldiers who
occupied Bath in 1643. See J. Adair,
Roundhead General, pp. 31–2 (illust.
opp. p. 64); K. Esdaile, *Engl. church
monuments*, pp. 20, 53, 55, 76.
2. The heads of a king and a bishop,
on the capital of two pillars on the n.
side of the nave of the Cathedral. 'It
was fore-told, that when a King
should be like that King, and a Bishop
like that Bishop; that Abbots should
be put down, and Nuns should marry.
. . . This Prophecy was Writ in
Parchment, and hung in a Table on
one of those Pillars, before the Civil-
Wars. . . . It was Prophecy'd 300
years before the Reformation.
Bishop *Knight*, was Bishop here at the
Reformation, and the Picture (they
say) did resemble him': John Aubrey,
Miscellanies (1696), p. 95.

Before I took coach I went to make a boy⎫
dive in the King's bath _____⎭   0- 1- 0

⟨I paid also for my coach and ⟨a⟩ horse
to *Bristoll*   1- 1- 6⟩

Took coach and away without any of
the company of the other ⟨stage⟩ coaches
that go out of this town today and rode
all day with some trouble for fear of being
out of our way over the *downes* (where
the life of the shepherds is in fair weather
⟨only⟩ pretty).   In the afternoon came
to *Abebury*[1] where seeing great stones like
those of Stonage standing up I stepped
and took a countryman of the town and
he carried me and showed me a place
trenched in like Old Sarum almost with
great stones pitched in it some bigger then
those at *Stonage* in figure to my great
admiration and he told me that most
people of learning coming by do come
and view them and that the King did so.
And that the *Mount* cast hard by is called
Selbury from one King *Seale* buried there
as tradition says.[2]   I did give this man__   0- 1- 0
So took coach again (seeing one place
with great high stones pitched round
which I believe was once some perticular
fine building like that in some measure
like that of Stonag).   But about a mile
on it was prodigious to see how full the
downes are of great stones and all along
the valleys stones of considerable bigness
most of them growing certainly out of
the ground so think thick as to cover the

---

1. The common spelling of Ave-
bury (Wilts.) until the 19th century.
2. A contemporary account of both
Avebury and Silbury (with illust.) is in
John Aubrey's *Topog. Collections* (ed.
Jackson, 1862), pp. 314–33. Charles II
had visited both places in 1663 under
Aubrey's guidance: op. cit., p. 316.
Of Silbury, Aubrey wrote (p. 332):

'No History gives us any account of it:
the tradition only is, that King Sil, or
Zel as the countrey folke pronounce,
was buried here on horseback, and
that the hill was raysed while a posset
of milk was seething'. See also W.
Stukeley, *Abury, a temple of the
British Druids* (1724); VCH, *Wilts.*, i.
31–6, 324–6.

ground. Which makes me think the less
of the wonder of Stonage for hence they
might undoubtedly supply themselfs
with stones as well as those at *Abebery*.[a][1]

June. In my way did give to the poor and
menders of the highway_____ 00 – 3 – 0.
Before night came to *Marlborough* and lay
at the *Hart*[2] a good house and there a fair
a pretty fair town for a street or two and
what is most singular is their houses on
one side having their penthouses supported with pillars which makes it a good
walk.[3] My wife pleased with all this
evening reading of Mustapha[4] to me till
supper and then to supper and had music
whose innocence pleased me and I did
give them   0 – 3 – 0.
So to bed and lay well all night and long
so as all the five coaches that came this day
from *Bath* as well as we were gone out of
the town before us. So paying the

Tuesday 16[b] reckoning   0 – 14 – 04
              & servants   0 – 2 – 00
              poor   0 – 1 – 0
Set out and overtook one coach and kept
a while company with it till one of our
horses c losing a shoe we stopped and
drank and spent   0 – 1 – 00
So on and passing through a good part
of this country of *Wiltshire* and saw good

a end of page '5'   *b* repl. '15'

---

1. All the Avebury stones and most
of those at Stonehenge were of local
sarsen.

2. The White Hart; no longer in
existence.   It is said to have occupied
the corner between the Green and St
Martin's.

3. A few pillars of the penthouses
still remain on the n. side of the main
street.   Much of the town had been
recently rebuilt after the disastrous
fire of 1653.

4. A tragedy by the Earl of
Orrery; see above, vi. 73, n. 1. (A).

house of *Alex. Pophams*[1] and another of
my Lord *Cravens* I think in *Barkeshire*[2]
we came to *Newbery* and there dined
which cost me[a]
and music which a song of the old
Courtier of Q. *Eliz.* and how he was
changed upon the coming in of the King
did please me mightily and I did cause
WH to write it out[3] _____   0 – 3 – 6
Then comes the reckoning ⟨forced to
change gold⟩   0 – 8 – 7
   Servants ⟨and poor⟩_____   0 – 1 – 6
So out and lost our way which made me
vexed but came into it again.   And in the
evening betimes came to *Reding* and there
heard my wife read more of *Mustapha*.
Then to supper and then I to walk about
the town which is a very great one I
think bigger then *Salsbury*.   A river runs
it through it behind in seven branches and
unite in one at the end in one part of the
town[4] and runs into *Thames* a half mile off.
One odd sign of The *Broad face*.[5]   *WH*
troubled with the head *ake* we had none
of his company last night nor all this day

---

a   no sum entered

---

1. Littlecote House, nr Ramsbury;
a mainly Elizabethan building.   Pop-
ham (M.P. for Bath) was a relative of
the Mountagus, and a political associate of the Crews.

2. Hampstead Marshall, Benham,
nr Newbury, Berks.; said to have
been designed by Balthasar Gerbier
(after Heidelberg Castle); built 1625–
65; destroyed by fire, 1718: VCH,
Berks., iv. 179.   Craven was a distinguished soldier and a prominent
figure at court.

3. 'The Queen's Old Courtier' (and
other titles), sung on a single note.   It
was not the old courtier but his son

who in James I's time was 'changed'
(i.e. came to typify a new style in
manners and morals).   See C. M.
Simpson, *Brit. broadside ballad*, pp.
591+.   (E).

4. At Swan Bridges: see Speed's
map (1610) in J. Man, *Hist. . . .
Reading* (1816), pl. vi.   The Kennet
was later canalised and the site is now
built over.

5. An inn in High St pulled down
shortly before 1934: *Berks. Chron.*,
26 January 1934.   The sign (cf. 'The
Happy Man') was a rare one: there
was another at this time (and still is) in
Abingdon.

nor night to talk. Then to my *inn* and so to bed.

Wedn. 17ᵗʰ Rose and paying the reckoning _____⎤   0 – 12 – 6
            Servants ⟨and poor⟩ _____⎦   0 – 2 – 6
Music the worst we have had came to our chamber door but calling us by wrong names we gave him nothing[a]

June. So set out with one coach in company and through *Mydenhead* which I never saw before to *Colebrooke*[1] by noon the way mighty good. And there dined and fitted ourselfs a little to go through London anon. Somewhat out of humour all day reflecting on my wife's neglect of things and impertinent humour got by this liberty of being from me which she is never to be trusted with for she is a fool.

Thence pleasant way to London before night ⟨and find all very well to great content⟩ and there to walk with my wife. And saw ~~Mr.~~ Sʳ W P who is well again. ~~I hear~~ Hear of the ill news by the great fire at *Berbedos*.[2]

By and by home and there with my people to supper all in pretty good humour though I find my wife hath something in her gizzard that which waits an opportunity of being provoked to bring up. But I will not for my content sake give it. So I to bed glad to find all so well here. And slept well.[b]

a end of page '2'   *b* end of page '3'

---

1. Colnbrook, Bucks.; a coach stage between Maidenhead and London.
2. At St Michael's (now Bridge-town) on 18 April; the magazine had been destroyed, together with most of the town: *CSPCol: Am. & W. Indies 1661–8*, pp. 561, 563, 578.

18.*ᵃ*   Up betimes and to the office, there to set my papers in order and books, my office having been new-whited and windows made clean. And so to sit, where all the morning; and did receive a hint or two from my Lord Anglesy, as if he thought much of my taking the ayre as I have done – but I care not a turd. But whatever the matter is, I think he hath some ill-will to me, or at least ⟨an⟩ opinion that I am more the servant of the Board then I am. At noon home to dinner, where my wife*ᵇ* still in a melancholy fusty humour, and crying; and doth not tell me plainly what it is, but I by little words find that she hath heard of my going to plays and carrying people abroad every day in her absence; and that I cannot help, but the storm will break out, I know, in a little time. After dinner, carried her by coach to St. James's, where she sat in the coach till I to my Lady Peterborough; who tells me, among other things, her Lord's good words to the Duke of York lately about my Lord Sandwich, and that the Duke of York is kind to my Lord Sandwich – which I am glad to hear. My business here was about her Lord's pension from Tanger.[1] Here met with Povy, who tells me how hard Creed is upon him,[2] though he did give him, about six months since I think he said, 50 pieces in gold. And one thing there is in his accounts that I fear may touch me; but I shall help it, I hope.[3] So, my wife not speaking a word going nor coming, nor willing to go to a play, though a new one, I to the office and did much business. At night home, where supped Mr. Turner and his wife, and Betty and Mercer and Pelling, as

---

a Roughly from this point onwards to the end of the diary, the effects of Pepys's eyestrain are visible in the MS. The symbols and lines are more widely spaced, and the handwriting larger: this becomes marked after early February 1669. The MS. is also less impeccable: the symbols often less neat, sometimes incomplete, and blots and errors more frequent.

b repl. 'my'

---

1. See above, viii. 459 n. 3.

2. Povey, whom Pepys had succeeded as Treasurer of the Tangier Committee in 1665, was putting his accounts into order. Creed was the Committee's secretary.

3. See below, p. 371.

merry as the ill melancholy humour that my wife was in would
let us; which vexed me, but I took no notice of it, thinking that
will be the best way, and let it wear away itself.

After supper, parted and to bed; and my wife troubled all
night, and about one a-clock goes out of the bed to the girl's
bed; which did trouble me, she crying and sobbing, without
telling the cause.   By and by comes back to me, and still crying;
I then rose and would have sat up all night, but she would have
me come to bed again.   And being pretty well pacified, we to
《19》 sleep; when between*a* 2 and 3 in the morning, we were
waked with my maids crying out, "Fire! Fire! in Marke
lane!" so I rose and looked out, and it was dreadful; and strange
apprehensions in me, and us all, of being presently burnt: so
we all rose, and my care presently was to secure my gold and
plate and papers, and could quickly have done it, but I went
forth to see where it*b* was, and the whole town was presently in
the streets; and I found it in a new-built house*c* that stood alone
in Minchin-lane, over against the Clothworkers-hall – which
burned furiously, the house not yet quite finished.[1]   And the
benefit of brick was well seen, for it burnt all inward and fell
down within itself – so no fear of doing more hurt; so homeward and stopped at Mr. Mills, where he and she at the door,
and Mrs. Turner and Betty and Mrs. Hollworthy; and there I
stayed and talked, and up to the*d* church leads and saw the fire,
which spent and spent itself, till all fear over; I home, and there
we to bed again and slept pretty well.   And about 9 rose; and
then my wife fell into her blubbering again and at length had ⟨a⟩
request to make to me, which was that she might go into France
and live there out of trouble: and then all came out, that I
loved pleasure and denied her any, and a deal of do; and I find

a	repl. 'about'	*b*	blot above symbol
c	MS. 'us'	*d*	repl. 'l'-

---

1. The house was apparently burnt
down deliberately. In October a
beggar was condemned and hanged
for causing the fire.   It was alleged
that he did it because the owner of the
house had refused him alms, but
'many think he was hired to do it':
newsletters, 20, 29 October (BM,
Add. 36916, ff. 116*r*, 117*r*).

that there have been great fallings-out between my father and her, whom for ever hereafter I must keep asunder, for they cannot possibly agree. And I said nothing; but with very mild words and few suffered*ª* her*ᵇ* humour to spend, till we begin to be very quiet and I think all will be over, and friends; and so I to the office, where all the morning doing business. Yesterday I heard how my Lord Ashly is like to die, having some imposthume in his breast, that he hath been fain to be cut into the body.[1]

At noon home to dinner; and thence by coach to White-hall, where we*ᶜ* attended the Duke of York in his closet upon our usual business. And thence out and did see many of the Knights of the Guarter with the King and Duke of York, going into the Privy-chamber to elect the Elector*ᵈ* of Saxony into the Order; who I did hear the Duke of York say was a good drinker; I know not upon what score this compliment is done him.[2] Thence with W. Penn, who is in great pain of the gowte, by coach round by Hoborn home, he being at every kennel full of pain. There home; and by and by comes in my wife and Deb, who*ᵉ* have been at the King's House today, thinking to spy me there; and saw the new play, *Evening Love* (of Dryden's);[3] which

---

a   repl. ? 'e'-   b   repl. 'er'   c   repl. 'sp'-
d   repl. 'Duke'   e   MS. 'whom'

---

1. The trouble was caused by a cyst on the liver, and an abscess had been removed on 12 June by cautery (a hot knife). For the rest of his life he carried a silver pipe in the wound. K. H. D. Haley, *Shaftesbury*, pp. 202+.

2. John George II of Saxony (d. 1680) was now elected in the place of the late Lord Treasurer, the Earl of Southampton. He was invested at Dresden on 13 April 1669 and installed by proxy two years later: W. A. Shaw, *Knights*, i. 36. His election was one of the moves made by Arlington to attach the Protestant powers of the Empire and of N. Europe to the anti-French cause. The King of Sweden (already a member of the Protestant Triple Alliance formed in January) was elected at the same meeting.

3. *An evening's love, or The mock astrologer*, a comedy by Dryden, first acted in June 1668 and published in 1671. The cast listed in *The comedies, tragedies, and operas, written by John Dryden* (1701, i. 283) includes Hart as Wildblood, Shatterel as Maskal, Burt as Don Lopez, Nell Gwyn as Donna Jacintha, and Mrs Knepp as Beatrix. (A).

though the world commends, she likes not. So to supper and talk, and all in good humour; and then to bed – where I slept not well, from my apprehensions of some trouble about some business of Mr. Povy's he told me of the other day.¹

20. Up, and talked with wife, all in good humour; and so to the office, where all the morning; and then home to dinner. And so she and I alone to the King's House. And there I saw this new play my wife saw yesterday; and do not like it, it being very smutty, and nothing so good as *The Maiden Queen* or *The Indian Imperour*,² of his making, that I was troubled at it; and my wife tells me is wholly (which he confesses a little in the epilogue) taken out of the *Illustr. Bassa*.³ So she to Un-thankes, and I to Mr. Povy and there settled some business; and here talked of things, and he thinks there will be great revolutions* and that Creed will be a great man, though a rogue, he being a man of the old strain, which will now be up again.

So I took coach, and set Povy down at Charing-cross and took my wife up; and calling at the New Exchange at Smith's shop, and kissed her pretty hand; and so we home, and there able to do nothing by candlelight, my eyes being now constantly so bad that I must take present advice or be blind.

So to supper, grieved for my eyes, and to bed.

21. *Lords day*. Up, and to church; and home and dined with my wife and Deb alone, but merry and in good humour; which is, when all is done, the greatest felicity*ª* of all. And after dinner, she to read in the *Illustr. Bassa* the plot of yesterday's play, which is most exactly the same. And so to church, I alone, and thence to see Sir W. Penn, who is ill again; and then home – and there get my wife to read to me till supper, and then to bed.

22. Up, and with Balty to St. James's and there presented him to Mr. Wren about his being muster-maister this year;

a repl. 'fis'-

---

1. See above, p. 244 & n. 3.
2. Two tragedies: see above, viii. 91 & n. 2; 14 & n. 2. (A).

3. *Ibrahim, ou L'illustre Bassa*, by Madame de Scudéri (first published 1641). (A).

which will be done.[1]   So up to wait on the Duke of York; and thence with W. Coventry walked to White-hall: good discourse about the Navy, where want of money undoes us. Thence to Harp and Ball, I to drink; and so to the Coffee-house in Covent-garden, but met with nobody but Sir Ph. Howard, who shamed me before the whole house there, in commendation of my speech in Parliament;[2] and thence I away home to dinner alone, my wife being at her tailor's; and after dinner comes Creed, whom I hate, to speak with me, and before him comes Mrs. Daniel about business and yo did tocar su cosa with mi mano.   She gone, Creed and I to the King's playhouse and saw an act or two of the new play again, but like it not. Calling this day at Herringman's,[3] he tells me Dryden doth himself call it but a fifth-rate play.   Thence with him to my Lord Bruncker's, where a Council of the Royal Society;[4] and there heard Mr. Harry Howards noble offers about ground for our College, and his intentions of building his own house there – most nobly.[5]   My business was to meet Mr. Boyle, which I did, and discoursed about my eyes; and he did give me the best advice he could, but refers me to one[a] Turberville of Salsbury, lately come to town, which I will go to.[6]   Thence home, where

a blot in MS.

---

1. He seems to have been appointed in July: *CSPD 1668-9*, pp. 175, 309. He had held a similar appointment in 1667-8: above, pp. 158-9 & n.

2. See above, p. 103 & n. 1.   Sir Philip Howard was member for Carlisle.

3. Dryden's publisher.

4. Birch (ii. 299-300) has a report of this meeting.   Pepys was not a member of the Council until 1672.

5. Henry Howard was later (1677) Duke of Norfolk.   The plans – both abortive – concerned Arundel House and Gardens, south of the Strand.   For that concerning the Royal Society (which was already occupying part of the house), see above, p. 28, n. 1. For that concerning the house, see

Evelyn, iii. 234 & n. 4; *Archaeologia*, 72/255-6.   A private act for its construction was obtained in 1671 and some existing buildings pulled down c. 1676-80, but no new house was built.

6. Robert Boyle was much interested in optics (cf. his essay on 'vitiated sight' in *Works*, 1744, iv. 551-6). Daubigny Turberville was the most successful practising oculist of his day, and paid periodic visits to London. He later successfully treated Princess Anne: W. Pope, *Life of Seth Ward* (1697), p. 101.   'He generally prescribed to all, shaving their Heads and taking Tobacco which he had often known to do much good, and never any harm to the Eyes': ib., p. 103.

the streets full at our end of the town, removing their wine against the Act begins, which will be two days hence, to raise the price.[1] I did get my store in of Batelier this night. So home to supper and to bed.

23. Up, and all the morning at the office. At noon home to dinner; and so to the office again all the afternoon, and then to Westminster to Dr. Turberville about my eyes; whom I met with, and he did discourse I thought learnedly about them, and takes time, before he did prescribe me anything,[a] to think of it. So I away with my wife and Deb, whom I left at Unthankes; and so to Hercules-Pillars, and there we three supped on cold powdered beef; and thence home and in the garden walked a good while with Deane, talking well of the Navy miscarriages and faults. So home to bed.

24. Up, and Creed and Collonell Atkins comes to me about sending coals to Tanger, and upon that most of the morning.[2] Thence Creed and I to Alderman Backewell's about Tanger business of money; and thence I by water (calling and drinking, but not besando, at Michells) to Westminster; but it being holiday, did no business[3] – only, to Martins and there yo did hazer la cosa con her; and so home again by water and busy till dinner; and then with wife, Mercer, Deb, and W. Hewer to the Duke of York's playhouse, and there saw *The Impertinents,*[4] a pretty good play; and so by water to Spring-garden and there supped; and so home, not very merry; only, when we came home, Mercer and I sat and sung in the garden a good while. And so to bed.

a   repl. 'think'

---

1. The act recently passed on 9 May (19–20 Car. II c. 6) raising the duty on wine and other liquors; operative from 24 June 1668 to 24 June 1670.

2. Tangier was in constant need of coal since the Moors hemmed in the garrison and prevented their foraging for wood. Samuel Atkins of Stepney often supplied it.

3. St John the Baptist's day; an Exchequer holiday.

4. See above, p. 183, n. 2. (A).

25. Up, and to the office all the morning; and after dinner at home, to the office again and there all the afternoon, very busy till night; and then home to supper and to bed.

26. All the morning doing business at the office. At noon, with my fellow-officers to the Dolphin, at Sir G Carteret's charge, to dinner, he having some accounts examined this morning. All the afternoon we all at Sir W. Penn's with him about the Victuallers' accounts; and then in the evening to Charing-cross, and there took up my wife at her tailor's and so home and to walk in the garden; and then to sup and to bed.

27. At the office all the morning; at noon dined at home; and then my wife and Deb and I to the King's playhouse and saw *The Indian Queene*; but do not dote up[on] Nan Marshall's acting therein as the world talks of her excellence therein.[1] Thence with my wife to buy some linen, 13*l* worth, for sheets, &c., at the new shop over against the New Exchange,[2] come out of London since the fire; who says his and other tradesmen's retail trade is so great here, and better then it was in London, that they believe they shall not return,*a* nor the City be ever so great for retail as heretofore. So home and to my business and supper, and to bed.

28. *Lords day.* Up, and to church; and then home to dinner, where Betty Turner, Mercer, and Captain Deane. And after dinner, to sing, Mr. Pelling coming. Then they gone, Deane and I all the afternoon till night to talk of Navy matters and ships, with great pleasure; and so at night,*b* he gone, I to supper, Pelling coming again and singing a while; then to bed.

Much talk of the French setting out their fleet afresh; but I

---

a repl. symbol badly formed   *b* repl. ? 'noon'

---

1. She played the leading role of Zemboalla, the Queen, in this heroic tragedy by Sir Robert Howard and Dryden; q.v. above, v. 29, n. 1. (A).

2. In the Strand.

hear nothing that our King is alarmed at it at all; but rather making his fleet less.[1]

29. Called up by my Lady Peterborough's servant about some business of hers, and so to the office. Thence by and by with Sir J. Mennes toward St. James's; and I stop at Dr Turbervilles and there did receive a direction for some physic, and also a glass of something to drop into my eyes; who gives me hopes that I may do well. Thence to St. James's and thence to White-hall, where find the Duke of York in the Council-chamber, where the Officers of the Navy were called in about Navy business, about calling in of more ships; the King of France having, as the Duke of York says, ordered his fleet to come in, notwithstanding what he had lately ordered for their staying abroad.[2] Thence to the Chapel, it being St. Peter's day, and did hear an Anthem of Silas Taylors making – a dull old-fashion thing of six and seven parts that nobody could understand; and the Duke of York, when he came out, told me that he was a better store-keeper then Anthem-maker – and that was bad enough too.[3] ⟪This morning, Mr. May showed me the King's new buildings at White-hall,[4] very fine; and among other things, his ceilings and his houses of office.⟫ So home to dinner, and then with my wife to the King's playhouse: *The Mulbery Garden*,[5] which she had not seen. And so by coach to Islington and round by Hackney home with[a] much pleasure. And to supper and bed.

a repl. 'which'

---

1. Sir Thomas Allin had heard of a squadron of French warships sighted off Ushant on the night of 25–26 June: Allin, ii. 18. For the English preparations to pay off ships, see *CSPD 1667–8*, p. 463 (Coventry to Pepys, 28 June). The French in fact did nothing in European waters this year except to maintain a fleet at intervals off their w. coasts in the early summer: C. de la Roncière, *Hist. marine française*, v. 474+.

2. On 1/11 July Beaufort's force had returned to harbour: *London Gazette*, 16 July. For the previous order for the ships to stay out, see ib., 22 June.

3. Taylor (Navy Storekeeper at Harwich) probably got his compositions performed through his friendship with professionals. None were published. The King told Aubrey that he liked his anthems: *Brief Lives* (ed. Clark), ii. 254. (E).

4. Some were by the river. They included a bedchamber, a laboratory and a library. LCC, *Survey of London*, xiii (pt 2), pp. 75–6.

5. A comedy by Sedley; see above, p. 189, n. 4. (A).

30. Up and at the office all the morning. Then home to dinner, where a stinking leg of mutton*ᵃ* – the weather being very wet and hot*ᵇ* to keep meat*ᶜ* in. Then to*ᵈ* the office again all the afternoon; we met about the Victualler's new contract. And so up, and to walk all the evening with my wife and Mrs. Turner in the garden till supper, about 11 at night; and so after supper parted and to bed – my eyes bad but not worse; only, weary with working. But however, I very melancholy under the fear of my eyes being spoilt and not to be recovered; for I am come that I am not able to read out a small letter, and yet my sight good, for the little while I can read, as ever they were I think.

a repl. 'motum'   *b* repl. 'bad'   *c* repl. 'd'-
d blot over symbol

JULY

1. Up, and all the morning we met at the office about the Victualler's contract. At noon home to dinner; Cosen Roger, come newly to town, dined with us, and mighty importunate for our coming down to Impington – which I think to do this Sturbridge-Fair.[1] Thence I set him down at the Temple; and Commissioner Middleton dining the first time with me, he and I on to White-hall and so to St. James's, where we met and much business with the Duke of York; and I find the Duke of York very hot for regulations in the Navy,* and I believe is put on it by W. Coventry and I am glad of it; and perticularly, he falls heavy on Chatham-yard and is vexed that Lord Anglesy did the other day complain at the Council-table of disorders in the Navy, and not to him.[2] So I to White-hall to Committee of Tanger; and there vexed with the importunity and clamours of Alderman Backewell for my acquittance for money by him supplied the garrison, before I have any order for paying it.[3] So home, calling at several places; among others,*a* the Change, and on Cooper to know when my wife shall come and sit for her picture – which will be next week;[4] and so home and to walk with my wife; and then to supper and to bed.

a repl. 'others I'

---

1. The Cambridge fair held annually from 24 August to 28 September. Cf. above, ii. 181, n. 3.

2. For the malpractices at Chatham, see Rawl. A 195a, f. 72 (report, 3 June); below, p. 258 & n. 3. For the Duke's new regulations for the Navy Office, see below, p. 289 & n. 1. The Council's Navy Committee (established in February 1668) was attracting some business normally dealt with by the Admiral alone.

3. The order was issued this day: *Econ. Hist.*, ii. 502–3.

4. This miniature has not been traced. Mrs Pepys first sat to Samuel Cooper on 6 July; six further sittings, or visits by Pepys to Cooper's studio, took place in July. On 10 August Pepys saw Cooper finish it and mentions the price of the miniature and its setting. (OM).

2. Called up by a letter from W. Coventry, telling me that the Comissioners of Accounts intend to summon me about W Warren's Hamburg contract;[1] and so I up and to W. Coventry (he and G. Carteret and I being the party concerned in it); and after conference with him about it, to satisfaction, I home again to the office. At noon home to dinner; and then all the afternoon busy, to prepare answer to this demand of the Comissioners of Accounts, and did discourse with Sir W. Warren about it; and so in the evening with my wife and Deb by coach to take ayre to Mile-end; and so home and I to bed, vexed to be put to this frequent trouble in things we deserve best in.

3. Betimes to the office, my head full of this business. Then by coach to Commissioners of Accounts at Brooke house, the first time I ever there. And there Sir W Turner in the chair; and present, Lord Halifax, Thomson, Gregory, Dunster, and Osborne. I long with them, and see them hot set on this matter; but I did give them proper[a] and safe answers. Halifax, I perceive, was industrious on my side, on behalf[b] of his uncle Coventry, it being the business of Sir W Warren – vexed only at their denial of a copy of what I set my hand to and swore. Here till almost 2 a-clock; and then home to dinner and set down presently what I had done and said this day;[2] and so abroad by water, I to Eagle Court in the Strand and there to a ale-house; met Mr. Pierce the surgeon and Dr. Clerke, Waldron, Turberville my physician for the eyes, and Lowre,[3] to dissect several Eyes of sheep and oxen, with great pleasure – and to my great information; but strange that this Turberville should be so great a man, and yet to this day had seen no eyes dissected, or

a repl. 'good'   b preceded by blot

1. The mast contract of 1664: q.v. below, p. 378 & n. 2. For correspondence between the Brooke House Committee and the Board on this subject in July and August, see PRO, Adm. 106/16, ff. 275+, 348, 377; Adm. 106/2886, pt I, passim.

2. This memorandum has not been traced. The committee had ended by desiring Pepys to send 'more particular answers' later: Adm. 106/2886 (3 July).

3. All were physicians; Richard Lower the most distinguished of them.

but once, but desired this Dr. Lowre to give him the opportunity to see him dissect some. Thence to Unthankes to my wife and carried her home, and there walked in the garden; and so to supper and to bed.

4. Up, and to see Sir W. Coventry and give him account of my doings yesterday; which he well liked of, and was told thereof by my Lord Halifax before. But I do perceive he is much concerned for*a* this business – gives me advice to write a smart letter to the Duke of York about the want of money in the Navy,[1] and desire him to communicate it to the Commissioners of the Treasury; for he tells me he hath hot work sometimes to contend*b* with the rest for the Navy, they being all concerned for some other part of the King's expense, which they would prefer to this of the Navy. He showed me his closet, with his round table for him to sit in the middle, very*c* convenient.[2] And I borrowed several books of him to collect things out of of the Navy which I have not. And so home and there busy sitting all the morning; and at noon dined, and then all the afternoon busy till night; and then to Mile-end with my wife and girl, and there eat and drank a Jole of salmon at the Rose and Crown, our old house; and so home to bed.

5. *Lords day.* About 4 in the morning took*d* four pills of Dr. Turberville's prescribing for my eyes, and they wrought pretty well most of the morning, and I did get*e* my wife to spend the morning reading of Wilkins's *Reall Character*.[3] At noon comes W How and Pelling, and young Michell and his wife, and dined with us. And most of the afternoon talking; and then at night, my wife to read again and to supper and to bed.

---

a repl. 'in'   *b* repl. 'content'   *c* repl. full stop
d repl. 't'–   *e* MS. 'give'

---

1. Untraced; possibly not written; but many of the Admiralty in-letters for this period have disappeared.
2. The table 'turns to him (as he sitts still) several sorts of business':

BM, Lansdowne 1010, f. 383*v*. Coventry's enemies later used the table in a play intended to ridicule him: below, p. 471 & nn. 2, 3.
3. See above, p. 200, n. 7.

6. Up, and to St. James and there attended the Duke of York; and was there by him himself told how angry he was and did declare to my Lord Anglesy, about his late complaining of things of the Navy to the King in Council, and not to him.[1] And I perceive he is mightily concerned at it, and resolved to reform things*a* therein.

Thence with W. Coventry, walked in the park together a good while, he mighty kind to me. And hear many pretty stories of my Lord Chancellor's being*b* heretofore made sport of – by Peter Talbot the priest in his story of the death of Cardinall Bleau[2] – my*c* Lord Cottington in his *Dolor de las Tripas*[3] – and Tom Killigrew, in his being bred in Ram Ally and now bound prentice to Lord Cottington, going to Spain with 1000*l* and two suits of clothes.[4] Thence home to dinner; and thence to Mr. Cooper's and there met my wife and W Hewers and Deb; and there my wife first set for her picture, but he is a most admirable workman – and good company. Here comes Harris, and first told us how Betterton is*d* come again upon the stage; whereupon my wife and company to that house to see *Henry*

---

a   repl. same symbol badly formed   b   repl. same symbol
c   MS. 'by'   d   repl. 'of'

---

1. See above, p. 253 & n. 2.
2. Like Clarendon, Cardinal Jean Balue (d. 1491), Louis XI's minister, had been hated for his riches and power, and, like Clarendon, had been accused, but never convicted, of treason. Talbot (Almoner to the Queen and an enemy of Clarendon) had presumably been referring not to the Cardinal's death but to his imprisonment (1469–1480). The story – for which there is only doubtful authority – was that he was imprisoned in a cage in which it was impossible for him to stand or sit.
3. Cottington, one of the pro-

Spanish courtiers of Charles I, had died a Catholic at Valladolid in 1652. He was said to have declared himself a Roman Catholic whenever he was seriously ill and reverted to Protestantism every time he recovered. The story was based on an incident in 1623: see M. J. Havran, *Cottington*, pp. 76–7.
4. Ram Alley was a debtors' sanctuary off Fleet St. Presumably Killigrew was taken into Cottington's service in the autumn of 1629 when the latter went on a mission to Spain. He would then have been 17.

the 5th;[1] while I to attend the Duke of York at the Committee of the Navy at the Council, where some high dispute between him and W. Coventry about settling pensions upon all flag-officers while unimployed – W. Coventry against it – and I think with reason.[2] Thence I to the playhouse and saw a piece of the play, and glad to see Betterton; and so with wife and Deb to Spring-garden and eat a lobster; and so home in the evening and to bed. Great doings at Paris, I hear, with their Triumphs for their late conquests.[3] The Duchess of Richmond sworn last week of the Queen's Bedchamber, and the King minding little else but what he used to do about his women.

7. Up, and to the office, where Kate Joyce came to me about some tickets of hers, but took no notice to me of her being married;[4] but seemed mighty pale, and doubtful what to say or do,*a* expecting, I believe, that I should begin; and not finding me beginning, said nothing; but with trouble in her face, went

a MS. 'to'

---

1. Pepys is probably referring not to Shakespeare's play, but to *The history of Henry the Fifth*, a heroic drama by Roger Boyle, Earl of Orrery; see above, v. 240 & n. 2. Betterton, Pepys's favourite actor, had been ill; he now played the part of Owen Tudor. (A).

2. The Duke's view prevailed, and on 17 July a council order to this effect was issued: PC 2/60, f. 197*v* (copies in PL 2867, pp. 477–8, PL 2902, pp. 22–3; BM, Add. 9318, f. 1*v*). It established for the first time the principle of continuous employment for naval officers which already governed the employment of officers in the army. Applied at first to flag-officers only (who received a peace-time 'pension' proportionate to their wartime pay), it was extended to further classes of officers in the Third

Dutch War, 1672–4. It is not known on what grounds Coventry and Pepys now disagreed with the pro-posal; Pepys himself later regarded it as an essential reform. See *Cat.*, i. 145–7; M. Lewis, *England's Sea-officers*, pp. 64+. For the Commit-tee of the Navy, see above, p. 67, n. 3.

3. By the peace of Aix-la-Chapelle Spain had been forced to concede important territory to France. The French celebrations in Paris, Ver-sailles and elsewhere from 1 July onwards, were marked by a magnifi-cence 'digne du plus grand Monarque du Monde'. See *Gazette de Paris*, no. 83 (14 July), pp. 670–1, 695–6.

4. Pepys (somewhat to his surprise) had not been consulted about her re-marrying: above, p. 195. As an inn-keeper, she cashed seamen's tickets (at a discount).

away and said nothing.   At the office all the morning; and after dinner, also all the afternoon; and in the evening with my wife and Deb and Betty Turner to Unthankes, where we are fain to go round by Newgate because of Fleet bridge being under rebuilding.[1]   They stayed there, and I about some business; and then presently back and brought them home and supped; and Mrs. Turner the mother comes to us, and there late; and so to bed.

8.   Betimes by water to Sir W. Coventry and there discoursed of several things; and I find him much concerned in the present inquiries now on foot of the Commissioners of Accounts, though he reckons himself and the rest very safe; but vexed to see[a] us liable to these troubles in things wherein we have laboured to do best.   Thence, he being to go out of town tomorrow to drink Banbury waters[2] – I to the Duke of York to attend him about business of the Office; and find him mighty free to me, and how he is concerned to mend things in the Navy himself, and not leave it to other people.   So home to dinner; and then with my wife to Coopers and there saw her sit; and he doth do extraordinary things endeed.   So to White-hall; and there by and by the Duke of York comes to the Robe Chamber and spent with us three hours till night, in hearing the business of the Maisters Attendants of Chatham and the Storekeeper of Woolwich; and resolves to displace them all, so hot he is of giving proofs of his justice at this time – that it is their great fate now, to come to be questioned at such a time as this.[3]   Thence I

a MS. 'seem'

---

1. See above, p. 223 & n. 1.
2. There was a sulphur well at Banbury, and another near by at Astrop, Northants.: both had been recently discovered and were much recommended by Oxford physicians. See R. Plot, *Nat. hist. Oxfordshire* (1677), p. 44, *Verney Mem.*, ii. 244, 378, 453.   Coventry had a house at Minster Lovell, nr Witney, Oxon.
3. The Master-Attendants (John Brooke and William Rand), charged

with malpractices, were suspended by the Duke's order on 9 July, but restored on 15 August. They had escaped further punishment through the influence of Middleton, Commissioner at Chatham: below, p. 267. The Storekeeper (William Acworth), in trouble not for the first time, faced an enquiry and trial, but came off unscathed. PRO, Index 10704/2, n.pp. Cf. above, p. 253 & n. 2.

to Unthankes and took my wife and Deb home – and to supper
and bed.

9. Up, and to the office, where sat all the morning; and after
noon, to the office again till night, mighty busy getting Mr. Fist[a1]
to come and help me, my own clerks all busy; and so in the
evening, to ease my eyes, I with my wife and Deb and Betty
Turner by coach to Unthankes and back again; and then to
supper and to bed.

10. Up, and to attend the Council; but all in vain, the
Council spending all the morning upon a business about the
printing of The[b] Critickes, a dispute between the first printer, one
Bee, that is dead, and the Abstractor, who would now print his
abstracts, one Poole.[2] So home to dinner; and thence to[c]
Hawards to look upon an Espinettes; and I did come near the
buying of one, but broke off. I have a mind to have one. So
to Coopers and there find my wife (and W. Hewer and Deb)
sitting and painting; and here he doth work finely, though I fear
it will not be so like as I expected; but now I understand his
great skill in music, his playing and setting to the French lute[3]
most excellently – and speaks French; and endeed is an excellent

a repl. 'Fus'-   *b* repl. 'p'-   *c* repl. 'on'

1. Anthony Fist, lately Batten's clerk.
2. Cornelius Bee had in 1660 issued a vast collection of the works of biblical commentators (*Critici Sacri*; 9 vols), whose sale was now threatened by this proposal of Matthew Poole, a Nonconformist scholar. Poole argued that Bee had no rights in the work since he was not an author, and that his own work included abstracts of works other than those in the *Critici Sacri*. At this meeting the disputants were given 14 days in which to agree. The Council later declared in Poole's favour: his

Synopsis Criticorum came out in five volumes in 1669–70, and was often reissued. (Pepys kept the Utrecht edition of 1684: PL 2743.) PRO, PC 2/60, pp. 370, 382; PRO, SP 29/253, f. 55r; *CSPD 1667–8*, pp. 515–16; *London Gazette*, 27 August; BM, Add. 19526, ff. 163v–164v; pamphlets cited in *DNB*, s.n. 'Poole' (and which should probably be dated 1667, not 1677). Further lawsuits followed: see H. R. Plomer, *Dict. Booksellers, 1641–67*, p. 19. Bee did not die in fact until 1672: ib., loc. cit.
3. For the French lute, see above, viii. 530, n. 3. (E).

man.　Thence in the evening with my people in a glass hackney-coach[1] to*ᵃ* the park, but was ashamed to be seen; so to the Lodge and drank milk and so home to supper and to bed.

11.　At the office all the morning.　After dinner, to the King's playhouse to see an old play of Shirly's called *Hide parke*, the first day acted – where horses are*ᵇ* brought upon the stage,[2] but is but a very moderate play; only, an excellent Epilogue spoke by Becke Marshall.　So thence home and to my office, and then to supper and to bed – and overnight took some pills.

12.　which work with me pretty betimes, being*ᶜ* Lords day, and so I within all day – busy all the morning upon some accounts with W. Hewer; and at noon, an excellent dinner, comes Pelling and W How, and the latter stayed and talked with me all the afternoon; and in the evening comes Mr. Mills and his wife and supped and talked with me; and so to bed.　⟨This last*ᵈ* night, Betty Michell about midnight cries out; and my wife goes to her, and she brings forth a girl; and this afternoon is christened, and my wife godmother again to a Betty.⟩*ᵉ*[3]

13.　Up, and to my office; and thence by water to Whitehall to attend the Council, but did not; and so home to dinner; and so out with my wife and Deb and W. Hewer towards Coopers; but I light and walked to Ducke-lane, and there to the bookseller's at the Bible, whose moher yo have a mind to,[4] but ella no era dentro; but I did there look upon and buy some

a repl. 'but was'　　　*b* repl. 'there'　　　*c* repl. 'been'
　　　　d repl. 'day'　　　*e* addition crowded in

---

1. For the introduction of glass windows in coaches, see above, viii. 446, n. 1.
2. The play was a comedy, licensed in 1632 and published in 1637.　The horse-spectacle is not demanded by Shirley's stage directions; it had probably been added to the scene at the races in Hyde Park in Act IV.　(A).

3. The previous Betty was also a child of the Mitchells.　Christened on 5 May 1667, she had died just over a month later: above, viii. 202, 277.
4. The bookseller was William Shrewsbury: Pepys had kissed his wife ('moher') on 10 April.

books, and made way for coming again to the^a man; which pleases me. Thence to Reeves's and there saw some, and bespoke a little, perspective – and was mightily pleased with seeing objects in a dark room.[1] And so to Coopers and spent the afternoon with them;^b and it will be an excellent picture. Thence my people all by water to Deptford to see Balty, while I to buy my Espinette which I did now agree for; and did at Hawards meet with Mr. Thacker and heard him play on the Harpsicon, so as I never heard man before I think.[2] So home, it being almost night, and there find in the garden Pelling, who hath brought Tempest, Wallington, and Pelham to sing; and there had most excellent music, late in the dark, with great pleasure. Made them drink and eat; and so with much pleasure to bed, but above all with little Wallington. This morning I was let blood, and did bleed about 14^c ounces, towards curing my eyes.[3]

14. Up, and to my office, where sat all the morning. At noon home to dinner; and thence all the afternoon hard at the office, we meeting about the Victualler's new contract; and so into the garden, my Lady Pen, Mrs. Turner and her daughter, my wife and I, and there supped in the dark and were merry; and so to bed. This day Bosse finished his copy^d of my picture, which I confess I do not admire, though^e my wife prefers him to Browne; nor do I think it like.[4] He doth it for W Hewers, who hath my wife's also; which I like less. This afternoon my Lady Pickering came to see us; I busy,^f saw her not. But how natural it is for us to slight people out of power, and

a repl. ? 'him'	*b* repl. same symbol	*c* repl. '16'
d repl. 'pic'-	*e* preceded by blot	*f* repl. 'busied'

---

1. Through a camera obscura.
2. Thacker has not been identified as a professional musician. (E).
3. Cf. above, iii. 77, n. 1.
4. This copy of the portrait of Pepys by Hayls cannot be identified: see D. Piper, *Cat. 17th-cent. portraits in*

Nat. Port. Gall. (1963), p. 270. Bosse is probably to be identified with the artist of this name whom Hooke, on 6 February 1674, saw drawing 'Mr. Hill's picture': *Diary* (ed. Robinson and Adams), p. 85. (OM).

for people out of power to stoop to see those that while in power they contemned.[1]

15. Up, and all the morning busy at the office to my great content, tending to the settling of papers there, that I may have the more rest in winter for my eyes by how much[a] I do the more in the settling of all things in the summer by daylight. At noon home to dinner, where is brought home the Espinette I bought the other day of Haward; costs me 5*l.* So to St. James's, where did our ordinary business with[b] the Duke of York. And so to Unthankes to my wife, and with her and Deb to visit Mrs. Pierce, whom I do not now so much affect since she paints.[2] But[c] stayed here a while, and understood from her how my Lady Duchess of Monmouth is still lame, and likely alway to be so – which is a sad chance for a young [lady] to get, only by trying of tricks in dancing.[3] So home, and there Captain Deane came and spent the evening with me, to draw some finishing lines on his fine draft of the *Resolution*,[4] the best ship, by all report, in the world. And so to bed. Wonderful hot all day and night, and this the first night that I remember in my life that ever I could lie with only a sheet and one rug; so much I am now stronger then ever I remember myself to be, at least since before I had the stone.

16. Up, and to the office, where Yeabsly and Lanyon[5] came to town and to speak with me about a matter wherein they are accused of cheating the King before the Lords-Commissioners of Tanger; and I doubt it true, but I have no hand [in] it; but will serve them what I can. All the morning at the office; and at noon dined at home, and then to the office again, where we met

---

a MS. 'which'   *b* repl. full stop   *c* repl. 'By'

---

1. Lady Pickering was Sandwich's sister-in-law. Her husband, Sir Gilbert (now retired into private life) had been a Councillor of State and Lord Chamberlain under the Protectorate.
2. Cf. above, viii. 439 & n. 2.
3. See above, p. 191 & n. 3.

4. For the ship, see below, p. 330 & n. 3. There is some information about this drawing in *Further Corr.*, pp. 195, 198. It does not appear to survive.
5. Victualling agents, of Plymouth.

to finish the draft of the Victualler's contract; and so I by water with my Lord Brouncker to Arundell-house to the Royal Society, and there saw an experiment of a dog's being tied through the back about the spinal Artery, and thereby made void of all motion; and the artery being loosened again, the dog recovers.[1] Thence to Coopers and saw his advance on my wife's picture, which will be endeed very fine. So with her to the Change to buy some things, and here I first bought of the seam-stress next my bookseller's, where the pretty young girl is that will be a great beauty.[2] So home, and to supper with my wife in the garden, it being these two days excessive hot. And so to bed.

17. Up, and fitted myself to discourse before the Council about business of tickets.[3] So to White-hall, where waited on the Duke of York, and then the Council about that business, and I did discourse to their liking; only, was too high an asserter that nothing could be invented to secure the King more in the business of tickets then there is; which the Duke of Buckingham did except against, and I could have answered, but forebore; but all liked very well. Thence home, and with my wife and Deb to the King's House to see a play revived called *The   *,[4] a sorry mean*a* play, that vexed us to sit in so much heat of the

a blot below symbol

---

1. Cf. Birch, ii. 306: 'July 16 1668. The experiment of Mr. Steno was tried, according to his method, before the Society by Dr. King, and suc-ceeded, so as the dog . . . was seen to be deprived of all motion below the part, where the descending artery was tied, which was upon the top of the spine by a needle passed through between the 8th. and 9th. ribs.'

2. Probably the Betty mentioned below, pp. 511, 534.

3. On 8 July the Council, in an effort to meet parliamentary criticism of the use of pay-tickets, had asked the Navy Board to find some means of putting an end to them. The Board reported on the 10th, giving reasons why they were indispensable: PRO, PC 2/60, ff. 196*v*–197*v*; Penn, *Memorials*, ii. 507–9. Pepys's notes of the 'Heads of discourse prepared to satisfie the Councill this day', are in NWB, p. 146; copies in BM, Add. 11602, f. 341*r* (in Pepys's hand); PL 2581, p. 146 (in Gibson's).

4. Probably James Shirley's *Hyde Park* (q.v. above, p. 260 & n. 2): see *The London stage, 1660–1800* (ed. W. van Lennep), i. 139. (A).

weather to hear it.   Thence to see Betty Michell newly lain in,
and after a little stay we took water and to Spring Garden,[1] and
there walked and supped and stayed late, and with much pleasure
home and to bed.   The weather excessive hot, so as we were
forced to lie in two beds, and I only with a sheet and rug, which
is colder than ever I remember I could bear.

18.   At the office all the morning.   At noon dined at home,
and Creed with me, who I do really begin to hate, and do use
him with some reservedness.   Here was also my old acquaintance Will Swan to see me, who continues a factious fanatic still;
and I do use him civilly, in expectation that those fellows may
grow great again.   Thence to the office, and then with my wife
to the Change and Unthankes, after[a] having been at Coopers
and sat there for her picture; which will be a noble picture,
but yet I think not so like as Hales's is.[2]   So home and to my
office, and then to walk in the garden, and home to supper and
to bed.   They say the King of France is making a war again in
Flanders with the King of Spain, the King of Spain refusing to
give him all that he says[b] was promised him in the treaty.[3]
Creed told me this day how when the King was at my Lord
Cornwallis, when he went last to Newmarket,[4] that being there
on a Sunday, the[c] Duke of Buckingham did in the afternoon, to
please the King, make a bawdy sermon to him out of the Canticles.[5]
And that my Lord Cornwallis did endeavour to get the King a
whore, and that must be a pretty girl, the daughter of the parson

a   repl 'and so home'   b   repl. 'was p'-
c   repl. 'he'

1. At Vauxhall.
2. For Hayls's portrait of Mrs Pepys, see above, p. 138 & n. 2. (OM).
3. This was untrue.   The story was put about by France's enemies, especi- ally by Castel-Rodrigo, Governor of the Spanish Netherlands: A. Legrelle, La diplom. française et la succession d'Espagne, i. 151.   For the treaty, see above, p. 257, n. 3.

4. In May: above, p. 209 & n. 2.
5. Mimicry of sermons was a fashionable game (cf. Aubrey, ii. 143), and its prevalence at court was noted with regret by Clarendon: Life, ii. 351-2.   The King's host was the 2nd Baron Cornwallis, Gentleman of the Privy Chamber, whose home was at Culford, Suff.   The story which follows has not been traced elsewhere.

of the place; but that she did get away, and leaped off of some place and killed herself – which*a* if true, is very sad.

19. *Lords day.* Up, and to my chamber; and there and up and down in the house; spent the morning getting things ready against noon, when comes Mr. Cooper, Hales, Harris, Mr. Butler that wrote *Hudibras*, and Mr. Cooper's cousin Jacke;*b* and by and by comes Mr. Reeves and his wife, whom I never saw before, and there we dined; a good dinner, and company that pleased me mightily – being all eminent men in their way.[1] Spent all the afternoon in talk and mirth, and in the evening parted; and then my wife and I to walk in the garden; and so home to supper, Mrs. Turner and husband and daughter with us; and then to bed.

20. Up and to the office, where Mrs. Daniel comes and I could not tocar su cosa, she having ellos sobre her. All the morning at the office – where all the morning. Dined at home. Then with Mr. Colvill to the new Excise Office in aldersgate-street. And thence back to the Old Exchange to see a*c* very noble fine lady I spied as I went through in coming – and there took occasion to buy some gloves and admire her, and a mighty fine fair lady endeed she was. Thence, idling all the afternoon, to Duck-lane and there saw my bookseller's moher,[2] but could get no ground there yet. And here saw Mrs. Michell's daughter, married newly to a bookseller,[3] and she proves a comely little grave woman. So to visit my Lord Crew, who is very sick, to great danger, by an Irisipulus – the first day I heard of it. And so home and took occasion to buy a Rest* for my spinet at the ironmonger's by Holborn Conduit,*d* where the fair pretty

a repl. 'and'   *b* l.h. repl. l.h. 'Jak'   *c* repl. 'him'
  d repl. same symbol badly formed and full stop

---

1. Besides Samuel Butler the author, Pepys's guests were Samuel Cooper the miniaturist, John Hayls the portrait painter, Henry Harris the actor and Richard Reeve, foremost among English makers of optical instruments.
2. See above, p. 260, n. 4.
3. The Mitchells were themselves booksellers, in Westminster Hall.

woman is that I have lately observed there, and she is pretty pretty, and yo creo vain enough. Thence home and busy till night, and so to bed.

21.*a* Up, and to St. James, but lost labour, the Duke of York abroad. So home to the office,*b* where all the morning; and so to dinner and then all the afternoon at the office; only, went to my plat-maker's and there spent an hour about contriving my little plats for my book of the King's four yards.[1] At night walked in the garden, and supped and to bed, my eyes bad.

22.*c* All the morning at the office. Dined at home; and then to White-hall with Symson the Joyner; and after attending at the Committee of the Navy about the old business of tickets,[2] where the only expedient they have found is to bind the Commanders and Officers by oaths – the duke of York told me how the Duke of Buckingham, after the Council the other day, did make mirth at my position about the sufficiency of present rules in the business of tickets. And here I took occasion to desire a private discourse with the Duke of York, and he granted it me on Friday next. So to show Symson the King's new lodgings, for his chimneys,[3] which I desire to*d* have one built in that mode. And so I home; and with little supper, to bed. ⟨This day, a falling-out between my wife and Deb about a hood lost; which vexed me.⟩

23. Up, and all day long but at dinner at the office, at work till I was almost blind, which makes my heart sad.

a repl. '20'   *b* repl. 'ol'
c repl. '21'   *d* repl. 'have'

---

1. The four yards were those at Chatham, Woolwich, Deptford and Portsmouth. (Harwich was only a temporary yard used in the late war.) The plates are not in the PL.

2. See above, viii. 538, n. 1. For the Committee of the Navy, see above, p. 67, n. 3.

3. For the lodgings, see above, p. 251, n. 4. Thomas Simpson (master-joiner at Woolwich and Deptford yards) had in 1666 made Pepys's book-cases: above, vii. 214 & n. 4. The 'chimneys' were chimney-pieces.

24. Up, and by water to St. James (having by the way shown Symson Sir W. Coventry's chimny-pieces, in order to the making me one); and there, after the Duke of York was ready, he called me to his closet, and there I did long and largely show him the weakness of our office, and did give him advice to call us to account for our duties; which he did take mighty well, and desired me to draw up what I would have him write to the office.[1] I did lay open the whole failings of the office, and how it was his duty to find them and to find fault with them, as Admiral, especially at this time – which he agreed to – and seemed much to rely on what I said. Thence to White-hall and there waited to attend the Council, but was not called in; and so home, and after dinner back with Sir J. Mennes by coach, and there attended, all of us, the Duke of York, and had the hearing of Mr. Pett's business, the maister-shipwright at Chatham; and I believe he will be put out.[2] But here Commissioner Middleton did, among others, show his good-nature and easiness to the Maisters-Attendants by mitigating their faults, so as I believe they will come in again.[3] So home and to supper and to bed, the Duke of York staying with us till almost night.

25.[a] Up and at the office all the morning; and at noon after dinner to Coopers, it being a very rainy day, and there saw my wife's picture go on, which will be very fine endeed. And so home again to my letters; and then to supper and to bed.

26. *Lords day.* Up, and all the morning and, after dinner, the afternoon also, with W. Hewer in my closet, setting right my Tanger accounts, which I have let alone[b] these six months

a repl. '24'   b repl. 'again'

---

1. This prompted what Pepys came to call 'the Duke's great letter': see below, p. 289, n. 1; p. 305, n. 1.
2. Phineas Pett was accused of fraudulent practices and was dismissed on 28 September: *CSPD 1667–8*, pp. 501–2, 607. But he was reinstated in November, and thereafter prospered, becoming Navy Commissioner and Comptroller of the Stores (1680–5), and Commissioner at Chatham (1685–9). He was knighted in 1680.
3. See above, p. 258 & n. 3.

and more; but find them very right, and is my great comfort.   So in the evening*a* to walk with my wife; and to supper and to bed.

27.   Busy all the morning at my office.   At noon dined; and then I out of doors to my bookseller in Duck-lane, but su moher not at home.[1]   And it was pretty here to see a pretty woman pass by with a little wanton look; and yo did sequi her*b* round about the street from Duck-lane to Newgate-market, and then ella did turn back and yo did lose her.*c*   And so to see my Lord Crew, who I find up and did wait on him; but his face sore,[2] but in hopes to [do] now very well again.   Thence to Coopers, where my wife's picture almost done, and mighty fine endeed. So over the water with my wife and Deb and Mercer to Spring-garden, and there eat and walked, and observe how rude some of the young gallants of the town are become, to go into people's arbors where there are not men, and almost force the women – which troubled me, to see the confidence of the vice of the age: and so we away by water, with much pleasure home.

This day my plat-maker*d* comes with my four little plats of the four yards, cost me 5*l*; which troubles me, but yet doth please*e* me also.

28.*f*   All the morning at the office; and after dinner, with my wife and Deb to the Duke of York's playhouse and there saw *The Slighted Maid*,[3] but a mean play; and thence home, there being little pleasure now in a play, the company[4] being but little. Here we saw Gosnell, who is become very*g* homely, and sings meanly I think, to*h* what I thought she did.[5]

---

a symbol blotted	*b* garbled s.h.	*c* garbled s.h.
d repl. 'makers'	*e* symbol blotted	*f* repl. '27'
	g repl. 'but'	*h* repl. 'what'

---

1. Cf. above, p. 260, n. 4.
2. Cf. above, p. 265.
3. A comedy by Sir Robert Stapylton; see above, iv. 56 & n. 1. (A).
4. I.e. the audience. (A).
5. (?) Winifred Gosnell, now an actress, had briefly served as Mrs Pepys's companion in December 1662. She was referred to as 'that old hag' in Sir Carr Scroope, *In defense of satire*, l. 300 (*Poems on affairs of state*, vol. i, *1660–78*, ed. G. deF. Lord, p. 369).

29.   Busy all the morning at the office.   So home to dinner, where Mercer; and there comes Mr. Swan, my old acquaintance, and dines with me, and tells me for a certainty that Creed is to marry Betty Pickering and that the thing is concluded; which I wonder at – and am vexed for.[1]   So he gone, I with my wife and two girls to the King's House and saw *The Mad Couple*,[2] a mean play altogether; and thence to Hyde-park, where but few coaches; and so to the New Exchange and thence by water home with much pleasure; and then to sing in the garden, and so home to bed, my eyes for these four days being my trouble, and my heart thereby mighty sad.

30.   Up, and by water to White-hall; there met with Mr. May, who was giving directions about making a close way for people*a* to go dry from the gate up into the House,[3] to prevent their going through the galleries; which will be very good. I stayed and talked with him about the state of the King's offices in general, and how ill he is served, and do still find him an excellent person; and so back to the office.   So, close at my office all the afternoon till evening; and then out with my wife to the New*b* Exchange, and so back again.

31.   Up, and at my office all the morning.   About noon, with Mr. Ashburnham to the new Excise Office;[4] and there discoursed about our business and I made him admire my drawing a*c* thing presently in shorthand; but God knows, I have paid dear for it in my eyes.   Home and to dinner; and then my wife and Deb and I with Sir J. Mennes to White-hall, she going thence*d* to New Exchange; and the Duke of York not being in the way, J.

a repl. 'coaches'   *b* repl. same symbol (blot in MS.)
      c blot under symbol   *d* MS. 'to thence'

1. They were married in the following October.
2. A comedy by James Howard;
see above, viii. 443 & n. 1.   (A).
3. The New Gallery, running
from Whitehall Gate to the King's
Guard Chamber, and finished in 1669.

LCC, *Survey of London*, xiii (pt 2),
pp. 44, 63.   Hugh May was Comptroller of the King's Works.
4. In Bloomsbury Sq., where it had
moved after the Fire.   William Ashburnham was Cofferer of the King's
Household.

Mennes and I to her and took them two to the King's House to
see the first day of Lacy's *Monsieur Ragou*,[1] now new-acted.   The
King and Court all there, and mighty merry: a Farce.   Thence,
Sir J. Mennes giving us like a gentleman his coach, hearing we
had some business, we to the park,*a* and so home; little pleasure
there, there being little company.   But mightily taken with a
little chariot that we saw in the street, and which we are resolved
to have ours like it.   So home to walk in the garden a little, and
then to bed.

The month ends mighty sadly with me, my eyes being now
past all use almost;[2] and I am mighty hot upon trying the late
printed experiment of paper Tubes.[3]

a   repl. 'Chan'-

---

1. John Lacy's farcical comedy, *The
old troop, or Monsieur Raggou*, was first
acted about 1663, and published in
1672. (A).

2. Cf. above, p. 244, note *a*.

3. 'An extract of a letter concerning
an Optical Experiment, conducive to

a decayed sight, communicated by
a Worthy person, who found the
benefit of it himself': *Philos. Trans.*
no. 37, 13 July 1668, iii. 727–31, 765,
802. Cf. R. Hooke, *Diary* (ed.
Robinson and Adams), p. 102.

AUGUST

1. All the morning at the office. After dinner, my wife and Deb and [I] to the King's House again, coming too late yesterday to hear the prologue, and do like the play better now then before; and endeed there is a great deal of true wit in it – more then in the common sort of plays; and so home to my business – and at night to bed – my eyes making me sad.

2. *Lords day.* Up and at home all the morning, hanging and removing of some pictures in my study and house. At noon Pelling dined with me. After dinner, I and Tom my boy by water up to Putney and there heard a sermon, and many fine people in the church. Thence walked to Barne elmes; and there, and going and coming, did make the boy read to me several things, being nowadays unable to read myself anything for above two lines together but my eyes grow weary. Home about night, and so to supper and then to bed.

3. Up, and by water to White-hall and St. James's, where I did much business. And about noon, meeting Dr. Gibbons,[1] carried him to the Sun tavern in King's Street and there made him and some friends of his drink; among others, Captain Silas Taylor[2] – and here did get Gibbons to promise me some things for two flagelettes. So to the ⟨Old⟩ Exchange and then home to dinner. And so Mercer dining with us, I took my wife and her and Deb out to Unthankes, while I to White-hall to Commissioners of the Treasury; and so back to them and took them out to Islington, where we met with W Joyce and his wife and boy and there eat and drank, and a great deal of his idle

---

1. Christopher Gibbons, court organist and composer. (E).   2. Antiquary and composer. (E).

talk; and so we round by Hackney home, and so to sing a little in the garden; and then to*a* bed.

4. Up, and to my office a little, and then to White-hall about a Committee for Tanger – at my Lord Arlington's; where, by Creeds being out of town, I have the trouble given me of drawing up answers to the complaints of the Turks of Algier,[1] and so I have all the papers put into my hand. Here till noon, and then back to the office, where sat a little; and then to dinner and presently to the office, where came to me Lord Bellasses, Lieu-tenant-Collonell Fitzgerald, newly come from Tanger, and Sir Arth. Basset, and there I received their informations; and so they being gone, I with my clerks and another of Lord Brouncker's, Seddon, sat up till 2 in the morning, drawing up my answers*b* and writing them fair; which did trouble me mightily to sit up so long, because of my eyes.

5. So to bed about 2 a-clock, and then up about 7 and to White-hall, where read over my report to Lord Arlington and Berkely and then afterward at the Council Board, with great good liking; but Lord, how it troubled my eyes, though I did not think I could have done it, but did do it, and was not very bad afterward. So home to dinner, and thence out to the Duke of York's House and there saw *The Guardian*, formerly the same, I find, that was called *Cutter of Coleman street*,[2] a silly play. And thence to Westminster-hall, where I met Fitzgerald; and with him to a tavern to consider of the instructions for Sir Tho. Allen against his going to Algier, he and I being designed to go

a repl. 'home'   *b* repl. 'answer'

---

1. The Algerian authorities had complained that the English at Tangier had refused them watering facilities, and had protected ships of powers with which they were at war: Allin, vol. ii, pp. xxxviii, 46–7; Routh, p. 134. John Creed was secretary to the Tangier committee. Pepys's mem-orandum has not been traced.

2. Abraham Cowley's revision of an earlier play of his, *The Guardian*; q.v. above, ii. 234, n. 3. (A).

down to Portsmouth by the Council's order;[1] and by and by he and I went to the Duke of York, who orders me to go down tomorrow morning; so I away home and there bespeak a coach; and so home and to bed, my wife being abroad with the Mercers, walking in the fields and upon the water.

6. Wake betimes; and my wife, at an hour's warning, is resolved to go with me; which pleases me, her readiness. But before ready, comes a letter from Fitzgerald that he is seized upon last night by an order of the Generalls by a file of musqueteers, and kept prisoner[a] in his chamber. The Duke of York did tell me of it today; it is about a quarrel between him and Witham, and they fear a challenge.[2] So I to him, and sent my wife by the coach round to Lambeth. I lost my labour, going to his lodgings and he in bed; and staying a great while for him, I at last grew impatient and would stay no longer; but to St. James's to Mr. Wren to bid him God be with you, and so over the water to Fox-hall; and there my wife and Deb comes and took me up, and we away to Gilford, losing our way for three or four mile about Cobham. At Gilford[b] we dined, and I showed them the Hospitall there of Bishop Abbot's,[3] and his tomb in the

a repl. 'up'   b name blotted

---

1. Allin's instructions had been revised by the Privy Council on this day. He was to compose the disputes between Algiers and Tangier and to confirm the peace he had made with Algiers in 1664: PRO, PC 2/60, ff. 410, 416. The Council's order about the journey mentions Fitzgerald (late Deputy-Governor of Tangier) but not Pepys. Cf. Tanner 44, ff. 116–18; Allin, ii. 33; *CSPD 1667-8*, p. 531; *Bulstrode Papers*, i. 53–4. Allin sailed from St Helen's Road on 16 August and renewed the peace with Algiers on 30 October.

2. Both had served in the Tangier garrison. Fitzgerald had been Deputy-Governor until 1666; Witham, a cavalry captain now back in England to bring a report on the state of the fortifications and the mole, had been made redundant by the reduction of the garrison in March 1668. PRO, SP 29/253, f. 41*v*; Routh, pp. 313–14 & n.

3. The Hospital of The Blessed Trinity, on the n. side of High St.; founded (1619–22) by George Abbot (d. 1633), Archbishop of Canterbury and a native of the town.

church; which, and the rest of the tombs there, are kept mighty
clean and neat, with curtains before them.[1]　So to coach again
and got to Lippock late, over Hindehead, having an old man a
guide in the coach with us; but got thither with great fear of
being out of our way, it being 10 at night.　Here, good honest
people; and after supper, to bed.　This day yo did first with my[a]
hand tocar la cosa[a] de our Deb in the coach – ella being troubled
at it – but yet did give way to it.　To bed.

7.　Up, and to coach and with a guide to Petersfield, where I
find Sir Tho. Allen and Mr. Tippets[b][2] come; the first about the
business, the latter only in respect to me – as also Fitzgerald, who
came post all last night, and newly arrived here.　We four sat
down presently to our business, and in an hour despatch all our
talk and did inform Sir Tho. Allen well in it; who I perceive,
in serious matters is a serious man – and tells me he wishes all
we are told be true in our defence; for he finds by all, that the
Turkes have to this day been very civil to our merchantmen
everywhere;[3] and if they would have broke with us, they never
had such an opportunity over our rich merchantmen as lately,
coming out of the Streights.　Then to dinner, and pretty merry;
and here was Mr. Martin the purser – and dined with us and
wrote some things for us.　And so took coach again back,
Fitzgerald with us; whom I was pleased with all the day with his
discourse of his observations abroad, as being a great soldier and
of long standing abroad and knows all things and persons abroad
very well, I mean the great soldiers of France and Spain and
Germany, and talks very well.　Came at night to Gilfford, where
the Red Lyon[4] so full of people, and a wedding, that the maister

a–a　garbled s.h.: see above, viii. 244, note a　　　　b　repl. 'P'-

1. For the tombs in Holy Trinity
church, opposite the Hospital, see
I. Nairn and N. Pevsner (rev. Cherry),
Buildings of Engl.: Surrey, pp. 271–2.
Abbot's large marble tomb was designed by Gerard Christmas and
erected in 1640.

2. John Tippetts was Master-Ship-
wright (later, from February 1669,
Commissioner) at Portsmouth.

3. Cf. Sir Godfrey Fisher, *Barbary
Legend*, esp. p. 241.

4. See above, ii. 94, n. 1.

of the house did get us a lodging over the way at a private house, his landlord, mighty neat and fine; and there supped and talked with the landlord and his wife; and so to bed – with great content – Fitzgerald lay at the Inne. So to bed.

8. Up, and I walked out and met Uncle Wight (whom I sent to last night) and Mr. Wight coming to see us; and I walked with them back to see my aunt at Katherine hill,[1] and there walked up and down the Hill and places about; but a dull place, but good ayre – and the house dull. But here I saw my aunt after many days not seeing her, I think a year or two, and she walked with me to see my wife; and here at the Red Lyon we all dined together, and mighty merry; and then parted, and we home to Fox-hall, where Fitzgerald and I light, and by water to White-hall; where, the Duke of York being abroad, I by coach and met my wife, who went round; and after doing at the office a little, and finding all well at home, I to bed.

I hear that Colbert the French Imbassador is come, and hath been at Court incognito. When he hath his audience, I know not.[2]

9. *Lords day.* Up, and walked to Holborne, where got John Powell's[3] coach at the Black Swan, and he attended me to St. James's, where waited on the Duke of York; and[a] both by him and several of the Privy-Council, beyond expectation, I find that

a repl. 'of'

---

1. Uncle Wight (half-brother of Pepys's father) had a house at St Catherine's Hill, nr Guildford. 'Mr. Wight' was possibly his son William.

2. Charles Colbert, Marquis de Croissy, was ambassador-extraordinary, later ambassador-in-ordinary, until 1674. He had now taken up residence at Leicester House: *Bulstrode Papers*, i. 54. His official audience did not take place until 19 August: *CSP Ven. 1666–8*, p. 252. This incognito visit (the first of two)

excited the suspicion that France was anxious to break up the understanding between England and Holland and could not wait for the formalities of public entry and public audience to be completed before making a *démarche*: ib., pp. 250, 251, 252–3. His instructions were dated 2 August; for his arrival, see *CSPD 1667–8*, p. 531; for his public entry, see below, pp. 281–2 & n.

3. Navy Office messenger.

my going to Sir Tho. Allen was looked upon as a thing necessary, and I have got some advantage by it among them. Thence to White-hall and thence to visit Lord Brouncker; and back to White-hall, where saw the Queen and ladies; and so with Mr. Slingsby to Mrs.*ᵃ* Williams's, thinking to dine with Lord Brouncker there but did not, having promised my wife to come home; though here I met Knipp to my great content. So home; and after dinner, I took wife and Deb round by Hackny, and up and down to take the ayre; and then home and made visits to Mrs. Turner and Mrs. Mercer and Sir W. Penn, who is come from Epsum not well, and Sir J. Mennes, who is not well neither. And so home to supper and to set my books a little right, and then to bed. This day, Betty Michell came and dined with us, the first day after her lying in – whom I was glad to see.

10. Up, and by water to White-hall, and thence to Sir W. Coventry, but he is gone out of town this morning; so thence to my Lord Arlington's house,*ᵇ* the first time I there since he came thither, at Goring-house, a very fine noble place;[1] and there he received [me] in sight of several Lords with great respect. I did give him an account of my journey. And here, while I waited for him a little, my Lord Orery took notice of me, and begun discourse of hangings and of the improvement of shipping: I not thinking that he knew me, but did then discover it, with a mighty compliment of my abilities and ingenuity – which I am mighty proud of; and he doth speak most excellently. Thence to Westminster-hall, and so by coach to the Old Exchange and there did several businesses; and so home to dinner, and then abroad to Duck-lane, where I saw my belle femme of the book-vendor[2] but had no opportunity para hablar con her;*ᶜ* so away to Coopers, where I spent all the afternoon with my wife and girl, seeing him make an end of her picture; which he did to my

a repl. 'Lord Brouncker's'　　　*b* repl. 'lodg'-
　　　　　c garbled s.h.

1. The house (standing roughly where Buckingham Palace now stands) had been bought by Arlington on his marriage in 1665. Pepys had visited it on 12 July 1666. It was burnt down in 1674 and rebuilt.

2. See above, p. 260, n. 4.

great content, though not so great as, I confess, I expected, being not satisfied in the greatness of the resemblance – nor*a* in the blue garment; but [it] is most certainly a most rare piece of work as to the painting.¹ He hath 30*l* for his*b* work, and the crystal and case and gold*c* case comes to 8*l*–3*s*–4*d*; and which I sent him this night, that I might be out of debt. Thence, my people home and I to*d* Westminster-hall about a little business; and so by water home, supper, and my wife to read a ridiculous book I bought today, of the history of the Taylors Company;² and all the while Deb. did comb my head and I did tocar her with my mano*e* para mi great*e* pleasure; and so to bed.

11. Up, and by water to Sir W. Coventry to visit him, whom I find yet troubled at the Commissioners of Accounts about this business of Sir W. Warren;³ which is a ridiculous thing – and can come to nothing but contempt. And thence to West-minster-hall, where the Parliament met enough to adjourne, which they did, to*f* the 10th of November next;⁴ and so I by water home to the office, and so to dinner; and thence at the office all the afternoon till night, being*g* mightily pleased with a little trial I have made of the use of a Tube=spectacall of paper, tried with my right eye. This day, I hear that to the great joy of the nonconformists, the time is out of the Act against them, so that they may meet;⁵ and they have declared that they will

a repl. 'but is'   *b* repl. 'the'   *c* repl. 'silver'
      d 'I to' repeated   *e–e* garbled s.h.
f preceded by blot   *g* repl. 'and so a little abroad'

---

1. See above, p. 138, n. 3. (OM).

2. William Winstanley, *The honour of Merchant-Taylors, wherein is set forth the noble acts, valliant deeds, and heroick performances of Merchant-Taylors in former ages. Their honourable loves, and knightly adventures* . . . (1668). Pepys retained it, bound in a volume of what he entitled his *Vulgaria*; PL 1193 (13).

3. See above, p. 254 & n. 1.

4. *CJ*, ix. 97.

5. The Conventicle Act of 1664 was due to expire at the end of this parliamentary session. The King did not in fact end the session until 1 March 1669, but no further meetings of parliament were held. Noncon-formists in London now met fairly freely until the summer of 1669: cf. below, pp. 385, 501–2 & nn.; M. Sylvester, *Reliq. Baxt.* (1696), bk i, pt iii. 22; Rugge, ii, f. 225*v*; BM, Add. 36916, f. 107.

have a morning lecture¹ up again, which is pretty strange; and
they are connived*ᵃ* at by the King everywhere I hear, in city
and country. So to visit W Penn, who is yet ill; and then
home, where W Batelier and Mrs. Turner came and sat and
supped with us; and so they gone, we to bed.

This afternoon, my wife and Mercer and Deb went with
Pelling to see the Gipsys at Lambeth and have their fortunes told;
but what they did, I did not enquire.²

12. Up, and all the morning busy at my office. Thence to
the Excise Office, and so to the Temple to take counsel about
Major Nicholls's business for the King.³ So to several places
about business; and among others, to Dromblebys about the
molds for my paper*ᵇ* Tubes,⁴ and so to the Change and home.
Met Captain Cocke, who tells me that he hears for certain the
Duke of York will lose the authority of an Admiral and be
governed by a Committee,⁵ and all our Office changed; only,
they are in dispute whether I shall continue or no – which puts
new thoughts in me, but know not whether to be glad or sorry.
Home to dinner, where Pelling dines with us and brings some
patriges with him, very good meat; and after dinner, I and wife
and Mercer and Deb to the Duke of York's House and saw
Mackbeth,⁶ to our great content; and then home, where the

a repl. 'conv'-   b MS. 'taper'

---

1. A service consisting mostly of
a sermon and beginning often at
6 a.m. Lectures had been a popular
form of worship among city puritans
in the 1650s. According to one
report, this lecture had already been
revived some weeks earlier – taking
'its course round the City, staying a
fortnight at a place': newsletter (4
July) in BM, Add. 36916, loc. cit.

2. Norwood, in Lambeth parish,
was a favourite resort of gipsies until
the late 19th century. 'Gipsy Hill'
preserves the memory.

3. Maj. Henry Nicolls had in May
contracted with the Board to clear the
Medway of the wrecks sunk there in
1667 as part of the river's defences.
Disputes had arisen about the work.
See NWB, pp. 109–10; *CSPD
1667–8*, passim, esp. p. 401.

4. The tubes were for his eyes:
above, p. 270 & n. 2. Drumbleby
was a maker of flageolets etc.

5. The Duke was not replaced by a
commission until the Test Act forced
his resignation in 1673.

6. Probably Davenant's adaptation:
see above, v. 314, n. 3. (A).

women went to the making of my Tubes, and I to the office; and then comes Mrs. Turner and her husband to advise about their son the Chaplain,[1] who is turned out of his ship, a sorrow to them; which I am troubled for, and do give them the best advice I can; and so they gone, we to bed.

13. Up, and Greeting comes and there he and I tried some things of Mr. Lockes for two flagelettes,[2] to my great content; and this day my wife begins again to learn of him,[3] for I have a great mind for her to be able to play a part with me. Thence I to the office, where all the morning*a*; and then to dinner, where W How dined with me, who tells me for certain that Creed is like to speed in his match with Mrs. Betty Pickering. Here dined with me also Mr. Hollier, who is mighty vain in his pretence to talk Latin. So to the office again all the afternoon till night, very busy; and so with much content home at night, and made my wife sing and play on the*b* flagelette to me till I slept with great pleasure in bed.

14. Up, and by water to White-hall and St. James's, and to see W. Coventry and discourse about business of our office, telling him my trouble there to see how things are ordered. I told him also what Cocke told me the other day;[4] but he says there is not much in it, though he doth know that this hath been in the eye of some persons to compass, for the turning all things in the Navy; and that it looks so like a popular thing, as that he thinks something may be done in it; but*c* whether so general or no as I tell it him, he knows not.

Thence to White-hall and there wait at the Council-chamber door a good while, talking with one or other; and so home by water, though but for a little while, because I am to return to White-hall. At home, I*d* find Symson putting up my new

---

a MS. 'afternoon'   *b* blot above symbol
c repl. 'wh'-   *d* repl. 'my'

---

1. Probably Thomas Turner, jun. His father was a senior clerk at the Navy Office.
2. Possibly from PL 2065–7. (E).
3. Cf. above, pp. 25, 94. (E).
4. About the appointment of an Admiralty commission: above, p. 278 & n. 5.

chimney-piece[1] in our great chamber; which is very fine, but
will cost great deal*a* of money; but it is not flung away.

So back to White-hall; and after the council up, I with Mr.
Wren by invitation to Sir St. Fox's to dinner, where the Cofferer
and Sir Edw. Savage – where many good stories of the antiquity
and estates of many families at this day in Cheshire[2] and that
part of the kingdom, more then what is on this side near London.

My Lady dined with us; a very good lady, and a family
governed so nobly and neatly as doth me good to see it.

Thence, the Cofferer, Sir Steph. and I to the Commissioners of
the Treasury about business;[3] and so I up to the Duke of York,
who enquired for what I had promised him about my observations of the miscarriages of our office; and I told him he should
have it next week, being glad he called for it; for I find he is
concerned to do something, and to secure himself thereby I
believe; for the world is labouring to eclipse him I doubt; I
mean, the factious part of the Parliament. The office met this
afternoon as usual, and waited on him; where among*b* other
things, he talked a great while of his intentions of going to Dover
soon, to be sworn as Lord Warden, which is a matter of great
ceremony and state.[4] And so I to the Temple with Mr. Wren
to the Atturney's chamber about business, but he abroad; and so
I home and there spent the evening talking with my wife and
piping, and pleased with our chimney-piece; and so to bed.

15. Up, and to the office, where all the morning busy. After
dinner, with my wife, Mercer and Deb to the King's play-

---

a repl. 'dead'   *b* MS. 'like'

---

1. Cf. above, p. 266.

2. This was a boast frequently
repeated: see e.g. W. Camden,
Britannia (1695 ed.), p. 555; Defoe,
Tour (ed. Cole), p. 472. Savage
(Gentleman of the Privy Chamber)
came of a prolific Cheshire family.

3. See *CTB*, ii. 413.

4. He had been appointed Lord
Warden of the Cinque Ports and
Constable of Dover Castle in 1660,
but was not sworn in until 3 September 1668. On that day the Lord-
Lieutenant of Kent and a force of the
county militia attended him to Dover
where the ceremony of installation
was held in a tent: *CSPD 1667-8*,
p. 574; *London Gazette*, 3 September.

house, and there saw *Love's Mistresse*[1] revived; the thing pretty good, but full of variety of divertisement. So home and to my business at the office, my eyes bad again; and so to bed.

16. *Lords day.* All the morning at my[a] office with W. Hewer, there drawing up my report to the Duke of York, as[b] I have promised, about the faults of this office, hoping therein to have opportunity of doing myself [some good]. At noon to dinner; and again with him, to work all the afternoon till night, till I was weary and had despatched a good deal of business. And so to bed, after hearing my wife read a little.

17. Up, and by water to White-hall, and so to St. James's; and thence with Mr. Wren by appointment in his coach to Hamsted, to speak with the Atturny general, whom we met in the fields by his old route and house.[2] And after a little talk about[c] our business of Ackeworth,[3] went and saw the Lord Wotton's house and garden, which is wonderful fine; too good for the house, the gardens are; being endeed the most noble that ever I saw – and rare Orange and lemon trees.[4] Thence to Mr. Chichly's[5] by invitation, and there dined with Sir John, his father not coming home. And while at dinner, comes by the French Embassador Colbert's Mules (the first I ever saw) with their sumpter-cloths mighty rich, and his coaches, he being to have his entry today; but his things, though rich, are not new – supposed to be the same his brother had the other day at the

---

a repl. 'the'   *b* blot below symbol   *c* repl. 'between'

---

1. An allegorical drama by Thomas Heywood; see above, ii. 48, n. 2. (A).

2. The Attorney-General was Sir Geoffrey Palmer; for his house and manor at Hampstead, see PCC, Penn, 81.

3. See above, p. 123, n. 4.

4. Evelyn (2 June 1676) described the gardens as 'very large, but ill kept'. The house was Belsize House,

an Elizabethan mansion rebuilt soon after 1660 by the rich Irish courtier Daniel O'Neill, and leased since 1667 to his stepson Lord Wotton. It was pulled down shortly after 1745. D. Lysons, *Environs* (1792–1811), ii. 532+, v. 179–80; J. J. Park, *Topog. Hampstead* (1818), pp. 136+; J. Kennedy, *Hampstead*, pp. 27–8.

5. In Great Queen St.

treaty at Aix la chapelle in Flanders.[1]   Thence to the Duke of York's house and there saw *Cupid's Revenge*, under the new name of *Love despised*;[2]   that hath something very good in it, though I like not the whole body of it.   This day, the first time acted here.   Thence home and there with Mr. Hater and W. Hewer late, reading over all the Principal Officers' instructions[3] in order to my great work upon my hand.   And so to bed – my eyes very ill.

18.   Up, and to my[a] office about my great business betimes. And so to the office, where all the morning.   At noon dined; and then to the office all the afternoon also; and in the evening to Sir W. Coventry's; but he not within, I took coach alone to the park to try to meet him there, but did not; but there was few coaches, but among the few, there was in two coaches our two great beauties, my Lady Castlemaine and Richmond; the first time I saw the latter since she had the smallpox.   I had much pleasure to see them, but I thought they were strange one to another.   Thence going out, I met a coach going which I thought had Knipp in it; so I went back, but it was not she. So back to White-hall and there took water, and so home and busy late about my great letter to the Duke of York.   And so to supper and to bed.   This night yo did hazer Deb[b] tocar mi thing with her hand[b] after yo was in lecto – with great pleasure.

a   repl. 'the'   b–b   garbled s.h.

---

1. A mistake: Charles Colbert, Marquis de Croissy, had himself been the French plenipotentiary at Aix. (His brother Jean-Baptiste Colbert, was Louis XIV's principal adviser.) His state entry (described e.g. in *CSP Ven. 1666–8*, p. 252) took the usual form of a journey by royal barge from Greenwich to the Tower, followed by a procession of coaches through the principal streets to his residence at Leicester House. The affair was complete even to a punctili-ous dispute about the order of precedence for the coaches.   There were six sumpter mules with bells: *CSPD 1667–8*, p. 540.

2. *Cupid's Revenge* is a tragedy by Beaumont and Fletcher, written c. 1608 and published in 1615.   This is the first record of a post-Restoration performance.   Downes (p. 29) notes the revival but not the new name. (A).

3. See above, iii. 24, n. 1.

19. Up betimes; and all day and afternoon, without going out, busy upon my great letter to the Duke of York, which goes on to my content. W Hewer and Gibson I imploy with me in it. This week my people wash over the water,[1] and so I little company at home. In the evening, being busy above, a*a* great cry I hear, and go down; and what should it be but Jane, in a fit of direct raveing which lasted half-an-hour; beyond four or five of our strength to keep her down. And when all came to all, a fit ,of jealousy about Tom, with whom she is in love. So at night, I and my wife*b* and W Hewer called them to us, and there I did examine all the thing, and them in league. She in love,*c* and he hath got her to promise him*d* to marry, and he is now cold in it – so that I must rid my hands of them. Which troubles me, and the more because my head is now busy upon other greater things. I am vexed also to be told by W Hewer that he is summoned to Commissioners of Accounts about receiving a present of 30*l* from Mr. Mason the timber merchant[2] – though there be no harm in it that will appear on his part – he having done them several lawful kindnesses and never demanded anything, as they themselfs have this day declared to the Commissioners, they being forced up by the discovery of somebody that they in confidence had once told it to. So to supper, vexed and my head full of care; and so to bed.

20. Betimes at my business again. And so to office, and dined with Brouncker and J. Mennes at Sir W. Penn's at a bad pasty of venison;*e* and so to work again, and at it till past 12 at night, that I might get my great letter to the Duke of York ready against tomorrow; which I shall do, to my great content. So to bed.

21. Up betimes and with my people again to work, and finished all before noon; and then I by water to White-hall and

---

a repl. 'comes'   *b* MS. 'night and I wife'   *c* MS. 'and love'
      d MS. 'her'   *e* repl. 'venson'

---

1. At Lambeth: cf. above, viii.   2. Cf. above, p. 90 & n. 3.
383 & n. 5.

there did tell the Duke of York that I had done; and he hath to my great content desired[a] me to come to him at Sunday next in the afternoon to read it over, by which I have more time to consider and correct it.   So back home and to the Change, in my way calling at Morris's my vinter's, where I love to see su moher, though no acquaintance hasta this day[b] con her.[b]   Did several things at the Change, and so home to dinner.

After dinner, I by coach to my bookseller's in Duck-lane and there did spend a little time and regarder su moher;[c1] and so to St. James's, where did a little ordinary business; and by and by comes Monsieur Colbert the French Imbassador to make his first visit to the Duke of York, and then to the Duchess.[2]   And I saw it: a silly piece of ceremony, he saying only a few formal words. A comely man, and in a black suit and cloak of silk; which is a strange fashion now, it hath been so long left off.[3]   This day I did first see the Duke of York's room of pictures of some Maids of Honour, done by Lilly; good,[d] but not like.[4]   Thence to Reeves and bought a reading-glass; and so to my bookseller's again, there to buy a *Book of Martyrs*,[5] which I did agree for;

---

a repl. 'bid'   *b–b* garbled s.h.
c repl. symbol rendered illegible   *d* repl. 'was of'

---

1. See above, p. 260, n. 4.

2. The Venetian resident enviously noted the number of audiences accorded to his French colleague. On this day, he had already had a long audience of the King and Queen. Colbert achieved this by bringing letters from the Queen Mother addressed to the Queen and the Duchess: *CSP Ven. 1666–8*, pp. 252, 256. These formal visits occurred several days after the incognito visits at which the real business of the embassy was broached.

3. Cloaks had been out of fashion in England (except for riding) since the Restoration.

4. This set of portraits of court beauties was commissioned by the Duchess of York and had probably been painted by Lely c. 1662–5. In June 1674 they were hanging in the White Room at Whitehall: MS. Bodl. 891, f 7v. The series now consists of ten canvases, but may have originally contained a portrait of the Duchess's sister Frances. For many years the portraits hung at Windsor, but they have been at Hampton Court since at least June 1835. See O. Millar, *Tudor, Stuart and early Georgian pictures in coll. H.M. Queen* (1962), nos 257–66.   (OM).

5. John Foxe's *Acts and monuments*, usually known as his *Book of martyrs*, was first published in 1562–3. This copy was probably PL 2536–8 (1641, folio).

and so after seeing and beginning acquaintance con his*ᵃ* femme,*ᵃ* but very little, away home; and there busy very late at the correcting my great letter to the Duke of York; and so to bed.

22. Up betimes, at it again with great content, and so to office I, where all the morning; and did fall out with W. Penn about his slight performance of his office; and so home to dinner, fully satisfied that this office must sink or the whole service be undone. To the office all the afternoon again; and then home to supper and to bed, my mind being pretty well at ease, my great letter being now finished to my full content; and I thank God I have opportunity of doing it, though I know it will set the office and me by the ears for ever.

This morning Captain Cocke comes and tells me that he is now assured that it is true what he told me the other day, that our whole office will be turned out, only me; which, whether he says true or no, I know not nor am much concerned, though I should be better contented to have it thus then otherwise.

This afternoon, after I was weary in my business of the office, I went forth to the Change, thinking to have spoke with Captain Cocke, but he was not within. So I home, and took London-bridge in my way, walking down Fish-street and Gracious-street to see how very fine a descent they have now made down the hill, that it is become very easy and pleasant.[1] And going through Leaden-hall, it being market-day, I did see a woman ketched that had stolen a shoulder of mutton off of a butcher's stall, and carrying it wrapped up in a cloth in a basket. The jade was surprized, and did not deny it; and the woman so silly that took it as to let her go, only taking the meat.

23. *Lords day.* Up betimes, my head busy on my great letter,

---

a–a garbled s.h.

---

1. The gradient of the streets running northwards from Thames St between Tower Dock and St And- rew's Hill was reduced: see T. F. Reddaway, *Rebuilding of London*, p. 291.

and I did first hang up my new map of Paris[1] in my green room –
and changed others in other places.   Then to Captain Cocke's,
thinking to have talked more of what he told me yesterday, but
he was not within; so back to church and heard a good sermon of
Mr. Gifford's at our church, upon "Seek ye first the Kingdom of
Heaven and its righteousness, and all these things shall be added
to you."[2]   A very excellent and persuasive, good and moral
sermon; showed[a] like a wise man that righteousness is a surer
moral way of being rich then sin and villainy.   Then home to
dinner, where Mr. Pelling, who brought us a hare, which we had
at dinner, and W How.   After dinner to the office, Mr. Gibson
and I, to examine my letter to the Duke of York; which to my
great joy, I did very well by my paper tube, without pain to my
eyes.   And I do mightily like what I have therein done; [and]
did, according to the Duke of York's order, make haste to St.
James'; and about 4 a-clock got thither, and there the Duke of
York was ready to expect me, and did hear it all over with extraordinary content and did give me many and hearty thanks, and in
words the most expressive tell me his sense of my good endeavours, and that he would have a care of me on all occasions, and did
with much inwardness tell me what was doing, suitable almost to
what Captain[b] Cocke tells me, of design to make alterations in
the Navy; and is most open to me in them, and with utmost
confidence desires my further advice on all occasions.   And he
resolves to have my letter transcribed and sent forthwith to the
office.[3]   So, with as much satisfaction as I could possibly or did
hope for, and obligation on the Duke of York's side professed to
me, I away into the park, and there met Mr. Pierce and his
wife and sister and brother and little boy, and with them to
Mullbery-garden and spent 18s on them; and there left them, she
being again with child, and by it, the least pretty that ever I saw

a   MS. 'should'   b   repl. 'of'

---

1. Possibly the 1665 edition of
Gomboust's map (q.v. above, vii. 379
& n. 2).

2. A loose recollection of Luke, xii.

31. George Gifford was Rector of
St Dunstan-in-the-East, and Professor
of Divinity at Gresham College.

3. See below, p. 289 & n. 1.

her; and so I away and got a coach and home; and there with wife and W Hewers talking all the evening, my mind running on the business of the office, to see what more I can do to the rendering myself acceptable and useful to all and to the King: we to supper and to bed.

24. Up, and to the office, where all the morning upon considerations on the Victualler's contract; and then home to dinner, where my wife is upon hanging the long chamber, where the girl lies, with the sad stuff that was in the best chamber, in order to the hanging that with tapestry; and so to dinner and then to the office again – where all the afternoon, till night, we met to discourse upon the alterations which are propounded to be made in the draft of the victualler's contract which we did lately make.[1] And then we being up, there comes Mr. Child, Papillion and Littleton, his parteners, to discourse upon this matter with me; which I did, and spent all the evening*a* with them at the office; and so they being gone, I home to supper and talk with my wife, and so to bed.

25. Up, and by water to St. James's and there with Mr. Wren did discourse about my great letter; which the Duke of York hath given him and he hath set it to be transcribed by Billup his man, whom, as he tells me, he can most confide in for secrecy. And is much pleased with it, and earnest to have it with us; and he and I are like to be much together in the considering how to reform the Office, and that by the Duke of York's command. Thence I, mightily pleased with this success, away to the*b* office, where all the morning, my head full of this business; and it is pretty how Lord Brouncker this day did tell me how he hears that a design is on foot to remove us out of the office, and proposes that we two do agree to draw up a form of a new constitution of the

a repl. 'm'-
b repl. 'Lord Brouncker, who I find within and doth not intend'

---

1. The contract was to be put to tender, and several of the competitors had objected to certain clauses in the Navy Board's draft: *CTB*, ii. 420 (20 August).

office, there*ᵃ* to provide remedies for the evils we are now under, that so we may be beforehand with the world – which I agreed to, saying nothing of my design.   And the truth is, he is the best man of them all, and I would be glad, next myself, to save him; for as he deserves best, so I doubt he needs his place most.   So home to dinner at noon, and all the afternoon busy at the office till night;   and then, with my mind full of businesses now in my head, I to supper and to bed.

26.   Up, and to the office, where all the morning almost, busy about business against the afternoon;   and we met a little, to sign two or three things at the Board of moment.   And thence at*ᵇ* noon home to dinner, and so away to White-hall by water, in my way to the Old Swan finding a great many people gathered together in Cannon-street*ᶜ* about a man that was working in the ruins, and the*ᵈ* ground did sink under him, and he sunk in and was forced to be dug out again, but without hurt.   Thence to White-hall;   and it is strange to see with what speed the people imployed do pull down Paul's steeple* – and with what ease.   It is said that it and the Quire are to be taken down this year, and another church begun in the room thereof the next.[1]   At White-hall we met at the Treasury-chamber, and there before the Lords did debate our draft of the victualling contract with the several bidders for it – which were Sir D. Gawden – Mr. Child and his fellows, and Mr. Dorrington and his – a poor variety in a business of this value.[2]   There till after candle-lighting, and so home by coach with Sir D Gawden, who by the way tells me how the

a   blot below symbol
b   repl. 'I to White-hall to the Council-chamber'
c   MS. 'Cannot street'   d   repl. 'his'

1. On 25 July 1668 a royal warrant had been issued for the demolition of what remained of the old East end, choir and Tower down to the line of the foundations, on which a temporary choir was to be built: Sir W. Dugdale, *Hist. St Paul's* (ed. Ellis, 1818), p. 129; J. Lang, *Rebuilding St Paul's*, p. 41.   The building of Wren's church was begun in 1673 and ended in 1716.

2. The Board was now directed to alter certain details of their draft contract and to meet the Treasury Commissioners and the merchants again: *CTB*, ii. 423.

City doth go on in several things toward the building of the public places; which I am glad to hear, and gives hope that in a few years it will be a glorious place. But we met with several stops and new troubles in the way in the streets, so as makes it bad to travel in the dark now through the City. So I to Mr. Bateliers by appointment, where I find my wife and Deb and Mercer – Mrs. Pierce and her husband, son and daughter; and Knipp and Harris; and W. Batelier and his sister Mary and cousin Gumbleton, a good-humoured, fat young gentleman, son to the Jeweller, that dances well. And here danced all night long, with a noble supper; and about 2 in the morning, the table spread again for a noble breakfast, beyond all moderation, that put me out of countenance – so much and so good. Mrs. Pierce and her people went home betimes, she being big with child; but ⟪27⟫ Knipp and the rest stayed till almost 3 in the morning, and then broke up and Knipp home with us; and I to bed and rose about 6 – mightily pleased with this night's mirth; and away by water to St. James's and there with Mr. Wren did correct his copy of my letter; which the Duke of York hath signed in my very words, without alteration of a syllable.[1] And so, pleased therewith, I to my Lord Brouncker, who I find within, but hath business and so comes not to the office today; and so I by water to the office, where we sat all the morning; and just as the Board rises, comes the Duke of York's letter; which I knowing, and the Board not being full and desiring rather to have the Duke of York deliver himself to*a* us, I suppressed it for this day,

a blot above symbol

---

1. This letter (Duke of York to Navy Board, 26 August) is one of Pepys's most masterly compositions, and proved to be the starting-point of several reforms. It traced the roots of maladministration to the failure of Principal Officers to observe the Duke's Instructions of 1662, and blamed particularly the Comptroller (first and foremost), the Treasurer and the Surveyor. Pepys did not attribute any specific faults to himself. The Duke altered nothing in the draft beyond omitting a single phrase. Copies both of the draft and of the letter (with its covering letter) are in PL 2242, pp. 25+ (in Gibson's hand) and PL 2867, pp. 484+ (in Hayter's). Other copies are in Adm. Lib. MS. 9, ff. 54+; BM, Harl. 6003, ff. 146+; ib. 6287, ff. 35+; Add. 36782, ff. 70+; HMC, *Portland*, ii. 106; ib., iii. 307. For a summary, see *Cat.*, i. 28–31.

my heart beginning to falsify in this business – as being doubtful
of the trouble it may give me by provoking them; but however,
I am resolved to go through it, and it is too late to help it now.
At noon to dinner to Captain Cocke's, where I met with Mr.
Wren, my going being to tell him what I have done; which he
likes – and to confer*a* with Cocke about our office; who tells me
that he is confident the design of removing our officers doth
hold, but that he is sure that I am safe enough – which pleases me;
though I do not much show it to him, but as a thing indifferent.
So away home, and there met at Sir Rd. Ford's with the Duke of
York's Commissioners about our prizes,[1] with whom we shall
have some trouble before*b* we make an end with them.   And
thence, staying a little with them, I with my wife and W Batelier*c*
and Deb; carried them to Bartholomew fayre,[2] where we saw
the dancing of the ropes and nothing else, it being late; and so
back home to supper and to bed – after having done at my*a*
office.

28. Busy at the office till towards 10 a-clock; and then by
water to White-hall, where attending the Council's call all the
morning with Lord Brouncker, W. Penn, and the rest, about the
business of supernumerarys*e* in the fleet[3] – but were not called in.
But here the Duke of York did call me aside and told me that
he must speak with me in the afternoon with Mr. Wren, for
that now he hath got the paper from my Lord Keeper about the
exceptions taken against the management of the Navy,[4] and so
we are to debate upon answering them.   At noon, I home with
W. Coventry to his house and there dined with him, and talked
freely with him and did acquaint him with what I have done;
which [he] is well pleased with and glad of – and doth tell me that

a   repl. same symbol badly formed   *b*   repl. 'again'
c   repl. 'Mercer'   *d*   repl. same symbol badly formed
e   l.h. repl. s.h. 'super'–

---

1. I.e. those taken by the privateer
the *Flying Greyhound.* The Duke's
commissioners (governing his household and finances) were concerned to
collect the Admiral's 'tenths' due to
him.

2. See above, ii. 166, n. 2.
3. This concerned the payment of
the summer fleet. The papers are
summarised in *CSPD 1667-8,* pp.
553–4; see below, p. 350 & n. 4.
4. See below, pp. 291–2 & n.

there are endeavours on foot to bring the navy into new, but he fears worse hands. After much talk with great content with him, I walked to the Temple and stayed at Starky's my bookseller's (looking over Dr. Heylins new book of the life of Bishop Laud, a strange book of the church history of his time)[1] till Mr. Wren comes by, and by appointment we to Atturny Generalls chamber and there read and heard the witnesses in the business of Ackeworth,[2] most troublesome, and perplexed by the counterswearing of the witnesses one against the other. And so with Mr. Wren away thence to St. [James's] for his papers, and so to White-hall; and after the Committee was done at the Councilchamber about the business of supernumerarys, wherein W. Penn was to do all, and did, but like an ignorant illiterate coxcomb – the Duke of York fell to work with us (the Committee being gone) in the Council-chamber; and there with his own hand did give us his long letter, telling us that he had received several from us, and now did give us one from him, taking notice of our several duties and failures; and desired answer to it,[a] as he therein desired. This pleased me well. And so fell to other business and then parted; and the Duke of York and Wren and I, it being now candle-light, into the Duke of York's closet in Whitehall[b] and there read over this paper of my[c] Lord Keeper's; wherein is laid down the faults of the Navy,* so silly and the remedies so ridiculous, or[d] else the same that are now already provided, that we thought it not to need any answer, the Duke of York being

a repl. 'do'   b blot above symbol
c MS. 'Lord'   d repl. 'and'

1. Peter Heylyn's posthumous *Cyprianus Anglicus, or The history of the life and death of William Laud, Archbishop of Canterbury* (1668); PL 2222. In the Introduction he defended Laudianism, justifying ceremonies, confession and absolution. On p. 4 he quoted with approval James I's aphorism: 'That no Church ought further to separate it self from the Church of Rome, either in Doctrine or ceremony, then she had

departed from her self, when she was in her flourishing and best estate.' Heylyn had already published two sharp attacks on Fuller's *Church History* of which Pepys was so fond. Pepys bought this book and had it read to him in November: for his later comments, see below, pp. 308, 379.

2. The Woolwich storekeeper accused of embezzlement: above, p. 123 & n. 4.

able himself to do it[1] – that so it makes us admire* the confidence
of these men to offer things so silly, in a business of such moment.
But it is a most perfect instance of the complexions of the times,
and so the Duke of York said himself – who I perceive is mightily
concerned in it – and doth again and again recommend it to Mr.
Wren and me together, to consider upon remedies fit to provide
for him to propound to the King, before the rest of the world,
and perticularly the Commissioners of Accounts, who are men of
understanding and order, do[a] find our faults and offer remedies
of their own – which I am glad of, and[b] will endeavour to do
something in it.[2]   So parted, and with much difficulty by candle-
light walked over the Matted Gallery, as it is now, with the
mats and boards all taken up, so that we walk over the rafters.[3]
But strange to see what hard matter the plaster of paris[c] is that is
there taken up, as hard as stone – and pity to see Holben's work
in the ceiling[4] blotted on, and only whited over.   Thence, with
much ado, by several coaches home and to supper, and to bed –
my wife having been this day with Hales, to sit for her hand to be
mended in her picture.

29.   Up, and all the morning at the office ⟪where the Duke
of York's long letter was read, to their great trouble and their
suspecting me to have been the writer of it⟫;   and at noon
comes, by appointment, Harris to dine with me;   and after
dinner, he and I to Chyrurgeon's-hall, where they are building it
new, very fine,[5] and there to see their Theatre, which stood all the

a MS. 'to'   *b* repl. 'and'   *c* l.h. repl. s.h.

---

1. It listed nine items of alleged
mismanagement: copy (in Hewer's
hand) in Rawl. A 195a, ff. 64–5.
Pepys endorsed it as the work of the
Duke of Buckingham 'and other the
present reformers'. He drafted replies in detail to all nine charges, which
the Duke accepted, altering only one
phrase: ib., f. 65*v*.
2. See below, p. 374 & n. 3. For
the Commissioners' proposals, see
above, viii. 559, n. 2.
3. For these alterations, see LCC,
Survey of London, xiii (pt 2), p. 84.
4. There is no documentary evidence for work by Holbein in the
Matted Gallery. E. Croft-Murray,
*Decorative painting in Engl., 1537–
1837*, i. 161. (OM).
5. The new hall cost £4,292 and
was completed by c. 1674.

fire, and (which was our business) their great picture of Holben's,[1] thinking to have bought it, by*a* the help of Mr. Pierce, for a little money; I did think to give 200*l* for it, it being said to be worth 1000*l* – but it is so spoiled that I have no*b* mind to it, and is not a pleasant, though a*c* good picture. Thence carried Harris to his playhouse, where though 4 a-clock, so few people there at *The Impertinents*[2] as I went out; and do believe they did not act, though there was my Lord Arlington and his company there. So I out, and met my wife in a coach and stopped her going thither to meet me; and took her and Mercer and Deb to Bartholomew-fair, and there did see a ridiculous, obscene little stage-play called *Mary Andrey*,[3] a foolish thing but seen by everybody; and so to Jacob Hall's dancing of the ropes, a thing worth seeing and mightily fallowed; and so home and to the office, and then to bed – writing to my father tonight not to*d* unfurnish our house in the country for my sister, who is going to her own house,[4] because I think I may have occasion myself to come thither; and so I do, by our being put out of the office; which doth not at all trouble me to think of.

30. *Lords day.* Walked to St. James and Pell Mell, and read over with Sir W. Coventry my long*e* letter to the Duke of York and what the Duke of York hath from mine wrote to the Board; wherein he is mightily pleased, and I perceive to put great value upon me. And did talk very openly on all matters of State,

a repl. same symbol badly formed   *b* repl. same symbol
c repl. 'me'-   *d* blot below symbol   *e* repl. 'l'-

---

1. A large panel still in the possession of the Company, showing Henry VIII and the Barber-Surgeons; painted from a cartoon by Holbein and begun, but not completed, by him. It contains allusions to the unification of the Barbers' Company and the Guild of Surgeons in 1540. Recent examination confirms that it was damaged in the Fire. See R. Strong in *Burl. Mag.*, 105/4+; id.,

Holbein and Henry VIII. Cf. above, iv. 59 & n. 3. (OM).
2. A comedy by Shadwell; see above, p. 183, n. 2. Henry Harris acted at the LIF. Performances usually began at 3.30 p.m. (A).
3. 'Merry Andrew' (clown); probably a puppet play. (A).
4. On her marriage to John Jackson, Paulina moved to Ellington, Hunts.

and how some people have got the bitt into their mouths (meaning
the Duke of Buckingham and^a his party) and would likely run
away with all.   But what pleased me mightily, was to hear the
good Character he did give of my Lord Falmouth for his gener-
osity, good-nature, desire of public good, and low thoughts of his
own wisdom; his employing his interest in the King to do good
office to all people, without any other fault then the freedom he
did learn in France, of thinking himself obliged to serve his King
in his pleasures – and was W. Coventry's perticular friend; and
W. Coventry doth tell me very odde circumstances about the
fatality of his death,¹ which are very strange.

Thence to White-hall to chapel and heard the Anthemne, and
did dine^b with the Duke of Albemarle in a dirty manner as ever.
All the afternoon, I sauntered up and down the House and park;
and there was a Committee of Tanger met, wherein Lord
Middleton would I think have found fault with me for want of
Coles;² but I slighted it and he made nothing of it, but was
thought to be drunk; and I see that he hath a mind to find [fault]
with me and Creed, neither of us having yet applied ourselfs to
him about anything.   But doth talk of his profits and perquisites
taken from him, and garrison reduced, and that it must^c [be]
encreased, and such things, as I fear he will be just such another as
my Lord Tiviott and the rest, to ruin the place.   So I to the park
and there walk an hour or two; and in the King's garden and
saw the Queen and ladies walk; and I did steal some apples off
the trees; and here did see my Lady Richmond, who is I believe
of a noble person as ever I see, but her face worse then it was
considerably, by the smallpox.³   Her sister⁴ is also very handsome.

---

a repl. closing bracket   *b* MS. 'dined'   *c* repl. 'was'

---

1. Coventry had been present at
the Battle of Lowestoft (June 1665)
when Falmouth had been killed by
chain-shot. For some details, see
above, vi. 122–3 & nn. Falmouth
had been an unpopular royal favourite – 'a man of too much pleasure

to do the King any good' (above, vi.
123–4).

2. Cf. above, p. 249, n. 2.

3. Cf. above, pp. 134–5 & n.

4. Sophia Stewart, a younger sister;
later married to Henry Bulkeley,
Master of the Horse.

Coming into the park, and the door kept strictly, I had opportunity of handing in the little, pretty, squinting girl of the Duke of York's House; but did not make*ᵃ* acquaintance of her, but let her go, and a little girl that was with her, to walk by themselfs.

So to White-hall in the evening, to the Queen's side, and there met the Duke of York; and he did tell me and W. Coventry, who was by me, how that Lord Anglesy did take notice of our reading his[1] long and sharp letter to the board; but that it was the better, at least he said so. The Duke of York, I perceive, is earnest in it and will have good effects of it – telling W. Coventry that it was a letter that might have come from the Commissioners of Accounts, but it was better it should come first from him. I met Lord Brouncker, who I perceive, and the rest, doth smell that it came from me, but dare not find fault with [it]; and I am glad of it, it being my glory and defence that I did occasion and write it.

So by water home, and did spend the evening with W Hewers, telling him how we are all like to be turned out, Lord Brouncker telling me this evening that the Duke of Buckingham did within few hours say that he had enough to turn us all out; which I am not sorry for at all, for I know the world will judge me to go for company; and my eyes are such as I am not able to do the business of my office as I used, and would desire to do while I am in it. So with full content, declaring all our content in being released of my imployment, my wife and I to bed; and W. Hewer home and so all to bed.

31. Up, and to my office, there to set my Journall for all the last week; and so by water to Westminster to the Exchequer; and thence to the Swan and there drank and did besar la fille there. And so to the New Exchange and paid for some things, and so to Hercules-Pillars and there dined all alone while I sent my shoe to have the heel fastened at Wotton's. And thence to

a MS. 'take'

---

1. The Duke of York's.

White-hall to the Treasury-chamber, where did a little business;[1] and thence to the Duke of York's playhouse and there met my wife and Deb and Mary Mercer and Batelier, where also W Hewers and Batelier was also; and saw *Hamlett*, which we have not seen this year before or more, and mightily pleased with it; but above all with Batterton, the best part, I believe, that ever man acted.[2] Thence to the Fayre and saw *Polichinelle*;[3] and so home and after a little supper, to bed. This night lay the first night in[a] Deb's chamber, which is now hung with that that hung our great chamber, and is now a very handsome room. This day Mrs. Batelier did give my wife a mighty pretty spaniel-bich, Flora, which she values mightily, and is pretty; but as a new-comer, I cannot[b] be fond[c] of her.

a 'in' repeated (over page) *b* repl. 'do not like'
c blot over symbol

---

1. See *CTB*, ii. 425-6.

2. In ch. iv of his *Apology*, Colley Cibber gives an excellent firsthand description of Betterton's Hamlet. (A).

3. A popular puppet-play of Italian origin, now performed at Bartholomew Fair. The puppeteer was probably Antonio Devoto; see G. Speaight, *Hist. Engl. puppet theatre*, p. 77. (A).

SEPTEMBER

1. Up, and all the morning at the office, busy. And after dinner, to the office again, busy till about 4; and then I abroad (my wife being gone to Hales's about drawing her hand new in her picture)*a*1 and to see Betty Michell; which I did, but su marido was dentro – and no pleasure. So to the Fair and there saw several sights; among others, a Mare that tells money and many things to admiration; and among others, came to me when she was bid to go to him of the company that most loved a pretty wench in a corner. And this did cost me 12*d* to the horse, which I had flung him before, and did give me occasion*b* to besar a mighty belle fille that was in the house, that was exceeding plain but forte belle. At night, going home, I went to my bookseller's in Ducke-lane,2 and found her weeping in the shop, so as yo could not have any discourse con her*c* nor ask the reason; so departed and took coach home; and taking coach, was set on by a wench that was naught, and would have gone along with me to her lodging in Shoe-lane, but yo did donner her*d* a shilling and hazer her tocar mi cosa and left her;*e* and home, where after supper, W Batelier with us, we to bed. ⟨This day Mrs. Martin came to see us, and dined with us.⟩

2. Fast day for the burning of London strictly observed.3 I at home at the office all day, forenoon and afternoon, about the Victualler's contract and other things; and at night home to supper (having had but a cold dinner), Mr. Gibson with me. And this evening comes Mr. Hill to discourse with me about

a closing-bracket repl. full stop   b repl. 'opportunity'
c garbled s.h.: see above, viii. 244, note a   d garbled s.h.
e garbled s.h.

---

1. For this portrait, see above, p. 138 & n. 2. (OM).
2. See above, p. 260, n. 4.

3. This day was the anniversary of the Fire. For the fast-day, see above, vii. 316, n. 3.

Yeabsly and Lanyon's business;[1] wherein they are troubled, and I fear they have play[ed] the knaves too far for me to help or think fit*ᵃ* to appear for them. So he gone, and after supper, to bed – being troubled with a summons, though a kind one, from Mr. Jessop, to attend the Commissioners of Accounts tomorrow.

3. Up, and to the office, where busy till it was time to go to the Commissioners of Accounts – which I did about noon, and there was received with all possible respect, their business being only to explain the meaning of one of their late demands to us, which we had not answered in our answer to them;[2] and this being done, away with great content, my mind being troubled before; and so to the Exchequer and several places, calling on several businesses, and perticularly my bookseller's, among others, for Hobbs's *Leviathan*, which is now mightily called for; and what was heretofore sold for 8s I now give 24s at the second hand, and is sold for 30s, it being a book the Bishops will not let be printed again.[3] And so home to dinner, and then to the office all the afternoon; and towards the evening, by water to the Commissioners of the Treasury; and presently back again and there met a little with W. Penn and the rest about our Prize-accounts, and so W. Penn and Lord Brouncker and I at the lodging of the latter to read over our new draft of the victualler's contract;[4] and so broke up, and home to supper and to bed.

4.*ᵇ* Up, and met at the office all the morning; and at noon, my

a repl. 'to'   *b* repl. '5'

---

1. See above, p. 262. They were victualling agents for Tangier.

2. This concerned the accounts of Sir W. Warren, the timber merchant: see PRO, Adm. 106/2886, pt I, *sub* 26 August.

3. The hostility to Hobbes and Hobbism was now at its height: in this year publication of *Behemoth* was stopped. The *Leviathan* had been first published in 1651, and the licensers had prevented its being openly printed in English thereafter.

But it is possible that one of the editions with the imprint 1651 dates in fact from later: Hugh Macdonald and M. Hargreaves, *Thomas Hobbes, a bibliography*, pp. 27–9. Pepys kept his copy (PL 2037); it is one of the genuine 1651 editions. On the flyleaf he wrote 'September 1668 – 30s.'

4. At their meeting earlier in the day the Treasury Commissioners had ordered Pepys to have the final draft ready by the 7th: *CTB*, ii. 431.

wife and Deb and Mercer and W. Hewer to the Fair, and there at the old house did eat a pig[1], and was pretty merry; but saw no sights, my wife having a mind to see the play, *Bartholomew fayre* with puppets; which we did, and it is an excellent play; the more I see it, the more I love the wit of it; only, the business of abusing the puritans begins to grow stale, and of no use, they being the people that at last will be found the wisest.[2] And here Knipp came to us and sat with us, and thence took coach in two coaches; and losing one another, my wife and Knipp and I to Hercules-Pillars and there supped, and I did take from her both the words and notes of her song of the Larke,[3] which pleases me mightily. And so set her at home, and away we home, where our company came home before us. This[a] night, Knipp tells us that there is a Spanish woman, lately come over, that pretends to sing as well as Mrs. Knight; both[b] of which I must endeavour to hear. So after supper, to bed.

5. Up, and at the office all the[c] morning. At noon home to dinner, and to the office to work all the afternoon again, till the evening; and then by coach to Mr. Hales's new house, where I find he hath finished my wife's hand, which is better then the other.[4] And here I find Harris's picture, done in his habit of *Henery the 5th*;[5] mighty like a player, but I do not think the picture near so good as any yet he hath made for me; however,[d] it is pretty well. And thence through the Fair home, but saw nothing, it being late; and so home to my business at the office. And thence to supper and to bed.

---

a repl. 'and pretends to' *b* repl. 'which'
c repl. 'day' *d* repl. 'whom'

---

1. Cf. above, viii. 421 & n. 4.
2. This was the comedy by Ben Jonson (q.v. above, ii. 117, n. 1) acted at the TR; with a performance of the puppet show which forms part of the fifth act. For some details of the anti-Puritan satire, see above, ii. 174, n. 1. (A).

3. Possibly John Wilson's setting of Davenant's words, 'The lark now leaves his watery nest': Bodl., Mus. b. 1, ff. 128*v*–129*r*; Wilson, *Cheerfull ayres or ballads* (1660), pp. 54–6. (E).
4. See above, p. 138 & n. 2. (OM).
5. See above, loc. cit. (OM).

6. *Lords day.* Up betimes and got myself ready to go by water; and about 9 a-clock took boat with Hen. Russell[1] to Gravesend, coming thither about one, where at the Ship I dined; and thither came to me Mr. Hosier,[2] whom I went to speak with about several businesses of work that he is doing, and I would have him do, of writing work for me. And I did go with him to his lodging and there did see his wife, a pretty tolerable woman, and do find him upon an extraordinary good work of designing a method of keeping our storekeepers' accounts in the Navy.[3] Here I should have met with Mr. Willson,[4] but he is sick and could not come from Chatham to me. So having done with Hosier, I took boat again the beginning of the flood, and came home by 9 at night – with much pleasure, it being a fine day. Going down I spent reading of the *Five Sermons of Five Several Styles*;[5] worth comparing one with another, but I do think when all is done, that contrary to the design of the book, the Presbyterian style and the Independent are the best of the five for sermons to be preached in; this I do by the best of my present judgment think. And coming back I spent reading of the book of warrants of our office in the first Dutch war,[6] and do find that my letters and warrants and method will be found another-gate's business than[a] this that the world so much adores – and I am glad for my own sake to find it so. My boy was with me, and read to me all day, and we sang a while together; and so home to supper a little, and so to bed.

a MS. 'that'

---

1. Waterman to the Navy Board.
2. Muster-Master, Gravesend; late Clerk of the Cheque, Harwich.
3. See below, p. 374 & n. 1.
4. Thomas Wilson, late Surveyor of Victualling in the port of London. Pepys wrote to him on this day: *Further Corr.*, p. 194.
5. Abraham Wright, *Five sermons in five several styles* . . . (duodecimo, 1656; PL 151), containing two genuine sermons by Lancelot Andrewes and

Joseph Hall, and three parodies of the Presbyterians and Independents, together with a defence of the Anglican style, and particularly of the academic style as compared with that of the city preachers. See A. Wood, *Ath. Oxon.*, iii. 277; W. Fraser Mitchell, *Engl. pulpit oratory*, pp. 365–7. Pepys had usually disliked the Puritan style.
6. Cromwell's war, 1652–4.

7. At the office all the morning; we met and at noon dined at home; and after dinner carried my wife and Deb to Un-thankes, and I to White-hall with Mr. Gibson, where the rest of our officers met us, and to the Commissioners of the Treasury about the Victualling contract[1] – but stayed not long; but thence sending Gibson to my wife, I with Lord Brouncker (who was this day in an unusual manner merry, I believe with drink) J. Mennes and W. Penn to Bartholomew-Fair and there saw the dancing mare again (which today, I find her to act much worse then the other day, she forgetting many things, which her master did beat her for and was mightily vexed). And then the dancing of the ropes and also the little stage-play,[2] which is very ridiculous; and so home to the office with Brouncker, W. Pen, and myself (J. Mennes being gone home before, not well); and so after a little talk together, I home to supper and to bed.

8. Up and by water to White-hall and to St. James's, there to talk a little with Mr. Wren about the private business we are upon in the office,[3] where he tells me he finds that they all suspect me to be the author of the great letter;[a][4] which I value not – being satisfied that it is the best thing I could ever do for myself. And so after some discourse of this kind more, I back to the office, where all the morning; and after dinner, to it again all the after-noon[b] and very late; and then home to supper, where met W Batelier and B. Turner; and after some talk with them, and[c] supper, we to bed. This day, I received so[d] earnest an[e] invitation again from Roger Pepys to come to Sturbridge-Fair, that I resolve to let my wife go, which she shall do the next week; and so to bed. This day I received two letters from the Duke of Richmond about his Yacht, which is newly taken into the

---

a repl. incomplete symbol   *b* MS. 'night'   *c* repl. 'we and'
        d rep. 'to'   *e* repl. 'an'

---

1. See *CTB*, ii. 433.
2. See above, p. 293 & n. 3. (A).
3. A draft of reforms of the office: above, p. 289 & n. 1; p. 291.

4. See above, p. 289, n. 1.

King's service,[1] and I am glad of it, hoping hereby to oblige him
and to have occasions of seeing his noble Duchess, which I adore.

9. Up, and to the office; and thence to the Duke of Richmond's lodgings by his desire, by letter yesterday. I found him
at his lodgings in the little building in the Bouling-green at
White-hall, that that was begun to be built by Captain Rolt.[2]
They are fine rooms. I did hope to see his Lady, the beautiful
Mrs. Stuart; but she, I hear, is in the country. His business[a]
was about his Yacht, and seems a mighty good-natured man,
and did presently write me a warrant for a Doe from Cobham[3]
when the season comes, bucks season being past. I shall make
much of this acquaintance, that I may live to see his Lady near.
Thence to Westminster to Sir R. Long's office; and going, met
Mr. George Mountagu, who talked and complimented me
mightily; and long discourse I had with him – who, for news,
tells me for certain that Trevor doth come to be Secretary at
Michaelmas and that Morris goes out, and he believes without
any compensation.[4] He tells me that now Buckingham does rule
all; and the other day, in the King's Journy he is now in, at
Bagshot and that way,[5] he caused Prince[b] Rupert's horses to be
turned out of an Inne, and caused his own to be kept there;
which the Prince complained of to the King, and the Duke of
York seconded the complaint but the King did over-rule it for
Buckingham; by which there are high displeasures among them –
and Buckingham and Arlington rule all.   Thence by water home

a repl. 'dis'-   *b* repl. 'the Duke of'

---

1. The *Richmond*. The work of
refitting her proved difficult, and it
was not until 1672 that she was put
into the royal service: *CSPD 1667–8*,
p. 575; *Cat.*, i. 295.

2. Edward Rolt had been a Gentleman of the Bedchamber to Oliver
Cromwell. The building has not
been identified.

3. Cobham Hall, Kent.

4. John Trevor was appointed on

22 September, but did in fact pay
£8000 to Morice for the office:
CSPD 1667–8, p. 595; *Bulstrode
Papers*, i. 61.

5. The King, the Duke of York,
Rupert, and others of the court had
been away since 3 September hunting
in Windsor Forest and the New
Forest. They returned on the 10th.
London Gazette, 7 September; BM,
Add. 36916, f. 113r.

and to dinner; and after dinner by water again to White-hall, where Brouncker, W. Penn and I attended the Commissioners of the Treasury about the victualling contract – where high words between Sir Tho. Clifford and us, and myself more per-ticularly, who told him that something that he said was told him about this business was a flat untruth. However, we went on to our business in the examination of the draft, and so parted, and I vexed at what happened.[1] And Brouncker, W. Penn and I home in a hackney-coach – and I all the night so vexed, that I did not sleep almost all night; which shows how unfit I am for trouble. So after a little supper, vexed and spending a little time melancholy in making a base to the Lark's song,[2] I to bed.

10.[a] Up, and by water to White-hall, and there to Sir W. Coventry's house; where I stayed in his dining-room two hours, thinking[b] to speak with him, but I find Garraway and he are private; which I am glad of[3] – Captain Cocke bringing them this day together. Cocke came out and talked with me till it was too late for me to stay longer; and therefore to the Treasury chamber, where the rest met, and W. Coventry came presently after; and we spent the morning in finishing the Victualler's contract,[4] and so I by water home. And there dined with me,

a repl. '9' *b* preceded by blot

---

1. The Treasury minute runs: 'My Lords [of the Treasury] say to the Commissioners [of the Navy] that they did not give notice to the proposers [the contractors about to make tenders]. Mr. Pepys says that they [the proposers] desired them-selves that the matters should be drawn up by the Navy Commis-sioners. Mr. Child says that the matters are drawn up worse than before [i.e. worse than in the first draft of the contract] and wholly im-practicable. The victualling debate adjourned until tomorrow.' *CTB*, ii. 435.

2. For the song, see above, p. 299 & n. 3. The bass has not been traced. (E).

3. William Garraway (M.P. for Chichester, Suss.) was a leading critic of the administration in parlia-ment, but his considerable influence was occasionally used in the govern-ment's interest. Coventry seems to have known him well and to have thought highly of him. Cf. above, vii. 310–11 & n.

4. *CTB*, ii. 436.

Batelier and his wife, and Mercer and my people, at a good
venison-pasty; and after dinner, I and W How (who came to see
me) by water to the Temple and met our four women, my wife,
M. Batelier, Mercer, and Deb, at the Duke's play-house, and
there saw *The Maid in the Mill*[1] revived, a pretty harmless old
play.   Thence to Unthankes and Change, where wife did a little
business while Mercer and I stayed in the coach; and in quarter
of an hour I taught her the whole Lark's song[2] perfectly – so
excellent an eare she hath.   Here we at Unthanke's light and
walked them to White-hall; my wife mighty angry at it and did
give me ill words before Batelier, which vexed me but I made no
matter of it – but vexed to myself.   So landed them, it being fine
moonshine, at the Bear, and so took water on the other side and
home; and I to the office, where a child is laid at Sir J. Mennes's
door, as there was one heretofore.   So being good friends again,
my wife seeking it, by my being silent I overcoming her,[3] we
to bed.

11.[a]   Up, and at my[b] office all the morning.   And after dinner,
all the afternoon in my house with Batelier shut up, drawing up
my defence to the Duke of York upon his great letter, which I
have industriously take[n] this opportunity of doing for my future
use.[4]   At it late, and my mind and head mighty full on it all
night.

12.   At it again in the morning; and then to the office, where
till noon; and I do see great whispering among my Brethren
about their replies to the Duke of York; which vexed me,
though I know no reason for it – for I have no manner of ground
to fear them.   At noon home to dinner; and after dinner, to
work all the afternoon again; at home late and so to bed.

a repl. 'io'   *b* repl. 'the'

---

1. A comedy by Fletcher and
Rowley; see above, ii. 25, n. 4.   (A).
2. See above, p. 299, n. 3.   (E).
3. Cf. his similar ruse: above, viii.
250-1.

4. Pepys and the other Principal
Officers had been enjoined to reply to
the 'great letter' of 26 August within
fourteen days.   A copy of Pepys's
reply (13 September, in Gibson's
hand), is in PL 2242, pp. 94+.

13. *Lords day.* The like all this morning and afternoon, and finished it to my mind. So about 4 a-clock walked to the Temple, and there by coach to St. James's and met, to my wish, the Duke of York and Mr. Wren; and understand the Duke of York hath received answers from Brouncker, W. Penn and J. Mennes; and as soon as he saw me, he bid Mr. Wren read them over with me. So having no opportunity of talk with the Duke of York, and Mr. Wren some business to do, he puts them into my hand like an idle companion, to take home with me before himself had read them; which doth give me great opportunity of altering my answer, if there was cause. So took a hackney and home; and after supper made my wife to read them all over, wherein she is mighty useful to me. And I find*a* them all evasions, and in many things false, and in few to the full purpose.*b* Little said reflective on me, though W. Penn and J. Mennes do mean me in one or two places, and J. Mennes a little more plainly would lead the Duke of York to question the exactness of my keeping my records – but all to no purpose. My mind is mightily pleased by this, if I can but get them to have a copy taken of them for my future use; but I must return them tomorrow.[1] So to bed.

14. Up betimes, and walked to the Temple and stopped, viewing the Exchange and Paul's and St. Fayth's; where strange how the very sight of the stones falling from the top of the steeple* doth make me sea-sick. But no hurt, I hear, hath yet happened*c* in all this work of the steeple – which is very much.[2] So from the Temple, I by coach to St. James, where I find Sir

a MS. 'fear'. Errors now multiply in the MS: cf. above, p. 244, note *a*.
    b repl. 'purse'   *c* repl. 'been'

---

1. Pepys kept copies of the replies (in Gibson's hand) in PL 2242, pp. 50+; see below, p. 344. The original of Mennes's elaborate reply (13 September) is in Tanner 44, ff. 29+. He and his colleagues alleged in their defence the custom of their predecessors and the circumstances of the war, the Plague and the Fire.
2. For the rebuilding of St Paul's, see above, p. 288, n. 1.

W. Penn and Lord Anglesey, who delivered this morning his answer to the Duke of York,[1] but I could not see it.   But after being above with the Duke of York, but said nothing, I down with Mr. Wren; and he and I read them all over that I had and I expounded them to him, and did so order it that I had them home with me, so that I shall to my heart's wish be able to take a copy of them.   After dinner, I by water to White-hall and there with the Cofferer and Sir St. Fox attended the Commissioners of the Treasury about bettering our fund, and are promised it speedily.[2]   Thence by water home, and so all the afternoon and evening late, busy at the office; and then home to supper, and Mrs. Turner comes to see my wife before her journey tomorrow but she is in bed; and so sat talking to little purpose with me a great while; and she gone, I to bed.[a]

15.   Up mighty betimes, my wife and people, Mercer lying[b] here all night, by 3 a-clock and I about 5; and they before and I after them to the Coach[c] in Bishopsgate-street; which was not ready to set out, so took wife and Mercer, Deb and W. Hewer (who all set out this day for Cambridge to Cosen Rogr. Pepys's to see Sturbridge fayre) and I showed them the Exchange, which is very finely and carried on with good despatch.[3]   So walked back and saw them gone, there being only one man in the coach besides them; and so home to the office, where Mrs. Daniel came and stayed talking to little purpose with me, to borrow money, but I did not lend her any, having not opportunity para hazer alieno[d] thing mit her.[e]   At the office all the morning and at

a   followed by two blank pages
b   MS. 'liking'   c   repl. 'Carriers'
d   garbled s.h.   e   doubtful reading (symbol blotted)

---

1. PL 2242, pp. 50-5 (Anglesey to Duke of York, 12 September; copy).

2. Assignments were to be drawn on the excise for the payment of Tangier, the Guards, and the Household.   The fund was already over-drawn to the extent of two years' net income.   The official Treasury min-ute records no promise as positive as the one Pepys mentions: CTB, ii. 438.

3. The reference here is to the rebuilding after the Fire.   The inner quadrangle was finished by September 1669 but the rebuilding was not com-pleted until 1671.

noon dined with my people at home; and so to the office again a while and so by water to the King's playhouse to see a new play, acted but yesterday, a translation out of French by Dryden called *The Ladys a la Mode*;[1] so mean a thing, as when they came to say it would be acted again tomorrow, both he that said it, Beeson,[2] and the pit fell a-laughing – there being this day not a quarter of the pit full. Thence to St. James's and White-hall to wait on the Duke of York, but could not come to speak to him till time to go on; and so by water home and there late at the office and my chamber, busy; and so after a little supper, to bed.

16. Up; and dressing myself, I did begin para tocar the breasts of my maid*a* Jane, which ella did give way to more*a* then usual heretofore, so as I have a design to try more what I can bring it to. So to the office, and thence to St. James's to the Duke of York – walking it to the Temple; and in my way observe that the Stockes[3] are now pulled quite down, and it will make the coming into Cornhill and Lumber-street mighty noble. I stopped too at Paul's, and there did go into St. Fayth's church and also into the body of the west part of the church, and do see a hideous sight, of the walls of the church ready to fall, that I was in fear as long as I was in it. And here I saw the great vaults underneath the body of the church. No hurt, I hear, is done yet, since their going to pull down the church and steeple; but one man, on Monday this week, fell from the top to a piece*b* of the roof of the east end

---

a–a garbled s.h.   *b* repl. 'rope of'

---

1. Pepys appears to have been misinformed about the authorship of this play, which was probably Richard Flecknoe's comedy, *The damoiselles à la mode*, published in 1667. If this identification is correct, this is the first record of a performance. The King's Company had planned to use it for the opening performance at the Theatre Royal, Drury Lane, in November 1666, but did not do so. The 1667 edition lists the intended cast, which includes Cartwright as Bonhomme, Hart as Valerio, Lacy as Sganarelle, Mohun as Mascarillo, and the Marshall sisters, Mary and Anne, as the '*Damoiselles à la mode*'. (A).

2. William Beeston. (A).

3. A market building at the junction of Cornhill, Threadneedle St and the Poultry; once the site of the city stocks. It was now rebuilt further back from the cross-roads. (R).

that stands next the steeple, and there broke himself all to pieces.
It is pretty here, to see how the last church was but a case brought*a*
over the old church; for you may see the very old pillars standing
whole within the wall of this.[1]   When I came to St. James's, I
find the Duke of York gone with the King to see the muster of
the Guards in Hyde Park; and their colonel, the Duke of Monmouth, to take his command this day of the King's Life-Guard,
by surrender of my Lord Gerard's.[2]   So I took a hackney-coach
and saw it all; and endeed, it was mighty noble and their firing
mighty fine, and the Duke of Monmouth in mighty rich clothes;
but the well-ordering of the men I understand not.   Here, among
a thousand coaches that*b* was there, I saw and spoke to Mrs.
Pierce; and by and by Mr. Wren hunts me out and gives me my
Lord Anglesy's answer to the Duke of York's letter, where I
perceive he doth do what he can to hurt me, by bidding the
Duke of York call for my books;[3] but this will do me all the right
in the world, and yet I am troubled at it.   So away out of the
park and home, and there Mr. Gibson and I to dinner; and all
the afternoon with him, writing over anew, and a little altering,*c*
my answer*d* to the Duke of York, which*e* I have not yet delivered and so have the opportunity of doing it after seeing all
their answers, though this doth give me occasion to alter very
little.   This done, he to write it over and I to the office, where
late; and then home and he had finished it; and then he to read
to me the *Life of Archbishopp Laud*, wrote by D. Heylin; which
is a shrowd book, but that which I believe will do the Bishops
in general no great good, but hurt – it pleads for so much
Popish.[4]   So after supper, to bed.   This day, my father's letters
tell me of the death of poor Fancy in the country, big with

a ? 'wrought'   *b* repl. 'was'   *c* repl. 'cor'-
        d repl. 'letter'   *e* MS. 'to which'

1 There were two earlier and smaller churches (of the 7th and 10th
centuries) on the site of Old St Paul's.
    2. Monmouth's commission is
dated this day: *CSPD 1667–8*, p. 586.
(He was said to have paid £15,000 to
Gerard for it: *Bulstrode Papers*, i. 55

etc.; W. Westergaard, ed., *First
Triple Alliance*, pp. 17–18.) Description of ceremony in Westergaard, loc.
cit.
    3. PL 2242, pp. 54–5. Cf. above,
p. 289, n. 1.
    4. See above, p. 291, n. 1.

puppies, which troubles me, as being one of my oldest acquaintances and servants.[1] Also, Goody Stankes[2] is dead.

17. Up, and all the morning sitting at the office, where
everybody grown mighty cautious in what they do or omit to do.
And at noon comes Knepp, with design to dine with Lord
Brouncker; but she being undressed, and there being much
company, dined with me; and after dinner, I out with her and
carried her to the playhouse, and in the way did give her five
guineas as a fairing, I having given her nothing a great while,
and her coming hither sometimes having been matter of cost to
her. And so I to St. James's, but missed of the Duke of York;
and so went back to the King's playhouse and saw *Rollo, Duke of
Normandy*,[3] which, for old acquaintances, pleased me pretty well.
And so home and to my business, and to read again and to bed.
⟨This evening Batelier came to tell me he was going down to
Cambridge to my company, to see the Fair; which vexed me,
and the more because I fear he doth know that Knepp did dine
with me today.⟩*a*

18. Up, and to St. James's and there took a turn or two in the
park; and then up to the Duke of York and there had opportunity
of delivering my answer to his late letter;[4] which he did not
read but give to Mr. Wren, as looking*b* on it as a thing I needed
not have done, but only that I might not give occasion to the
rest to suspect my communication with the Duke of York against
them. So now I am at rest in that matter, and shall*c* be more
when my copies are finished of their answers, which I am now
taking with all speed. Thence to my several booksellers and
elsewhere, about several arrands; and so at noon home, and after
dinner by coach to White-hall; and thither comes the Duke of
York to us, and by and by met at the robe-chamber upon our

a addition crowded in   *b* MS. loo[k]ing'   *c* repl. 'when'

1. Cf. above, v. 239.
2. Wife of Will Stankes of Brampton. Her husband acted as bailiff for
Pepys's property there. She had been
buried on 3 July.

3. A tragedy by John Fletcher and
several others: see above, ii. 62, n. 1.
(A).
4. See above, p. 304 & n. 4.

usual business; where the Duke of York I find somewhat sower –
and perticularly angry with Lord Anglesy for his not being there
now, nor at other times – so often as he should be with us.   So
to the King's House and saw a piece of *Henry the 4th*[1] at the end
of the play, thinking to have gone abroad with Knepp; but it
was too late, and she to get her part against tomorrow in *The
Silent Woman*;[2] and so I only set her at home, and away home
myself and there to read again and sup with Gibson; and so
to bed.

19.   Up, and to the office, where all the morning busy; and
so dined with my people at home, and then to the King's playhouse and there saw *The Silent Woman*; the best comedy, I think,
that was ever wrote; and sitting by Shadwell the*a* poet, he was
big*b* with admiration of it.[3]   Here was my Lord Brouncker
and W. Penn and their ladies in the box, being grown mighty
kind of a sudden – but God knows, it will last but a little while,
I dare swear.   Knepp did her part mighty well; and so home
straight and to write;*c* and perticularly to my Cosen Roger,
who, W Hewers and my wife writes me, doth use them with
mighty plenty and noble entertainment.   So home to supper and
to bed.

All the news now is that Mr. Trevor is for certain now to be
Secretary in Secretary Morris's place,[4] which the Duke of York
did himself tell me yesterday*d* – and also that Parliament is ⟨to be⟩
adjourned to the first of March;[5]   which doth please me well,
hoping thereby to get my things in a little better order then I
should have done – and the less attendances at that end of the
town in Winter.   So home to supper and to bed.

a repl. 'he'   *b* repl. 'over'   *c* MS. 'work'
             d repl. 'two days since'

---

1. Probably Part I of Shakespeare's
play: see above, i. 325 & n. 1. (A).
2. The comedy by Ben Jonson: see
above, i. 171, n. 2. Mrs Knepp
played Epicoene, the title-role:
Downes, p. 4. (A).
3. Thomas Shadwell's own realistic

plays were strongly influenced by
Jonson's. (A).
4. Cf. above, p. 302 & n. 4.
5. It was adjourned by proclamation, 19 September: Steele, no. 3517.
It had stood adjourned since 9 May.

20. *Lords day.* Up, and to set some papers to rights in my chamber, and the like in my office; and so to church – at our own church; and heard but a dull sermon of one Dr. Hicks, who is a suitor to Mrs. Howell, the widow of our Turner of the Navy.[1] Thence home to dinner, staying till past one a-clock for Harris, whom I invited, and to bring Shadwell the poet with him; but they came not, and so a good dinner lost through my own folly. And so to dinner alone, having since church-time heard my boy read over Dryden's reply to Sir R. Howard's answer about his *Essay of Poesy* – and a letter in answer to that, the last whereof is mighty*a* silly in behalf of Howard.[2] Thence walked forth and got a coach, and to visit Mrs. Pierce, with whom, and him, I stayed a little while and do hear how the Duchesse of Monmouth is at this time in great trouble of the shortness of her lame leg, which is likely to grow shorter and shorter, that she will never recover it.[3] Thence to St. Margaret's church, thinking to have seen Betty Michell*b* – but she*b* was not there. So back and walked to Grays Inn walks a while, but little company; and so over the fields to Clerkenwell to see whether I could find that the fair Botelers do live there still, I seeing Frances the other day in a coach with Cary Dillon, her old servant, but know not where she lives.[4] So walked home and there walked in the garden an hour, it being mighty pleasant weather; and so took my Lady Pen

a MS 'my'   *b–b* garbled s.h.

---

1. Dr Edward Hickes, Rector of St Margaret Pattens, was a widower. A licence for his marriage to Sarah Howell had been issued three days before. She was the widow of Richard Howell, who had supplied turnery to the navy.

2. Dryden's defence of the use of rhyme in drama (*Essay of dramatic poesy*, 1668) had been criticised by Sir Robert Howard in the preface to his play *The Duke of Lerma* (1668). Dryden had replied in *A defence of an essay . . .* (1668); the 'letter in ans-

wer to that' referred to by Pepys was probably *A letter from a gentleman to the Hon. Ed. Howard, Esq.* (1668), signed 'R.F.' (? Richard Flecknoe). Neither is in the PL. (A).

3. She had dislocated her hip at a dance: above, p. 191 & n. 3.

4. Pepys had much admired Frances Boteler and her sister in 1660–1: Frances he sometimes thought the loveliest woman he knew. Dillon (later 5th Earl of Roscommon) had once been betrothed to her: he never married her.

and Mrs. Markham home and sent for Mrs. Turner; and by and by comes Sir W. Penn and supped with me, a good supper, part of my dinner today. They gone, Mrs. Turner stayed an hour talking with me and yo did now the first time tocar her cosa with my hand*a* and did make her do the like con su hand*a* to my thing, whereto neither did she show any averseness really, but a merry kind of opposition, but yo did do both*b* and yo do believe I might have hecho la cosa too mit her.*c*   So parted, and I to bed.

21. Up, and betimes Sir D Gawden with me, talking about the Victualling business which is now under dispute for a new contract, or whether it shall be put into a commission.¹ He gone, comes Mr. Hill to talk with me about Lanyon's business; and so being in haste, I took him to the water with me, and so to White-hall and there left him; and I to W. Coventry and showed him my answer to the Duke of York's great letter, which he likes well; we also discoursed about the victualling business, which he thinks there is a design to put into a way of commission – but doth look upon all things to be managed with faction, and is grieved under it.   So to St. James and there the Duke of York did of his own accord come to me and tell me that he had read and doth like of my answers to the*d* Objections which he did give me the other day about the Navy.   And so did W. Coventry too, who told me that the Duke of York had shown him them.²   So to White-hall a little and the Chequer, and then by water home to dinner with my people, where Tong was also this day with me, whom I shall imploy for a time;³

a–a garbled s.h.   b garbled s.h.
  c garbled s.h.   d repl. 'the'

1. Victualling had been put under the direct management of a commission during 1642–51 and 1655–60. For the crisis in victualling affairs at this time, see *Cat.*, i. 155; for its solution, see below, p. 316, n. 1, pp. 317–18 & n.

2. Cf. above, pp. 291–2 & n.

3. Thomas Tong, once a purser, was now a ropemaker. In November he was employed in the discovery of embezzlements at Portsmouth: *CSPD 1668–9*, p. 57.

and so out*a* again and by water to Somerset-house; but when
come hither, I turned back and to Sowthworke-Fair,[1] very dirty,
and there saw the Puppet-show of Whittington,[2] which was
pretty to see; and how that idle thing doth work upon people
that see it, and even myself too. And thence to Jacob Hall's
dancing on the ropes, where I saw such action as I never saw
before, and mightily worth seeing. And here took acquaintance
with a fellow that carried*b* me to a tavern, whither came the
music of this booth, and by and by Jacob Hall himself, with
whom I had a mind to speak to hear whether he had ever any
mischief by falls in his time; he told me, "Yes, many; but never
to the*c* breaking of a limb." He seems a mighty strong man.

So giving them a bottle or two of wine, I away with Payne
the waterman; he, seeing me at the play, did get a link to light me,
and so light me to the Beare, where Bland my waterman waited
for me with gold and other things he kept for me, to the value
of 40*l* and more, which I had about me for fear of my pockets
being cut. So by link-light through the Bridge, it being mighty*d*
dark, but still water; and so home – where I find my draght of the
Resolucion[3] come finished from Chatham; but will cost me, one
way or other, above 12*l* or 13*l* in the board, frame, and garnishing;
which is a little too much – but I will not be beholding to the
King's officers that do it. So to supper, and the boy to read to
me, and so to bed. ⟨This day I met Mr. Moore in the New
Exchange and had much of talk of my Lord's concernments.
This day also came out first the new 5*l*-pieces in gold coined by
the Guinea Company,[4] and I did get two pieces of Mr. Holder.⟩*e*

---

        a MS. 'home'   *b* blot in MS.
c repl. 'do'   *d* MS. 'my'   *e* addition crowded in

---

1. See above, i. 242, n. 2.

2. The legendary version of the
history of Dick Whittington (en-
shrined in street-ballads, chapbooks,
plays and puppet-shows like this one)
had been popular in London since
at least the early years of James I.
Whittington (d. 1423) had been a rich
Lord Mayor whose munificence had
left a lasting impression on Londoners,

but the details of the legend bore
almost no relation to the historical
facts of his career. For the puppet-
play, see G. Speaight, *Hist. Engl.
puppet theatre*, pp. 77, 94, 101, 108–9.

3. See above, p. 262 & n. 4.

4. These were five-'guinea' pieces
(so-called from the name of the
Company). Thomas Holder was
Treasurer of the Guinea Company.

22. Up, and to the office, where sitting all the morning. At noon home to dinner with my people, and so to the office again, where busy all the afternoon. And in the evening spent my time walking in the dark in the garden, to favour my eyes, which*a* I find nothing*b* but ease to help. In the garden there comes to me my Lady Pen and Mrs. Turner and Markham, and we sat and talked together, and I carried them home and there eat a bit of something; and by and by comes Sir W. Penn and eat with us, and mighty merry, in appearance at least – he being on all occasions glad to be at friendship with me, though we hate one another, and know it on both sides. They gone, Mrs. Turner and I to walk in the garden, and there yo did the second part of Sunday night last, tocando su cosa and making her tocar mi thing, but no mas – which she did bear with very merrily, but with a seeming remorse. So led her home, and I back to bed. ⟨This day Mr. Wren did give me at the Board Commissioner Middleton's answer to the Duke of York's great letter;[1] so that now I have all of them.⟩

23. At my office busy all the morning. At noon comes Mr. Eveling to me about some business with the office,[2] and there in discourse tells me of his loss, to the value of 500*l*, which he hath met with in a*c* late attempt of making of Bricks upon an adventure with others, by which he presumed to have got a great deal of money[3] – so that I see the most ingenious men may sometimes be mistaken.*d*   So to the Change a little, and then home to dinner;

a symbol repeated   b repl. 'of'
c repl. 'at'   d repl. 'com'-

---

1. Chatham, 19 September; copy (in Gibson's hand) in PL 2242, pp. 90+.
2. Evelyn had been one of the Commissioners for the Sick and Wounded, 1664–7.
3. Evelyn had joined with Sir Jan Kievit (a Dutch political exile) in a scheme to embank the Thames from the Temple to the Tower and to con-struct wharves there, in accordance with the provisions of the city's first Rebuilding Act (February 1667). The scheme was abandoned, as was the later scheme (under the second act, 1670) to embank the section from the Tower to London Bridge. See Evelyn, iii. 471, 476, 477–8; T. F. Reddaway, *Rebuilding of London*, pp. 221+.

and then by water to White-hall to attend the Commissioners of the Treasury with*a* Alderman Backwell about 10000*l* he is to lend*b* us for Tanger.[1] And then up to a committee of the Council, where was the Duke of York; and they did give us, the Officers of the Navy, the proposals of the several bidders for the victualling of the Navy, for us to give them*c* our answer to which is the best, and whether it be better to victual by commission or contract – and to bring them our answer by Friday afternoon – which is a great deal of work. So thence back with Sir J. Mennes home, and came after us Sir W. Penn and Lord Brouncker, and we fell to the business; and I late when they were gone, to digest something of it; and so to supper and to bed.

24. Up betimes, and Sir D. Gawden with me and I told him all; being very desirous, for the King's sake as well as my own, that he may be kept in it. And after consulting him, I to the office, where we met again and spent most of the morning about this business and no other; and so at noon home to dinner and then close with Mr. Gibson till night, drawing up our answer, which I did the most part by 7 at night; and so to Lord Brouncker and the rest at his lodgings to read it, and they approved of it. So back home to supper, and made my boy read to me a while and then to bed.

25. Up, and Sir D Gawden with me betimes to confer again about this business; and he gone, I all the morning finishing our answer, which I did by noon; and so to dinner, and W Batelier with me, who is lately come from Impington, beyond which I perceive he was not, whatever his pretence at first was. And so he tells me how well and merry all are there, and how nobly used by my cousin.[2]

---

a repl. 'about'   *b* repl. 'advance'   *c* MS. 'us'

---

1. Sir John Shaw was to join Backwell in lending the money, which was to be secured on the customs. According to the Treasury Books, this business was discussed on the 22nd, but not at the meeting held on the 23rd: *CTB*, ii. 442-3.

2. Roger Pepys, who had inherited the Impington property on the death of his father Talbot in 1666.

He gone after dinner, I to work again; and Gibson having wrote our answer fair, and got Brouncker and the rest to sign it,[1] I by coach to White-hall to the Committee of the Council, which met late, and Brouncker and J. Mennes with me and there the Duke of York present (but not W. Coventry, who I perceive doth wholly avoid to have to do publicly in this business, being shy of appearing in any Navy business; which I telling him the other day that I thought the King might suffer by it, he told me that the occasion is now so small that it cannot be fatal to the service, and for the present it is better for him not to appear; saying*a* that it may fare the worse for his appearing in it, as things are now*b* governed); where our answer was read and debated, and some hot words between the Duke of York and Sir T. Clifford; the first for and the latter against Gawden. But the whole put off to tomorrow's Council*c* – for till the King goes out of town the next week, the Council sits every day. So with the Duke of York and some others to his closet, and Alderman Backwell, about a Committee of Tanger, and there did agree upon a price for pieces-of-eight at 4s 6d.[2] Present, the Duke of York, Arlington, Berkely, J Minnes, and myself. They gone, the Duke of York did tell me how hot Clifford is for Child and for removing of old*d* officers (he saying plainly tonight, that though D. Gawden was a*e* man that had done the best service that he believed any man, or any ten men, could have done, yet that it was for the

a repl. closing bracket   *b* repl. 'gl'-   *c* repl. full stop
d repl. 'odd'   *e* repl. 'as'

---

1. Navy Board to Privy Council, 25 September: copies (in Hayter's hand) in PRO, SP 46/137, no. 154 (summarised in *CSPD Add. 1660–85*, pp. 275–6); Rawl. A 216, ff. 105–12; BM, Add. 11602, ff. 337+; ib., 9311, ff. 176+. The Navy Board, presenting their answers to questions addressed to them by the Privy Council, concluded in favour of management by contract rather than by direct control, and, of the tenders put in by four applicants, recommended Gauden's as the cheapest and best. For the award of the contract to him, see below, p. 318. It was not until December 1683 that the Board adopted the system of direct management introduced in the Civil War.

2. I.e. this was to be the price at Tangier: see a summary of Pepys's statement to the Treasury Commissioners (4 May 1668) in *CTB*, ii. 312.

King's interest not to let it lie too long in one hand, lest nobody should be able to serve him but one).[1] But the Duke of York did openly tell him that he was not for removing of old servants that have done well, neither in this place nor in any other place – which is very nobly said. It being 7 or 8 at night, I home with Backewell by coach; and so walked to D. Gawden's, but he not at home. And so back to my chamber, the boy to read to me; and so to supper and to bed.

26. Could sleep but little last night for my concernment in this business of the victualling for Sir D Gawden. So up in the morning and he comes to me, and there I did tell him all and give him my advice; and so he away, and I to the office, where we met and did a little business; and I left them, and by water to attend the Council, which I did all the morning, but was not called in; but the Council meets again in the afternoon on purpose about it. So I at noon to Westminster-hall and there stayed a little, and at the Swan also, thinking to have got Doll Lane thither, but ella did not understand my signs;[a] and so I away and walked to Charing-cross, and there into the great new ordinary[2] by my Lord Mulgrave's, being led thither by Mr. Beale, one of Oliver's and now of the King's Guards;[3] and he sat with me while I had two grilled pigeons, very handsome, and good meat; and there he and I talked of our old acquaintances, W. Clerke[4] and others, being a very civil man; and so walked[b] to Westminster and there parted, and I to the Swan again but did nothing; and so to White-hall and there attended the King

a garbled s.h.   *b* repl. same symbol

---

1. Gauden had been navy victualler since 1660. He remained associated with the victualling until 1677.

2. Adam Lockett's, often mentioned in the plays of Cibber and Vanbrugh, on the w. side of Charing Cross, assessed (1674) on 14 hearths: LCC, *Survey of London*, xvi. 89. (R).

3. Simon Beale was now one of the King's fourteen trumpeters-in-ordinary. He had been a favourite trumpeter of Oliver Cromwell's and had played at his funeral.

4. Sir William Clarke (d. 1666); Monck's secretary before the Restoration, and Secretary at War, 1661-6.

and Council, who met and heard our answer; I present and then withdrew, and they spent two hours at least afterwards about it, and at last rose; and to my great content, the Duke of York at coming out told me that it was carried for D. Gawden at 6*d*. 8*d*. and 8¾*d*,[1] but with great difficulty I understand, both from him and others; so much, that Sir Edwd. Walker[2] told me that he prays to God he may never live to need to plead his merit for D. Gawden's sake, for that it*a* hath stood him in no stead in this business at all, though both he and all the world that speaks*b* of him, speaks of him as the most deserving man of any servant of the King's in the whole na-ion – and so I think he is. But it is done, and my heart is glad at it. So I took coach and away; and in Holborne overtook D. Gawden's coach, and stopped and went home, and Gibson too in his, and to my house, where D. Gawden did talk a little; and he doth mightily acknowledge my kindness to him,*c* and I know I have done the King and myself good service in it. So he gone, and myself in mighty great content in what is done, I to the office a little; and then home to supper, and the boy to read to me; and so to bed. This*d* noon I went to my Lady Peterborough's house and talked with her about the money due to her Lord;[3] and it gives me great trouble, her importunity and impertinency*e* about it. ⟨This afternoon, at Court, I met with Lord Hinchingbrooke, newly come out of the country; who tells me that Creed's business with Mrs. Pickering will do, which I am neither troubled nor glad at.⟩[4]

---

a repl. 'he'   *b* repl. 'tell' (blotted)   *c* MS. 'me'
     d repl. 'that'   *e* repl. 'folly'

---

1. These were the three rates of daily allowance for each man for harbour-victuals, ordinary sea-victuals, and foreign sea-victuals respectively. Three other contractors had been in competition with Gauden: Josiah Child, King and Dodington. The drafting of the contract gave rise to difficulties (see below, p. 428 & n. 4) and in its final form (the indenture was signed on 18 March 1669) Sir William Penn and Benjamin Gauden were included as Gauden's partners: Rawl. A 216, pp. 217+ (draft in BM, Add. 9296, ff. 173+).

2. One of the four Clerks of the Privy Council.

3. His pension as ex-Governor of Tangier.

4. For their match, see below, p. 332 & n. 3.

27. *Lords day.* Up, and to my office to finish my journall for five days past; and so abroad and walked to White-hall, calling in at Somerset-house chapel, and also at the Spanish Imbassador's at York-house and there did hear a little Masse; and so to White-hall and there, the King being gone to chapel, I to walk all the*ᵃ* morning in the park; where I met Mr. Wren and he and I walked together in the Pell-Mell, it being most summer weather that ever was seen. And here talking of several things: of the corruption of the Court, and how unfit it is for ingenious men, and himself perticularly, to live in it; where a man cannot live but he must spend, and cannot get suitably without breach of his honour; and did thereupon up and tell me of the basest thing of my Lord Berkely, as of the basest thing that ever was heard of of a man. Which was this – how the Duke of York's Commissioners have*ᵇ* let his wine-licenses at a bad rate; and being offered a better, they did persuade the Duke of York to give some satisfaction to the former to quit it, and let it to the latter; which being done, my Lord Berkely did make the bargain for the former to have 1500*l* a year to quit it; whereof, since, it is come to light that they were to have but 800*l*, and himself 700*l*;*ᶜ* which the Duke of York hath ever since for some years paid, though this second bargain hath been broke, and the Duke of York lost by it of what the first was.[1]

He told me that there hath been a seeming accomodacion between the Duke of York and the Duke of Buckingham and Lord Arlington, the two latter desiring it; but yet that there is not true agreement between them, but they do labour to bring in all new creatures into play,[2] and the Duke of York doth oppose it, as perticularly in this of Sir D Gawden.

Thence, he gone, I to the Queen's Chapel and there heard some good singing; and so to White-hall and saw the King and

---

a repl. 'in'   *b* MS. 'of' (phonetic spelling)   *c* repl. '500'

---

1. The Duke had in 1661 been granted the revenue from the sale of licences to retail wine, the business being managed for him by commissioners who let it out to farm.

Berkeley of Stratton (Steward of his Household) boasted in 1663 that he (Berkeley) had already made £50,000 since the Restoration: above, iv. 331.

2. Cf. below, pp. 340–1.

Queen at dinner; and thence with Sir St. Fox to dinner, and the
Cofferer with us, and there mighty kind usage – and good discourse.   Thence, spent all the afternoon walking in the park;
and then in the evening at Court, on the Queen's side, and there
met Mr. Godolphin, who tells me that the news is true we heard
yesterday, of my Lord Sandwiches being come to Mounts bay
in Cornwall;[a1] and so I heard this afternoon at Mrs. Pierce's,
whom I went to make a short visit to.   This night, in the Queen's
drawing-room, my Lord Brouncker told me the difference that is
now between the three Imbassadors here, the Venetian,[b] French,
and Spaniard, the third not being willing to make a visit to the
first, because he would not receive him at the door; who is
willing to give him as much respect as he did to the French,
who was used no otherwise, and who refuses now to take more
of him, upon being desired thereto,[c] in order to the making an
accomodacion in this matter – which is very pretty.[2]   So, a boat
staying for me all this evening, I home in the dark about 8 at
night, and so over the ruins from the Old Swan home, with great
trouble.   And so to hear my boy read a little, and supper and to
bed.   ⟨This evening I found at home Pelling and Wallington
and one Aldrige, and we supped and sung.⟩[d]

28.   Up betimes, and Knepp's maid comes to me to tell[e] me
that the women's day at the playhouse[3] is today, and that therefore I must be there to encrease their profit.   I did give the pretty
maid Betty that comes to me half-a-crown for coming, and had

---

a   MS. 'Cornhill'   b   repl. 'Ventian'   c   repl. 'into'
   d   addition crowded in   e   repl. 'desire'

---

1. Cf. F. Bellott to Williamson,
Pendennis, 23 September (*CSPD
1667–8*, pp. 596–7), reporting that the
Greenwich frigate with Sandwich
aboard was anchored in Mount's Bay
because of contrary winds.   She had
sailed from Tangier on 29 August:
Harris, ii. 159.

2. The dispute is described in a
despatch (2/12 October) from the
Venetian resident: *CSP Ven. 1666–8*,
pp. 290–3.   The French ambassador,
paying his first visit of ceremony to
the new Venetian resident, had been
received half-way up the stairs, and
now insisted that the Spanish ambassador should not be accorded the
superior courtesy of a reception at the
door.

3. The actresses' benefit day.   (A).

a besar or dos, ella being mighty jolie; and so I about my business
by water to St. James's, and there had good opportunity of
speaking with the Duke of York, who desires me again, talking
on that matter, to prepare something for him to do for the better
managing of our office, telling me that my Lord Keeper and he
talking about it yesterday, my Lord Keeper did advise him to do
so, it being better to come from him then*a* otherwise – which I
have promised to do.   Thence to my Lord Burlington's house,[1]
the first time I ever was there, it being the house built by Sir
Jo. Denham, next to Clarendon-house.   And here I visited my
Lord Hinchingbrooke and his Lady, Mr. Sidny Mountagu being
come last night, come to town unexpectedly from Mounts bay,
where he left my Lord well eight days since; so as we may now
hourly expect to hear of his arrivall at Portsmouth.   Sidny is
mightily grown;[2] and I am glad I am here to see him at his first
coming, though it cost me dear, for here I come to be necessitated
to supply them with 500*l* for my Lord:[3] he sent him up with a
declaration to his friends of the necessity of his being presently
suppli[ed] with two thousand pounds, but I do not think he will
get one; however, I think it becomes my*b* duty to my Lord to do
something extraordinary in this,*c* and the rather because I have
been remiss in writing to him during this voyage – more then
ever I did in my life, and more indeed then was fit for me.   By
and by comes Sir W. Godolphin to see Mr. Sidny, who I perceive
is much dissatisfied that he should come to town last night and not
yet be with my Lord Arlington, who, and all the town, hear of his
being come to town; and he did it seems take notice of it to

a MS. 'and' *b* repl. 'might' *c* repl. 'the'

1. Burlington House, Piccadilly.
Burlington was Hinchingbrooke's
father-in-law. (R).
2. Sydney, Sandwich's second son,
was 18.
3. Pepys immediately sent £500 to
Portsmouth by a letter of credit from
Edward Backwell drawn on Hugh
Salisbury of Portsmouth: Pepys to

Sandwich, 29 September (Rawl. A
174, ff. 424, 427; printed Bray-
brooke, 1854, iv. 197+). Sandwich,
recording its receipt on 30 September
remarked that it was 'absolutely
necessary for my occasions and noe
more': Sandwich MSS, Journals, viii.
546.

Godolphin this morning. So that I perceive this remissness in affairs doth continue in my Lord's managements still – which I am sorry for – but above all, to see in what a condition my Lord is for money, that I dare swear he doth not know where to take up 500*l* of any man in England at this time upon his word, but of myself, as I believe by the sequel hereof it will appear. Here I first saw and saluted my Lady Burlington, a very fine-speaking lady – and a good woman, but old and not handsome – but a brave woman in her parts. Here my Lady Hinchingbrooke tells me that she hath bought most of the wedding-clothes for Mrs. Pickering, so that the thing is gone through and will be soon ended – which I wonder at; but let them do as they will. Here I also, standing by a candle that was brought for sealing of a letter, do set my periwigg a-fire; which made such an odd noise, nobody could tell what it was till they saw the flame, my*a* back being to the candle. Thence to Westminster-hall and there walked a little, and to the Exchequer and so home by water; and after eating a bit, I to my vintner's and there did only look*b* upon su wife, which is mighty handsome.*b* And so to my glove and ribbon shop in Fanchurch-street and did the like there; and there stopping against the door of the shop Mrs. Horsfall, now a late Widdow, in a coach, I to her and shook her by the hand; and so she away and I by coach towards the King's playhouse; and meeting W How, took him with me and there saw *The Citty Match*,[1] a play not acted these 30 years, and but a silly play. The King and Court there. The*c* house, for the women's sake, mighty full. So I to White-hall, and there all the evening on the Queen's side; and it being a most summerlike day and a fine warm evening, the Italians came in a barge under the leads*d* before the Queen's drawing-room, and so the Queen and ladies went out*e* and heard it for almost an hour; and it was endeed very good together but yet there was but one voice that alone did appear considerable, and that was Seignor Joanni.[2] This done,

---

a   repl. 'by'   b–b garbled s.h.   c   repl. 'So'
d   repl. symbol rendered illegible   e   repl. 'home'

---

1. A farcical comedy by Jasper Mayne, acted in 1637 or 1638, and published in 1639. (A).
2. Possibly   Giovanni   Battista

Draghi (cf. above, viii. 54 & n. 4); later organist in Queen Catherine's chapel. (E)

by and by they went in; and here I saw Mr. Sidny Mountagu kiss the Queen's[a] hand; who was mighty kind to him – and the ladies looked mightily on him, and the King came by and by and did talk to him. So[b] I away by coach with Alderman Backewell home, who is mighty kind to me, more then ordinary, in his expressions. But I do hear this day what troubles me: that Sir W. Coventry is quite out of play, the King seldom speaking to him; and that there is a design of making a Lord Treasurer and that my Lord Arlington shall be the man;[1] but I cannot believe it – but yet the Duke of Buckingham hath it in his mind, and those with him, to make a thorough alteration in things; and among the rest, Coventry to be out.[2] The Duke of York did this day tell me how hot the whole party was in the business of Gawden – and perticularly, my Lord Anglesy tells me, the Duke of Buckingham for Child against Gawden; but the Duke of York did stand stoutly to it. So home to read and sup; and to bed.

29. 〈*Tuesday*〉 *Michaelmas day.* Up and to the office, where all the morning.[3]

---

a repl. 'King and Queen's hands'   *b* repl. 'So'

---

1. Cf. above, viii. 96 & n. 2.

2. Coventry was now upheld only by the Duke of York's support, and resigned in March 1669.

3. The rest of this page and the following twelve pages are left blank (except for the headline 'October' on the twelfth page), and the diary entries resumed twelve days later. No rough notes are inserted, as was done on two similar occasions previously (above, pp. 160+, 224+): whether Pepys kept them is not known. It is possible however to recover a few facts about his movements during the blank period. Sandwich's journal (Sandwich MSS, Journals, viii. 546–8) shows that on 1 October Pepys travelled to Southwick, Hants., with Viscount Hinchingbrooke and other members of Sandwich's family and household to welcome Sandwich back

from Spain. The party stayed at Guildford on the 2nd and returned to London on the 3rd, where Sandwich stayed until he left on the 10th to present himself at court, then at Audley End. A few days earlier, Pepys (perhaps taking advantage of the reduction in office business caused by the Duke of York's absence with the court) had himself travelled to E. Anglia. He paid a visit to the King, then staying at Little Saxham, Suffolk, on the evening of 7 October: below, p. 336 & n. 5. Afterwards it seems that he called at Impington, near Cambridge, for his wife, who (with Mercer, Deb and Will Hewer) had been visiting Roger Pepys there since 15 September, in order to see Sturbridge Fair: above, p. 306. They returned to London on the 10th: *Further Corr.*, p. 195.

11. *Lords day.* Up and to church, where I find Parson Mills come to town and preached, and the church full, most people being now come home to town, though the season of year is as*a* good as summer in all respects.[1] At noon dined at home with my wife all alone, and busy all the afternoon in my closet, making up some papers with W. Hewer; and at night comes Mr. Turner and his wife, and there they tell me that Mr. Harper is dead at Deptford, and so now all his and my care is how to secure his being Storekeeper in his stead. And here, they and their daughter, and a kinswoman that came along with them, did sup with me, and pretty merry; and then they gone, and my wife to read to me, and to bed.

12. Up, and with Mr. Turner by water to White-hall, there to think to enquire when the Duke of York will be in town, in order to Mr.*b* Turner's going down to Audly-end[2] about his place; and here I met in St. James's park with one that told us that the Duke of York would be in town tomorrow, and so Turner parted and went home, and I also did stop my intentions of going to the Court also this day, about securing Mr. Turner's place of Petty Pourveyor to Mr. Hater. So I to my Lord Brouncker's, thinking to have gone and spoke to him about it, but he is gone out of town till night. And so meeting a gentle-man of my Lord Middleton's looking*c* for me about the payment of the 1000*l* lately ordered to his Lord in advance of his pay, which shall arise upon his going governor to Tanger, I did go*d* to his Lord's lodgings, and there spoke the first time with him and find

a repl. 'almost'   *b* repl. 'his going'
c repl. 'in looking'   *d* repl. 'good'

---

1. Cf. above, p. 150, n. 1.
2. The court had been at Audley End, Essex (and elsewhere in E.
Anglia) since 6 October: *London Gazette*, 8 October.

him a shrowd man, but a drinking man I think, as the world says –
but a man that hath seen much of the world, and is a Scott.[1]
I offered him my service, though I can do him little, but he sent
his man home with me; where I made him stay till I had gone
to Sir W Pen to bespeak him*a* about Mr. Hater; who, contrary
to [my] fears, did appear very friendly, to my great content, for I
was afeared of his appearing for his man Burroughs; but he did
not.   But did declare to me afterward his intentions to desire an
excuse in his own business, to be eased of the business of the
Controller[2] – his health not giving him power to stay always in
town, but he must go into the country.   I did say little to him
but compliment, having no leisure to think of his business, or any
man's but my own; and so away and home,*b* where I find Sir
H. Cholmly come to town, and*c* is come hither to see me.   And
he is a man that I love mightily, as being, of a gentleman, the most
industrious that ever I saw.[3]   He stayed with me a while, talking
and telling me his obligations to my Lord Sandwich; which I
was glad of.   And that the Duke of Buckingham is now chief of
all men in this Kingdom; which I knew before.   And that he
doth think the Parliament will hardly ever meet again; which is a
great many men's thoughts, and I shall not be sorry for it.   He
being gone, I with my Lord Middleton's servant to Mr. Colvill's,
but he was not in town; and so he parted, and I home and
there to dinner, and Mr.*d* Pelling with us; and thence my wife
and Mercer and W. Hewer and Deb to the King's playhouse,
and I afterward by water after them, and there we did hear the
Eunuch (who it seems is a Frenchman, but long bred in Italy)

a repl. 'with'   *b* repl. 'with'
c repl. 'to'   *d* repl. 'after dinner'

---

1. Appointed to the post in May
1668, Middleton was not sent there
until October 1669. He had served
in both parliamentarian and royalist
armies in England and Scotland, had
been in exile with the court in France
and elsewhere, and had been High
Commissioner to the Scottish parliament in 1660–3.

2. Since November 1666 Penn

(with Brouncker) had assisted Mennes
as Comptroller.

3. Sir Hugh Cholmley was in
charge of the building of the mole at
Tangier. He had also built a pier
at Whitby, Yorks. His industry is
plain to see in his letter-books, now
in the N. Yorkshire County R. O.,
Northallerton.

sing;[1] which I seemed to take as new to me, though I saw on Saturday last but said nothing of it.   But such action and singing I could never have imagined to have heard – and doth make good whatever Tom Hill used to tell me.   Here we met with Mr. Batelier and his sister; and so they home with us in two coaches, and there at my house stayed and supped; and this night my bookseller, Shrewsbury, comes and brings my *Books of Martyrs*,[2] and I did pay him for them, and did this night make the young women before supper to open all the volumes for me; and so to supper, and after supper to read a ridiculous nonsensical book set out by Will Pen for the Quakers; but so full of nothing but nonsense that I was ashamed[a] to read in it.[3]   So they gone, we to bed.

13.   Up and to the office; and before the office, did speak with my Lord Brouncker and there did get his ready assent to T. Hater's having of Mr. Turner's place, and so Sir J. Mennes also. But when we came to set down at the Board, comes to us Mr. Wren this day to town, and tells me that James Southern doth petition the Duke of York for the Store-keeper's place of Deptford; which did trouble me much, and also the Board, though upon discourse after he was gone, we did resolve to move hard for our Clerks, and that places of preferment may go according to Seniority and merit.[4]   So, the Board up, I home with my people

a   repl. 'afeared'

1. Possibly Baldassare Ferri. Pepys's reference to 'the Eunuch' two days later (p. 329) makes it clear that the play was Fletcher's *The faithful shepherdess*. (A).

2. See above, p. 284, n. 5.

3. This was a short unlicensed tract (18 pp.), just issued; written from Newgate, where Penn was imprisoned: *Truth exalted; in a short, but sure, testimony against those religions, faiths and worships that have been formed and followed in the darkness of apostacy. By William Penn the Younger, whom Divine Love constrains in a holy contempt to trample on Egypt's glory, not fearing the King's wrath, having beheld the Magisty of him who is invisible.* It was Penn's first book, in which he attacked everybody ('Princes, Priests and People') except Quakers; an immature and worthless work; not in the PL.

4. James Southerne was one of the clerks in the Admiral's office. (He became Clerk of the Acts in 1677.) Thomas Turner (clerk to Mennes and Purveyor of Petty Provisions in the Navy Office) was now appointed to the storekeeper's place on 14 October.

to dinner; and so to the office again and there, after doing some business, I with Mr. Turner to the Duke of Albemarle's at night, and there did speak to him about his appearing to Mr. Wren a friend to Mr. Turner, which he did take kindly from me;[1] and so away thence, well pleased with what we had now done; and so I with him home, stopping at my Lord Brouncker's and getting his hand to a letter I wrote to the Duke of York for T. Hater,[2] and also at my Lord Middleton's to give him an account of what I had done this day with his man at Alderman Backwell's, about the getting of his 1000*l* paid. And here he did take occasion to discourse about the business of the Dutch war, which he says he was alway an enemy to; and did discourse very well of it, I saying little, but pleased to hear him talk and to see how some men may by age come to know much, and yet by their drinking and other pleasures render themselfs not very considerable. I did this day find by discourse with somebody, that this gentleman was the great Major-Generall Middleton, that was of the Scots army in the beginning of the late war against the King.[3] Thence home and to the office to finish my letters; and so home and did get my wife to read to me, and then ⟨Deb⟩ to comb my head; and here I had the pleasure para touch the cosa of her*a* and all about, with a little opposition; and so to bed.

14. Up, and by water, stopping at Michell's; and there saw Betty, but could have no discourse with her, but there drank. To White-hall and there walked to St. James, where I find the Court mighty full, it being the Duke of York's birthday; and he mighty fine, and all the music, one after another, to my great content. Here I met with Sir H Cholmly, and he and I to walk and to my Lord Berkely's new house,[4] there to see a new

a garbled s.h.: see above, viii. 244, note *a*

1. Albemarle was well disposed towards Turner. In 1660 he had tried to get him appointed Clerk of the Acts instead of Pepys: above, vii. 31 & n. 1.
2. Untraced.

3. Until 1648 Middleton had been one of the leaders of the Covenanters, playing a prominent part in the battle of Philiphaugh (1645) and the campaign of 1646 against Montrose.
4. In Piccadilly.

experiment of a Cart, which by having two little wheeles fastened to the axle tree is said to make it go with half the ease and more, then*a* another cart; but we did not see the trial made.¹ Thence I home; and there after dinner to St. James's and there met my Brethren; but the Duke of York being gone out, and tonight being a play there and a great festival,² we would not stay, but went all of us to the King's playhouse and there saw *The Faythfull Shepherdess*³ again, that we might hear the French Eunuch sing; which we did, to our great content, though I do admire his action as much as his singing, being both beyond all I ever saw or heard. Thence with W. Penn*b* home, and there to get my people to read and to supper, and so to bed.

15. Up and all the morning at the office, and at home at dinner; where after dinner, my wife and I and Deb out by coach to the Upholster's in Long-lane, Alderman Reeves, and then to Alderman Crow's, to see variety of Hangings; and were mightily pleased therewith and spent the whole afternoon thereupon; and at last, I think we shall pitch upon the best suit of Apostles, where three pieces for my room will come to almost 80*l.*⁴ So home and to my office, and then home to supper and to bed. ⟨This day at the Board came, unexpected, the warrants*c* from the Duke of York for Mr. Turner and Hater for the places they desire;⁵ which contents me mightily.⟩*d*

---

a MS. 'that'   *b* repl. 'W. Coventry'
c repl. same symbol   *d* addition crowded in

---

1. For some of his earlier (1665) experiments with 'chariots', see Birch, ii. 63, 66.
2. For an account, see the despatch of the Swedish resident (14 October), in W. Westergaard (ed.), *First Triple Alliance*, p. 28.
3. A pastoral drama by John Fletcher; see above, iv. 182, n. 3. (A).
4. The prices both of this and of the suit which Pepys in fact bought (on the 16th) suggest that they were

either second-hand or imitation tapestries made of painted or stained cloth. The 'Acts of the Apostles' was a favourite design, based on cartoons by Raphael and manufactured e.g. at the Mortlake tapestry works (with which both Sir Sackville and Sir Richard Crow were connected, 1661–7): Whinney and Millar, pp. 126–7, 129–30.
5. See above, p. 327 & n. 4. Turner's warrant (14 October) is in PRO, Adm. 106/17, p. 170.

16.   Up and busy at the office all the morning; and before*a*
noon I took my wife by coach, and Deb, and showed her Mr.
Wren's hangings and bed at St. James's and Sir W. Coventry's
in the Pell-Mell, for our satisfaction in what we are going to
buy.   And so by Mr. Crow's home about his hangings, and do
pitch upon buying his second suit*b* of Apostles, the whole suit,
which comes to 83*l* – and this we think the best for us, having
now the whole suit to*c* answer any other rooms or service.   So
home to dinner, and with Mr. Hater by water to St. James's;
there Mr. Hater do give Mr. Wren thanks for his kindness about
his place that he hath lately granted him, of petty-purveyor of
petty emptions,[1] upon the removal of Mr. Turner to be Storekeeper at Deptford on the death of Harper.   And then we all up
to the Duke of York and there did our usual business; and so
I with J. Mennes home; and there finding my wife gone to my
aunt Wight's to see her the first time after her coming to town,
and endeed the first time I think these two years (we having
been great strangers one to the other for a*d* great while),[2] I to
them and there mighty kindly used and had a barrel of oysters;
and so to look up and down their house, they having hung a
room since I was there, but with hangings not fit to be seen with
mine, which I find all come home tonight.   And here staying
an hour or two, we home and there to supper and to bed.

17.   Up and to the office, where all the morning sitting; and
at noon home to dinner and to the office all the afternoon; and
then late home and there with much pleasure getting Mr. Gibbs,
that writes well, to write the name upon my new draft of the
Resolution;[3] and so set it up and altered the situation of some of

a repl. 'at'	*b* repl. 'sort'
c repl. full stop	*d* repl. 'many days'

---

1. This officer had charge of all
purchases made on behalf of the
Board without warrant from the
Navy Treasurer.
2. Uncle Wight had in May 1664
made an improper proposal to Mrs
Pepys. According to the diary, Mrs
Pepys had not been to his house since

28 May 1666. The Wights had a
country house near Guildford, Surrey.
3. The drawing was by Anthony
Deane: above, p. 262 & n. 4. The
Resolution was a 3rd-rate built in 1667
at Harwich. Gibbs was a Navy
Office clerk.

my pictures in my closet, to my extraordinary content, and at it with much pleasure till almost 12 at night. Mr. Moore and Seamour were with me this afternoon, who tell me that my Lord Sandwich was received mighty kindly by the King,[1] and is in exceeding great esteem with him and the rest about him; but I doubt it will be hard for him to please both King and Duke of York; which I shall be sorry for. Mr. Moore tells me the sad condition my Lord is in in*ª* his estate and debts and the way he now lives in, so high, and so many vain servants about him, that he must be ruined if he doth not take up; which by the grace of God, I will put him upon when I come to see him.

18. *Lords day.* Up and with my boy Tom all the morning, altering the places of my pictures with great pleasure; and at noon to dinner, and then comes Mr. Shales to see me, and I with him to recommend him to my Lord Brouncker's service;[2] which I did at Madam Williams's, and my Lord receives him. Thence with Brouncker to Lincoln's Inn and Mr. Ball, to visit Dr. Wilkins, now newly Bishop of Chester; and he received us mighty kindly and had most excellent discourse from him about his book of *reall Character;*[3] and so I with Lord Brouncker to White-hall and there saw the Queen and some ladies; and with Lord Brouncker back again,*ᵇ* it being a rainy evening, and so my*ᶜ* Lord forced [to] lend me his coach till I got a hackney; which I did, and so home and to supper, and got my wife to read to me and so to bed.

19. Up and to my office to set down my Journall for some days past, and so to other business. At the office all the morning

---

a repl. 'for'   *b* MS. 'it again'
       c repl. 'me'

---

1. On 11 October, at Audley End: Sandwich MSS, Journals, viii. 548. Henry Moore had helped to look after Sandwich's affairs during his absence; John Seymour had been with him in Madrid.

2. John Shales had been a victual-ling agent at Portsmouth. He now entered Brouncker's service: *CSPD 1668–9*, p. 264.

3. His book on a universal language: see above, p. 200, n. 7. Wilkins had been made Bishop of Chester on 26 September.

upon some business of Sir W. Warren's[1] and at noon home to
dinner; and thence out by coach with wife and Deb and Mr.
Harman the upholster, and carried him to take measure of Mr.
Wren's bed at St. James's, I being resolved to have just such
another made me; and thence set him down in the Strand, and
my wife and I to the Duke of York's playhouse and there saw,
the first time acted, *The Queene of Arragon*, an old Blackfriars'
play but an admirable one,[2] so good that I am astonished at it
and wonder where it hath lain asleep all this while, that I have
never heard of it before.   Here met W. Batelier and Mrs. Hunt,
Deb's aunt, and saw her home; a very witty woman and one
that knew this play, and understands a play mighty well.   Left
her at home in Jewen-street; and we home and to supper, and
my wife to read to me and so to bed.

20.   Up and to the office all the morning; and then home to
dinner, having this day a new girle come to us in the room of
Nell, who is lately, about four days since, gone away, being
grown lazy and proud.   This girl to stay only till we have a
boy, which I intend to keep when I have a coach; which I am
now about.   At this time, my wife and I mighty busy laying out
money in dressing up our best chamber and thinking*a* of a coach
and coachman and horses &c, and the more because of Creed's
being now married to Mrs. Pickering; a thing I could never
have expected, but it is done about seven or ten days since – as I
hear out of the country.[3]   At noon home to dinner, and my wife
and Harman and girl abroad to buy things; and I walked out to

a   repl. 'and making'

---

1. Warren's figures for the abate-
ment to be made (for short length) on
his bill for New England masts had
recently been challenged by a report
from the Deptford yard: Tanner 44,
ff. 40, 44.

2. The play was a tragicomedy by
William Habington; acted and published in 1640.   It was 'an old Blackfriars play' in that it was the property

of the King's Men, who used the
Blackfriars Theatre from c. 1608 until
1642.   (A).

3. Betty Pickering was Sandwich's
niece; she and John Creed had been
married at Tichmarsh, Northants., on
6 October.   Pepys greatly resented
Creed's 'devilish presumption' in
aspiring to her: above, vi. 88; cf. also
above, p. 269.

several places to pay debts, and among other things to look out for a coach; and saw many, and did light on one, for which I bid 50l,[1] which doth please me mightily – and I believe I shall have it. So to my tailor's and the New Exchange, and so by coach home; and there, having this day bought[a] the *Queene of Arragon* play,[2] I did get my wife and W Batelier to read it over this night by 11 a-clock, and so to bed.

21.[b] Lay pretty long, talking with content with my wife about our coach and things; and so to the office, where Sir D Gawden was to do something in his accounts. At noon to dinner to Mr. Batelier's, his mother coming this day a'house-warming to him, and several friends of his, to which he invited us. Here mighty merry, and his mother the same; I heretofore took her for a gentlewoman, and understanding. I rose from table before the rest, because under an obligation to go to my Lord Brouncker's, where to meet several gentlemen of the Royal Society to go and make a visit to the French Embassador Colbert at Licester-house, he having endeavoured[c] to make one or two to my Lord Brouncker, as our President, but he was not within.[3] But I came too late, they being gone before; but I fallowed to Leicester-house, but they are gone in and up before me; and so I away to the New Exchange and there stayed for my wife; and she come,[d] we to cow-lane and there I showed her the coach which I pitch on, and she is out of herself for joy almost; but[e] the man not within, so did nothing more towards an agreement; but to Mr. Crow's about a bed, to have his advice; and

      a repl. 'brought'   *b* repl. '20'
c repl. 'made'   *d* repl. 'gone I away'   *e* repl. 'and'

---

1. Pepys's ambition to own a coach went back at least to April 1667: above, viii. 173–4. For prices, see J. Parkes, *Travel in Engl. in 17th cent.*, p. 73. In 1665 Sir Edward Harley paid £38 for the cheapest coach and harness he could buy in London: HMC, *Portland*, iii. 290.

2. No longer in the PL. (A).
3. The visit is briefly noticed in a newsletter of 21 October: *Bulstrode Papers*, i. 69. The writer states that Colbert had already visited Brouncker twice.

so home and there had my wife to read to me, and so to supper
and to bed. *Memorandum*: that from Crows, we went back to
Charing-cross and there left my people at their tailor's while I to
my Lord Sandwiches lodgings, who came to town the last night
and is come thither to lie – and met with him within; and among
others, my new Cosen Creed, who looks mighty soberly; and
he and I salute one another with mighty gravity, till we came to
a little more freedom of talk about it. But here I hear that Sir
Gilb. Pickering is lately dead, about three days since, which
makes some sorrow there; though not much, because of his
being long expected to die, having been in a Lethargy long.[1] So
waited on my Lord to Court, and there stayed and saw the ladies
awhile; and thence to my wife and took them up; and so home
and to supper and bed.

22. Up, and W Batelier's Frenchman, a periwig-maker,
comes and brings me a new one, which I liked and paid him
for*a* – a mighty gentile fellow. So to the office, where sat all
the morning. And at noon home to dinner; and thence with
wife and Deb to Crows and there did see some more beds;
and we shall, I think, pitch upon a Camlott one when all is done.
Thence sent them home, and I to Arundell-house, where the first
time we have met since the vacation;[2] and not much company,
but here much good discourse; and afterward, my Lord and
others and I to the Devil tavern and there eat and drank; and so
late with Mr. Colwell home by coach; and at home took him
with me and there found my uncle Wight and aunt, and Woolly
and his wife, and there supped and mighty merry. And anon
they gone; and Mrs. Turner stayed, who was there also, to talk
of her husband's business; and the truth is, I was the less pleased
to talk with her for that she hath not yet owned, in any fit manner

a repl. 'a'

1. Pickering was Creed's new
father-in-law. He died aged about
55 at his house at Tichmarsh,
Northants., and had been buried on
the 17th.

2. The Royal Society on this day
resumed its meetings after ten weeks'
vacation: Birch, ii. 313.

of thanks, my late and principal service to her husband about his place,[1] which I alone ought to have the thanks for, if they know as much as I do – but let it go: if they do not own it, I shall have it in my hand to teach them to do it. So to bed. ⟨This day, order came for all the Principal Officers to bring them[2] their patents; which I did in the afternoon, by leaving it at their office, but am troubled at what should be their design therein.⟩*a*

23. Up, and plasterers at work and painter[s] about my house.[3] Collonell Middleton and I to St. James's, where with the rest of our company we attended on our usual business the Duke of York. Thence I to White-hall to my Lord Sandwiches, where I find my Lord within but busy, private; and so I stayed a little, talking with the young gentlemen;[4] and so away with Mr. Pierce the surgeon toward Tyburne to see the people executed, but came too late, it being done, two men and a woman hanged;[5] and so I back again and to my coachmaker's, and there did come a little nearer agreement for the coach; and so to Duck-lane and there my bookseller's[6] and saw his moher, but ella is so big*b*-bellied that ella is not worth seeing.*b* So home and there all alone to dinner, my wife and W. Hewer being gone to Deptford to see her mother; and so I to the office all the afternoon. In the afternoon comes my cousin Sidny Pickering to bring my wife and me his sister's favour for her wedding;[7] which is kindly done. And he gone, I to business again; and in the evening home, there made my wife read till supper time, and so to bed. This day Pierce doth tell me, among other news, the late frolic and Debauchery of Sir Ch. Sidly and Buckhurst, running up and down all the night with their*c* arses bare through the streets,

---

a   addition crowded in at bottom of page   *b–b*   garbled s.h.
c   MS. 'the'

---

1. See above, p. 328 & n. 1.
2. The Brooke House Committee.
3. The plasterer's bill (£6 19s. 6d.) is recorded in the Navy Treasurer's ledgers: PRO, Adm. 20/12, p. 21, no. 5.
4. Sandwich's twin sons, John and Oliver, now (probably) at Westminster school.
5. Not identified.
6. William Shrewsbury.
7. With Creed: see above, p. 332 & n. 3.

and at last fighting and being beat by the watch and clapped up all night; and how the King takes their parts and my Lord Chief Justice Keeling hath laid the constable by the heels to answer it next sessions – which is a horrid shame.[1] How the King and these gentlemen did make the fiddlers of Thetford, this last progress,[2] to sing them all the bawdy songs they could think of. How*a* Sir W. Coventry was brought the other day to the Duchesse of York by the Duke of York*b* to kiss her hand; who did acknowledge his unhappiness to occasion her so much sorrow,[3] declaring his intentions in it and praying her pardon; which she did give him upon his promise to make good his*c* pretences of innocence to her family by his faithfulness to his master,*d* the Duke of York. That the Duke of Buckingham is now all in all, and will ruin Coventry if he can; and that W. Coventry doth now rest wholly upon the Duke of York for his standing; which is a great turn. He tells me that my Lady Castlemayne, however, is a mortal enemy to the Duke of Buckingham; which I understand not, but it seems she doth disgust his greatness and his ill usage of her. That the King was drunk at Saxam[4] with*e* Sidly, Buckhurst, &c. the night that my Lord Arlington came thither, and would not give him audience, or could not – which is true, for it was that night that I was there and saw the King go up to his chamber, and was told that the King had been drinking.[5] He tells me too, that the Duke of York did the next day chide Bab. May for his occasioning the King's giving*f* himself up to these gentlemen, to the neglecting of my Lord Arlington; to which he answered merrily, that, by God, there was no man in England

---

a repl. 'So'   *b* repl. 'Duke'   *c* repl. 'the'
d repl. same symbol   *e* repl. 'the night that'   *f* repl. 'not'

---

1. The incident has not been traced elsewhere. Cf. their similar offence, above, iv. 209–10.

2. See above, p. 323, n. 3.

3. By his part in the fall of Clarendon, her father, in October 1667.

4. Little Saxham, nr Bury St Edmund's, Suff.; the home of Lord Crofts.

5. The King was there on the night of 7–8 October: *Bulstrode Papers*, i. 67. Arlington wrote to Williamson from Bury on the 7th reporting that he had failed to see the King 'by reason of the uncertainty of his motions': *CSPD 1668–9*, p. 8.

that had heads to lose, durst do what they do every day with the King; and asked the Duke of York's pardon – which is a sign of a mad world. God bless us out of it.

24. This morning comes to me the coachmaker, and agreed with me for 53*l*, and stand to the courtesy for what more I should give him upon the finishing of it. He is likely also to fit me with a coachman. There comes also to me Mr. Shotgrave, the Operator of our Royal Society, to show me his method of making the Tubes for Eyes, which are clouterly done, so that mine are better; but I have well informed myself in several things from him and so am glad of speaking with him. So to the office, where all the morning, and then to dinner; and so all the afternoon late at the office; and so home, and my wife to read to me; and then with much content to bed. ⟨This day, Lord Brouncker tells me that the making Sir J. Mennes a bare Commissioner is now in doing, which I am glad of; but he speaks of two new Commissioners, which I do not believe.⟩*a*1

25. *Lords day.* Up, and discoursing with my wife about our house and many new things we are doing of; and so to church I, and there find*b* Jack Fen come, and his wife, a pretty black* woman; I never saw her before, nor took notice of her now. So home and to dinner; and after dinner, all*c* the afternoon got my wife and boy to read to me. And at night W Batelier comes and sups with us; and after supper, to have my head combed by Deb, which occasioned the greatest sorrow to me that ever I knew in this world; for my wife, coming up suddenly, did find me imbracing the girl con my hand*d* sub su coats; and endeed, I was with my main in her cunny.*d* I was at a wonderful loss upon it, and the girl also; and I endeavoured to put it off,

---

a addition crowded in at bottom of page   b MS. 'fine'
c repl. 'by water to White-hall'   d–d garbled s.h.

---

1. Nothing came of these proposals. No new commissioners were now appointed, and Mennes kept the comptrollership until his death in 1671, by which time he had held office for a longer period than any other Principal Officer except Pepys himself.

but my wife was struck mute and grew angry, and as her voice came to her, grew quite out of order; and I do*ᵃ* say little, but to bed; and my wife said little also, but could not sleep all night; but about 2 in the morning waked me and cried, and fell to tell me as a great secret that she was a Roman Catholique and had received the Holy Sacrament;[1] which troubled*ᵇ* me but I took no notice of it, but she went on from one thing to another, till at last it appeared plainly her trouble was at what she saw; but yet I did not know how much she saw and therefore said nothing to her. But after her much crying and reproaching me with inconstancy and preferring a sorry girl*ᶜ* before her, I did give her no provocations but did promise all fair usage to her, and love, and foreswore any hurt that I did with her – till at last she seemed to be at ease again; and so toward morning, a little

《26》 sleep; and so I, with some little repose and rest, rose, and up and by water to White-hall, but with my mind mightily troubled for the poor girl, whom I fear I have undone by this, my [wife] telling me that she would turn her out of door. However, I was obliged to attend the Duke of York, thinking to have had a meeting of Tanger today, but had not; but*ᵈ* he did take me and Mr. Wren into his closet, and there did press me to prepare what I had to say upon the answers of my fellow-officers to his great letter; which I promised to do against his coming to town again the next week; and so to other discourse, finding plainly that he is in trouble and apprehensions of the reformers,[2] and would be found to do what he can towards re-forming himself. And so thence to my Lord Sandwich; where after long stay, he being in talk with others privately, I to him; and there he taking physic*ᵉ* and keeping his chamber, I had an hour's talk with him about the ill posture of things at this time, while the King gives*ᶠ* countenance to Sir Ch. Sidly and Lord Buckhurst, telling him their late story of running up and down the streets a little while since all night, and their being beaten

---

a MS. 'to'   *b* repl. same word struck through twice   *c* repl. 'slut'
     d repl. 'and'   *e* repl. 'his'   *f* repl. same symbol

---

1. She more than once threatened   2. Cf. above, pp. 291-2 & n.
to become a Catholic, but never did:
cf. above, v. 92, n. 2.

and clapped up all night by the constable, who is since chid and imprisoned for his pains.

He tells me that he thinks his matters do stand well with the King – and hopes to have despatch to his mind; but I doubt it, and do see that he doth fear it too. He told me my Lady Carteret's trouble about my writing of that letter of the Duke of York's lately to the office; which I did not own, but declared to be of no injury to G. Carteret, and that I would write a letter to him to satisfy him therein. But this I am in pain how to do without doing myself wrong, and the end I had, of preparing a justification to myself hereafter, when the faults of the Navy come to be found out. However, I will do it in the best manner I can.

Thence by coach home and to dinner, finding my wife mightily discontented and the girl sad, and no words from my wife to her. So after dinner, they out with me about two or three things; and so home again, I all the evening busy and my wife full of trouble in her looks; and anon to bed – where about midnight, she wakes me and there falls foul on me again, affirming that she saw me hug and kiss the girl; the latter I denied, and truly; the other I confessed and no more. And upon her pressing me, did offer to give her under my hand that I would never see Mrs. Pierce more, nor Knepp, but did promise her perticular demonstrations of my true love to her, owning some indiscretion in what I did, but that there was no harm in it. She at last on these promises was quiet, and very kind we were, and so to sleep; and in the morning up, but with my mind troubled for the poor girl, with whom I could not get opportunity to speak; but to the office, my mind mighty full of sorrow for her,[a] where all the morning, and to dinner with my people and to the office all the afternoon; and so at night home and there busy to get some things ready against tomorrow's meeting of Tanger; and that being done and my clerks gone, my wife did towards bedtime begin to be in a mighty rage from some new matter that she had got in her head, and did most part of the night in bed rant at me in most high terms, of threats of publishing my shame; and when I offered to rise, would have rose too, and caused a candle to be lit, to burn by

《27》

a followed by 'to the office

her all night in the chimney while she ranted; while [I], that knew
myself to have given some grounds for it, did make it my business
to appease her all I could possibly, and by good words and fair
promises did make her very quiet; and so rested all night and
rose with perfect good peace, being heartily afflicted for this
folly of mine that did occasion it; but was forced to be silent
about the girl, which I have no mind to part with, but much
《28》   less that the poor girl should be undone by my folly. So
up, with mighty kindness from my wife and a thorough
peace; and being up, did by a note advise the girl what I had
done and owned, which note I was in pain for till*a* she told me
that she had burned it. 《This evening, Mr. Spong came and
sat late with me, and first told me of the instrument called
Parrallogram,[1] which I must have one of, showing me his practice
thereon by a map of England.》

So by coach with Mr. Gibson to Chancery-lane, and there
made oath before a Maister of Chancery to my Tanger account
of Fees; and so to White-hall, where by and by a Committee
met; my Lord Sandwich there, but his report was not received,
it being late; but only a little business done, about the supplying
the place with victuals; but I did get, to my great content, my
account allowed of Fees, with great applause by my Lord Ashly
and Sir W. Penn. Thence home, calling at one or two places,
and there about our workmen,*b* who are at work upon my wife's
closet and other parts of my house, that we are all in dirt. So
after dinner, with Mr. Gibson all the afternoon in my closet;
and at night*c* to supper and to bed, my wife and I at good
peace, but yet with some little grudgeings of trouble in her, and
more in me, about the poor girl.

29. At the office all the morning, where Mr. Wren first tells
us of the order from the King, come last night to the Duke of
York, for signifying his pleasure to the Sollicitor generall for
drawing up a commission for suspending of my Lord Anglesy

a repl. 'it while'   *b* repl. 'walk'   *c* repl. 'sup'-

---

1. Pantograph; an instrument for copying maps etc. on the same or on
an altered scale.

and putting in Sir Tho. Littleton and Sir Tho. Osborne (the former a creature of Arlington's, and the latter of the Duke of Buckingham's) during the suspension.[1] The Duke of York was forced to obey, and did grant it, he being to go to Newmarket this day with the King, and so the King pressed for it. But Mr. Wren doth own that the Duke of York is the most wounded in this in the world, for it is done and concluded without his privity, after his appearing for him[2] – and that it is plain that they do ayme to bring the Admiralty into commission too, and lessen the Duke of York.[3] This doth put strange apprehensions into all our Board; only, I think I am the least troubled at it, for I care not at all for it – but my Lord Brouncker and Pen do seem to think much of it. So home to dinner, full of this news; and after dinner to the office, and so home all the afternoon to do business towards my drawing up an account for the Duke of York of the answers of this office to his late great letter, and late at it; and so to bed, with great peace from my wife and quiet, I bless God.

30. Up betimes, and Mr. Povy comes to even accounts with me; which we did, and then fell to other talk;[4] he tells me, in short, how the King is made a child of by Buckingham and Arlington, to the lessening of the Duke of York, whom they cannot suffer to be great, for fear of my Lord Chancellors return; which therefore they make the King violent against. That he believes it is impossible these two great men can hold together long – or at least that the ambition of the former is so great that he will endeavour to master all, and bring into play as many as he can. That Anglesy will not lose his place easily, but will contend in law with whoever comes to execute it.[5] That

---

1. There was some difficulty involved in dismissing Anglesey outright since he had been appointed for life by patent; but he was 'suspended and discharged' on 2 November: *CSPD 1671*, p. 498. For the political explanation of the new appointment, see A. Browning, *Danby*, i. 64–5.

2. I.e. for Anglesey. This is con-

firmed by James's own account: *Life* (ed. Clarke, 1816), i. 436.

3. For this rumour, see above, p. 278 & n. 5.

4. Thomas Povey knew the Duke of York's household well, having been the Duke's Comptroller until 1666.

5. See below, p. 362, n. 1.

the Duke of York, in all things but in his codpiece,[a] is led by the nose by his wife.   That W. Coventry is now, by the Duke of York, made friends with the Duchess – and that he is often there, and waits on her.   That he doth believe that these present great men will break in time, and that W. Coventry will be a great man again; for he doth labour to have nothing to do in matters of the State, and is so useful to the side that he is on, that he will stand, though at present he is quite out of play.   That my Lady Castlemaine hates the Duke of Buckingham.   That the Duke of York hath expressed himself very kind to my Lord Sandwich; which I am mighty glad of.   That we are to expect more changes if these men stand.   This done, he and I to talk of my coach, and I got him to go see it; where he finds most infinite fault with it, both as to being out of fashion and heavy; with so good reason, that I am mightily glad of his having corrected me in it; and so I do resolve to have one of his build, and with his advice, both in coach and horses, he being the fittest man in the world for it.   And so he carried me home and said the same to my wife.   So I to the office and he away; and at noon I home to dinner and all the afternoon late, with Gibson at my chamber late, about my present great business; only, a little in the afternoon at the office about Sir D. Gawden's accounts; and so to bed and slept heartily; my wife and I at good peace, but my heart troubled and her mind not at ease I perceive, she against and I for the girl; to whom I have not said anything these three days – but resolve to be mighty strange in appearance to her.

This night, W Batelier came and took his leave of us, he setting[b] out for France to-morrow.[1]

31.   Up, and at the office all the morning.   At noon home to dinner with my people; and afternoon, to[c] the office again, and then to my chamber with Gibson to do more about my great answer for the Duke of York; and so at night, after supper, to bed, well pleased with my advance thereon.   This day Lord Anglesy was at the office and doth seem to make nothing of

a repl. 'cop'-   b repl. 'going'   c repl. 'home'

---

1. He was a wine merchant in the Bordeaux trade.

this business of his suspension, resolving to bring it into Council, where he seems not to doubt to have right, he standing upon his defence and patent – and hath put in his Caveats to the several offices; so as soon as the King comes back again, which[a] will be on Tuseday next, he will bring it into the Council.

So ends this month, with some quiet to my mind, though not perfect, after the greatest falling out with my poor wife, and through my folly with the girl, that ever I had; and I have reason to be sorry and ashamed of it – and more, to be troubled for the poor girl's sake; whom I fear I shall by this means prove the ruin of – though I shall think myself concerned both to love and be a friend to her. This day, Rogr. Pepys and his son Talbot, newly come to town, came and dined with me, and mighty glad I am to see them.

a repl. 'he will'

NOVEMBER

1. *Lords day.* Up, and with W Hewers at my chamber all this morning,[a] going further in my great business for the Duke of York; and so at noon to dinner, and then W. Hewer to write fair what he had writ, and my wife to read to me all the afternoon; till anon Mr. Gibson came, and he and I to perfect it to my full mind. And so to supper and to[b] bed – my mind yet at disquiet that I cannot be informed how poor Deb stands with her mistress, but I fear she will put her away; and the truth is, though it be much against my mind and to my trouble, yet I think it will be fit that she be gone, for my wife's peace and mine; for she cannot but be offended at the sight of her, my wife having conceived this jealousy of me with reason. And therefore, for that, and other reasons of expense, it will be best for me to let her go – but I shall love and pity her. This noon Mr. Povy sent his Coach for my wife and I to see; which we like mightily, and will endeavour to have him get us just such another.

2. Up, and a cold morning, by water through bridge without a cloak; and there to Mr. Wren at his chamber at White-hall, the first time of his coming thither this year, the Duchess coming thither tonight.[1] And there he and I did read over my paper that I have with so much labour drawn up about the several answers of the Officers of this office to the Duke of York's reflections, and did debate a little what advice to give the Duke of York when he comes to town upon it.[2] Here came in Lord Anglesy, and I perceive he makes nothing of this order for his

a repl. 'day' and full stop   *b* repl. 'we'

---

1. The Duke and Duchess of York usually moved from Whitehall to St James's during the summer.
2. A l.h. copy (mostly in Pepys's hand), both of Pepys's draft and of the Duke's letter of 25 November based on it, is in PL 2242, pp. 122+.

suspension, resolving to contend*ᵃ* and to bring it to the Council on Wednesday when the King is come to town tomorrow. And Mr. Wren doth join with him mightily in it, and doth look upon the Duke of York as concerned more in it then he. So I to visit Creed at his chamber, but his wife not come thither yet; nor doth he tell me where she is, though she be in town at Stepny, at Atkins's. So to Mr. Povy's to talk about a coach, but there I find my Lord Sandwich and Peterborough and Hinchingbrooke, Ch. Herbert and Sidny Mountagu; and there I was stopped, and dined mighty nobly at a little table, with one little dish at a time upon it – but mighty merry; I was glad to see it, but sorry, methought, to see my Lord hath so little reason to be merry, and yet glad for his sake to have him cheerful. After dinner, up, and looked up and down the house, and so to the cellar and thence I slipped away without taking leave; and so to a few places about business; and among others, to my bookseller's in Duck-lane; and so home, where the house still full of dirt by painters and others, and will not be clean a good while. So to read and talk with my wife, till by and by called to the office about Sir W. Warren's business;[1] where we met a little, and then home to supper and to bed. This day I went by Mr. Povy's direction to a coachmaker near him[2] for a coach just like his, but it was sold this very morning.

3. Up and all the morning at the office. At noon to dinner; and then to the office and*ᵇ* there busy till 12 at night, without much pain to my eyes; but I did not use them to read or write, and so did hold out very well. So home, and there to supper; and I observed my wife to eye my eyes whether I did ever look upon Deb; which I could not but do now and then (and to my grief did see the poor wretch look on me and see me look on her, and then let drop a tear or two; which doth make my heart relent at this minute that I am writing this, with great trouble of

a repl. 'content'   *b* repl. 'and so home

1. See above, p. 332, n. 1.
2. Povey lived in Lincoln's Inn Fields. Long Acre was celebrated both now and later for its coach-makers.

mind, for she is endeed my sacrifice, poor girl); and my wife did tell me in bed, by the by, of my looking on other people, and that the only way is to put things out of sight; and this I know she means by Deb, for she tells me that her aunt[1] was here on Monday and she did tell her of her desire of parting with Deb; but in such kind terms on both sides, that my wife is mightily taken with her. I see it will be, and it is but necessary; and therefore, though it cannot but grieve me, yet I must bring my mind to give way to it. We had a great deal of do this day at the office about Clutterbucke, I declaring my dissent against the whole Board's proceedings; and I believe*a* I shall go near to show W. Penn a very knave in it, whatever I find my Lord Brouncker.[2]

4. Up, and by coach to White-hall; and there I find the*b* King and Duke of York come the last night, and everybody's mouth full of my Lord Anglesy's suspension being sealed; which it was, it seems, yesterday;*c* so that he is prevented in his remedy at the Council; and it seems the two new Treasurers did kiss the King's hand this morning, brought in by my Lord Arlington.[3] They walked up and down together the Court this day, and several people joyed them. But I avoided it, that I might not be seen to look either way. This day also, I hear that my Lord Ormond is to be declared in Council no more Deputy-Governor of Ireland, his commission being expired, and the King is prevailed with to take it out of his hands; which people do

---

     a   repl. same symbol badly formed
     b   repl. 'ever'-   *c*   repl. 'last'

---

1. Mrs Hunt: above, viii. 569, n. 1.

2. Thomas Clutterbuck, consul at Leghorn, had presented a bill for the victualling of ships which had not been authorised by the Board or by the commander of the station. Pepys made notes on 1 December in his memorandum book about the 'foule play . . . lately observed by mee' in the management of these accounts by Penn and Brouncker: NWB, pp. 122–4.

3. The order for Anglesey's suspension was sealed on the 2nd, not the 3rd: above, p. 341, n. 1. It did not prevent his petitions to the King from being heard in Council: below, p. 351. The new Treasurers were Sir Thomas Littleton and Sir Thomas Osborne, who remained Joint-Treasurers of the Navy until 1671.

mightily admire,* saying that he is the greatest subject of any prince in Christendome, and hath more acres of land then any – and hath done more for his prince then ever any yet did. But all will not do; he must down it seems – the Duke of Buckingham carrying all before him.¹ But that that troubles me most, is that they begin to talk that the Duke of York's regiment is ordered to be disbanded; and more, that undoubtedly his Admiralcy will fallow;² which doth shake me mightily, and I fear will have ill consequences in the nation, for these counsels are very mad. The Duke of York doth, by all men's report, carry himself wonderful submissive to the King, in the most humble*a* manner in the world; but yet it seems nothing must be spared that tends to the keeping out of the Chancellor, and that is the reason of all this. The great discourse now is that the Parliament shall be dissolved, and another called which shall give the King the Deane and Chapters lands; and that will put him out of debt.³ And it is said that Buckingham doth knownly meet daily with Wildman and

---

a   repl. same symbol badly formed

---

1. Ormond (another victim of Buckingham and the anti-Clarendonians) was not dismissed until 14 March 1669. His appointment in 1661 had not in fact been limited to any term of years: *CSP Ireland 1660–2*, pp. 454, 685. Cf. his own account in T. Carte, *Ormonde* (1736), v. 103+. He was held in universally high regard and there could have been no greater contrast than that between him and the irresponsible and disreputable Buckingham. For Ormond's estates, see Clarendon, *Life*, ii. 24; Carte, ii, App. 132–3. For his own account of his dismissal, see ib., v. 103+.

2. James's influence had suffered eclipse since Clarendon's fall: the recent changes in the Treasurership of the Navy had been made without his consent, and it was put about that it was dangerous to have so much military and naval power in the hands of one man. Cf. his own account: *Life* (ed. Clarke), i. 433–5. He was not in fact deprived of his commands or of his admiralty.

3. Cf. the similar report (newsletter, 18 November) in BM. Add. 36916, f. 119*r*. The project (dating from the beginning of the year – see above, pp. 35–6, 44–5 & nn.) was widely canvassed, along with other fiscal schemes of Buckingham, during the following months, until parliament met in October 1669. See e.g. the French ambassador's despatches (March 1669): PRO, PRO 31/3/121, ff. 82+, and the newsletters (November 1668, May 1669) in *CSPD 1668–9*, p. 320. Nothing came of it.

other Commonwealths-men;[1] and that when he is with them, he makes the King believe that he is with his wenches. And something looks like the Parliament's being dissolved, by Harry Brouncker's being now come back;[2] and appears this day the first day at White-hall, but hath not been yet with the King – but is secure that he shall be well received, I hear. God bless us, when such men as he shall be restored. But that that pleases me most, is that several do tell me that Pen is to be removed; and others, that he hath resigned his place; and perticularly, Spragge tells me for certain that he hath resigned it and is become a partener with Gawden in the victualling – in which I think he hath done a very cunning thing, but I am sure I am glad of it, and it will be well for the King – to have him out of this office.[3]

Thence by coach, doing several errands, home; and there to dinner and then to the office, where all the afternoon till late at night; and so home. Deb hath been abroad today with her friends,* poor girl; I believe toward the getting of a place.

This day a boy is sent me out of the country from Impington, by my Cousin Roger Pepys's getting; whom I visited this morning at his chamber in the Strand and carried him to West-minster-hall, where I took a turn or two with him and Sir Jo. Talbot, who talks mighty high for my Lord of Ormond; and I perceive this family of the Talbots hath been raised by my Lord.[4]

When I came home tonight, I find Deb not come home, and do doubt whether she be not quite gone or no; but my wife is silent to me in it, and I to her, but fell to other discourse; and

1. Cf. the comment made in a newsletter of 18 February: 'The Duke of Buckingham is the great favourite, and his cabal are Major Wildman, Dr. Owen, and the rest of that fraternity, so that some say we are carried in Oliver's basket': *CSPD 1667–8*, p. 238.

2. He had fled to escape impeachment: see above, p. 170 & n. 4.

3. Penn joined Gauden in the victualling (below, p. 350 & n. 2), and resigned from the Navy Board shortly after the new victualling contract was signed in February 1669.

4. The Talbots associated in Ireland with Ormond were a Catholic 'Old English' family. (There were five brothers of whom one became Archbishop of Dublin in 1669 and another, in 1685, the Earl, later Duke, of Tyrconnel.) Sir John Talbot of Lacock Abbey, Wilts. (M.P. for Knaresborough, Yorks.) belonged to an English branch of the family and was descended from the 1st Earl of Shrewsbury (d. 1453).

endeed am well satisfied that my house will never be at peace between my wife and I unless I let her go, though it grieves me to the heart.

My wife and I spent much time this evening talking of our being put out of the office and my going to live at Deptford at her brother's till I can clear my accounts and rid my hands of the town – which will take me a year or more; and I do think it will be best for me to do so, in order*a* to our living cheap and out of sight.

5. Up, and Willet came home in the morning; and God forgive me, I could not conceal my content thereat, by smiling, and my wife observed it; but I said nothing, nor she, but away to the office.* Presently, up by water to White-hall, and there all of us to wait on the Duke of York; which we did, having little to do. And then I up and down the House, till by and by the Duke of York (who had bid me stay) did come to his closet*b* again, and there did call in me and Mr. Wren; and there my paper[1] that I have lately taken pains to draw up was read, and the Duke of York pleased therewith; and we did all along conclude upon answers to my mind for the Board, and that that, if put in execution, will do the King's business. But I do now more and more perceive the Duke of York's trouble, and that he doth lie under great weight of mind from the Duke of Buckingham's carrying things against him; and perticularly when I advised that he would use his interest that a seaman might come into the room of W. Penn, who is now declared to be gone from us to that of the Victualling, and did show how the office would now be left without one seaman in it but the Surveyor and the Controller,[2] who is so old as to be able to do nothing. He told me plainly that I knew his mind well enough as to seamen, but that it must be as others will. And Wren did tell it me as a secret, that when the Duke of York did first [tell] the King about Sir

《*Look over the leaf for my mistake》

---

a repl. same symbol badly formed   *b* repl. 'lodg'-

---

1. See above, p. 344 & n. 2.
2. I.e. Middleton and Mennes.

Brouncker was doing most of the latter's work.

W. Penn's leaving of the place, and that when the Duke of York did move the King that either Captain Cox or Sir Jer. Smith might succeed him, the King did tell him that that was a matter fit to be considered of, and would not agree to either presently; and so the Duke of York could not prevail for either, nor knows who it shall be.   The Duke of York did tell me himself, that if he had not carried it privately when first he mentioned Pen's leaving his place to the King, it had not been done; for the Duke of Buckingham and those of his party do cry out upon it, as a strange thing to trust such a thing into the hands of one that stands accused in Parliament.   And that they have so far prevailed upon the King, that he would not have*a* him named in Council, but only take his name to the Board; but I think he said that only D Gawden's name shall go in the patent; at least, at the time when Sir Rd. Browne[1] asked the King the*b* names of D. Gawden's security, the King told him it was not yet necessary for him to declare them.[2]   And by and by, when the Duke of York and we had done, and Wren brought into the closet Captain Cox and James Temple about business of the Guinea Company, and talking something of the Duke of Buckingham's concernment therein, "Nay," says the Duke of York, "I will give the Devil his due, as they say; the Duke of Buckingham hath paid in his money to the Company,"[3] or something of that kind, wherein he would do right to him.   The Duke of York told me how these people do begin to cast dirt upon the business that passed the Council lately touching Supernumerarys,[4] as passed by virtue of his

a repl. 'name'   b repl. 'he'

---

1. One of the four Clerks of the Privy Council.

2. Penn's name and that of Gauden's son, Benjamin, were added to the patent appointing the victuallers.

3. The Royal African Company, founded under the aegis of the Duke of York in 1663, was now virtually bankrupt, and had to be refounded in 1672. For the efforts to collect subscriptions at this time, see G. F. Zook, *Company of R. Adventurers trading into Africa*, p. 22.   Buckingham had subscribed £500: ib., pp. 12, 22; K. G. Davies, *R. African Co.*, p. 65.

4. On 18 September the Council had at the Duke's request approved the payment of certain supernumeraries in the summer fleet beyond the number authorised by the Navy Board, which acted under a regulation of 10 May 1666. PRO, PC 2/61, pp. 18–20.

authority there, there being not liberty for any*ᵃ* man to withstand what the Duke of York advises there; which he told me they bring only as an argument to insinuate the putting of the Admiralty into commission – which by all men's discourse is now designed, and I perceive the same by him. This being done, and gone from him, I up and down the House to hear news; and there everybody's mouth full of changes; and among others, that the Duke of York's regiment of Guards, that was raised during the late war at sea, is to be disbanded;[1] and also that this day the King doth intend to declare that the Duke of Ormond is no*ᵇ* more Deputy of Ireland, but that he will put it into commission. This day our new Treasurer's did kiss the King's hand, who complimented them, as they say, very highly; that he had for a long time been abused in his treasure and that he was now safe in their hands. I saw them walk up and down the Court together all this morning, the first time I ever saw Osborne, who is a comely gentleman. This day I was told that my Lord Anglesy did deliver a petition on Wednesdy in Council to the King, laying open that whereas he had heard that his Majesty had made such a disposal of his place, which he had formerly granted*ᶜ* him for life upon a valuable consideration, and that without anything laid to his charge,*ᵈ* and during a Parliament session,[2] he prayed that his Majesty would be pleased to let his case be heard before the Council and the Judges of the land, who were his proper counsel in all matters of Right; to which, I am told the King, after my Lord's being withdrawn, concluded upon his giving him an answer some few days hence; and so he was called in and told so – and so it ended.[3]

Having heard all this, I took*ᵉ* coach and to Mr. Povy's, where I

---

a repl. 'him to'   *b* repl. same symbol badly formed
        c repl. 'obt'-   *d* MS. 'charged'
        e repl. same symbol badly formed

---

1. The Duke's Maritime Regiment continued in being until disbanded in 1689. The practice of raising and maintaining military regiments for wartime service with the fleet was again adopted under William III and Anne, when they were given the title of 'Marines'.

2. He was here pleading his privilege as a peer.

3. For the petition and the King's reply, see below, p. 362 & n. 1.

hear [he] is gone to the Swedes Resident[1] in Covent-garden, where
he is to dine. I went thither, but he is not come yet; so I to
White-hall to look* him, and up and down walking there,
I met with Sir Rob. Holmes; who asking news, I told him of Sir
W Pens going from us, who ketched at it, so as my heart misgives
me that he will have a mind to it; which made me heartily sorry
for my words. But he invited me and would have me go to
dine with him at the Treasurer's, Sir Tho. Clifford, where I did
go and eat some oysters; which while we were at, in comes my
Lord Keeper and much company, and so I thought it best to
withdraw; and so away and to the Swedes Agents and there met
Mr. Povy; where the Agent would have me stay and dine, there
being only them and Jos. Williamson and Sir Tho. Clayton, but*
what he is, I know not.[2] Here much extraordinary noble discourse of foreign princes, and perticularly the greatness of the
King of France, and of his being fallen into the right way of
making that Kingdom great; which [none] of his Ancestors ever
did before. I was mightily pleased with this company and their
discourse, so as to have been seldom so much in all my life;
and so after dinner, up into his upper room and there did see a
piece of perspective, but much inferior to Mr. Povy's.[3] Thence
with Mr. Povy spent all the afternoon going up and down
among the coachmakers in Cow lane, and did see several, and at
last did pitch upon a little Chariott, whose body was framed but
not Covered, at the widow's*b* that made Mr. Lowther's fine coach.
And we are mightily pleased with it, it being light, and will be
very gent and sober – to be covered with leather, but yet will
hold four. Being much satisfied with this, I carried him to
White-hall; and so by coach home, where give my wife a good
account of my day's work; and so to the office and there*c* late,
and so to bed.*d*

a repl. full stop   b repl. 'woman'   c repl. 'late'
      d followed by a blank space of approximately three lines

───────────────

1. Johan   Barckmann,   Baron   sic at Oxford, M.P. for the university,
Leijonbergh.   and Warden of Merton College.
   2. Clayton was Professor of Phy-   3. See above, iv. 18 & n. 1. (OM).

6.ᵃ Up, and presently my wife up with me, which she professedly now doth every day to dress me, that I may not see Willett; and doth eye me whether I cast my eye upon her or no. And doth keep me from going into the room where she is among the Upholsters at work in our blue chamber. So abroad to White-hall by water, and so on for all this day, as I have by

《*Look back on left for my mistake.》

mistake set down in the fifth day after this mark * – in the room of which, I should have said that I was at the office all the morning; and so to dinner, my wife with me, but so as I durst not look upon the girl; though God knows, notwithstanding all my protestations, I could not keep my mind from desiring it. After dinner to the office again and there did some business; and then by coach to see Roger Pepys at his lodgings next door to Arundell-house, a barber's. And there I did see a book which my Lord Sandwich hath promised one to me of – a description of the Escuriall in Spain;¹ which I have a great desire to have, though I took it forᵇ a finer book when he promised it me. With him to see my Cosen Turner and The, and there sat and talked, theyᶜ being newly come out of the country; and here pretty merry, and with The to show her a coach at Mr. Povy's man's, she being in want of one; and so back again with her and then home by coach, with my mind troubled and finding no content, my wife being still troubled, nor can be at peace while the girl is there; which I am troubled at on the other side. We passed the evening together, and then to bed and slept ill, she

---

a number blotted   *b* MS. 'for it'
c repl. 'she'

---

1. Probably Francisco de los Santos, *Descripcion breve del monasterio de S. Lorenzo el real del Escorial . . .* (Madrid, 1667); a folio, with engravings. The copy in the PL (PL 2123) has no inscription indicating that it was a gift. This was the second edition of a popular work which had first appeared in 1657, and of which an English abstract (by 'a servant of the Earl of Sandwich' on his Spanish embassy) appeared in 1671: *The Escurial, or A description of that wonder of the world for architecture and magnificence of structure: built by K. Philip the IIᵈ of Spain and lately consumed by fire. . . .*

being troubled and troubling me in the night with talk and complaint upon the old business.[1]

This is the day's work of the 5th, though it stands under*a* the 6th, my mind being now so troubled that it is no wonder that I fall into this mistake more then ever I did in my life before.

---

7. Up, and at the office all the morning; and so to it again after dinner and there busy late, choosing to imploy myself rather then go home to trouble with my wife, whom, however, I am forced to comply with; and endeed I do pity her, as having cause enough for her grief.   So to bed, and there slept ill because of my wife.   ⟨This afternoon I did go out toward Sir D Gawden's, thinking to have bespoke a place for my coach and horses, when I have them, at the Victualling Office; but find the way so bad and long that I returned and looked up and down for places elsewhere in an Inne, which I hope to get with more convenience then there.⟩*b*

8. *Lords day*.   Up, and at my chamber all the morning, setting papers to rights with my boy.   And so to dinner at noon, the girl with us; but my wife troubled thereat to see her, and doth tell me so; which troubles me, for I love the girl.   At my*c* chamber*d* again to work all the afternoon till night, when Pelling comes, who wonders to find my wife so dull and melancholy; but God knows, she hath too much cause.   However, as pleasant as we can, we supped together; and so made the boy read to me, the poor girl not*e* appearing at supper, but hides herself in her chamber – so that I could wish in that respect that she was out of the house, for our peace is broke to all of us while she is here. And so to bed – where my wife mighty unquiet all night, so as my bed is become burdensome to me.

---

a repl. 'up'   *b* addition crowded into bottom of page
            c repl. 'the'   *d* repl. 'office'
                e repl. incomplete symbol

---

1. Presumably their recent quarrel over Deb, but possibly their separa- tion early in their married life (cf. above, ii. 153 & n. 3).

9.   Up, and I did, by a little note which I flung to Dcb, advise her that I did continue to deny that ever I kissed her, and so she might govern herself.   The truth [is], that I did adventure upon God's pardoning me this lie, knowing how heavy a thing it would be for me to be the ruin of the poor girl; and next, knowing that if my wife should know all, it were impossible ever for her to be at peace with me again – and so our whole lives would be uncomfortable.   The girl read, and as I bid her, returned me the note, flinging it to me in passing by.   And so I abroad by [coach] to White-hall, and there to the Duke of Yorke's*a* to wait on him; who told me that Sir W. Penn had been with him this morning to ask whether it would be fit for him to sit at the Office now because*b* of his resolution to be gone and to become concerned in the Victualling.   The Duke of York answered, "Yes, till his contract was signed."   Thence I to Lord Sandwich, and there to see him; but was made to stay so long, as his best friends are; and when I came to him, so little pleasure, his*c* head being full of his own business I think, that I have no pleasure to give him.   Thence to White-hall with him to the Committee of Tanger, a day appointed for him to give an account of Tanger and what he did and found there;[1] which though he had admirable matter for it, and his doings there was good and would have afforded a noble account, yet he did it with a mind so low and mean, and delivered in so poor a manner, that it appeared nothing at all, nor anybody seemed to value it; whereas, he might have shown himself to have merited extraordinary thanks, and been held to have done a very great service; whereas now, all the cost the*d* King hath been at [for] his Journy through Spain thither seems to be almost lost.   After we were up, Creed and I walked together and did talk a good while of the weak report my Lord made, and were troubled for it – I fearing that either his mind and judgment are depressed, or that

---

a   repl. 'my Lord Sandwich'   b   repl. 'or stay till the
        c   repl. 'is'   d   repl. ? 'the'

---

1. Sandwich's private account of the visit to Tangier and of his conclusions is in Sandwich MSS, Journals, viii. 395+, 512+; summary in Harris, ii. 165-6. Cf. above, p. 135 & n. 3.

he doth it out of his general neglect and so may fear that he doth all the rest of his affairs accordingly. So I stayed about the Court a little while; and then to look for a dinner, and had it at Hercules-Pillars very late, all alone, costing me 10*d*; and so to the Excize Office, thinking to meet*ᵃ* Sir St. Fox and the Cofferer, but the former was gone and the latter I met going out, but nothing done; and so I to my bookseller's, and also to Crows and there saw [a] piece of my bed, and I find it will please us mightily. So home, and there find my wife troubled, and I sat with her talking; and so to bed, and there very unquiet all night.

10. Up, and my wife still every day as ill as she is all night; will rise to see me out doors, telling me plainly that she dares not let me see the girl; and so I out to the office, where all the morning; and so home to dinner, where I find my wife mightily troubled again, more then ever, and she tells me that it is from her examining the girl and getting a confession now from her of all, even to the very tocando su thing*ᵇ* with my hand*ᵇ* – which doth mightily trouble me, as not being able to foresee the consequences of it as to our future peace together. So my wife would not go down to dinner, but I would dine in her chamber with her; and there, after mollifying her as much as I could, we were pretty quiet and eat; and by and by comes Mr. Hollier, and dines there by himself after we had dined. And he being gone, we to talk again, and she to be troubled, reproaching*ᶜ* me with my un-kindness and perjury, I having denied my ever kissing her – as also with all her old kindnesses to me, and my ill-using of her from the beginning, and the many temptations she hath refused out of faithfulness to me; whereof several she was*ᵈ* perticular in, and especially from my Lord Sandwich by the sollicitation of Captain Ferrer; and then afterward, the courtship of my Lord Hinching-brooke, even to the trouble of his Lady. All which I did acknow-ledge and was troubled for, and wept; and at last pretty good friends again, and so I to my office and there late, and so home to supper with her; and so to bed, where after half-an-hour's slumber, she wakes me and cries out that she should never sleep more, and so kept raving till past midnight, that made me cry

and weep heartily all the while for her, and troubled for what she
reproached me with as before; and at last, with new vows, and
perticularly that I would myself bid the girl be gone and show my
dislike to her – which I shall endeavour to perform, but with
much trouble.   And so, this appeasing her, we to sleep as well
as we could till morning.

11.   Up, and my wife with me as before; and so to the office,
where by a special desire, the new Treasurer's came and there did
show*ᵃ* their Patent, and the Great Seal for the suspension of my
Lord Anglesy.   And here did sit and discourse of the business of
the office; and brought Mr. Huchinson with them, who*ᵇ* I hear
is to be their paymaster in the room of Mr. Waith;¹ for it seems
they do turn out every servant that belongs to the present
Treasurer; and so for Fenn, do bring in Mr. Littleton, Sir Tho's
brother² – and out all the rest.   But Mr. Huchinson doth already
see that his work now will be another kind of thing then before,
as to the trouble of it.   They gone (and endeed, they appear both
of them very intelligent men) I home to dinner, and there with
my people dined; and so to my wife, who would not dine with
[me], that she might not have the girl come in sight, and there
sat and talked a while with her; and pretty quiet, I giving no
occasion of offence, and so to the office*ᶜ* [and then
《All this*ᵈ* be-   by coach to my Cosen Roger Pepys, who did,*ᵉ*
longs to to-   at my last being with him this day sennit, move
morrows in   me as to the supplying him with 500*l* this term
the after-   and 500*l* the next for two year upon a Mortgage,
noon》   he having that sum to pay, a debt left him by his
father; which I do agree to, trusting to his honesty and ability,

a repl. 'see'   *b* repl. ? 'him'
c followed by 'a while' struck through
d i.e. the passage which Pepys puts in square brackets
e repl. 'continues his desire'

---

1. Richard Hutchinson had been
Treasurer of the Navy, 1651–60.
Waith continued in office jointly with
him: *CSPD 1668–9*, p. 605.

2. James Littleton replaced John
Fenn as cashier to the Treasurer.

and am resolved to do it for him, that I may not have all I have lie in the King's hands. Having promised him this, I returned home again, where to the office]; and there having done, I home and to supper and to bed; where after lying a little while, my wife starts up, and with expressions of affright and madness, as one frantic, would rise; and I would not let her, but burst out in tears myself; and so continued almost half the night, the moon shining so that it was light; and after much sorrow and reproaches and little ravings (though I am apt to think they were counterfeit from her), and my promise again to discharge the girl myself, all was quiet again, and so to sleep.

12. Up, and she with me as heretofore; and so I to the office, where all the morning; and at noon to dinner, and Mr. Wayth, who being at my office about business, I took him with me to talk and understand his matters; who is in mighty trouble from the Committee of Accounts about his contracting with this office for sail-cloth,[1] but no hurt can be laid at his door in it, but upon us for doing it, if any, though we did it by the Duke of York's approval. And by him I understand that the new Treasurers do intend to bring in all new instruments.* And so having dined, we parted, and I to my wife and to sit with her a little; and then called her and Willet to my chamber, and there did with tears in my eyes, which I could not help, discharge her and advise her to be gone as soon as she could, and never to see me or let me see her more while she was in the house; which she took with tears too, but I believe understands me to be her friend; and I am apt to believe, by what my wife hath of late told me, is a Cunning girl, if not a slut. Thence, parting kindly with my wife, I away by coach to my Cosen Roger, according as by mistake (which the trouble of my mind for some days hath occasioned, in this and another case a day or two before) is set down in yesterday's notes. And so back again, and with Mr. Gibson late at my chamber, making an end of my draft of a letter for the Duke of York, in answer to the answers of this office;[2] which

---

1. Robert Waith was paymaster to the Navy Treasurer and, like all officials, was forbidden to trade with the office. Several of his contracts

for canvas are in *CSPD 1663-4,* pp. 132, 134, 135.

2. See below, p. 374, n. 3.

I have now done to my mind, so as, if the Duke of York likes it, will I think put an end to a great deal of the faults of this office, as well as my trouble*a* for them.   So to bed, and did lie now a little better then formerly, with but little and yet with some trouble.

13. Up, and with Sir W. Penn by coach to White-hall, where to the Duke of York and there did our usual business; and thence I to the Commissioners of the Treasury, where I stayed and heard an excellent case argued between my Lord Gerard and the Town of Newcastle, about a piece of ground which that Lord hath got a grant of under the Exchequer Seal, which they were endeavouring to get of the King under the Great Seal.[1]   I liked mightily the counsel for the Town, Shaftow their Recorder, and Mr. Offly; but I was troubled, and so the Lords, to hear my Lord fly out against their great pretence of merit from the King for their sufferings and Loyalty; telling them that they might thank him for that repute which*b* they have for their Loyalty, for that it was he that forced them to be so, against their wills, when he was there.[2]   And moreover, did offer a paper to the Lords to read from the Town, sent in 1648,*c* but the Lords would not read it; but I believe it was something about bringing the King to trial, or some such thing, in that year.[3]   Thence I to the Three Tuns tavern by Charing-cross and there dined with W. Penn, Sir J. Mennes, and Commissioner Middleton, and

a repl. 'mind'   *b* repl. 'of'   *c* repl. '1648'

---

1. See *CTB*, ii. 483–4 (official minute).   The castle and its precincts ('Castle Garth') had been leased by the King in 1664 to Gerard who had been nominated Constable of the city. The corporation (owners of the property, 1652–60, and now Crown tenants) eventually obtained the reversion in 1685: Eneas MacKenzie, *Newcastle-upon-Tyne* (1827), p. 94.

2. Gerard had been an active royalist commander in the Civil War but there is no evidence that he ever held any military command, or any post

of authority, in Newcastle.   It is possible that he was referring to the events of 1640 when he served in the war against the Scots.   But he was then only a captain.

3. A petition from the mayor and corporation, presented to parliament on 10 October 1648, 'requiring speedy and impartial justice to be done upon the greatest offenders and incendiaries': *CJ*, vi. 49; cf. Roger Howell, *Newcastle and the Puritan Rebellion*, p. 203 & n. 2.

as merry as my mind could be, that hath so much trouble upon it at home. And thence to White-hall, and there stayed in Mr. Wren's chamber with him, reading over my draft of a letter, which Mr. Gibson then attended me with; and there he did like all, but doubted whether it would be necessary for the Duke to write in so sharp a style to the Office as I had drawn it in – which I yield to him, to consider the present posture of the times and the Duke of York, and whether it were not better to err on that hand then the other. He told me that he did not think it was necessary for the Duke of York to do, and that it would not suit so well with his nature nor greatness – which last, perhaps, is true, but then doth too truly show the effects of having princes in places where order and discipline should be. I left it to him to do as the Duke of York pleases; and so fell to other talk, and with great freedom, of public things; and he told me, upon my several enquiries to that purpose, that he did believe it was not yet resolved whether the Parliament should ever meet more or no, the three great rulers of things now standing thus – the Duke of Buckingham is absolutely against their meeting, as moved thereto by his people that he advises with, the people of the late times – who do never expect to have anything done by this Parliament for their religion, and who do propose that by the sale of the Church lands they shall be able to put the King out of debt.[1] My Lord Keeper is utterly against putting away this and choosing another Parliament, lest they prove worse then this and will make all the King's friends, and the King himself, in a desperate condition. My Lord Arlington knows not which is best for him, being to seek whether this or the next will use him worst. He tells me that he believes that it is intended to call this Parliament and try them with a sum of money; and if they do not like it, then to send them going and call another who will, at the ruin of the Church perhaps, please the King with what he will for a time. And he tells me, therefore, that he doth believe that this policy will be endeavoured by the Church and their friends: to seem* to promise the King money when it shall*a* be propounded, but

a repl. 'will'

---

1. Cf. above, p. 347, n. 3.

make the King and these great men buy it dear before they have it. He tells me that he is really persuaded that the design of the Duke of Buckingham is, by bringing the state into ⟨such⟩ a condition as,*a* if the King doth die without issue, it shall upon his death break into pieces again and so put by the Duke of York, who they have disobliged, they know, to that degree as to despair of his pardon. He tells me that there is no way to rule the King but by brisknesse, which the Duke of Buckingham hath above all men; and that the Duke of York having it not, his best way is what he practises, that is to say, a good temper, which will support him till the Duke of Buckingham and Lord Arlington fall out, which cannot be long; first, the former knowing that the latter did, in the time of the Chancellor, endeavour with*b* the Chancellor to hang him at that time when he was proclamed against[1] – and here, by the by, he told me that the Duke of Buckingham did by his friends treat with my Lord Chancellor, by the mediation of Matt Wren and Matt Clifford,[2] to fall in with my Lord Chancellor; which he tells me he did advise my Lord Chancellor to accept of, as that that, with his own interest and the Duke of York's, would undoubtedly have secured all to him and his family; but that my Lord Chancellor was a man not to be advised, thinking himself too high to be counselled; and so all is come to nothing – for by that means, the Duke of Buckingham became desperate, and was forced to fall in with Arlington, to his[3] ruin. Thence I home, and there to talk, with great pleasure, all the evening with my wife, who tells me that Deb hath been abroad today, and is come home and says she hath got a place to go to, so as she will be gone tomorrow morning. This troubled me; and the truth is, I have a great mind for to have the maiden-head*c* of*d* this girl, which I should not doubt to have if yo could get time para be con her – but she will be gone and I know not

a repl. 'of'   *b* repl. 'to'   *c* garbled s.h.
d repl. same symbol

---

1. In February 1667, when Buckingham was charged with treason: above, viii. 86 & n. 3.
2. Their secretaries respectively.

'Matt' Clifford is a mistake for 'Martin'.
3. Clarendon's. Cf. above, viii. 330; Clarendon, *Life*, iii. 297–8.

whither.*ᵃ* Before*ᵇ* we went to bed, my wife told me she would not have me to see her or give her her wages; and so I did give my*ᶜ* wife 10*l* for her year and half-a-quarter's wages, which she went into her chamber and paid her; and so to bed, and there, blessed be God, we did sleep well and with peace, which I had not done in now almost twenty nights together. This afternoon I went to my coachmaker and Crows, and there saw*ᵈ* things go on to my great content.

This morning at the Treasury-chamber, I did meet Jacke Fenn; and there he did show me my Lord Anglesy's petition and the King's answer. The former, good and stout, as I before did hear it; but the latter, short and weak – saying that he was not, by what the King had done, hindered*ᵉ* from taking the benefit of his laws, and that the reason he had to suspect his mismanagement of his money in Ireland did make him think it unfit to trust him with his treasure in England till he was satisfied in*ᶠ* the former.[1]

14.*ᵍ* Up, and had a mighty mind to have seen or given a note to Deb or to have given her a little money; to which purpose I wrapped up 40*s* in a paper, thinking to give her; but my wife rose presently, and would not let me be out of her sight; and went down before me into the kitchen, and came up and told me that she was in the kitchen, and therefore would have me go round the other way; which she repeating, and I vexed at it,

---

a garbled s.h.　　*b* repl. ? 'with'　　*c* repl. 'her'
d repl. same symbol badly formed　　*e* repl. 'inhib'-
f symbol repeated　　*g* repl. '12'

---

1. Anglesey's petition (undated, presented on 4 November) and the King's reply (11 November) are in PRO, PC 2/61, f. 55*v*; cf. also Sandwich MSS, Journals, ix. 18–22. Two later petitions of Anglesey (5 December 1668 and 24 November 1669) are in *CSPD 1668–9*, pp. 90, 589. He had relinquished his vice-treasureship of Ireland in July 1667, on his appointment as Treasurer of the Navy, but an enquiry into his Irish administration was still proceeding. He later brought an action against his successors in the navy post (T. Carte, *Ormond*, 1851, iv. 340), but in 1672 accepted a pension in lieu of office: *CSPD 1672*, p. 273.

answered her a little angrily; upon which she instantly flew out
into a rage, calling me dog and rogue, and that I had a rotten
heart; all which, knowing that I deserved it, I bore with; and
word being brought presently up that she was gone away by
coach with her things, my wife was friends; and so all quiet,
and I to the office with my heart sad, and find that I cannot forget
the girl, and vexed I know not where to look for her – and more
troubled to see how my wife is by this means likely for ever to
have her hand over me, that I shall for ever be a slave to her;
that is to say, only in matters of pleasure, but in other things she
will make her business, I know, to please me and to keep me
right to her – which I will labour to be endeed, for she deserves
it of me, though it will be I fear a little time before I shall be able
to wear Deb out of my mind. At the office all the morning,
and merry at noon at dinner; and after dinner to the office,
where all the afternoon and doing much business late; my mind
being free of all troubles, I thank God, but only for my thoughts
of this girl, which hang after her. And so at night home to
supper, and there did sleep with great content with my wife.
I must here remember that I have lain*a* with my*b* moher as a
husband more*b* times since this falling-out then in I believe twelve
months before – and with more pleasure to her then I think in
all the time of our marriage before.

15.*c* *Lords day.* Up, after long lying with pleasure talking
with my wife; and then up to look up and down our house;
which will, when our upholster hath done, be mighty fine. And
so to my chamber and there did do several things among my
papers, and so to the office to write down my journall for six or
seven days, my mind having been so troubled as never to get
time to do it before – as may appear a little by the mistakes I*d*
have made in this book within these few days.*e* At noon comes
Mr. Sheply to dine with me, and W How, and there dined and
pretty merry; and so after dinner, W How to tell me what hath
happened between him and the Commissioners of late, who are
hot again, more then ever, about my Lord Sandwiches business of

<hr>

a garbled s.h.   b–b garbled s.h.   c repl. '13'
d repl. 'with'   e see esp. those at 5, 6, 11 November

prizes;[1] which I am troubled for, and the more because of the
great security and neglect which I think my Lord doth look
upon this matter, that may yet, for aught I know, undo him.
They gone, and Balty being*a* come from the Downs not very well,
is*b* come this day to see us, I to talk with him, and with some
pleasure, hoping that he will make a good man; I in the evening
to my office again to make an end of my journall, and so home
to my chamber with W Hewers to settle some papers, and so to
supper and to bed, with my mind pretty quiet; and less troubled
about Deb then I was, though yet I am troubled I must confess,
and would be glad to find her out – though I fear it would be
my ruin. This evening there came to sit with us Mr. Pelling,
who wondered to see my wife and I so dumpish; but yet it went
off only as my wife's not being well; and poor wretch, she hath
no cause to be well, God knows.

16.*c* Up, and by water to White-hall, and there at the Robe-
chamber at a Committee for Tanger; where some of us, my
Lord Sandwich, Sir W. Coventry, and myself, with another or
two, met to debate the business of the Molle and there draw up
reasons for the King's taking of it into his own hands and managing of it upon accounts with Sir H Cholmly.[2] This being done,
I away to Holborne about Whetstones-park, where I never was
in my life before, where I understand by my wife's discourse
that Deb is gone; which doth trouble me mightily, that the poor
girl should be in a desperate condition forced to go thereabouts;
and there, not hearing of any such man as Allbon, with whom
my wife said she now was, I to the Strand and there, by sending
of Drumbleby's boy, my flagelette-maker, to Eagle-court, where
my wife also by discourse lately let fall that he did lately live,
I found that this Dr. Allbon is a kind of a poor broken fellow
that dare not show his head nor be known where he is gone;
but to Lincoln's Inn-fields I went, to Mr. Povy's, but missed him;

a repl. same symbol badly formed   *b* repl. 'to'
c repl. '14'

1. See above, vi. 231, n. 1.   2. See above, p. 199 & n. 2.

and so hearing only that this Allbon is gone to Fleet-street, I did only call at Martins my bookseller's, and there bought *Cassandra*[1] and some other French books for my wife's closet; and so home, having eat nothing but two pennorth of Oysters, opened for me by a woman in the Strand while the boy went to and again to inform me about this man; and therefore home and to dinner, and so all the afternoon at the office and there late, busy; and so home to supper and, pretty pleasant with my wife, to bed – and rested pretty well.

17.[a] Up, and to the office all the morning, where the new Treasurers came their second time; and before they sat down, did discourse with the Board, and perticularly my Lord Brouncker, about their place which they challenge, as hav[ing] been heretofore due and given to their predecessor; which at last my Lord did own it hath been given him only out of courtesy to his quality, and that he did not take it as of right at the Board; so they for the present sat down and did give him the place, but I think with an intent to have the Duke of York's directions about it. My wife and maids busy now to make clean the house above stairs, the Upholsters having done there in her closet and the blue room; and are mighty pretty. At my[b] office all the afternoon and at night, busy; and so home to my wife, and pretty pleasant and at mighty ease in my mind, being in hopes to find Deb, and without trouble or the knowledge of my wife. So to supper at night, and to bed.

18.[c] Lay long in bed, talking with my wife, she being unwilling to have me go abroad, being and declaring herself jealous of my going out, for fear of my going to Deb; which I do deny – for which God forgive me, for I was no sooner out about noon but I did go by coach directly to Somerset-house and there

---

1. The romance by La Calprenède, first published in ten volumes in 1642; not in the PL.

enquired among the porters there[1] for Dr. Allbun; and the first
I spoke with told me he knew him, and that he was newly gone
into Lincoln's Inn fields, but whither he could not tell me, but
that one of his fellows, not then in the way, did carry a chest of
drawers thither with him, and that when he comes he would ask
him.   This put me in some hopes; and I to White-hall and thence
to Mr. Povy's, but he at dinner; and therefore I away and walked
up and down the Strand between the two turnstiles,[2] hoping to
see her out of a window; and then imployed a porter, one
Osbeston, to find out this Doctors lodgings thereabouts; who by
appointment comes to me to Hercules-pillars, where I dined alone,
but tells me that he cannot find out any such but will enquire
further.   Thence back to White-hall to the Treasury a while,
and thence to the Strand; and towards night did meet with the
porter that carried the chest of drawers with this Doctor, but
he would not tell me[a] where he lived, being his good maister he
told me; but if I would have a message to him, he would deliver
it.   At last, I told him my business was not with him, but a
little gent[le]woman, one Mrs. Willet, that is with him; and sent
him to see how she did, from her friend in London, and no other
token.   He goes while I walk in Somerset-house – walk there
in the Court; at last he comes back and tells me she is well, and
that I may see her if I will – but no more.   So I could not be
commanded by my reason, but I must go this very night; and
so by coach, it being now dark, I to her, close by my tailor's;
and there she came into the coach to me, and yo did besar her[b]
and tocar her thing,[b] but ella was against it and laboured with
much earnestness,[c] such as I believed to be real; and yet at last yo
did[d] make her tener mi cosa in her mano, while mi mano was
sobra her pectus, and so did hazer with grand delight.[d]   I did
nevertheless give her the best counsel I could, to have a care of

---

a   repl. 'of'   b–b   garbled s.h.: see above, viii. 244, note *a*
c   repl. 'seeming'   d–d   garbled s.h.

---

1. Street-porters: cf. above, i. 38,
n. 2.
2. Possibly two of the narrow cuts

running south from the Strand had
turnstiles at their heads to prevent use
save by foot-passengers.   (R).

her honour and to fear God and suffer no man para haver to do*a*
con her – as yo have done*a* – which she promised.   Yo did give
her 20s and directions para laisser sealed in paper at any time the
name of the place of her being, at Herringman's my bookseller*b*
in the Change – by which I might go*c* para her.*c*   And so bid
her good-night, with much content to my mind and resolution
to look after her no more till I heard from her.   And so home,
and there told my wife a fair tale, God knows, how I spent the
whole day; with which the poor wretch was satisfied, or at least
seemed so; and so to supper and to bed, she having been mighty
busy all day in getting of her house in order against tomorrow,
to hang up our new hangings and furnishing our best chamber.

19.   Up, and at the office all the morning, with my heart full
of joy to think in what a safe condition all my matters now stand
between my wife and Deb and me; and at noon, running upstairs
to see the upholsters, who are at work upon hanging my best
room and setting up my new bed, I find my wife sitting sad in the
dining-room; which inquiring into the reason of, she begun to
call me all the false, rotten-hearted rogues in the world, letting me
understand that I was with Deb yesterday; which, thinking
impossible for her ever to understand, I did a while deny; but at
last did, for the ease of my mind and hers, and for ever to discharge my heart of this wicked business, I did confess all; and
above-stairs in our bed-chamber there, I did endure the sorrow
of her threats and vows and curses all the afternoon.   And which
was worst, she swore by all that was good that she would slit the
nose of this girl, and be gone herself this very night from me;
and did there demand 3 or 400*l* of me to buy my peace, that she
might be gone without making any noise, or else protested that
she would make all the world know of it.   So, with most perfect
confusion of face and heart, and sorrow and shame, in the greatest
agony in the world, I did pass this afternoon, fearing that it will
never have an end; but at last I did call for W Hewers, who I
was forced to make privy now to all; and the poor fellow did cry
like a child [and] obtained what I could not, that she would be
pacified, upon condition that I would give it under my hand

a–a garbled s.h.   *b* garbled s.h.   *c–c* garbled s.h.

never to see or speak with Deb while I live, as I did before of
Pierce and Knepp;[1] and which I did also, God knows, promise for
Deb too, but I have the confidence to deny it, to the perjuring of
myself. So before it was late, there was, beyond my hopes as
well as desert, a*a* tolerable peace; and so to supper, and pretty kind
words, and to bed, and there yo did hazer con ella to her*b* content;
and so with some rest spent the night in bed, being most absolutely
resolved, if ever I can maister this bout, never to give her occasion
while I live of more trouble of this or any other kind, there being
no curse in the world so great as this of the difference between
myself and her; and therefore I do by the grace of God promise
never to offend her more, and did this night begin to pray to
God upon my knees alone in my chamber; which God knows
I cannot yet do heartily, but I hope God will give me the grace
more and more every day to fear Him, and to be true to my poor
wife. This night the Upholsters did finish the hanging of my
best chamber, but my sorrow and trouble is so great about this
business, that put me out of all joy in looking upon it or minding*c*
how it was.

20.*d* This morning up, with mighty kind words between my
poor wife and I; and so to White-hall by water, W. Hewer with
me, who is to go with me everywhere until my wife be in condition to go out along with me herself; for she doth plainly
declare that she dares not trust me out alone, and therefore made
it a piece of our league that I should alway take somebody with
me, or her herself; which I am mighty willing to, being, by the
grace of God resolved never to do her wrong more.
    We landed at the Temple, and there I did bid him call at my
Cosen Roger Pepys's lodgings, and I stayed in the street for him;
and so took water again at the Strand-stairs and so to White-hall,
in my way I telling him plainly and truly my resolutions, if I
can get over this evil, never to give new occasion for it. He is,
I think, so honest and true a servant to us both, and one that loves

---

a MS. 'as'   *b* garbled s.h.
c repl. 'mind'- badly formed   *d* figure blotted

---

1. See above, p. 339.

us, that I was not much troubled at his being privy^a to all this, but rejoiced in my heart that I had him to assist in the making us friends; which he did do truly and heartily, and with good success – for I did get him to go to Deb to tell her that I had told my wife all of my being with her the other night, that so, if my wife should send, she might not make the business worse by denying it. While I was at White-hall with the Duke of York doing our ordinary business with him, here being also the first time the new Treasurers, W. Hewer did go to her and come back again; and so I took him into St. James's park,^b and there he did tell me he had been with her and found what I said about my manner of being with her true, and had given her advice as I desired. I did there enter into more talk about my wife and myself, and he did give me great assurance of several perticular cases to which my wife had from time to time made^c him privy of her loyalty and truth to me after many and great temptations, and I believe them truly. I did also discourse the unfitness of my leaving of my imployment now in many respects, to go into the country as my wife desires – but that I would labour to fit myself for it; which he thoroughly understands, and doth agree with me in it; and so, hoping to get over this trouble, we about our business to Westminster hall^d to meet Roger Pepys; which I did, and did there discourse of the business of lending him 500*l* to answer some occasions of his, which I believe to be safe enough; and so took leave of him and away by coach home, calling on my coach-maker by the way, where I like my little coach mightily. But when I came home, hoping for a further degree of peace and quiet, I find my wife upon her bed in a horrible rage afresh, calling me all the bitter names; and rising, did^e fall to revile me in the bitterest manner in the world, and could not refrain to strike me and pull my hair; which I resolved to bear with, and had good reason to bear it. So I by silence and weeping did prevail with her a little to be quiet, and she would not eat her dinner without me; but yet by and by into a raging fit she fell again worse then before, that she would slit the girl's nose; and at last W. Hewer came in and came up, who did allay her fury,

---

a repl. 'p'-   *b* repl. 'the park'   *c* repl. 'my'
d l.h. repl. s.h. 'the coach'   *e* repl. 'there'

I flinging myself in a sad desperate condition upon the bed in the blue room, and there lay while they spoke together; and at last it came to this, that if I would call Deb "whore" under my hand, and write to her that I hated her and would never see her more, she would believe me and trust in me – which I did agree to; only, as to the name of "whore" I would have excused, and therefore wrote to her sparing that word; which my wife thereupon tore it, and would not be satisfied till, W. Hewer winking upon me, I did write so, with the name of a whore, as that I did fear she might too probably have been prevailed*a* upon to have been a whore by her carriage to me, and therefore, as such, I did resolve never to see her more.   This pleased my wife, and she gives it W. Hewer to carry to her, with a sharp message from her.   So from that minute my wife begun to be kind to me, and we to kiss and be friends, and so continued all the evening and fell to talk of other matters with great comfort, and after supper to bed.

This evening comes Mr. Billup to me to read over Mr. Wren's alterations of my draft of a letter for the Duke of York to sign, to the Board; which I like mighty well, they being not considerable, only in mollifying some hard terms which I had thought fit to put in.[1]   From this to other discourse; I do find that the Duke of York and his maister Mr. Wren do look upon this service of mine as a very seasonable service to the Duke of York, as that which he will have to show to his enemies in his own justification of his care of the King's business.   And I am sure I am heartily glad of it – both for the King's sake and the Duke of York's, and my own also – for if I continue, my work, by this means, will be the less, and my share in the blame also.

He being gone, I to my wife again and so spent the evening with very great joy, and*b* the night also, with good sleep and rest, my wife only troubled in her rest, but less then usual – for which the God of Heaven be praised.   I did this night promise to

---

a   repl. 'persuaded'   *b*   repl. 'and the night'

---

1. Cf. above, p. 360. The draft and the letter (25 November) are reproduced in parallel columns in PL 2242, pp. 122+. See below, p. 374 & n. 3, p. 377 & n. 3; PL 2867, p. 510; PRO, Index 10704/1, p. 13; Adm. Lib. MS. 9, ff. 61+. Summary in *Cat.*, i. 32.   Thomas Billop was Wren's clerk.

my wife never to go to bed without calling upon God upon my knees by prayer; and I begun this night, and hope I shall never forget to do the like all my life – for I do find that it is much the best for my soul and body to live pleasing to God and my poor wife – and will ease me of much care, as well as much expense.

21. Up, with great joy to my wife and me, and to the office, where W. Hewer did most honestly bring me back that part of my letter under my hand to Deb wherein I called her "whore", assuring me that he did not show it her – and that he did only give her to understand that wherein I did declare my desire never to see her, and did give her the best Christian counsel he could; which was mighty well done of him. But by the grace of God, though I love the poor girl and wish her well, as having gone too far toward the undoing her, yet I will never enquire after or think of her more – my peace being certainly to do right to my wife.

At the office all the morning; and after dinner, abroad with W. Hewer to my Lord Ashly's, where my Lord Berkely and Sir Tho. Ingram met upon Mr. Povy's account; where I was in great pain about that part of his account wherein I am concerned, above 150*l* I think; and Creed hath declared himself dissatisfied with it, so far as to desire to cut his *Examinatur* out of the paper, as the only condition upon which he would be silent in it.[1] This, Povy had the wit to yield to; and so when it came to be enquired into, I did avouch the truth of the account as to that perticular, of my own knowledge, and so it went over as a thing good and just; as endeed, in the bottom of it it*ᵃ* is; though in strictness, perhaps, it would not so well be understood.

This Committee rising, I with my mind much satisfied herein, I away by coach home, setting Creed into Southampton-buildings. And so home and there ended my letters, and then home to my wife; where I find my house clean now from top to bottom, so as I have not seen it many a day, and to the full satisfaction of my mind – that I am now at peace as to my poor

a repl. 'is'

1. Cf. above, p. 244.

wife – as to the dirtiness of my house – and as to seeing an end, in a great measure, of my present great disbursements upon my house and coach and horses.

22. *Lords day.* My wife and I lay long, with mighty content, and so rose, and she spent the whole day making herself clean, after four or five weeks being in continued dirt.   And I knocking up nails and making little settlements in my house, till noon; and then eat a bit of meat in the kitchen, I all alone, and so to the office to set down my Journall, for some days leaving it imperfect, the matter being mighty grievous to me and my mind from the nature of it.   And so in to solace myself with my wife, whom I got to read to me, and so W. Hewer and the boy; and so after supper, to bed.

This day, my boy's Livery is come home, the first I ever had of Greene lined with red;[1] and it likes me well enough.

23. Up, and called upon by W How, who went with W Hewers with me by water to the Temple.   His business was to have my advice about a place he is going to buy – the Clerk of the Patent's place[2] – which I understand not, and so could say little to him – but fell to other talk; and setting him in at the Temple, we to White-hall, and there I to visit Lord Sandwich, who is now so reserved, or moped rather, I think with his own business, that he bids welcome to no man, I think, to his satisfaction.   However, I bear with it, being willing to give him as little trouble as I can and to receive as little from[a] him, wishing only that I had my money in my purse that I have lent him – but however, I show no discontent at all.   So to White-hall, where a

a repl. 'from the'

---

1. Previously the colours had been those of Pepys's arms: see above, iii. 50 & n. 3.
2. Howe probably meant to buy the deputy-clerkship (the clerkship at this time being held by Sir Richard Pigott: *CTB*, ii. 258; cf. HMC, *Lindsey*, pp. 180-1), and may have

been consulting Pepys about the purchase price.   On 21 March 1669 he asked Pepys for a loan of £500 for what is probably this same purchase: below, p. 492 & n. 4.   His brother John held a clerkship there.   The Patent Office was part of Chancery.

Committee of Tanger expected, but none met. I met with Mr. Povy, who I discoursed with about public business; who tells me that this discourse which*a* I told him of, of the Duke of Monmouth being made Prince*b* of Wales,¹ hath nothing in it; though he thinks there are all the endeavours used in the world to overthrow the Duke of York. He would not have me doubt of my safety in the Navy, which I am doubtful of from the reports of a general removal; but he will endeavour to inform me what he can gather from my Lord Arlington. That he doth think that the Duke of Buckingham hath a mind rather to overthrow all the Kingdom and bring in a Commonwealth, wherein he may think to be General of their Army, or to make himself King; which he believes he may be led to by some*c* advice he hath had with conjurors which he doth affect.²

Thence*d* with W Hewers (who goes up and down with me like a jaylour, but yet with great love and to my great good liking, it being my desire above all things to please my wife therein). I took up my wife and boy at Unthanks, and from thence to Hercules-Pillars and there dined; and thence to our Upholsters about some things more to buy, and so to see our coach, and so to the looking-glass man's by the New Exchange, and so to buy a picture for our blue-chamber chimney, and so home; and there I made my boy to read to me most of the night, to get through the *Life of the Archbishop of Canterbury*.³ At supper comes Mary Battelier, and with us all the evening prettily talking, and very innocent company she is; and she gone, we with much content to bed and to sleep, with mighty rest all night.

24. Up and at the office all the morning; and at noon home to dinner, where Mr. Gentleman the cook and an old woman, his

a repl. 'where I'   *b* repl. 'Duke'   *c* repl. 's'-
d page-heading corrected from 'Navy Office' to 'November'

---

1. Possibly during their conversation on 30 October. Cf. above, iii. 238, n. 4.
2. Buckingham's association with John Heydon the astrologer was notorious: cf. above, viii. 93–4 & n.

Letters had been discovered in Heydon's papers in which Buckingham was addressed as 'prince': John H. Wilson, *A rake and his times*, p. 62.
3. Heylyn's biography of Laud: see above, p. 291, n. 1.

third or fourth wife,*a* comes and dined with us, to enquire about a
ticket of his son's that is dead.   And after dinner, I with Mr.
Hosier to my closet to discourse of the business of balancing
Storekeepers accounts, which he hath taken great pains in
reducing to a method, to my great satisfaction; and I shall be
glad, both for the King's sake and his, that the thing may be
put in practice, and will do my part to promote it.[1]   That done,
he gone, I to the office, where busy till night; and then with
comfort to sit with my wife, and get her to read to me; and so to
supper and to bed – with my mind at mighty ease.

25.   Up, and by coach with W. Hewer to see W. Coventry,
but he gone out, I to White-hall and there waited on Lord
Sandwich; which I have little encouragement to do, because of
the difficulty of seeing him and the little he hath to say to me
when I do see him, or to anybody else but his own idle people
about him, Sir Ch. Herbert,[2] &c; thence walked with him to
White-hall, where to the Duke of York; and there the Duke of
York and Wren and I by appointment in his closet, to read
over our letter to the office; which he heard, and signed it;[3]
and it is to my mind, M. Wren having made it somewhat
sweeter to the Board, and yet with all the advice fully that I
did draw it up with.   He said little more to*b* us now, his head

a repl. same symbol   *b* repl. full stop

1. Francis Hosier, Muster-Master
at Gravesend, had been recently
employed as an accountant in the
office of the Navy Treasurer. His
proposals were adopted in March
1669: below, p. 474 & n. 1.   Copies
of three letters he wrote at this time to
Pepys on the subject are in PL 1788.
Storekeepers' accounts were difficult
to balance since they involved so
many goods and services both at
home and overseas.   See Pepys's observations made in his evidence to the
Brooke House Committee (November 1669) in PL 2874, pp. 457+,

531+.   Thomas Turner also made
proposals (26 January 1669): Tanner
44, ff. 1-2, 78.
2. Sir Charles Harbord, jun.; a
close companion of Sandwich's since
at least the Bergen expedition in
1665; appointed Paymaster, Tangier,
in 1669, by Sandwich's influence (and
against Pepys's opposition).
3. Cf. above, p. 370 & n. 1; dated
this day: copies in PL 2242, pp. 122+
(in Hayter's hand); BM, Harl. 6003,
ff. 156+; ib., 6287, ff. 43+; Add.
9311, ff. 28+; ib., 36782, ff. 67+.

being full of other business. But I do see that he doth continue to put a value upon my advice; and so M. Wren and I to his chamber and there talked, and he seems to hope that these people, the Duke of Buckingham and Arlington, will run themselfs off of their legs, they being forced to be always putting the King upon one ill thing or other, against the easiness of his nature; which he will never be able to bear, nor they to keep him to, and so will lose themselfs; and for instance of their little progress, he tells me that my Lord of Ormond is like yet to carry it, and to continue in his command in Ireland; at least, they cannot get the better of him yet. But he tells me that the*a* Keeper is wrought upon, as they say, to give his opinion for the dissolving of the Parliament – which he thinks will undo him in the eyes of the people. He doth not seem to own the hearing or fearing of anything to be done in the Admiralty to the lessening of the Duke of York, though he hears how the town talk's full of it. Thence I by coach home,*b* and there find my cousin Roger come to dine with me and to seal his mortgage for the 500*l* I lend him. But he and I first walked to the Change, there to look for my uncle Wight and get him to dinner with us; so home, buying a barrel of oysters at my old oyster-woman's in Gracious-street,[1] but over the way to where she kept her shop before. So home, and there merry at dinner; and the money not being ready, I carried R Pepys to Holborn-conduit and there left him going to Stradwicke's,[2] whom we avoided to see because of our long absence; and my wife and I to the Duke of York's House to see *The Duchesse of Malfy*, a sorry play;[3] and sat with little pleasure, for fear of my wife's seeing me look about; and so I was uneasy all the while – though I desire and resolve never to give her trouble of that kind more. So home, and there busy at the office a while; and then home, where my wife to read to me; and so to supper and to bed. ⟨This evening, to

a repl. 'my'   *b* repl. 'to'

———————

1. A 'fine woman': above, vi. 307.
2. Thomas Stradwick, grocer; a cousin by marriage.
3. Webster's tragedy. Pepys had enjoyed reading it in 1662: above, iii. 209 & n. 1. (A).

my great content, I got Sir Rd. Ford to give me leave to set my
coach in his yard.⟩*a*

26. Up and at the office all the morning, where I was to
have delivered the Duke of York's letter of advice to the Board,
in answer to our several answers to his great letter; but Lord
Brouncker not being there, and doubtful to deliver it before the
new Treasurers, I forbore it to next sitting. So home at noon to
dinner, where I find Mr. Pierce and his wife, but I was forced to
show very little pleasure in her being there, because of my vow
to my wife; and therefore was glad of a very bad occasion for
my being really troubled, which is W. Hewer's losing of a Tally of
1000*l* which I sent him this day to receive of the Commissioners
of Excise; so that though I hope at the worst I shall be able to
get another, yet I made use of this to get away as soon as I had
dined; and therefore out with him to the Excise Office to make
a stop of its payment, and so away to the*b* coachmaker's and
several other places; and so away home, and there to my business
at the office; and thence home, and my wife to read to me and
W. Hewer to set some matters of accounts right at my chamber;
to bed.

27. Up and with W. Hewer to see W. Coventry again, but
missed him again by*c* coming too late, the man of the world that I
am resolved to preserve an interest in. Thence to White-hall,
and there at our usual waiting*d* on the Duke of York;*e* and that
being done, I away to the Exchequer to give a stop and take some
advice about my lost tally, wherein I shall have some remedy,
with trouble. And so home, and there find Mr. Povy by
appointment to dine with me, where a pretty good dinner; but
for want of thought*f* in my wife, it was but slovenly dressed up.
However, much pleasant discourse with him, and some serious;
and he tells me that he would by all means have me get to be a
Parliament-man the next Parliament; which he believes*g* there

a addition crowded in   *b* repl. 'do'
c blot below symbol   *d* repl. 'mee'-
e repl. 'W. Coventry'   *f* repl. 'care'
          g repl. symbol rendered illegible

will be one – which I do resolve of.[1] By and by comes my cousin
Roger and dines with us; and after dinner, did seal his Morgage,
wherein I do wholly rely on his honesty,[a] not having so much as
read over what he hath given me for it, nor minded it, but do
trust to his integrity therein. They all gone, I to the office, and
there a while and then home to ease my eyes and make my wife
read to me.

28.[b] Up, and all the morning at the office; where, while I
was sitting, one comes and tells me that my Coach is come[2] – so I
was forced to go out; and to Sir Rd. Ford's, where I spoke to
him, and he is very willing to have it brought in and stand there;
and so I ordered it, to my great content, it being mighty pretty;
only, the horses do not please me, and therefore resolve to have
better. At noon home to dinner; and so to the office again all
the afternoon and did a great deal of business; and so home to
supper and to bed, with my mind at pretty good ease, having
this day presented to the Board the Duke of York's letter; which
I perceive troubled Sir W. Penn, he declaring himself meant in
the part that concerned excuse by sickness;[3] but I do not care,
but am mightily glad that it is done, and now I shall begin to be
at pretty good ease in the office. ⟨This morning, to my great
content, W Hewers tells me that a porter is come, who found
my tally in Holborne and brings it him, for which he gives
him 20s.⟩[c]

a repl. 'hosty'   b figure blotted
c addition crowded in

---

1. Pepys's parliamentary ambitions
had been roused by the success of his
speech to the Commons on 5 March
1668.   There was no new Parliament
until 1679, but Pepys stood, unsuccessfully, at a bye-election for Alde-
burgh, Suff., in the summer of 1669.
He sat for Castle Rising, Norf., 1673–
9 and for Harwich in 1679 and 1685–7,
unsuccessfully contesting the latter
again in 1689.   For his parliamentary
career, see B. McL. Ranft in *Journ.
Mod. Hist.*, 24/368+.

2. Cf. above, p. 333 & n. 1.

3. PL 2242, p. 122.   Pepys's point
was that 'want of health' was an
allowable excuse, but that the invalid
had the duty to arrange for his work
to be done by deputy.   Penn had
been ill of the gout for much of this
year. (Cf. NWB, p. 236.)

29. *Lords day.* Lay long in bed with pleasure [with my wife], with whom I have now a great deal of content; and my mind is in other things also mightily more at ease, and I do mind my business better then ever and am more at peace; and trust in God I shall ever be so, though I cannot yet get my mind off from thinking now and then of Deb. But I do, ever since my promise a while since to my wife, pray to God by myself in my chamber every night, and will endeavour to get my wife to do the like with me ere long; but am in much fear of what she hath lately frighted me with about her being a Catholique[1] – and dare not therefore move*a* her to go to church, for fear she should deny me. But this morning, of her own accord, she spoke of going to church the next Sunday; which pleases me mightily. This morning my coachman's clothes comes home, and I like my livery mightily; and so I all the morning at my chamber, and dined with my wife and got her to read to me in the afternoon, till Sir W Warren by appointment comes to me, who spent two hours or three with me about his accounts of Gottenbrough;[2] which are so confounded, that I doubt they will hardly ever pass without my doing something; which he desires of me, and which, partly from fear and partly from unwillingness to wrong the King and partly from its being of no profit to me, I am backward to give way to, though the poor man doth endeed deserve to be rid of this trouble that he hath lain so long under from the negligence of this Board.[3] We afterward fell into other talk; and he tells me, as soon as he saw my coach yesterday, he wished that the owner might not contract envy by

a repl. 'more'

1. See above, p. 338 & n. 1.
2. They concerned a contract of July 1664 to supply 1000 masts shipped from Gothenburg (Göteborg), Sweden: see above, v. 215–16 & n. Some correspondence in early December about the accounts is in

Tanner 44, ff. 64–5. Pepys blamed Mennes for the delays: PL 2874, pp. 397–8.
3. A certificate for the payment to Warren of £1729 9s. 8d. was issued by the Board on 12 December: HMC, *Lindsey*, p. 116.

it;[1] but I told him it was now manifestly for my profit to keep a coach, and that after imployments[a] like mine for eight years, it were hard if I could not be justly thought to be able to do that.

He gone, my wife and I to supper; and so she to read and made an end of the *Life of Archbishop Laud*,[2] which is worth reading, as informing a man plainly in the posture of the Church, and how the things of it were managed with the same self-interest and design that every other thing is, and have succeeded accordingly. So to bed.

30. Up betimes, and with W. Hewer, who is my guard, to White-hall to a Committee of Tanger, where the business of Mr. Lanyon took up all the morning, and where, poor man, he did manage his business with so much folly, and ill fortune to boot, the Board before his coming in inclining of their own accord to lay his cause aside and leave it to the law; but he pressed that we would hear it, and it ended to the making him appear a very knave, as well, as it did to me, a fool also – which I was sorry for.[3] Thence by water, Mr. Povy, Creed and I, to Arundell-house and there I did see them choosing their Council, it being St. Andrews-day; and I had his[b] cross set on my hat, as the rest had, and cost me 2s.[4] And so leaving them, I away by coach home to dinner; and my wife after dinner went the first time abroad, to take the maidenhead of her coach, calling on Rogr. Pepys and visiting Mrs

a repl. 'an'   *b* repl. 'my'

---

1. In 1679 Pepys's coach (a later one) attracted the scorn of the anonymous pamphleteer who attacked him and Hewer during the Popish Plot in *A hue and cry after P. and H.* (p. 3): 'You had upon the Fore-part of your Chariot, Tempestuous Waves, and Wracks of Ships: On your Left-hand, Forts and great Guns, and Ships a fighting: On your Right-hand, was a fair Harbor and Town, with Ships and Galleys riding with their Flags and Penants. . . . Behind it were high Curl'd Waves and Ships a

sincking; and here and there, an Appearance of some Bits of Land.'

2. See above, p. 291, n. 1.

3. John Lanyon, a victualling agent for Tangier, lay under a charge of having underfreighted the *Tiger: CSPD 1668-9*, p. 138.

4. Evelyn mentions the wearing of St Andrew's crosses of ribbon on 30 November 1663. For the choice of St Andrew's Day as the anniversary day of the Royal Society, see Sir H. G. Lyons, *Royal Soc. 1660-1940*, p. 44.

Creed and my Cousin Turner – while I at home all the afternoon and evening, very busy and doing much work to my great content. Home at night, and there comes Mrs. Turner and Betty to see us, and supped with us; and I showed them a cold civility, for fear of troubling my wife; and after supper, they being gone, we to bed.

Thus ended this month with*a* very good content, that hath been the most sad to my heart and the most expenseful to my purse on things of pleasure, having furnished my wife's closet and the best chamber, and a coach and horses, that ever I yet knew in the world; and doth put me into the greatest condition of outward state that ever I was in, or hoped ever to be, or desired – and this at a time when we do daily expect great changes in this office and, by all reports, we must all of us turn out. But my eyes are come to that condition that I am not able to work; and therefore, that, and my wife's desire, makes me have no manner of trouble in my thoughts about it – so God do his will in it.

a repl. 'that hath'

DECEMBER

1. Up and to the office, where sat all the morning; and at noon with my people to dinner, and so to the office again, very busy till night; and then home and made my boy read to me Wilkins's *Reall Character*,[1] which doth please me mightily. And so after supper to bed – with great pleasure and content with my wife. ⟨This day I hear of poor Mr. Clerke the solicitor's being dead of a Cold, after being not above two days ill; which troubles me mightily, poor man.⟩[a][2]

2. Up and at the office all the morning upon some accounts of Sir D Gawden; and at noon abroad with W. Hewer, thinking to have found Mr. Wren at Captain Cox, to have spoke something to him about doing a favour for Will's Uncle Stevenson,[3] but missed[b] him; and so back home and abroad with my wife, the first time that ever I rode in my own coach; which doth make my heart rejoice and praise God, and pray him to bless it to me and continue it. So she and I to the King's playhouse, and there sat to avoid seeing of Knepp in a box above, where Mrs. Williams happened to be; and there saw *The Usurper*, a pretty good play in all but what is[c] designed to resemble Cromwell and Hugh Peters, which is mighty silly.[4] The play done, we to White-hall; where [my] wife stayed, while I up to the Duchesses and Queenes

---

a addition crowded in
b repl. 'came'   *c* repl. 'whose'

---

1. See above, p. 200 & n. 7.
2. Clarke was a solicitor employed by the Navy Board.
3. See below, p. 382 & n. 4.
4. The play was a tragedy by Edward Howard: see above, v. 3, n. 2. Damocles was supposed to

represent Cromwell; and Hugo de Petro, Peters, the most prominent of Cromwell's army chaplains. According to Genest (i. 72), Cleomenes may have been intended as Monck. (A).

side to speak with the Duke of York; and here saw all the ladies and heard the silly discourse of the King with his people about him, telling a story of my Lord of Rochester's having of his clothes stole while he was with a wench, and his gold all gone but his clothes found afterward, stuffed into a feather-bed by the wench that stole them.   I spoke with the Duke of York, just as he was set down to supper with the King, about our sending of victuals to Sir Tho. Allens fleet hence to Cales to meet him.[1]   And so back to my wife in my coach, and so with great content and joy home – where I made my boy to make an end of the *Reall Character*, which I begun a*ᵃ* great while ago and doth please me infinitely, and endeed is a most worthy labour – and I think mighty easy, though my eyes makes me unable to attempt anything in it.[2]   So after supper, to bed.

Today I hear that Mr. Ackworth's cause went for him at Guildhall against his accusers; which I am well enough pleased with.[3]

3.   Up betimes and by water with W. Hewer to White-hall; and there to Mr. Wren, who gives me but small hopes of the favour I hoped for Mr. Stevenson, Will's uncle, of having leave, being upon the point of death, to surrender his place;[4] which doth trouble me, but I will do what I can.   So back again to the office, Sir Jer. Smith with me, who is a silly, prating, talking man, but he tells me what he hears: that Holmes and Spragg now rule all with the Duke of Buckingham as to sea-business, and will be great men.   But he doth prophesy what will be the fruit of it – as I do.   So to the office, where we sat all the morning; and at

---

a   repl. 'ag'-

---

1. Allin in fact took the victuals on board not at Cadiz, but at Tangier, on 15 February 1669: Allin, ii. 85.

2. In this work (q.v. above, p. 200 & n. 7), John Wilkins attempted to construct in symbols a non-mathematical scientific language which would be universally understood.

3. For this case, see above, p. 123, n. 4; *CSPD 1668–9*, p. 71. (Records of cases at the Guildhall are defective for this period.)

4. He was trying to get permission to surrender his office to a nominee. In 1663 he was a purser: above, iv. 151.

noon home to dinner, and then abroad again with wife to the Duke of York's playhouse and saw *The Unfortunate Lovers*;[1] a mean play I think, but some parts very good, and excellently acted. We sat under the boxes and saw the fine ladies; among others, my Lady Kerneguy,[2] who is most devilishly painted. And so home, it being mighty pleasure to go alone with my poor*a* wife in a coach of our own to a play; and makes us appear mighty great, I think, in the world; at least, greater then ever I could, or my friends for me, have once expected, or I think then ever any of my family ever yet lived, in my memory, but my Cosen Pepys in Salsbury-court.[3] So to the office, and thence home to supper and to bed.

4. Up and with W. Hewer by water to White-hall, and there did wait as usual upon the Duke of York; where, upon discoursing something touching the Ticket-Office, which by letter[4] the Board did give the Duke of York their advice to be put upon Lord Brouncker, Sir J. Mennes did foolishly rise up and complain of the office and his being made nothing of – and this before Sir Tho. Littleton, who would be glad of this difference among us; which did trouble me mightily, and therefore did forbear*b* to say what I otherwise would have thought fit for me to say on this occasion, upon so impertinent* a speech as this doting fool made – but I say, I let it alone and contented myself that it went as I advised, as to the Duke of York's judgment in the thing disputed. And so thence away, my coach meeting me there and carrying me to several places to do little jobbs, which is a mighty convenience; and so home, where by invitation I find my aunt Wight, who looked over all our house and is mightily pleased with it; and endeed, it is now mighty handsome, and rich in furniture. By and by comes my uncle, and then to dinner, where a venison pasty and very merry; and after dinner, I carry

---

a repl. same symbol   *b* repl. 'avoid'

---

1. A tragedy by Davenant; see above, v. 77, n. 2. (A).

2. Lady Carnegie: cf. above, pp. 154-5 & n.

3. John Pepys (d. ?1652), secretary to Lord Chief Justice Coke.

4. Untraced.

my wife and her to Smithfield, where they set in the coach, while Mr. Pickering, who met me there, and I and W. Hewer and a friend, a jockey,* of his, did go about to see several pairs of horses for my coach; but it was late, and we agreed on none but left it to another time; but here I do see instances of a piece of craft and cunning that I never dreamed of concerning the buying and choosing of horses. So Mr. Pickering (to whom I am much beholden for his kindness herein) and I parted; and I with my people home – where I left them, and I to the office to meet about some business of Sir W. Warren's accounts,[1] where I vexed to see how ill all the Controller's business is likely to go as long as ever Sir J. Mennes lives. And so troubled I was, that I thought it a good occasion for me to give my thoughts of it in writing; and therefore wrote a letter at the Board, by the help of a tube, to Lord Brouncker, and did give it him; which I kept a copy of, and may be of use to me hereafter to show in this matter.[2]   This being done, I home to my aunt, who supped with us, and my uncle also; and a good-humoured woman she is, so that I think we shall keep her acquaintance; but mighty proud she is of her wedding-ring, being lately set with Diamonds; cost her about 12*l.*   And I did commend it mightily to her, but do not think it very suitable for one of our quality.   After supper, they home and we to bed.

5.   Up, after a little talk with my wife which troubled me, she being ever since our late difference mighty watchful of sleep and dreams, and will not be persuaded but I do dream of Deb, and doth tell me that I speak in my dream and that this night I did cry "Huzzy!" and it must be she – and now and then I start otherwise then I used to do, she says; which I know not, for I do not know that I dream of her more then usual, though I cannot deny that my thoughts waking do run now and then, against my will and judgment, upon her, for that only is wanting to undo me, being now in every other thing as to my mind most

1. Concerning his contract for New England masts: NWB, pp. 129, 147.

2. The copy (in Gibson's hand; with two memoranda of 4 and 11 December on the same subject) is in NMM, LBK/8, pp. 549–50; printed in *Further Corr.*, pp. 199–201.

happy – and may still be so but for my own fault, if I be ketched loving anybody but my wife again. So up and to the office; and at noon to dinner and thence to office, where late, mighty busy and despatching much business, settling papers in my own office; and so home to supper and to bed. No news stirring but that my Lord of Ormond is likely to go to Ireland again,[1] which doth show that the Duke of Buckingham doth not rule all so absolutely – and that, however, we shall speedily have more changes in the Navy. And it is certain that the non=conformists do now preach openly in houses in many places, and among others, the house that was heretofore Sir G Carteret's in Leadenhall-street, and have ready access to the King.[2] And now the great dispute is whether this Parliament or another; and my great design, if I continue in the Navy, is to get myself to be a Parliament-man.[3]

6. *Lords day.* Up, and with my wife to church; which pleases me mightily, I being full of fear that she would never go to church again after she had declared to me that she was a Roman Catholique.[4] But though I do verily think she fears God, and is truly and sincerely virtuous, yet I do see she is not so strictly so a Catholique as not to go to church with me; which pleases me mightily. Here Mills made a lazy sermon upon Moses's meekenesse; and so home, and my wife and I alone to dinner; and then she to read a little book concerning Speech in general, a translation late out of French,[5] a most excellent piece as ever I read, proving a soul in man and all the ways and secrets by which Nature teaches speech in man – which doth please me

---

1. See above, p. 347, n. 1.

2. Between the lapse of the First Conventicle Act in May 1668 and the summer of 1669, Dissenters enjoyed some liberty: cf. above, p. 277 & n. 5. In September 1668 a deputation of London Presbyterian ministers had thanked the King for their freedom: M. Sylvester, *Reliq. Baxt.* (1696), bk i, pt iii. 36. There are records of three Independent congregations meeting in Leadenhall St in 1669: G. Lyon Turner (ed.), *Orig. records early Nonconformity*, ii. 980–1.

3. Cf. above, pp. 376–7 & n.

4. See above, p. 338 & n. 1.

5. *A philosophicall discourse concerning speech, conformable to the Cartesian principles . . . Englished out of French* (1668); PL 385; a translation of L. G. de Cordemoy, *Discours physique de la parole . . .* (1668).

most infinitely to read. By and by my wife to church, and I to my office to complete my journall for the last three days; and so home to my chamber to settle some papers, and so to spend the evening with my wife and W. Hewer, talking over the business of the office, and perticularly my own office, how I will make it; and it will become in a little time an office of ease, and not slavery, as it hath for so many years been. So to supper and to bed.

7. Up by candlelight, the first time I have done so this winter; but I had lost my labour so often to visit Sir W. Coventry, and not visited him so long, that I was resolved to get time enough; and so up, and with W. Hewer, it being the first frosty day we have had this winter, did walk it very well to W. Coventry's; and there alone with him an hour talking of the Navy, which he pities, but says he hath no more mind to be found meddling with it, lest it should do it hurt, as well as him, to be found to meddle with it. So to talk of general things; and telling him that with all these doings, he, I thanked*a* God, stood yet, he told me "Yes," but that he thought his continuing in did arise from his enemies, my Lord of Buckingham and Arlington's, seeing that he cared so little if he was out. And he doth protest to me that he is as weary of the Treasury as ever he was of the Navy. He tells me that he doth believe that their heat is over almost, as to the Navy, there being now none left of the old stock but my Lord Brouncker (J. Mennes, who is ready to leave the world) and myself. But he tells me that he doth foresee very great wants and great disorders by reason thereof – insomuch, as he is represented to the King by his enemies as a melancholy man, and one that is still prophesying ill events, so as the King called him *Visionaire;*[1] which being told him, he says he answered the party, that whatever he foresaw, he was not afeared as to*b* himself of anything, nor perticularly of

a repl. 'thank'   *b* repl. 'him'-

1. In March 1669 he was satirised in a play as 'Sir Cautious Trouble-all': below, p. 471 & nn. 2, 3.

my Lord Arlington so much as the Duke of Buckingham hath been, nor of the Duke of Buckingham so much as my Lord Arlington at this time is. But he tells me that he hath been always looked upon as a melancholy man; whereas, others that would please the King do make him believe that all is safe; and so he hath heard my Lord Chancellor openly say to the King, that he was now a glorious prince and in a glorious condition, because of some one accident that hath happened, or some one rub that hath been removed; "when", says W. Coventry, "they reckoned their one good meal, without considering that there was nothing left in the cupboard for tomorrow." After this and other discourse of this kind, I away; and walked to my Lord Sandwiches and walked with him to White-hall, and took a quarter of an hour's walk in the garden with him, which I had not done so much time with him since his coming in to England; and talking of his own condition, and perticularly of the world's talk of his going to Tanger[1] – I find, if his conditions can be made profitable and safe as to money, he would go, but not else; but however, will seem not averse to it, because of facilitating his other accounts now depending, which he finds hard to get through but yet hath some hopes, the King, he says, speaking very kindly to him. Thence to a Committee of Tanger; and so with W. Hewer to Westminster to Sir R. Long's office; and so to the Temple, but did nothing, the*a* auditor not being within; and so home to dinner, and after dinner out again with my wife to the Temple, and up and down to do a little business and back again; and so to my office and did a little business; and so home, and W. Hewer with me, to read and talk; and to supper and then to bed in mighty good humour. ⟨This afternoon, passing through Queen's-street, I saw pass by our coach on foot, Deb; which God forgive me, did put me into some new thoughts of her and for her, but durst not show them; and I think my wife did not see her, but I did get my thoughts free of her as soon as I could.⟩*b*

a repl. 'my'   *b* addition crowded into bottom of page

---

1. He never became Governor of Tangier. There had been a similar rumour in 1664: above, v. 313.

8. Up, and Sir H. Cholmly betimes with me about some accounts and moneys due to him;[1] and he gone, I to the office, where sat all the morning; and here, among other things, breaks out the storm W. Hewer and I have long expected from the Surveyor, about W. Hewer's conspiring to get a contract, to the burdening of the stores with Kerseys and Cottons, of which he hath often complained, and lately more then ever; and now he did it by a most scandalous letter to the Board, reflecting on my office;[2] and by discourse, it fell to such high words between him and I as can hardly ever be forgot, I declaring I would believe W. Hewer as soon as him, and laying the fault, if there be any, upon himself; he, on the other hand, vilifying of my word and W. Hewer's, calling him knave, and that if he were his clerk, he should lose his ears; at last, I closed the business for this morning with making the thing ridiculous, as it is; and he swearing that the*a* King should have right in it, or he would lose his place. The office was cleared of all but ourselfs and W. Hewer; but however, the world did by the beginning see what it meant, and it will I believe come to high terms between us; which I am sorry for, to have any blemish laid upon me or mine at this time, though never so unduly, for fear of giving occasion to my real discredit; and therefore I was*b* not only all the rest of the morning

a repl. 'with'   *b* repl. 's'-

---

1. For his work on the construction of the mole at Tangier: see below, p. 536 & n. 1.

2. The allegation of the Surveyor (Middleton) related to stores at Chatham. Pepys immediately started an enquiry, asking the Clerk of the Cheque there for copies of the letters in which Hewer was said to have pressed for the bills to be made out, and adding: 'I desire you by noe means to with=hold any light from me that should informe me in this matter; For as I shall give him my utmost protection while he is innocent, Soe Ile be found the forwardest of the Board in the promoteing of his

punishment when he shalbe found blameable' (Pepys to Thomas Wilson, 11 December: NMM, LBK/8, p. 553; in Hewer's hand; printed *Further Corr.*, p. 203). On 16 December Pepys wrote to the Board a powerful letter vindicating Hewer's conduct: below, p. 393 & n. 3. The Board found unanimously in Hewer's favour on 18 December, and on the same day the Surveyor in the presence of his colleagues burnt his letter of 7 December to which Pepys had taken objection. On Pepys's direction Hewer made a collection of the papers relating to the affair: NMM, PLA/19.

vexed, but so went home to dinner – where my wife tells me of my Lord Orrery's new play, *Tryphon*,[1] at the Duke of York's House; which, however, I would see, and therefore put a bit of meat in our mouths and went thither; where, with much ado, at half-past one we got into a blind hole in the 18*d* place above stairs,[2] where we could not hear well; but the house infinite full; but the prologue most silly,[3] and the play, though admirable, yet no pleasure almost in it, because just the very same design and words and sense and plot as every of his plays have,[4] any one of which alone would be held admirable, whereas so many of the same design and fancy do but dull one another; and this, I perceive, is the sense of everybody else, as well as myself – who therefore showed but little pleasure in it. So home, mighty hot and my mind mightily out of order, so as I could not eat any supper nor sleep almost all night; though I spent till 12 at night with W. Hewer to consider of our business, and we find it not only most free from any blame of our side, but so horrid scandalous on the other, to make so groundless a complaint and one so shameful to him, that it could not but[a] let me see that there is no need of my being troubled. But such is the weakness of my nature, that I could not help it – which vexes me, showing me how unable I am to[b] live with difficulties.

9. Up and to the office but did little there, my mind being still uneasy, though more and more satisfied that there is no occasion for it. But abroad with my wife to the Temple, where I met with Auditor Wood's clerk and did some business with him; and so to see Mr. Spong, and found him out by Southampton-market and there carried my wife, and up to his chamber, in a by-place but with a good prospect to the fields; and there I

a MS. 'be'   *b* repl. 'not'

---

1. A tragedy, published in 1669. This is the first record of its being performed. (A).

2. I.e. in the middle gallery, the tier of seats between the boxes and the upper gallery. (A).

3. It is in dialogue. According to the 1672 edition of the play, it was spoken 'by Mr. *Nokes* and Mr. *Angel*.' (A).

4. Cf. Pepys's similar criticism above, p. 144 & n. 1. (A).

had most infinite pleasure not only with his ingenuity in general, but in perticular with his showing me the use of the Paralelogram,[1] by which he drow in a quarter of an hour before me, in little from a great, a most neat map of England; that is, all the outlines – which gives me infinite pleasure and foresight of pleasure I shall have with it, and therefore dcsire to have that which I have bespoke made.   Many other pretty things he showed us, and did give me a glass bubble to try the strength of liquors with.[2]   This done, and having spent 6*d* in ale in the coach at the door of the Bull Inn with the innocent master of the house, a Yorkshireman, for his letting us go through his house, we away to Hercules-Pillars and there eat a bit of meat: and so with all speed back to the Duke of York's House, where very full again; but we came time enough to have a good place in the pit, and did hear this new play again; where, though I*a* better understood it then before, yet my sense of it, and pleasure, was just the same as yesterday and no more, nor anybody's else about us. So took our coach and home, having now little pleasure to look about me to see the fine faces, for fear of displeasing my wife, whom I take great comfort now, more then ever, in pleasing – and it is a real joy to me.   So home and to my office, where spend an hour or two; and so home to my wife to supper and talk, and to bed.

10.   Up and to the office, where busy all the morning. Middleton not there, so no words or looks of him.   At noon home to dinner; and so to the office and there all the afternoon busy; and at night W. Hewer home with me, and we think we have got matter enough to make Middleton appear a coxcomb; but it troubled me to have Sir W. Warren meet me at night, going out of the office home, and tell me that Middleton doth intend to complain to the Duke of York.   But upon consideration of the business, I did go to bed satisfied that it was best

a   repl. 'it'

---

1. Pantograph; q.v. above, p. 340, n. 1.
2. A hydrometer; a new inven-

tion.   Boyle had exhibited one of his own design to the Royal Society in May 1662: Birch, i. 82.

for me that he should; and so my trouble was over, and to bed and sleep well.

11. Up and with W. Hewer by water to Somerset-house; and there I to my Lord Brouncker before he went forth to the Duke of York, and there told him*a* my confidence that I should make*b* Middleton appear a fool; and that it was, I thought, best for me to complain of the wrong he hath done; but brought it about that my Lord desired me I would forbear, and promised that he would prevent Middleton's till I had given in my answer to the Board which I desired; and so away to White-hall and there did our usual attendance, and no word spoke before the Duke of York by Middleton at all; at which I was glad to my heart – because by this means*c* I have time to draw up my answer to my mind. So with W. Hewer by coach to Smithfield, but met not Mr. Pickering, he being not come; and so he and I to a cook's*d* shop in Aldersgate-street and dined well for 19½*d* upon roast-beef, pleasing ourselfs with the infinite strength we have to prove Middleton a coxcomb; and so having dined, we back to Smithfield and there met Pickering, and up and down all the afternoon about horses, and did see the*e* knaveries and tricks of Jockys.* Here I met W Joyce, who troubled me with his impertinencies a great while, and the like Mr. Knepp, who it seems is a kind of a Jocky and*f* would fain have been doing something for me; but I avoided him, and the more for fear of being troubled thereby with his wife, whom I desire but dare not see – for my vow to*g* my wife.*g* At last went away and did nothing; only, concluded upon giving 50*l* for a fine pair of black horses we saw this day sennit.[1] And so set Mr. Pickering down near his house (whom I am much beholden to for his care herein, and he hath admirable skill, I perceive, in this business); and so home and spent the evening talking and merry, my mind at good ease; and so to bed.

---

a MS. 'me'   *b* repl. 'appear'
c repl. same symbol badly formed
d repl. same symbol badly formed
e repl. 'a'   *f* repl. 'but'   *g–g* garbled s.h.

---

1. For prices of coach-horses, see above, vi. 180 & n. 1.

12.   Up and to the office, where all the morning; and at [noon] home to dinner, and so the like, mighty busy, late all the afternoon, that I might be ready to go to the drawing up my answer to Middleton tomorrow; and therefore home to supper and to bed.

I hear this day that there is fallen down a new house, not quite finished, in Lumberdstreet, and that there have been several so, they making use of bad mortar and bricks; but no hurt yet, as God hath ordered it. ⟨This day was brought home my pair of black coach-horses, the first I ever was maister of; they cost me 50*l*, and are a fine pair.⟩*a*

13.   *Lords day.*   Up and with W. Hewer to the office, where all the morning; and then home to a little dinner, and presently to it again all alone till 12 at night, drawing up my answer to Middleton, which I think I shall do to very good purpose; at least, I satisfy myself therein.   And so to bed, weary with walking in my office dictating to him.   In the night, my wife very ill; vomited, but was well again by and by.

14.*b*   Up and by water to White-hall to a Committee of Tanger; where, among other things, a silly account of a falling-out between Norwood at Tanger and Mr. Bland the Mayor, who is fled to Cales.[1]   His complaint is ill-worded; and the other's defence, the most ridiculous that ever I saw – and so everybody else that was there thought it.   But never did I see so great an instance of the use of grammar and knowledge how to tell a man's tale as this day, Bland having spoiled his business by ill-telling it; who had work to have made himself notorious*c* * by his mastering Norwood his enemy, if he had known how to

a   addition crowded in
     b   repl. '13'   *c*   repl. 'famous'

---

1. This quarrel between the military and civil authorities (Norwood being Deputy-Governor) had culminated in a dispute over the right to issue licences for the sale of wine.   See BM, Sloane 3510, ff. 4+, 69+; Routh, pp. 122–3.   A copy of Bland's wordy letter of complaint to Norwood (28 October 1668) is in Rawl. C 423, f. 139*r*.   Norwood wrote a sprightly letter (10 November) to Ormond, appealing for his support: HMC, *Ormonde*, n.s. iii. 288.   Bland later returned to Tangier.

have used. Thence, calling* Smith the Auditors clerk at the Temple, I by the Exchange home and there looked over my Tanger accounts with him; and so to dinner, and then set him down again by*a* a hackney, my coachman being this day about breaking of my horses to the coach, they having never yet drawn. Left my wife at Unthanks, and I to the Treasury, where we waited on the Lords-Commissioners about Sir D. Gawden's matters;[1] and so took her up again at night, and home to the office; and so home with W. Hewer, and to talk about our quarrel with Middleton; and so to supper and to bed.

This day I hear and am glad that the King hath prorogued the Parliament to October next; and among other reasons, it will give me time to go to France I hope.[2]

15. Up and to the office, where sat all the morning, and the new Treasurers there; and, for my life, I cannot keep Sir J. Mennes and others of the Board from showing our weakness, to the dishonour of the Board, though I am not concerned – but it doth vex me to the heart to have it before these people, that would be glad to find out all our weaknesses. At noon home to dinner, Mrs. Mary Batelier with us; and so after dinner, I with W. Hewer all the afternoon till night begins, to draw up our answer to Middleton; and it proves troublesome, because*b* I have so much in my head at a time to say; but I must go through with it. So at night to supper and to bed.

16. I did the like all day long, only a little at dinner; and so to work again, and were at it till 2 in the morning; and so W Hewer, *c* who was with me all day, home to his lodging, and I to bed – after we had finished it.[3]

---

a repl. 'in'   *b* repl. 'but yet'   *c* repl. 'home to'

---

1. Both his new contract and his Lent accounts were dealt with: *CTB*, ii. 506–07.

2. Pepys is mistaken about parliament. It now stood adjourned from 10 November 1668 until 1 March 1669. It was then prorogued until 19 October 1669: *CJ*, ix. 97. For his journey to France, see below, p. 462, n. 3.

3. Pepys to Navy Board, 16 December: copy (in Gibson's hand) in NMM, PLA/19, n.p. For Middleton's allegations against Hewer, see above, p. 388 & n. 2.

17.   Up and set my man Gibson and Mr. Fist to work to write it over fair, while I all the morning at the office, sitting.   At noon home to them, and all the afternoon looking over them and examining with W. Hewer; and so about 10 at night, I to bed, leaving them to finish the writing it fair, which they did by sitting up most of the night; and so home to bed.[a]

18.   All the morning at the office about Sir W. Warren's accounts[1], my mind full of my business, having before we met gone to Lord Brouncker and got him to read over my paper; who owns most absolute content in it, and the advantage I have in it and the folly of the Surveyor.   At noon home to dinner and then again to the office a while, and so by hackney-coach to Brooke house and there spoke with Collonell Thomson, I by order carrying them our contract-books from the beginning to the end of the late war.[2]   I found him finding of errors in a ship's book, where he showed me many; which must end in the ruin, I doubt, of the Controller, who found them not out in the pay of the ship, or the whole office.   But I took little notice of them to concern myself in them; but so leaving my books, I home to the office, where the office met and after some other business done, fell to mine with the Surveyor; begun to be a little brisk at the beginning, but when I came to the point to touch him, which I had all the advantages in the world to do, he became as calm as a lamb and owned, as the whole Board did, their satis-faction, and cried excuse; and so all made friends and their acknowledgment put into writing[3] and delivered into Sir J. Mennes's hand, to be kept there for the use of the Board, or me when I shall call for it; they desiring it might be so, that I might not make use of it to the prejudice of the Surveyor, whom I had an advantage over by his extraordinary folly in this matter. But besides this, I have no small advantage got by this business, as I have put several things into my letter which I should other-

----

a   MS. 'beds'

----

1. Cf. above, p. 378 & n. 2.
2. For the contract books, see above, iii. 65, n. 2. Col. George

Thomson was a member of the Brooke House Committee.
3. Now untraced.

wise have wanted an opportunity of saying – which pleases me mightily. So Middleton desiring to be friends, I forgave him; and all mighty quiet and fell to talk of other stories; and there stayed, all of us, till 9 or 10 at night (more then ever we did in our lives before together); and so home – where*a* I have a new*b* fight to fight with my wife, who is under new trouble by some news she hath heard of Deb's being mighty fine, and gives out that she hath a friend that gives her money; and this my wife believes to be me, and poor wretch, I cannot blame her. And therefore she run into mighty*c* extremes; but I did pacify all, and were mighty good friends and to bed; and I hope it will be our last struggle from this business, for I am resolved never to give any new occasion – and great peace I find in my mind by it. So to supper, she and I, and to bed.

19. Up, and to the office, where all the morning; and at noon, eating very little dinner, my wife and I by hackney to the King's playhouse and there, the pit being full, sat in a box above and saw *Catelin's Conspiracy*[1] – yesterday being the first day – a play of much good sense and words to read, but that doth appear the worst upon the stage, I mean the least divertising, that ever I saw any, though most fine in clothes[2] and a fine Scene*d* of the Senate and of a fight, that ever I saw in my life – but the play is only*e* to be read. And therefore home with no pleasure at all, but only in sitting next to Betty Hall, that did belong to this House and was Sir Ph. Howard's mistress; a mighty pretty wench, though my wife will not think so, and I dare neither commend nor be seen to look upon her or any other now, for

1. *Catiline*; a tragedy by Ben Jonson; q.v. above, v. 349, n. 4. According to the 1669 edition, Hart played Catiline; Mohun, Cethegus; Burt, Cicero; Mrs Carey, Sempronia. Downes (p. 8) says that it had been revived by the King's Company before 1663, but there is no specific record of a post-Restoration performance before this one of Pepys's. (A).

2. The robes (provided by the King) were a style of costume 'à la Romaine', including the conventional cuirass and helmet. The toga was not used as early as this. (A).

fear of offending her.   So, our own coach coming for us, home
and to end letters; and so home, my wife to read to me out of
The Siege of Rhodes;¹ and so to supper and to bed.

20.   *Lords day.*   Up and with my wife to church, and then
home; and there found W. Joyce come to dine with me, as
troublesome a talking coxcomb as ever he was – and yet once
in a year I like him well enough.   In the afternoon, my wife and
W. Hewer and I to White-hall, where they set me down and
stayed till I had been with the Duke of York, with the rest of us
of the office, and did a little business; and then the Duke of
York in good humour did fall to tell us many fine stories of the
wars in Flanders, *ᵃ* and how the Spaniards are the [best] discip-
lined foot in the world² – will refuse no extraordinary service if
commanded, but scorn to be paid for it, as in other countries,
though at the same time they will beg in the streets.   Not a
soldier will carry you a cloak-bag for money*ᵇ* for the world,
though he will beg a penny, and will do the thing if commanded
by his commander.   That in the citadel of Antwerp, a soldier
hath not a liberty of begging till he hath served three years.
They will cry out against their King and commanders and
generals, none like them in the world, and yet will not hear a
stranger say a word of them but he will cut his throat.   That
upon a time, some of the commanders of their*ᶜ* army exclaiming*ᵈ*
against their generals, and perticularly the Marquis de Caranene,³
the confessor of the Marquis coming by and hearing them, he
stops and gravely tells them that the three great trades of the
world are, the Lawyer[s], who govern the world – the Church-
men, who enjoy the world – and a sort of fools whom they call

---

a   repl. 'Fr'-   b   repl. 'me'
c   repl. 'the'   d   repl. 'falling out'

---

1. I.e. from Davenant's text of
this opera; q.v. above, ii. 130, n. 2.
PL 2347 (1673 ed.). (A).
2. The Duke had served with the
Spaniards in two campaigns in 1657–8.

3. **Caracena** (d. 1667/8), Spanish
soldier and proconsul; commander,
under Don Juan, of the Spanish forces
in the Netherlands, 1656–9; Governor
of the Netherlands, 1658–64.

Souldiers, who make it their work to defend the world.[1]   He told us too, that Turein being now become a Catholique, he is likely to get over the head of Colbert, their interests being contrary;[2] the latter to promote Trade and the sea (which, says the Duke of York, is that that we have most cause to fear); and Turin to imploy the King and his forces by land, to encrease his conquests.   Thence to the coach to my wife and so home; and there with W. Hewer to my office to do some business, and so set down my journall for four or five days; and then home to supper and read a little, and to bed.

W. Hewer tells me today that he hears that the King of France hath declared in print that he doth intend this next summer to forbid his commanders to strike to us, but that both we and the Dutch shall strike to him.[3]   And that he hath made his captains swear it already, that they will observe it – which is a great thing if he doth it, as I know nothing to hinder him.

21.   My own coach carrying me and my boy Tom, who goes with me in the room of W. Hewer who could not, and I dare not go alone, to the Temple and there set me down – the first time ⟨my fine horses⟩[a] ever carried me, and I am mighty proud of them; and there took a hackney and to White-hall, where a Committee of Tanger, but little to do; and so away home, calling at the Exchange and buying several little things; and so home and there dined with my wife and people; and then she and W. Hewer and I by appointment out with our coach, but the

---

a   repl. 'they'

---

1. This appears to be a version of a widespread late-medieval proverb. One variant runs: 'The King rules all; the ploughman works for all; the priest prays for all; the soldier fights for all.'

2. Turenne (under whom the Duke had served in 1652–5) had become a Roman Catholic in the previous October.   His political influence never rivalled that of Colbert.

3. No such declaration has been traced. (Cf. the similar, unfounded, report current in October: *Bulstrode Papers*, i. 66.) Negotiations were now on foot which led to an agreement between Charles and Louis in the summer of 1669 by which the ships of neither country were to demand salutes from each other in the Mediterranean.   See below, p. 560 & n. 2.

old horses, not daring yet to use them too much, but only to
enter them – and to the Temple, there to call* Talbt. Pepys;[1]
and took him up, and first went*a* into Holborne and there saw
the woman that is to be seen with a Beard;[2] she is a little plain
woman, a Dane, her name, Ursula Dyan, about forty years old,
her voice like a little girl's, with a beard as much as any man I
ever saw, as black almost, and grizzly.   They offered [to] show
my wife further satisfaction if she desired it, refusing it to men*b*
that desired it there.   But there is no doubt but by her voice she is
a woman; it begun to grow at about seven years old – and was
shaved not above seven months ago, and is now so big as any
man almost that ever I saw, I say, bushy and thick.   It was a
strange sight to me, I confess, and what pleased me mightily.
Thence to the Duke's playhouse and saw *Mackbeth*;[3] the King
and Court there, and we sat just under them and my Lady
Castlemayne, and close*c* to the woman that comes into the pit, a
kind of a loose gossip, that pretends to be like her, and is*d* so
something.   And my wife, by my troth, appeared I think as
pretty as any of them, I never thought so much before; and so
did Talbot and W. Hewer, as they said, I heard, to one another.
The King and Duke of York minded me, and smiled upon me at
the handsome woman near me: but it vexed me to see Mall
Davis, in the box over his and my Lady Castlemaynes head, look
down upon the King and he up to her; and so did my Lady
Castlemayne once, to see who it was; but when she saw her, she
blushed like fire; which troubled me.[4] The play done, took
leave of Tall. who goes into the country this Christmas; and

---

	a repl. 'carry'	*b* repl. 'me'
c repl. incomplete symbol		*d* repl. 'doth'

---

1. Son of Roger, now a student at
the Middle Temple.

2. Probably the woman seen by
Evelyn on 15 September 1657. She
was Barbara Ursler, wife of Michael
van Beck, born in 1629 in Germany.
Several portraits survive: see Evelyn,
iii. 198, n. 1.

3. Probably Davenant's adaptation:
see above, v. 314, n. 3. (A).

4. Moll Davis had left the Duke
of York's Company to become the
King's mistress: see above, p. 19,
n. 3. (A).

so we home, and there I to work at the office late; and so home to supper and to bed.

22. At the office all the morning; and at noon to the Change, thinking to meet with Langford[1] about my father's house in Fleet-street but I came too late; and so home to dinner, and all the afternoon at the office busy; and at night home to supper and talk, and with mighty content, with my wife; and so to bed.

23. Met at the office all the morning; and at noon to the Change and there met with[a] Langford and Mr. Franke, the land-lord of my father's house in Fleet-street, and are come to an arbitration what my father shall give him to be freed of his lease and building the house again. Walked up and down the Change; and among others, discoursed with Sir Jo. Bankes, who thinks this prorogation[2] will please all but the Parliament itself, which will, if ever they meet, be vexed with Buckingham, who yet governs all. He says the nonconformists are glad of it, and he believes will get the upperhand in a little time, for the King must trust to them or nobody; and he thinks the King will be forced to it.[3] He says that Sir D. Gawden is mightily troubled at Pen's being put upon him by the Duke of York, and that he believes he will get clear of it;[4] which, though it will trouble[b] me to have Pen still at the office, yet I shall think D. Gawden doth well in it, and what I would advise him to, because I love him. So home to dinner; and then with my wife alone abroad with our new horses, the beautifullest almost that ever I saw, and the first time they ever carried her at all, and me

a   followed by erasure and blot   *b*   repl. 'troubled'

---

1. William Langford, a tailor, had taken over the remainder of the lease in 1664 when Tom Pepys (the diarist's brother) had died. In 1665 the house had been destroyed in the Fire.

2. See above, p. 393 & n. 2.

3. Banks, now a moderate Angli-can, had once been a moderate Presby-terian: see D. C. Coleman, *Sir J.*

Banks, pp. 143+. He was one of the leading merchants of the day.

4. Penn had been joined with Sir Denis Gauden and his son Benjamin Gauden in the contract for navy victualling, as a means of providing some official check on the victualler: *CSPD 1668–9*, p. 208.

but once. But we are mighty proud of them. To her tailor's
and so to the Change*a* and laid out three or four pound in lace*
for her and me; and so home, and there I up to my Lord
Brouncker at his lodgings and sat with him an hour on purpose
to talk over the wretched state of this office at present, according
to the present hands it is made up of; wherein he doth fully
concur with me, and that it is our parts not*b* only to prepare for
defending it and ourselfs against the consequences of it, but to
take the best ways we can to make it known to the Duke of
York – for till Sir J. Mennes be removed, and a sufficient man
brought into W. Penn's place when he is gone, it is impossible
for this office ever to support itself. So home to supper and
to bed.

24. A cold day. Up and to the office, where all the morning
alone at the office, nobody meeting, being the Eve of Christmas.
At noon home to dinner and then to the office, busy all the
afternoon, and at night home to supper; and it being now very
cold, and in hopes of a frost, I begin this night to put on a Wastecoate,* it being the first winter in my whole memory that ever I
stayed till this day before I did so. So to bed, in mighty good
humour with my wife, but sad in one thing, and that is for my
poor eyes.

25. *Christmas day.* Up, and continued on my waistcoat, the
first day this winter. And I to church, where Alderman Backewell coming in late, I beckoned to his lady to come up to us;
who did, with another lady; and after sermon I led her down
through the church to her husband and coach – a noble, fine
woman, and a good one – and one my wife shall be acquainted
with. So home and to dinner alone with my wife, who,
poor wretch, sat undressed all day till 10 at night, altering and
lacing of a black petticoat – while I by her, making the boy
read to me the life of Julius Caesar[1] and Des Cartes book of

a MS. 'changed'   *b* repl. 'on'-

1. Probably the *Life* prefaced to   of *C. Julius Caesar*; a translation first
Clement Edmonds, *The commentaries*   published in 1600; PL 2221 (1655 ed.).

music[1] – the latter of which I understand not, nor think he did well that writ it, though a most learned man. Then after supper made the boy play upon his lute, which I have not done twice before sence he came to me; and so, my mind in mighty content, we to bed.

26. Lay long, with pleasure prating with my wife; and then up, and I a little to the office, and my head busy setting some papers and accounts to rights; which being long neglected because of my eyes, will take me up much time and care to do, but it must be done. So home at noon to dinner; and then abroad with my wife to a play at the Duke of York's House; the house full of ordinary citizens; the play was *Women pleased*,[2] which we had never seen before; and though but*a* indifferent, yet there is a good design for a good play. So home, and there to talk and my wife to read to me, and so to bed.

27. *Lords day.* Walked to White-hall and there saw the King at chapel; but stayed not to hear anything, but went to walk in the park with W. Hewer, who was with me; and there, among others, met with Sir G*b* Downing and walked with him an hour, talking of business and how the late war was managed, there being nobody to take care of it; and telling how when he was in Holland,[3] what he offered the King to do if he might have power; and they would give him power,*c* and then upon the least word, perhaps of a woman, to the King, he was contradicted again, and perticularly to the loss of all that we lost in Guinny.[4]

a repl. 'ind'- *b* repl. 'D' *c* repl. 'and'

---

1. Probably Brouncker's translation: see above, p. 167, n. 3. (E).

2. A tragicomedy by John Fletcher, acted c. 1620, and published in 1647. This is the first record of a post-Restoration performance. (A).

3. He was envoy-extraordinary to the United Provinces, 1661–5.

4. In September 1664 Downing informed his home government of a rumour that the Dutch intended to send a naval force to W. Africa: Lister, *Clarendon*, iii. 344–5, 353. But on the vital matter of which force was to be sent and from where, he was completely deceived by de Witt, who (keeping his plan secret even from the Estates-General) arranged for de Ruyter to sail from the Mediterranean. See J. Beresford, *Godfather of Downing St*, pp. 172–4.

He told me that he had so good spies, that he hath had the*a* keys taken out of De Witts pocket when he was a-bed, and his closet opened and papers brought to him and left in his hands for an [hour], and carried back and laid in the place again and the keys put into his pocket again.   He says he hath alway had their*b* most private debates, that have been but between two or three of the chief of them, brought to him in an hour after, and an hour after that hath sent word thereof to the King[1] – but nobody here regarded them.   But he tells me the sad news that he is out of all expectations that ever the debts of the Navy will be paid, if the Parliament doth not enable the King to do it by money; all they can hope for to*c* do out of the King's revenue being but to keep our wheels a-going on present services, and, if they can, to cut*d* off the growing Interest – which is a sad story, and grieves me to the heart.[2]

So home, my coach coming for me, and there find Balty and Mr. How, who dined with me; and there my wife and I fell out a little about the foulness of the linen of the table, but were friends presently; but she cried, poor heart, which I was troubled for, though I did not give her one hard word.

Dinner done, she to church, and W. How and I all the afternoon talking together about my Lord Sandwiches suffering his business of the prizes to be managed by Sir R. Cuttance; who is so deep in the business, more then my Lord knows of, and such a loggerhead, and under*e* such prejudice, that he will, we doubt, do my Lord much wrong.[3]   In the evening, he gone, my wife

a repl. 'papers'   *b* repl. symbol rendered illegible
c repl. 'being but to'   *d* repl. 'give'   *e* repl. 'lies'

---

1. Downing (who had once been Scoutmaster-General to Cromwell's army) regarded himself as an expert in espionage. In the United Provinces his spy-system throve on the cumbrousness and party divisions of the government.

2. A more cheerful (but less accurate) impression is conveyed by a despatch (15 January 1669) of Lindenov, the Danish envoy: W.

Westergaard (ed.), *First Triple Alliance*, p. 70. Downing was now Secretary to the Treasury.

3. For the prize-goods scandal, see above, vi. 231, n. 1.   Cuttance attended the Brooke House Committee on Sandwich's behalf; some of his letters to Sandwich are in Sandwich MSS, Letters from Ministers, ii. ff. 52r, 54r etc. He was very critical of Howe's part in the affair.

to read to me and talk, and spent the evening with much pleasure; and so to supper and to bed.

28. Up, called up by drums and trumpets; these things and boxes having cost me much money this Christmas already, and will do more. My wife down by water to see her mother,[1] and I with W Hewers all day together in my closet, making some advance in the settling of my accounts, which have been so long unevened that it troubles me how to set them right, having not the use of my eyes to help*a* me. My wife at night home, and tells me how much her mother prays for me and is troubled for my eyes; and I am glad to have friendship with them, and believe they are truly glad to see their daughter come to live so well as she doth. So spent the night in talking, and so to supper and to bed.

29. Up, and at the office all the morning; and at noon to dinner, and*b* there by a pleasant mistake find my uncle and aunt Wight, and three more of their company, come to dine with me today, thinking that they had been invited; which they were not, but yet we did give them a pretty good dinner, and mighty merry at the mistake. They sat most of the afternoon with us, and then parted; and my wife and I out, thinking to have gone to a play, but it was too far begun; and so to the Change, and there she and I bought several things; and so home, with much pleasure talking, and then to reading; and so to supper and to bed.

30. Up, and vexed a little to be forced to pay 40*s* for a glass of my coach which was broke the other day, nobody knows how, within the door while it was down; but I do doubt that I did break it myself – with my knees. After dinner, my wife and I to the Duke's playhouse and there did see *King Harry the 8th*,[2] and was mightily pleased, better then I ever expected,

a repl. 'cause'   *b* repl. 'and then'

---

1. Her parents apparently now lived with her brother Balty and his wife (above, vii. 291), who were now settled at Deptford (above, p. 349).

2. A spectacular production of Shakespeare's play: see above, iv. 411, n. 5. (A).

with the history and shows of it. We happened to sit by Mr. Andrews our neighbour and his wife, who talked so fondly to his little boy. Thence my wife and I to the Change; but in going, our neere-horse did fling himself, kicking of the coachbox over the poale; and a great deal of trouble it was to get him right again, and we forced to light and in great fear of spoiling the horse, but there was no hurt. So to the Change and then home and there spent the evening talking; and so to supper and to bed.

31. Up and at the office all the morning. At noon Captain Ferrer and Mr. Sheres comes to me to dinner, who did, and pretty pleased with their talk of Spain.[1] But my wife did not come down, I suppose[a] because she would not, Captain Ferrer being there – to oblige me by it.[2] They gone after dinner, I to the office; and then in the evening home, being the last day of the year, to endeavour to pay all bills and servants' wages &c, which I did almost to 5*l*, that I know that I owe in the world but to the public. And so with great pleasure to supper and to bed. And blessed be God, the year ends, after some late very great sorrow with my wife by my folly; yet ends, I say, with great mutual peace and content – and likely to last so by my care, who am resolved to enjoy the sweet of it which I now possess, by never giving[b] her like cause of trouble. My greatest trouble is now from the backwardness of my accounts, which I have not[c] seen the bottom of now near these two years, so that I know not in what condition I am in the world; but by the grace of God, as fast as my eyes will give me leave, I will do it.

a corrected from 'supposed' *b* repl. 'give' badly formed
c repl. 'never'

---

1. Both had served in Sandwich's embassy.
2. It was Ferrer who had made advances to her on Sandwich's behalf; above, p. 356.

1. Up, and presented from Captain Beckford with a noble silver warming-pan, which I am doubtful whether to take or no.[1] Up, and with W. Hewer to the New Exchange, and there he and I to the cabinet-shops to look out, and did agree for a Cabinett to give my wife for a New-year's gift; and I did buy one, cost me 11*l*, which is very pretty, of Walnutt-tree,[2] and will come home tomorrow.[3] So back to the Old Exchange and there met my uncle Wight; and there walked and met with the Houblons and talked with them, gentlemen whom I honour mightily. And so to my uncles and met my wife, and there, with W. Hewer, we dined with his family and had a very good dinner, and pretty merry; and after dinner my wife and I with our coach to the King's playhouse and there in a box saw *The Mayden Queene*.[4] Knepp looked upon us, but I durst not show her any countenance and, as well as I could carry myself, I found my wife uneasy there, poor wretch. Therefore I shall avoid that House as much as I can. So back to my aunts and there supped and talked, and stayed pretty late, it being dry and moonshine; and so walked home, and to bed in very good humour.

2. Up and at the office all the morning; and at noon*a* home

a repl. 'home'

---

1. Thomas Beckford was a slop-seller to the navy. He shortly afterwards petitioned successfully for permission to sell his wartime stock of clothing at higher prices than those allowed by regulation: Duke of York, *Mem. (naval)*, pp. 187–8.

2. Walnut was only just coming into use.

3. This is the first occasion on which Pepys records giving a New Year gift to his wife. On 4 January he agreed to give her an annual allowance. His guilt about Deb Willett was having its effects.

4. *Secret Love, or The maiden queen*, a tragicomedy by Dryden (q.v. above, viii. 91, n. 2), in which Mrs Knepp played the part of Asteria. (A).

to dinner, where I find my Cabinett come home and paid for it, and it pleases me and my wife well. So after dinner, all the afternoon busy late at the*ª* office, and so home and to bed.

3. *Lords day.* Up, and busy all the morning, getting rooms and dinner ready for my guests; which were my uncle and aunt Wight and two of their cousins, and an old woman and Mr. Mills and his wife; and a good dinner and all our plate out, and mighty fine and merry – only I a little vexed at burning a new table-cloth myself, with one of my trencher-salts. Dinner done, I out with W. Hewer and Mr. Spong, who by accident came to dine with me, and good talk with him, to White-hall by coach and there left him, and I with my Brethren to attend the Duke of York; and then up and down the House till the evening hearing how the King doth intend this frosty weather, it being this day the first and very hard frost that hath come this year, and very cold it is.*ᵇ* So home and to supper and read; and there my wife and I treating about coming to an allowance to my wife for clothes, and there I, out of my natural backward-ness, did hang off; which vexed her and did occasion some dis-contented talk in bed when we went to bed – and also in the morning; but I did recover all in the morning.

4.*ᶜ* Lay long talking with my wife, and did of my own accord come to an allowance of her of 30*l* a year for all expenses, clothes and everything; which she was mightily pleased with, it being more then ever she asked or expected; and so rose with much content, and up and with W. Hewer to White-hall, there to speak with Mr. Wren; which I did, about several things of the office entered in my memorandum-books;¹ and so about noon, going homeward with W. Hewer, he and I went in and saw the great tall woman that is to be seen, which is but twenty-one

---

a repl. 'home' and full stop
b repl. symbol rendered illegible; the sentence being left incomplete
c page heading corrected from 'December' to 'January'

---

1. The conversation was about finance, and Mennes's inefficiency: NWB, pp. 136–40; cf. *Further Corr.*, pp. 205–06. For the memorandum books, see above, p. 91 & n. 2.

years old and I do easily stand under her arms.[1] Then going
further, The Turner called me out of her coach, where her
mother &c was, and invited me by all means to dine with them
at my Cosen Roger's mistress, the Widdow Dickenson; so I went[a]
to them afterward and dined with them, and mighty handsomely
treated; and she a wonderful merry, good-humoured, fat but[b]
plain woman, but I believe a very good woman – and mighty civil
to me.[2] Mrs. Turner the mother, and Mrs. Dike and The and
Betty was the company, and a gentleman of their acquaintance.
Betty I did long to see, and she is indifferent pretty, but not what
the world did speak of her; but I am mighty glad to have one
so pretty of our kindred. After dinner I walked with them to
show them the great woman, which they admire,* as well they
may; and so back with[c] them, and left them and I to White-
hall, where a Committee of Tanger met, but little to do there;
but I did receive an instance of the Duke of York's kindness to
me, and the whole Committee, that they would not order anything about the Treasurer for the Corporation now in establishing
without my assent and considering whether it would be to my
wrong or no.[3] Thence up and down the House, and to the
Duke of York's side and there in the Duchess's presence; and
was mightily complimented by my Lady Peterborough in my
Lord Sandwiches presence, whom she engaged to thank ⟨me⟩
for my kindness to her and her Lord.[4] By and by I met my Lord

a repl. 'dined with them and'
b repl. 'and'   *c* repl. 'them'

---

1. She was a Dutchwoman on
display in Holborn: see below, p. 440.
Evelyn saw her on 29 January and
says she came from 's Hertogenbosch.
She was 6 ft 10 ins tall (according to
Evelyn), or 6 ft 5 ins (according to
Pepys, below, loc. cit. The latter
figure would make Pepys c. 5 ft 1 in.).
On 3 May Cosmo III of Tuscany, on
his visit to England, 'had the con-
descension' to receive her: Magalotti,
p. 196.

2. Esther Dickenson and Roger
Pepys were married on 2 February
1669.
3. Pepys was Treasurer for the
garrison. Regulations for the organ-
isation of civil government under the
new municipal corporation were
issued on 20 January by the Privy
Council: see Routh, pp. 124–5. See
also below, p. 417.
4. About his pension: see above,
viii. 459, n. 3.

Brouncker; and he and I to the Duke of York alone and dis-coursed*a* over the carriage of the present Treasurers, in opposition, or at least independency, on the Duke of York or our Board – which the Duke of York is sensible of, and all remember I believe, for they do carry themselfs very respectlessly of*b* him – and us. We also declared our minds together to the Duke of York about Sir Jo. Minnes's incapacity to do any service in the*c* office, and that it is but to betray the King to have any business of trust committed to his weakness[1] – so that the Duke of York was very sensible of it and promised to speak to the King about it. That done, I with W. Hewer took up my wife at Unthankes'; and so home and there with pleasure to read and talk; and so to supper and put into writing, in merry terms, our agreement between her and me about the 30*l* a year; and so to bed. This was done under both our hands merrily, and put into W. Hewer's to keep.[2]

5. Up and to the office all the morning, the frost and cold continuing. At noon home with*d* my people to dinner, and so to work at the office again. In the evening comes Creed to me, and tells me his wife is at my house; so I in, and spent an hour with them – the first time she hath been here, or I have seen her, sence she was married.[3] She is not overhandsome, though a good lady and one I love. So after some pleasant discourse, they gone, I to the office again and there late; and then home to supper to my wife, who is not very well of those; and so sat talking till past one in the morning, and then to bed.

6. *Twelfth day.* Up, and to look after things against dinner today for my guests. And then to the office to write down my

---

a repl. 'discourse'   *b* MS. 'on'   *c* repl. symbol rendered illegible
d MS. 'to with'

---

1. In his evidence to the Brooke House Committee and the Council Pepys put the principal blame on Mennes for the wartime failures of the Navy Board. Cf. PL 2874, pp. 394–5.

2. The document does not appear to have survived.

3. They had been married in October: see above, p. 332, n. 3.

journall for five or six days backward, and so home to look after dinner, it being now almost noon. At noon comes Mrs. Turner and Dike and Mrs. Dickenson, and then comes The. and Betty Turner, the latter of which is a very pretty girl – and then Creed and his wife, whom I sent for by my coach. These were my guests, and Mrs. Turner's friend, whom I saw the other day, Mr. Wickam; and very merry we were at dinner, and so all the afternoon, talking and looking up and down my house; and in the evening I did bring*a* out my cake, a noble cake, and there cut into pieces, with wine and good drink; and after a new fashion, to prevent spoiling the cake, did put so many titles into a hat and so drow cuts; and I was Queene and The Turner, King; Creed, Sir Martin Marrall; and Betty, Mrs. Millicent.[1]   And so we were mighty merry till it was night; and then, being moonshine and fine frost, they went home, I lending some of them my coach to help to carry them; and so my wife and I spent the rest of the evening in talk and reading, and so with great pleasure to bed.

7.   Up and to the office, where busy all the morning; and then at noon home to dinner; and thence, my wife and I to the King's playhouse and there saw *The Island princesse*, the first time I ever saw it; and it is a pretty good play, many good things being in it – and a good scene of a town on fire.[2]   We sat

---

a   repl. 'have'

---

1. For Twelfth-Night cakes, see above, i. 10, n. 3. In one of Pepys's favourite comedies, *Sir Martin Marrall*, by John Dryden and the Duke of Newcastle (see above, viii. 387 & n. 1), Sir Martin persistently commits blunders to his own discomfiture. He courts Millisent but she tricks him into marrying a lady's maid. (A).

2. This was a tragicomedy by John Fletcher, first acted about 1621, and published in 1647. The version which Pepys saw now and later this year (pp. 441, 532) was an anonymous adaptation (published in 1669), with some cuts but few alterations of the text. The cast listed in this 1669 edition includes Hart as Armusia, Mohun as Rudyas, Burt as Soza, Mrs Marshall as Quisara, Mrs Corey as Quisana, and Mrs Hughes as Panura. The fire scene occurs in Act II, sc. iii, where the chief town of Ternata is set on fire. Burning sulphur and aqua vitae were used to imitate conflagrations on the Restoration stage, but Pepys is probably referring here to a painted drop-scene. An engraving in Beaumont and Fletcher, *Works* (1711), vi. 3005, may be a representation of what he saw. (A).

in an*ᵃ* upper box, and that jade Nell came and sat in the next box, a bold merry slut, who lay laughing there upon people, and with a comrade of hers of the Duke's House that came in to see the play. Thence home and to the office to do some business; and so home to supper and to bed.

8. Up and with Collonell Middleton in his coach, and Mr. Tippets, to White-hall and there attended the Duke of York with the rest; where the Duke of York was mighty plain with the Treasurers, according to the advice my Lord Brouncker and I did give him the other night; and he did it fully, and so as I believe will make the Treasurers careful of themselfs, unless they do resolve upon defying the Duke of York. Thence with W. Hewer home and to dinner; and so out again, my wife and I and Mr. Hater, to White-hall, where she set us down; and she up and down to buy things, while we at the Treasury-chamber, where I alone did manage the business of the *Leopard* against the whole Committee of the East India Company, with Mr. Blackburne with them – and to the silencing of them all, to my great*ᵇ* content.[1] Thence walked to my wife, and so set out for home in our coach, it being very cold weather; and so to the office to do a little business, and then home to my wife's chamber, my people having laid the cloth and got the rooms all clean above-stairs tonight for our dinner tomorrow – and therefore I to bed.

9. Up, and at the office all the morning; and at noon my Lord Brouncker, Mr. Wren, Jos. Williamson, and Captain Cocke dined with me. And being newly sat down, comes in, by an*ᶜ* invitation of Williamson's, the Lieutenant of the Tower – and he brings in with him young Mr. Whore, whose father, of the

---

a repl. 'the'   *b* MS. 'no great'   *c* repl. 'my'

---

1. Cf. above, p. 37 & n. 3. In this dispute (dating back to 1663) one of the issues was whether the company was responsible for the under- freighting of the *Leopard*. For this meeting, see *CTB*, iii. 4. Robert Blackborne was Secretary to the company.

Tower, I know.[1]   And here I had a neat dinner, and all in so good manner and fashion and with so good company and everything to my mind, as I never had more in my life – the company being to my heart's content, and they all well pleased. So continued looking over my books and closet till the evening, and so I to the office and did a good deal of business; and so home to supper and to bed, with my mind mightily pleased with this day's management, as one of the days of my life of fullest content.

10.   *Lords day.*   Accidentally, talking of our maids before we rose, I said a little word that did give occasion to my wife to fall out, and she did most vexatiously almost all the morning, but ended most perfect good friends; but the thoughts of the unquiet which her ripping up of old faults will give me did make me melancholy all day long.   So about noon, past 12, we rose; and to dinner and then to read and talk, my wife and I alone, after Balty was gone, who came to dine with us; and then in the evening comes Pelling to sit and talk with us, and so to supper and pretty merry discourse; only, my mind a little vexed at the morning's work, but yet without any appearance; so after supper, to bed.

11.   Up and with W. Hewer, my guard,[2] to White-hall, where no Committee of Tanger met; so up and down the House talking with this and that man; and so home, calling at the New Exchange for a book or two to send to Mr. Sheply;[3] and thence home, and thence to the Change and there did a little business; and so walked home to dinner and then abroad with my wife to King's playhouse and there saw *The Joviall Crew*, but ill acted to what it was heretofore in Clun's time and when Lacy could

---

1. James   Hoare,   sen.,   was Comptroller of the Mint (and later founder of what became Hoare's Bank). His son (also James) succeeded him in his business as gold-smith-banker. The Lieutenant of the Tower was Sir John Robinson.

2. Pepys was still being kept on a short leash because of his affair with Deb.

3. Sandwich's steward at Hinching-brooke.

dance.[1] Thence to the New Exchange to buy some things; and among others, my wife did give me my pair of gloves, which by contract she is to give me in her 30*l.* a year. Here Mrs. Smith tells us of the great murder thereabouts[a] on Saturday last, of one Captain Brombrige by one Symons, both of her acquaintance, and hectors that were at play and in drink; the[b] former is killed, and is kinsman to my Lord of Ormond; which made him speak of it with so much passion, as I overheard him this morning, but could not make anything of it till now.[2] But would they would kill more of them. So home; and there at home all the evening, and made Tom to prick down some little conceits and notions of mine in Musique, which doth mightily encourage me to spend some more thoughts about it; for I fancy, upon good reason, that I am in the right way of unfolding the mystery of this matter better then ever yet.[3]

12. Up and to the office, where by occasion of a message from the Treasurers that the Board found fault with Commissioner Middleton, and I went up from the Board to the Lords of the Treasury to meet our Treasurers; and did, and there did dispute the business, it being about the manner of paying a little money to Chatham-yard;[4] wherein I find the Treasurers mighty supple, and I believe we shall bring them to reason; though they begin mighty upon us, as if we had no power of directing[c] them, but they us. Thence back presently home to dinner, where I discern my wife to have been in pain

a repl. 'at'   *b* repl. 'he'   *c* repl. 'com'-

---

1. The play was a comedy by Richard Brome: see above, ii. 141, n. 1. Walter Clun, a versatile actor, had been murdered on 2 August 1664, and John Lacy, a popular comedian and dancer, had been ill: see above, viii. 334. (A).

2. The murder had been committed in the Bear, a Drury Lane tavern. Symonds (who served in the Queen Mother's Household) fled abroad with his two accessories. The victim had served in the Spanish army and was visited on his death-bed by the Spanish ambassador. *Bulstrode Papers*, i. 83, 84; HMC, *Ormonde*, n.s., iii. 440. Mrs Smith was a sempstress in a mercer's shop in the New Exchange, Strand.

3. Cf. above, p. 125 & n. 2. (E).

4. Cf. *CTB*, iii. 4.

where I have been, but said nothing to me; but I believe did send W. Hewer to seek*ª* me, but I take no notice of it – but am vexed. So to dinner with my people, and then to the office, where all the afternoon, and did much business and at it late; and so home to supper and to bed.

This day, meeting Mr. Pierce at White-hall, he tells me that his boy hath a great mind to see me, and is going to school again; and Dr. Clerke, being by, doth tell me that he is a fine boy; but I durst not answer anything, because I durst not invite him to my house for fear of my wife,[1] and therefore to my great trouble was forced to neglect that discourse. But here Mr. Pierce, I asking him whither he was going, he told me as a great secret that he was going to his Maister's*ᵇ* mistress, Mrs. Church-hill,[2] [with] some physic; meaning for the pox I suppose, or else that she is got with child; but I suppose the former, by his manner of speaking it.

This evening I observed my wife mighty dull; and I myself was not mighty fond, because of some hard words she did give me at noon, out of a jealousy at my being abroad this morning; when, God knows, it was upon the business of the office un-expectedly; but I to bed, not thinking but she would come after me; but waking by and by out of a slumber, which I usually fall into presently*ᶜ* after my coming*ᵈ* into the bed, I found she did not prepare to come to bed, but got fresh candles and more wood for her fire, it being mighty cold too. At this being troubled, I after a while prayed her to come to bed, all my people being gone to bed; so after an hour or two, she silent, and I now and then praying her to come to bed, she fell out into a fury, that I was a rogue and false to her; but yet I could perceive that she was to seek what to say; only, she invented, I believe, a business that I was seen in a hackney-coach with the glasses up with Deb, but could not tell the time, nor was sure I was he.*ᵉ* I did, as I might

a repl. 'know' *b* l.h. repl. s.h. *c* repl. 'p'-
d repl. incomplete symbol *e* repl. 'she'

---

1. Mrs Pepys was jealous of Mrs Pearse.
2. Arabella Churchill, sister of John Churchill, later 1st Duke of Marl-borough. She was the mistress of the Duke of York, whom Pearse served as surgeon.

truly, deny it, and was mightily troubled; but all would not serve. At last, about one a-clock, she came to my side of the bed and drow my curtaine open, and with the tongs, red hot at the ends, made as if she did design to pinch me with them; at which in dismay I rose up, and with a few words she laid them down and did by little and little, very sillily, let all the discourse fall; and about 2, but with much seeming difficulty, came to bed and there lay well all night, and long in bed talking together with much pleasure; it being, I know, nothing but her doubt of my going out yesterday without telling her of my going which did vex her, poor wretch, last night: and I cannot blame her jealousy, though it doth vex me to[a] the heart.

13. So up, and by coach to Sir W. Coventry's, but he gone out; so I to White-hall and thence walked out into the park, all in the snow, with the Duke of York and the rest; and so ⟨after visiting my Lady Peterborough⟩ home and there by invitation find Mr. Povy, and there was also Talbt. Pepys, newly come from Impington,[b] and dined with me; and after dinner and a little talk with Povy about public matters, he gone, and I and my wife and Tall. towards the Temple, and there to the King's playhouse and there saw, I think, *The Maiden Queene*;[1] and so home and to supper and read; and so to bed. ⟨This day came home the instrument I have so long longed for, the *Paralellogram*.⟩[2]

14. Up and to the office, where all the morning busy; and so home to dinner, where Goodgroome[3] with us, and after dinner, a song; and then to the office, where busy till night; and then home to work there with W. Hewer to get ready some Tanger papers against tomorrow; and so to supper and to bed.

a repl. 'me'   *b* repl. 'Brampton'

---

1. It was Jonson's *Catiline*, not Dryden's *Maiden Queen*, which was performed on this day: Nicoll, p. 344. (A).

2. The pantograph ordered on 9 December 1668.

3. Theodore Goodgroome, singing-master. (E).

15. Up and by coach to Sir W. Coventry; where with him a good while in his chamber, talking of one thing or another; where, among others, he told me of the great factions at Court at this day, even to the sober engaging of great persons and differences, and making the King cheap and ridiculous. It is about my Lady Harvy's being offended at Doll Common's acting of Sempronia to imitate her – for which she got my Lord Chamberlain, her kinsman, to imprison Doll;[1] which my Lady Castlemayne made the King to release her, and to order her to act it again worse then ever the other day*a* where the King himself was. And since, it was acted again, and my Lady Harvy provided people to hiss her and fling oranges at her. But it seems the heat is come to a great heighth, and real troubles at Court about it. Thence he and I out a-doors, but he to Sir J Duncomb's and I to White-hall through the park, where I met the King and Duke of York and so walked with them; and so to White-hall, where the Duke of York met the office and did a little business, and I did give him thanks for his favour to me yesterday at the Committee of Tanger in my absence (Mr. Povy having given me advice of it, of the discourse there, of doing something as to the putting the payment of the garrison into some undertakers hand, Alderman Backewell, which*b* the Duke of York would not suffer to go on without my presence at the debate) and he answered me just thus: that he ought to have a care of him that doth the King's business in the manner that I do, and words of more force then that. ⟨Then down with Lord

a repl. 'yesterday' *b* repl. closing bracket

1. Lady Harvey (Hervey), whose influence at court, especially with the Queen, infuriated Lady Castlemaine, was said to boast of having made one secretary of state (Trevor), of having control of the other (Arlington), and of having placed her husband (Sir Daniel) as ambassador to Turkey and her brother (Ralph Mountagu) as ambassador to France: Sandwich MSS, Journals, ix. 122–4. 'Doll Common' was the name given to Mrs Corey of the King's Company, from the character in Jonson's *Alchemist*. Sempronia (a character in Jonson's *Catiline*) was an ageing courtesan who posed as 'a great stateswomen'. When examined by the Lord Chamberlain (Manchester, Lady Harvey's second cousin), Mrs Corey, according to Sandwich, was 'bold and Sawcye'.

Brouncker to Sir R. Murray into the King's little elaboratory
under his closet, a pretty place, and there saw a great many
Chymicall glasses and things, but understood none of them.⟩ᵃ¹
So I home and to dinner; and then out again and stop with my
wifeᵇ at my cousin Turner's, where I stayed and satᶜ a while
and carried The and my wife to the Duke of York's House to
Mackbeth,² and myself to White-hall to the Lords of the Treasury
about Tanger business; and there was by at much merry discourse
between them and my Lord Anglesy, who made sport of our
new Treasurers and called them his Deputys,³ and much of that
kind. And having done my own business, I away back and
carried my cousin Turner and sister Dike to a friend's house,
where they were [to] sup, in Lincoln's Inn fields; and I to the
Duke of York's House and saw the last two acts; and so carried
The thither, and so home with my wife, who read to me late;
and so to supper and to bed. This day, The Turner showed me
at the play my Lady Portman, who was grown out of my
knowledge.⁴

16. Up and to the office all the morning. Dined at home
with my people, and so all the afternoon till night at the office
busy; and so home to supper and to bed. This morning Creed,
and in the afternoon, comes Povy to advise with me about my
answer to the Lords of Tanger about the propositions for the
Treasurership there – which I am not much concerned for.⁵ But
the latter, talking of public things, told me, as Mr. Wren also did,
that the Parliament is likely to meet again, the King being frighted

---

a   addition crowded into bottom of page
b   repl. 'set my wife down'   c   MS. 'stayed'

---

1. Charles was interested in several
branches of science, particularly chem-
istry and anatomy. Sir Robert
Moray seems to have had charge of
the King's laboratory.

2. Probably   by   Shakespeare –
Davenant: see above, v. 314, n. 3.
(A).

3. Anglesey, suspended from the
office of Treasurer to the Navy, had
not yet been dismissed.

4. She was Elizabeth, daughter of a
rich E. India Company merchant, Ald.
Sir John Cutler, and had married Sir
William Portman (M.P. for Taunton)
in 1661.

5. See above, p. 407 & n. 3.

with what the Speaker hath put him in mind of, of his promise not
to prorogue but only to adjourne them.[1]   They speak mighty
freely of the folly of the King in this foolish woman's business of
my Lady Harvy.   Povy tells me that Sir W. Coventry was with
the King alone an hour this day.   And that my Lady Castlemayne is now in a higher command over the King then ever;
not as a mistress, for she scorns him, but as a tyrant to command
him.[2]   And says that the Duchess of York and the Duke of
York are mighty great with her;   which is a great interest to my
Lord Chancellor's family.   And that they do agree to hinder all
they like[a] the proceedings of the Duke of Buckingham and
Arlington.   And so we are in the old mad condition, or rather
worse then any – no man knowing what the French intend to do
the next summer.

17.   *Lords day*.   To church myself, after seeing everything
fitted for dinner.   And so after church, home;   and thither comes
Mrs. Batelier and her two daughters to dinner to us, and W
Hewer and his mother, and Mr. Spong.[3]   We were very civilly
merry, and Mrs. Battelier a very discreet woman, but mighty
fond* in the stories she tells of her son Will.   After dinner, Mr.
Spong and I to my closet, there to try my instrument Paralello-
gramm, which doth mighty well, to my full content;   but only a
little stiff, as being new.   Thence, taking leave of my guests,
he and I and W. Hewer to White-hall;   and there parting with
Spong, a man that I mightily love for his plainness and ingenuity –
I into the Court, and there up and down and spoke with my Lord
Bellasses and Peterbrough about the business now in dispute,
about my deputing a Treasurer to pay the garrison at Tanger;
which I would avoid and not be accountable, and they will
serve me therein.   Here I met Hugh May,[4] and he brings me to

a   ? error for 'can

---

1. Parliament had stood adjourned
since 9 May 1668.   See below, p. 426
& n. 1.

2. On 19 January she was granted a
life-pension of £4700 p.a. from Post

Office revenues: G. S. Steinman,
Duchess of Cleveland, pp. 116–17.

3. An instrument maker.

4. Comptroller of the King's
Works.

the knowledge of Sir Harry Capell, a Member of Parliament and brother of my Lord of Essex, who hath a great value it seems for me; and they appoint a day to come and dine with me and see my books and papers of the office; which I shall be glad to show them and have opportunity to satisfy them therein.¹ Here, all the discourse is that now the King is of opinion to have the Parliament called, notwithstanding his late resolutions for the proroguing them; so unstable are his counsels, and those about him. So staying late talking in the Queen's side, I away with W. Hewer home; and there to read and talk with my wife, and so to bed.

18. Up by candlelight, and with W. Hewer walked to the*ᵃ* Temple; and thence took coach, and to Sir W. Coventry's and there discoursed the business of my Treasurer's place at Tanger; wherein he consents to my desire and concurs therein, which I am glad of, that I may not be accountable for a man so far off. And so I to my Lord Sandwiches and there walk with him through the garden to White-hall, where he tells me what he had done about this Treasurer's place (and I perceive the whole thing did proceed from him): that finding it would be best to have the Governour have nothing to do with the pay of the garrison, he did propose to the Duke of York alone that a paymaister should be there; and that being desirous to do a courtesy to Sir Ch. Herberd,² and to prevent the Duke of York's looking out for anybody else, he did name him to the Duke of York. That when he come the other day to move this to the Board of Tanger, the Duke of York, it seems, did readily reply that it was fit to have Mr. Pepys satisfied therein first, and that it was not good to make places for persons. This my Lord in great confidence tells me that he doth take very ill from the Duke of York, though nobody knew the meaning of these words but him; and that he did take no notice of them, but bit his lip,

a repl. 'Sir'

---

1. For the visit, see below, pp. 527–8. Capel seems to have been curious about Pepys since hearing his speech to the Commons in March 1668.

2. Harbord (who had served in the Tangier garrison) was not appointed. Pepys thought him an idle young fellow: above, p. 374 & n. 2.

being satisfied that the Duke of York's care of me was as desirable
to him as it could be to have Sir Ch. Herberd; and did seem
industrious to let me see that he was glad that the Duke of York
and he might come to contend who shall be kindest to me;
which I owned as his great love, and so I hope and believe it is –
though my Lord did go a little too far in this business, to move
it so far without consulting me. But I took no notice of that,
but was glad to see this competition come about, that my Lord
Sandwich is apparently jealous of my thinking that the Duke of
York doth mean me more kindness then him. So we walked
together and I took this occasion to invite him to dinner one day
to my house; and he readily appointed Friday next, which I
shall be glad to have over to his content – he having never yet
eat a bit of my bread. Thence to the Duke of York on*a* the
King's side[1] with our Treasurers of the Navy, to discourse some
business of the Navy about the pay of the yards; and there I was
taken notice of by many Lords being there in the room, of the
Duke of York's conference with me; and so away, and meeting
Mr. Sidny Mountagu and Sheres, a small invitation served their
turn to carry them to London; where I paid Sheres his 100*l*,
given him for his pains in drawing the plat of Tanger fortifications, &c;[2] and so home to my house to dinner, where I had a
pretty handsome sudden dinner, and all well pleased; and thence,
we three and my wife, to the Duke of York's playhouse and there
saw *The Witts*,[3] a medley of things, but some similes mighty good,
though ill mixed; and thence with my wife to the Exchange and
bought some things; and so home, after*b* I had been at White
Hall and there in the Queen's withdrawing-room invited my
Lord Peterborough to dine with me with my Lord Sandwich –

a repl. 'and told him my mind, who I fear'
b repl. 'after I had been at White-hall and in the Queen's drawing-room
invited my'

---

1. I.e. of Whitehall Palace.
2. Untraced: a 'Prospect of Tangier' was in the possession of the Pepys Cockerell family in 1824 (Harvard, Houghton Lib., b. MS. Eng. 991). He had been ordered to conduct a survey of the fortifications and mole in the previous autumn: Sir H. Cholmley, *Short account of . . . mole* (? 1680), p. 3.
3. A comedy by Davenant; see above, ii. 155, n. 1. (A).

who readily accepted it.   Thence back and took up my wife at
the Change, and so home.   This day at noon, I went with my
young gentlemen (thereby to get a little time while W. Hewer
went home to bid them get a dinner ready) to the Popes-head
tavern, there to see the fine[a] painted room which Rogerson[1] told
me of, of his doing; but I do not like it at all, though it be good
for such a public room.

19.   Up and at the office all the morning.   At noon eat a
mouthful, and so with my wife to Madam Turner's and find her
gone, but The stayed for us; and so to the King's House to see
Horace;[2] this the third day of its acting – a silly Tragedy; but
Lacy hath made a farce of several dances, between each act, one.[3]
But his words are but silly, and invention not extraordinary as to
the dances; only some Dutchmen come out of the mouth and
tail of a Hamburgh sow.   Thence, not much pleased with the
play, set[b] them at home in the Strand; and my wife and I home,
and there to do a little business at the office, and so home – to
supper and to bed.

20.   Up, and my wife and I and W. Hewer to White-hall,
where she set us down; and there I spoke with my Lord Peterborough to tell him of the day for his dining with me being
altered by my Lord Sandwich from Friday to Saturday next.
And thence, heard at the Council-board the City, by their single
counsel Symson, and the company of Strangers Merchants, debate

a MS. 'find'   *b* MS. 'sem'

---

1. No painter of this name is at
present known. It is conceivable that
Pepys was talking of Robert Robinson
(d. 1706), a painter who specialised
in painting panels of interiors with
decorative fantasies. His most important surviving work is the series of
panels (1696) now in Sir John Cass's
School, painted in No. 5, Botolph
Lane: E. Croft-Murray, *Decorative
painting in England, 1537–1837*, i.
223–5. (OM).

2. By Pierre Corneille (1640); the
first four acts translated by Mrs
Katherine Philips, the last by Sir John
Denham. This version was first
acted by amateurs at Court in 1668,
after being published in Katherine
Philips's *Poems* (1667). (A).

3. Nell Gwyn assisted John Lacy in
this entertainment. (A).

the business of Water baylage, a tax demanded upon all goods by the City, imported and exported – which these Merchants oppose; and demanding leave to try the justice of the City's demand by a *Quo Warranto*, which the City opposed, the*a* Merchants did quite lay the City on their backs, with great tryumph – the City's cause being apparently too weak.[1] But here I observed Mr. Gold the Merchant to speak very well and very sharply against the City. Thence to my wife at Unthankes and with her and W. Hewer to Hercules-Pillars, calling to do two or three things by the way, and there dined; and thence to the Duke of York's House and saw *Twelfth Night*, as it is now revived, but I think one of the weakest plays that ever I saw on the stage.[2] ⟨This afternoon, before the play, I called with my wife at Dancre's[3] the great lanskip-painter, by Mr. Povy's advice, and have bespoke him to come to take measure of my dining*b*-room panels; and there I met with the pretty daughter of the Coate-seller's that lived in Cheapside, and now in Covent-garden, who hath her picture drawn here, but very poorly; but she is a pretty woman, and now I perceive married, a very pretty black woman.⟩*c* So the play done, we home, my wife letting fall some words of her observing my eyes too mightily imployed in the playhouse; meaning, upon women, which did vex me; but however, when we came home we were good friends; and so to read and to supper, and so to bed.

21. Up and walked to the Temple, it being frosty; and there

a repl. 'did'   *b* repl. 'b'-
c The addition is crowded (in square brackets) at the bottom of this page and the top of the next, between 'we' and 'home' in the following sentence.

---

1. This was one of several disputes about this tax lasting until 1680, when the King caused a *nolle prosequi* to be entered on the verdict now given against the City: LRO, Repert. 73, f. 11*v*; ib., 74, f. 118*r*; Journals 47, f. 20*r*; ib., 49, ff. 34*r*, 98*r*; PRO, PC 2/61, pp. 12, 105, 122, 169, 175, 181; *CTB*, iii. 1040, 1079.

2. Pepys perseveres in his low opinion: cf. above, ii. 177; iv. 6. Shakespeare's romantic comedies were not popular at this time and the version Pepys saw may have been much altered: cf. H. Spencer, *Shakespeare Improved*, pp. 27, 71–2. (A).

3. Danckerts: see below, p. 423, n. 1. (OM).

took coach, my boy Tom with me, and so to White-hall to [a]
Committee of Tanger; where they met by and by and till twelve
at noon upon business; among others, mine, where my desire
about being eased of appointing and standing accountable for a
Treasurer there was*ᵃ* well accepted, and they will think of some
other way.¹   This I was glad of, finding reason to doubt that I
might in this (since my Lord Sandwich made me understand
what he had said to the Duke of York herein) fear to offend,
either the Duke of York by denying it, for he seem[ed] on Sunday
night last, when I first made known my desire to him herein,
to be a little amused* at it, though I knew not then the reason – or
else offend my Lord Sandwich by accepting it, or denying it in a
manner*ᵇ* that might not forward his desire for Sir Ch. Harberd.
But I thank God, I did it to my great content, without any offence
I think to either.   Thence in my own coach home, where I find
Madam Turner, Dike, and The – and had a good dinner for them,
and merry; and so carried them to the Duke of York's House (all
but Dyke, who went away on other business) and there saw *The
Tempest*; but it is but ill done, by Gosnell in lieu of Mall Davis.²
Thence set them at home, and my wife and I to the Change;
and so home, where my wife mighty dogged; and vexed to see
it, being mightily troubled of late at her being out of humour,
for fear of her discovering any new matter of offence against me;
though I am conscious of none, but do hate to be unquiet at
home.   So late up, silent and not supping, but hearing her utter
some words of discontent to me with silence; and so to bed weeping to myself for grief – which she discerning, came to bed and
mighty kind; and so, with great joy on both sides, to sleep.

22.   Up and with W. Hewer to White-hall, and there attended
the Duke of York; and thence to the Exchange, in the way
calling at several places on occasions relating to my feast tomorrow, on which my mind is now set – as, how to get a new

---

a repl. 'shall'   *b* repl. 'matter none'

---

1. Cf. above, pp. 415, 418.
2. Mary Davis had left this company to become the King's mistress.

Gosnell (or her sister) had once been
lady's maid to Mrs Pepys. (A).

looking-glass for my dining-room, and some pewter and good wine against tomorrow. And so home, where I had the looking-glass set up; cost me 6*l* 7*s* 6*d*. And here at*a* the Change I met with Mr. Dancre, the famous lanskip painter – with whom I was on Wednesdy; and he took measure of my panels in my dining-room, where in the four I intend to have the*b* four houses of the King – White-hall, Hampton-court, Greenwich – and Windsor.[1] He gone, I to dinner with my people, and so to my office*c* to despatch*d* a little business; and then home to look after things against tomorrow. And among *e* other things, was mightily pleased with the fellow that came to lay the cloth and fold the napkins – which I like so well, as that I am resolved to give him 40*s*. to teach my wife to do it. So to supper, with much kindness between me and my wife, which nowadays is all my care; and so to bed.

23. Up, and again to look after the setting things right against dinner, which I did to very good content; and so to the office, where all the morning till noon, when word brought me to the Board that my Lord Sandwich was come; so I presently rose, leaving the Board ready to rise, and there I found my Lord Sandwich, Peterburgh, and Sir Ch. Herberd; and presently after them come my Lord Hinchingbrooke, Mr. Sidny, and Sir Wm. Godolphin; and after greeting them, and some time spent in talk, dinner was brought up, one dish after another, but a dish at a time;[2] but all so good, but above all things, the variety of wines, and excellent of their kind, I had for them, and all in so

---

a repl. 'came'   b MS. 'a'   c repl. 'people'
d repl. beginning of same symbol badly formed   e repl. 'so'

---

1. Hendrick Danckerts (the Dutch painter) now specialised in topographical pictures and classical landscapes. His view of Hampton Court still survives in the royal collection (O. Millar, *Tudor, Stuart and early Georgian pictures in coll. H.M. Queen*, no. 397), and he is known also to have painted Windsor and Hampton Court for the Crown. There is a view of Greenwich almost certainly by him in the National Maritime Museum there. On 31 March Pepys decided to have a view of Rome instead of the picture of Hampton Court. (OM).

2. The division of a meal into courses in this way – a French fashion – was still a novelty.

good order, that they were mightily pleased, and myself full of content at it; and endeed it was, of a dinner of about six or eight dishes, as noble as any man need to have I think – at least, all was done in the noblest manner that ever I had any, and I have rarely seen in my life better anywhere else – even at the Court. After dinner, my Lords to cards, and the rest of us sitting about them and talking, and looking on my books and pictures and my wife's drawings, which they commend mightily; and mighty merry all day long, with exceeding great content, and so till 7 at night; and so took their leaves, it being dark and foul weather. Thus was this entertainment over, the best of its kind, and the fullest of honour and content to me that ever I had in my life, and shall not easily have so good again. The truth is, I have some fear that I am run behind-hand in the world for these last two years, since I have*ᵃ* not, or for some time could not, look after my accounts; which doth a little allay my pleasure, but I do trust in God I am pretty well yet, and resolve in a very little time to look into my accounts and see how they stand. So to my wife's chamber, and there supped and got her cut*ᵇ* my hair and look* my shirt, for I have itched mightily these six or seven days; and when all came to all, she finds that I am louzy, having found in my head and body above*ᶜ* 20 lice, little and great; which I wonder at, being more then I have had I believe almost these 20 years. I did think I might have got them from*ᵈ* the little boy, but they did presently look him, and found none – so how they came, I know not; but presently did shift myself, and so shall be rid of them, and cut my hayre close to my head. And so, with much content to bed.

24. *Lords day.* An order brought me in bed for the Principal Officers to attend the King at my Lord Keepers this afternoon – it being resolved late the last night;*ᵉ* and by that warrant, I find my Lord Keeper did not then know the cause of it, the messenger being ordered to call upon him to tell it him by the way, as he came to us. So I up, and to my office to set down my journall for*ᶠ* yesterday; and so home and with my wife to church. And

---

  a repl. 'like'   *b* repl. 'to read'   *c* repl. 'about'
  d repl. 'of'   *e* symbol repeated   *f* repl. **'of'**

then *a* home and to dinner; and after dinner, out with my wife by coach to my cousin Turner's, where she and The gone to church; but I left my wife with Mrs. Dike and Joyce Norton, whom I have not seen till now since their coming to town (she is become an old woman, and with as cunning a look as ever); and thence I to White-hall and there walked up and down till the King and Duke of York were ready to go forth. And here I met Will Battelier,[1] newly come post from France, his boots all dirty – he brought letters to the King; and I glad to see him, it having been reported that he was drowned for some days past; and then he being gone, I to talk with Tom Killigrew, who told me and others, talking about the playhouses, that he is fain to keep*b* a woman on purpose, at 20*s* a week, to satisfy eight or ten of the young men of his House,[2] whom till*c* he did so he could never keep to their business, and now he doth. By and by the King comes out, and so I took coach and fallowed his coaches to my Lord Keepers at Essex-house, where I never was before since I saw my old Lord Essex lie in state when he was dead – a large but ugly house.[3] Here all the Officers of the Navy attended, and by and by were called in to the King and Cabinet, where my Lord, who was ill, did lie upon the bed, as my old Lord Treasurer or Chancellor heretofore used to.[4] And the business was to know in what time all the King's ships might be repaired fit for service; the*d* Surveyor answered, "In two years and not sooner." I did give them hopes that with supplies of money suitable, we might

a repl. 'at noon'   *b* repl. 'give'   *c* repl. 'other'   *d* repl. 'so'

---

1. Wine merchant.
2. The TR, Drury Lane, of which Killigrew was manager. (A).
3. The house lay to the south of the Strand. The 3rd Earl of Essex (the parliamentary general) had died on 15 September 1646. For an account of the house, and views, see Lethaby in *Archaeologia*, 73/1+; P. H. Hulton (ed.), *Drawings of Engl. in 17th cent.*, ii, pl. 26. Since the Restoration the

larger part of it had been used as a private residence, and was now occupied by the Lord Keeper, Sir Orlando Bridgeman. For some time after the Fire it also housed Doctors' Commons and the Court of Arches.
4. Bridgeman had, like Southampton and Clarendon, suffered serious and prolonged attacks of gout: cf. HMC, *Rep.*, 7/485.

have them all fit for sea some part of the summer after this. Then they demanded in what time we could set out 40 ships: it was answered, as they might be chosen of the newest and most ready, we could, with money, get 40 ready against May.   The King seemed mighty full* that we should have money to do all that we desired, and satisfied that without it nothing could be done; and so, without determining anything, we were dismissed; and I doubt all will end in some little fleet this year, and those of hired merchantmen; which would endeed be cheaper to the King, and have many conveniences attending it, more then to fit out the King's own.   And this I perceive is designed, springing from Sir W. Coventry's counsel; and the King and most of the Lords, I perceive, full of it, to get the King's fleet all at once in condition for service.   Thence I with Mr. Wren in his coach to my cousin Turner's for discourse sake; and in our way he told me how the business of the Parliament is wholly*a* laid aside, it being overruled now, that they shall not meet but must be prorogued; upon this argument chiefly, that all the differences between the two Houses, and things on foot that were matters of difference and discontent, may be laid aside; and must begin again if ever the House shall have a mind to pursue them – they must begin all anew.[1]   Here he set me down, and I to my cousin Turner and stayed and talked a little; and so took my wife and home, and there to make her*b* read, and then to supper and to bed.   ⟨At supper came W. Batelier and supped with us, and told us many pretty things of France and the greatness of the present King.⟩*c*

25.   Up and to the Committee of Tanger, where little done. And thence I home by my own coach, and busy after dinner at

a repl. 'h'-   *b* repl. 'r'-   *c* addition crowded in

---

1. The Houses had been adjourned in May 1668 after hot disputes between the Lords and Commons over the case of Skinner v. E. India Company (see above, pp. 182–3 & n.), and did not meet again until 19 October 1669. Wren's evidence here is of interest since it was his master, the Duke of York, who, with Buckingham, principally opposed the recall of parliament.

my office, all the afternoon till late at night, that my eyes were tired. So home, and my wife showed me many excellent prints of Nantueil's and others, which W Batelier hath at my desire brought me out of France of the King's and Colberts and others, most excellent, to my great content.¹ But he hath also brought over*ᵃ* a great many gloves perfumed, of several sorts; but all too big by half for her, and yet she will have two or three dozen of them, which vexed me and made me angry; so she at last, to please me, did come to take what alone I thought fit; which pleased me. So after a little supper,*ᵇ* to bed – my eyes being very bad.

26. Up and to the office, where busy sitting all the morning. Then to the office again, and then to White-hall, leaving my wife at Unthankes; and I to the Secretary's chamber, where I was by perticular order this day summoned to attend, as I find Sir D. Gawden also was, and here was the King and the Cabinet met; and being called in among the rest, I find my Lord Privy Seale, whom I never before knew to be in so much play as to be of the Cabinet.² The business is that the Algerins have broke the peace with us, by taking out some Spaniards and goods out of an English ship which had the Duke of York's pass – of which advice came this day; and the King is resolved to stop Sir Tho. Allen's fleet from coming home till he hath amends made him for this affront, and therefore sent for us to advise about

a repl. 'her'   *b* repl. 'supped'

---

1. Robert Nanteuil (d. 1678) was the best-known portrait draughtsman and engraver of his day in France. Pepys later lost these prints in the Navy Office fire of 1673, but replaced some of them (including those of the portraits of Louis XIV and Colbert) with the help of John Brisbane, secretary to the Paris embassy. In his final collection there were 47 prints

by Nanteuil. See *Further Corr.*, pp. 279–81; J. Charrington, *Cat. engraved portraits in library of S. Pepys*. For the prints of Louis XIV and Colbert, see C. Petitjean and C. Wickert, *Cat. de l'œuvre gravé de R. Nanteuil* (Paris), nos 138, 139, 54. (OM).

2. In May Lord Robartes was appointed Lord-Lieutenant of Ireland while still retaining the Privy Seal.

victuals to be sent to that fleet, and some more ships[1] – wherein
I answered them to what they demanded of me, which was but
some few mean things; but I see that on all these occasions they
seem to rely most upon me. And so this being done, I took
coach and took up my wife, and straight home and there late at
the office busy; and then home, and there I find W Batelier hath
also sent the books which I bade him bring me out of France;
among others, *L'estat de France*,[2] *Marnix*,[3] &c., to my great
content; and so I was well pleased with them and shall take a
time to look them over, as also one or two printed music-books
of songs; but my eyes are now too much out of tune to look
upon them with any pleasure. Therefore, to supper and to bed.

27. Up and with Sir J. Mennes in his coach to White-hall,
where first we waited on the Lords of the Treasury about finishing
the victualling contract;[4] and there also I was put to it to make
good our letter complaining against my Lord Anglesy's failing
us in the payment of the moneys assigned us upon the Customes[5] –
where Mr. Fenn was, and I know will tell my Lord; but it is no

1. The Algerines, claiming that the
treaty of 1664 did not cover foreigners
or foreign goods carried in English
ships, had taken '60 Spaniards, many
friars and a person of quality' from
the *William* of London, and demanded a ransom of 100,000 pieces of
eight. Allin's account of this and
other incidents (Algiers, 2 February)
is in *CSPD 1668–9*, pp. 179–80 ('All
our ships are foul, and we have but 7
weeks' provisions, at short allowance;
all our boatswains' and carpenters'
stores are expended, and very little
money left. These and other difficulties make one grey-headed').
Two ships were immediately fitted
out for despatch to the Straits (*CSPD
1668–9*, p. 171) and Allin was able to
impose another treaty on the Algerines
(February 1670). For his instructions
from the Duke (28 January), see Allin,
ii. 228–30.

2. Nicolas Besongne, *L'etat de la
France, où l'on voit tous les princes, ducs
et pairs, maréchaux de la France, et
autres officiers de la couronne: les
évêques, les cours* etc. (2 vols, Paris,
1669); not in the PL.

3. Probably Philippe de Marnix,
Le tableau des differens de la religion
(first published 1599–1605; 3 vols);
not in the PL. Marnix (d. 1598) was
one of the leaders of the revolt of the
Netherlands against Spain, and his
book one of the most influential attacks of its time on Roman Catholicism.

4. Alterations, for which the Board
had to have Treasury approval, were
to be made in the new contract: *CTB*,
iii. 14–15. It was signed on 24
February: *CSPD 1668–9*, p. 208.

5. Anglesey had diverted money
assigned for naval stores: *CTB*, loc.
cit.

matter, I am over-shoes already, and therefore must not fear.
Then we up to a committee of the Council for*a* the Navy about
a business of Sir D. Gawden's relating to the victualling; and
thence I by hackney to the Temple and there to the Auditors man,
and with him to a tavern to meet with another under-auditor to
advise about the clearing of my Lord Bellasses[1] accounts without
injuring myself and perplexing my accounts. And so thence
away to my cousin Turners, where I find Roger Pepys came last
night to town, and here is his mistress, Mrs. Dickenson; and by
and by comes in Mr. Turner (a worthy, sober, serious man;
I honour him mightily)[2] and there we dined, having but an
ordinary dinner; and so after dinner, she and I, and Roger and
his mistress, to the Duke of York's playhouse and there saw
The Five Hours Adventure[3] – which hath not been acted a good
while before, but*b* once, and is a most excellent play I must
confess. My wife and The came after us, after they had been to
buy some things abroad; and so after the play done, we to see
them home and then home ourselfs – and home, my wife to read
to me; and so to supper and to bed.

28. Up and to the office, where all the morning,*c* also after
dinner, and there late, despatching much business; and then home
to supper with my wife, and to get her to read to me. And here
I did*d* find that Mr. Sheres hath, beyond his promise, not only
got me a candlestick made me, after a form he remembers to
have seen in Spain, for keeping the light from one's eyes, but*e*
hath got it done in silver, very neat, and designs to give it me in
thanks for my paying him his 100*l* in money for his service at
Tanger which was ordered him.[4] But I do intend to force him to

---

a repl. 'about'	*b* repl. 'the'	*c* MS. 'afternoon'
d repl. 'find' badly formed		*e* repl. 'hath'

---

1. Governor of Tangier, 1665–7.
2. John Turner (who had married Jane Pepys) was a barrister of the Middle Temple, and Recorder of York. He became a King's Serjeant in 1669.

3. *The adventures of five hours*, a comedy by Sir Samuel Tuke; see above, iv. 8, n. 2. (A).
4. The payment was for work on the mole.

make me [pay] for it.   But I yet, without his direction, cannot tell
how it is to be made use of.   So after a little reading, to bed.

29.   Up, and with W. Hewer in Collonell Middleton's coach
to White-hall, and there to the Duke of York to attend him;
where among other things, I did give a severe account of our
proceedings, and what we found in the business of Sir W
Jenings's demand of supernumerarys; I thought it a good occasion
to make an example of [him], for he is a proud, idle fellow, and
it did meet with the Duke of York's acceptance and well-liking;
and he did call him in after I had done, and did not only give him
a sound rebuke, but condemns him to pay both their victuals and
wages, or right himself of the purser.[1]   This I was glad of, and
so were all the rest of us, though I know I have made myself an
immortal enemy by it.   Thence home by hackney, calling Roger
Pepys at the Temple-gate in the bookseller's shop, and to the
Old Exchange, where I stayed a little to invite my uncle Wight;
and so home and there find my aunt Wight and her husband
come presently, and so to dinner; and after dinner, Roger and I
and my wife and aunt to see Mr. Cole, but he nor his wife was
within; but we looked upon his picture of Cleopatra,[2] which I
went*a* principally to see, being so much commended by ⟨my⟩
wife and aunt; but I find it a base copy of a good originall, that
vexed me to hear so much commended.   Thence to see Creeds
wife, and did so and stayed a while, where both of them within;
and here I met Mr. Bland, newly come from Cales after his
differences with Norwood.[3]   And think him a foolish, light-
headed man; but certainly he hath been abused in this matter

a   repl. 'that'

---

1. Jennens of the *Sapphire* had
(between April 1667 and November
1668) taken on board more men than
those allowed him, and had attempted
to cast the blame on his purser.   He
had been known to commit the same
offence in an earlier command, and
the Board now stopped his pay.
The papers in the case are summarised

in *CSPD 1668-9*, pp. 215-16. Pepys
has some notes on it in NWB, pp.
165-9.
    2. Not identified.   (OM).
    3. John Bland was the Mayor of
Tangier;   Henry Norwood,   the
Deputy-Governor.   For their dispute, see above, p. 392 & n. 1.

by Collonell Norwood.   Here Creed showed me a copy of some
propositions which Bland and others, in the name of the Corporation of Tanger, did present to Norwood for his opinion in, in
order to the King's service; which were drawn up very humbly,
and were really good things; but his answer to them were*a* in
the most shitten proud, carping, insolent, and ⟨ironically⟩*b* profane style that ever I saw in my life[1] – so as I shall never*c* think the
place can do well while he is there. Here, after some talk,
and Creeds telling us that he is upon taking the next house to his
present lodgings, which is next to that that my Cosen Tom Pepys
once lived in in Newport-street in Covent-garden, and is in a
good place – and then I suppose he will keep his coach.   So,
setting Roger down at the Temple, who tells that he is now
concluded in all matters with his widow,[2] we home; and there
hired my wife to make an end of Boyles book of Forms[3] tonight
and tomorrow; and so fell to read and sup, and then to bed.

This day Mr. Ned Pickering brought his lady to see my wife,
in acknowledgment for a little present of oranges and Olives
which I sent her for his kindness to me in the buying of my horses;
which was very civil.   She is old, but hath I believe been a pretty
comely woman.

30.   Lay long in bed, it being a fast-day for the murther of the
late King; and so up and to church, where Dr. Hicks made a
dull sermon;[4] and so home, and there I find W Battelier and
Balty and they dined with us; and I spent all the afternoon with
my wife and W Battelier talking and then making them read,
and perticularly made an end of Mr. Boyl's book of Formes,
which I am glad to have over; and then fell to read a French
discourse which he hath brought over with him for me, to invite

a repl. 'with'   *b* repl. 'prof'-   *c* MS. 'ever'

---

1. The proposals, and Norwood's
answer, are in BM, Sloane 3510, ff. 4,
48, 49.
2. Esther Dickenson, whom he
married on 4 February.

3. See above, p. 144, n. 2.
4. Dr Edward Hickes was Rector
of St Margaret Pattens. For the
service, see above, ii. 26, n. 1.

the people of France to apply themselfs to Navigacion;[1] which it doth do very well, and is certainly their interest, and what will undo us in a few years if the[a] King of France goes on to fit up his Navy and encrease it and his trade, as he hath begun.[2] At night to supper; and after supper, and W. Battler gone, my wife begun another book I lately bought, a new book called *The State of England*, which promises well and is worth reading;[3] and so after a while to bed.

31. *Lords day.* Lay long, talking with pleasure, and so up,[b] and I to church and there did hear the Doctor that is lately turned Divine, I have forgot his name, I met him[c] a while since at Sir D. Gawden's at dinner, Dr. Waterhouse;[4] he preaches in devout manner of way, not elegant nor very persuasive, but seems to mean well and that he would preach holily, and was mighty

a repl. 'he goes'   *b* repl. 'to bed'   *c* repl. 'time'

─────────────

1. Probably either *Le commerce honorable ou Considerations Politiques. Contenant les motifs de necessité, d'honneur, et de profit, qui se treuvent à former des compagnies de personnes de toutes conditions pour l'entretien du negoce de mer en France. Composé par un habitant de la ville de Nantes* (Nantes, 1646; PL 1674); or *Relation de l'establissement de la Compagnie Françoise pour le commerce des Indes Orientales* (Paris, 1666; PL 106).

2. Colbert's efforts to turn the energies of France towards maritime achievement were now at their height. In 1673–8 Pepys, as Secretary to the Admiralty, was to be more concerned about this than about any other issue.

3. Edward Chamberlayne, *Angliæ Notitia; or The present state of England: together with divers reflections upon the antient state thereof*; duodecimo; three editions 1669. A discursive little handbook of political and other information (one section of the Table of Contents reads 'Suffragan Bishops; Buggery; Buildings'), and the first of a series which continued until 1755 (the title changing in 1708 to *Magnæ Britanniæ notitia*), founded on the model of *L'etat nouveau de la France* (Paris, 1661). This is probably the first, anonymous, edition, licensed 18 July 1668, and announced in the Michaelmas lists at 2*s.* 6*d.* bound: *Trans. Stat. Reg.*, ii. 389; Arber, *Term Cat.*, i. 2. See also *N. & Q.*, 13 February 1886, pp. 123+. In the PL are the volumes for 1687 (both parts), 1692, 1694, 1700 and 1702: PL 537, 910, 788, 965, 997.

4. See above, p. 215 & n. 1. According to Wood, he was 'a cockbrain'd man', who became 'a fantastical preacher': *Fasti Oxon.* (ed. Bliss), ii. 163.

passionate against people that make a scoff of religion. And the truth is, I did observe Mrs. Hallworthy smile often, and many others of the parish, who I perceive have known him and were in mighty expectation of hearing[a] him preach, but could not forbear smiling; and she perticularly upon me, and I on her. So home to dinner; and before dinner, to my office to set down my journal for this week, and then home to dinner – and after dinner, to get my wife and boy, one after another, to read to me – and so spent the afternoon and the evening; and so after supper, to bed.

And thus ended this month, with many different days of sadness and mirth, from differences between me and my wife, from her remembrance of my late unkindness to her with Willet, she not being able to forget it, but now and then hath her passionate remembrance of it, as often as prompted to it by any occasion; but this night we are at present very kind. And so ends this month.[b]

a   repl. 'him'
b   Last paragraph crowded into bottom of page.   One blank page follows.

1. Up and by water from the Tower to White-hall, the first time that I have gone to that end of the town by water for two or three months I think, since I kept a coach*a* – which God send propitious to me – but it is a very great convenience. I went to a Committee of Tanger, but it did not meet; and so I meeting Mr. Povy, he and I away to Dancres to speak something touching the pictures I am getting him to make for me.[1] And thence he carried me to Mr. Streeters the famous history-painter over the way, whom I have often heard of but did never see him before; and there I found him and Dr. Wren and several virtuosos*b* looking upon the paintings which he is making for the new Theatre at Oxford; and endeed, they look as they would be very fine, and the rest thinks better then those of Rubens in the Banqueting-house at White-hall, but I do not so fully think so – but they will certainly be very noble, and I am mightily pleased to have the fortune to see this man and his work, which is very famous – and he a very civil little man and lame, but lives very handsomely.[2] So thence to my Lord Bellasses and met him within; my business only to see a chimney-piece of Dancre's doing in distemper with egg to keep off the glaring of the light, which I must have done for my room; and endeed it is pretty, but I must confess I do think it is not altogether so beautiful as the oyle

---

a repl. 'good'   *b* l.h. repl. s.h. 'virt'-

---

1. See above, p. 423 & n. 1. (OM).

2. The Sheldonian, designed by Wren, was now nearing completion, the first Encaenia being held there in the following July. Robert Streeter's ceiling (which is still in position) represents Truth descending upon the Arts and Sciences: see Whinney and Millar, pp. 292–3; E. Croft-Murray,

Decorative painting in England, 1537–1837, i. 44–5, 227. It was painted in sections on canvas and taken to Oxford by water: MS. Bodl. 898, f. 183*v*. Rubens's ceiling in the Banqueting House at Whitehall (also still in position) had been painted for Charles I. (OM).

pictures;[1] but I will have some of one and some of another. Thence set him down at Little Turnstile, and so I home; and there eat a little dinner, and away with my wife by coach to the King's playhouse, thinking to have seen *The Heyresse*, first acted on Saturday last;[2] but when we came thither, we find no play there – Kinaston, that did act a part therein in abuse to Sir Charles Sidly, being last night exceedingly dry-beaten with sticks by two or three that assaulted him – so as he is mightily bruised, and forced to keep his bed.[3] So we to the Duke of York's playhouse, and there saw *Shee Would if She Could.*[a][4] And so home and to my office to business, and then to supper and to bed. ⟨This day, going to the play, The. Turner met us and carried us to her mother at my Lady Mordants; and I did carry both mother and daughter with us to the Duke of York's playhouse at next door.⟩[b]

2. Up and to the office, where all the morning; and home to dinner at noon, where I find Mr. Sheres; and there made a short dinner and carried him with us to the King's playhouse, where *The Heyresse*, notwithstanding Kinaston's being beaten,

---

a repl. 'The Five Hours Adventure'
b addition crowded into bottom of page

---

1. The use of tempera ('distemper') – a medieval practice – was now being revived under the sponsorship of the Royal Society: Croft-Murray, op. cit., i. 276. It consisted of egg mixed with shredded figleaves, and enabled paint to dry quickly and several degrees lighter in tone than the wet pigment. (OM).

2. As that Saturday was the fast-day for Charles I, Pepys may have been mistaken: see E. L. Avery in *Research studies of State Coll. Washington,* 13/253. At 2 February Pepys ascribes the play to the Duke of Newcastle: below, p. 436. (A).

3. Edward Kynaston was proud of his resemblance to Sedley and was strolling in St James's Park wearing the clothes in which he had impersonated Sedley on the stage when the assault was committed. Sedley ordered his bravo to give Kynaston the impression that he thought he was Sedley and to thrash him for an insult which he was to pretend to have received from Sedley. Kynaston, as Pepys records, was unable to act again until 9 February. For details, see V. de Sola Pinto, *Sedley,* pp. 111, 112, 318. (A).

4. A comedy by Etherege: see above, p. 53, n. 3. (A).

is acted; and they say the King is very angry with Sir Ch. Sidly for his being beaten; but he doth deny it.   But his part is done by Beeston, who is fain to read it out of a book all the while, and thereby spoils the part*a* and almost the play, it being one of the best parts in it; and though the design is in the first conception of it pretty good, yet it is but an indifferent play – wrote, they say, by my Lord Newcastle.[1]   But it was pleasant to see Beeston come in with others, supposing it to be dark and yet he is forced to read his part by the light of the candles.   And this I observing to a gentleman that sat by me, he was mightily pleased therewith and spread it up and down; but that that pleased me most in the play is the first*b* song that Knepp sings (she singing three or four); and endeed, it was very finely sung,*c* so as to make the whole house clap her.   Thence carried Sheres to White-hall, and there I stepped in and looked out Mr. May, who tells me that he and his company cannot come to dine with me tomorrow, whom I expected only to come to see the manner of our office and books[2] – at which I was not very much displeased, having much business at the office; and so away home, and there to the office about my letters; and then home to supper and to bed, my wife being in mighty*d* ill humour all night; and in the morning, I found it to be from her observing Knepp*e* to wink and*f* smile on me, and she says I smiled on her; and poor wretch, I did perceive that she did, and doth on all such occasions, mind my eyes.   I did with much difficulty pacify her, and were friends, she desiring that hereafter at that House we might always sit either above in a box or, if there be room, close up to the lower boxes.[3]

a repl. 'pl'-   *b* s.h. repl. l.h. 'K'-   *c* repl. 'song'
d repl. same symbol badly formed   *e* repl. 'him'   *f* repl. 'on'

---

1. There is no play entitled *The Heiress* among the published works of the Duke of Newcastle. The play was evidently one of which he was only part-author, for in a letter written by John Evelyn's wife on 10 February she mentions a play 'of my Lord of Newcastle's, for which printed apologies are scattered in the assembly by Briden's order, either for himself who had some hand in it, or for the author most; I think both had right to them': see *Diary and corresp. of Evelyn* (ed. Bray), iv. 14. (A).

2. Cf. above, pp. 417–18 & n.

3. I.e. at the very back of the pit. (A).

[3.] So up, and to the office till noon and then home to a little dinner; and thither again till*a* night, mighty busy, to my great content doing a great deal of business; and so home to supper and to bed – I finding this day that I may be able to do a great deal of business by dictateing, if I do not read myself or write, without spoiling my eyes, I being very well*b* in my eyes after a great day's work.

4. Up and at*c* the office all the morning. At noon, home with my people to dinner; and then after dinner comes Mr. Spong to see me, and brings me my parrallogram[1] in better*d* order then before, and two or three drafts of ⟨the port of⟩ Brest,[2] to my great content: and I did call Mr. Gibson to take notice of it, who is very much pleased therewith. And it seems this is not, as Mr. Sheres would the other day have persuaded me, the same as a Protractor – which doth so much the more make me value it; but*e* of itself it is a most useful instrument. Thence out with my wife and him, and carried him to a instrument-maker's shop in Chancery-lane that was once a prentice of Greatorex's,[3] but the master was not within; and there he showed me a paralellogram in brass, which I like so well that I will buy, and therefore bid it be made clean and fit for me. And so to my cousin Turner's and there just spoke with The, the mother not being at home; and so to the New Exchange and thence home to my letters; and so home to supper and to bed. ⟨This morning I made a slip from the office to White-hall, expecting Povys business at a Committee of Tanger at which I would be, but it did not meet and so I presently back.⟩*f*

5. Up betimes; by coach to Sir W. Coventry's and with him by coach to White-hall; and there walked in the garden,

a repl. 'will'   *b* repl. 'weather'   *c* repl. 'close'
d repl. 'order'   *e* repl. 'of'   *f* addition crowded in

1. See above, p. 340 & n. 1.
2. These have not survived in the PL.
3. Probably Henry Wynne, at the

Pope's Head, Chancery Lane: see Eva G. R. Taylor, *Math. Practitioners*, pp. 242–3.

talking of several things, and by my visit to keep fresh my interest in him; and there he tells me how it hath been talked that he was to go one of the Commissioners to Ireland, which he was resolved never to do, unless directly commanded; for he told me that for to go thither, while the Chief Secretary of State was his*a* professed enemy,*b* was to undo himself;[1] and therefore it were better for him to venture being unhappy here, then go further off to be undone by some obscure instructions, or whatever other way of mischief his enemies should cut out for him. He mighty kind to me; and so parted and thence*c* home, calling in two or three places; among others, Dancre's, where I find him beginning of a piece for me, of Greenwich,[2] which will please me well; and so home to dinner and very busy all the afternoon; and so at night home to supper and to bed.

6.   Up and to the office, where all the morning, and thence after dinner to the King's playhouse and there in an upper box (where came in Collonell Poynton and Doll Stacy, who is very fine, and by her wedding ring I suppose he hath married her at last) did see *The Moore of Venice*, but ill acted in most parts; Moone (which did a little surprize me) not acting Iago's part by much so well as Clun used to do, nor another*d* Hart's, which was Cassio's; nor endeed Burt doing the Moor's so well as I once thought he did.   Thence home, and just at Holburne-Conduit the bolt broke that holds the fore-wheels to the perch, and so the horses went away with them and left the coachman and us; but being near our coach-makers, and we staying in a little iron-monger's shop, we were presently supplied with another; and so home and there to my letters at the office, and so to supper and to bed.

a   repl. 'is'   *b*   repl. same symbol   *c*   repl. 'and there being no'
                    d   repl. 'Beeto'-

1. Arlington and Coventry had been at odds since Clarendon's fall. Rumours had been current for some time that Ormond would be replaced in Ireland by a commission (BM, Add. 36916, ff. 117, 118); in fact Lord Robartes was appointed Lord Lieutenant in his place on 14 February.

2. See above, p. 423 & n. 1. (OM).

7. *Lords day.* My wife mighty peevish in the morning about my lying unquietly a-nights,*a* and she will have it that it is a late practice, from my evil thoughts in my dreams; and I do often find that in my dreams she doth lay her hand upon my cockerel to observe what she can. And mightily she is troubled about it, but all blew over; and I up and to church, and so home to dinner, where she in a worse fit, which lasted all the afternoon, and shut herself up in her closet; and I mightily grieved and vexed, and could not get her to tell me what ayled her,*b* or to let me into her closet; but at last she did, where I found her crying on the ground, and I could not please her; but I did at last find that she did plainly expound it to me: it was that she did believe me false to her with Jane, and did rip up three or four most silly circumstances, of her not rising till I came out of my chamber and her letting*c* me thereby see her dressing herself, and that I must needs go into her chamber and was naught with*d* her; which was so silly, and so far from truth, that I could not be troubled at it, though I could not wonder at her being troubled, if she had these thoughts. And therefore she would lie from me, and caused sheets to be put on in the blue room and would have Jane to lie with her, lest I should come to her. At last, I did give her such satisfaction, that we were mighty good friends and went to bed betimes, where yo did hazer very well con her,*e* and did this night by chance the first*f* time poner my digito en her*g* thing, which did do her*g* much pleasure; but I pray God that ella doth not think that yo did know before – or get a trick of liking it. So para sleep.*h*

8. Up and dressed myself, and by coach with W. Hewer and my wife to White-hall, where she set us two down; and in the way, our little boy, at Martin my bookseller's shop going to light, did fall down; and had he not been a most nimble boy

---

        a repl. 'at'   *b* repl. 'here'
  c repl. 'see'   *d* repl. 'was'   *e* garbled s.h.
  f repl. 'fr'-   *g–g* garbled s.h.   *h* garbled s.h.

(I saw how he did it, and was mightily pleased with him for it), he had been run over by the coach. I to visit my Lord Sandwich; and there, while my Lord was dressing himself, did see a young Spaniard that he hath brought over with him, dance; which he is admired for, as the best*a* dancer in Spain; and endeed, he doth with mighty mastery, but I do not like his dancing as the English, though my Lord commends it mightily. But I will have him to my house, and show it my wife. Here I met with Mr. Moore, who tells me the state of my Lord's accounts of his imbassy; which I find not so good as I thought – for though it be past the King and his Caball (the Committee for Foreign Affairs as they are called),[1] yet they have cut off from 19000*l* full 8000*l*, and have now sent it to the Lords of the Treasury; who, though the Committee have allowed the rest, yet they are not obliged to abide by it.[2] So that I do fear this account may yet be long ere it be passed; much more, ere the sum be paid. I am sorry for the family, and not a little for what it owes me. So to my wife; took her up at Unthankes, and in our way home did show her the tall woman in Holburne which I have seen before.[3] And*b* I measured her and she is, without shoes, just 6 feet-5 inch high, and they say not above 21 years old. Thence home and there to dinner, and my wife in a wonderful ill humour, and after dinner I stayed with her alone, being not able*c* to endure this life, and fell to some angry words together; but by and by were mighty good friends, she telling me plainly it was still about Jane – whom she cannot believe but I am base with; which I made a matter of mirth at, but at last did call up Jane and confirmed her mistress's directions for her being gone at

a repl. 'most'   *b* repl. 'but'   *c* repl. 'ab'-

---

1. A Committee of Foreign Affairs, nine in number, had been constituted in February 1668, and served as a Cabinet.

2. The Treasury quickly confirmed the lower figure: *CTB*, iii. 22–4. For the subsequent disputes, see Harris, ii. 162–5. For a summary of the accounts, see *CSPD 1668–9*, pp. 54, 191–2, 454. In August 1669 Sandwich agreed to the reductions, and the accounts passed. The Foreign Affairs Committee cut down his weekly allowance from £133 to £100, and agreed to pay £4000 (instead of £6000) for travelling and other costs.

3. See above, p. 407 & n. 1.

Easter: which I find the wench willing to be, but directly prayed that Tom might go with her; which I promised, and was but what I designed; and she being thus spoke with and gone, my wife and I good friends and mighty kind, I having promised, and I will perform it, never to give her for the time to come ground of new trouble; and so I to the office with a very light heart, and there close at my business all the afternoon.

This day I was told by Mr. Wren that Captain Cox, Master-Attendant at Deptford, is to be one of us very soon, he and Tippets being to take their turns for Chatham and Portsmouth; which choice I like well enough – and Captain Annesly is to come in his room at Deptford.[1]

This morning also, going to visit Rogr. Pepys at the poticary's in King's-street, he tells me that he is gone to his wife's, so that they have been married, as he tells me, ever since the middle of last week. It was his design, upon good reasons, to make no noise of it; but I am well*a* enough contented*b* that it is over.[2]

Despatched a great deal of business at the office, and there pretty late, till finding myself very full of wind by my eating no dinner today, being vexed, I was forced to go home; and there supped, W Batelier with us, and so with great content to bed.

9. Up and all the morning busy at the office; and after dinner, abroad with my wife to the King's playhouse and there saw *The Island Princesse*,[3] which I like mighty well, as an excellent play; and here we find Kinaston to be well enough to act again, which he doth very well, after his beating by Sir Ch. Sidly's appointment.[4] And so thence home, and there to my business at the office; and after my letters done, then home to supper

a repl. 'gl'-   *b* repl. 'with'

---

1. John Cox was made Commissioner at Chatham on 29 March 1669: *CSPD, Add. 1660–70*, p. 734. John Tippets had served in the same office at Portsmouth since February 1668: *CSPD 1667–8*, p. 258. Abraham Ansley had been Cox's deputy at Deptford.

2. See above, p. 431, n. 2. She was his fourth wife.

3. See above, p. 409, n. 2. (A).

4. According to Genest (i. 93), Kynaston played the King of Tidore. For the attack on him, see above, p. 435 & n. 3. (A)

and to bed – my mind being mightily eased by my having this morning delivered to the office a letter of advice about our answers to the Commissioners of Accounts, whom we have neglected;[1] and I have done this as a record in my justification hereafter, when it shall come to be examined.

10. Up, and with my wife and W. Hewer; she set us down at White-hall, where the Duke of York was gone a-hunting; and so after I had done a little business there, I to my wife, and with her to the Plasterer's at Charing-cross that casts heads and bodies in plaster, and there I had my whole face done;[2] but I was vexed first to be forced to daub all my face over with Pomatum, but it was pretty to feel how saft and easily it is done on the face, and by and by, by degrees, how hard it becomes, that you cannot break it, and sits*a* so close that you cannot pull it off, and yet so easy that it is as soft as a pillow, so safe is everything where many parts of the body do bear alike.   Thus was the mold made; but when it came off, there was little pleasure in it as it looks in the mold, nor any resemblance whatever there will be in the figure when I come to see it cast off – which I am to call for a day or two hence; which I shall long to see.   Thence to Hercules-

a repl. 'set'

---

1. Pepys to the Navy Board, 9 February: copy (in unidentified clerical hand) in NMM, LBK/8, pp. 572–3 (printed in *Further Corr.*, pp. 221–2). This was a reply to the enquiries made by the Brooke House Committee almost a year before: above, p. 34 & n. 4.   Pepys began by stating that as the 'daily remembrancer' of the Board, he had kept a journal of its proceedings in the matter of the Committee's enquiries. (It is now PRO, Adm. 106/2886, pt I.)   He enclosed 'an abstract of whatever hitherto has been by them Demanded, and thereto [in] distinct Columnes added a

view of what thereof is answered, what not, what the Board has joyntly done preparative to it, and on what hands the delay thereof (for now more than 12 moneths in some perticulers) seemes chargeable'.   Later he wrote a long vindication of the office himself (27 November 1669; copy, in Hayter's hand, in Rawl. A 457; 73 pp.).

2. The artist has been identified by Mrs K. A. Esdaile as William Larson, jun., modeller and caster: *Times Lit. Supp.*, 2 October 1943, p. 480.   The cast does not survive.   (OM).

Pillars, and there my wife and W. Hewer and I dined. So^{*a*} to White-hall, where I stayed till the Duke of York came from hunting, which he did by and by; and when dressed, did come out to dinner, and there I waited; and he did tell me that to-morrow was to be the great day that the business of the Navy would be discoursed of before the King and his Caball; and that he must stand on his guard and did design to have had me in readiness by, but upon second thoughts did think it better to let it alone. But they are now upon entering into the Æconimicall part of the Navy. Here he dined, and did mightily magnify his Sawce which he did then eat with everything, and said it was the best universal sauce in the world – it being taught him by the Spanish Imbassador – made of some parsley and a dry toast, beat in a mortar together with vinegar, salt, and a little pepper. He eats it with flesh or fowl or fish. And then he did now mightily commend some new sort of wine lately found out, called Navarr wine;¹ which I tasted, and is I think good wine; but I did like better the notion of the Sawce and by and by did taste it, and liked it mightily. After dinner I did what I went for, which was to get his consent that Balty might hold his muster-maister's place by deputy, in his new imployment which I design for him about the Store-keeper's accounts; which the Duke of York did grant me, and I was mighty glad of it. Thence home, and there I find Povy and W Bateler by appointment met to talk of some merchandise of wine and linen; but I do not like of their troubling my house to meet in, having no mind to their pretences of having their randezvous here. But however, I was not much troubled, but went to the office, and there very busy and did much business till late at night; and so home to supper, and with great pleasure to bed.

This^{*b*} day at dinner, I sent to Mr. Spong to come to me to

---

a repl. 'and back to White-hall, calling upon Dancres at the way, who was on our picture; and it begins to appear mighty fine, he beginning with Green-wich in distemper.' This visit is reported at 12 February.
    b date '11' struck through in margin

---

1. Possibly Jurançon, a rare orange-coloured dessert wine, made near Pau: A. L. Simon, *Dict. wine*; G. S. Thomson, *Life in a noble household*, p. 195.

Hercules-pillars; who came to us, and there did bring with him my new Parallellogram of brass, which I was mightily pleased with; and paid for it 25*s*, and am mightily pleased with his ingenious and modest company.

11. Up and to the office, where sat all the morning; and at noon home and heard that the last night, Collonell Middleton's wife died*ᵃ* – a woman I never saw since she came hither, having never been within their house since. Home at noon to dinner, and thence to work all the afternoon with great pleasure, and did bring my business to a very little compass in my day-book,¹ which is a mighty pleasure. And so home to supper, and get my wife to read to me, and then to bed.

12. Up and my wife with me to White-hall, and Tom,*ᵇ* and there she sets us down; and there to wait on the Duke of York, with the*ᶜ* rest of us, at the Robes; where the Duke of York did tell us that the King would have us prepare a draft of the present Administracion of the Navy, and what it was in the late times – in order to his being able to distinguish between the good and the bad; which I shall do, but to do it well will give me a great deal of trouble.² Here we showed him Sir J. Mennes's propositions*ᵈ* about balancing*ᵉ* storekeepers*ᶠ* accounts; and I did show him Hosiers,³ which did please him mightily, and he will have it showed the Council and King anon, to be put in practice. Thence the Treasurer's; and I and Sir J. Mennes and Mr. Tippets down to the Lords Commissioners of the Treasury, and there had a hot debate from Sir Tho. Clifford and my Lord Ashly (the latter of which, I hear, is turning about as fast as he can to the Duke of Buckingham's side, being in danger, it seems, of being otherwise out of play, which would not be convenient

---

a followed by 'a' struck through   *b* repl. 'WH'   *c* repl. 'that'
d repl. 'propos'–   *e* MS. 'balancings'   *f* repl. 'storekeep'–

---

1. The daybooks for this period are not extant: above, v. 117, n. 4.
2. See below, p. 525 & n. 1. The Duke transmitted the order to the Board on the 13th: BM, Add. 36782, f. 81*r*.
3. See below, p. 474 & n. 1.

for him) against Sir W. Coventry and Sir J Duncomb, who did uphold our*a* office against an accusation of our Treasurers, who told the Lords that they found that we had run the King in debt 50000*l* or more, more then the money appointed for the year would defray[1] – which they declared like fools, and with design to hurt us, though the thing is in itself ridiculous. But my Lords Ashly and Clifford did most horribly cry out against the want of method in the office. At last it came that it should be put in writing what they had to object; but I was devilish mad at it, to see us thus wounded by our own members; and so away vexed, and called* my wife and to Hercules-Pillars, [with] Tom, and there dined; and here, there coming a Frenchman by with his Shew, we did make him show it us; which he did, just as Lacy acts it[2] – which made it mighty pleasant to me. So after dinner, we away and to Dancres and there saw our picture of Greenwich[3] in doing, which is mighty pretty; and so to White-hall, my wife to Unthankes – and I*b* attended, with Lord Brouncker, the King and Council about the proposition of balancing storekeepers accounts: and there presented Hosier's book and it was mighty well resented* and approved of. So the Council being up, we to the Queen's side with the King and Duke of York, and the Duke of York did take me out to talk of our Treasurers, whom he is mighty angry with; and I perceive is mighty desirous to bring in as many good motions of profit and reformation in the Navy as he can, before the Treasurers do light upon them; they being desirous, it seems, to be thought the great reformers – and the Duke of York doth well. But to my great joy, he is mighty open to me in everything; and by this means I know his whole mind, and shall be able to secure myself if he stands. Here

a repl. 'the'   *b* repl. 'we'

---

1. Cf. *CTB*, iii. 25–6.

2. Evidently a puppet-show containing a part similar to one played by John Lacy, the leading comedian of the King's Company, probably the dancing master in the play that Pepys calls *The French Dancing Master* (see above, iii. 87, n. 5, & 88, n. 1), though the 'shew' may have been based on one of his more recent parts (see above, viii. 384 & n. 3: ix. 178 & n. 1). (A).

3. See above, p. 423 & n. 1. (OM).

tonight, I understand by my Lord Brouncker that at last it is
concluded on by the King and Buckingham that my Lord of
Ormond shall not hold his government of Ireland;[1] which is a
great stroke, to show the power of Buckingham and the poor
spirit of the King and little hold that any man can have of him.
Thence I homeward; and calling my wife, called at my cousin
Turner's and there met our new Cosen Pepys (Mrs. Dickenson)[2]
and Bab and Betty,[3] come yesterday to town, poor girls; whom[a]
we have reason to love, and mighty glad we are to see them;
and there stayed and talked a little, being also mightily pleased
to see Betty Turner, who is now in town, and her brother[s]
Charles and Will,[b] being come from school to see their father; and
there talked a while and so home, and there Pelling hath got me
W. Pen's book against the Trinity; I got my wife to read it to
me, and I find it so well writ, as I think it too good for him
ever to have writ it[4] – and it is a serious sort of book, and not fit
for everybody to read. And so to supper and to bed.

13. Up, and all the morning at the office; and at noon home
to dinner, and thence to the office again, mighty busy to my
great content till night; and then home to supper and my eyes
being weary, to bed.

a repl. 'which'　　　*b* repl. 'John'

---

1. The announcement that Ormond was to be replaced by Robartes
was made by the King at the Committee for Foreign Affairs at Essex House
on the afternoon of the 14th, in
Ormond's presence: PRO, SP 104,
f. 119r.

2. Roger Pepys's new (fourth)
wife.

3. Bab and Betty were Roger
Pepys's daughters by his second wife.

4. This was *The sandy foundation
shaken: or, Those so generally believed
and applauded doctrines, of one God, sub-
sisting in three distinct and separate
persons, the impossibility of God's*
*pardoning sinners, without a plenary
satisfaction, the justification of impure
persons by an imputative righteousness
refuted, from the authority of Scripture
testimonies, and right reason. By W.P.j.
a builder on that foundation which cannot
be moved* (1668); not in the PL.
Attacks on the doctrine of the Trinity
were regarded as blasphemy, and it
was for publishing this pamphlet that
Penn was kept a close prisoner in the
Tower, December 1668–August 1669.
See W. C. Braithwaite, *Second period
of Quakerism*, pp. 61–4. It is odd that
Pepys never mentions Penn's imprisonment in the diary.

14. *Lords day.* Up and by coach to Sir W. Coventry; and there, he taking physic, I with him all the morning, full of very good discourse of the Navy and public matters, to my great content; wherein I find him doubtful*a* that all will be bad; and for his part, he tells me he takes no more care for anything more then in the Treasury; and that that being done, he goes to cards and other delights, as plays, and in summer time to Bowles; but here he did show me two or three old books of the Navy of my Lord Northumberland's times,[1] which he*b* hath taken many good notes out of for justifying the Duke of York and us in many things wherein perhaps precedent will be necessary to produce – which did give me great content. At noon home, pleased mightily with my morning's work; and coming home, do find a letter from Mr. Wren, to call me to the Duke of York after dinner; so dined in all haste, and then*c* W. Hewer and my wife and I out; and we*d* set her at my cousin Turner's, while we to White-hall, where the Duke of York expected me, and in his closet, Wren and I, did tell me how the King hath been acquainted with the Treasurers' discourse at the Lords-Commissioners of the Treasury the other day, and is dissatisfied with our running him in debt; which I removed, and he did carry me to the King and I did satisfy him also; but his satisfaction is nothing worth, it being easily got and easily removed – but I do purpose to put it in writing that shall make the Treasurers ashamed. But the Duke of York is horrid angry against them; and he hath cause, for they do all they can to bring dishonour upon his management, as doth plainly appear in all they do. Having done with the Duke of York, who doth repose all in me, I with Mr. Wren to his chamber to talk; where he observed that these people are all of them a broken sort of people, that have not much to lose and therefore will venture all to make their fortunes better. That Sir Tho Osborne is a beggar, having 11 or 1200*l* a year but owes above

a repl. same symbol, incomplete   *b* repl. 'will'   *c* MS. 'there'
     d repl. 'she set us'

1. The 10th Earl of Northumber-land had been Lord High Admiral, 1638–42. The books appear to have been the tracts by Sir William Monson referred to below, p. 524 & n. 2.

10000*l*.[1] That the Duke of Buckingham's condition is shortly
this: that he hath about 19600*l* a year, of which he pays away
about 7000*l* a year in interest, about 2000*l* in Fee-farm rents to the
King, about 6000*l* in wages and pensions; and the rest to live
upon, and pay taxes for the whole.[2] Wren says that for the
Duke of York to stir in this matter as his quality might justify,
would but make all things worse, and that therefore he must
bend and suffer all, till time works it out. That he fears they
will sacrifice the Church,[3] and that [Buckingham] will take anything, and so he [will][a] hold up his head a little longer, and then
break in pieces. But Sir W. Coventry did today mightily
magnify my late Lord Treasurer[4] for a wise and solid, though
infirm man. And among other thing[s], that when he hath said
it was impossible in nature to find this or that sum of money,
and my Lord Chancellor hath made sport of it and tell the King
that when my Lord hath said it [was] impossible, yet he hath made
shift to find it, and that was by Sir G. Carteret's getting credit,
my Lord did once in his hearing say thus, which he magnifies as a
great Saying: "That impossible would be found impossible at
last" – meaning, that the King would run himself out, beyond
all his cred[it] and Fonds, and then we should too late find it impossible – which is, he says, now come to pass; for that Sir W.
Coventry says they could borrow what money they would, if
they had assignments and Fonds to secure it with, which before
they had enough of, and then must spend it as if it would never
have an end.

a For these errors, etc., see above, p. 244, note *a*.

---

1. Osborne's father's estate had
been valued in 1646 at £970 p.a., and
to this he had added by his marriage:
A. Browning, *Danby*, i. 17–19, 30.
His indebtedness had been increased
since 1668 by his maintaining a London establishment as well as his
Yorkshire home: ib., pp. 68–9.

2. Buckingham's estates were
valued in 1651, when parliament
confiscated them, at £26,000 p.a.:
DNB; Cal. Comm. Compounding, iii.
2182–92. His debts were so heavy
that by 1671 he had settled all or most
of his estates on trustees: H. J.
Habbakuk in *Studies in social hist.* (ed.
J. H. Plumb), p. 145.

3. Cf. above, p. 347, n.3.

4. Southampton.

From White-hall to my cousin Turners, and there took up my wife; and so to my uncle Wights and there sat and supped and talked pretty merry; and then walked home and to bed.

15.*ᵃ* Up and with Tom to White-hall, and there at a Committee of Tanger, where a great instance of what a man may lose by the neglect of a friend. Povy never had such an opportunity of passing his accounts, the Duke of York being there, and everybody well disposed and in expectation of them; but my Lord Ashly, on whom he relied and for whose sake this day was pitched on, that he might be sure to be there among the rest of his friends, stayed too long, till the Duke of York and the company thought unfit to stay longer; and so the day lost, and God knows when he will ever have so good a one again as long as he lives. And this was the man of the whole company that he hath made most interest to gain, and now most depended upon him.

So up and down the House a while; and then to the Plasterers and there saw the figure of my face taken from the Mold; and it is most admirably like, and I will have another made before I take it away; and therefore I away and to the Temple, and thence to my cousin Turner's; where, having the last night been told by*ᵇ* her that she had drawn me for her Valentine, I did this day call at the New*ᶜ* Exchange and bought her a pair of green silk stockings¹ and garters and shoe-strings, and two pair of Jessimy-gloves, all coming to about 28*s* – and did give them her this noon. At the Change, I did at my bookseller's shop accidentally fall into talk with Sir Sam. Tuke about Trees and Mr. Evelings garden;² and I do find him, I think a little conceited but a man of very fine discourse as any I ever heard almost – which I was mighty glad of.

a repl. '14'   *b* repl. 'my'   *c* repl. 'Ch'-

---

1. The Duke of York at about this time said that there was no hope for a leg unless it was clothed in green: Gramont, p. 176.

2. Tuke (an original F.R.S.; a friend of John Evelyn and a relative of his wife) was the author of the play *The adventures of five hours*, which Pepys saw later that day. Evelyn's gardens at Sayes Court were among the finest in England: see above, vi. 97 & n. 1.

I dined at my cousin Turner's, and my wife also, and her
husband there; and after dinner my wife and I endeavoured to
make a visit to Ned Pickering, but he not at home nor his lady.
And therefore back again and took up my cousin Turner, and
to my cousin Roger's lodgings and there*a* find him pretty well
again, and his wife mighty kind and merry and did make mighty
much of us; and I believe he is married to a very good woman.
Here was also Bab and Betty,[1] who have not their clothes yet,
and therefore cannot go out; otherwise I would have had them
abroad tomorrow; but the poor girls mighty kind to us, and we
must show them kindness also. Here, in Suffolke-street, lives
Mall Davis;[2] and we did see her coach come for her to her door,
a mighty pretty fine coach. Here we stayed an hour or two,
and then carried Turner home and there stayed and talked a while;
and then my wife and I to White-hall and there, by means of
Mr. Cooling, did get into the play, the only one we have seen
this winter;[3] it was *The Five Hours Adventure*;[4] but I sat so
far, I could not hear well, nor was there any pretty women that
I did see but my wife, who sat in my Lady Foxe's pew[5] with her.
The house very full; and late before done, so that it was past 11
before we got home – but we were well pleased with seeing it;
and so to supper (where it happened that there was no bread in
the house, which was an unusual case) and so to bed.

16. Up and to the office, where all the morning, my head
full of business of the office now at once on my hand; and so at
noon home to dinner, where I find some things of W Batelier's
come out of France; among which, some clothes for my wife,
wherein she is likely to lead me to the expense of so much money

a repl. 'with'

---

1. See above, p. 446, n. 3.

2. The actress who had left the
Duke of York's Company to become
the King's mistress: above, p. 24.
(A).

3. I.e. the only private performance
at Whitehall (probably staged in the
Great Hall). Richard Cooling was
secretary to the Lord Chamberlain.
(A).

4. See above, iv. 8 & n. 2. (A).

5. As Clerk of the Green Cloth Sir
Stephen Fox had a private seat or
box.

as vexed me; but I seemed so, more then I at this time was, only to prevent her taking too much – and she was mighty calm under it. But I was mightily pleased with another picture of the King of France's head, of Nantueil's, bigger then the other which he brought over,[1] that pleases me infinitely. And so to the office, where busy all the afternoon, though my eyes mighty bad with the light of the candles last night; which was*a* so great as to make my eyes sore all this day, and doth teach me, by a manifest experiment, that it is only too much light that doth make my eyes sore.

Nevertheless, with the help of my Tube, and being desirous of easing my mind of five or six days Journall, I did adventure to write it down from ever since this day sennit, and I think without hurting my eyes any more then they were before; which was very much. And so home to supper and to bed.

17. Up, and with W. Hewer with me to Lincoln's Inne by appointment, to have spoke with Mr. Pedly about Mrs. Goldsborough's business and Mrs. Weavers,[2] but he was gone out; and so I (with Mr. Castle, the son-in-law of Weaver) to Whitehall to look for him, but did not find him; but here I did meet with several and talked, and do hear only that the King dining yesterday at the Duch Embassadors, after dinner they drank and were pretty merry; and among the rest of the King's company, there was that worthy fellow my Lord of Rochester and T. Killigrew, whose mirth and raillery offended the former so much, that he did give T. Killigrew a box on the ear in the King's presence; which doth*b* much give offence to the people here at Court, to see how cheap the King makes himself, and the more for*c* that the King hath not only passed by the thing and pardoned it to Rochester already, but this very morning the King did publicly walk up and down, and Rochester I saw with him, as free

a repl. 'troub'-   *b* repl. 'did'   *c* repl. 'from'

---

1. See above, p. 427 & n. 1. The 'bigger head' of Louis XIV is PL 2978, no. 227 (Petitjean and Wickert, no. 138). (OM).

2. Concerning Pepys's Brampton property. Nicholas Pedley was a lawyer who acted for Pepys in several matters of this sort.

as ever, to the King's everlasting shame to have so idle a rogue his companion.[1]   How T. Killigrew takes it, I do not hear.

I do also this day hear that my Lord Privy Seale doth accept to go Lieutenant into Ireland; but whether it be true or no, I cannot tell.[2]   So calling at my shoemaker's and paying him to this day, I home*a* to dinner; and in the afternoon to Collonell Middleton's house to the burial*b* of his wife, where we are all invited, and much more company, and had each of us a ring.[3] And so towards evening to our church, where there was a sermon preached by Mills; and so home.   At church, there was my Lord Brouncker and Mrs. Williams in our pew, the first time they were ever there or that I knew that either of them would go to church.   At home comes Castle to me, to desire me to go to Mr. Pedly this night, he being to go out of town tomorrow morning – which I therefore did by hackney-coach, first going to White-hall to meet with Sir W. Coventry, but missed him; but here I had a pleasant *rancontre* of a lady in mourning, that by the little light I had seemed handsome;   I passing by her, I did observe she looked back again and again upon me, I suffering her to go before, and it being now duske.   I observed*c* she went into the little passage towards the privy water-gate, and I fallowed but missed her;   but coming back again, I observed she returned and went to go out of the Court.   I fallowed her, and took occasion in the new passage now built, where the walke is to be,[4] to take her by the hand to lead her through;   which she willingly accepted, and I led her to the great gate and there left her, she

---

a repl. same symbol blotted   *b* repl. 'birth'   symbol blotted

---

1. According to an account by Sandwich (Sandwich MSS, Journals, ix. 116–18), Killigrew had railed at Rochester for keeping his wife in the country. Rochester was forbidden the court and took himself off to France. See also newsletter accounts in BM, Add. 36916, f. 127r; *Bulstrode Papers*, i. 91.

2. Lord Robartes had accepted the

office, while still remaining Lord Privy Seal, on 14 February. He was formally appointed Lord-Lieutenant on 3 May 1669.

3. The burial was on the 16th: *Harl. Soc. Reg.*, 46/207; cf. *CSPD 1668–9*, p. 195. For funeral rings, see above, ii. 74, n. 2.

4. Cf. above, p. 269 & n. 3.

telling me*ᵃ* of her own accord that she was going as far as Charing-
cross; but my boy was at the*ᵇ* gate, and so yo durst not go out con
her – which vexed me; and my mind (God forgive me) did run
après her todo the night,*ᵇ* though I have reason to thank God,
and so I do now, that I was not tempted to go further. So to
Lincoln's Inne,*ᶜ* where to Mr. Pedly, with whom I spoke and
[did] my business presently. And I find him a man of very good
language and mighty civil, and I believe very upright. And so
home, where W Batelier was and supped with us; and I did
reckon this night what I owed him,[1] and I do find that the things
my wife, of her own head, hath taken (together with my own,
which comes*ᵈ* not to above 5*l*) comes to above 22*l*. But it is the
last, and so I am the better contented – and they are things that
are not trifles, but clothes, gloves, shoes, hoods, &c; so after
supper, to bed.

18. Up, and to the office; and at noon home, expecting to
have this day seen*ᵉ* Babb and Betty Pepys here, but they came
not; and so after dinner, my wife and I to the Duke of York's
House to a play, and there saw *The Mad lover*, which doth not
please me so well as it used to do; only, Baterton's part still
pleases me.[2] But here, who should we have come to us but
Bab and Betty and Talbot,[3] the first play they were yet at;
and going to see us, and hearing by my boy, whom I sent to
them, that we were here, they came to us hither and happened
all of us to sit by my cousin Turner and The. And we carried
them home first, and then took Bab and Betty to our house,
where they lay and supped, and pretty merry; and very fine with
their new clothes, and good comely girls they are enough, and
very glad I am of their being with us; though I could very well
have been contented to have been without that charge. So they
to bed and we to bed.

a repl. 'him'   *b–b* garbled s.h.   *c* repl. 'cham'-
        d repl. same symbol   *e* repl. 'brought'

---

1. For the goods he had brought
back from France.
2. Betterton played the part of
Memnon in this tragi-comedy by
Fletcher; q.v. above, ii. 34, n. 3.   (A).
3. Children of Roger Pepys.

19.   Up, and after seeing the girls, who lodged in our bed
with their Mayd Martha (who hath been their father's*ᵃ* maid these
twenty years and more), I with Lord Brouncker to White-hall,
where all of us waited on the Duke of York; and after our usual
business done, W. Hewer and I to look my wife at the Black
Lion, Mercer's, but she is gone home; and so I home and there
dined, and W Battelier and W. Hewer with us; and all the
afternoon I at the office while the young people went to see
Bedlam;¹ and at night home to them to supper, and pretty
merry; only, troubled with a great cold at this time – and my
eyes very bad, ever since Monday night last that the light of the
candles spoiled me.   So to bed.

This morning, among other things, talking with Sir W.
Coventry, I did propose to him my putting in to serve in Parliament, if there should, as the world begins to expect, be a new
one chose.   He likes it mightily, both for the King's and service's
sake, and the Duke of York's, and will propound it to the Duke
of York.   And I confess, if there be one, I would be glad to be in.²

20.   Up, and all the morning at the office, and then home to
dinner; and after dinner, out with my wife and my two girls
to the Duke of York's House and there saw *The Gratefull Servant*,
a pretty good play, and which I have forgot that ever I did see.³
And thence with them to Mrs. Gotiers, the Queen's tire-woman's,
for a pair of locks for my wife (she is a oldish French woman,
but with a pretty hand as most I have seen); and so home and to
supper, W Battelier and W. Hewer with us; and so my cold
being great, and the greater by my having left my coat at my

a   repl. 'mother's'

---

1. The hospital for lunatics, situated
near Bishopsgate; commonly visited
by sight-seers: cf. James Yonge,
Journal (ed. Poynter), p. 158 [1678].
2. For Pepys's parliamentary career,
see above, pp. 376–7 & n.
3. The play was a tragicomedy by
James Shirley, licensed in 1629 and
published in 1630. There is no
previous notice of it in the diary.
Downes (p. 27) notes that the title-
role, Dulcino, was played by Mrs
Long, and that this, her first appearance 'in Man's Habit, prov'd as
Beneficial to the Company, as several
succeeding new Plays'.   (A).

tailor's tonight and come home in a thinner that I borrowed there, I went to bed before them, and slept pretty well.

21. *Lords day.* Up, and with my wife and two girls to church, they very fine; and so home, where comes my Cosen Roger and his wife (I*ᵃ* having sent for them) to dine with us, and there comes in by chance also Mr. Sheply, who is come to town with my Lady Paulina, who is desperately sick and is gone to Chelsy to the old house where my Lord himself was once sick – where I doubt my Lord means to visit her, more for young Mrs. Beck's sake then for hers.[1] Here we dined with W Battelier, and W. Hewer with us (these two girls making it necessary that they be always with us, for I am not company light enough to be always merry with them); and so sat talking all the afternoon, and then Sheply went away first, and then my cousin Roger and his wife; and so I to my office to write down my journall, and so home to my chamber to do a little business there, my papers being in mighty disorder and likely so to continue while these girls are with us. In the evening comes W Batelier and his sisters and*ᵇ* supped and talked with us, and so spent the evening, myself being somewhat out of order because of my eyes, which have never been well since last Sundy's reading at Sir W. Coventry's chamber. And so after supper to bed.

22. Up and betimes to White-hall; but there the Duke of York is gone abroad a-hunting and therefore, after a little stay there, I into London with Sir H. Cholmly, talking all the way of Tanger matters, wherein I find him troubled from some reports lately from Norwood[2] (who is his great enemy and I doubt an ill man) of some decay of the Molle and a breach made therein by the Sea, to a great value. He set me down at the end of Leadenhall-street, and so I home and after dinner with my wife (in her morning-gown) and the two girls dressed, to Unthankes, where my wife dresses herself, having her gown this day laced, and a new

a repl. 'having'   *b* repl. 'Mary'

---

1. Betty Becke had been Sand-wich's mistress, c. 1662–3.

2. Deputy-Governor of Tangier.

petticoat, and so is endeed very fine; and in the evening I do carry them to White-hall, and there did without much trouble get them into the playhouse there, in a good place among^a the Ladies of Honour, and myself also sat in the pit; and there by and by comes the King and Queen, and they begun – *Bartholomew fayre*[1] – but I like no play here so well as at the common playhouse.[2]   Besides that, my eyes being very ill since last Sunday and this day sennit with the light of the candles, I was in mighty pain to defend myself now from the light of the candles.[3]   After the play done, we met with W Batelier and W. Hewer and Tall. Pepys, and they fallow us in a hackney-coach; and we all stopped at Hercules-Pillars and there I did give them the best supper I could, and pretty merry; and so home between 11 and 12 at night and so to bed, mightily well pleased with this day's work.

23.   Up, and to the office, where all the morning.   And then home and put a mouthful of victuals in my mouth; and by a hackney-coach fallowed my wife and the girls, who are gone by 11 a-clock, thinking to have seen a new play at the Duke of York's House;[4] but I do find them staying at my tailor's, the play not being today, and therefore I now took them to Westminster Abbey and there did show them all the tombs very finely,

a repl. 'by'

---

1. The comedy by Ben Jonson (q.v. above, ii. 117, n. 1), acted probably in the Great Hall, which, as Pepys records at 20 April 1665, had been converted into a theatre for private performances. (A).
2. There were good reasons for this opinion. The acoustics were not good: above, vii. 347 & n. 4. Unlike the public theatres, it had neither an apron stage nor proscenium doors (see E. Boswell, *Restoration court stage*, pp. 38–9), and as most Elizabethan and Restoration plays were written for stages equipped with these structures,

it would not always be easy to present them there. (A).
3. The chandeliers, which, together with footlights, were the chief means of illuminating the stage. (A).
4. The theatres usually opened at noon, though performances did not begin until 3.30 p.m. Early attendance was necessary to secure a seat when a new play was being performed. The play intended to have its premiere on this day was probably Shadwell's *The Royal Shepherdess*, first acted on 25 February. (A).

having one with us alone (there being other company this day to see the tombs, it being Shrove Tuesday); and here we did see, by perticular favour, the body of Queen Katherine of Valois, and had her upper part of her body in my*a* hands.[1] And I did kiss her mouth, reflecting upon it that I did kiss a Queen, and that this was my birthday, 36 year old, that I did first kiss a Queen. But here this man, who seems to understand well, tells me that the saying is not true that says she was never buried, for she was buried; only, when Henry the 7th built his chapel, it was taken up and laid in this wooden coffin; but I did there see that in it, the body was buried in a leaden one, which remains under the body to this day.

Thence to the Duke of York's playhouse, and there finding*b* the play begun, we homeward to the glass-house and there showed my cousins the making*c* of glass,[2] and had several things made with great content; and among others, I had one or two singing-glasses made, which make an echo to the voice, the first that ever I saw; but so thin that the very breath broke one or two of them.[3] So home, and thence to Mr. Batelier's, where we

---

a repl. 'our'   *b* repl. 'saw'   *c* repl. 'work'

---

1. She was the beautiful Queen of Henry V and had died in 1437 at the age of 36. She had been buried in the Lady Chapel which was pulled down by Henry VII, and her coffin now rested on the s. side of the tomb of Henry V at the e. end of the Confessor's chapel. It contained 'part of [her] *skelleton* and parched body . . . (from the waste upwards) . . . which is not frequently shown to any, but as an especial favour by some of the Chief Officers of the Church': H. Keepe, *Monumenta Westmonasterium* (1682), pp. 155–6. Dart (1742) reported that it was still to be seen: 'the Bones firmly united, and thinly cloth'd with Flesh, like Scrapings of tann'd Leather . . .': *Westmonasterium*, ii. 39. After at

least two further moves the body came to rest in Henry V's chantry in 1878.

2. There were glasshouses at various times on each side of the Fleet river and near the playhouse here mentioned. Glass House Alley (north out of Tudor St) still bears witness to them. In 1696 there were said to be 24 glasshouses in London and Southwark, making a variety of glass: looking-glass, crown-glass, flint- and bottle-glass etc. See J. Houghton, *Coll. for improvement husbandry and trade*, 15 May 1696. (R).

3. The glasses vibrated in sympathy when certain notes were sung, their sound continuing after the voice ceased. Cf. Birch, ii. 453. (E).

supped, and had a good supper; and here was Mr. Gumbleton, and after supper some fiddles and so to dance; but my eyes were so out of order that I had little pleasure this night at all, though I was glad to see the rest merry.[1]   And so about midnight home and to bed.

24.   Lay long in bed, both being sleepy and my eyes bad, and myself having a great cold, so as I was hardly able to speak; but however, by and by up and to the office; and at noon home[a] with my people to dinner; and then I to the office again and there till the evening, doing of much business; and at night my wife sends for me to W Hewer's lodging, where I find two[b] most [fine] chambers of his, so finely furnished and all so rich and neat, that I was mightily pleased with him and them;[2] and here only my wife and I and the two girls, and had a mighty neat dish of custards and tarts, and good drink and talk; and so away home to bed, with infinite content at this[c] his treat, for it was mighty pretty and everything mighty rich.

25.   All the morning at the office; at noon home and eat a bit myself, and then fallowed my wife and girls to the Duke of York's House and there before one, but the house infinite full; where by and by the King and Court comes, it being a new play, or an old one new-vamp[ed] by Shadwell, called *The Royall Shepheardesse*;[3] but the silliest for words and design, and every-

----

a repl. 'to'   b repl. 'a'   c repl. 'his'

----

1. This occasion (rather than that reported at 25 February 1664) appears to be the one which Pepys recalled in 1677, when he set down an account of his health.   He wrote then that it was after exposing his eyes to the brightness of the flames of the glasshouse that he began to suffer attacks of pain when reading: Rawl. A 185, f. 208*v* (printed in Bryant, ii. 407).
2. These were possibly the same fine lodgings, at William Mercer's

house, St Olave's parish, which Pepys had admired on 6 June 1666.   By this time Hewer was rich enough to offer diamonds to Elizabeth Pepys and to buy portraits for himself: above, pp. 7, 261.
3. A pastoral tragicomedy by Shadwell, published in 1669.   This is the first record of a performance.   It was based on John Fountains's *The rewards of virtue*, published in 1661. (A).

thing, that ever I saw in my whole life – there being nothing in the world pleasing in it but a good martiall dance of pike-men, where Harris and another do handle their pikes in a dance to admiration – but never less satisfied with a play in my life. Thence to the office I, and did a little business; and so home to supper with my girls, and pretty merry; only my eyes, which continue very bad, and my cold, that I cannot speak at all, do trouble me.

26. Was forced to send my excuse to the Duke of York for my not attending him with my fellows this day, because of my cold;[1] and was the less troubled because I was thereby out of the way to offer my proposals about pursers till the Surveyor hath delivered his notions; which he is to do today, about something hc hath to offer relating to the Navy in general, which I would be glad to see and peruse before I offer what I have to say.

So lay long in bed, and then up and to my office; and so to dinner, and then, though I could not speak, yet I went with my wife and girls to the King's playhouse to show them that, and there saw *The Faythfull Shepherdess*;[2] but Lord, what an empty house, there not being, as I could tell the people, so many as to make up above 10*l* in the whole house – the being of a new play at the other House, I suppose, being the cause; though it be so silly a play, that I wonder how there should be enow people to go thither two days together and not leave more to fill this house. The emptiness of the house took away our pleasure a great deal, though I liked it the better; for that I plainly discern the music is the better, by how much the House the emptier.

Thence home, and again to W Hewer's; and had a pretty little treat and spent an hour or two my voyce being wholly taken away with my cold; and so home and to bed.

27. Up and at the office all the morning, where I could speak but a little. At noon home to dinner, and all the afternoon till

1. The hour of the meeting had been advanced to 8.30 a.m., it being a sermon-day at court: *CSPD 1668-9*, p. 210.

2. A pastoral drama by Fletcher; see above, iv. 182, n. 3. (A).

night busy at the office again, where forced to speak low and dictate. But that that troubles me most is my eyes, which are still mighty bad, night and day. And so home at night to talk and sup with my cousins;[1] and so all of us in mighty good humour to bed.

28. *Lords day.* Up, and got my wife to read to me a copy of what the Surveyor offered to the Duke of York on*a* Friday, he himself putting it into my hand to read; but Lord, it is a poor silly thing ever to think to bring it in practice in the King's Navy; it is to have the Captains to endent for all stores and victuals; but upon so silly grounds to my thinking, and ignorance of the present instructions of Officers, that I am ashamed to hear it.[2] However, do take a copy of it for my future use and answering; and so to church, where God forgive me, I did most of the time gaze on the fine milliner's wife in Fanchurch-street,[3] who was at our church today; and so home to dinner. And after dinner, to write down my journall and then abroad by coach with my cousins to their father's, where we are kindly received; but he is in great pain for his Man Arthur, who he fears is now dead, having been desperately sick, and speaks so much of him, that my Cozen his wife[4] and I did make mirth of it, and call him Arthur of Bradly.[5] After staying here a little, and eat and drank, and she*b* gave me some ginger-bread made in cakes like chocolatte,

a repl. 'yesterday'　　　　*b* repl. 'he'

---

1. Roger Pepys's daughters, Bab and Betty, who had been staying with Pepys since 18 February.

2. Middleton's memorandum has not been traced. The experiment had been tried in 1651–5, without success. Writing about a similar proposal made c. 1673, Pepys commented, 'Tis too troublesome and small a matter for the commanders to be charged with finding . . . fire and candle etc.': *Cat.*, i. 163–4; PL 2871, pp. 736–7. Cf. Thomas Wilson to

Pepys (undated memo.): Rawl. A 174, f. 267r.

3. Later identified as Mrs Clerke: below, p. 518.

4. Esther, newly-married wife of Roger Pepys.

5. The hero of a popular ballad. The refrain ran, 'With oh! brave Arthur O'Bradley! O, rare Arthur O'Bradley! Arthur O'Bradley, oh!': W. Chappell and J. W. Ebsworth (ed.), *Roxburghe Ballads*, vii. 312+.

very good, made by a friend, I carried him and her to my cousin Turners, where we stayed, expecting her coming from church; but she coming not, I went to her husband's chamber in the Temple and thence fetched her, she having been there alone ever since sermon, staying till the evening to walk home on foot,*a* her horses being ill. This I did, and brought her home; and after talking there a while and agreeing to be all merry at my house on Tuesdy next, I away home; and there spent the evening talking and reading with my wife and Mr. Pelling, and yet much troubled with my cold, it hardly suffering me to speak, we to bed.

a repl. 'h'-

MARCH.

1. Up and to White-hall to the Committee of Tanger, but it did not meet. But here I do hear first that my Lady Paulina Montagu did die yesterday;[1] at which I went to my Lord's lodgings, but he is shut up with sorrow and so not to be spoken with; and therefore I returned and to Westminster hall, where I have not been I think in some months; and here the Hall was very full, the King having, by commission to some Lords, this day prorogued the Parliament till the 19th. of October next;[2] at which I am glad, hoping to have time to go over to France this year.[3] But I was most of all surprized this morning by my Lord Bellasses, who by appointment met me[a] at Auditor Wood's at the Temple and[b] tells me of a Duell designed between the Duke of Buckingham and my Lord Halifax or Sir W. Coventry – the challenge being carried by Harry Savill, but prevented by my Lord Arlington and the King told of it. And this was all the discourse at Court this day. But I meeting Sir W. Coventry in the Duke of York's chamber, he would not own it to me, but told me that he was a man of too much peace to meddle with fighting; and so it rested. But the talk is full in the town

a repl. 'at'   b repl. 'of'

---

1. She was Sandwich's second daughter and had died of 'a consumption': *Bulstrode Papers*, i. 93. 'Dear sweet . . . Paulina, in her 20th year . . .', Sandwich wrote, had died at 9 a.m. 'at the upper Chelsey at Mrs Becks. house': Sandwich MSS, Journals, ix. 120.

2. *LJ*, xii. 249–50.
3. He went with his wife and her brother Balty in late August, travelling through Holland and the Spanish Netherlands to Paris, and returning on 20 October. (The last date is given in PL 2874, f. 387r.) Parliament reassembled on 19 October.

of the business.[1] Thence, having walked some turns with my Cosen Pepys,[2] and most people by their discourse believing that this Parliament will never sit more, I away to several places to look after things against tomorrow's feast; and so home to dinner and thence, after noon, my wife and I out by hackney-coach and spent the afternoon in several places, doing several things at the Change and elsewhere against tomorrow; and among others, I did also bring home a piece of my Face cast in plaster, for to make a vizard upon for my eyes; and so home, where W Batelier came and sat with us; and there, after many doubts, did resolve to go on with our feast and dancing tomorrow; and so after supper left the maids to make clean the house and to lay the cloth and other things against tomorrow, and we to bed.

2. Up and at the office till noon, when home; and there I find my company come – *viz*, Madam Turner, Dike, The and Betty Turner, and Mr. Bellwood, formerly their father's clerk but now set up for himself,[3] a conceited silly fellow but one they make mightily of – my Cosen Roger Pepys and his wife and two daughters. And I had a noble*ᵃ* dinner for them as I almost ever

a repl. 'f'-

---

1. It was Coventry who was involved in this abortive duel and it led to his disgrace. The quarrel was provoked by Buckingham's plan to ridicule Coventry and his friends in a play (*The country gentleman*) written by himself and Sir Robert Howard: see below, p. 471 & n. 2. The King caused the offending scene to be cut out. At a Council meeting on the 3rd, the challenge which Coventry had sent to Buckingham was construed as a conspiracy to cause the death of a privy councillor, and therefore as felony under a statute of 3 Henry VII. Coventry and his second, Henry Savile (his nephew),

were imprisoned on the 4th; on the 5th Coventry was relieved of his offices. The King was delighted to be rid of him. The confusion about whether the challenger was Coventry or Halifax was common at the time (see e.g. HMC, *Portland*, iii. 311). Coventry's peaceableness was well-known. PRO, PC 2/61, p. 230; BM, Add. 36916, ff. 128r, 129r; C. H. Hartmann, *The King my brother*, p. 245; W. D. Christie, *Shaftesbury*, ii. 3–4.

2. Roger Pepys, M.P. for Cambridge borough.

3. As a lawyer.

had, and mighty merry; and perticularly, myself pleased with
looking on Betty Turner – who is mighty pretty.   After dinner
we fell one to one talk, and another to another, and looking over
my house and closet and things, and The Turner to write a letter
to a lady in the country, in which I did now and then put in
half a dozen words, and sometimes five or six lines, and then
she as much, and made up a long and good letter, she being
mighty witty really, though troublesome-humoured with it.
And thus till night, that our music came and the office ready, and
candles; and also W Batelier and his sister Susan came, and also
Will How and two gentlemen more, strangers, which at my
request yesterday he did bring to dance, called Mr. Ireton and
Mr. Starkey; we fell to dancing and continued, only with intermission for a good supper, till 2 in the morning, the music being
Greeting and another most excellent violin and Theorbo, the
best in town; and so, with mighty mirth and pleased with their
dancing of Jiggs afterward, several of them, and among others
Betty Turner, who did it mighty prettily; and lastly, W. Batelier's blackmore and blackmore-maid, and then to a country-
dance again; and so broke up with extraordinary pleasure, as
being one of the days and nights of my life spent with the greatest
content, and that which I can but hope to repeat again a few
times in*a* my whole life.   This done, we parted, the strangers
home, and I did lodge my cousin Pepys and his*b* wife in*c* our blue
chamber – my cousin Turner, her sister, and The in our best
chamber – Babb, Betty, and Betty Turner in our own chamber;
and myself and my wife in the maid's bed, which is very good –
our maids*d* in the coachman's bed – the coachman with the boy
in his settle-bed; and Tom where he uses to lie; and so I did to
my great content lodge at once in my house, with great ease,
fifteen, and eight of them strangers of quality. ⟨My wife
this day put on first her French gown, called a *Sac*,¹ which
becomes her very well, brought her over by W. Batelier.⟩*e*

---

a repl. 'in life' and full stop   *b* repl. 'is'   *c* repl. 'our'
d repl. 'best'   *e* addition crowded into bottom of page

---

1. An early mention of this style, fashionable at various times.

3. Up after a very good night's rest, and was called upon by Sir H. Cholmly, who was with me an hour; and though acquainted, did not yet stay to talk with my company I had in the house, but away. And then I to my guests and got them to breakfast, and then parted by coaches, and I did in mine carry my ⟨she⟩-cousin Pepys and her*a* daughters home, and there left them. And so to White-hall, where W. Hewer met me; and he and I took a turn in St. James's park and in the Mall did meet Sir W. Coventry and Sir J Duncomb and did speak with them about some business before the Lords of the Treasury; but I did find them more then usually busy, though I knew not then the reason of it, though I guess it by what fallowed tomorrow. Thence to Dancres the painter's and there saw my picture of Greenwich,[1] finished to my very good content, though this manner of distemper doth make the figures not so pleasing as in oyle.[2] So to Unthankes and there took up my wife and carried her to the Duke of York's playhouse and there saw an old play, the first time acted these 40 years, called *The Lady's tryall*, acted only by the young people of the House,[3] but the House*b* very full. But it is but a sorry play, and the worse by how much my head is out of humour by being a little sleepy and my legs weary since last night. So after the play, we to the New Exchange and so called at my cousin Turner's; and there meeting Mr. Bellwood, did hear how my Lord Mayor, being invited this day to dinner at the Reader's at the Temple, and endeavouring to carry his sword upp, the students did pull it down and forced him to go and stay all the day in a private counsellor's chamber until the Reader himself could get the young gentlemen to dinner; and then my Lord Mayor did retreat out of the Temple by

a repl. 'his'
b repl. same symbol badly formed

---

1. See above, p. 423 & n. 1. (OM).
2. Cf. above, pp. 434–5 & n. (OM).
3. I.e. by the junior members of the company. The play was a tragi-comedy by John Ford, first acted in 1638, and published in 1639. (A).

stealth, with his sword upp.[1] This doth make great heat among the students; and my Lord Mayor did send to the King, and also I hear that Sir Rd. Browne did cause the drums to beat for the train-bands; but all is over, only I hear that the students do resolve to try the Charter of the City. So we home, and betimes to bed and slept well all night.

4. Up, and a while at the office; but thinking to have Mr. Povy's business today at the Committee for Tanger, I left the Board and away to White-hall; where in the first court I[a] did meet Sir Jere. Smith, who did tell me that Sir W. Coventry was just now sent to the tower about the business of his challenging the Duke of Buckingham, and so was also Harry Savill to the Gate-house – which, as a gentleman and of the Duke of York's bed-chamber, I heard afterward that the Duke of York is mightily incensed at, and doth appear very high to the King that he might not be sent thither, but to the Tower – this being done only in contempt to him.[2] This news of Sir W Coventry did strike me to the heart; and with reason, for by this and my Lord of Ormond's business, I do doubt that the Duke of Buckingham will be so fleshed, that he will not stop at anything but be forced to do anything now, as thinking it not safe to end here; and Sir W. Coventry being gone, the King will have never a good counsellor, nor the Duke of York any sure friend to stick

a   repl. 'a'

---

1. The Lord Mayor was Sir William Turner; the Reader Christopher Goodfellow; the inn, Inner Temple; the counsellor, John Phillips (Phelps), Auditor of the Receipt in the Exchequer.   The Temple claimed immunity from civic jurisdiction by virtue of its origin as an ecclesiastical liberty.   For the dispute, see below, pp. 511-12 & n.; LRO, Repert. 74, ff. 116, 232; ib., Historical Papers, 109 ('Narrative of the Temples disorder'); the French ambassador's account in PRO, PRO 31/121, ff. 201+; BM, Egerton 2539, f. 329; ib., Add. 19526, f. 182*v*; HMC, *Le Fleming*, p. 62; *Bulstrode Papers*, i. 93, 97; John B. Williamson, *Hist. Temple*, pp. 478-81.

2. Savile, who had carried Coventry's challenge, was this day transferred 'for honours sake' to the Tower: HMC, *Portland*, iii. 311; *CSPD 1668-9*, p. 222. Both he and Coventry were released on the 20th: *CSPD*, op. cit., p. 240.

to him – nor any good man will be left to advise what is good. This, therefore, doth heartily trouble*a* me, as anything that ever I heard. So up into the House and met with several people, but the Committee did not meet. And the whole House I find full of this business of Sir W. Coventry's, and most men very sensible of the cause and effects of it. So meeting with my Lord Bellasses, he told me the perticulars of this matter; that it arises about a quarrel which Sir W. Coventry had with*b* the Duke of Buckingham about a design between him*c* and Sir Rob. Howard to bring him into a play at the King's House;[1] which W. Coventry not enduring, did by H. Savill send a letter to the Duke of Buckingham that he had a desire to speak with him – upon which, the Duke of Buckingham did bid Holmes (his champion ever since my [Lord] of Shrewsbury's business)[2] go to him to know the business; but H. Savill would not tell it to any but himself, and therefore did go presently to the Duke of Buckingham and told him that his Uncle Coventry was a person of honour, and was sensible of his Grace's liberty taken of abusing him and that he had a desire of satisfaction*d* and would fight with him. But that here they were interrupted by my Lord Chamberlains coming in, who was*e* commanded to go to bid the Duke of Buckingham to come to the King, Holmes having discovered* it. He told me that the King did last night at the Council ask the Duke of Buckingham, upon his honour, whether he received any challenge*f* from W. Coventry; which he confessed that he had. And then the King*g* asking W. Coventry, he told him that he did not owne what the Duke of Buckingham had said, though it was not fit for him to give him a direct contradiction. But being by the King put upon declaring upon his honour the matter, he answered that he had understood that many hard questions had upon this business been moved to some

a repl. 'afflict'   b MS. 'to'   c repl. 'B'
d repl. 'just'–   e repl. 'had'
f repl. 'I'–   g MS. 'here'

---

1. For the play, see below, p. 471, nn. 2, 3. (A).

2. The duel fought over the Countess: see above, pp. 26–7 & n.

lawyers,[1] and that therefore he was unwilling to declare anything that might from his own mouth render him obnoxious* to his Majesty's displeasure, and therefore prayed to be excused – which the King did think fit to interpret to be a confession, and so gave warrant that night for his commitment to the Tower.[2] Being very much troubled at this, I away by coach*a* homeward, and directly to the Tower, where I find him in one Mr. Bennet's house, son to Major*b* Bayly, one of the Officers of the Ordnance, in the Bricke-tower – where I find him busy with my Lord Halifax and his brother;[3] so I would not stay to interrupt them, but only to give him comfort and offer my service to him; which he kindly and cheerfully received, only owning his being troubled for the King his master's displeasure, which I suppose is the ordinary form and will of persons in this condition; and so I parted, with great content that I had so earlily seen him there; and so going out, did meet Sir Jer. Smith going to meet me, who had newly been with Sir W. Coventry; and so he and I by water to Redriffe, and so walked to Deptford, where I have not been I think these twelve months; and there to the Treasurer's house,[4] where the Duke of York is,*c* and his Duchesse; and there we find them at dinner in the great room, unhung, and there was with them my Lady Duchess of Monmouth, the Countess of Falmouth, Castlemayne, Henrietta Hide my Lady Hinching-brooke's sister, and my Lady Peterbrough. And after dinner, Sir Jer. Smith and I were invited down to dinner with some of the Maids of Honour; *viz.*, Mrs. Ogle, Blake,[5] and Howard (which did me good to have the honour to dine with and look on); and the Mother of the Maids,[6] and Mrs. Howard,*d* the mother of the Maid of Honour of that name, and the Duke's house-keeper here. Here was also Monsieur Blancfort, Sir Rd. Powell,

a repl. 'l'-   *b* repl. 'Mr'.   *c* repl. 'his'
d repl. 'house'

---

1. The challenge had been construed as a felony: above, p. 463, n. 1.
2. Secretary's warrant, 3 March: *CSPD 1668–9*, p. 222.
3. Henry Coventry, the diplomatist, was Sir William's brother; Halifax his nephew.

4. An official residence used normally by the Navy Treasurer.
5. Margaret Blagge, the young friend of Evelyn.
6. Lucy Wise. For the office of 'Mother', see above, iii. 83, n. 6.

Collonell Villers, Sir Jona. Trelany, and others. And here drank most excellent and great variety and plenty of wines, more then I have drank at once these seven years, but yet did me no great hurt. Having dined and very merry, and understanding by Blancfort how angry the Duke of York was about their offering to send Savill to the Gate-house among the rogues – and then observing how this company, both the ladies and all, are of a gang and did drink a health to the union of the two brothers[1] – and talking of others as their enemies – they parted; and so*a* we up, and there I did find the Duke of York and Duchess with all the great ladies, sitting upon a carpet on the ground, there being no chairs, playing at "I love my love with an A because*b* he is so and so; and I hate him with an A because of this and that;"*c*[2] and some of them, but perticularly the Duchess herself and my Lady Castlemaine, were very witty. This done, they took barge, and I with Sir J. Smith to Captain Cox's and there to talk, and left them and other company to drink while I slunk out to Bagwells and there saw her and her mother and our late*d* maid Nell,[3] who cried for joy to see me; but I had no time for pleasure there nor could stay; but after drinking, I back to the yard, having a month's mind para have had*e* a bout with Nell – which I believe I could have had – and may another time.*e* So to Cox's and thence walked with Sir J. Smith back to Redriffe, and so by water home; and there my wife mighty angry for my absence and fell mightily out; but not being certain of anything, but think[s] only that Pierce or Knepp were there, and did ask me, and I perceive the boy, many questions, but I did answer her; and so after much ado, did go to bed and lie quiet all night; but had another bout with me in the morning, but I did

---

a repl. 'that'   b repl. 'and'
c quotation enclosed in large square brackets   d repl. 'lade'
e–e garbled s.h.

---

1. The King and the Duke of York, now estranged by Coventry's dismissal.

2. A game later said to have been introduced 'at the Restoration . . . when nothing was thought of but Pleasure

and Gallantry . . .': *Gent. Mag.*, 8/80 (February 1738).

3. Pepys had employed several Nells; this was almost certainly Nell Payne: cf. above, viii. 276.

make shift to quiet her; but yet she was not fully satisfied, poor
wretch, in her mind, and thinks much at my taking so much
pleasure from her; which endeed is a fault, though I did not design
or foresee it when I went.

5. Up, and by water*a* to White-hall, where did a little
business with the Duke of York at our usual attending him;
and thence to my wife, who was with my coach at Unthankes,
though not very well of those upon her, and so home – to dinner.
And after dinner, I to the Tower, where I find Sir W. Coventry
with abundance of company with him; and after sitting a while
and hearing some merry discourse, and among others, of Mr.
Brouncker's being this*b* day summoned to Sir Wm. Morton –
one of the judges, to give in security for his good behaviour,
upon his words the other day to Sir John Morton, a Parliament-
[man], the other day at White-hall, who had heretofore spoke
very highly against Brouncker in the House.¹ I away and to All-
gate,*c* and walked forward toward White-chapel till my wife
overtook me with the coach,*d* it being a mighty fine afternoon;
and there we went the first time out of town with our coach and
horses, and went*e* as far as Bow, the spring beginning a little now
to appear, though the way be dirty; and so with great pleasure,
with the fore-part of our coach up, we spent the afternoon;
and so in the evening home and there busy at the office a while;
and so to bed, mightily pleased with being at peace with my
poor wife and with the pleasure we may hope to have with our
coach this summer, when the weather comes to be good.

                    a repl. 'coach'   *b* repl. 'carry'
         c repl. 'my wife'   *d* MS. 'c'-   *e* repl. 'so'

---

1. This day Henry Brouncker and
Sir John Morton had drawn swords
on each other in Whitehall and
Brouncker had been wounded: PRO,
SP 29/253, f. 17r. Morton was M.P.
for Poole, Dorset; he was not related
to the judge of King's Bench (Sir
William Morton) who now bound
his adversary to good behaviour.
There had been a sharp exchange in
the Commons between Sir John and
Brouncker on 18 April 1668, shortly
before Brouncker had been expelled
the House for his share in the naval
miscarriages of 1665: see Grey, i. 141;
above, p. 170.

6. Up and to the office, where all the morning. Only before the office, I stepped to Sir W. Coventry at the Tower and there had a great deal of discourse with him – among others, of the King's putting him out of the Council yesterday – with which he is well contented, as with what else*ᵃ* they can strip him of – he telling me, and so hath long, that he is weary and surfeited*ᵇ* of business.[1] But he joins with me in his fears that all will go to naught as matters are now managed. He told me the matter of the play that was intended for his abuse[2] – wherein they foolishly and sillily bring in two tables like that which he hath made, with a round hole in the middle, in his closet,*ᶜ* to turn himself in; and he is to be in one of them as maister, and Sir J. Duncomb in the other as his man or imitator – and their discourse in those tables, about the disposing of their books and papers, very foolish.[3] But that that he is offended with, is his being made so contemptible, as that any should dare to make a gentleman a subject for the mirth of the world; and that therefore he had told Tom. Killigrew[4] that he should tell his actors, whoever they were, that did offer at anything like representing him, that he would not complain to my Lord Chamberlain, which was too weak, nor get him beaten, as Sir Ch. Sidly is said to do,[5] but that he would

---

a repl. 'all'   *b* repl. 'surf'- badly formed   *c* MS. 'close'

---

1. He shortly afterwards retired to Minster Lovell in Oxfordshire, and for the rest of his life (he died in 1686), although serving in parliament, never returned to ministerial office.

2. This was *The country gentleman*, written jointly by Buckingham and Sir Robert Howard; banned before performance and never printed. A complete scribal copy has been discovered in the Folger Lib., Washington (MS. V. b. 228); see A. H. Scouten and R. D. Hume in *Times Lit. Supp.*, 28 September 1973, pp. 1105–6. Coventry was represented as the solemn and conceited Sir Cautious Trouble-all who is duped into marrying a barber's daughter. The practice of including caricatures in plays had grown of late: cf. above, p. 191 & n. 1; p. 435 & n. 3. (A).

3. In a scene contributed by Buckingham to Act III Sir Cautious Trouble-all (Coventry) demonstrates the use of his table to Sir Gravity Empty (Sir John Duncomb), showing how he opens it, sits on a swivel-stool in the middle, and consults papers about various parts of the world arranged on the periphery of the table. Pepys has a reference to the table at 4 July 1668: above, p. 255 & n. 2. (A).

4. Manager of the Theatre Royal, Bridges St, Drury Lane. (A).

5. See above, p. 435. (A).

cause his nose to be cut.   He told me the passage at the Council
much like what my Lord Bellasses told me.   He tells me how
the Duke of Buckingham did himself some time since desire to
join with him, of all men in England, and did bid him propound
to himself to be Chief Minister of State, saying that he would
bring it about; but that he refused to have anything to do with
any faction; and that the Duke of Buckingham did within these
few days say that of all men in England he would have chosen
W. Coventry to have joined intire with.   He tells me that he
fears their prevailing against the Duke of York; and that their
violence will force them to it, as being already beyond his pardon.
He repeated to me many examples of challengings of Privy-
Councillors and others; but never any proceeded against with
that severity which he is, it never amounting to others to more
then a little confinement.   He tells me of his being weary of the
Treasury; and of the folly, ambitions, and desire of popularity
of Sir Tho. Clifford, and yet the rudeness of his tongue and
passions when angry.[1]   This and much more discourse being
over, I with great pleasure came home to the office, where all
the morning; and at noon home to dinner and thence to the
office again, where very hard at work all the afternoon till night;
and then home to my wife to read to me, and to bed – my cold
having been now almost for three days quite gone from me.
This day,[a] my wife made it appear to me that my late entertainment this week cost me above 12l, a expense which I am almost
ashamed of, though it is but once in a great while, and is the end
for which in the most part we live, to have such a merry day
once or twice in a man's life.

7.   *Lords day*.   Up and to the office, busy till church time;
and then to church, where a dull sermon; and so home to dinner

---

a In the margin is '7' struck through.   Apparently the rest of this day's
entry was added when the next day's entry was begun.

---

1. This was not far from being the
general opinion of Clifford, though
not all would have agreed he was
foolish: cf. C. H. Hartmann, *Clifford*
of the Cabal, pp. 305+.   Even Evelyn,
who admired him, wrote of him as
'bold', 'ambitious' and 'Passionate':
iii. 470; iv. 20.

all alone with my wife, and then to even my journall to this day; and then to the Tower to see Sir W. Coventry, who had H. Jermin and a great many more with him, and more, while I was there, came in; so that I do hear that there was not less then 60 coaches there yesterday and*ª* the other day – which I hear also, that there is great exception taken at by the King and the Duke of Buckingham, but it cannot be helped. Thence home, and with our coach out and to Suffolke-street to see my cousin Pepys, but neither the old nor young at home; so to my cousin Turners and there stayed talking a little, and then back to Suffolke-street – where they not being yet come home, I to White-hall and there hear that there is letters come from Sir Tho. Allen that he hath made some kind of peace with Argier,[1] upon which the King and Duke of York, being to go out of town tomorrow, are met at my Lord Arlington's; so I there, and by Mr. Wren was desired to stay to see if there were occasion for their speaking with me; which I did, walking without with Ch. Porter,[2] talking of a great many things; and I perceive all the world is against the Duke of Buckingham his acting thus high, and do prophesy nothing but ruin from it. But he doth well observe that the Church lands cannot certainly come to much, if the King shall be persuaded to take*ᵇ* them,[3] they being leased out for long leases. By and by, after two hours' stay, they rose, having as Wren tells me resolved upon sending six ships to the Streights forthwith, not being contented with that peace upon the terms they demand; which is, that all our ships, where any Turks or Moore's shall be found slaves, shall be prize: which will imply that they must be searched.[4] I hear that tomorrow the King and Duke of York set out for Newmarket by 3 in the morning to some foot and horse-races, to be abroad ten or twelve days.[5] So

---

a repl. full stop   *b* repl. 'give them'

---

1. Allin to Williamson, Algiers, 2 February: *CSPD 1668–9*, pp. 179–81. For the agreement (2/12 February), see Allin, ii. 227; for the occasion of it, see above, pp. 427–8 & n.

2. Solicitor to the Duke of York.

3. Cf. above, p. 347 & n. 3.

4. For this clause of the agreement, see Allin, vol. ii, p. xl. The council order about the despatch of the ships was made on the 3rd: PRO, PC 2/61, p. 223.

5. They returned on the 20th: *London Gazette*, 22 March.

I [away] without seeing the Duke of York; but Mr. Wren
showed me the Order of Council about the balancing storekeepers
accounts, passed the Council in the very terms I drow it; only,
I did put in my name as he that presented that book of Hosiers
preparing, and that is left out; I mean, my name, which is no
great matter.[1] So to my wife to Suffolke-street, where*a* she
was gone, and there I find them at supper and I eat a little with
them; and so home and there to bed, my cold being pretty well
gone.

8.   Up and with W. Hewer by hackney-coach*b* to White-
hall, where the King and Duke of York is gone by 3 in the
morning and had the misfortune to be overset with the Duke of
York, the Duke of Monmouth, and the Prince, at the King's-
gate in Holborne; and the King all dirty, but no hurt.   How it
came to pass I know not, but only it was dark and the torches did
not, they say, light the coach as they should do.   I thought
this morning to have seen my Lord Sandwich before he went out
of town, but I came half an hour too late; which troubles me,
I having not seen him since my Lady Pall died.   So W. Hewer
and I to the Harp and Ball to drink my morning draught, having
come out in haste; and there met with King the Parliament-
man, with whom I had some impertinent* talk; and so to the
Privy Seal Office to examine what records I could find there for
my help in the great business I am put upon, of defending the
present constitution of the Navy;[2] but there could not have
liberty without order from one*c* that is in present waiting, Mr.
Bickerstaffe, who is out of town.   This I did after I had walked
to the New Exchange and there met Mr. Moore, who went with
me thither; and I find him the same discontented poor man as

---

a MS. 'which'   *b* repl. 'water'   *c* repl. 'him'

---

1. The order (12 February; PRO,
PC 2/60, f. 47*r*-*v*) provided for the
appointment of five extra clerks for
the purpose – one at the Navy Board,
to assist Mennes, and four at the yards.
It referred to the 'method prepared by

one Francis Hosier, a Navy Clerke'.
Hosier presented a beautifully-written
copy of his scheme to Pepys, who
bound and preserved it: PL 1788.
Cf. above, p. 374 & n. 1.

2. See below, p. 525 & n. 1.

ever. He tells me that Mr. Sheply is upon being turned away from my Lord's family, and another sent down;[1] which I am sorry for, but his age and good-fellowship have almost made him fit for nothing. Thence, at Unthankes my wife met me, and with our coach to my cousin Turner's and there dined; and after dinner, with my wife alone to the King's playhouse and there saw[a] *The Mocke Astrologer*,[2] which I have often seen, and but an ordinary play. And so to my cousin Turners again, where we met Roger Pepys his wife and two daughters and there stayed and talked a little; and then home and there my wife to read to me, my eyes being sensibly hurt by the too great lights of the playhouse. So to supper and to bed.

9. Up, and to the tower and there find Sir W. Coventry alone, writing down his journall, which he tells me he now keeps of the material things; [upon] which I told him, and he is the only man that I ever told it to I think,[3] that I have kept it most strictly these eight or ten years; and I am sorry almost that I told it him – it not being necessary, nor may be convenient to have it known. Here he showed me the petition[4] he had sent to the King by my Lord Keeper; which was not to desire any admittance to imployment, but submitting himself therein humbly to his Majesty; but prayed the removal of his displeasure and that he might be set free. He tells me that my Lord Keeper did acquaint the King with the substance of it, not showing him the petition; who answered that he was disposing of his imployments, and when that was done, he might be led to discharge him – and this is what he expects and what he seems to desire. But by this discourse he was pleased to take occasion to show me and read to

---

a repl. 'sat but with the fewest people in the House that I almost ever saw to'

---

1. Edward Shipley had been Sandwich's steward at Hinchingbrooke throughout the diary period. Lowd (? Laud) Cordell was his steward in 1672: Harris, ii. 286.

2. A comedy by Dryden; see above, p. 246, n. 3. (A).

3. In fact at 11 April 1660 Pepys records having made a similar confidence to a naval lieutenant. Coventry's diary has not survived among his MSS either at Longleat or in the BM.

4. Untraced.

me his account,ᵃ which he hath kept by him under his own hand, of all his discourse and the King's answers to him upon the great business of my Lord Clarendon;¹ and how he had first moved the Duke of York with it twice, at good distance, one after another, but without success – showing me thereby the simplicity and reasons of his so doing and the manner of it, and the King's accepting it, telling him that he was not satisfied in his management, and did discover* some dissatisfaction against him for his opposing the laying aside of my Lord Treasurer at Oxford; which was a secret the King hath not discovered.² And really, I was mighty proud to be privy to this great transaction, it giving me great conviction of the noble nature and ends of Sir W. Coventry in it, and considerations in general of the consequences of great men's actions, and the uncertainty of their estates, and other very serious considerations. From this to other discourse; and so I to the office, where we sat all the morning; and after dinner, by coach to my cousin Turner's, thinking to have taken the young ladies to a play, but The was let blood today; and so my wife and I toward the King's playhouse, and by the way found Betty³ and Bab and Betty Pepys staying for us; and so took them all to see *Claracilla*,⁴ which doth not please me almost at all, though there are some good things in it; and so to my cousin Turner's again and there find my Lady Mordant and her sister Johnson,⁵ and by and by comes in a gentleman, Mr. Overbury, a pleasant man who plays most excellently on the Flagelette, a little one that sounded as low as one of mine⁶, and mighty pretty.

a repl.'jour'-

---

1. This account has not been traced.
2. In the autumn of 1665, when parliament met at Oxford, Coventry and Arlington had attempted to persuade the King to replace Southampton by commissioners. Clarendon had successfully opposed the suggestion. Clarendon, *Life*, iii. 1, 29, 32.
3. Daughter of John and Jane Turner.

4. A tragicomedy by Thomas Killigrew; see above, ii. 132, n. 2. (A).
5. Her maiden sister; probably the one who, after marriage, as Mrs Stewart, later became, with Lady Mordaunt, one of Pepys's greatest friends.
6. Probably his 'low and saft' flageolet: above, p. 30. (E).

Hence by and by away, and with my wife and Bab. and Betty
Pepys and W Hewers, whom I carried all this day with me, to
my Cosen Stradwicks, where I have not been ever since my
brother Tom died, there being some difference between my father
and them upon the account of my cousin Scott.[1] And I was
glad of this opportunity of seeing them, they being good and
substantial people, and kind.[2] And here met my cousin Rogr.
and his wife and my cousin Turner; and here, which I never
did before, I drank a glass, of a pint I believe, at one draught, of
the juice of Oranges of whose peel they make comfits; and here
they drink the juice as wine, with sugar, and it is very fine drink;[3]
but it being new, I was doubtful whether it might not do me
hurt; and having stayed here a while, my wife and I back with my
cousin Turner &c to her house, and there we took our leaves of
my cousin Pepys, who goes with his wife and two daughters for
Impington tomorrow. They are very good people, and people
I love and am much obliged to, and shall have great pleasure in
their friendship, and perticularly in hers – she being a understanding and good woman. So away home; and there, after
signing my letters, my eyes being bad, to supper and to bed.

10. Up and by hackney-coach to Auditor Beales office in
Holborne to look for records of the Navy; but he was out of
the way, and so forced to go next to White-hall to the Privy
Seal; and after staying a little there, then to Westminster, where
at the Exchequer I met with Mr. Newport and Major Halsey;
and after doing a little business with Mr. Burges, we by water
to White-hall, where I made a little stop; and so with them by
coach to Temple-Barr, where at the Suger Loaf we dined, and
W. Hewer with me, and there comes a companion of theirs,
Collonell Vernon*a* I think they called him, a merry good-fellow,

a repl. 'Byron'

---

1. A dispute over the administration of the estate of Pepys's brother
Tom: above, v. 124-5 & n.
2. Thomas Strudwick was a provision merchant.
3. Both orange- and lemon-juice
were drunk only rarely. Lemonade
is said to have been first mentioned in
Thomas Killigrew's *Parson's Wedding*
(1663), IV, 5; see M. Summers's edition.

and one that was very plain in cursing the Duke of Buckingham and discoursing of his designs to ruin us, and that ruin must fallow his counsels, and that we are an undone people – to which the other concurred but not so plain; but all vexed*a* at Sir W. Coventry's being laid aside, but Vernon, he is concerned, I perceive, for my Lord Ormonds being laid aside.[1] But their company, being all old Cavaliers, were very pleasant to hear how they swear and talk. But Halsey, to my content, tells me that my Lord Duke of Albemarle says that W. Coventry being gone, nothing will be well done at the Treasury, and I believe it. But they do all talk as that Duncomb, upon some pretence or other, must fallow him.[2] Thence to Auditor Beales his house and office, but not to be found; and therefore to the Privy Seal at White-hall, where with W. Hewer and Mr. Gibson, who met me at the Temple, I spent the afternoon till evening, looking over the books there; and did find several things to my purpose, though few of those I designed to find, the books being kept there in no method at all. Having done there, we by water home and there find my cousin Turner and her two daughters come to see us; and there, after talking a little, I had my coach ready, and my wife and I, they going home, we out to*b* White-chapel to take a little ayre, though yet the dirtiness of the road doth prevent most of the pleasure which should have from this tour. So home, and my wife to read to me till supper, and to bed.

11. Up and to Sir W. Coventry to the Tower, where I walked and talked with him an hour alone, from one good thing to another; who tells me that he hears that the Commission is gone down to the King with a blank to fill for his place in the Treasury; and he believes it will be filled with one of our Treasurers of the Navy, but which he knows not, but he believes

a repl. 's'-   *b* MS. 'at'

---

1. Edward Vernon was a servant of Ormond.
2. Cf. the similar rumour in BM, Add. 36916, f. 131r (newsletter,

18 March). The Treasury commiss-ion was reduced to four members on 20 March, but Duncombe retained his place.

it will be Osborne.¹ We walked down to the Stone Walk,
which is called, it seems, "My Lord of Northumberland's
Walk," being paved by some of that title that was prisoner there;
and at the end of it there is a piece of Iron upon the wall with his
armes upon it, and holes to put in a peg for every turn that they
make upon that walk.² So away to the office, where busy all
the morning, and so to dinner; and so very busy all the afternoon
at my office late, and then home, tired, to supper, with content
with*ᵃ* my wife; and so to bed – she pleasing me, though I dare
not own it, that she hath hired a chambermaid; but she, after
many commendations, told me that she had one great fault,
and that was that she was very handsome; at which I made
nothing, but let her go on; but many times tonight she took
occasion to discourse of her handsomeness and the danger she
was in by taking her, and that she did doubt yet whether it would
be fit for her to take her. But I did assure her of my resolutions
to having nothing to do with her maids, but in myself I was glad
to have the content to have a handsome one to look on.

12. Up, and abroad with my own coach to Auditor Beales
house; and thence with W. Hewer to his office and there with
great content spent all the morning, looking over the Navy
accounts of several years and the several patents of the Treasurers,
which was more then I did hope*ᵇ* to have found there. About
noon I ended there, to my great content; and giving the*ᶜ* clerks
there 20*s* for their trouble, and having sent for W How to me
to discourse with him about the Patent Office records, wherein I

a repl. 'to'   *b* MS. 'home'   *c* repl. 'them'

---

1. Coventry's place was not in fact
filled: a new commission was issued
on 20 March which simply omitted
his name: *CSPD 1668-9*, p. 240.
The appointment of Osborne had
been scotched by Arlington, who
feared an increase in Buckingham's
interest: A. Browning, *Danby*, i. 67.
   2. The 9th Earl of Northumberland

(d. 1632) was imprisoned in the
Tower, 1605-21, on suspicion of
complicity in the Gunpowder Plot.
The walk named after him still remains (though the piece of iron has
disappeared), and runs from Martin
Tower, where he lived in some state,
to Brick Tower. See G. R. Batho in
Hist. Today, 6/344+.

remembered his Brother to be concerned,[1] I took him in my coach with W. Hewer and myself toward Westminster, and there he carried me to Nott's, the famous bookbinder that bound[a] for my Lord Chancellor's library. And here I did take occasion for[b] curiosity to bespeak a book to be bound, only that I might have one of his binding.[2] Thence back to Grayes-Inn; and at the next door, at a[c] cook's-shop of How's acquaintance, we bespoke dinner, it being now 2 a-clock; and in the meantime he carried us into Gray's[d]-Inn to his chamber, where I never was before; and it is very pretty, and little and neat, as he was always. And so after a little stay and looking over a book or two there we carried a piece of my Lord Cooke with us, and to our dinner, where after dinner he read at my desire a chapter in my Lord Cooke about Perjury, wherein I did learn a good deal touching oaths.[3] And so away to the Patent Office in Chancery-lane, where his Brother Jacke, being newly broke by running[e] in debt and growing an idle rogue, he is forced to hide himself, and W How doth look after the office; and here I did set a clerk to look out for some things for me in their books, while W Hewers and I to the Crowne Office,[4] where we met with several good things that I most wanted and did take short notes of the Dockets; and so back to the Patent Office and did the like there, and by candle-light ended; and so home, where thinking to meet my wife with content, after my pains all this day, I find her in her closet, alone in the dark, in a hot fit of railing against me, upon some news she hath this day heard of Deb's living very fine, and with black spots, and speaking ill words of her mistress; which with good reason might[f] vex her, and the baggage is to blame; but God knows, I know nothing of her nor what she doth nor

---

<table>
<tr><td>a MS. 'bind'</td><td>b repl. 'to'</td><td>c repl. 'an'</td></tr>
<tr><td>d repl. same symbol</td><td>e MS. 'ruining'</td><td>f repl. 'doth'</td></tr>
</table>

---

1. John How was a clerk there.

2. Mr H. M. Nixon writes: 'This is almost certainly R. Doleman [Robert Parsons], *A conference about the next succession to the crown of Ingland* (1594); PL 518. The binder was William Nott.'

3. Sir Edward Coke, *Institutes*, pt

iii, ch. 74. Pepys was particularly interested in the oaths taken by the Commissioners of the Navy, with a view to his report on the constitution of the office: below, p. 525, n. 1.

4. Like the Patent Office, a division of Chancery; situated in the Temple.

what becomes of her; though God knows, my devil that is within me doth wish that I could. Yet God I hope will prevent me therein – for I dare not trust myself with it, if I should know it. But what with my high words, and slighting it and then serious, I did at last bring her to very good and kind terms, poor heart; and I was heartily glad of [it], for I do see there is no man can be happier then myself, if I will, with her. But in her fit she did tell me what vexed me all the night, that this had put her upon putting off her handsome maid and hiring another that was full of the small-pox – which did mightily vex me, though I said nothing, and doth still. So down to supper, and she to read to me, and then with all possible kindness to bed.

13. Up and to the Tower to see Sir W. Coventry, and with him talking of business of the Navy all alone an hour, he taking physic. And so away to the office, where all the morning; and then home to dinner with my people and so to the office again. And there all the afternoon till night, when comes by mistake my cousin Turner and her two daughters (which loves such freaks) to eat some anchoves and ham of bacon with me, by mistake instead of noon at dinner, when I expected them; but however, I had done my business before they came and so was in good humour enough to be with them; and so home to them to supper, and pretty merry – being pleased to see Betty Turner, which hath something mighty pretty. But that which put me in good humour, both at noon and night, is the fancy that I am this day made a Captain of one of the King's ships, Mr. Wren having this day sent me the Duke of York's commission to be Captain*a* of the *Jerzy*, in order to my*b* being of a Court Martiall for examining the loss of the *Defyance*, and other things[1] –

a repl. same symbol   *b* repl. 'be'-

1. Pepys (together with Middleton) acted as expert assessors, not as full members of the court. Court-martials were governed at this time by an act of 1661 (13 Car. II, c. 9). For the trial, see below, pp. 488–9, 497–8, 505, 508. The *Defiance* was a 3rd-rate which had been destroyed by fire at Chatham in the previous December: *CSPD 1668–9*, p. 91. The trial had been ordered shortly afterwards (Penn, ii. 520–1), but the warrant constituting the court was not issued until 10 March: NMM, MS. M.14.

which doth give me occasion of much mirth, and may be of
some use to me; at least, I shall get a little money by it for the
time I have it, it being designed that I must really be a Captain
to be able to sit in this Court. They stayed till about 8 at night,
and then away; and my wife to read to me, and then to bed in
mighty good humour, but for my eyes.

14. *Lords day.* Up, and to my office with Tom, whom I
made to read to me the books of Propositions in the time of the
Grand Comission,[1] which I did read a good part of before church;
and then with my wife to church, where I did see my milliner's
wife[2] come again, which pleased me: but I durst not be seen to
mind her for fear of my wife's seeing me – though the woman
I did never speak twenty words to, and that but only in her
husband's shop – but so fearful I am of discontenting my wife
or giving her cause of jealousy. But here we heard a most
excellent good sermon of Mr. Gifford's,[3] upon the righteousness
of Scribes and Pharisees. So home to dinner and to work again,
and so till dinner, where W How came and dined with me,
and stayed and read in my Lord Cooke upon his chapter of
Perjury again, which pleased me; and so parted, and I to my
office and there made an end of the books of Proposicions; which
did please me mightily to hear read, they being excellently writ
and much to the purpose, and yet so as I think I shall make good
use of in defence of our present constitution. About 4 a-clock,
took coach and to visit my cousin Turner, and I out with her to
make a visit, but the lady she went to see was abroad; so back
and to talk with her and her daughters, and then home and she
and I to walk in the garden, the first time this year, the weather
being mighty temperate; and then I to write down my journall
for the last week, my eyes being very bad; and therefore I forced

1. The report of the reforming
commission of 1618 (cf. above, iv. 96
& n. 4); in Pepys's view the best
available analysis of the problems of
naval administration: cf. *Naval Minutes*, pp. 277–8. It had a strong influence on Pepys's own Special Commission of 1686–8.
2. See above, p. 460 & n. 3.
3. George Gifford, Rector of St
Dunstan-in-the-East.

to find a*ᵃ* [way] to use by turns with my tube, one after another; and so home to supper and to bed. ⟨Before I went from my office this night, I did tell Tom my resolution not to keep him after Jane was gone, but*ᵇ* shall do well by him – which pleases him; and I think he*ᶜ* will presently marry her and go away out of my house with her.⟩*ᵈ¹*

15. Up, and by water with W. Hewer to the Temple; and thence to the Chapel of Rolles, where I made enquiry for several Rolles and was soon informed in the manner of it; and so spent the whole morning with W. Hewer, he taking*ᵉ* little notes in short-hand,² while I hired a clerk there to read to me about twelve or more several rolls which I did call for: and*ᶠ* it was great pleasure to me to see the method wherein their Rolles are kept; that when the Master of the Office, one Mr. Case, doth call for them (who is a man that I have heretofore known by coming to my Lord Sandwiches) he did most readily turn to them. At noon they shut up, and W. Hewer and I did walk to the Cocke at the end of Suffolke-street, where I never was, a great ordinary, mightily cried up, and there bespoke a pullet; which while dressing, he and I walked into St. James's park, and thence back and dined very handsome, with a good Soup and a pullet, for 4*s*–6*d* the whole. Thence back to the Rolles and did a little more business; and so by water from White-hall, whither I went to speak with Mr. Williamson (that if he hath any papers relating to the Navy, I might see them, which he promises me);³ and so by water home, with great content for what I have this day found, having got almost as much as I desire of the history of the Navy from 1618 to 1642, when the King and Parliament fell out. So home, and did get my wife to read, and so to supper and to bed.

a repl. 'to' *b* repl. 'which' *c* repl. 'they will'
d addition crowded into margin and end of paragraph
e repl. 'reading' *f* repl. 'it'

---

1. Tom Edwards and Jane Birch were married on 26 March.
2. For Hewer's knowledge of shorthand, see above, vii. 374 & n. 1.

3. Joseph Williamson, of the Secretary of State's office and Keeper of State Papers: for the papers he produced, see below, p. 486 & n. 1.

16.　Up and to the office, after having visited Sir W. Coventry at the Tower and walked with him upon the Stone Walk alone,[a] till other company came to him, and had very good discourse with him.　At noon home, where my wife and Jane gone abroad, and Tom, in order to their buying of things for their wedding; which, upon my discourse the last night, is now resolved to be done[b] upon the 26 of this month, the day of my solemnity for my cutting of the stone, when my Cosen Turner must be with us.　My wife therefore not at dinner; and in comes to me Mr. Evelin of Deptford, a worthy good man, and dined with me, but a bad dinner; who is grieved for, and speaks openly to me his thoughts of the times and our ruin approaching, and all by the folly of the King.　His business to me was about some ground of his at Deptford, next to the King's yard.[1]　And after dinner we parted, my sister Michell coming also this day to see us – whom I left there; and I away down by water with W. Hewer[c] to Woolwich, where I have not been I think more then a year or two; and here saw, but did not go on board, my ship the *Jerzy*, she lying at the wharf under repair.　But my business was to speak with Ackworth about some old things and passages in the Navy,[2] for my information therein in order to my great business now, of stating the [hi]story of the Navy.　This I did, and upon the whole do find that the late times, in all their management were not more husbandly then we,[3] and other things of good content to me.　His wife was sick, and so I

---

a repl. full stop　　　*b* repl. 'd'- badly formed　　　*c* repl. 'Tom'

---

1. In August 1668 John Evelyn had been granted a lease of a strip of ground in Brick Close, which lay to the east of his house, Sayes Court, and in June of this year he built a long wall enclosing it: PRO, Adm. 106/3520, f. 36r; *CTB*, ii. 228–30, 418; Evelyn, iii. 482, n. 4, 530. Cf. *CSPD 1660–85*, pp. 185–6.

2. William Acworth had been Storekeeper at Woolwich since at least 1650.

3. Cf. Pepys's undated memorandum (Rawl. A 181, f. 36r): 'The Expence of the Navy for 7 yeares, beginning the 1st of Jan: 1652 compared with its expence for 7 yeares, beginning the 1st of July 1660'; showing that the latter was less by £1,166,168 10s. 8d. Some of the material Pepys used is in Rawl. A 195a, f. 241r (naval expenses, 1652–9). For a similar calculation made in 1666, see above, vii. 307 & n. 5.

could not see her. Thence, after seeing Mr. Sheldon, I to
Greenwich by water, and there landed at the King's house,
which goes on slow, but is very pretty.[1] I to the park, there to
see the prospect of the hill to judge of Dancre's picture which he
hath made thereof for me;[2] and I do like it very well – and is a
very pretty place.   Thence to Deptford but stayed not, Uthwayte
being out of the way; and so home and there to the Ship tavern,
Morrice's, and stayed till W. Hewer fetched his uncle Blackburne
by appointment to me, to discourse of the business of the Navy
in the late times; and he did do it by giving me a most exact
account, in writing, of the several turns in the Admiralty and
Navy of the persons imployed therein, from the beginning of the
King's leaving the Parliament to his son's coming in[3] – to my
great content; and now I am fully [in]formed in all I at present
desire.   We fell to other talk, and I find by him that the Bishops
must certainly fall, and their Hierarchy; these people[4] have got*a*
so much ground upon the King and Kingdom as is not to be got
again from them – and the Bishops do well deserve it.   But it is
all the talk, I find, that Dr. Wilkins my friend, the Bishop of
Chester, shall be removed to Winchester and be Lord Treasurer;
though this be foolish talk – yet I do gather that he is a mighty
rising man, as being a Latitudinarian – and the Duke of Buckingham his great friend.[5]   Here we stayed talking till 10 at night,
where I did never*b* drink before since this man came to the house;

a repl. 'gone'   *b* repl. same symbol badly formed

---

1. For the building operations at
Greenwich Palace, see above, v. 75
& n. 3.
2. See above, p. 423, n. 1. (OM).
3. Robert Blackborne had been
Secretary to the Admiralty Commissioners, c. 1653–60. His memorandum has not been traced.
4. Nonconformists such as Blackborne.
5. This and similar rumours were
rife: Buckingham was now at
Newmarket with the King, and big

changes were expected on their
return. The Treasury commission
had been weakened by the removal of
Coventry and the incapacity (through
illness) of Albemarle.   Some believed
Arlington would become Treasurer,
with Clifford succeeding him in as
Secretary of State: PRO, PRO
731/3/121, ff. 216, 224, 225. Wilkins's liberal churchmanship was a link
with Buckingham, but he had no
political ambitions. None of the
rumoured changes in fact took place.

though for his pretty wife's sake, I do fetch my wine from this, whom I could not nevertheless get*a* para see tonight – though her husband did seem*a** to call for her.   So parted here, and I home and to supper and to bed.

17.   Up and by water to see Mr. Wren and then Mr. Williamson, who did show me the very original Bookes of propositions made by the Commissioners for the Navy in 1618,[1] to my great content – but no other Navy papers he could now show me. Thence to Westminster by water and to the Hall, where Mrs. Michell doth surprize me with the news that Doll. Lane is suddenly brought to bed at*b* her sister's lodgings, and gives it out that she is married; but there is no such thing certainly, she never mentioning it before; but I have cause to rejoice that I have not seen her a great while, she having several times desired my company, but I doubt to an evil end.   Thence to the Exchequer, where W. Hewer came to me; and after a little business, did go by water home, and there dined and took my wife by a hackney to the King's playhouse and saw *The Coxcomb*,[2] the first time acted; but an old play and a silly one, being acted only by the young people.[3]   Here met Cosen Turner and*c* The.   So parted there from them, and home by coach and to my letters at the office, where pretty late; and so to supper and to bed.

18.   Up, and to see Sir W. Coventry, and walked with him a good while in the Stone Walk; and brave discourse about my Lord Chancellor and his ill managements – and mistakes – and several things of the Navy; and thence to the office, where we sat all the morning; and so home to dinner, where my wife

---

a–a garbled s.h.   *b* repl. 'of the'   *c* repl. full stop

---

1. These are probably those now in PRO, SP 14/101. Pepys kept copies: Rawl. A 215, ff. 251+; ib., A 455, ff. 33+ (both in Hayter's hand); PL 2735 (in an unidentified clerical hand). For the commission, see above, p. 482 & n. 1.

2. A comedy by Beaumont and Fletcher, acted c. 1608, and published in 1647. This is the first record of a post-Restoration performance. (A).

3. I.e. by the less eminent members of the company, who had probably been given special permission to perform on a Wednesday in Lent: cf. above, viii. 122 & n. 2. (A).

mighty finely*a* dressed, by*b* a maid that she hath taken and is to come to her when Jane goes, and the same she the other day told me of to be so handsome.[1] I therefore longed to see her, but did not till after dinner, that my wife and I going by coach, she went with us to Holburne, where we set her down. She*c* is a mighty proper maid and pretty comely, but so-so – but hath a most pleasing tone of a voice and speaks handsomely, but hath most great hands, and I believe ugly, but very well dressed in good clothes; and the maid I believe will please me well enough. Thence to visit Ned Pickering and his lady, and Creed and his wife; but the former abroad and the latter out of town, gone to my Lady Pickering's in Northamptonshire upon occasion of the late death of their Brother Oliver Pickering, a youth that is dead of the small-pox.[2] So my wife and I to Dancre's to see the pictures[3] and thence to Hide-park, the first time we were there this year, or*d* ever in our own coach – where with mighty pride rode up and down; and many coaches there, and I thought our*e* horses and coach as pretty as any there, and observed so to be by others. Here stayed till night, and so home and to the office, where busy late; and so home to supper and to bed with great content, but much business in my head of the office, which troubles me.

19. Up and by water to White-hall; there to the Lords of the Treasury and did some business; and here Sir Th. Clifford did speak to me, as desirous that I would sometime come and confer with him about the Navy; which I am glad of, but will take the direction of the Duke of York before I do it, though I would be glad to do something to secure myself, if I could, in my imployment. Thence to the plasterer's[4] and took my face and my Lord Duke of Albemarle's home with me by coach, they being done

---

a repl. 'f'- *b* repl. 'being'
c repl. 'Sho' *d* repl. 'and' *e* MS. 'I our'

---

1. Matt; she began work on 29 March.

2. He was buried at Tichmarsh (near Thrapston) on the 17th.

3. See above, p. 423 & n. 1. (OM).

4. See above, p. 442 & n. 2.

to my mind; and mighty glad I am of understanding this way
of having the pictures of any friends.   At home to dinner where
Mr. Sheres dined with us; but after dinner I left him and my
wife, and with Commissioner Middleton and Kempthorne to a
Court Martiall to which, by virtue of my late Captainshipp, I am
called, the first I was ever at – where many commanders, and
Kempthorne president.[1]   Here was tried a difference between Sir
L. van Hemskirke, the Dutch captain who commands the *Nonsuch*, built by his direction, and his Lieutenant; a drunken kind
of silly business.[2]   We ordered the Lieutenant to ask him pardon,
and have resolved to lay before the Duke of York what concerns
the Captain, which was striking of his Lieutenant and challenging
him to fight,[3] which comes not within any Article of the laws-
Martiall.   But upon discourse the other day with Sir W.
Coventry, I did advise Middleton, and he and I did forbear to
give judgment; but after the debate, did withdraw into another
cabin (the Court being held in one of the Yachts,[4] which was on
purpose brought up over against St. Katharines), it being to be
feared that this precedent of our being made Captains in order
to the trying of the loss of the *Defyance*,[a5] wherein we are the
proper persons to enquire out the want of instructions while ships
do lie in Harbour, evil use might be hereafter made of the precedent, by putting the Duke of Buckingham or any of these
rude fellows that now are uppermost to make packed Courts,
by Captains made on purpose to serve their turns.   The other
cause was of the loss of the *Providence* at Tanger; where the
Captain's being by chance[b] on shore may prove very incon-
venient to him, for example sake, though the man be a good
man, and one whom for Norwood's sake I would be kind to;

a   repl. 'Royall Katharine'   b   repl. 'absence'

---

1. Cf. above, p. 481 & n. 1;
CSPD Add. 1660–85, pp. 286–7.
The court consisted of a President and
seven captains, Pepys and Middleton
serving as assessors.

2. For the ship, see above, p. 171 &
n. 2.   The dispute had arisen over the
action of the lieutenant (William
Dawson) in confining the master-
carpenter to his cabin: PRO, SP
46/137, no. 181.

3. The challenge had been made on
shore.

4. The *Henrietta*.

5. See below, pp. 497–8 & n.

but I will not offer anything to the excusing such a miscarriage.[1] He is at present confined, till he can bring better proofs on his behalf of the reasons of his being on shore. So Middleton and I away to the office; and there I late busy, making my people, as I have done lately, to read Mr. Holland's discourse of the Navy[2] and what other things I can get to inform me fully in all. And here late, about 8 at night, comes Mr. Wren to me, who had been at the Tower to visit Sir W. Coventry. He came only to see how matters go; and tells me as a secret, that the last night the Duke of York's closet was broken open, and his cabinets, and shut again, one of them. That the rogue that did it hath left plate and a watch behind him, and therefore they fear that it was only for papers; which looks like a very malicious business, in design to hurt the Duke of York; but they cannot know the truth till the Duke of York comes to town about the papers, and therefore make no words of it.[3] He gone, I to work again; and then to supper at home and to bed.

20. Up and to the Tower to W. Coventry, and there walked with him alone on the Stone Walk till company came to him; and there about the business of the Navy discoursed with him, and about my Lord Chancellor and Treasurer; that they were against the war at first – declaring, as wise men and statesmen at first to the King, that they thought it fit to have a war with them at some time or other, but that it ought not to be till we found the Crowns of Spain and France together by the eares;[4]

---

1. She was a fireship which had been stranded near Tangier. She had just brought back prisoners released by the recent treaty with Algiers: HMC, *Eliot Hodgkin*, p. 170; Routh, p. 134.

2. John Hollond, Surveyor of the Navy 1649–52, had written two MS. discourses on naval administration, in 1638 and in 1659 (see above iii. 145, n. 1), of which copies were kept in the office. Pepys is probably referring to the earlier one.

3. Cf. the similar report in HMC, *Rutland*, i. 11 (Lady Chaworth to Lord Roos, ?31 March), where the affair is referred to as 'the great talke and amazement of the wholle towne'. Some said (she added) that the culprit was the Duchess, searching for love-letters. It was discovered on the Duke's return that the loss was simply that of 700 gold pieces: PRO, SP 29/253, f. 21*v*.

4. Clarendon and Southampton had expected France and Spain to fall out over Flanders (as indeed they did, in 1667). There is no lack of evidence for their opposition to the war.

the want of which did ruin our Warr.   But then he told me, that a great deal before the Warr, my*a* Lord Chancellor did speak of a Warr with some heat, as a thing to be desired,[1] and did it upon a belief that he could with his speeches make the Parliament give what money he pleased, and do what he would or would make the King desire; but he found himself soon deceived of that, the Parliament having a long time before his removal been cloyed with his speeches and good words – and were come to hate him.   Sir W. Coventry did tell me it, as the wisest thing that ever was said to the King by any statesman of his time, and it was by my Lord Treasurer that is dead,[2] whom I find he takes for a very great statesman; that when the King did show himself forward for passing the Act of Indemnity, he did advise the King that he would hold his hand in doing it, till he had got his power restored that had been diminished by the late times, and his revenue settled in such a manner as he might depend on himself, without resting upon Parliaments, and then pass it.   But my Lord Chancellor, who thought he could have the command of Parliaments for ever, because for the King's sake they were awhile willing to grant all the King desire[d], did press for its being done; and so it was, and the King from that time able to do nothing with the Parliament almost.[3]

Thence to the office, where sat all the forenoon; and then home to dinner and so to the office, where late busy; and so home, mightily pleased with the news brought me tonight, that the King and Duke of York are come back this afternoon to town, and no sooner come but a Warrant was sent to the Tower for the releasing Sir W. Coventry;[4] which doth put me in some hopes that there may be, in this absence, some accommodation made

a repl. 'the'

----

1. There appears to be no substantial evidence for this allegation.

2. Southampton.

3. Clarendon, on the other hand, says there was no division of opinion between King and ministers or between ministers over the need for passing the bill of indemnity with all

speed in 1660, because nothing could be done with parliament (e.g. no progress made in disbanding the Cromwellian army) until that matter was settled: *Life*, i. 470–1.

4. The warrant was dated this day: *CSPD 1668–9*, p. 240. The royal party had returned from Newmarket.

between the Duke of York and the Duke of Buckingham and Arlington. So home to supper and to bed.

21. *Lords day.* Up, and by water over to Southworke; and thence, not getting a boat, I forced to walk to Stangate and so over to White-hall in a scull, where up to the Duke of York's dressing-room; and there met Harry Savill and do understand that Sir W. Coventry is come to his house last night. I understand by Mr. Wren that his friends having by Secretary Trevor and my Lord Keeper applied to the King upon his first coming home, and a promise made that he should be discharged this day, my Lord Arlington did anticipate them by sending a warrant presently for his discharge, which looks a little like kindness or a desire of it; which God send, though I fear the contrary. However, my heart is glad that he is out.

Thence up and down the House; met with Mr. May, who tells me the story of his being put by Sir John Denham's place (of Surveyor of the King's Works, who*ᵃ* it seems is lately dead)[1] by the unkindness of the Duke of Buckingham, who hath brought in Dr. Wren – though he tells me he hath been his servant for twenty years together, in all his wants and dangers, saving him from want of bread by his care and management, and with a promise of having his help in his advancement, and an*ᵇ* engagement under his hand for 1000*l* not yet paid; and yet the Duke of Buckingham is so ungrateful as to put him by[2] – which is an ill thing – though Dr. Wren is a worthy man.[3] But he tells me that the King is kind to him, and hath promised him a

---

a repl. 'which'   *b* repl. 'a'

---

1. Denham had died on 20 March. Hugh May had been his deputy since 1660.

2. May had helped to transfer some of Buckingham's works of art to Holland, where they were sold to maintain him in exile during the revolution. He had served under the Duke at the battle of Worcester: T. Blount, *Boscobel* (1662), p. 24.

3. Christopher Wren served as Surveyor of the King's Works from 24 November 1669 until his resignation in 1718: *CSPD 1668–9*, p. 615; *DNB*. Denham had made him deputy during his (Denham's) life on 6 March: ib., pp. 224, 227.

pension of 300*l* a year out of the Works,[1] which will be of more content to him then the place, which under their present wants of money is a place that disobliges most*a* people, being not able to do what they desire to their lodgings.*b*

Here meeting with Sir H. Cholmly and Povy, that tell me that my Lord Middleton is resolved in the Caball that he shall not go to Tanger and that Sir Edwd. Harlow, whom I know not, is propounded to go; who was Governor of Dunkirke and they say a most worthy brave man;*c* which I shall be very glad of.[2]

So by water (H. Russell[3] coming for me) home to dinner, where W. How comes to dine with me, and after dinner propounds to me my lending him 500*l* to help him to purchase a place – the Master of the Patent Office, of Sir Rd. Piggott.[4] I did give him a civil answer, but shall think twice of it; and the more because of the changes we are like to have in the Navy, which will not make it fit for me to divide the little I have left more then I have done – God knowing what my condition is, I having not attended and now not being able to examine what my state is of my accounts and being in the world, which troubles me mightily.

He gone, I to the office to enter my journell for a week.

News are lately come of the Algerins taking 13000*l* in money out of one of our Company's East India ships, outward bound, which will certainly make the war last;[5] which I am sorry for, being so poor as we are – and broken in pieces.

a repl. 'more'   *b* followed by 'thence' struck through
c repl. 'the'

---

1. The pension was granted on 24 March: *CSPD 1668–9*, p. 245.

2. The official minute of the meeting has no reference to this matter: PRO, SP 104/176, f. 130. Middleton in fact took up the appointment: see below, p. 504. 'Harlow' was Harley, father of Robert Harley, 1st Earl of Oxford, the statesman.

3. Waterman to the office.

4. Cf. above, p. 372 & n. 2. It is possible that Howe did not obtain

any post in the Patent Office since he later emigrated to Barbados.

5. I.e. the punitive expedition against the Algerines led by Sir Thomas Allin: see above, p. 428, n. 1. The *Morning Star* had been attacked off Cadiz and had recently come into Falmouth. The loss was valued by the company at £11,000; *Cal. court mins E. India Co., 1668–70* (ed. Sainsbury), pp. 169, 174.

At night, my wife to read to me and then to supper, where Pelling comes to see and sup with us, and I find that he is assisting to my wife in getting a licence to our young people[1] to be married this Lent, which is resolved shall be done upon Friday next, my great day or feast for my being cut of the stone. So after supper, to bed, my eyes being very bad.

22. Up and by water with W. Hewer to White-hall, there to attend the Lords of the Treasury; but before they set I did make a stop*a* to see Sir W. Coventry at his house, where, I bless*b* God, he is come again; but in my way I met him, and so he took me into his coach and carried me to White-hall and there set me down where he ought not; at least, he hath not yet leave to come, nor hath thought fit yet to ask it, hearing that Harry Savill is not only denied to kiss the King's hand, but the King, being asked it by the Duke of York, the King did deny it and directed that he shall not receive him to wait upon him in his chamber till further order. Sir W. Coventry told me that he was going to visit Sir Jo Trevor,[2] who hath been kind to him; and he showed me a long list of all his friends that he must this week make visits to, that came to visit him in the Tower. And seems mighty well satisfied with his being out of business; but I hope he will not long be so. At least, do believe that all must go to wrack, if the King doth not come to see the want of such a servant. Thence to the Treasury-chamber; and there all the morning, to my great grief, put to do Sir G Dow[n]ing's work of dividing the Customes for this year between the Navy, the Ordnance, and Tanger;[3] but it did so trouble my eyes, that I had rather have given 20*l* then have had it to do; but I did thereby oblige Sir Tho. Clifford and Sir J Duncomb, and so am glad of the opportunity to recommend myself to the former; for the latter, I need not, he loving me well already. At it till noon, here being several of my Bretheren with me, but doing nothing, but I all; but this day I did*c* also represent to our Treasurers, which

a MS. 'step'   *b* repl. 'thank'   *c* repl. 'day'

---

1. Tom Edwards and Jane Birch, Pepys's servants.   2. Secretary of State.   3. *CTB*, iii. 39.

was read here, a state of the charge of the Navy, and what the
expense of it this year would likely be;[1] which is done so as
will appear well done and do me honour, for so the Lords did
take it – and I oblige the Treasurers by doing it at their request.

Thence with W. Hewer at noon at Unthankes, where my
wife stays for me; and so to the Cocke, where there was no
room; and thence to King's-street to several cooks' shops, where
nothing to be had. And at last to the corner shop going down
Ivy-lane by my Lord of Salsbury['s], and there got a good dinner,
my wife and W. Hewer and I; and after dinner, she with her
coach home and he and I to look over my papers for the East
India Company against the afternoon; which done, I with them
to White-hall, and there to the Treasury-chamber, where the
East India Company and three counsellors pleaded against me
alone for three or four hours, till 7 at night, before the Lords;
and the Lords did give me the*a* conquest on behalf of the King,
but could not come to any conclusion, the Company being stiff;
and so I think we shall go to law with them.[2] This done, and
my eyes mighty bad with this day's work, I to Mr. Wren's,
and then up to the Duke of York; and there with Mr. Wren did
propound to him my going to Chatham tomorrow with Commissioner Middleton, and so this week to make the pay there, and
examine the business of the *Defyance* being lost, and other
businesses; which I did the rather, that I might be out of the
way at the wedding and be at a little liberty myself for a day or
two, to find a little pleasure and give my eyes a little ease. The
Duke of York mightily satisfied with it; and so away home,
where my wife troubled*b* at my being so late abroad, poor
woman, though never more busy; but I satisfied her, and so
begun to put things in order for my journey tomorrow; and so
after*c* supper, to bed.

---

a repl. 'v'-   *b* repl. 'mad'   *c* MS. 'to after'

---

1. Copy (21 March, in Hayter's
hand) in NMM, LBK/8, pp. 583+;
printed in *Further Corr.*, pp. 226+.

2. This dispute concerned the
Leopard (see above, p. 410 & n. 1), and
a Treasury minute of this day directed
a trial at law. 'Pepis is to attend the
Attorney-General in order to it':
CTB, iii. 41.

23. Up and to my office to do a little business there; and so my things being all ready, I took coach with Commissioner Middleton, Captain Tinker, and Mr. Huchinson, a hackney-coach, and over the bridge, and so out towards Chatham; and dined at Dartford, where we stayed an hour or two, it being a cold day; and so on and got to Chatham just at night, with very good discourse by the way; but mostly of matters of religion, wherein Huchinson his vein lies.[1] After supper we fell to talk of spirits and apparitions, whereupon many pretty perticular stories were told,[2] so as to make me almost afeared to lie alone, but for shame I could not help it; and so to bed, and being sleepy, fell soon to rest and so rested well.

24. Up and walked about in the garden, and find that Mrs. Tooker hath not any of her daughters here as I expected. And so walked to the yard, leaving Middleton at the pay; and there I only walked up and down the yard, and then to the Hill-house and there did give order for the coach to be made ready and got Mr. Gibson, whom I carried with me, to go with[a] me and Mr. Coney the surgeon towards Maydston, which I had a mighty mind to see; and took occasion in my way, at St. Margetts, to pretend to call to see Captain Allen, to see whether Mrs. Jowles his daughter was there;[3] and there his wife came to the door, he being at London, and through a window I spied Jowles, but took no notice of her; but made excuse till night, and then promised to come[b] and see Mrs. Allen again; and so away, it being a mighty cold and windy, but clear day, and had the pleasure of seeing the Medway running, winding up and down mightily, and a very fine country; and I went a little way out of the way to have visited Sir Jo. Bankes, but he at London; but here I had a sight of his seat and house, the outside, which is an old abbey just like Hinchingbrooke, and as good at least, and mighty finely placed

a repl. 'to'   *b* repl. 'be'

---

1. Richard Hutchinson had been Navy Treasurer during the puritan revolution. He was now paymaster in the office of which he had been the head.

2. There was said to be a ghost at Hill House, Chatham: above, ii. 68.

3. A 'very handsome' young woman whom Pepys had flirted with in 1661: above, ii. 68, 71.

by the river; and he keeps the grounds about it, and walls and
the house, very handsome – I was mightily pleased with the sight
of it.[1]   Thence to Maydstone, which I had a mighty mind to see,
having never been there; and walked all up[a] and down the town,
and up to the top of the steeple* and had a noble view, and then
down again and in the town did see an old man beating of Flax,
and did step into the barn and give him money and saw that piece
of husbandry, which I never saw, and it is very pretty.   In the
street also, I did buy and send to our Inne, the Bell,[2] a dish of fresh
fish; and so having walked all round the town, and find it very
pretty as most towns I ever saw, though not very big, and
people of good fashion in it,[3] we to our Inne to dinner, and had a
good dinner; and after dinner a barber came to me and there
trimmed me, that I might be clean[b] against night to go to Mrs.
Allen; and so staying till about 4 a–clock, we set out, I alone in
the coach going and coming; and in[c] our way back, I light out
of the way to see a Saxon monument,[4] as they say, of a king; which
is three stones staying upright and a great round one lying on

a repl. ? 'up'   b repl. 'fine'   c repl. 'our'

---

1. Banks was a prosperous E. India
merchant, and was later to become a
close friend of Pepys.   The house was
The Fryers, Aylesford; originally a
Carmelite friary, founded in 1240,
and acquired by Banks in 1657.
Illust. in D. C. Coleman, *Sir J. Banks*,
opp. p. 51.   In 1949 it was restored to
the Carmelite order.   Sir John had a
London house in Lincoln's Inn Fields.
Coleman, pp. 43+.

2. At the top of Gabriel's Hill:
J. M. Russell, *Hist. Maidstone*, p. 241.

3. In 1639 Peter Mundy wrote of
Maidstone: 'For Many Miles aboutt
London there is Not a handsomer and
cleanlier place': Mundy, iii. 40.   To
Celia Fiennes (c. 1697) it was 'a very
neate market town as you shall see in
the Country, its buildings are mostly
of timber worke the streets are large

. . . very pretty houses about the
town look like the habitations of rich
men, I believe its a wealthy place
. . .': *Journeys* (ed. Morris), p. 130.
Defoe called it 'a Town of very great
business and Trade, and yet full of
Gentry, of Mirth, and of good
Company': *Tour* (ed. Cole), i. 115.
Its staple trade was the making of linen
thread.

4. Kit's Coty House, one of a number of neolithic megaliths in the
Aylesford district; a burial chamber,
once at the end of a long barrow;
reputed by popular tradition to be
associated with the Saxon king Horsa,
or with Catigern, killed at the battle
of Aylesford (455).   E. Hasted, *Hist.
Kent* (1797–1801), iv. 420–2; *Arch.
Cant.*, 63/63+; ib., 62/133+.

them, of great bigness, although not so big as those on Salsbury-plain, but certainly it is a thing of great antiquity, and I mightily glad to see it; it is near to Alesford, where Sir Jo. Bankes lives. So homeward*a* and stopped again at Captain Allen's and there light, and sent the coach and Gibson home and I and Cony stayed; and there comes to us Mrs. Jowles, who is a very fine proper lady as most I know, and well dressed. Here was also a gentleman, one Major Manly, and his wife, neighbours; and here we stayed and drank and talked, and set Cony and him to play while Mrs. Jowles and I to talk, and there had all our old stories up; and there I had the liberty to salute her*b* often and pull off her glove,*c* where her hand mighty moist; and she mighty free in kindness to me, and yo do not at all doubt*d* but I might have had*d* todo that yo would have desired de ella had I had time to have carried her to Cobham; as she, upon ⟨my⟩ proposing it, was willing to go, for ella is a whore,*e* that is certain, but a very brave and comely one. Here was a pretty cousin of hers came in to supper also, of a great fortune, daughter-in-law to this Manly; mighty pretty, but had now such a cold, she could not speak. Here mightily pleased with Mrs. Jowles, and did get her to the street-door in the dark, and there tocar su breasts and besar her*f* without any force, and creo that I might*g* have hecho algo else; but it was not time nor place. Here stayed till almost 12 at night; and then with a lanthorn from thence walked over the fields, as dark as pitch, and mighty cold and snow, to Chatham, and Mr. Cony with great kindness with me; and there all in bed before I came home, and so I presently to bed.

25.*h* Up, and by*i* and by, about 8 a-clock, comes Rere-Admirall Kempthorne and seven captains more by the Duke of York's order, as we expected, to hold the Court Martiall about the loss of the *Defyance*;[1] and so presently, we by boat to the *Charles*,

---

a repl. 'to'   b repl. 'o'-   c repl. 'gl'- badly formed
d–d garbled s.h.: see above, viii. 244, note a   e garbled s.h.
f garbled s.h.   g garbled s.h.   h repl. '24'   i repl. 'at'

---

1. See above, p. 481 & n. 1. For the court's proceedings, see PRO, SP 46/137, nos 183, 184.

which lies over against Upnor Castle, and there we fell to the business; and there I did manage the business, the Duke of York having by special order directed them to take the assistance of Commissioner Middleton and me, forasmuch as there might be need of advice in what relates to the government of the ship in Harbour; and so I did lay the law open to them, and rattle the Maister-Attendants out of their wits almost,[1] and I made the trial last till 7 at night, not eating a bit all the day; only, when we had done examination and I given my thoughts that the neglect of the gunner*a*[2] of the ship was as great as I thought any neglect could be, which might*b* by*c* the law deserve death, but Commissioner Middleton did declare that*d* he was against giving the sentence of death, we withdrew, as not being of the Court,[3] and so left them to do what they pleased; and while they were debating it, the bosun of the ship did bring us out of the Kettle a piece of hot salt beef and some brown bread and brandy; and there we did make a little meal, but so good as I never would desire to eat better meat while I live – only, I would have cleaner dishes. By and by they had done, and called us down from the quarter-deck; and there we find they do sentence that the gunner of the *Defyance* should stand upon the *Charles*[e] three hours, with his fault writ upon his breast and with a halter about his neck, and so be made uncapable of any office. The truth is, the man doth seem, and is I believe, a good man; but his neglect, in trusting a girle to carry fire into his cabin, is not to be pardoned.

This being done, we took boat and home; and there a good supper was ready for us, which should have been our dinner. The Captains, desirous to be at London, went away presently for

---

a l.h. repl. s.h. 'bosun'   *b* repl. 'mighty'   *c* MS. 'be'
    d MS. 'that that'   *e* l.h. repl. s.h. 'Ch'-

---

1. Some of the court's questions (written in Gibson's hand) were: 'Q*r* have they at any time and how often mustered this shipp by night? Q*r* have they ever satisfy'd themselves that the Clerke of the Cheque did his Duty, And whither they have ever directed the Clerk of the Cheque?

. . . What their Practice has beene . . . in Lodging by turnes upon some of the Kings shipps at least every third night?': ib., no. 184.

2. The master-gunner, Robert Waymouth.

3. Cf. above, p. 488, n. 1.

Gravesend, to get thither by this night's tide. And so we to supper, it having been a great snowy and mighty cold foul day; and so after supper, to bed.

26. Up and with Middleton all the morning at the Docke, looking over the storehouses and Comissioner Pett's house, in order to Captain Cox's coming to live there in his stead, as Commissioner. But it is a mighty pretty house; and pretty to see how everything is said to be out of repair for this new man, though 10*l* would put it into as good condition in everything as it ever was in – so free everybody is of the King's money.[1]

By and by to Mr. Willson's, and there drank but did not see his wife, nor any woman in the yard. And so to dinner at the Hill-house; and after dinner, till 8 at night, close, Middleton and I examining the business of Mr. Pett about selling a boat, and we find him a very knave;[2] and some other quarrels of his, wherein, to justify himself, he hath made complaints of others. This being done, we to supper and so to talk, Commissioner Middleton being mighty good company upon a journey; and so to bed – thinking how merry my*ª* people are at this time, putting Tom and Jane to bed, being to have been married this day, it being also my feast for my being cut of the stone; but how many years I do not remember, but I*ᵇ* think it to be about ten or eleven.[3]

27. Up, and did a little business, Middleton and I; then after drinking a little buttered ale, he and Huchinson and I took coach, and exceeding merry in talk, to Dartford, Middleton finding

a MS. 'mighty'   *b* repl. 'it'

---

1. John Cox was appointed on 29 March: *CSPD 1670* (*Add. 1660–70*), p. 734. For the practice of embellishing dockyard officers' houses, see above, ii. 13, n. 2.

2. According to the memorandum made after this examination by Middleton and Pepys, Phineas Pett, master-shipwright at Chatham yard,

admitted to lending boats from the Chatham store, but denied giving away or selling any. He could not swear, however, that all had been returned. *CSPD 1668–9*, pp. 250–1.

3. It was eleven: cf. Pepys's similar doubt about the number of years he had been married: above, vii. 318 & n. 1.

stories of his own life at Berbados and up and down, at Venice and elsewhere,[1] that are mighty pretty and worth hearing; and he is a strange good-companion and droll upon the road, more then ever I could have thought to have been in him. Here we dined and met Captain Allen of Rochester, who dined with us and so went on his journey homeward. And we by and by took coach again, and got home about 6 at night, it being all the morning as cold, snowy, windy, and rainy day as any in the whole winter past, but pretty clear in the afternoon. I find all well, but my wife abroad with Jane, who was married yesterday; and I to the office busy, till by and by my wife comes home; so home and there hear how merry they were yesterday; and I glad at it, they being married it seems very handsomely, at Islington, and dined at the old house[2] and lay in our blue chamber, with much company and wonderful merry. The Turner and Mary Battalier bridemaids, and Talb. Pepys and W Hewers bridemen.[a] Anon to supper and to bed, my head a little troubled with the muchness of business I have upon me at present. So to bed.

28. *Lords day.* Lay long, talking with pleasure with my wife, and so up and to the office with Tom, who looks mighty smug upon his marriage, as Jane also doth, both of whom I did give joy. And so Tom and I at work at the office all the morning till dinner, and then dined, W Battelier with us; and so after dinner to work again,[b] and sent for Gibson and kept him also till 8 at night, doing much business; and so, that being done and my journall writ, my eyes being very bad and every day worse and worse, I home. But I find it most certain that strang drinks do make my eyes sore, as they have done heretofore always, when I was in the country, when[c] my eyes were at the best – there strang beere would make my eyes sore.

So home to supper – and by and by to bed.

---

a repl. 'bridegrooms'   *b* repl. 'and'
   c repl. same symbol badly formed

---

1. At his death in 1672 Middleton left land in Barbados, Antigua and New England.

2. The King's Head. The wedding had been at the parish church, St Mary's.

29. Up and by water to White-hall, and there to the Duke of
York to show myself after my journey to Chatham, but did no
business today with him. Only, after gone from him, I to Sir
T. Clifford's and there, after an hour's waiting, he being alone in
his closet, I did speak with him and give him the account he
gave me to draw up,[1] and he did like it very well; and then
fell to talk of the business of the Navy; and giving me good
words, did fall foul of the constitution, and did then discover
his thoughts that Sir J. Mennes was too old, and so was Collonell
Middleton, and that my Lord Brouncker did mind his mathematics too much. I did not give much encouragement to that of
finding fault with my fellow-officers, but did stand up for the
constitution, and did say that what faults there was in our[a]
office would be found not to arise from the constitution, but from
the failures of the officers in whose hands it was. This he did
seem to give good ear to. But did give me of myself very[b]
good words; which pleased me well, though I shall not build
upon them anything. Thence home; and after dinner, by water
with Tom down to Greenwich, he reading to me all the way,
coming and going, my collections out of the Duke of York's old
manuscript of the Navy, which I have bound up and doth please
me mightily.[2] At Greenwich I came to Captain Cock's, where
the house full of company at the burial of James Temple,[3] who it
seems hath been dead these five days. Here I had a very good
ring, which I did give my wife as soon as I came home. I spent
my time there walking in the garden, talking with James Pierce;
who tells me that he is certain that the Duke of Buckingham had
been with his wenches all the time that he was absent, which was
all the last week, nobody knowing where he was. The great

---

a repl. same symbol badly formed   *b* repl. 'a'

---

1. See above, p. 493 & n. 3.
2. 'Navall Collections out of a
Miscellaneous Manuscript Lent me by
His Royall Highness then Lord High
Admirall of England. Anno Dom.
1668', once in Pepys's library and now
in the Bodleian (Rawl. C 846). The

Duke's MS. survives in the PL:
'Jamys Humphreys's Miscellaneous
Collections relating to the Admiralty
and Navy of England, 1568' (PL
1266).
3. Goldsmith; a business associate
of Cocke.

talk is of the King's being hot of late against Conventicles, and to see whether the Duke of Buckingham's being returned will turn the King[1] – which will make him very popular; and some think it is his plot to make the King thus, to show his power in the making him change his mind.   But Pierce did tell me that the King did certainly say that he that took one stone from the Church did take two from his crown.[2]   By and by the Corps came out; and I with Sir Rd. Browne and Mr. Eveling in their coach to the church, where Mr. Plume preached; but I, in the midst of the sermon, did go out and walked all alone round to Deptford, thinking *para* have seen*ᵃ* the wife of Bagwell; which I did at her door, but I could not conveniently go*ᵇ* into her house, and so lost my*ᵃ* labour.   And so to the King's-yard, and there my*ᶜ* boat by order met me, and home, where I made my boy to finish the reading of my manuscript; and so to supper and to bed. This day our new chamber-maid*ᵈ* that comes in the room of Jane, is come, Jane and Tom lying at their own lodging this night.   The new maid's name is Matt, a proper and very comely maid; so as when I was in bed,*ᵉ* the thoughts *de ella* did*ᵉ* make me *para hazer in mi mano.*   This day also, our cook-maid Bridget went away, which I was sorry for; but just at her going, she was found to be a thief, and so I was the less troubled for it. But now our whole house will in a manner be new; which, since Jane is gone, I am not at all sorry for, for that my late differences with my wife about poor Deb will not be remembered. So to bed after supper, I to sleep with great content.

30.   Up, and to Sir W. Coventry to see and discourse with

a–a garbled s.h.   *b* repl. same symbol badly formed
c MS. 'by'   *d* repl. 'maid came'   *e–e* garbled s.h.

---

1. The period of Buckingham's dominance had coincided with a period of lenity towards Nonconformists: see above, p. 277 & n. 5. But on 21 March the judges of assize had been instructed to enquire about unlawful preachers, and on the 26th and 29th council orders had been issued against the meeting of conventicles in London: PRO, SP 104/176, f. 130r; ib., SP 29/253, f. 23v; BM, Add. 36916, f. 134.

2. This saying has not been traced elsewhere.

him; and he tells me that he hath lately been with my Lord
Keeper and had much discourse about the Navy; and perticularly,
he tells me that he finds that they are divided touching me
and my Lord Brouncker; some are for removing, and some for
keeping us. He told my Lord Keeper that it should cost the
King 10000*l* before he hath made another as fit to serve him in
the Navy as I am; which, though I believe is true, yet I am much
pleased to have that character given me by W. Coventry, whatever be the success of it; but I perceive they do think that I
know too much and shall impose upon whomever shall come
next, and therefore must be removed; though he tells me that
Sir T. Clifford is inclined well enough to me, and Sir T. Osborne;
by what I have lately done, I suppose.[1] This news doth a little
trouble me; but yet when I consider it, it is but what I ought
not to be much troubled for – considering my incapacity, in
regard to my eyes, to continue long at this work – and this,
when I think of and talk with my wife, doth make me the less
troubled for it. After some talk of the business of the Navy
more with him, I away and to the office, where*a* all the morning,
and Sir W. Penn, the first time that he hath been here since
his being last sick, which I think is two or three months; and I
think will be the last that he will be here as one of the Board,[2]
he now inviting us all to dine with him, as a parting dinner,
on Thursday next – which I am glad of, I am sure, for he is a
very villain. At noon home to dinner; where, and at the office
all the afternoon, troubled at what I have this morning heard;
at least, my mind full of thoughts upon it. And so at night, after
supper, to bed.

31. Up and by water to W. Coventry, there to talk with
him about business of the Navy, and received from him direction
what to advise the Duke of York at this time; which was, to
submit and give*b* way to the King's naming a man or two that
the people about him have a mind should be brought into the

        a repl. 'which'   *b* repl. 'suf'-

---

1. In undertaking work normally
done by the Treasury: above, p. 493
& n. 3.

2. He was about to resign on his
becoming a navy victualler: above,
p. 348, n. 3.

Navy, and perhaps that may stop their fury in running further
against the whole – and this he believes will do it.   After much
discourse with him, I walked out with him into St. James's
park; where being afeared to be seen with*a* him (he having not
leave yet to kiss the King's hand, but notice taken, as I hear, of
all that go to him) I did take the pretence of my attending
Tanger Committee to take my leave; though to serve him, I
should I think stick at nothing.   At the Committee this morning,
my Lord Middleton declares at last his being*b* ready to go as soon
as ever money can be made ready to pay the garrison.   And so I
have orders to get money, but how soon I know not.

Thence home and there find Mr. Sheres, for whom I find my
moher of late to talk with mighty kindness; and perticularly, he
hath shown himself to be a poet, and that she doth*c* mightily value
him for.[1]   He did not stay to dine with us; but we to dinner,
and then in the afternoon, my wife being very well dressed by
her new maid, we abroad to make a visit to Mrs. Pickering;
but she abroad again, and so we never yet saw her.   Thence to
Dancre's and there saw our pictures which are in doing,[2] and I
did choose a view of Rome instead of Hampton Court – and
mightily pleased I shall be in them.   Here was Sir Ch. Cotterell
and his son, bespeaking something; both ingenious men I hear.[3]
Thence my wife and I to the park, and pretty store of company,
and so home with great content: and so ends the month – my
mind in pretty good content for all things but the designs on foot
to bring alterations in the Office; which troubles me.

     a repl. 'I did'   *b* repl. same symbol badly formed
                              c repl. 'did'

1. Henry Sheeres published several
books, mostly in prose.   Of his published verse there survives *A song in
the play call'd Oroonoko* (1700), composed for Southern's play in 1696.

2. See above, p. 423 & n. 1.
(OM).

3. Sir Charles Cotterell (Master of
Ceremonies to the King) was a friend
of Sandwich; his son Clement had
served in Sandwich's embassy to
Spain.

APRILL.

1. Up and with Collonell Middleton (at the desire of Rere=
Admirall Kempthorne, the President, for our assisting them[a]) to
the Court Martiall on board a yacht in the River, here to try the
business of the purser's complaints (Baker against Trevanion his
commander of the *Dartmouth*).[1]   But Lord, to see what wretched
doings there was among all the commanders to ruin the purser
and defend the captain in all his rogueries, be it to the prejudice
of the King or purser, no good man could bear.   I confess I was
pretty high, which [they] did not, at least the young gentlemen-
commanders, like; and Middleton did the like – but could not
bring it to any issue this day, sitting till 2 a-clock; and therefore,
we being sent for, went to Sir W Pen's by invitation to dine;
where my wife was, and my Lord Brouncker and his mistress
and Sir J. Mennes and his niece.   And here a bad dinner and little
mirth, I being little pleased with my host.   However,[b] I made
myself sociable; and so after dinner, my wife and I, with my
Lord Brouncker and his mistress, they set us down at my cousin
Turner's, and there we stayed a while and talked; and perticularly, here we met with Dr. Ball,[2] the parson of the Temple,
who did tell me a great many pretty stories about the manner of
the parsons being paid for their preaching at Pauls heretofore
and now, and the ground of the Lecture, and how heretofore the

a repl. closing bracket   *b* repl. 'How'-

1. The captain was charged with
assault; he counter-charged the purser with fraud. 'It appears by the
captain's confession that he caned the
said purser with a little Japan, which
he usually carries, but not in the manner the purser pretends nor was it
without intolerable provocation . . .
He had used reproachful and provok-

ing language, saying his captain durst
not strike him, for, if he should, he
would give him three blows for one
. . .': *CSPD Add. 1660–85*, pp. 288,
290.   The trial was aboard the *Merlin*
yacht.
2. Richard Ball, Master of the
Temple and Rector of St Mary
Woolchurch.

names of the founders thereof, which were many, at some 5s, some 6s per annum towards it, had*a* their names read in the pulpit every sermon, among those*b* holy persons that the Church doth order a Collect for giving God thanks for.[1]   By and by comes, by my desire, Commissioner Middletons coach and horses for us, and we went with it towards the park, thinking to have met The Turner and Betty, but did not; so turned back again to their lodging, and there found them and Mr. Batelier; and there after a little talk we took leave, and carry Batelier home with us.   So to supper and so to bed.

2.   Up and by water to White-hall, and there with the Office attended the Duke of York, and stayed in White-hall till about noon; and so with W. Hewer to the Cock, and there he and I dined alone with great content, he reading to me, for my memory sake, my late collections of the history of the Navy,[2] that I might represent the same by and by to the Duke of York; and so after dinner he and I to White-hall and there to the Duke of York's lodgings, whither he by and by, by his appointment, came; and alone with him an hour in his closet, telling him mine and W. Coventry's advice touching the present posture of the Navy,[3] as the Duke of Buckingham and the rest do now labour to make changes therein; and that it were best for him to suffer the King to be satisfied with the bringing in of a man or two which they

a   repl. 'were'   *b*   repl. 'and'

---

1. These were sermons founded in the 14th century, preached on Sunday mornings and at festivals, and regularly attended by the Lord Mayor and Corporation. The preacher (appointed by the Bishop) was paid 45s. and given four days' diet at the house of a person who was also appointed by the Bishop and was called 'the Shunamite'. The sermons (originally given at Paul's Cross but since 1660 in the Cathedral) attracted great crowds at Eastertide. The endowments (created largely by bequests of much greater sums than 4s. or 5s: see list in R. Newcourt, *Repertorium*, i. 4–5) were controlled by the City. The sermons are still given and the City still pays the preachers. See BM, Harl. 417, f. 132; M. Maclure, *Paul's Cross sermons, 1534–1642*.

2. See above, p. 483; below, p. 525, n. 1.

3. Pepys gives another, longer, account of this interview in NWB, pp. 181–3. He once again criticised Mennes for incompetence.

desire.   I did also give the Duke of York a short account of the history of the Navy, as to our Office, wherewith he was very well satisfied; but I do find that he is pretty stiff against their bringing in of men against his mind, as the Treasurers were, and perticularly against Child's coming in, because he is a merchant.*a1* After much discourse with him, we parted; and he to the Council, while I stayed, I waiting for his telling me when I should be ready to give him a written account of the administration of the Navy.   This caused me to wait the whole afternoon till night.   In the meantime, stepping to the Duchesse of York's side to speak with Lady Peterborough, I did see the young Duchess,*2* a little child in hanging sleeves, dance most finely, so as almost to ravish me, her airs*b* were so good – taught by a Frenchman*3* that did heretofore teach the King and all the King's children, and the Queen-Mother herself, who doth still dance well.   Thence to the Council-door, and Mr. Chevins took me into the back-stairs, and there with his friend Mr. Fowkes,*4* for whom he is very solicitous in some things depending in this office – he did make me, with some others that he took in, among others Alderman Bucknell,*5* eat a pickled herring, the largest I ever saw, and drink variety of wines, till I was almost merry; but I did keep in good tune, and so after the Council was up, I home and there find my wife not yet come home from Deptford, where she hath been all this day to see her mother – but she came by and by.   And so to talk and supper, and to bed.   This night*c* I did bring home from the King's potticary's in White-hall, by Mr. Cooling's direction, a water that he says did him mighty good for his eyes;*6* I pray God it may do me good, but by his description,

---

a repl. 'merant'   *b* MS. 'ears'   *c* repl. 'day this day'

---

1. Josiah Child; now proposed for a commissioner's place (below, p. 550 & n. 1). It was a rule that no officer of the Board should have an interest in trading with the navy.

2. Princess Mary, now a few days under seven.

3. Antoni Robert. (Inf. from R. Luckett.)

4. Thomas Foulkes, Groom of the Buckhounds. 'Chevins' was Will Chiffinch, Page of the Backstairs.

5. A rich brewer and excise-farmer.

6. Richard Cooling was secretary to the Lord Chamberlain; the King's apothecary was John Chase.

his disease was the same as mine, and this doth encourage me to use it.

3. Up and to the council-of-war again with Middleton; but the proceedings of the commanders so devilishly bad, and so professedly partial to the captain, that I could endure it no longer, but took occasion to pretend business at the office and away, and Collonell Middleton with me; who was of the same mind, and resolved to declare our minds freely to the Duke of York about it.[1] So to the office, where we sat all the morning. Then home to dinner, and so back to the office, where busy late till night; and so home to supper and to bed.

4. *Lords day.* Up, and to church, where Alderman Backewell's wife, by my invitation with my[a] head, came up with her mother and sat with us; and after sermon I did walk with them home, and there left them and home to dinner; and after dinner, with Sir J. Mennes and T. Middleton to White-hall by appointment; and at my Lord Arlingtons, the Office did attend the King and Caball to discourse the further quantity of victuals fit to be declared for – which was 2000 men for six months;[2] and so without more ado or stay there, hearing no news but that Sir Tom. Allen is to be expected every hour at home with his fleet, or news of his being gone back to Algier, and so home, where got my wife to read to me, and so after supper to bed. The Queene-Mother hath been of late mighty ill, and some fears of her death.[3]

a   repl. 'h'-

1. Cf. above, p. 505 & n. 1. Judgement was given *nem. con.* this day – the purser being fined and dismissed the service, and the commander merely fined £17 5s.

2. This was a meeting of the Foreign Affairs Committee of Council (i.e. the cabinet): for the official minute, see PRO, SP 104/176, ff. 135-6. The supplies were for the fleet which was now preparing for a voyage to the Mediterranean. On 5 April the Council directed the Duke of York to order the victuals from Gauden, and the Board to prepare an estimate: PRO, PC 2/61, p. 254.

3. Henrietta-Maria was at Colombes, near Paris, where she died on 21/31 August of this year.

5. Up, and by coach, it being very cold, to White-hall, expecting a meeting of Tangier, but it did not [meet] – but however, did wait there all the morning. And among other things, I spent a little time with Creed, walking in*a* the garden and talking about our office and Childs coming in to be a Commissioner; and being his friend, I did think he might do me a kindness, to learn of him what the Duke of Buckingham and that faction do design touching me, and to instil good words concerning me; which he says, and I believe, he will – and it is but necessary – for I have not a mind endeed at this time to be put out of my office if I can make any shift that is honourable to keep it; but I will not do it by deserting the Duke of York. At noon by appointment comes Mr. Sheres, and he and I to Unthankes, where my wife stays for us in our coach, and Betty Turner with her; and we to the Mullberry-garden, where Sheres is to treat us with a Spanish *Oleo*[1] by a cook of his acquaintance that is there, that was with my Lord in Spain. And without any other company, he did do it, and mighty nobly; and the *Oleo* was endeed a very noble dish, such as I never saw better, or any more of. This, and the discourse he did give us of Spain, and description*b* of the Escuriall, was a fine treat. So we left other good things that would keep till night for a collation – and with much content took coach again and went five or six miles towards Branford: the Prince of Tuscany, who comes into England only to spend money and see our country, comes into the town today, and is much expected; and we met him, but the coach passing by apace, we could not see much of him, but he seems a very jolly and good comely*c* man.[2]

a MS. 'with'   *b* repl. 'discour'-   *c* repl. 'comp'-

---

1. A stew of assorted meats (*olla podrida*).

2. Cosimo de' Medici (d. 1723), Grand Duke (as Cosimo III) in 1670, was travelling incognito. He was said to have undertaken a long tour in an attempt to overcome an unrequited passion for his wife: C. H. Hartmann, *The King my brother*, p. 261. His travels in England were described in an account written by his secretary, and published in English (with engravings of English scenes) in 1821: L. Magalotti, *Travels of Cosmo III* . . . His portrait appears as frontispiece. Magalotti (pp. 161–2) tells how the visitors dined at Brentford and were there greeted by the Lord Chamberlain (Earl of Manchester) and other royal officials.

By the way we overtook Captain Ferrers[1] upon his fine Spanish horse; and he is a fine horse endeed, but not so good, I think, as I have seen some. He did ride by us most of the way, and with us to the park and there left us, where we passed the evening; and meeting The Turner, Talbt., W Batelier and his sister in a coach, we anon took them with us to the Mullbery-garden; and there, after a walk, to supper upon what was left at noon, and very good; only, Mr. Sheres being taken suddenly ill for a while did spoil our mirth; but by and by was well again, and we mighty merry. And so broke up,*a* and left him at Charing-cross; and so calling*b* only*c* at my cousin Turner's, away home, mightily pleased with that day's work: and this day*d* came another new mayd for a middle-maid, but her name I know not yet – and for a cook-maid, we have ever since Bridget went used a black-moore of Mr. Batelier's (Doll), who dresses our meat mighty well, and we mightily pleased with her.[2] So by and by to bed.

6. Up and to the office; and thence to the Excise Office about some business; and so back to the office and sat till late; and thence to Mr. Bateliers to dinner, where my*e* cousin Turner and both her daughters and Tall Pepys and my wife, and a mighty fine dinner. They at dinner before I came; and when I had dined, I away home and*f* thence to White-hall, where the Board waited on the Duke of York to discourse about the dis-posing of Sir Tho. Allen's fleet, which is newly come home to Portsmouth;[3] and here Middleton and I did in plain terms acquaint the Duke of York what we thought and had observed

a repl. 'the'   *b* repl. 'them'   *c* symbol repeated
d repl. 'night'   *e* repl. 'Mrs. T'-
f repl. 'and with Commissioner Middleton'

---

1. Robert Ferrer, Master of the Horse to Sandwich, whom he (like Sheeres) had accompanied to Spain.

2. Negro servants were not un-commonly employed, especially in London. Bridget had left on 29 March.

3. Allin's fleet had returned from an expedition to Algiers: above, p. 428, n. 1. It had anchored off the Isle of Wight on the 4th and off Spithead on the 6th: Allin, ii. 95.

in the late Court Martiall, which the Duke of York did give ear to; and though he thinks not fit to revoke what is already done in this case by a Court Martiall, yet it shall bring forth some good laws in the behaviour of captains to their under-officers for the time to come.¹

Thence home; and there, after a while at the office, I home; and there came home my wife, who hath been with Bateliers late and been dancing with the company; at which I seemed* a little troubled, not being sent for thither myself; but I was not much so, but went to bed well enough pleased.

7. Up and by coach to my cousin Turner's, and invited them to dine at the Cock today with my wife and me; and so to the Lords of the Treasury I, where all the morning, and settled matters to*ᵃ* their*ᵇ* liking about the assignments on the Customs between the Navy Office and Victualler, and to that end spent most of the morning there with D Gawden;² and thence took him to the Cock and there left him and my clerk Gibson together, evening their reckonings, while I to the New Exchange to talk with Betty my little seamstress;³ and so to Mrs. Turner's to call them to dinner; but my wife not come, I back again, and was over-taken by a porter with a message from my wife that she was ill and could not come to us; so I back again to Mrs. Turner's and find them gone, and so back again to the Cock and there find Mrs. Turner, Betty, and Talbt. Pepys, and they dined with myself,*ᶜ* Sir D. Gawden and Gibson; and mighty merry, this house being famous for good meat, and perticularly pease-porridge. And after dinner broke up, and they away and I to the Council-chamber and there heard the great complaint of the City tried, against the gentlemen of the Temple for the late Riott, as they would have it, when my Lord Mayor was there.⁴ But upon hearing the whole business, the City was certainly to blame

---

a MS. 'to Lord' *b* repl. 'l' (incomplete, badly formed symbol)
  c repl. 'us'

---

1. For the case, see above, p. 505 & n. 1. For its sequel, below, p. 547 & n. 1.

2. *CTB*, iii. 53.
3. Betty Smith.
4. See above, pp. 465–6 & n.

to charge them in this manner, as a Riott; but the King and Council did forbear to determine anything in it till the other business of
the Title and privilege be decided, which is now under dispute at
law between them – whether the Temple be within the liberty
of the City or no.[1]   But I was sorry to see the City so ill advised
as to complain in a thing where their proofs were so weak.
Thence to my cousin Turner's, and thence with her and her
daughters and her sister Turner (I carrying Betty in my lap) to
Tall's[a] chamber at the Temple – where by agreement the poor
rogue had a pretty dish of anchoves and sweetmeats for them;
and hither came Mr. Eden, who was in his mistress's disfavour
ever since the other night that he came in thither fuddled, when
we were there; but I did make them friends by my buffoonery
and bringing up a way of spelling their names, and making
"Theophila" spell "Lamton", which The would have to be the
name of Mr. Edens mistress.[2]   And mighty merry we[b] were, till
late; and then I by coach home, and so to bed – my wife being ill
of those, but well enough pleased with my being with them.
This day I do hear that Betty Turner is to be left at school at
Hackny; which I am mightily pleased with, for then I shall now
and then see her.   She is pretty, and a girl for that, and her relation, that I love.[3]

8.   Up, and to White-hall to the King's side to find Sir
T. Clifford, where the Duke of York came and found me;
which I was sorry for, for fear he should think I was making
friends on that side.   But I did put it off the best I could, my
being there; and so by and by had opportunity alone to show
Sir T. Clifford the fair account I had drawn up of the Customs;
which he liked, and seemed mightily pleased with me; and so

---

a MS. 'the Tall's'   b repl. 'were'

---

1. The council debate is summarised
in PRO, PC 2/61, p. 258.   The city in
fact never took the dispute to court,
and to this day the issue has never
been tested in the courts.

2. Margaret Lambton later married

Robert Eden (d. 1720), the first
baronet.   Both came of distinguished
co. Durham families.

3. Sc. 'a girl whom I love both
because she is pretty and because she
is a relative'.

away to the Excise-Office to do a little business there, and so to the office, where all the morning. At noon home to dinner, and then to the office again till the evening; and then with my wife by coach to Islington to pay what we owe there for the late dinner at Jane's wedding; and so round by Kingsland and Hogsden[1] home, pleased with my wife's singing with me by the way; and so to the office again a little and then home to supper and to bed.

《Going this afternoon through Smithfield, I did see a coach run over the coachman's neck and stand upon it, and yet the man rose up and was well after it, which I thought a wonder.》

9. Up and by water to White-hall and there with the Board attended the Duke of York, and Sir Tho. Allen with us (who came to town yesterday); and it is resolved another fleet shall go to the Straights forthwith, and he command it. But his coming home is mighty hardly talked on by the merchants, for leaving their ships there to the mercy of the Turks – but of this, more in my White booke.[2] Thence out, and slipped out by water to Westminster-hall and there thought to have spoke with Mrs. Martin, but she was not there – nor at home; so back again, and with W. Hewer by coach home and to dinner; and then to the office, and out again with W. Hewer to the Excise-Office and to several places; among others, to Mr. Faythurne's to have seen an instrument which he was said to have for[a] drawing perspectives, but he had it not;[3] but here I did see his workhouse and the best things of his doing he had by him; and so to other places, and among others to Westminster-hall; and I took

a MS. 'of'

---

1. Hoxton. For the wedding, see above, p. 483 & n. 1.
2. NWB, pp. 190–1. (For Pepys's 'Navy White Book', see above, v. 116, n. 1.) Several English ships had been plundered by the Algerines after Allin's departure: *CSPD 1668–9*, p. 101. The merchants complained that he and his captains had hurried home

because they were more interested in transporting goods (trade of this sort being common at the time) than in commanding men-of-war. He sailed again for the Straits on 20 July 1669: Allin, ii. 98.
3. Pepys later got one from another shop: below, pp. 537–8 & n.

occasion to make a step to Mrs. Martins, the first time I have been
with her since her husband went last to sea, which is I think a
year since; but yo did now hazer con ella what I would, though
she had ellos upon her;*a* but yo did algo.   But Lord, to hear how
sillily she tells the story of her sister Doll's being a widow and
lately brought to bed, and her husband, one Rowland Powell,
drowned, that was at sea with her husband, but by chance dead*b*
at sea, cast away – when, God knows, she hath played the whore,
and is sillily forced at this time, after she was brought to bed, to
forge this story.

Thence, calling at several places by the way, we home and
there to the office; and then home to supper and to bed.

10.   Up and to the Excise-Office, and thence to White-hall a
little; and so back again to the Change, but nobody there, it
being over; and so walked home and to dinner; and after dinner
comes Mr. Seamour to visit me, a talking fellow, but I hear by
him that Captain Trevanion doth give it out everywhere that I
did over-rule the whole Court Martiall against him as long as I
was there.[1]   And perhaps I may receive at this time some wrong
by it; but I care not, for what I did was out of my desire of doing
justice.   So to the office, where late, and then home to supper
and to bed.

11.   *Lords day. Easter day.*   Up, and to church, where
Alderman Backewell's wife and mother and boy and another
gentlewoman did come and sit in our pew – but no women of
our own there, and so there was room enough.   Our parson
made a dull sermon; and so home to dinner, and after dinner
my wife and I out by coach, and Balty with us, to Loton the
lanskip-drawer,[2] a Dutchman living in St. James's-market, but
there saw no good pictures; but by accident he did direct us to a
painter that was then in the house with him, a Dutchman newly

a garbled s.h.   *b* repl. 'died'

---

1. Cf. above, pp. 505, 508 & nn.   2. Jan Looten (d. 1681); in London
John Seymour was a customs officer   since c. 1662; much influenced by
in the port of London.   Ruysdael. (OM).

come over,[a] one Everelst,[1] who took us to his lodging close by
and did show us a little flower=pott of his doing, the finest thing
that ever I think I saw in my life – the drops of Dew hanging on
the leaves, so as I was forced again and again to put my finger
to it to feel[b] whether my eyes were deceived or no. He doth
ask 70*l* for it; I had the vanity to bid him 20*l* – but a[c] better picture
I never saw in my whole life, and it is worth going twenty miles
to see. Thence, leaving Balty there, I took my wife to St.
James's and there carried her to the Queen's Chapel, the first
time I ever did it[2] – and heard excellent music, but not so good
as by accident I did hear there yesterday as I went through the
park from White-hall to see Sir W. Coventry; which I have
forgot to set down in my journal yesterday. And going out of
the Chapel, I did see the Prince of Tuskany come out, a comely
black, fat man, in a mourning-suit[3] – and my wife and I did see
him this[d] afternoon through a window in this Chapel. All that
Sir W. Coventry yesterday did tell me new was that the King
would not yet give him leave to come to kiss his hand, and he
doth believe that he will not in a great while do it, till those about
him shall see fit – which I am sorry for.

Thence to the park, my wife and I; and here Sir W. Coventry
did first see me and my wife in a coach of our own, and so did
also this night the Duke of York, who did eye my wife mightily.
But I begin to doubt that my being so much seen in my own
coach at this time may be observed to my prejudice – but I must

a repl. 'one'   *b* repl. 'see'
c repl. 's'-   *d* repl. 'too'

---

1. Simon Verelst (d. 1710); a
specialist in flower painting who also
painted portraits of the King and
members of his immediate circle. He
seems to have been extremely successful and to have owed much to the
patronage of the Duchess of Portsmouth and the Duke of Buckingham.
Pepys's reference here appears to
constitute the earliest evidence of
Verelst's presence in London. (OM).

2. Perhaps because the services
were Roman Catholic.
3. On the 9th he had gone into
mourning for his grandmother, the
late Grand-Duchess Maria Maddalena,
widow of Cosimo II of Tuscany and
sister of the Emperor Ferdinand II:
Magalotti, p. 166.

venture it now. So home; and by night home and so to my
office and there set down my journal, with the help of my left
eye through my tube, for fourteen days past; which is so much,
as I hope I shall not run in arrear again, but the*a* badness of my
eyes doth force me to it.[1]

So home to supper and to bed.

12. Up and by water to White-hall, where I of the whole
office attended the Duke of York at his meeting with Sir Tho.
Allin and several flag-officers to consider of the manner of
managing the war with Algier; and it being a thing I was wholly
silent in, I did only*b* observe; and find that their manner of discourse on this weighty affair was very mean and disorderly, the
Duke of York himself being the man that I thought spoke most
to the purpose. Having done here, I up and down the House,
talking with this man and that; and then meeting Mr. Sheres,
took him to see the fine Flower pott I saw yesterday, and did
again offer 20*l* for it, but he insists upon 50*l*. Thence I took him
to St.*c* James, but there was no music; but so walked to White-
hall, and by and by to my wife at Unthankes, and with her was
Jane, and so to the Cocke, where they and I and Sheres and Tom
dined, my wife having a great*d* desire to eat of their Soup made
of pease – and dined very well; and thence by water to the
Bear-Garden and there happened to sit by Sir Fretch. Hollis, who
is still of his vain-glorious and profane talk. Here we saw a
prize fought between a soldier and a country fellow, one Warrell,
who promised the least in his looks, and performed the most of
valour in his boldness and evenness of mind and smiles in all he
did that ever I saw, and we were all both deceived and infinitely
taken with him. He did soundly beat the soldier, and cut him
over the head.[2] Thence back to White-hall, mightily pleased all
of us with this sight, and perticularly this fellow, as a most

a repl. 'it'   *b* repl. same symbol badly formed   *c* repl. 'the'
d repl. 'des'-

1. For the effects on the MS., see   2. For prize-fighting, see above, iv.
above, p. 244, note *a*.   167–8 & n.

extraordinary man for his temper and evenness in fighting; and there leaving Sheres, we by our coach home; and after sitting an hour thruming upon my viall and singing, I to bed, and left my wife to do something to a waistcoat and petticoat she is [to wear] tomorrow.

This evening, coming home, we overtook Alderman Backewells coach and his lady, and fallowed them to their house and there made them the first visit, where they received us with extraordinary civility and owning the obligation. But I do, contrary to my expectation, find her something a proud and vainglorious woman in telling the number of her servants and family and expense. He is also so, but he was also ever of that strain. But here he showed me the model of his houses that he is going to build in Cornhill and Lumbard-street; but he hath purchased so much there, that it looks like a little town,*a* and must have cost him a great deal of money.[1]

13. Up, and at the office a good while; and then my wife going down the River to spend the day with her mother at Deptford, I abroad, and first to the milliner's in Fanchurch-street over against Rawlinsons; and there meeting both him and her in the shop, I bought a pair of gloves and fell to talk, and found so much freedom that I stayed there the best part of the morning till towards noon, with great pleasure, it being a holiday; and then against my will away and to the Change, where I left W. Hewer, and I by hackney-coach to the Spittle and heard a piece of a dull sermon to my Lord Mayor and Aldermen[2] and then saw them all take horse and ride away, which I have not seen together many a day; their wifes also went in their coaches –

a   repl. 'time

---

1. On 9 December 1670 Backwell obtained from the heirs of the late Charles Everard a 51 years' lease of 6576 sq. ft of ground intermingled with his holdings at £130 p.a. rent, and by July 1672 had rebuilt a number of houses: BM, Add. 5091 (11), 5100 (55). He enlarged his own house from 13 hearths to 21: PRO, E 179/252/23, n.f. For the purchases he had made here just before the Fire, see above, iv. 214 & n. 3; J. B. Martin, 'The Grasshopper' in Lombard St, pp. 185, 186. (R).

2. For the Spital sermons (in Spital Sq.), see above, iii. 58, n. 1.

and endeed the sight was mighty pleasing. Thence took
occasion to go back to this milliner's, whose name I now understand to be Clerke; and there, her husband inviting me up to the
Balcony to see the sight go by to dine at Cloathworker's-hall,[1]
I did go up, and there saw it go by; and then, there being a good
piece of ⟨cold⟩ roast-beef upon the table, and one Margetts, a
young merchant that lodges there and is likely to marry a sister
of hers, I stayed and eat and had much good conversation[a] with
her, who hath the vanity to talk of her great friends and father,
one Wingate,[2] near Welling, that hath been a Parliament-man.
Here also was Stapely the rope-merchant, and dined with us.
And after spending most of the afternoon also, I away home;
and there sent for W. Hewer and he and I by water to White-
hall to look, among other things, Mr. May, to unbespeak his
dining with me tomorrow. But here, being with him in the
Court-yard, as God would have it I spied Deb. which made my
heart and head to work; and I presently could not refrain, but
sent W. Hewer away to look for Mr. Wren (W. Hewer, I
perceive, did see her, but whether he did see me see her I know
not, or suspect my sending him[b] away I[c] know not) but my heart
could not hinder me. And I run after her and two women and a
man, more ordinary people, and she in her old clothes; and
after hunting a little, find them in the lobby of the Chapel below-
stairs; and there I observed she endeavoured to avoid me, but I
did speak to her and she to me, and did get[d] her para docere me ou
she demeures now. And did charge her para say nothing of me
that I had vu elle – which she did[d] promise; and so, with my
heart full of surprize and disorder,[e] I away; and meeting with
Sir H. Cholmley, walked into the park with him and back again,
looking to see if I could spy her again in the park, but I could not.
And so back to White-hall, and then back to the park with Mr.
May, but could see her no more; and so with W. Hewer, who I
doubt by my countenance might see some disorder in me, we

a repl. 'company'   *b* repl. 'me'   *c* repl. closing bracket
     d-d garbled s.h.   *e* repl. 'distr'-

home by water; and there I find Talb. Pepys and Mrs. Turner, and Betty too, come to invite us to dinner on Thursday; and after drinking, I saw them to the water-side, and so back home through Crutched-Friars, and there saw Mary Mercer and put off my hat to her on the other side the way; but it being a little darkish, she did not, I think, know me well. And so to my office to put my*a* papers in order, they having been removed for my closet to be made clean; and so home to my wife, who is come home from*b* Deptford. But, God forgive me, I hardly know how to put on confidence enough to speak as innocent, having had this passage today with Deb, though only, God knows, by accident. But my great pain is lest God Almighty shall suffer me to find out this girl, whom endeed I love, and with a bad*c* amour; but I will pray to God to give me grace to forbear it.

So home to supper, where very*d* sparing in my discourse, not giving occasion of any enquiry where I have been today, or what I have done; and so, without any trouble tonight more then my fear, we to bed.

14. Up and with W. Hewer to White-hall; and there I did speak with the Duke of York, the Council sitting in the morning, and it was to direct me to have my business ready of the Administracion of the Office against Saturday next, when the King would have a hearing of it. Thence home, W. Hewer with me, and then out with my own coach to the Duke of York's playhouse and there saw *The Impertinents*,[1] a play which pleases me well still; but it is with great trouble that I now see a play, because of my eyes, the light of the candles making it very troublesome to me. After the play, my wife and I toward the park; but it being too late, we to Creeds, and there find him and her together alone in their new house, where I never was before, they lodging before at the next door. And a pretty house it is, but I do not see that they intend to keep any coach. Here they treat us like

a repl. 'it'   b repl. full stop   c garbled s.h.
d repl. 'after'

---

1. A comedy by Shadwell; see above, p. 183, n. 2. (A).

strangers, quite according to the fashion, nothing to drink or eat, which is a thing that will spoil our ever having any acquaintance with them; for we do continue the old freedom and kindness of England to all our friends. But they do here talk mightily of my Lady Paulina's making a very good end[1] and being mighty religious in her lifetime, and hath left many good notes of sermons and religion, wrote with her own hand, which nobody ever knew*a* of – which I am glad of; but she was alway a peevish lady. Thence home, and there to talk and to supper and to bed, all being yet very safe as [to] my seeing of poor Deb yesterday.

15. Up and to the office; and thence, before the office sat, to the Excise Office with W. Hewer, but found some occasion to go another way to the Temple upon business; and I, by Deb's direction, did know whither in Jewen-street to direct my hackney*b*-coachman, while I stayed in the coach in Aldgate-street, to go thither first to enquire whether Mrs. Hunt her aunt was in town, who brought me word she was not; I thought this was as much as I could do at once, and therefore went away, troubled though that I could do no more; but to the office I must go, and did, and there all the morning; but coming thither, I find Bagwell's wife, who did give me a little note into my hand, wherein I find her*c* para invite me para meet her in Moorfields this noon, where I might speak with her;*c* and so after the office was up, my wife being gone before by invitation to my cousin Turner's to dine, I to that place; and there, after walking up and down by the windmills,*d* I did find her and talk with her; but it being holiday and the place full of people, we parted, leaving further discourse and doing to another time: thence I away and through Jewen-street, my mind, God knows, running that way, but stopped not; but going down Holburn-hill by the Conduit, I did see Deb on foot going up the hill; I saw her, and she me, but she made no stop, but seemed unwilling to speak to me; so I away on, but

a repl. 'hear'   *b* repl. 'coachman'
c–c garbled s.h.   *d* MS. 'wild-mills'

---

1. Lady Paulina Mountagu, Sandwich's unmarried daughter, had died on 28 February.

then stopped and light and after her, and overtook her at the end
of Hosier-lane in Smithfield; and without standing in the street,
desired her to fallow me, and I led her into a little blind alehouse
within the walls; and there she and I alone fell to talk and besar
la and tocar su mamelles; but she mighty coy, and*a* I hope
modest; but however, though with great force, did hazer ella
con su hand*b* para tocar mi thing, but ella was in great pain para
be brought para it. I did give her in a paper 20*s*, and we did
agree para meet*b* again in the Hall at Westminster on Monday
next; and so, giving me great hopes by her carriage that she
continues modest and honest, we did there part, she going home
and I to*c* Mrs. Turner's; but when I came back to the place where
I left my coach, it was gone, I having stayed too long, which did
trouble me to abuse a poor fellow so; but taking another coach,
I did direct him to find out the fellow and send him to me.
At my cousin Turner's, I find they are gone all to dinner to
Povey's; and thither I, and there they were all, and W. Batelier
and his sisters, and had dined; but I had good things brought
me, and then all up and down the house, and mightily pleased to
see the fine rooms:[1] but the truth is, there are so many bad
pictures, that to me make the good ones lose much of the pleasure
in seeing them. The and Betty Turner in new flowered-tabby
gowns, and so we were pretty merry; only, my fear upon me
for what I had newly done doth keep my content in. So about
5 or 6 a-clock away, and I took my wife and the two Bateliers
and carried them homeward; and W. Batelier lighting, I carried
the women round by Islington and so down Bishopsgate-street
home, and there to talk and sup, and then to bed.

16. Up and to my chamber, where with Mr. Gibson all the
morning, and there by noon did almost finish what I had to
write about the Administracion of the Office to present to the
Duke of York; and my wife being gone abroad with W. Hewer
to see the new play today at the Duke of York's House, *Guzman*,[2]

a repl. 'or I'   *b–b* garbled s.h.   *c* repl. 'by c'-

---

1. Cf. above, v. 161–2.
2. A comedy by the Earl of Orrery,
published in 1693. This is the first
record of its being performed. (A).

I dined alone with my people; and in the afternoon, away by coach to White-hall, and there the Office attended the Duke of York; and being despatched pretty soon and told that we should not wait on the King as intended till Sundy, I thence presently to the Duke of York's playhouse, and there in the 18*d* seat[1] did get room to see almost three acts of the play; but it seemed[a] to me but very ordinary. After the play done, I into the pit and there find my wife and W. Hewer, and Sheres got to them; which, so jealous is my nature, did trouble me, though my judgment tells me there is no hurt in it on neither side. But here I did meet with Shadwell the poet, who to my great wonder doth tell[b] me that my Lord of [Orrery] did write this play, trying what he could do in comedy, since his Heroique plays could do no more wonders. This doth trouble me, for it is as mean a thing, and so he says, as hath been upon the stage a great while; and Harris, who hath no part in it, did come to me and told me in discourse that he was glad of it, it being a play that will not take.[2] Thence home and to my business at the office, to finish it; but was in great pain about yesterday still, lest my wife should have sent her porter to enquire anything; though for my heart, I cannot see it possible how anything could be discovered of it; but yet, such is fear, as to render me full of doubt[c] and disquiet. At night, to supper and to bed.

17. Up and to the office, where all the morning. At noon home to dinner, and there find Mr. Pierce the surgeon, and he dined with us; and there hearing that *The Alchymist* was acted, we did go and took him with us, at the King's House; and is still a good play, it having not been acted for two or three years

a   repl. same symbol   *b*   repl. same symbol badly formed
                    c   repl. 'd'-

1. In the middle gallery, between the boxes and the upper gallery. (A).
2. Downes, on the other hand, records (p. 28) that the play 'took very well'. (A).

before; but I do miss Clun for the*ᵃ* Doctor¹ – but more, my eyes
will not let me enjoy the pleasure I*ᵇ* used to have in a play.
Thence with my wife in hackney to Sir W. Coventry's; who
being gone to the park, we drove after him; and there met him
coming out and fallowed him home, and there sent my wife to
Unthankes while I spent an hour with him, reading over first
my draft of the Administracion of*ᶜ* the Navy,² which he doth
like very well. And so fell to talk of other things; and among
the rest, of the story of his late disgrace,*ᵈ* and how basely and
in a mean manner the Duke of Buckingham hath proceeded
against him, not like a man of honour. He tells me that the
King will not give other answer about his coming to kiss his
hands then "not yett". But he says that this that he desires, of
kissing the King's hand, is only to show to the world that he is
not a discontent, and not in any desire to come again into play;
though I do perceive that he speaks this with less earnestness then
heretofore; and this, it may [be], is from what he told me lately,
that the King is offended at what is talked: that he hath declared
himself desirous not to have to do with any imployment more.
But he doth tell me that the leisure he hath yet had doth not at all
begin to be burdensome to him, he knowing how to spend his
time with content to him; and that he hopes shortly to contract
his expense, so as that he shall not be under any straits in that
respect neither – and so seems to be in very good condition of
content.

Thence I away over the park, it being now night, to White-
hall, and there in the Duchess's chamber to find the Duke of
York; and upon my offer to speak with him, he did come to me;
and withdrew to his closet and there did hear and approve my

---

a	s.h. repl. l.h. 'Face'	*b*	repl. 'to'
c	symbol repeated	*d*	repl. 'dist'–

---

1. Walter Clun, one of Pepys's
favourite actors, had regularly played
the title-role of Subtle in Jonson's
comedy. After Clun's murder on 2
August 1664 (see above, v. 232), he was
missed so much that the King's Company did not present *The Alchemist*
after the evening of his death until
this occasion. In the cast listed by
Downes (pp. 4–5), Wintersel played
Subtle; Mohun, Face; Cartwright,
Sir Epicure Mammon; Lacy, Ananias;
and Mrs Corey, Doll Common. (A).

2. See below, p. 525, n. 1.

paper of the Administration of the Navy; only, did bid me alter these words, "upon the rupture between the late King and the Parliament,"[a] to these, "the beginning of the late Rebellion;"[a] giving it me as but reason to show that it was with the Rebellion that the Navy was put by out of its old good course into that of a Commission.[1]   Having done this, we fell to other talk; he with great confidence telling me how matters go among our adversaries in reference to the Navy, and that he thinks they do begin to flag. But then beginning to talk in general of the excellency of old constitutions, he did bring out of his cabinet, and made me read it, an extract out of a book of my late Lord of Northumberlands, so prophetic of the business of Chatham as is almost miraculous.[2] I did desire and he did give it me to copy out, which pleased me mightily.[3]   And so it being late, I away and to my wife and by hackney home.   And there, my eyes being weary with reading so much, but yet not so bad as I was afeared they would, we home and to supper and to bed.

18.   *Lords day*.   Up, and all the morning till 2 a-clock at my office with Gibson and Tom, about drawing up fair my discourse of the Administracion of the Navy.   And then Mr. Spong being

a   quotation enclosed in large square brackets

1. It was in 1642 that the first of the commissions replacing the Navy Office was appointed. The Office was restored in June 1660.

2. This was a passage in Bk V of the MS. 'Tracts' written by the admiral, Sir William Monson (d. 1643), which had been in the possession of the 10th Earl of Northumberland, Lord High Admiral, 1638–42. In it Monson warned that given an easterly wind the Dutch might bring ships upriver as far as Gravesend without striking sail, and make a landing at Upnor. A fleet riding in the Medway would then be at their mercy. Monson recommended the fortification of Upnor Castle and the building of defence-works across the river. Pepys refers to this prophetic passage later (c. 1684) in his *Naval Minutes* (pp. 204–5). See *Naval tracts of Monson* (ed. Oppenheim), esp. v. 13–15. (None of the tracts were in print at this time but several copies circulated in MS.)

3. The copy of the extract (in Hewer's hand) survives in Rawl. A 195a, ff. 124–5. Pepys there states that it was communicated to him on the 16th, not the 17th, and that on 19 May the Duke of York told him that he had discovered that the author was Monson.

come to dine with me, I in to dinner and then out to my office again to examine the fair draft; and so borrowing Sir J. Mennes's coach, he going with Commissioner Middleton, I to White-hall, where we all met and did sign it; and then to my Lord Arlington's, where the King and Duke of York and Prince Rupert, as also Ormond and the two Secretaries, with my Lord Ashly and Sir T. Clifford, was; and there, by and by being called in, Mr. Williamson did read over our paper, which was in a letter to the Duke of York, bound up in a book with the Duke of York's book of Instrùctions.[1] He read it well; and after read, we were bid to withdraw, nothing being at all said to it. And by and by we were called in again, and nothing said to that business but another begun, about the state of this year's Action and our wants of money, as I had stated the same lately to our Treasurers – which I was bid, and did largely and with great content, open;[a] and having so done, we all withdrew and left them to debate our supply of money; after[b] which, being called in and referred[c] to attend on the Lords of the Treasury, we all departed; and I only stayed in the House till the Council rose, and then to the Duke of York, who in the Duchess's chamber came to me and told me that the book was there left with my Lord Arlington, for any of the Lords to view that had a mind, and to[d] prepare and present to the King what they had to say in writing to any

a   repl. 'op'- badly formed   b   MS. 'to'
c   repl. ? 'ref'-   d   blot under symbol

---

1. The letter, dated 17 April, was bound together with three other *pièces justificatives* besides the Duke's Instructions of 1662 (q.v. above, iii. 24, n. 1). In a memorandum of 3 May which Pepys attached to the office-copy, he refers to this meeting as one of the King and Cabinet, which Ashley and Clifford attended in order to deal with the question of supply for the navy. The letter was in substance a defence of the existing constitution of the Navy Board, and argued that it combined the virtues of government by commission in which all or most officers had general duties, with those of government by specialist officers with specific duties. The Board had both types of member. The office-copy of the letter (in Gibson's hand) is in NMM, LBK/8, pp. 589–93; printed in *Further Corr.*, pp. 230–5. Other copies in PL 2735, pp. 110+; BM, Add. 36782, ff. 81+ (printed in J. Charnock, *Hist. marine architecture*, 1801, ii. 404+). Summary in HMC, *Rep.*, 11/7/8. The original, in Hayter's hand, is in the Duke of Leeds MSS (Yorks. Archaeol. Soc., DD5/12/10).

part of it; which is all we can desire, and so that rested.[1] The
Duke of York then went to other talk; and by and by comes the
Prince of Tuscany to visit him and the Duchess, and I find that
he doth still remain Incognito, and so intends to do all the time
he stays here – for avoiding trouble to the King and himself,
and expense also to both.

Thence I to White-hall-gate, thinking to have found Sir J.
Mennes's coach staying for me; but not being there, and this
being the first day of rain we have had many a day, the streets
being as dusty as in summer, I forced to walk to my cousin
Turner's, and there find my wife newly gone home, which vexed
me; and so I having kissed and taken leave of Betty, who goes
to Putny to school tomorrow, I walked through the rain to the
Temple and there with much ado got a coach; and so home and
there to supper, and Pelling comes to us; and after much talk we
parted, and to bed.

19.   Up, and with Tom (whom, with his wife, I and my wife
had this morning taken occasion to tell that I did intend to give
him 40*l* for himself and 20*l* to his wife toward their setting out
in the world, and that my wife would give her 20*l* more, that so
she might have as much to begin with as he)[2] by coach to White-
hall; and there having set him work in the robe-chamber to write
something for me, I to Westminster-hall and there walked from
10 a-clock*a* to past 12, expecting to have met Deb; but whether
she had been there before, and missing me went away, or is
prevented in coming and hath no mind to come to me (the last
whereof, as being most pleasing, as showing most modesty, I
should be most glad of) I know not; but she not then appearing,
I being tired with walking went home; and my wife being all
day at Jane's, helping her as she said to cut out linning and other
things belonging to her new*b* condition, I after dinner out again;

a repl. ? 'my'   *b* repl. 'self'

---

1. On 3 May Williamson told
Pepys that no-one had by that time
consulted it: *Further Corr.*, pp. 235–6.
2. Earlier (in February 1668) Pepys

had intended to give Jane £50:
above, p. 64. But that may have
been meant for both of them.

and calling for my coach, which was at the coachmaker's and
hath been for these two or three days, to be new painted and the
window-frames gilt against May-day, went*a* on with my hackney
away to White-hall; and thence by water to Westminster-hall
and there did beckon to Doll. Lane, now Mrs. Powell as she would
have herself called, and went to her sister Martin's lodgings, the
first time I have been there these eight or ten months I think;
and her sister being gone to Portsmouth to her husband, I did
stay and talk with and drink with Doll and hazer ella para tocar
mi thing;*b* and yo did the like*b* para her, but ⟨did⟩ not the thing
itself, having not opportunity enough; and so away and to
White-hall and there took my own coach, which was now
come; and so away home and there to do business; and my
wife being come home, we to talk and to sup, there having been
nothing yet like discovery in my wife of what hath lately passed
with me about Deb, and so with great content to bed.

20. Up and to the office, and my wife abroad with Mary
Batelier with our own coach, but borrowed Sir J. Mennes's
coachman, that so our own might stay at home to attend at
dinner, our family being mightily disordered by our little boy's
falling sick the last night, and we fear it will prove the small-pox.
At noon comes my*c* guest, Mr. Hugh May, and with him Sir
Henry Capell, my old Lord Capells son, and Mr. Packer; and I
had a pretty dinner for them,*1* and both*d* before and after dinner
had excellent discourse, and showed them my closet*e* and my
office and the method of it, to their great content; and more
extraordinary manly discourse, and opportunity of showing
myself and learning from others, I have not in ordinary discourse
had in my life – they being all persons of worth; but especially
Sir H. Capell, whose being a Parliament-[man] and hearing my

a repl. 'took her and'   *b–b* garbled s.h.
c repl. 'our'   *d* repl. 'before'   *e* repl. 'ch'-

---

1. This was the dinner party arranged on 17 January and postponed
on 2 February. May was Comptroller
of the King's Works; Capel (M.P.
for Tewkesbury, Glos.) a close friend
of his, and Philip Packer Paymaster of
the Works.

discourse in the Parliament-house hath, as May tells me, given
him a long desire to know and discourse with me.   In the afternoon we walked to the old Artillery-ground near the Spitalfields,
where I never was before; but now, by Captain Deanes invitation, did go to see his new gun tryed, this being the place where
the officers of the Ordnance do try all their great guns; and
when we came, did find that the trial had been made, and they
going away with extraordinary report of the proof of his gun,
which, from the shortness and bigness, they do call "*punchinello*".[1]
But I desired Collonell Legg to stay and give us a sight of her
performance, which he did; and there, in short, against a gun
more then as long and as heavy again, and charged with as much
powder again, she carried the same bullet as strong to the mark,
and nearer*a* and above the mark at a point-blank then theirs, and is
more easily managed and recoyls no more then that – which is a
thing so extraordinary, as to be admired for the happiness of his
invention, and to the great regret of the old gunners and officers
of the Ordinance that were there; only, Collonel Legg did do her
much right in his report of her.   And so having seen this great
and first experiment, we all parted, I seeing my guests into a
hackney coach, and myself, with Captain Deane, taking a hackney, did go out toward Bow and went as far as Stratford, and all
the way talking of this invention, and he offering me a third of
the profit of the invention; which, for aught I know or do at
present think, may prove matter considerable to us; for either
the King will give him a reward for it, if he keeps it to himself,
or he will give us a patent to make our profit of it; and no
doubt but it will be of profit to merchantmen and others, to
have guns*b* of the same force at half the charge.   This was our
talk; and then to talk of other things of the Navy in general;
and among other things, he did tell me that he doth hear how
the Duke of Buckingham hath a spite at me, which I knew before

a repl. 'as'   *b* repl. 'the'

---

1. Nothing more appears to be
known of this gun.   It was presumably a naval piece.   Anthony Deane
was a shipwright: for his interest in
explosives, see above, viii. 358 & n. 1.

For naval guns at this time and the
efforts made to improve them, see
Ehrman, pp. 23+. '*Punchinello*' or
'punch' was now a fashionable word:
see below, p. 538.

but value it not; and he tells me that Sir T. Allen is not my friend; but for all this I am not much troubled, for I know myself so useful, that, as I believe, they will not part with me; so I thank [God],*a* my condition is such that I can retire and be able to live with comfort, though not with abundance. Thus we spent the evening with extraordinary good discourse, to my great content; and so home to the office and there did some business; and then home, where my wife doth come home, and I vexed at her staying out so late; but she tells me that she hath been at home with M. Batelier a good while, so I made nothing of it – but to supper and to bed.

21. Up, and with my own coach as far as the Temple; and thence sent it to my cousin Turner, who, to ease her own horses that are going with her out of town, doth borrow mine today. So I to Auditor Woods, and there to meet and met my Lord Bellasses upon some business of his accounts;[1] and having done that, did thence go to White-hall and attended the Duke of York a little, being*b* the first time of my waiting on him at St. James's this summer, whither he is now newly gone; and thence walked to White-hall, and so by and by to the Council-chamber and heard a remarkable cause pleaded, between the Farmers of the Excise of Wiltshire in complaint against the Justices of Peace of Salsbury, and Sir H. Finch were for the former;*c* but Lord, to see how he did with his admirable eloquence word the matter is not to be conceived almost – so pleasant a thing it is to hear him plead.[2] Thence at noon by coach home, and thither by and by

---

a no blank in MS.   *b* repl. 'and so to the Council-chamber'
c repl. same symbol badly formed

---

1. As ex-Governor of Tangier.

2. This case was due to be heard at 9 a.m. The excise-farmers accused three aldermen of Salisbury of helping the brewers of the city to evade payment of the duty on beer by giving twenty-two 'erroneous and false' judgements. The aldermen were discharged from custody on the 23rd. PRO, PC 2/61, pp. 260, 265, 280; ib.,

SP 29/253, f. 31 *v*; *CTB*, iii. 19, 20, 47 etc. There are several similar cases recorded in the Privy Council registers at about this time: excise duties were profoundly unpopular. Cf. below, p. 532 & n. 2. Sir Heneage Finch was Solicitor-General; Pepys often admired his eloquence: cf. above, v. 140 & n. 2.

comes my cousin Turner and The and Joyce in their riding-
clothes, they being come from their lodgings to her husband's
chamber at the Temple, and there do lie and purpose to go out of
town on Friday next.　And here I had a good dinner for them.
And after dinner, by water to White-hall, where the Duke of
York did meet our Office and went with us to the Lord-Com-
missioners of the Treasury; and there we did go over all the
business of the state I had drawn up, of this*a* year's action and
expense; which I did do to their satisfaction, and convincing
them of the necessity of providing more money, if possible, for
us.[1]　Thence, the Duke of York being gone, I did there stay
walking with Sir H. Cholmly in the Court, talking of news;
where he told me that now the great design of the Duke of
Buckingham is to prevent the meeting, since he cannot bring
about with the King the dissolving, of this Parliament, that the
King may not need it; and therefore my Lord St. Albans is
hourly expected, with great offers of a million of money, to
buy our breach with the Dutch;[2] and this they do think may
tempt the King to take the money, and thereby be out of a
necessity of calling the Parliament again – which these people
dare not suffer to meet again.　But this he doubts, and so do I,
that it will be to the ruin of the nation if we fall out with Holland.
This we were discoursing, when my boy comes to tell me that
his mistress was at the gate with the coach; whither I went and
there find my wife and the whole company; so she and Mrs.
Turner and The and*b* Talbot in mine, and Joyce, W Batelier,
and I in a hackney to Hyde-park, where I was ashamed to be
seen; but mightily pleased, though troubled with a drunken
coachman that did not remember, when*c* we came to light, where

a repl. 'the'　　　*b* MS. 'this'
c repl. 'where'

---

1. Cf. *CTB*, iii. 56–7: 'Mr Pepys
opens the present occasions of the
Navy for money.'
2. St Albans (English ambassador-
extraordinary in France, February–
April 1669) left Paris on 23 April/
3 May, but brought no large bribes:

cf. below, p. 536 & nn. 2, 3.　The
French ambassador to England (Colbert de Croissy) was said to have
brought 800,000 crowns with him in
August 1668: *CSPVen. 1666–8*, p.
263.

it was that he took us up; but said at Hammersmith, and thither he was carrying of us when*a* we came first out of the Park. So I carried them all to Hercules-Pillars and there did treat them; and so about 10 at night parted, and my wife and I and W. Batelier home; and he gone, we to bed.

22.   Up and to the office, where all the morning. At noon home to dinner, and Captain Deane with us and very good discourse, and perticularly about my getting a book for him to draw his whole Theory of shipping,[1] which at my desire he hath gone far in, and hath shown me what he hath done therein, to admiration. I did give him a Parallellogram,[2] which he is mightily taken with; and so after dinner to the office, where all the afternoon till night late, and then home, vexed at my wife's not being come home, she being gone again abroad with M. Batelier and came not home till 10 at night, which vexed me, so that I to bed and lay in pain awake till past one, and then to sleep.

23.   Going to rise without saying anything, my wife stopped me; and after a little angry talk, did tell me how she spent all yesterday with M. Batelier and her sweetheart, and seeing a play at the new Nursery which is set up at the House in Lincoln's [Inn] fields[3] which was formerly the King's House; so that I was mightily pleased again and rose with great content; and so up and by water to White-hall, and there to the Council-chamber and heard two or three causes; among others, that of the complaint of Sir Ph. Howard and Watson, the inventors, as they pretend, of the business of Vernashing and Lack[er]worke, against

---

a repl. full stop

---

1. In 1670 Anthony Deane completed a large folio treatise entitled (in 1675, when bound) 'Sir Ant. Deane's Doctrine of Naval Architecture' (PL 2910). It was illustrated with drawings of ships of every rate. Evelyn later wrote of it: 'I esteeme this one booke above any of the *Sybillas*, & it is an extraordinary Jewel' (iv. 271).

2. See above, p. 340, n. 1.
3. A theatre for the training of young actors: see above, p. 14, n. 2. The one used on this occasion was the theatre in Vere St, which had been headquarters of the King's Company, 8 November 1660 – 7 May 1663: see above, iv. 126, n. 2. (A).

the Company of Painters, who take upon them to do the same thing – where I saw a great instance of the weakness of a young counsel, not used to such an audience, against the Sollicitor general and two more able counsel used to it.[1] Though he had the right of his side and did prevail for what he pretended to against the rest, yet it was with much disadvantage and hazard. Here I also heard*a* Mr. Papillion make his defence to the King against some complaints of the Farmers of the Excise; but it was so weak, and done only by his own seeking, that it was to his injury more then profit, and made his case the worse – being ill managed, and in a cause against the King.[2] Thence at noon, the Council rising, I to Unthankes and there by agreement met my wife; and with her to the Cocke and did give her a dinner, but yet both of us but in ill humour, whatever was the matter with her; but thence to the King's playhouse and saw *The Generous Portugalls*,[3] a play that pleases me better and better every time we see it; and I thank God it did not trouble my eyes so much as I was afeared it would. Here by accident, we met Mr. Sheres, and yet I could not but be troubled, because my*b* wife doth so delight to talk of him and to see him. Nevertheless, we took him with us to our Mercer's and to the Exchange, and [he] helped me to choose a

a repl. 'made'   *b* repl. 'by'

---

1. Pepys was mistaken in the date: this case and the one which follows were heard on the 21st. (On 25 April he wrote up 12 days' arrears.) Howard and Francis Watson had been granted a patent on 2 March 1669 for making a 'gilt' varnish or lacquer without the use of gold. Certain members of the Company of Painters had infringed the patent, which was then confirmed by a council award of 28 May. PRO, PC 2/61, pp. 269, 313–14. For the interest in lacquer at this time, see above, iv. 153, n. 2.

2. The dispute was over the double duty charged under the excise acts of 1660 and 1668 on brandy, which was often made in England from imported wine on which both customs and excise duties had already been paid. In a test-case in the Court of Exchequer the verdict had gone against Thomas Papillon, and he and his colleagues in the trade had recently petitioned parliament. PRO, PC 2/61, p. 265; Grey, i. 237+; Milward, pp. 244–5, 251.

3. *The island princess, or The generous Portugal*, a tragicomedy by Fletcher with some alterations and additions; see above, p. 409, n. 2. (A).

summer-suit of coloured Camelott, coat and breeches, and a flowered tabby vest, very rich. And so home, where he took his leave and down to Greenwich, where he hath some friends, and I to see[a] Collonell Middleton, who hath been ill for a day or two, or three; and so home to supper and to bed.

24. Up and to the office, where all the morning; and at noon home to dinner, Mr. Sheres dining with us by agreement, and my wife, which troubled me, mighty careful to have a handsome dinner for him. But yet I see no reason to be troubled at it, he being a very civil and worthy man I think; but only, it doth seem to imply some little neglect of me.

After dinner to the King's House and there saw *The Generall*[1] revived, a good play, that pleases me well; and thence, our coach coming for us, we parted and home, and I busy late at the office and then home to supper and to bed – well pleased tonight to have Lead the vizard-maker bring me home my vizard with a Tube fastened in it, which I think will do my business, at least in a great measure, for the easing of my eyes.

25. *Lords day.* Up and to my office awhile, and thither comes Lead with my vizard, with a Tube fastened within both eyes; which, with the help which he prompts me to, of a glass[b] in the Tube, doth content me mightily. So to church, where a stranger made a dull sermon, but I mightily pleased to look upon Mr. Buckworths little pretty daughters; and so home to dinner, where W How came and dined with us; and then I to my office, he being gone, to write down my journall for the last twelve days; and did it with the help of my vizard and Tube fixed to it, and do find it mighty manageable; but how helpful to my eyes, this[c] trial will show me.

So abroad with my wife in the afternoon to the park – where very much company, and the weather very pleasant. I carried my wife to the Lodge, the first time this year, and there in our

a repl. 'the'   b s.h. repl. l.h. 'tub'-   c repl. 'my'

1. A heroic drama by Orrery; see above, v. 282, n. 1. (A).

coach eat a cheese-cake and drank a tankard of milk. I showed her this day also first the Prince of Tuscany, who was in the park – and many very fine ladies. And so home, and after supper to bed.

26. Up, having lain long; and then by coach with W. Hewer to the Excise Office, and so to Lilly's the varnisher, who is lately dead and his wife and brother keep up the trade, and there I left my French prints[1] to be put on boards; and while I was there, a fire burst out in a chimney of a house just over against his house – but it was with a gun quickly put out. So to White-hall and did a little business there at the Treasury-chamber; and so homeward, calling at the laceman's for some lace for my new suit, and at my tailor's. And so home, where to dinner, and Mr. Sheres dined with us, who came hither today to teach my wife the rules of perspective; but I think, upon trial, he thinks it too hard to teach her, being ignorant of the principles of lines. After dinner comes one Collonell Macknachan, one that I see often at Court, a Scotchman, but know him not; only, he brings me a letter from my Lord Middleton, who he says is in great distress for 500*l* to relieve my Lord Morton with (but upon what account I know not);[2] and he would have me advance it, without order, upon his pay for Tanger; which I was astonished at, but had the grace to deny him with an excuse. And so he went away, leaving me a little troubled that I was thus driven on a sudden to do anything herein. But Creed coming just now to see me, he approves of what I have done. And then to talk of general matters; and by and by, Sheres being gone, my wife and he and I out, and I set him down at Temple-bar, and myself and wife went down the Temple upon seeming business, only to put him off. And just at the Temple-gate, I spied Deb with another gentlewoman, and Deb winked on me and smiled, but un-discovered, and I was glad to see her. So my wife and I to the Change about things for her; and here at Mrs. Barnett's shop I am told by Betty, who was all undressed, of a great fire happened in Durham-yard last night, burning the house of one

---

1. See above, p. 427 & n. 1.
2. The 9th Earl of Morton was Middleton's son-in-law. Alexander
Macnachan (who had served in the royalist army) was a friend of Mor-ton: Whitear, p. 126.

Lady Hungerford,[1] who was to come to town to it this night; and so the house is burned, new furnished, by carelessness of the girl sent to take off a candle from a bunch of candles, which she did by burning it off, and left the rest, as is supposed, on fire. The King and Court was here, it seems, and stopped[a] the fire by blowing up of the next house.

The King and Court went out of town to Newmarket this morning betimes, for a week.[2] So home and there to my chamber and got my wife to read to me a little; and so to supper and to bed.

Coming home this night, I did call at the coachmaker's, and do resolve upon having the standards of my coach gilt with this new sort of varnish; which will come but to 40s; and contrary to my expectation, the doing of the biggest coach all over comes not to above 6l – which is [not] very much.

27.[b] Up and to the office, where all the morning. At noon home to dinner, and then to the office again, where all the afternoon busy till late; and then home and got my wife to read to me again in *The Nepotisme*,[3] which is very pleasant, and so to supper and to bed. This afternoon was brought to me a fresh *Distringas*[4] upon the score of my Tanger accounts; which vexes me, though I hope it will not turn to my wrong.

a repl. 'save'-   *b* repl. '28'

---

1. The house was not Lady Hungerford's (Hungerford House), but one of those in the nearby Durham Yard built on a part of the former Durham House and grounds, owned, since 1641, by the Earls of Pembroke, and leased in building plots by the 5th Earl soon after the Restoration. By a coincidence the lessee of the one burnt was a Rachel Hungerford, widow: BM, Add. 5098 (60). (R).

2. They returned on 1 May: *London Gazette*, 3 May.

3. *Il nipotismo di Roma: or The history of the Popes nephews from the* time of Sixtus the IV to the death of the last Pope Alexander the VII. In two parts. Written originally in Italian, in the year 1667, and Englished by W. A. (1669); PL 986; an anecdotal account whose theme was the impermanence of the power and wealth acquired by papal families. The author is usually held to have been Gregorio Leti, and the translator W. Aglionby: *Camb. Bibliog. Eng. lit.* (ed. Bateson, 1940), ii. 811.

4. For the use of writs of distraint in Exchequer accounting, see above, viii. 180 & n. 2.

28.[a] Up, and was called upon by Sir H. Cholmly to discourse about some accounts of his of Tanger;[1] and then to other talk, and I find by him that it is brought almost to effect, the late endeavours of the Duke of York and Duchess, the Queen-Mother, and my Lord St. Albans, together [with] some of the contrary faction, my Lord Arlington, that for a sum of money we shall enter into a league with the King of France; wherein he says my Lord Chancellor is also concerned, and he believes that in the doing hereof, it is meant that he shall come in again, and that this sum of money will so help the King as that he will not need the Parliament; and that in that regard, it will be forwarded by the Duke of Buckingham and his faction, who dread the Parliament;[2] but hereby, we must leave the Dutch,[3] and that I doubt will undo us, and Sir H. Cholmly says he finds W. Coventry to think the like. My Lady Castlemayne is instrumental in this matter and, he says, never more great with the King then she is now.   But this is a thing that will make the Parliament and Kingdom mad, and will turn to our ruine – for with this money the King shall wanton away his time in pleasures, and think nothing of the main till it be too late.   He gone, I to the office, where busy till noon; and then home to dinner, where M. Batelier dined with us, and pretty merry; and so I to the office again.

This morning, Mr. Sheres sent me, in two volumes, Mariana

---

a repl. '29'

---

1. These accounts (for work on the Tangier mole), dated this day and covering 1665-8, are in Rawl. C 423, ff. 82-3.

2. These were the negotiations which led to the secret treaty of Dover in May 1670. It is significant that the rumour-mongers (of whom Charles declared himself afraid at this very time) had not suspected that Charles might promise in that treaty to declare himself a Catholic, and to restore Catholicism to his kingdom when he should judge the moment ripe, with the help of the French. Buckingham, informed of some part of the plan, knew nothing of this.   The rumour about the exiled Clarendon was quite beside the mark: he had nothing to do with the plot.   The rest of this account may stand, but it omits the real authors of the project: Charles, his sister Henrietta, and Louis. See C. H. Hartmann, *The King my brother*, pp. 252+ ; Feiling, pp. 289+.

3. An Anglo-Dutch alliance had been made in January 1668. See above, p. 30 & n. 4.

his history of Spaine in Spanish,[1] an excellent book and I am much obliged*a* for it to him.

29. Up and to the office, where all the morning; and at noon dined at home, and then to the office again, there to despatch as much business as I could, that I might be at liberty tomorrow to look after my many things that I have to do against May-day. So at night home to supper and to bed.

30. Up and by coach to the coachmaker's, and there I do find a great many ladies sitting in the body of a coach that must be ended by tomorrow; they were my Lady Marquess of Win-chester, Bellasses, and other great ladies, eating of bread and butter and drinking ale. I to my coach, which is silvered over, but no varnish yet laid on; so I put it in a way of doing, and myself about other business; and perticularly to see Sir W. Coventry, with whom I talked a good while to my great content; and so to other places, among others, to my tailor's and then to the belt-maker's, where my belt cost me 55s, of the colour of my new suit; and here, understanding that the mistress of the house, an oldish woman in a hat, hath some water good for the eyes, she did dress me, making my eyes smart most horribly, and did give me a little glass of it, which I will use and hope it will do me good. So to the Cutler's and there did give Tom, who was with me all day, a sword, cost me 12s, and a belt of my owne – and set my own silver-hilt sword a-gilding[2] against tomorrow.

This morning I did visit Mr. Oldenburgh and did*b* see the instrument for perspective made by Dr. Wren, of which I have

a repl. same symbol   *b* repl. 'he'

---

1. Juan de Mariana's *Historia general de España*, a pioneer work, was one of the greatest products of Spanish scholarship. First published in Latin in 1592, it was translated into Spanish by the author in 1601. Since then several editions had been published; Sheeres may now have given Pepys a copy of that of 1650. PL 2147 is a copy of a later edition (Madrid, 1678; 2 vols bound as one).

2. The silver and gold effects were usually produced by the use of silver- or gilt-wire wound around the grip. Silver remained fashionable well into the 18th century.

one making by Browne; and the*a* sight of this doth please me mightily.[1] At noon, my wife came to me at my tailor's; and I sent her home, and myself and Tom dined at Hercules-pillers; and so about our business again, and perticularly to Lillys the varnisher about my prints, whereof some*b* are pasted upon the boards, and to my full content. Thence to the frame-maker's, one Norris in Long-Acre[2] – who showed me several forms of frames to choose by; which was pretty, in little bits of mouldings to choose by. This done, I to my coachmaker's, and there vexed to see nothing yet done to my coach at 3 in the afternoon; but I set it in doing, and stood by it till 8 at night and saw the painter varnish it; which is pretty, to see how every doing it over doth make it more and more yellow. And it dries as fast in the sun as it can be laid on almost. And most coaches are nowadays done so, and it is very pretty when laid on well – and not too pale, as some are, even to show the silver. Here I did make the workmen drink, and saw my coach cleaned and oyled; and staying among poor people there in the ally, did hear them call their fat child "punch"; which pleased me mightily, that word being become a word of common use for all that is thick and short.[3] At night home, and there find my wife hath been making herself clean against tomorrow. And late as it was, I did send my coachman and horses to fetch home the coach tonight. And so we to supper, myself most weary with walking and standing*c* so much to see all things fine against tomorrow; and so to bed – God give a blessing to it.

---

a repl. 'it'   *b* repl. same symbol badly formed
                c repl. 'st'-

---

1. Christopher Wren's instrument 'invented divers years ago . . . for drawing the outlines of any Object in Perspective' had been recently described in *Philos. Trans.*, 25 March 1669 (iv. 898–9). John Browne was now making one from that description: below, p. 548. For Wren's work as a designer-maker of instruments, see Eva G. R. Taylor, *Math. Practitioners*, p. 241, no. 260. Henry Oldenburg was secretary of the Royal Society.

2. Probably Henry Norris. (OM).

3. Cf. above, p. 528 (where *'punchinello'* is used to describe a gun).

Meeting with Mr. Sheres, he*ᵃ* went with me up and down to several places; and among others, to buy a perriwig, but I bought none – and also to Dancre's, where he was about my picture of Windsor; which is mighty pretty, and so will the prospect of Rome be.[1]

a   repl. same symbol

---

1. See above, p. 423 & n. 1.   (OM).

MAY.

1. Up betimes, called up by my tailor, and there first put on a summer suit this*a* year – but it was not my fine one of flowered tabby vest and coloured camelott tunic, because it was too fine with the gold lace at the hands, that I was afeared to be seen in it – but put on the stuff-suit I made the last year, which is now repaired; and so did go to the office in it and sat all the morning, the day looking as if it would be fowle. At noon home to dinner, and there find my wife extraordinary fine with her flowered tabby gown*b* that she made two years ago, now laced exceeding pretty, and endeed was fine all over – and mighty earnest to go, though the day was very lowering, and she would have me put on my fine suit, which I did; and so anon we went alone through the town with our new Liverys of serge, and the horses' manes and tails tied with red ribbon and the standards thus gilt with varnish and all clean, and green raynes, that people did mightily look upon us; and the truth is, I did not see any coach more pretty, or*c* more gay, then ours all the day. But we set ⟨out⟩ out of humour; I because Betty, whom I expected, was not come to go with us; and my wife, that I would sit on the same seat with her, which she liked not, being so fine; and then expected to meet Sheres, which we did in the Pell Mell, and against my will I was forced to take him into the coach, but was sullen all day almost, and little complaisant; the day also being unpleasing, though the park*d* full of coaches; but dusty and windy and cold, and now and then a little dribbling rain; and what made it worst, there*e* were so many hackney-coaches as*f* spoiled the sight of the gentlemen's, and so we had

---

a repl. full stop   *b* repl. 'suit'
c MS. 'though'   *d* repl. 'c'–
e MS. 'that'   *f* repl. 'is'

little pleasure.[1] But here was W Batelier and his sister in a borrowed*a* coach by themselfs, and I took them and we to the Lodge, and at the door did give them a sullabub and other things, cost me 12*s*, and pretty merry; and so back to the coaches and there till the evening; and then home, leaving Mr. Sheres at St. James's gate, where he took leave of us for altogether, he being this night to set out for Portsmouth post, in his way to Tanger – which troubled my wife mightily, who is mighty, though not I think too fond of him. But she was out of humour all the evening, and I vexed at her for it; and she did not rest almost all the night, so as in the night I was forced to take her and hug her to put her to rest. So home, and after a little supper, to bed.

2. *Lords day.* Up, and by water to White-hall and there visit my Lord Sandwiches, who, after about two months absence at Hinchingbrooke, came to town last night. I saw him, and very kind; and I am glad he is so, I having not wrote to him all the time, my eyes endeed not letting me. Here, with Sir Ch. Herbert and my Lord Hinchingbrooke and Sidny, we looked upon the picture of Tanger designed by Ch. Herberd and drawn by Dancre,[2] which my Lord Sandwich admires, as being the truest picture that ever he saw in his life – and it is endeed very pretty, and I will be at the cost*b* of having one of them.

Thence with them to White-hall, and there walked out the sermon with one or other; and then saw the Duke of York after sermon and he talked to me a little; and so away back by water home, and after dinner got my wife to read; and then by coach, she and I, to the park and there spent the evening with much

---

a repl. 'g'-   *b* blot under symbol

---

1. For the May-Day 'tour' of Hyde Park, see above, iv. 95, n3.

2. Danckerts's view of Tangier is probably that still in the royal collection. Signed and dated 1669, it is a view of the town from the south-west. Danckerts is not known to have visited Tangier and may have based his view on drawings by Sir Charles Harbord. The version commissioned by Lord Sandwich, formerly at Hinchingbrooke, is also signed and dated 1669: O. Millar, *Tudor, Stuart, and early Georgian pictures in coll. of H.M. Queen,* no. 401. (OM).

pleasure, it proving clear after a little shower, and we mighty fine, as yesterday, and people mightily pleased with our coach as I perceived. But I had not on my fine suit, being really afeared to wear it, it being so fine with the gold lace, though not gay.

So home and to supper; and my wife to read, and Tom, my *Nipotisme*,[1] and then to bed.

3. Up and by coach to my Lord Brouncker's, where Sir G Carteret did meet Sir J. Mennes and me to discourse upon Mr. Deering's business; who was directed in the time of the war to provide provisions at Hambrough by Sir G. Carteret's direction; and now G. Carteret is afeared to own it, it being done without written order.[2] But by our meeting, we do all begin to recollect enough to preserve Mr. Deering I think – which, poor silly man, I shall be glad of, it being too much he should suffer for endeavouring to serve us.

Thence to St. James's,[a] where the Duke of York was playing in the Pell Mell;[3] and so he called me to him most part of the time that he played, which was an hour, and talked alone to me; and among other things, tells me how the King will not yet be got to name anybody in the room of Pen, but puts it off for three or four days;[4] from whence he doth collect that they are brewing something for the Navy, but what, he knows not, but I perceive is vexed that things should go so; and he hath reason, for he told me that it is likely they will do in this as in other things: resolve first, and consider it and the fitness of it afterward.

Thence to White-hall, and met with Creed and I took him to the Harp and Ball[b] and there drank a cup of ale, he and I alone, and discoursed of matters; and I perceive by him that he makes no doubt but that all will turn to the old religion,[5] for these

a repl. 'White h'-   *b* MS. 'Balls'

---

1. See above, p. 535, n. 3.
2. This business has not been traced.
3. For the game (after which the alley or avenue is named), see above, ii. 64, n. 2.

4. Cf. above, p. 348 & n. 3. For the new appointment, see below, p. 551 & n. 2.
5. Creed was a Puritan.

people cannot hold things in their hands, nor can prevent its coming to that – and by his discourse fits himself for it, and would have my Lord Sandwich do so too, and me. After a little*ᵃ* talk with him, and perticularly about the ruinous condition of Tanger,¹ which I have a great mind to lay before the Duke of York, but dare not because of his great kindness to Lord Middleton, before it be too late – we parted; and I homeward*ᵇ* but called at Povy's, and there he stopped me to dinner, there being Mr. Williamson, Lieutenant of the Tower, Mr. Childe, and several others. And after dinner, Povy and I together to talk of Tanger, and he would have me move the Duke of York in it, for [it] concerns him perticularly, more then any, as being the head of us; and I do think to do it.

Thence home, and at the office busy all the afternoon; and so to supper and to bed.

4. Up and to the office; and then my wife being gone with the coach to see her mother at Deptford, I, before the office sat, went to the Excise Office; and thence, being alone, stepped into Duck-lane and thence tried to have sent a porter to Deb's, but durst not trust him. And therefore, having bought a book to satisfy the bookseller for my stay there, a 12*d* book, *Andronicus* of Tom Fuller,² I took coach; and at the end*ᶜ* of Jewen-street next Red-cross-street,*ᵈ* I sent the coachman to her lodging, and understand she is gone to Greenwich to one Marys's, a tanner's; at which I was glad, hoping to have opportunity to find her out there. And so, in great fear of being seen, I to the office and there all the morning. Dined at home; and presently after

a repl. 'then'   *b* repl. 'to'
c repl. 'further'   *d* repl. 'Bishop'

---

1. The four-year programme of fortification begun in 1664 had been much hindered by lack of materials: Routh, pp. 74–5. Cf. Pepys's comment on the same difficulty in 1683: *Tangier Papers*, p. 25.

2. *Andronicus or The unfortunate politician, showing sin slowly punished,* *right surely secured*; published 1646, 1649, 1659; not in the PL. A study of tyranny allegedly in 12th-century Byzantium; in reality about the emergence of tyranny (founded on 'pretended religion') from the Civil War.

dinner comes home my wife, who I believe was jealous of my spending the day; and I had very good fortune in being at home, for if Deb had been to have been found, it is forty to one but I had been abroad – God forgive me.   So the afternoon at the office; and at night walked with my wife in the garden, and my Lord Brouncker with us, who is newly come to W Pen's lodgings. And by and by comes Mr. Hooke,[1] and my Lord and he and I into my Lord's lodging and there discoursed of*a* many fine things in philosophy,* to my great content;   and so home to supper and to bed.

5.   Up, and thought to have gone with Lord Brouncker to Mr. Hooke's this morning betimes;   but*b* my Lord is taken ill of the gowte, and says his new lodgings have infected him,[2] he having never had any symptoms of it till now.   So walked to Gresham College to tell Hooke that my Lord could not come;   and so left word, he being abroad;   and I to St. James's and thence with the Duke of York to White-hall, where the Board waited on him all the morning;   and so at noon with Sir Tho. Allen and Sir Ed. Scott and Lord Carlingford to the Spanish Embassadors, where I dined the first time – the *Oleo* not so good as Shere's.[3]   There was at the table, himself and a Spanish Countess, a good, comely, and witty lady – three fathers – and us.   Discourse good and pleasant;   and here was an Oxford scholar in a Doctor's of Laws gowne, where the Embassador lay when the Court was there, to salute him from the college before his return to Spain.[4]   This man,*c* though a gentle sort of scholar, yet sat like a fool for want of French or Spanish;   but only Latin, which he spoke like a Englishman to one of the fathers.[5]   And by and by, he and I to

a repl. 'on great'   b repl. 'with'   c repl. 'he'

---

1. Robert Hooke, scientist; curator of experiments to the Royal Society.
2. He had taken over the lodgings from Penn, who suffered from the gout.
3. Cf. above, p. 509 & n. 1.
4. The ambassador (the Conde de Molina) had lodged at New College when in 1665 the court went to Oxford during the Plague: Wood,

L. & T., ii. 46. He embarked for Spain in late June: *CSPD 1668–9*, p. 377.
5. The English (like the French) used their native accent in speaking Latin. Spaniards, in common with other Europeans, used an Italianate pronunciation. See Evelyn, iii. 288 & n. 1; F. Brittain, *Latin in church*.

talk, and the company very merry at my defending Cambridge
against Oxford: and I made much use of my French and Spanish
here, to my great content.   But the dinner not extraordinary at
all, either for quantity or quality.   Thence home, where my wife
ill of those upon the maid's bed, and troubled at my being
abroad.   So I to the office, and there till night; and then to her,
and she read to me the *Epistle of Cassandra*,[1] which is very good
endeed, and the better to her because recommended by Sheres.
So to supper, and I to bed.

6.   Up and by coach to W. Coventry's; but he gone out,
I by water back to the office and there all the morning; then to*ᵃ*
dinner and then the office again; and anon with my wife by
coach to take the ayre, it being a noble day, as far as the greene
Man,[2] mightily*ᵇ* pleased with our journey and our*ᶜ* condition of
doing it in our own coach; and so home and to walk in the
garden; and so to supper and to bed, my eyes being bad with
writing my journall, part of it, tonight.

7.   Up, and by Coach to W. Coventry's, and there to talk
with him a great deal, with great content; and so to the Duke of
York, having a great mind to speak to him about Tanger; but
when I came to it, his interest for my Lord Middleton is such
that I dare not.

So to the Treasury-chamber, and then walked home round
by the Excise Office, having by private vows last night, in
prayer to God Almighty, cleared my mind for the present of the
thoughts of going to Deb to Greenwich, which I did long after.
I passed by Guild hall, which is almost finished[3] – and saw a

---

a repl. 'after'   *b* repl. 'mily'   *c* repl. 'con'-

---

1. The letter ('L'autheur à Cas-
sandre') prefacing bk i, pt iii of La
Calprenède's romance: see above, p.
365 & n. 1.
2. Probably the fashionable tavern
on Stroud Green, nr Islington. (R).
3. Work in fact continued on it

and its ancillary buildings for many
years, but in November 1671 it was
so far complete that it was again used
for the elaborate ceremonies of the
Lord Mayor's feast: LRO, Repert.
76, f. 245r. (R).

poor labourer carried by, I think dead with a fall, as many there are I hear.

So home to dinner – and then to the office a little; and so to see my Lord Brouncker, who is a little ill of the gout; and there Madam Williams told me that she heard that my wife was going into France this year; which I did not deny, if I can get time, and I pray God I may;[1] but I wondering how she came to know it, she tells me a woman that my wife spoke to for a maid did tell her so, and that a lady that desires to go thither would be glad to go in her company. Thence with my wife abroad with our coach, most pleasant weather, and to Hackny and into the marshes, where I never was before, and thence round about to Old ford and Bow; and coming through the latter home, there being some young gentlewomen at a door and I seeming* not to know who they were, my wife's jealousy told me presently that I knew well enough, it was that damned place where Deb dwelt; which made me answer very angrily that it was false, as it was; and I carried back again to see the place, and it proved not it, so I continued out of humour a good while at it, she being willing to be friends, as I was by and by, saying no more of it. So home, and there met with a letter from Captain Silas Taylor; and with it, his written copy of a play that he hath wrote and intends to have acted. It is called *The Serenade, or Disappointment;*[2] which I will read, not believing he can make any good of that kind. He did once*a* ⟨offer to⟩ show Harris it,[3] but Harris telling him that he would judge by one Act whether it were good or no, which is endeed a foolish saying, and we see them out themselfs in the choice of a play after they have read the whole, it being sometimes found not fit to act above three times – nay, and some that have been refused at one House is found a good one at the other.[4] This made Taylor he would

a repl. same symbol badly formed

1. See above, p. 462, n. 3.
2. This play is not otherwise known. Silas Taylor (naval store-keeper at Harwich) was an antiquary and musician. (A).
3. Henry Harris, one of the leading actors in the Duke of York's Company. (A).
4. Pepys is here referring to the King's playhouse and the Duke's. (A).

not show it him; but is angry, and hath carried it to the other and he thinks it will be acted there, though he tells me they are not yet agreed upon it. But I will find time to get it read to me – and I did get my wife to begin a little tonight in the garden, but not so much as I could make any judgment on it.

So home to supper and to bed.

8. Up, and to the office and there comes Lead to me; and at last my vizards are done, and glasses got to put in and out as I will; and I think I have brought it to the utmost, both for easiness of using and benefit, that I can; and so I paid him 15*s* for what he hath done now last in the finishing them, and they, I hope, will do me a great deal of ease.

At the office all the morning; and this day the first time did alter my side of the table, after above eight years sitting on that next the fire. But now I am not able to bear the light of the windows in my eyes, I do go there; and I did sit with much more content then I had done on the other side for a great while, and in winter the fire will not trouble my*ᵃ* back.

At noon home to dinner; and after dinner, all the afternoon within with Mr. Hater, Gibson, and W. Hewer, reading over and drawing up new things in the instructions of commanders; which will be good, and I hope to get them confirmed by the Duke of York, though I perceive nothing will effectually perfect them but to look over the whole body of the instructions of all the officers of a ship, and make them all perfect together.[1] This being done, comes my bookseller and brings me home, bound, my collection of papers about my Addresse to the Duke of York

a repl. 'me'

---

1. The new instructions were issued in the following August: Rawl. D 794, f. 11; BM, Add. 36782, f. 82*v*. Pepys had been particularly anxious to reduce the powers of commanders in certain respects: see above, pp. 510–11 & n.

in August;[1] which makes me glad, it being that which shall do me more right many years hence then perhaps all I ever did in my life – and therefore I do, both for my own and the King's sake, value it much.

By and by also comes Browne the Mathematical-instrument maker, and brings me home my instrument for Perspective, made according to the description of Dr. Wren's in the late *Transactions*,[2] and he hath made it, I think, very well; and that that I believe will do the thing, and therein give me great content, but that I fear all the contents that must be received by my eyes are almost lost.

So to the office and there late at business, and then home to supper and to bed.

9. *Lords day.*[a] Up, and after dressed in my best suit with gold trimming, I to the office, and there with Gibson and Tom finishing against tomorrow my notes upon commanders' instructions; and when[b] church-time, to church with my wife, leaving them at work. Dr. Mills preached a dull sermon; and so we home to dinner – and thence by coach to St. Andrew, Holburne, thinking to have heard Dr. Stillingfleete preach, but we could not get a place; and so to St. Margaret, Westminster, and there heard a sermon and did get places,[c] the first time we have heard there these many years. And here at distance I saw Betty Michell, but she is become much a plainer woman then she was a

a From here onwards to 20 May (inclusive) the symbols and letters are heavily inked and often smudged.
                    b repl. 'of'   c repl. 'pl'-

1. 'Papers Conteyning my Addresse to his Royall Highnesse . . . by letter dated the 20 of August 1668. Humbly tendering him my advice touching the present state of the Office of the Navy. With his Royall Highness's proceedings upon the same, and their Result': PL 2242 (144 pp.; in Gibson's hand); copies of letters (20 August 1668–12 February 1669); memoranda of proceedings, and Pepys's summaries and analyses of his colleagues' self-exculpations. Other collections of papers concerning these transactions are in PL 2554 (in Gibson's hand); PL 2874, pp. 385–504, 509–81; Rawl. A 457 (in Hayter's hand). Cf. *Cat.*, i. 33–6. For the Duke's letter (26 August 1668, based on Pepys's draft of the 20th), see above, p. 289 & n. 1.
2. See above, p. 538 & n. 1.

girl. Thence*a* toward the park, but too soon to go in; so went on to Knightsbridge, and there eat and drank at the Worlds-end, where we had good things; and then back to the park and there till night, being fine weather and much company; and so home, and after supper, to bed. This day I first left off both*b* my waist-coats by*c* day, and my waistcoat by night, it being very hot weather, so hot as to make me break out here and there in my hands, which vexes me to see – but is good for me.

10. Troubled, about 3 in the morning, with my wife's calling her maid up, and rising herself, to go with her coach abroad to gather May-dew[1] – which she did; and I troubled for it, for fear of any hurt, going abroad so betimes, happening to her. But I to sleep again, and she came home about 6 and to bed again, all well. And I up, and with Mr. Gibson by coach to St. James and thence to White-hall, where the Duke of York met the office and there discoursed of several things, perticularly the instructions to commanders of ships. But here happened by chance a discourse of the Council of Trade, against which the Duke of York is mightily displeased, and perticularly Mr. Child;[2] against whom he speaking hardly, Captain Cox did second the Duke of York by saying that he was talked on for an unfayre dealer with masters of ships about freight – to which Sir T. Littleton very hotly and foolishly replied presently, that he never heard any honest man speak ill of Childe; to which the Duke of York did make a smart reply, and was angry – so as I was sorry to hear it come so far, and that I, by seeming to assent

a symbol blotted   *b* repl. 'all'   *c* repl. 'and'

---

1. Used as a cosmetic: cf. above, viii. 240 & n. 3.

2. Josiah Child, a member of the Council, was a prominent E. India merchant. The council had been established recently (by commissions issued on 20 October 1668 and 13 April 1669) under the Duke's presi-dency: C. M. Andrews, *British Committees etc. of Trade, 1622–75*, pp. 92–3.

to*a* Cox, might be observed too much by Littleton, though I said nothing aloud – for this must breed great heart-burning.[1]

After this meeting done, the Duke of York took the Treasurers into his closet to chide them, as Mr. Wren tells me, for that my Lord Keeper did last night at the Council say, when nobody was ready to say anything against the constitution of the Navy, that he did believe the Treasurers of the Navy had something to say – which was very foul on their part,*b* to be parties against us. They being gone, Mr. Wren took boat, thinking to dine with my Lord of Canterbury;[2] but when we came to Lambeth, the gate was shut, which is strictly done at 12 a-clock and nobody comes in afterward, so we lost our labour; and therefore back to White-hall and thence walked, my boy*c* Jacke with me, to my Lord Crew, whom I have not seen since*d* he was sick, which is eight months ago I think[3] – and there dined with him. He is mightily broke. A stranger, a country gentleman, was with him, and he pleased with my discourse accidentally about the decay of gentlemen's families in the country, telling us that the old rule was that a family might remain 50 miles from London 100 year, 100 mile off from London 200 years, and so, farther or nearer London, more or less years. He also told us that he hath heard his father say that in his time it was so rare for a country*e* gentleman to come to London, that when he did come, he used to make his will before he set*f* out.

Thence to St. James and there met the Duke of York, who told me with great content that he did now think*g*

---

a repl. 'did'   b MS. 'heart'   c MS. 'body' or 'bawdy'
    d repl. 'm'-   e repl. same symbol badly formed
        f repl. 'went'   g MS. 'he think'

---

1. Child had been put forward by Buckingham (to whose interest Littleton belonged) as Penn's successor on the Board, against the Duke of York's opposition. The King, who at first had been in his favour, now withdrew his support: NWB, p. 201.

2. Sheldon. The archbishops kept public dinners at Lambeth during the parliamentary session: cf. Milward, pp. 41 etc. See the description (1786) of the ceremony (which included a service) qu. D. Gardiner, *Story of Lambeth Palace*, pp. 233–4. The custom continued 'down to the time of Howley' (d. 1848): *DNB*, 'Sancroft'.

3. Cf. above, p. 265.

he should master our adversaries,[1] for that the King did tell
him that he was satisfied in the constitution*a* of the Navy, but
that it was well to give these people leave to object against it;
which they having not done, he did give*b* warrant to the Duke
of York to direct Sir Jeremy Smith to be a Commissioner
of the Navy in the room of Penn;[2] which, though he be an
impertinent fellow, yet I am glad of it, it showing that the
other side is not so strong as it was; and so, in plain terms,
the Duke of York did tell me that they were every day losing
ground – and perticularly, that he would take care to keep out
Childe. At all which I am glad, though yet I dare not think
myself secure, but the King may yet be wrought upon by these
people to bring changes in our office, and remove us ere it be
long. Thence I to White-hall, and there took boat to Westminster and to Mrs. Martins, who is not come to town from her
husband at Portsmouth; so drank only at Cragg's with her and
Doll, and so to the Swan and there besard a*c* new maid*c* that is
there; and so to White-hall again to a Committee of Tanger,
where I see all things going to wrack in the business of the
Corporation, and consequently in the place, by Middleton's
going.
   Thence walked a little with Creed, who tells me he hears how
fine my horses and coach are, and advises me to avoid being
noted for it; which I was vexed to hear taken notice of, it being
what I feared; and Povy told me of my gold-lace sleeves in the
park yesterday, which vexed me also, so as to resolve never to
appear in Court with it, but presently to have it taken off, as it is
fit I should. And so to my wife at Unthankes, and coach, and
called at my tailor's to that purpose; and so home, and after a
walk*d* in the garden, home to supper and to bed.

   11. My wife again up by 4 a-clock to go to gather May dew,
and so back home by 7 to bed; and by and by, I up and to the

---

a repl. 'const'-   *b* MS. 'give order to the Duke of York to give'
      c–c garbled s.h. repl. 'fal' 'fat'   *d* repl. 'little'

---

1. Buckingham's faction.   2. The Duke's warrant was issued
                                        on this day; the patent on 17 June.

office, where all the morning; and dined at noon at home*a* with my people, and so all the afternoon; in the evening, my wife and I all alone, with the boy,*b* by water up as high as Putney almost with the tide, and back again, neither staying, going nor coming; but talking and singing, and reading a foolish copy of verses up[on] my Lord Mayors entertaining of all the Bachelors, designed in praise to my Lord Mayor.[1] And so home, and to the office a little and then home to bed, my eyes being bad.

Some trouble at Court for fear of the Queens miscarrying, she being, as they all conclude, far gone with child.[2]

12. Up and to Westminster-hall, where the term is; and this the first day of my being there, and here by chance met Rogr. Pepys, come to town the last night. I glad to see him. After some talk with him and others, and among others, Sir Ch. Herberd and Sidny Mountagu, the latter of whom is to set out tomorrow toward Flanders and Italy, I invited them to dine with me tomorrow; and so to Mrs. Martin's lodging, who come to town last night, and there yo did hazer her,*c* she having been a month, I think, at Portsmouth with her husband, newly come home from the Streights. But Lord, how silly the woman talks of her great entertainment there, and how all the gentry came to visit her, and that she believes her husband is worth 6 or 700*l*;[3] which nevertheless I am glad of, but I doubt they will spend it as fast. Thence home; and after dinner, my wife and I to the Duke of York's playhouse, and there in the side balcone over

a MS. 'noon' *b* repl. same symbol badly formed
c garbled s.h: see above, viii. 244, note *a*

---

1. The Lord Mayor was Sir William Turner, a lifelong bachelor. (He was a brother of the lawyer John Turner who had married a cousin of Pepys.) On 5 May he had given a feast to 'a noble company' of London bachelors. The verses published (anonymously) on the occasion were by the puritan versifier Robert Wild, whose popular *Iter Boreale* (1660) had celebrated Monck's march from Scot-

land to restore the King. His present effort – *Upon the rebuilding the city . . . the Lord Mayor and the noble company of bachelors dining with him, May 5th 1669* (1669) – combined an encomium of the mayor with an attack on the papists for causing the Great Fire. It was republished, under the author's name, in *Iter Boreale* etc. (1670).

2. See below, p. 560 & n. 3.

3. He was a purser.

against the music,[1] did hear, but not see, a new play, the first day acted, *The Roman Virgin*, an old play[2] and but ordinary I thought; but the trouble of my eyes with the light of the candles did almost kill me.[3]

Thence to my Lord Sandwiches, and there have a promise from Sidny to come and dine with me tomorrow; and so my wife and I home in our coach, and there find my Brother John, as I looked for, come to town from Ellington; where, among other things, he tells me the first news that my sister*a* is with child and far gone;[4] which I know*b* not whether it did more trouble or please me, having no great care for my friends* to have children, though I love other people's.   So, glad to see him, we to supper and so to bed.

13.   Up and to the office, where all the morning, it being a rainy foul day.   But at noon comes my Lord Hinchingbrooke and Sidny and Sir Ch. Herberd and Rogr Pepys, and dined with me; and had a good dinner, and very merry, and with us all the afternoon, it being a farewell to Sidny; and so in the evening, they away and I to my business at the office; and so to supper and talk with my brother, and so to bed.

14.   Up, and to St. James's to the Duke of York and thence to

a MS. 'wife'   *b* smudge above symbol

1. The orchestra of the Restoration public theatre usually played in a small room situated above the middle of the proscenium arch. Hence Pepys on this occasion was evidently seated in one of the stage boxes on the same level as the upper gallery. (A).

2. Pepys's apparently contradictory use of the terms 'new' and 'old' is due to the fact that *The Roman virgin* was John Webster's tragedy, *Appius and Virginia* (published in 1654, but written twenty-five years earlier), as revised by Betterton: see Downes, p. 30; G. Langbaine, *Momus Triumphans* (1688), A 2ᵛ. Betterton's revision is

not extant.   This is the first record of its being performed. According to Downes (p. 30), Betterton played Virginius; Harris, Appius; and Mrs. Betterton, Virginia. (A).

3. Chandeliers were hung over the apron stage, where most of the acting took place. (A).

4. She had a son soon afterwards, who was christened Samuel in honour of the diarist. He lived to become the principal beneficiary under Pepys's will of 1701, but in that of 1703 was cut off with an annuity of £40 because he had made a match Pepys disapproved of.

White-hall, where we met about office business; and then at
noon to dinner with Mr. Wren to Lambeth, with the Archbishop
of Canterbury; the first time I was ever there, and I have long
longed for it – where a noble house, and well furnished with
good pictures and furniture, and noble attendance in good order,
and great deal of company, though an ordinary day,[1] and exceeding great cheer, nowhere better, or so much that ever I think I
saw for an ordinary table.   And the Bishop[2] mighty kind to me,
perticularly desiring my company another time, when less
company there. Most of the company gone, and I going, I
heard by a gentleman of a sermon that was to be there; and so I
stayed to hear it, thinking it serious, till by and by the gentleman
told me it was a mockery by one Cornet Bolton, a very gentle-
man-like*a* man, that behind a chair did pray and preach like a
presbyter-Scot that ever I heard in my life, with all the possible
imitation in grimaces and voice[3] – and his text about the hanging
up their harps upon the willows[4] – and a serious good sermon too,
exclaiming against Bishops and crying up of my good Lord
Eglington[5] – till it made us all burst; but I did wonder to have
the Bishop*b* at this time to make himself sport with things of
this kind, but I perceive it was shown him as a rarity. And he
took care to have the room-door shut, but there was about
twenty gentlemen there – and myself infinitely pleased with the
novelty.

So over to White-hall to a little Committee of Tanger; and
thence walking in the Gallery, I met Sir Tho. Osborne, who to
my great content did of his own accord fall into discourse with
me, with so much professions of value and respect, placing the
whole virtue of the office of the Navy upon me, and that for the

a repl. 'I'-   *b* MS. 'the Bishop make himself'

---

1. Sc. not a church festival. For
the building and its hall, see above,
vi. 164, n. 2.
2. William Sheldon, Archbishop.
3. Mimicry of preachers was a
popular parlour-trick: cf. above, p.
264 & n. 5. The mimic on this occasion appears to have been Richard
Bolton, commissioned ensign 1666:

C. Dalton, *Engl. army lists, 1661–
1714*, i. 69.
4. Ps., cxxxvii. 2.
5. 'Pious Eglintoun', the 6th Earl
(d. 1661). He had once served
penance for fornication: Burnet, i.
273; William Fraser, *Memorials of
Montgomeries*, i. 59+.

Controller's place, no man in England was fit for it but me when Sir J. Mennes, as he says it is necessary, is removed – but then, knows not what to do for a man in my place; and in discourse, though I have no mind to the other, did bring in Tom Hater to be the fittest man in the world for it – which he took good notice of.[1] But in the whole, I was mightily pleased, reckoning myself now 50 per cent securer in my place then I did before think myself to be. Thence to Unthankes and there find my wife, but not dressed; which vexed me, because of going to the park, it being a most pleasant day after yesterday's rain, which lays all the dust, and most people going out thither, which vexed me. So home, sullen; but then my wife and I by water, with my brother, as high as Fullam, talking and singing and playing the rogue with the western bargemen about the women of Woolwich, which mads them.[2] And so back home to supper and to bed.

15. Up and at the office all the morning. Dined at home, and Creed with me home, and I did discourse*a* about evening some reckonings with him in the afternoon; but I could not, for my eyes, do it, which troubled me and vexed him that I would not; but yet we were friends, I advancing him money without it; and so to walk all the afternoon together in the garden, and I perceive still he doth*b* expect a change in our matters, especially as to religion,[3] and fits himself for it by professing himself for it in his discourse. He gone, I to my business at my office, and so at night home to supper and to bed.

16. *Lords day.* My wife and I at church, our pew filled (which vexed me at her confidence) with Mrs. Backwell and six more that she brought with her. Dined at home, and W Batelier with us, and I all the afternoon drawing up a foul draft

a repl. 'even some reckonings in'   *b* repl. ? 'would'

1. Hayter became joint-Clerk of the Acts, with Pepys's brother John, when Pepys became Secretary to the Admiralty in 1673.

2. Cf. above, p. 221 & n. 4.
3. Cf. above, p. 542 & n. 5.

of my petition to the Duke of York about my eyes, for leave to spend three or four months out of the office, drawing it so as to give occasion to a voyage abroad; which I did to my pretty good liking.[1]   And then with my wife to Hyde-park, where a good deal of company, and good weather; and so home to supper and to bed.

17.   Up, and to several places doing business, and then home to dinner; and there my wife and I and brother John by coach to the King's playhouse and saw *The Spanish Curate*[2] revived, which is a pretty good play – but my eyes troubled with seeing it mightily.   Thence carried them and Mr. Gibson, who met me at my Lord Brouncker's with a fair copy of my petition, which I thought to show the Duke of York this night; but could not, and therefore carried them to the park, where they had never been; and so home – to supper and to bed.

Great the news now, of the French taking St. Domingo in Spaniola from the Spaniards; which troubles us, that they should have, and have the honour of taking it, when we could not.[3]

18.   Up, and to St. James and other places, and then to the office, where all the morning.[a]   At noon home and dined in my

---

a   repl. 'born'-

---

1. It was presented on 19 May; copy (in Gibson's hand) in NMM, LBK/8, pp. 599–600; printed in *Further Corr.*, pp. 237–9. The petitioner refers to the 'ill condition whereto the restless exercises of his Eyes requisite to the seasonable dispatching of the Worke of his Place dureing the late Warr have unhappily reduced him . . . [He has] fruitlessly made many Medicinall attempts . . ., [but is told by the doctors that] nothing but a considerable relaxation from Worke can bee depended upon either for recovery of what Portion of his Sight hee hath lost, or secureing the remainder'. For the journey which followed, see above, p. 462, n. 3; for the recovery of his eyesight, below p. 565, n. 1.

2. A comedy by Fletcher and Massinger; see above, ii. 54, n. 4. (A).

3. The French had taken not San Domingo (a town in Eastern Hispaniola under Spanish control), but the island of Tortuga (now Ile de la Tortue), thus denying to the Spaniards effective control of Western Hispaniola. In 1654–5 an English expedition under Penn and Venables had failed to take Hispaniola.

wife's chamber, she being much troubled with the tooth-ake; and I stayed till a surgeon of hers came, one Leeson, who hath formerly drawn her mouth. And he advised her to draw it; so I to the office, and by and by word is come that she hath drawn it – which pleased me, it being well done; so I home to comfort her, and so back to the office till night, busy, and so home[a] to supper and to bed.

19. With my coach to St. James, and there, finding the Duke of York gone to muster his men in Hyde-park,[1] I alone with my boy thither; and there saw more, walking out of my coach as other gentlemen did, of a soldier's trade then ever I did in my life – the men being mighty fine, and their commanders, perticularly the Duke of Monmouth; but methought their trade but very easy, as to the mustering of their men, and the men but indifferently ready to perform what was commanded in the handling their arms.

Here the news was first **talked** of Harry Killigrews' being wounded in nine places last night by footmen in the highway, going from the park in a hackney-coach toward Hammersmith to his house at Turnam-greene – they being supposed to be my Lady Shrewsbury's men – she being by in her coach with six horses. Upon an old grudge, of his saying openly that he had lain with her.[2]

Thence by and by to White-hall, and there I waited upon the King and Queen all dinner-time in the Queen's lodgings, she being in her white pinner and apern, like a woman with child; and she seemed handsomer, plain so, then dressed. And by and by, dinner done, I out and to walk in the Gallery for the Duke of York's coming out; and there meeting Mr. May, he took me down about 4 a-clock to Mr.[b] Chevins's lodgings, and all alone

---

a repl. 'to'   *b* symbol smudged

---

1. A muster of seven companies of the Foot Guards, with two troops of Horse Guards, was held in the morning: *London Gazette*, 20 May.
2. According to a newsletter (25 May), four footmen made the attack, having concealed their intention by attending on a mourning coach: HMC, *Le Fleming*, p. 64.

did get me a dish of cold chickens and good wine, and I dined like a prince, being before very hungry and empty. By and*ᵃ* by the Duke of York comes,*ᵇ* and readily took me to his closet and received*ᶜ* my petition, and discoursed it about my eyes and pitied me, and with much kindness did give me his consent to be absent, and approved of my proposition to go into Holland to observe things there of the Navy, but would first ask the King's leave; which he anon did, and did tell me that the King would be "a good maister to me" (these were his words about my eyes) and doth*ᵈ* like of my going into Holland, but doth advise that nobody should know of my going thither – but pretend that I did go into the country somewhither – which I liked well. Glad of this, I home; and thence took out my wife and to Mr. Holliards about a swelling in her cheek, but he*ᵉ* not at home; and so round by Islington and eat and drink; and so home and after supper, to bed.

In discourse this afternoon, the Duke of York did tell me that he was the most amazed at one thing just now that ever he was in his life; which was that the Duke of Buckingham did just now come into the Queen's bed-chamber, where the King and much mixed company, and among others Tom Killigrew, the father of Harry who was last night wounded so as to be in danger of death, and his man is quite dead – and there in discourse did say that he had spoke with some that was by (which all the world*ᶠ* must know that it must be his whore, my Lady Shrewsbury), who says that they did not mean to hurt, but beat him, and that he did run first at them with his sword – so that he doth hereby clearly discover* that he knows who did it, and is of conspiracy with them, being of known conspiracy with her; which the Duke of York did seem to be pleased with, and said it might perhaps cost him his life in the House of Lords[1] – and I find was mightily pleased with it – saying it was the most impudent thing, as well as foolish, that ever he knew man do in all his life.

a repl. 'and by'　　　*b* MS. 'comes and by'　　　*c* repl. 'my'
　　d repl. 'would'　　　*e* repl. same symbol
　　　　f repl. same symbol badly formed

---

1. Buckingham was not prosecuted.

20. Up and to the office, where all the morning. At noon, the whole office, Brouncker, J. Mennes, T. Middleton, S. Pepys, and Captain Cox, to dine with the parish at the Three Tuns, this day being Ascension-day[1] – where exceeding good discourse among the merchants. And thence back home, and after a little talk with my wife, to my office and did a great deal of business; and so, with my eyes mighty weary and my head full of care how to get my accounts and business settled against my journy, home to supper and to bed.

Yesterday, at my coming home, I found that my wife had on a sudden put away Matt[2] upon some falling out, and I doubt my wife did call her ill names, by my wife's own discourse; but I did not meddle to say anything upon it, but let her go; being not sorry, because now we may get one that speaks French to [go] abroad with us.

21. I waited with the office upon the Duke of York in the morning. Dined at home, where Lew. Phillips, with a friend of his, dined with me.[a] In the afternoon at the office. In the evening visited by Rogr. Pepys and Ph. Packer; and so home.

22. Dined at home. The rest of the whole day at the office.

23. *Lords day.* Called up by Rog. Pepys and his son, who to church with me and then home to dinner. In the afternoon, carried them to Westminster and myself to St. James; where not finding the Duke of York, back home and with my wife spent the evening taking the ayre about Hackny with great pleasure, and places we had never seen before.

24. To White-hall, and there all the morning, and thence home; and giving order for some business, and setting my

a MS. 'him'

---

1. For parish dinners, see above, p. 179, n. 1.
2. The 'very comely' maid who had come into their service on 29 March.

brother to making a catalogue of my books,[1] I back again to
W. Hewer to White-hall, where I attended the Duke of York
and was by him led to the King,*a* who expressed great sense of
my misfortune in my eyes, and concernment for their recovery;
and accordingly signified not only his assent to my desire therein,
but*b* commanded me to give them rest this summer, according
to my late petition to the Duke of York. W. Hewer and I
dined alone at the Swan, and thence, having thus waited on the
King, spent till 4 a-clock in St. James's-park, when I met my
wife at Unthankes and so home.

25. Dined at home, and the rest of the day, morning and
afternoon, at the office.

26. To White-hall, where all the morning. Dined with Mr.
Chevins with Alderman Backwell and Spragg; the Court full
of the news from Captain Hulbert of the *Milford*, touching his
being affronted in the Streights, shot at, and having eight men
killed him by a French man-of-war, calling him "English dog,"
and commanding him to strike; which he refused and, as knowing himself much too weak for him, made away from him.[2]
The Queen, as being*c* supposed with child, fell ill, so as to call
for Madam Nun, Mr. Chevins's sister, and one of her women,
from dinner from us, this being the last day of their doubtfulness
touching her being with child, and were therein well confirmed
by Her Majesty's being well again before night.[3]

a MS. 'Duke of York'   *b* repl. 'about'
c MS. 'as being' repeated

1. For Pepys's catalogues, see
above, vii. 412 & n. 2.
2. Evidence taken about this incident is in BM, Sloane 3510, ff. 58+;
there is no mention of any casualties.
It occurred on 13 April while the
Milford (Capt. John Hubbard) was
bound for Tangier from Malaga.
There was a rumour that the French
captain was ordered to be hanged:
CSPD 1668–9, p. 407. The English
and French soon afterwards agreed
that neither side should salute the

other in Mediterranean waters:
Charles II to Duke of York, 26 June,
CSPD 1668–9, p. 385; Duke of York,
Mem. (naval), pp. 173–4 (order, 6 July
1669); P. Clément (ed.), *Lettres . . .
de Colbert*, iii, pt 1, pp. 143–4. Cf.
T. W. Fulton, *Sovereignty of sea*,
p. 471 & n. 4.
3. The King described the symptoms in detail in a letter to his sister
Henrietta of 24 May: C. H. Hartmann, *The King my brother*, pp. 257–8.
She miscarried, however, in June.

One Sir Edmd. Bury Godfry, a woodmonger and Justice of Peace in Westminster, having two days since arrested*a* Sir Alex. Frazier for about 30*l* in firing, the baileys were apprehended, committed to the Porter's Lodge,[1] and there, by the King's command, the last night severely whipped – from which the Justice himself very hardly escaped (to such an unusual degree*b* was the King moved therein).[2] But he lies now in the Lodge, justifying his act as grounded upon the opinion of several of the judges, and among others, my Lord Chief-Justice[3] – which makes the King very angry with the Chief-Justice as they say; and the Justice doth lie and justify his act and says he will suffer in that cause for the people, and doth refuse to receive almost any nutriment.[4] The effects of it may be bad to the Court.

Expected a meeting of Tanger this afternoon, but failed. So home, met by my wife at Unthankes.

27. At the office all the morning. Dined at home, Mr. Hollier with me. Presented this day by Mr. Browne with a book of drawing by him, lately printed, which cost me 20*s* to him.[5] In the afternoon to the Temple to meet with Auditor Aldworth about*c* my interest account,[6] but failed of meeting

---

a MS. 'rested'   *b* repl. 'de'-   *c* repl. 'to'

---

1. A prison in Whitehall palace.

2. Frazier, as a royal physician, could be arrested only by the authority of the Lord Chamberlain. Godfrey claimed that he was forced to take action by the number of irrecoverable debts owing to him by the poor. See PRO, SP 29/353, ff. 44, 46; *Bulstrode Papers*, i. 101, 103; W. Westergaard (ed.), *First Triple Alliance*, pp. 121, 127; R. Turke, *Memoires of . . . Godfrey* (1682), pp. 36+.

3. Sir John Kelyng.

4. Godfrey was released after six days, having refused to petition for his liberty. He was the same Godfrey who later achieved fame as the

'Protestant magistrate' and whose death in violent and mysterious circumstances in 1678 detonated the explosion of anti-catholic panic in the Popish Plot. His careful display of public virtue on this occasion is perhaps typical of the man.

5. Alexander Browne, *Ars Pictoria, or An academy treating of drawing, painting, limning, etching . . .* (1669); announced in *Mercurius Librarius*, 28 June 1669, for publication at 10*s*. bound: Arber, *Term Cat.* i. 14; not in the PL. Browne had taught drawing to Mrs Pepys.

6. For Tangier.

him. To visit my cousin Creed and found her ill at home, being
with child, and looks poorly. Thence to her husband at Gresham
College upon some occasions of Tanger; and so home, with
Sir Jo. Bankes with me, to Mark-lane.

28. To St. James's, where the King's being with the Duke of
York prevented a meeting of the Tanger commission. But
Lord, what a deal of sorry discourse did I hear between the King
and several lords about him here – but very mean methought.
So with Creed to the Excise Office, and back to White-hall –
where in the park Sir G. Carteret did give me an account of his
discourse lately with the Commissioners of Accounts, who
except against many things but none that I find considerable –
among others, that of the officers of the Navy selling*a* of the
King's goods, and perticularly my providing him with calico
flags – which having been by order and but once, when necessity
and the King's apparent profit as conformable to my perticular
duty, it will prove to my advantage that it be enquired into.[1]
Nevertheless, having this morning received from them a demand
of an account of all monies within their cognizance*b* received and
issued by me, I was willing, upon this hint, to give myself rest,
by knowing whether their meaning therein might reach only to
my Treasurership for Tanger, or the monies imployed on this
occasion. I went therefore to them this afternoon, to understand what monies they meant; where they answered me by
saying the eleven-months tax, customs, and prize-money – without mentioning (any more*c* – then I demanding) the service they
respected therein; and so without further discourse, we parted
upon very good terms of respect and with few words – but my
mind not fully satisfied about the monies they mean. At noon
Mr. Gibson and I dined at the Swan; and thence, doing this at
Brooke-house and thence calling at the Excise Office for an

---

a repl. 'serving'   *b* repl. 'cog'-
c repl. same symbol badly formed

---

1. See above, v. 308 & n. 2. The
Brooke House Committee found that
Pepys had received £757 17s. 5¾d.
'for flags and cork': HMC, *Rep.*,
8/1/1/133*b*. Officials were forbidden
to trade in goods used by the Navy.

account of payment of my tallies of Tanger, I home. And thence with my wife and brother spent the evening on the water, carrying our supper with us, as high as Chelsea; so home, making sport with the Westerne bargees and my wife and I singing, to my great content. So home.

29. *The King's birth-day.* To White-hall, where all very gay; and perticularly, the Prince of Tuscany very fine, and is the first day of his appearing out of morning*ᵃ* since he came.¹ I heard the Bishop of Peterborough² preach, but dully; but a good anthem of Pelham's.³ Home to dinner, and then with my wife to Hyde-park, where all the evening great store of company, and great preparations by the Prince of Tuscany to celebrate the night with fireworks for the King's birthday;⁴ and so home.

30. *Whitsunday.ᵇ* By water to White-hall, and thence to Sir W. Coventry, where all the morning by his bedside, he being indisposed;*ᶜ* our discourse was upon the notes I had lately prepared for commanders' instructions;⁵ but concluded that nothing will render them effectual without an amendment in the choice of them, that they be seamen, and not gentlemen above*ᵈ* the command of the Admiral by the greatness of their relations at Court.⁶ Thence to White-hall and dined alone with Mr. Chevins his sister; whither by and by came in Mr. Progers and Sir Tho. Allen, and by and by fine Mrs. Wells,⁷ who is a great beauty and there I had my full gaze upon her, to my great content, she being a woman of pretty conversation.

Thence to the Duke of York, who, with the officers of the

---

a l.h. repl. s.h. 'm'-   *b* This day's entry is in a faltering hand.
      c repl. 'ind'-   *d* repl. 'about'

---

1. See above, p. 515 & n. 3.
2. Joseph Henshaw; Bishop of Peterborough, 1663–79; the sermon does not appear to have been printed.
3. Pelham Humfrey's. (E).
4. The display (by 'a machine with . . . fanciful artificial fireworks and squibs') was given in front of the house of the Earl of St Albans where the Prince lodged. Casks of Italian wine and of beer were distributed, 'which caused increased applause'. Magalotti, p. 371.
5. See above, p. 547 & n. 1.
6. Cf. above, vii. 11, n. 1.
7. Winifred Wells, Maid of Honour to the Queen.

Navy, made a good entrance on my draft of my new instructions
to commanders, as well expressing his general [views] of a
reformation among them, as liking of my humble offers towards
it. Thence, being called by my wife, Mr. Gibson and we to the
park, whence the rain sent us suddenly home.

31. [Up] very betimes, and so continued all the morning,
with W. Hewer, upon examining and stating my accounts, in
order to the fitting myself*a* to go abroad beyond sea, which the ill
condition of my eyes, and my neglect*b* for a year or two, hath
kept me behindhand in, and so as to render it very difficult now,
and troublesome to my mind to do it; but I this day made a
satisfactory entrance therein. Dined at home, and in the afternoon by water to White-hall, calling*c* by the way at Michell's,
where I have not been many a day till just the other day; and
now I met her mother there and knew her husband to be out of
town. And here yo did besar ella, but have not opportunity
para*d* hazer mas with her*e* as I would have offered if yo had
had*e* it. And thence had another meeting with the Duke of York
at White-hall with the Duke of York on yesterday's work, and
made a good advance; and so being called by my wife, we to the
park, Mary Batelier, a Duch gentleman, a friend of hers, being*f*
with us. Thence to the World's-end, a drinking-house by the
park, and there merry; and so home late.

And thus ends all that I doubt I shall ever be able to do with
my own eyes in the keeping of my journall, I being not able to do
it any longer, having done now so long as to undo my eyes
almost every time that I take a pen in my hand; and therefore,
whatever comes of it, I must forbear; and therefore resolve
from this time forward to have it kept by my people in longhand, and must therefore be contented to set down no more then
is fit for them and all the world to know; or if there be anything
(which cannot be much, now my amours to Deb*g* are past, and my
eyes hindering me in almost all other pleasures), I must endeavour
to keep a margin in my book open, to add here and there a note

---

a repl. 'f'-   *b* repl. 'l'-   *c* repl. 'called'
        d repl. 'at'   *e–e* garbled s.h.
    f repl. same symbol   *g* garbled s.h.

in short-hand with my own hand.[1] And so I betake myself to that course which [is] almost as much as to see myself go into my grave – for which, and all the discomforts that will accompany my being blind, the good God prepare me.

May. 31. 1669.   S. P.[a]

a   54 ruled pages and 3 unruled end-sheets are left blank.

---

1. He never kept any such record. His eyesight appears to have improved after his holiday abroad in the following autumn (q.v. above, p. 462 & n. 3), for from at least February 1670 he was able to make a limited use of shorthand (see e.g. *CSPD 1670*, p. 94; cf. also ib., pp. 480, 516, 639). He later composed journals (written up by clerks) for specific purposes – to record his examination by the Privy Council about the Brooke House Committee's report (3 January–17 February 1670; PL 2874, pp. 385–403), and to help him with his defence when accused of treason during the Popish Plot (20 May–June 1679, 24 January–10 April 1680; PL 2881, pp. 45–85;

ib., 2882, ff. 1189–1235), and to record the work of the Special Commission of 1686 (PL 1490, pp. 7–79). But he never again kept a personal diary for any length of time. What is sometimes called his 'second diary' is the short journal (30 July–1 December 1683), closely-written in shorthand, of his voyage to Tangier, when he went with the expedition which dismantled and evacuated it (Rawl. C 859 B and C; the accompanying memoranda of his observations are much longer than the journal itself). The best edition is by E. Chappell (Navy Rec. Soc., 1935). Being a *livre d'occasion* it is quite different in character and scale from the diary which now ends.

London
in the sixteen~sixties

Western half (omitting most minor streets & alleys)

| 0 | 220 | 440 | 600 yds |

Area of Great Fire

TO HAMPSTEAD

Tyburn Gibbet

TO OXFORD

1 St Martin-in-the-Fields
2 The Cockpit
3 Axe Yard
4 Holbein Gate
5 King St Gate
6 Westminster Hall
7 St Margaret's Church
8 The Gatehouse
9 The King's Playhouse, Drury Lane
10 The New Exchange
11 The Maypole
12 St Clement Danes Church
13 Clare Market
14 The Duke's Playhouse, Lincoln's Inn Fields
15 Temple Bar
16 St Dunstan-in-the-West
17 The Rolls Chapel
18 St Andrew's Church, Holborn

Burlington House

Clarendon House

Berkeley House

Piccadilly

St James's Fields (being developed)

TO KNIGHTSBRIDGE AND KENSINGTON

Berkshire House

St James's Palace

The Mall

St James's Park

Canal

Goring House

TO CHELSEA

Petty France

Based on a map prepared by the late Professor T. F. Reddaway

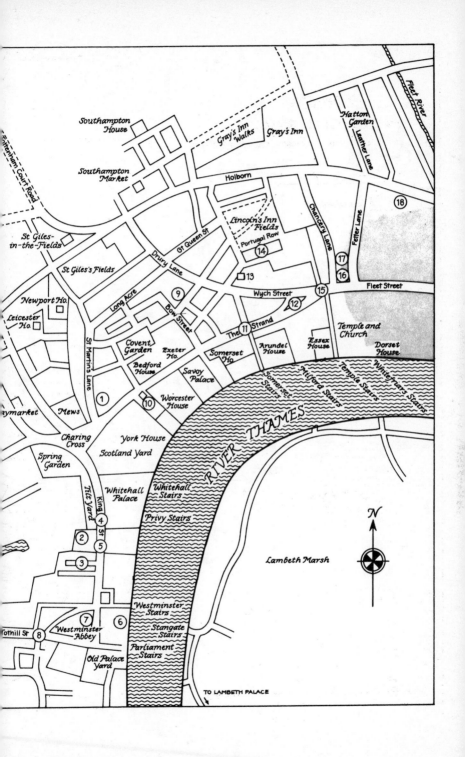

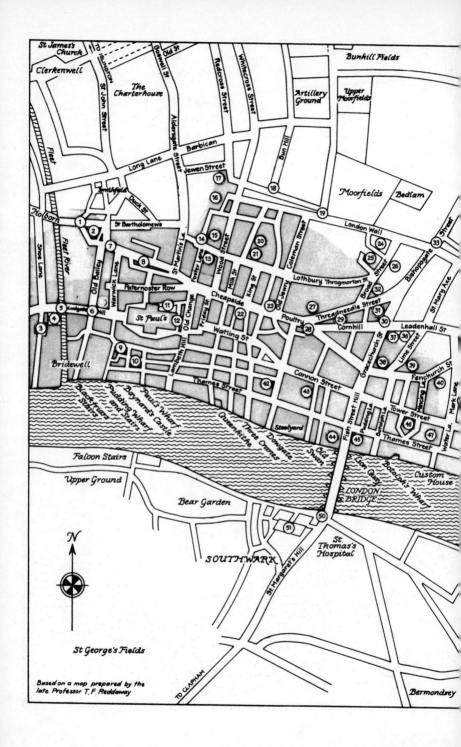

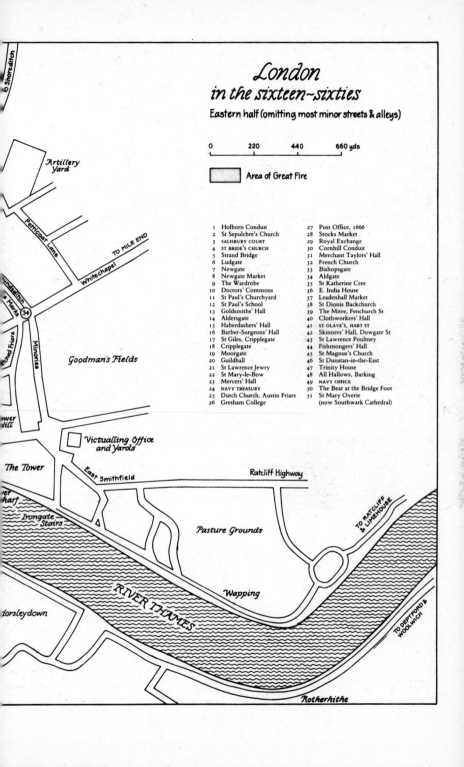

London
in the sixteen-sixties

Eastern half (omitting most minor streets & alleys)

```
0        220       440       660 yds
```

Area of Great Fire

1	Holborn Conduit	27	Post Office, 1666
2	St Sepulchre's Church	28	Stocks Market
3	SALISBURY COURT	29	Royal Exchange
4	ST BRIDE'S CHURCH	30	Cornhill Conduit
5	Strand Bridge	31	Merchant Taylors' Hall
6	Ludgate	32	French Church
7	Newgate	33	Bishopsgate
8	Newgate Market	34	Aldgate
9	The Wardrobe	35	St Katherine Cree
10	Doctors' Commons	36	E. India House
11	St Paul's Churchyard	37	Leadenhall Market
12	St Paul's School	38	St Dionis Backchurch
13	Goldsmiths' Hall	39	The Mitre, Fenchurch St
14	Aldersgate	40	Clothworkers' Hall
15	Haberdashers' Hall	41	ST OLAVE'S, HART ST
16	Barber-Surgeons' Hall	42	Skinners' Hall, Dowgate St
17	St Giles, Cripplegate	43	St Lawrence Poultney
18	Cripplegate	44	Fishmongers' Hall
19	Moorgate	45	St Magnus's Church
20	Guildhall	46	St Dunstan-in-the-East
21	St Lawrence Jewry	47	Trinity House
22	St Mary-le-Bow	48	All Hallows, Barking
23	Mercers' Hall	49	NAVY OFFICE
24	NAVY TREASURY	50	The Bear at the Bridge Foot
25	Dutch Church, Austin Friars	51	St Mary Overie
26	Gresham College		(now Southwark Cathedral)

Artillery Yard

Petticoat Lane

TO MILE END

Whitechapel

34

Goodman's Fields

Minories

Houndsditch

St Marks

Crutched Friars

Tower Hill

The Tower

Victualling Office and Yards

East Smithfield

Ratcliff Highway

Tower Wharf

Irongate Stairs

Pasture Grounds

TO RATCLIFF & LIMEHOUSE

Wapping

RIVER THAMES

Horsleydown

TO DEPTFORD & WOOLWICH

Rotherhithe

To Shoreditch

SELECT LIST OF PERSONS

ADMIRAL, the: James, Duke of York, Lord High Admiral of England

ALBEMARLE, 1st Duke of (Lord Monke): Captain-General of the Kingdom

ARLINGTON, 1st Earl of (Sir Henry Bennet): Secretary of State

ASHLEY, 1st Baron (Sir Anthony Ashley Cooper, later 1st Earl of Shaftesbury): Chancellor of the Exchequer

ATTORNEY-GENERAL: Sir Geoffrey Palmer

BACKWELL, Edward: goldsmith-banker

BAGWELL, Mrs: Pepys's mistress; wife of ship's carpenter

BALTY: Balthasar St Michel; brother-in-law; minor naval official

BATTEN, Sir William: Surveyor of the Navy

BETTERTON (Baterton), Thomas: actor in the Duke's Company

BIRCH, Jane: maidservant

BOOKSELLER, my: Joseph Kirton (until the Fire)

BOWYER, my father: Robert Bowyer, senior Exchequer colleague

BRISTOL, 2nd Earl of: politician

BROUNCKER (Bruncker, Brunkard, Brunkerd), 2nd Viscount: Commissioner of the Navy

BUCKINGHAM, 2nd Duke of: politician

CARKESSE (Carcasse), James: clerk in the Ticket Office

CARTERET, Sir George: Treasurer of the Navy and Vice-Chamberlain of the King's Household

CASTLEMAINE, Barbara, Countess of: the King's mistress

CHANCELLOR, the: see 'Lord Chancellor'

CHILD, the: usually Edward, eldest son and heir of Sandwich

CHOLMLEY, Sir Hugh: courtier, engineer

COCKE, George: hemp merchant

COFFERER, the: William Ashburnham

COMPTROLLER (Controller), the: the Comptroller of the Navy (Sir Robert Slingsby, 1660-1; Sir John Mennes, 1661-71)

COVENTRY, Sir William: Secretary to the Lord High Admiral, 1660-7; Commissioner of the Navy (occasionally called 'Mr.' after knighted, 1665)

CREED, John: household and naval servant of Sandwich

CREW, 1st Baron: Sandwich's father-in-law; Presbyterian politician

CUTTANCE, Sir Roger: naval captain

DEANE, Anthony: shipwright

DEB: see 'Willet, Deborah'

DOWNING, Sir George: Exchequer official, Envoy-Extraordinary to the United Provinces, and secretary to the Treasury Commission

DUKE, the: usually James, Duke of York, the King's brother; occassionally George (Monck), Duke of Albemarle

DUKE OF YORK: see 'James, Duke of York'

EDWARD, Mr: Edward, eldest son and heir of Sandwich

EDWARDS, Tom: servant

EVELYN, John: friend, *savant*; Commissioner of Sick and Wounded

FENNER, Thomas (m. Katherine Kite, sister of Pepys's mother): uncle; ironmonger

FERRER(s), Capt. Robert: army captain; Sandwich's Master of Horse

FORD, Sir Richard: Spanish merchant

FOX, Sir Stephen: Paymaster of the Army

GAUDEN, Sir Denis: Navy victualler

GENERAL(s), the: Albemarle, Captain-General of the Kingdom, 1660–70; Prince Rupert and Albemarle, Generals-at-Sea in command of the Fleet, 1666

GIBSON, Richard: clerk to Pepys in the Navy Office

GWYN, Nell: actress (in the King's Company) and King's mistress

HARRIS, Henry: actor in the Duke's Company

HAYTER, Tom: clerk to Pepys in the Navy Office

HEWER, Will: clerk to Pepys in the Navy Office

HILL, Thomas: friend, musician, Portuguese merchant

HINCHINGBROOKE, Viscount (also 'Mr Edward', 'the child'): eldest son of Sandwich

HOLLIER (Holliard), Thomas: surgeon

HOLMES, Sir Robert: naval commander

HOWE, Will: household and naval servant of Sandwich

JAMES, DUKE OF YORK: the King's brother and heir presumptive (later James II); Lord High Admiral

JANE: usually Jane Birch, maidservant

JOYCE, Anthony (m. Kate Fenner, 1st cousin): innkeeper

JOYCE, William (m. Mary Fenner, 1st cousin): tallow-chandler

JUDGE-ADVOCATE, the: John Fowler, Judge-Advocate of the Fleet

KNIPP (Knepp), Mrs: actress in the King's Company

LADIES, the young/ the two/ the: often Sandwich's daughters

LAWSON, Sir John: naval commander

LIEUTENANT OF THE TOWER: Sir John Robinson

L'IMPERTINENT, Mons.: [?Daniel] Butler, friend, ? clergyman

LORD CHAMBERLAIN: Edward Mountagu, 2nd Earl of Manchester; Sandwich's cousin

LORD CHANCELLOR: Edward Hyde, 1st Earl of Clarendon (often called Chancellor after his dismissal, 1667)

LORD KEEPER: Sir Orlando Bridgeman

LORD PRIVY SEAL: John Robartes, 2nd Baron Robartes (later 1st Earl of Radnor)

LORD TREASURER: Thomas Wriothesley, 4th Earl of Southampton

MARTIN, Betty (née Lane): Pepys's mistress; shopgirl

MENNES (Minnes), Sir John: Comptroller of the Navy

MERCER, Mary: maid to Mrs Pepys

MILL(E)S, Rev. Dr John: Rector of St Olave's, Hart St; Pepys's parish priest

MONCK (Monke), George (Lord): soldier. See 'Albemarle, 1st Duke of'

MONMOUTH, Duke of: illegitimate son of Charles II

MOORE, Henry: lawyer; officer of Sandwich's household

MY LADY: usually Jemima, wife of Sandwich

MY LORD: usually Sandwich

NELL, NELLY: usually Nell Gwyn

PALL: Paulina Pepys; sister (sometimes spelt 'pall')

PEARSE (Pierce), James: courtier, surgeon to Duke of York, and naval surgeon

PENN, Sir William: Commissioner of the Navy and naval commander (father of the Quaker leader)

PEPYS, Elizabeth (née St Michel): wife

PEPYS, John and Margaret: parents

PEPYS, John (unm.): brother; unbeneficed clergyman

PEPYS, Tom (unm.): brother; tailor

PEPYS, Paulina (m. John Jackson): sister

PEPYS, Capt. Robert: uncle, of Brampton, Hunts.

PEPYS, Roger: 1st cousin once removed; barrister and M.P.

PEPYS, Thomas: uncle, of St Alphege's, London

PETT, Peter: Commissioner of the Navy and shipwright

PICKERING, Mr (Ned): courtier, 1662–3; Sandwich's brother-in-law and servant

POVEY, Thomas: Treasurer of the Tangier Committee, 1663–5

PRINCE, the: usually Prince Rupert

QUEEN, the: (until May 1662) the Queen Mother, Henrietta-Maria, widow of Charles I; Catherine of Braganza, wife of Charles II (m. 21 May 1662)

RIDER, Sir William: merchant

ROBERT, Prince: Prince Rupert

RUPERT, Prince: 1st cousin of Charles II; naval commander

ST MICHEL, Alexandre and Dorothea: parents-in-law

ST MICHEL, Balthasar ('Balty'; m. Esther Watts): brother-in-law; minor naval official

SANDWICH, 1st Earl of: 1st cousin once removed, and patron; politician, naval commander and diplomat

SHIPLEY, Edward: steward of Sandwich's household

SIDNY, Mr: Sidney Mountagu, second son of Sandwich

SOLICITOR, the: the Solicitor-General, Sir Heneage Finch

SOUTHAMPTON, 4th Earl of: Lord Treasurer

SURVEYOR, the: the Surveyor of the Navy (Sir William Batten 1660–7; Col. Thomas Middleton, 1667–72)

TEDDEMAN, Sir Thomas: naval commander

THE: Theophila Turner

TREASURER, the: usually the Treasurer of the Navy (Sir George Carteret, 1660–7; 1st Earl of Anglesey, 1667–8); sometimes the Lord Treasurer of the Kingdom, the Earl of Southampton, 1660–7

TRICE, Tom: step-brother; civil lawyer

TURNER, John (m. Jane Pepys, distant cousin): barrister

TURNER, Betty and The[ophila]: daughters of John and Jane Turner

TURNER, Thomas: senior clerk in the Navy Office

VICE-CHAMBERLAIN, the: Sir George Carteret, Vice-Chamberlain of the King's Household and Treasurer of the Navy

VYNER, Sir Robert: goldsmith-banker

WARREN, Sir William: timber merchant

WARWICK, Sir Philip: Secretary to the Lord Treasurer

WIGHT, William: uncle (half-brother of Pepys's father); fishmonger

WILL: usually Will Hewer

WILLET, Deborah: maid to Mrs Pepys

WILLIAMS ('Sir Wms. both'): Sir William Batten and Sir William Penn, colleagues on the Navy Board

WREN, Matthew: Secretary to the Lord High Admiral, 1667–72

SELECT GLOSSARY

A Large Glossary will be found in the *Companion*. This Select Glossary is restricted to usages, many of them recurrent, which might puzzle the reader. It includes words and constructions which are now obsolete, archaic, slang or dialect; words which are used with meanings now obsolete or otherwise unfamiliar; and place names frequently recurrent or used in colloquial styles or in non-standard forms. Words explained in footnotes are not normally included. The definitions given here are minimal: meanings now familiar and contemporary meanings not implied in the text are not noted, and many items are explained more fully in *Companion* articles and in the Large Glossary. A few foreign words are included. The spellings are taken from those used in the text: they do not, for brevity's sake, include all variants.

ABLE: wealthy

ABROAD: away, out of doors

ACCENT (of speech): the accentuation and the rising and falling of speech in pronunciation

ACCOUNTANT: official accountable for expenditure etc.

ACHIEVEMENT: hatchment, representation of heraldic arms

ACTION: acting, performance

ACTOR: male or female theatrical performer

ADDES: adze

ADMIRAL SHIP: flagship carrying admiral

ADMIRATION; ADMIRE: wonder, alarm; to wonder at

ADVENTURER: investor, speculator

ADVICE: consideration

AFFECT: to be fond of, to be concerned

AFFECTION: attention

AGROUND: helpless

AIR: generic term for all gases

ALL MY CAKE WILL BE DOE: all my plans will miscarry

ALPHABET: index, alphabetical list

AMBAGE: deceit, deviousness

AMUSED, AMUZED: bemused, astonished

ANCIENT: elderly, senior

ANGEL: gold coin worth *c.* 10s.

ANGELIQUE: small archlute

ANNOY: molest, hurt

ANOTHER GATE'S BUSINESS: different altogether

ANSWERABLE: similar, conformably

ANTIC, ANTIQUE: fantastic

APERN: apron

APPRENSION: apprehension

APPROVE OF: criticise

AQUA FORTIS (FARTIS): nitric acid

ARTICLE: to indict

ARTIST: workman, craftsman, technician, practitioner

ASTED: Ashtead, Surrey

AYERY: airy, sprightly, stylish

BAGNARD: bagnio, prison, lock-up

BAILEY, BAYLY: bailiff

BAIT, BAŸTE: refreshment on journey (for horses or travellers). *Also* v.

BALDWICK: Baldock, Herts.

BALLET: ballad, broadside

BAND: neckband

BANDORE: musical instrument resembling guitar

BANQUET: course of fruits, sweets and wine; slight repast

BANQUET-, BANQUETING-HOUSE: summer-house

BARBE (s.): Arab (Barbary) horse

BARBE (v.): to shave

BARN ELMS: riverside area near Barnes, Surrey

BARRECADOS (naval): fenders

BASE, BASS: bass viol; thorough-bass

BASTE HIS COAT: to beat, chastise

BAVINS: kindling wood, brush-wood

BAYLY: see 'Bailey'

BAYT(E): see 'Bait'

BEARD: facial hair, moustache

BEFOREHAND, to get: to have money in hand

BEHALF: to behave

BEHINDHAND: insolvent

BELL: to throb

BELOW: downstream from London Bridge

BELOW STAIRS: part of the Royal Household governed by Lord Steward

BEST HAND, at the: the best bargain

BEVER: beaver, fur hat

BEWPERS: bunting, fabric used for flags

BEZAN, BIZAN (Du. *bezaan*): small yacht

BIGGLESWORTH: Biggleswade, Beds.

BILL: (legal) warrant, writ; bill of exchange; Bill of Mortality (weekly list of burials; see iii. 225, n. 2)

BILLANDER (Du. *bijlander*): bilander, small two-masted merchantman

BIRD'S EYE: spotted fabric

BIZAN: see 'Bezan'

BLACK (adj.): brunette, dark in hair or complexion

BLACK(E)WALL: dock on n. shore of Thames below Greenwich used by E. Indiamen

BLANCH (of coins): to silver

BLIND: out of the way, private, obscure

BLOAT HERRING: bloater

BLUR: innuendo; charge

BOATE: boot or luggage compartment on side of coach

BODYS: foundations, basic rules; structure; (of ship) sectional drawings

BOLTHEAD: globular glass vessel with long straight neck

BOMBAIM: Bombay

BORDER: *toupée*

BOTARGO: dried fish-roe

BOTTOMARYNE, BOTTUMARY, BUMMARY: mortgage on ship

BOWPOTT: flower pot

BRAINFORD: Brentford, Mdx.

BRAMPTON: village near Huntingdon in which Pepys inherited property

BRANSLE: branle, brawl, group dance in duple measure

BRAVE (adj.): fine, enjoyable

BRAVE (v.): to threaten, challenge

BREAK BULK: to remove part of cargo

BREDHEMSON, BRIGHTHEMSON: Brighton, Sussex

BRIDEWELL-BIRD: jailbird

BRIDGE: usually London Bridge; also jetty, landing stairs

BRIEF: collection authorised by Lord Chancellor for charity

BRIG, BRIGANTINE: small vessel equipped both for sailing and rowing

BRIGHTHEMSON: see 'Bredhemson'

BRISTOL MILK: sweet sherry

BROTHER: brother-in-law; colleague

BRUMLY: Bromley, Kent

BRUSH (s.): graze

BUBO: tumour

BULLEN: Boulogne

BULLET: cannon-ball

BUMMARY: see 'Bottomaryne'

BURNTWOOD: Brentwood, Essex

BURY (of money): pour in, salt away, invest

BUSSE: two- or three-masted fishing boat

CABALL: inner group of ministers; knot
CABARETT (Fr. *cabaret*): tavern
CALES: Cadiz
CALICE, CALLIS: Calais
CALL: to call on/for; to drive
CAMELOTT, CAMLET, CAMLOTT: robust, ribbed cloth made of wool or goat hair
CANAILLE, CHANNEL, KENNEL: drainage gutter (in street); canal (in St James's Park)
CANCRE: canker, ulcer, sore
CANNING ST: Cannon St
CANONS: boot-hose tops
CANTON (heraldic): small division of shield
CAPER (ship): privateer
CARBONADO: to grill, broil
CARESSE: to make much of
CARRY (a person): to conduct, escort
CAST OF OFFICE: taste of quality
CATAPLASM: poultice
CATCH: round song; (ship) ketch
CATT-CALL: whistle
CAUDLE: thin gruel made with wine
CELLAR: box for bottles
CERE CLOTH: cloth impregnated with wax and medicaments
CESTORNE: cistern
CHAFE: heat, anger
CHALDRON: $1\frac{1}{2}$ tons (London measure)
CHAMBER: small piece of ordnance for firing salutes
CHANGE, the: the Royal (Old) Exchange
CHANGELING: idiot
CHANNELL: see 'Canaille'
CHANNELL ROW: Cannon Row, Westminster
CHAPEL, the: usually the Chapel Whitehall Palace
CHAPTER: usually of Bible
CHARACTER: code, cipher; verbal portrait

CHEAP (s.): bargain
CHEAPEN: to ask the price of, bargain
CHEQUER, the: usually the Exchequer
CHEST, the: the Chatham Chest, the pension fund for seamen
CHILD, with: eager, anxious
CHIMNEY/CHIMNEY-PIECE: structure over and around fireplace
CHIMNEY-PIECE: picture over fireplace
CHINA-ALE: ale flavoured with china root
CHOQUE: a choke, an obstruction
CHOUSE: to swindle, trick
CHURCH: after July 1660, usually St Olave's, Hart St
CLAP: gonorrhoea
CLERK OF THE CHEQUE: principal clerical officer of a dockyard
CLOATH (of meat): skin
CLOSE: shutter; (of music) cadence
CLOUTERLY: clumsily
CLOWNE: countryman, clodhopper
CLUB (s.): share of expenses, meeting at which expenses are shared *Also* v.
CLYSTER, GLISTER, GLYSTER: enema
COACH: captain's state-room in large ship
COCK ALE: ale mixed with minced chicken
COCKPIT(T), the: usually the theatre in the Cockpit buildings, Whitehall Palace; the buildings themselves
COD: small bag; testicle
CODLIN TART: apple (codling) tart
COFFEE: coffee-house
COG: to cheat, banter, wheedle
COLEWORTS: cabbage
COLLAR DAY: day on which knights of chivalric orders wore insignia at court
COLLECT: to deduce
COLLIER: coal merchant; coal ship
COLLOPS: fried bacon
COLLY-FEAST: feast of collies (cullies, good companions) at which each pays his share

COMEDIAN: actor

COMEDY: play

COMFITURE (Fr. *confiture*): jam, marmalade

COMMEN, COMMON GUARDEN: Covent Garden

COMMONLY: together

COMPASS TIMBER: curved timber

COMPLEXION: aspect

COMPOSE: to put music to words. *Also* Composition

CONCEIT (s.): idea, notion

CONCLUDE: to include

CONDITION (s.): disposition; social position, state of wealth

CONDITION (v.): to make conditions

CONDITIONED: having a (specified) disposition or social position

CONGEE: bow at parting

CONJURE: to plead with

CONJUROR: wizard who operates by conjuration of spirits

CONSIDERABLE: worthy of consideration

CONSTER: to construe, translate

CONSUMPTION: (any) wasting disease. *Also* 'Consumptive'

CONTENT, by/in: by agreement, without examination, at a rough guess

CONVENIENCE: advantage

CONVENIENT: morally proper

CONVERSATION: demeanour, behaviour; acquaintance, society

COOLE: cowl

CORANT(O): dance involving a running or gliding step

COSEN, COUSIN: almost any collateral relative

COUNT: reckon, estimate, value

COUNTENANCE: recognition, acknowledgement

COUNTRY: county, district

COURSE, in: in sequence

COURSE, of: as usual

COURT BARON: manorial court (civil)

COURT-DISH: dish with a cut from every meat

COURT LEET: local criminal court

COUSIN: *see* 'Cosen'

COY: disdainful; quiet

COYING: stroking, caressing

CRADLE: fire-basket

CRAMBO: rhyming game

CRAZY: infirm

CREATURE (of persons): puppet, instrument

CRUSADO: Portuguese coin worth 3*s.*

CUDDY: room in a large ship in which the officers took their meals

CULLY: dupe; friend

CUNNING: knowledgeable; knowledge

CURIOUS: careful, painstaking, discriminating; fine, delicate

CURRANT: out and about

CUSTOMER: customs officer

CUT (v.): to carve meat

CUTT (s.): an engraving

DAUGHTER-IN-LAW: stepdaughter

DEAD COLOUR: preparatory layer of colour in a painting

DEAD PAYS: sailors or soldiers kept on pay roll after death

DEALS: sawn timber used for decks, etc.

DEDIMUS: writ empowering J.P.

DEFALK: to subtract

DEFEND: to prevent

DEFY (Fr.): to mistrust. *Also* Defyance

DELICATE: pleasant

DELINQUENT: active royalist in Civil War and Interregnum

DEMORAGE: demurrage, compensation from the freighter due to a shipowner for delaying vessel beyond time specified in charter-party

DEPEND: to wait, hang

DEVISE: to decide; discern

DIALECT: jargon

DIALL, double horizontal: instrument telling hour of day

DIRECTION: supervision of making; arrangement

DISCOVER: to disclose, reveal

DISCREET: discerning, judicious

DISGUST: to dislike

DISPENSE: outgoings

DISTASTE (s.): difference, quarrel, offence. *Also* v.

DISTINCT: discerning, discriminating

DISTRINGAS: writ of distraint

DOATE: to nod off to sleep

DOCTOR: clergyman, don

DOE: dough. *See* 'All my cake . . .'

DOGGED: determined

DOLLER: *see* 'Rix Doller'

DORTOIRE: dorter, monastic dormitory

DOTY: darling

DOWNS, the: roadstead off Deal, Kent

DOXY: whore, mistress

DRAM: timber from Drammen, Norway

DRAWER: tapster, barman

DRESS: to cook, prepare food

DROLL: comic song

DROLLING, DROLLY: comical, comically

DRUDGER: dredger, container for sweetmeats

DRUGGERMAN: dragoman, interpreter

DRY BEATEN: beaten without drawing blood

DRY MONEY: hard cash

DUANA: divan, council

DUCCATON: ducatoon, large silver coin of the Netherlands worth 5s. 9d.

DUCKET(T): ducat, foreign gold coin worth 9s.

DUKE'S [PLAY] HOUSE, the: playhouse in Lincoln's Inn Fields used by the Duke of York's Company from June 1660 until 9 November 1671; often called 'the Opera'. Also known as the Lincoln's Inn Fields Theatre (LIF)

DULL: limp, spiritless

EARTH: earthenware

EASILY AND EASILY: more and more slowly

EAST INDIES: the territory covered by the E. India Company, including the modern sub-continent of India

EAST COUNTRY, EASTLAND: the territory (Scandinavia and Baltic area) covered by the Eastland Company

EFFEMINACY: love of women

ELECTUARY: medicinal salve with a honey base

EMERODS: haemorrhoids

ENTENDIMIENTO (Sp.): understanding

ENTER (of horse): to break in

ENTERTAIN: to retain, employ

EPICURE: glutton

ERIFFE: Erith, Kent

ESPINETTE(S): spinet, small harpsichord

ESSAY: to assay

EVEN (adv.): surely

EVEN (of accounts): to balance

EVEN (of the diary): to bring up to date

EXCEPT: to accept

EXPECT: to see, await

FACTION: the government's parliamentary critics

FACTIOUS: able to command a following

FACTOR: mercantile agent

FACTORY: trading station

FAIN: to be forced; to like

FAIRING: small present (as from a fair)

FALCHON: falchion, curved sword

FAMILY: household (including servants)

FANCY (music): fantasia

FANFARROON: fanfaron, braggart

FARANDINE, FARRINDIN: *see* 'Ferrandin'

FASHION (of metal, furniture): design, fashioning

FAT: vat

FATHER: father-in-law (similarly with 'mother' etc.)

FELLET (of trees): a cutting, felling

FELLOW COMMONER: undergraduate

paying high fees and enjoying privileges

FENCE: defence

FERRANDIN, FARRINDIN, FARANDINE: cloth of silk mixed with wool or hair

FIDDLE: viol; violin

FINE (s.): payment for lease

FINE FOR OFFICE (v.): to avoid office by payment of fine

FIRESHIP: ship filled with combustibles used to ram and set fire to enemy

FITS OF THE MOTHER: hysterics

FLAG, FLAGGMAN: flag officer

FLAGEOLET: end-blown, six-holed instrument

FLESHED: relentless, proud

FLOOD: rising tide

FLUXED (of the pox): salivated

FLYING ARMY/FLEET: small mobile force

FOND, FONDNESS: foolish; folly

FOND: fund

FORCE OUT: to escape

FORSOOTH: to speak ceremoniously

FORTY: many, scores of

FOXED: intoxicated

FOX HALL: Vauxhall (pleasure gardens)

FOY: departure feast or gift

FREQUENT: to busy oneself

FRIENDS: parents, relatives

FROST-BITE: to invigorate by exposure to cold

FULL: anxious

FULL MOUTH, with: eagerly; openly, loudly

GALL: harass

GALLIOTT: small swift galley

GALLOPER, the: shoal off Essex coast

GAMBO: Gambia, W. Africa

GAMMER: old woman

GENERAL-AT-SEA: naval commander (a post, not a rank)

GENIUS: inborn character, natural ability; mood

GENT: graceful, polite

GENTILELY: obligingly

GEORGE: jewel forming part of insignia of Order of Garter

GERMANY: territory of the Holy Roman Empire

GET UP ONE'S CRUMB: to improve one's status

GET WITHOUT BOOK: to memorise

GHOSTLY: holy, spiritual

GIBB-CAT: tom-cat

GILDER, GUILDER: Dutch money of account worth 2s.

GIMP: twisted thread of material with wire or cord running through it

GITTERNE: musical instrument of the guitar family

GLASS: telescope

GLEEKE: three-handed card game

GLISTER, GLYSTER: see 'Clyster'

GLOSSE, by a fine: by a plausible pretext

GO TO ONE'S NAKED BED: to go to bed without night-clothes

GO(O)D BWYE: God be with ye, goodbye

GODLYMAN: Godalming, Surrey

GOODFELLOW: convivial person, good timer

GOODMAN, GOODWIFE (Goody): used of men and women of humble station

GOOD-SPEAKER: one who speaks well of others

GORGET: neckerchief for women

GOSSIP (v.): to act as godparent, to attend a new mother; to chatter. *Also* s.

GOVERNMENT: office or function of governor

GRACIOUS-STREET(E): Gracechurch St

GRAIN (? of gold): sum of money

GRAVE: to engrave

GREEN (of meat): uncured

GRESHAM COLLEGE: meeting-place of Royal Society; the Society itself
GRIEF: bodily pain
GRUDGEING, GRUTCHING: trifling complaint, grumble
GUEST: nominee; friend; stranger
GUIDE: postboy
GUILDER: *see* 'Gilder'
GUN: cannon, salute
GUNDALO, GUNDILOW: gondola
GUNFLEET, the: shoal off Essex coast

HACKNEY: hack, workhorse, drudge
HAIR, against the: against the grain
HALF-A-PIECE: gold coin worth *c.* 10s.
HALF-SHIRT: sham shirt front
HALFE-WAY-HOUSE: Rotherhithe tavern halfway between London Bridge and Deptford
HALL, the: usually Westminster Hall
HAND: cuff
HANDSEL: to try out, use for first time
HAND-TO-FIST: hastily
HANDYCAPP: handicap, a card game
HANG IN THE HEDGE: to be delayed
HANGER: loop holding a sword; small sword
HANGING JACK: turnspit for roasting meat
HANK: hold, grip
HAPPILY: haply, perchance
HARE: to harry, rebuke
HARPSICHON, HARPSICHORD: keyboard instrument of one or two manuals, with strings plucked by quills or leather jacks, and with stops which vary the tone
HARSLET: haslet, pigmeat (esp. offal)
HAT-PIECE: protective metal skull cap
HAVE A GOOD COAT OF [HIS] FLEECE: to have a good share
HAVE A HAND: to have leisure, freedom
HAVE A MONTH'S MIND: to have a great desire
HAWSE, thwart their: across their bows
HEAD-PIECE: helmet

HEART: courage
HEAVE AT: to oppose
HECTOR: street-bully, swashbuckler
HERBALL: botanical encyclopaedia; *hortus siccus* (book of dried and pressed plants)
HERE (Du. *heer*): Lord
HIGH: arrogant, proud, high-handed
HINCHINGBROOKE: Sandwich's house near Huntingdon
HOMAGE: jury of presentment at a manorial court
HONEST (of a woman): virtuous
HOOKS, off the: out of humour
HOPE, the: reach of Thames downstream from Tilbury
HOPEFUL: promising
HOUSE: playhouse; parliament; (royal) household or palace building
HOUSE OF OFFICE: latrine
HOY: small passenger and cargo vessel, fore-and-aft rigged
HOYSE: to hoist
HUMOUR (s.): mood; character, characteristic; good or ill temper
HUMOUR (v.): to set words suitably to music
HUSBAND: one who gets good/bad value for money; supervisor, steward
HYPOCRAS: hippocras, red or white wine (flavoured)

ILL-TEMPERED: out of sorts, ill-adjusted (to weather etc.; cf. 'Temper')
IMPERTINENCE: irrelevance, garrulity, folly. *Also* 'Impertinent'
IMPOSTUME: abscess
IMPREST: money paid in advance by government to public servant
INDIAN GOWN: loose gown of glazed cotton
INGENIOUS, INGENUOUS: clever, intelligent
INGENUITY: wit, intelligence; freedom
INGENUOUS: *see* 'Ingenious'

INSIPID: stupid, dull

INSTITUCIONS: instructions

INSTRUMENT: agent, clerk

INSULT: to exult over

INTELLIGENCE: information

INTRATUR: warrant authorising payment by Exchequer

IRISIPULUS: erysipelas

IRONMONGER: often a large-scale merchant, not necessarily a retailer

JACK(E): flag used as signal or mark of distinction; rogue, knave. *See also* 'Hanging Jack'

JACKANAPES COAT: monkey jacket, sailor's short close-fitting jacket

JACOB(US): gold sovereign coined under James I

JAPAN: lacquer, lacquered

JARR, JARRING: quarrel

JEALOUS: fearful, suspicious, mistrustful. *Also* Jealousy

JERK(E): captious remark

JES(S)IMY: jasmine

JEW'S TRUMP: Jew's harp

JOCKY: horse-dealer

JOLE (of fish): jowl, a cut consisting of the head and shoulders. *See also* 'Pole'

JOYNT-STOOL: stout stool held together by joints

JULIPP: julep, a sweet drink made from syrup

JUMBLE: to take for an airing

JUMP WITH: to agree, harmonise

JUNK (naval): old rope

JURATE (of Cinque Ports): jurat, alderman

JUSTE-AU-CORPS: close-fitting long coat

KATCH: (ship) ketch

KEEP A QUARTER: to make a disturbance

KENNEL: *see* 'Canaille'

KERCHER: kerchief, head-covering

KETCH (s.): catch, song in canon

KETCH (v.): to catch

KING'S [PLAY] HOUSE, the: playhouse in Vere St, Clare Market, Lincoln's Inn Fields, used by the King's Company from 8 November 1660 until 7 May 1663; the playhouse in Bridges St, Drury Lane, used by the same company from 7 May 1663 until the fire of 25 January 1672. Also known as the Theatre Royal (TR)

KITLIN: kitling, kitten, cub

KNEES: timbers of naturally angular shape used in ship-building

KNOT (s.): flower bed; difficulty; clique, band

KNOT (v.): to join, band together

KNOWN: famous

LACE: usually braid made with gold- or silver-thread

LAMB'S-WOOL: hot ale with apples and spice

LAMP-GLASS: magnifying lens used to concentrate lamp-light

LAST: load, measure of tar

LASTOFFE: Lowestoft, Suff.

LATITUDINARIAN: liberal Anglican

LAVER: basin of a fountain

LEADS: flat space on roof top, sometimes boarded over

LEAN: to lie down

LEARN: to teach

LEAVE: to end

LECTURE: weekday religious service consisting mostly of a sermon

LESSON: piece of music

LETTERS OF MART: letters of marque

LEVETT: reveille, reveille music

LIBEL(L): leaflet, broadside; (in legal proceedings) written charge

LIE UPON: to press, insist

LIFE: life interest

LIFE, for my: on my life

LIGHT: window

LIGNUM VITAE: hard W. Indian wood with medicinal qualities, often used for drinking vessels

LIMB: to limn, paint
LIME (of dogs): to mate
LINK(E): torch
LINNING: linen
LIPPOCK: Liphook, Hants.
LIST: pleasure, desire
LOCK: waterway between arches of bridge
LOMBRE: see 'Ombre'
LONDON: the city of London (to be distinguished from Westminster)
LOOK: to look at/for
LOOK AFTER: to have eyes on
LUMBERSTREETE: Lombard St
LUTE: pear-shaped instrument with six courses of gut strings and a turned-back peg-box; made in various sizes, the larger instruments having additional bass strings
LUTESTRING: lustring, a glossy silk
LYRA-VIALL: small bass viol tuned for playing chords

MAD: whimsical, wild, extravagant
MADAM(E): prefix used mainly of widows, elderly/foreign ladies
MAIN (adj.): strong, bulky
MAIN (s.): chief purpose or object
MAISTER: expert; professional; sailing master
MAKE (s.): (of fighting cocks) match, pair of opponents
MAKE (v.): to do; to copulate
MAKE LEGS: to bow, curtsey
MAKE SURE TO: to plight troth
MALLOWS: St Malo
MAN OF BUSINESS: executive agent, administrator
MANAGED-HORSE (cf. Fr. *manège*): horse trained in riding school
MANDAMUS: royal mandate under seal
MARGARET, MARGETTS: Margate, Kent
MARGENTING: putting margin-lines on paper
MARK: 13s. 4d.
MARMOTTE (Fr., term of affection): young girl

MARROWBONE: Marylebone, Mdx
MASTY: burly
MATCH: tinderbox and wick
MATHEMATICIAN: mathematical instrument-maker
MEAT: food
MEDIUM: mean, average
METHEGLIN: strong mead flavoured with herbs
MINCHIN-LANE: Mincing Lane
MINE: mien
MINIKIN: treble string of a viol
MISTRESS (MRS.): prefix used of unmarried girls and women as well as of young married women
MISTRESS: sweetheart
MITHRYDATE: drug used as an antidote
MODEST (of woman): virtuous
MOHER (Sp. *mujer*): woman, wife
MOIS, MOYS: menstrual periods
MOLD, MOLDE, MOLLE (archit.): mole
MOLEST: to annoy
MOND: orb (royal jewel in form of globe)
MONTEERE, MOUNTEERE: riding cap; close-fitting hood
MOPED: bemused
MORECLACK(E): Mortlake, Surrey
MORENA (Sp.): brunette
MORNING DRAUGHT: drink (sometimes with snack) usually taken mid-morning
MOTHER-IN-LAW: stepmother (similarly with 'father-in-law' etc.)
MOTT: sighting line in an optical tube
MOUNTEERE: see 'Monteere'
MOYRE: moire, watered silk
MUM: strong spiced ale
MURLACE: Morlaix, Brittany
MUSCADINE, MUSCATT: muscatel wine
MUSIC: band, choir, performers
MUSTY: peevish

NAKED BED: see 'Go to one's n.b.'
NARROWLY: anxiously, carefully
NAUGHT, NOUGHT: worthless, bad in condition or quality, sexually wicked

NAVY: Navy Office

NAVY OFFICERS: Principal Officers of the Navy – i.e. the Comptroller, Treasurer, Surveyor, Clerk of the Acts, together with a variable number of Commissioners; members of the Navy Board. Cf. 'Sea-Officers'

NEARLY: deeply

NEAT (adj.): handsome

NEAT(s.): ox, cattle

NEITHER MEDDLE NOR MAKE: to have nothing to do with

NEWSBOOK: newspaper (weekly, octavo)

NIBBLE AT: to bite at

NICOTIQUES: narcotics, medicines

NIGHTGOWN(E): dressing gown

NOISE: group of musical instruments playing together

NORE, the: anchorage in mouth of Thames

NORTHDOWNE ALE: Margate ale

NOSE: to insult, affront

NOTE: thing deserving of note, note of credit

NOTORIOUS: famous, well-known

NOUGHT: see 'Naught'

OBNOXIOUS: liable to

OBSERVABLE (adj.): noteworthy, notorious

OBSERVABLE (s.): thing or matter worthy of observation

OF: to have

OFFICE DAY: day on which a meeting of the Navy Board was held

OFFICERS OF THE NAVY: see 'Navy Officers'

OLEO (Sp. olla): stew

OMBRE (Sp. hombre): card game

ONLY: main, principal, best

OPEN: unsettled

OPERA: spectacular entertainment (involving use of painted scenery and stage machinery), often with music

OPERA, the: the theatre in Lincoln's Inn Fields. See 'Duke's House, the'

OPINIASTRE, OPINIASTREMENT (Fr.): stubborn, stubbornly

OPPONE: to oppose, hinder

ORDER: to put in order; to punish

ORDINARY (adj.): established

ORDINARY (s.): eating place serving fixed-price meals; peace-time establishment (of navy, dockyard, etc.)

OUTPORTS: ports other than London

OVERSEEN: omitted, neglected; guilty of oversight

OWE: to own

PADRON (?Sp., ?It. patrone): master

PAGEANT: decorated symbolic float in procession

PAINFUL: painstaking

PAIR OF OARS: large river-boat rowed by two watermen, each using a pair of oars. Cf. 'Scull'

PAIR (OF ORGANS/VIRGINALS): a single instrument

PALACE: New Palace Yard

PALER: parlour

PANNYARD: pannier, basket

PARAGON: heavy rich cloth, partly of mohair

PARALLELOGRAM: pantograph

PARCEL: share, part; isolated group

PARK, the: normally St James's Park (Hyde Park is usually named)

PARTY: charter-party

PASQUIL: a lampoon

PASSION: feeling, mood

PASSIONATE: touching, affecting

PATTEN: overshoe

PAY: to berate, beat

PAY A COAT: to beat, chastise

PAYSAN (Fr.): country style

PAY SAUCE: to pay dearly

PENDANCES, PENDENTS: lockets; earrings

PERPLEX: to vex

PESLEMESLE: pell-mell, early form of croquet

PETTY BAG: petty cash

PHILOSOPHY: natural science

PHYSIC: laxative, purge

PHYSICALLY: without sheets, uncovered

PICK: pique

PICK A HOLE IN A COAT: to pick a quarrel, complain

PICKAROON (Sp. *picarón*): pirate, privateer

PIECE: gold coin worth *c.* 20s.

PIECE (PEECE) OF EIGHT: Spanish silver coin worth 4s. 6d.

PIGEON: coward

PINK(E): small broad-beamed ship; poniard, pointed weapon

PINNER: coif with two long flaps; fill-in above low *décolletage*

PIPE: measure of wine (c. 120 galls.)

PIPE (musical): flageolet, after 16 Apr. 1668 usually a recorder, specified as such

PISTOLE: French gold coin worth 16s.

PLACKET: petticoat

PLAT(T): plate, plan, chart, map; arrangement; level; [flower] plot

PLATERER: one who works silver plate

PLAY (v.): to play for stakes

PLEASANT: comical

POINT, POYNT: piece of lace

POINT DE GESNE: Genoa lace

POLE: head; head-and-shoulder (of fish); poll tax

POLICY: government; cunning; self-interest

POLLARD: cut-back, stunted tree

POMPOUS: ceremonious, dignified

POOR JACK: dried salt fish

POOR WRETCH: poor dear

POSSET: drink made of hot milk, spices, and wine (or beer)

POST (v.): to expose, pillory

POST WARRANT: authority to employ posthorses

POSY: verse or phrase engraved on inside of ring

POWDERED (of meat): salted

PRACTICE: trick

PRAGMATIC, PRAGMATICAL: interfering, conceited, dogmatic

PRATIQUE: ship's licence for port facilities given on presentation of clean bill of health

PRESBYTER JOHN: puritan parson

PRESENT (s.): shot, volley

PRESENT, PRESENTLY: immediate, immediately

PRESS BED: bed folding into or built inside a cupboard

PREST MONEY (milit., naval): earnest money paid in advance

PRETTY (of men): fine, elegant, foppish

PREVENT: to anticipate

PRICK: to write out music; to list

PRICK OUT: to strike out, delete

PRINCE: ruler

PRINCIPLES (of music): natural ability, rudimentary knowledge

PRISE, PRIZE: worth, value, price

PRIVATE: small, secret, quiet

PRIZE FIGHT: fencing match fought for money

PROPRIETY: property, ownership

PROTEST (a bill): to record non-payment; represent bill after non-payment

PROUD (of animals): on heat

PROVOKE: to urge

PULL A CROW: to quarrel

PURCHASE: advantage; profit; booty

PURELY: excellently

PURL(E): hot spiced beer

PUSS: ill-favoured woman

PUT OFF: to sell, dispose of, marry off

PYONEER: pioneer (ditch digger, labourer)

QU: cue

QUARREFOUR: crossroads

QUARTERAGE: any salary or sum paid quarterly

QUARTRE: position in dancing or fencing

QUEST HOUSE: house used for inquests, parish meetings

QUINBROUGH: Queenborough, Kent

QUINSBOROUGH: Königsberg, E. Prussia

RACE: to rase, destroy

RAKE-SHAMED: disreputable, disgraceful

RARE: fine, splendid

RATE: to berate, scold

RATTLE: to scold

RATTOON: rattan cane

READY: quick, accomplished

REAKE: trick

RECEPI: writ of receipt issued by Chancery

RECITATIVO (*stilo r.*): the earliest type of recitative singing

RECONCILE: to settle a dispute, to determine the truth

RECORDER: family of end-blown, eight-holed instruments (descant, treble, tenor, bass)

RECOVER: to reconcile

RECOVERY (legal): process for re-establishment of ownership

REDRIFFE: Rotherhithe, Surrey

REFERRING: indebted, beholden to

REFORM: to disband

REFORMADO: naval/military officer serving without commission

REFRESH (of a sword): to sharpen

RELIGIOUS: monk, nun

REPLICACION (legal): replication, plaintiff's answer to defendant's plea

RESEMBLE: to represent, figure

RESENT: to receive

RESPECT: to mean, refer to

RESPECTFUL: respectable

REST: wrest, tuning key

RETAIN (a writ): to maintain a court action from term to term

REVOLUTION: sudden change (not necessarily violent)

RHODOMONTADO: boast, brag

RIDE POST: to travel by posthorse, to ride fast

RIGHT-HAND MAN: soldier on whom drill manoeuvres turn

RIGHTS, to: immediately, directly

RIS (v.): rose

RISE: origin

RIX DOLLER: Dutch or N. German silver coin (*Rijksdaalder, Reichsthaler*) worth c. 4s. 9d.

ROCKE: distaff

ROMANTIQUE: having the characteristics of a tale (romance)

ROUNDHOUSE: uppermost cabin in stern of ship

ROYALL THEATRE, the: *see* 'Theatre, the'

RUB(B): check, stop, obstacle

RUFFIAN: pimp, rogue

RUMP: remnant of the Long Parliament

RUMPER: member or supporter of the Rump

RUNLETT: cask

RUNNING: temporary

SACK: white wine from Spain or Canaries

SALT: salt-cellar

SALT-EELE: rope's end used for punishment

SALVE UP: to smooth over

SALVO: excuse, explanation

SARCENET: thin taffeta, fine silk cloth

SASSE (Du. *sas*): sluice, lock

SAVE: to be in time for

SAY: fine woollen cloth

SCALE (of music): key; gamut

SCALLOP: scalloped lace collar

SCALLOP-WHISK: *see* 'Whiske'

SCAPE (s.): adventure

SCAPE (v.): to escape

SCARE-FIRE: sudden conflagration

SCHOOL: to scold, rebuke

SCHUIT (Du.): canal boat, barge

SCONCE: bracket, candlestick

SCOTOSCOPE: spy-glass for use in dark

SCOWRE: to beat, punish

SCREW: key, screw-bolt

SCRUPLE: to dispute

SCULL, SCULLER: small river-boat rowed by a single waterman using one pair of oars. Cf. 'Pair of oars'

SEA-CARD: chart

SEA-COAL: coal carried by sea

SEA-OFFICERS: commissioned officers of the navy. Cf. 'Navy Officers'

SECOND MOURNING: half-mourning

SEEL (of a ship): to lurch

SEEM: to pretend

SENNIT: sevennight, a week

SENSIBLY: perceptibly, painfully

SERPENT: variety of firework

SERVANT: suitor, lover

SET: sit

SET UP/OFF ONE'S REST: to be certain, to be content, to make an end, to make one's whole aim

SEWER: stream, ditch

SHAG(G): worsted or silk cloth with a velvet nap on one side

SHEATH (of a ship): to encase the hull as a protection against worm

SHIFT (s.): trial; dressing room

SHIFT (v.): to change clothes; to dodge a round in paying for drinks (or to get rid of the effects of drink)

SHOEMAKER'S STOCKS: new shoes

SHOVE AT: to apply one's energies to

SHROUD: shrewd, astute

SHUFFLEBOARD: shovelboard, shove-ha'penny

SHUTS: shutters

SILLABUB, SULLYBUB, SYLLABUB: sweetened milk mixed with wine

SIMPLE: foolish

SIT: to hold a meeting

SIT CLOSE: to hold a meeting from which clerks are excluded

SITHE: sigh

SKELLUM: rascal, thief

SLENDERLY: slightingly

SLICE: flat plate

SLIGHT, SLIGHTLY: contemptuous; slightingly, without ceremony

SLIP A CALF/FILLY: to abort

SLOP(P)S: seamen's ready-made clothes

SLUG(G): slow heavy boat; rough metal projectile

SLUT (not always opprobrious): drudge, wench

SMALL (of drink): light

SNAP(P) (s.): bite, snack, small meal; attack

SNAP (v.): to ambush, cut down/out/off

SNUFF: to speak scornfully

SNUFFE, take/go in: to take offence

SOKER: old hand; pal; toper

SOLD(E)BAY: Solebay, off Southwold, Suff.

SOL(L)ICITOR: agent; one who solicits business

SON: son-in-law (similarly with daughter etc.)

SON-IN-LAW: stepson

SOUND: fish-bladder

SOUND, the: strictly the navigable passage between Denmark and Sweden where tolls were levied, but more generally (and usually in Pepys) the Baltic

SPARROWGRASS: asparagus

SPEAK BROAD: to speak fully, frankly

SPECIALITY: bond under seal

SPECIES (optical): image

SPEED: to succeed

SPIKET: spigot, tap, faucet

SPILT, SPOILT: ruined

SPINET: single-manual wing-shaped keyboard instrument with harpsichord action

SPOIL: to deflower; injure

SPOTS: patches (cosmetic)

SPRANKLE: sparkling remark, *bon mot*

SPUDD: trenching tool

STAIRS: landing stage

STAND IN: to cost

STANDING WATER: between tides

STANDISH: stand for ink, pens, etc.

STATE-DISH: richly decorated dish; dish with a round lid or canopy

STATESMAN: Commonwealth's-man

STATIONER: bookseller (often also publisher)

STEEPLE: tower

STEMPEECE: timber of ship's bow

STICK: blockhead

STILLYARD, the: the Steelyard

STIR(R): commotion

STOMACH: courage, pride; appetite

STOMACHFULLY: proudly

STONE-HORSE: stallion

STOUND: astonishment

STOUT: brave, courageous

STOWAGE: storage, payment for storage

STRAIGHTS, STREIGHTS, the: strictly the Straits of Gibraltar; more usually the Mediterranean

STRANG: strong

STRANGERS: foreigners

STRIKE (nautical): to lower the top-sail in salute; (of Exchequer tallies) to make, cut

STRONG WATER: distilled spirits

SUBSIDY MAN: man of substance (liable to pay subsidy-tax)

SUCCESS(E): outcome (good or bad)

SUDDENLY: in a short while

SULLYBUB: see 'Sillabub'

SUPERNUMERARY: seaman extra to ship's complement

SURLY: imperious, lordly

SWINE-POX: chicken-pox

SWOUND: to swoon, faint

SYLLABUB: see 'Sillabub'

SYMPHONY: instrumental introduction, interlude etc., in a vocal composition

TAB(B)Y: watered silk

TABLE: legend attached to a picture

TABLE BOOK: memorandum book

TABLES: board games

TAILLE, TALLE (Fr. *taille*): figure, shape (of person)

TAKE EGGS FOR MONEY: to cut one's losses, to accept something worthless

TAKE A CRAP: to defecate

TAKE OUT: to learn; perform

TAKE POST: to ride hired posthorses

TAKING (s.): condition

TALE: reckoning, number

TALL: fine, elegant

TALLE: see 'Taille'

TALLY: notched wooden stick used by the Exchequer in accounting

TAMKIN: tampion, wooden gun plug

TANSY, TANZY: egg pudding flavoured with tansy

TARGETT: shield

TARPAULIN: 'tar', a sea-bred captain as opposed to a gentleman-captain

TAXOR: financial official of university

TEAR: to rant

TELL: to count

TEMPER (s.): moderation; temperament, mood; physical condition

TEMPER (v.): to moderate, control

TENDER: chary of

TENT: roll of absorbent material used for wounds; (Sp. *tinto*) red wine

TERCE, TIERCE: measure of wine (42 galls.; one-third of a pipe)

TERELLA: terrella, spherical magnet, terrestrial globe containing magnet

TERM(E)S: menstrual periods

THEATRE, the: before May 1663 usually Theatre Royal, Vere St; afterwards usually Theatre Royal, Drury Lane (TR)

THEM: see 'Those'

THEORBO: large double-necked tenor lute

THOSE: menstrual periods

THRUSH: inflammation of throat and mouth

TICKELED: annoyed, irritated

TICKET(T): seaman's pay-ticket

TIERCE: *see* 'Terce'

TILT: awning over river-boat

TIMBER: wood for the skeleton of a ship (as distinct from plank or deals used for the decks, cabins, gun-platforms etc.)

TIRE: tier

TOKEN, by the same: so, then, and

TONGUE: reputation, fame

TOPS: turnovers of stockings

TOUCHED: annoyed

TOUR, the: coach parade of *beau monde* in Hyde Park

TOUSE: to tousle/tumble a woman

TOWN(E): manor

TOY: small gift

TOYLE: foil, net into which game is driven

TRADE: manufacture, industry

TRANSIRE: warrant allowing goods through customs

TRAPAN, TREPAN: (surg.) to perforate skull; cheat, trick, trap, inveigle

TREASURY, the: the Navy Treasury or the national Treasury

TREAT: to handle (literally)

TREAT, TREATY: negotiate, negotiation

TREBLE: treble viol

TREPAN: *see* 'Trapan'

TRIANGLE, TRYANGLE: triangular virginals

TRILL(O): vocal ornament consisting of the accelerated repetition of the same note

TRIM: to shave

TRUCKLE/TRUNDLE-BED: low bed on castors which could be put under main bed

TRYANGLE: *see* 'Triangle'

TRY A PULL: to have a go

TUITION: guardianship

TUNE: pitch

TURK, the: used of all denizens of the Turkish Empire, but usually here of the Berbers of the N. African coast, especially Algiers

TURKEY WORK: red tapestry in Turkish style

TURKY-STONE: turquoise

TUTTLE FIELDS: Tothill Fields

TWIST: strong thread

UGLY: unpleasant, offensive

UMBLES (of deer): edible entrails, giblets

UNBESPEAK: cancel, countermand

UNCOUTH: out of sorts or order, uneasy, at a loss

UNDERSTAND: to conduct oneself properly; (s.) understanding

UNDERTAKER: contractor; parliamentary manager

UNHAPPY, UNHAPPILY: unlucky; unluckily

UNREADY: undressed

UNTRUSS: to undo one's breeches, defecate

UPPER BENCH: name given in Interregnum to King's Bench

USE: usury, interest

USE UPON USE: compound interest

VAPOURISH: pretentious, foolish

VAUNT: to vend, sell

VENETIAN CAP: peaked cap as worn by Venetian Doge

VESTS: robes, vestments

VIALL, VIOL: family of fretted, bowed instruments with six gut strings; the bowing hand is held beneath the bow and the instrument held on or between the knees; now mostly superseded by violin family

VIRGINALS: rectangular English keyboard instrument resembling spinet; usually in case without legs

VIRTUOSO: man of wide learning

WAISTCOAT, WASTECOATE: warm undergarment

WAIT, WAYT (at court etc.): to serve a turn of duty (usually a month) as an official

WARDROBE, the: the office of the

King's Great Wardrobe, of which Lord Sandwich was Keeper; the building at Puddle Wharf containing the office; a cloak room, dressing room

WARM: comfortable, well-off

WASSAIL, WASSELL: entertainment (e.g. a play)

WASTCOATE: *see* 'Waistcoat'

WASTECLOATH: cloth hung on ship as decoration between quarter-deck and forecastle

WATCH: clock

WATER: strong water, spirits

WAY, in/out of the: accessible/inaccessible; in a suitable/unsuitable condition

WAYTES: waits; municipal musicians

WEATHER-GLASS(E): thermometer (or, less likely, barometer)

WEIGH (of ships): to raise

WELLING: Welwyn, Herts.

WESTERN BARGEMAN (BARGEE): bargee serving western reaches of Thames

WESTMINSTER: the area around Whitehall and the Abbey; not the modern city of Westminster

WHISKE: woman's neckerchief

WHITE-HALL: royal palace, largely burnt down in 1698

WHITSTER: bleacher, launderer

WIGG: wig, cake, bun

WILDE: wile

WIND (s.): wine

WIND LIKE A CHICKEN: to wind round one's little finger

WINDFUCKER: talkative braggart

WIPE: sarcasm, insult

WISTELY: with close attention

WITTY: clever, intelligent

WONDER: to marvel at

WOODMONGER: fuel merchant

WORD: utterance, phrase

WOREMOODE: wormwood

WORK: needlework. *Also* v.

WRETCH: *see* 'Poor wretch'

YARD: penis

YARE: ready, skilful

YILDHALL: Guildhall

YOWELL: Ewell, Surrey